READINGS IN PERSONALITY

READINGS IN PERSONALITY

Harriet N. Mischel

Walter Mischel

Stanford University

HOLT, RINEHART AND WINSTON, INC.
New York   Chicago   San Francisco   Atlanta
Dallas   Montreal   Toronto   London   Sydney

Library of Congress Cataloging in Publication Data

Mischel, Harriet N.   comp.
    Readings in personality.

    Includes bibliographies.
    1. Personality—Addresses, essays, lectures.
I. Mischel, Walter, joint comp. II. Title.
(DNLM: 1. Personality—Collected works. BF698 M621r
1973)
BF698.M553   155.2   73-8816
ISBN: 0-03-091625-9

TO OUR STUDENTS

PREFACE

In teaching courses in personality, social behavior, and personality theory over the past decade we often have wanted to expose our students to original source materials so that they could get first-hand views of some of the major ideas, methods, and findings in personality psychology. But although numerous readers are available, none adequately provided the organization and scope that we desired. Hence we confronted the task of choosing our own collection.

The present volume basically parallels the orientation and organization of Walter Mischel's text, *Introduction to Personality*. When used in conjunction with the *Introduction* text, this collection of readings should highlight some of the central topics and issues of the field as we see them. Some of the excerpts and articles in this reader are mentioned directly in *Introduction to Personality*, others add and expand important topics and themes.

While the present collection complements the Mischel text, it is designed to serve as a complete unit in its own right. Our aim has been to present the student with writings which are representative of major theories, issues, and research in the field. The task of selecting articles has been a difficult one, mainly because we have had to omit much that we would have liked to include, and pruning good works is an onerous task. When confronted by ten good articles on a topic when there is space to include only one, decision making becomes thorny at best. We therefore have had to sample, and the selection is of necessity incomplete.

For beginners we hope this volume will offer a realistic introduction to major original work in the field. And for more advanced students we hope the book will provide a glimpse of where the field has been, where it is moving and—most important—where it needs to forge ahead.

We are grateful to Janet Mailer for her invaluable assistance in all phases of the manuscript preparation, and to Barbara Pariser for her important contributions to the preparation of the index as well as for many helpful secretarial functions.

Stanford, California

Harriet N. Mischel
Walter Mischel

Coordination between *Readings in Personality* and Mischel's *Introduction to Personality**

The following comparison provides an overview of the relations between the units in the present volume and the chapters in W. Mischel's *Introduction to Personality* text:

Unit or Chapter	*Readings in Personality*	*Introduction to Personality*
1	Introduction to Part I	Introduction
2	Trait Theories	Type and Trait Theories
3	Trait Assessment—I	Psychodynamic Theories
4	Trait Assessment—II	Psychodynamic Behavior Theories
5	Psychodynamic Theories—I	Social Behavior Theories
6	Psychodynamic Theories—II	Phenomenological Theories
7	Psychodynamic Assessment	Trait Approaches to Assessment—I
8	Social Behavior Theories	Trait Approaches to Assessment—II
9	Social Behavior Assessment	Psychodynamic Approaches to Assessment
10	Phenomenological Theories	Behavioral Approaches to Assessment
11	Phenomenological Assessment	Phenomenological Approaches to Assessment
12	Introduction to Part II	Early Personality Development
13	Learning and Motivation	Learning, Emotion, and Motivation
14	Sex-typing and Personality Development	Sex-typing and Personality Development
15	Identification and Observational Learning	Identification and Observational Learning
16	Frustration and Aggression	Frustration and Aggression
17	Anxiety	Anxiety
18	Defense	Defense
19	Self-control	Self-control
20	Self-concepts	Self-concepts

While W. Mischel's *Introduction to Personality* presents personality theories and their associated assessment techniques sequentially (in two separate parts), this volume of readings presents them in juxtaposition within Part I. To coordinate the present readings completely with the sequence in the *Introduction* text, Units 2, 5, 6, 8, and 10 (personality theories) in the present volume may be read in conjunction with Chapters 1 through 6 (Personality Theories) of the *Introduction* text. Next, the present Units 3, 4, 7, 9, and 11 (assessment techniques) may be read in conjunction with Chapters 7 through 11 (personality assessment) of the *Introduction* text.

The present Units 13 through 20 deal with personality development and basic

* Holt, Rinehart and Winston, Inc., 1971.

processes and are coordinated exactly with Chapters 13 through 20 of the *Introduction* text. Each of these units in the *Readings* deals with the same topics as its corresponding chapter in *Introduction to Personality*. The present volume offers no readings to accompany Chapter 12 (Early Personality Development) and Chapters 21 and 22 (Abnormal Personality and Behavior Modification) of the *Introduction* text because of present space limitations and because these huge topics receive much more extensive coverage in available readers and related courses devoted specifically to child development, abnormal psychology, and behavior modification. Although not relegated to separate units, crucial issues from these domains, as they relate to personality psychology, are treated extensively in articles throughout this book.

CONTENTS

I | APPROACHES TO PERSONALITY: THEORY AND ASSESSMENT

1 | Introduction to Part I

Harriet N. Mischel

Part I provides samples of some of the major theoretical orientations to personality. Perhaps the most distinctive feature of modern personality study as a science is its concern with casting its theoretical speculations about man into testable form and studying them empirically. Indeed, each major theoretical approach has led to the development of distinctive methods of personality study and assessment. The findings and problems encountered with these methods in turn shed light on the theories that generated them. Efforts to measure and analyze behavior thus supply crucial information about the implications of the theoretical ideas that guided the measurement process. To highlight this close interaction, each theoretical approach is considered in juxtaposition with its accompanying assessment strategies.

Thus, in Part I, each theoretical orientation is followed by units on relevant assessment methods. The personality theories and assessment strategies selected have been categorized into four divisions. These are trait approaches (Units 2–4), psychodynamic approaches (Units 5–7), social behavior approaches (Units 8 and 9), and phenomenological approaches (Units 10 and 11).

TRAIT THEORIES (UNIT 2)

One of the earliest, yet still influential, approaches to personality is the trait approach, and no one has contributed more to it than Gordon Allport. Allport's paper (2.1) is an early statement (1937) of his conception of the structure and function of traits; the second excerpt is one of his final statements on this topic made twenty-nine years later. The emphasis on individual differences, a hallmark of the trait theoretical approach, is apparent throughout his writing. Allport believed that the structure of a person's traits (rather than the environment or stimulus conditions) determines that person's behavior. Traits, according to Allport, explain the often striking differences among individuals in response to the *same* stimuli and account for the apparent stability and consistency of behavior across time and in a variety of different situations. Traits are the units that Allport urges personality psychologists to discover.

Allport distinguishes between common and individual traits. He emphasizes that the latter are not amenable to scaling on a linear continuum for a general population and therefore have been neglected by investigators who use only quantitative, dimensional (rather than individual, clinical) measures. Allport divides traits into different kinds (for example, motivational and dynamic), but these are not rigid distinctions. Allport sees flexibility, and even contradiction and conflict, among traits as qualities of human personality.

In his second paper (Unit 2.2) Allport summarizes and comments upon the extensive criticisms and research that bear upon the concept of trait. In spite of many assaults Allport still finds the trait a viable concept and emphasizes that behaviors inconsistent with an hypothesized trait are not proof of the nonexistence of that trait, but rather demonstrate that traits occur in a complex web which must be untangled to understand such apparent contradictions. He questions whether a method like factor analysis (a mathematical procedure that helps to group test responses into clusters of units that are correlated with each other) has enough sensitivity to capture the individuality of personality. He urges that personality be studied at the individual (clinical) level in terms of personal structural dispositions.

J. P. Guilford's approach to personality (Unit 2.3) also emphasizes individual differences. He views the measurement of these differences on trait dimensions as central to the study of personality. Like Allport, he regards personality as an individual's unique pattern of traits. But unlike Allport, who stressed the need for the in-depth study of lives and was critical of many of the statistical methods and quantitative research strategies favored by other trait theorists, Guilford proposed that comparisons between individuals with respect to shared traits is the best way of understanding personality. Guilford regards this comparison of individuals as an analytical process, disclaiming the possibility of comparing one "person-as-a-whole" with another "person-as-a-whole." The aspects or properties that must be abstracted are traits. Guilford distinguishes between traits abstracted from behavior (behavior traits) and those abstracted from an individual's physical makeup (somatic traits).

Carl Jung's introversion-extroversion typology (unit 2.4), often mentioned but seldom quoted, has generated considerable research. The brief passage by Jung indicates the compatibility between the classification of individuals into polar types and the dynamic motivational concepts favored by psychodynamic theorists (Units 5 and 6). Trait concepts, especially motivational traits, have a definite place in psychodynamic approaches. For example, Freud devised an elaborate character typology which he related to fixation at various stages in his theory of psychosexual stages.

Hans Eysenck (2.5, 2.6), a British psychologist, has complemented and supplemented the work of American trait theorists in several important ways. Most important is his extension of the conception of personality dimensions into the area of abnormal behavior. Eysenck's sophisticated statistical methods underline one of the prominent features of the trait approach: its quantitative methodology. Eysenck and Rachman (Unit 2.6) have examined the relationship between an individual's position on a set of personality dimensions and his scores on a variety of other personality and intellectual measures. They use additional statistical techniques (especially factor analysis) to attempt to answer questions about what sorts of behaviors are most likely to occur together in order to obtain clues about the structure and organization of personality.

Eysenck contrasts his dimensional approach with what he calls the "hypothesis of discrete disease entities" used in traditional psychiatry. He proposes that the notion of discrete psychiatric disease entities is outmoded and erroneous. In his view it is imperative to supplant it with the concept of dimensional continuity and to measure testable relations between behaviors rather than to attempt psychiatric diagnostic classification.

TRAIT ASSESSMENT (UNITS 3 AND 4)

Traits are assumed to be general underlying dispositions that account for the observation that individuals confronted with the same event—the same final exam, the same party, the same teacher—react in different ways. Traits also are invoked to account for the apparently distinctive consistency in an individual's responses over a wide variety of events and over time. Trait theorists expect the individual who strives to achieve high standards of excellence to do so on the job and on the tennis courts as well as in the classroom, and they expect such a pattern to remain relatively stable throughout development.

The predominant research and assessment objective of the trait approach to personality is the identification and measurement of these hypothesized underlying broad dispositions. Emphasis is on the measurement of an individual's position on a particular dimension (or dimensions) in an objective way through the use of tests or other procedures administered under standard (uniform) conditions. Often, an individual is asked to respond to a questionnaire about himself, but whatever the behavior tested or sampled, the trait theorist views the person's responses as *signs* of his underlying traits. These signs are treated in a quantitative manner, for example, as additive scores, and are generally used to make comparisons among large numbers of people who have been sampled under uniform conditions.

In Units 3 and 4 some of the central issues and controversies stemming from the application of trait theoretical approaches are illustrated. Trait-oriented research and assessment often utilize questionnaires to study important attributes. The Manifest Anxiety Scale (MAS), devised by Janet Taylor, is probably the most popular anxiety test. Its items are borrowed from the Minnesota Multiphasic Personality Inventory (MMPI). The MMPI best exemplifies most features of the psychometric approach insofar as it relies on the subjects' self-reports, treats the responses as "signs" of underlying dispositions, and uses the scores additively to make comparisons between large groups of individuals. Taylor's paper (3.1) conveys the process involved in constructing a personality scale.

Passini and Norman (3.2) deal with the question of whether or not factor analysis can be used to reveal (discover) traits. In an influential study these authors demonstrate that trait dimensions may exist in the raters' heads rather than reflecting the organization of attributes in the persons being rated. They asked University of Michigan undergraduates, who had never seen each other prior to the experimental situation and had no opportunity to know each other except for fifteen minutes of superficial observations of physical appearance and manner, to rate each other on a set of personality scales. They were surprised to find that their data indicated the same five-factor structure that had been found in prior studies (using the same personality scales and instructions) conducted with raters who knew each other better, including one study in which professional psychologists were rating persons whom they had observed intensely. The authors suggest that their results may be due to an "implicit personality theory" which each rater brings to the situation.

The study reported by Ulrich, Stachnik, and Stainton (3.3) illustrates some hazards inherent in broadly stated personality impressions. They presented college students with individual "personality reports" supposedly derived from each student's scores on personality tests. In fact, they gave identical reports to all students. The majority enthusiastically accepted the descriptions as excellent, illustrating the ease with which personality impressions stated in broad terms may be endowed with extra meaning and adopted with confidence.

Campbell (3.4) sets forth some standards for inferring the traits which personality theorists guided by trait theory usually seek to discover. Construct or trait validation refers to the trait psychologist's efforts to elaborate the inferred traits which he hypothesizes are determining the individual's test responses. By "discriminant validity" Campbell means that when one introduces a measure of a trait, one has to show that the personality test provides new information, that it is not merely redundant with other better established or more parsimonious constructs. This caution is especially important with regard to intelligence tests, because numerous correlations have been found between them and personality tests. When a new personality measure involves self-description, Campbell urges that the test correlations (what the test is supposed to be measuring) be shown as *not* merely due to individual differences in the tendency to describe oneself on test items in a favorable light. Such a tendency is referred to as a "social desirability" response set. A "response set" is a tendency for individuals to answer test questions in a certain way independent of the content of the test questions. For example, an "acquiescence" response set is the tendency of some individuals to agree with the items in a questionnaire regardless of their content. Campbell has several recommendations to help avoid confusion between trait-specific content and response sets, although he does not rule out the possibility that a response set may be considered as a trait-like variable whose correlations with other personality indices may be meaningful.

It is important for the trait researcher to demonstrate not only that his test measures a new or different trait (rather than, for example, intelligence or a response set), but also that it measures that trait better than other measures; that better predictions about independent trait-appropriate or criterion measures can be made from his test than from self-description, stereotypes or self-ratings. Finally, Campbell notes the importance of using several methods of measuring a given trait and of measuring more than one trait by a given method. That is, two or more measures of the same trait should correlate decidedly more than the same measure of different traits, not just more than different measures of different traits. For example, measurements of dominance by the MMPI and by peer-group ratings should be more highly correlated than measurements of dominance and sociability by the MMPI. In showing that trait constructs are valid, it is just as important for some correlations to be low as it is for others to be high.

Traditionally, trait psychologists have generally assumed that personality traits are relatively stable, highly consistent attributes that exert widely generalized causal effects on behavior. The fundamental assumption has been that personality comprises broad underlying traits which pervasively influence the individual's behavior across many situations and which lead to consistency in his behavior. Guided by this assumption, trait-oriented personality research has been a quest for such underlying broad dimensions (or the basic "factors") that are characteristic of the individual and on which many persons may be compared to see how much of the disposition they possess. For this purpose hundreds of tests have been designed to infer consistent traits, yet the evidence for the existence of such broadly consistent global traits that manifest themselves pervasively has been seriously challenged. The essence of this controversy is the degree to which people have generalized personality traits. It is widely agreed that impressive consistencies often have been found for intellective features of personality and for behavior patterns (such as "cognitive styles") that are strongly correlated with intelligence. Consistency also often seems to be high when people rate their own traits on questionnaires and other self-reports. Likewise, stability over time (temporal continuity) has been obtained often when the individual's behavior is tested at different time periods but in similar situations. But, when one goes beyond cognitive variables to personality dimensions, and when one assesses personality by diverse methods and not just by self-report questionnaires, the data become much more controversial.

Thus the utility of generalized traits as the basic unit of personality is now being seriously questioned. Undermining the utility of traditional trait approaches has been evidence that indicates that much of the variance in personality measures comes from the situation and from complex interactions between the individual and the particular situation in which he finds himself. The paper by Endler and Hunt (4.1) deals with the issue of the relative importance of individual differences and of situations in determining responses. They chose the special case of anxiety to explore this controversy and sought to answer the question of whether variability in anxious behavior is due more to situationally evoked momentary states of anxiety or to a general personality trait of anxiousness.

Endler and Hunt devised a series of self-report anxiety inventories in which they separated situations and modes of responses. For example, the situations sampled by the questionnaire ranged from such innocuous ones as "you are starting on a long automobile trip" to "you are about to take the final examination for a course in which your status is doubtful." The response modes were also systematically varied to include a wide range of possible reactions. For example, the subject's perception of his physiological reaction ("hands trembling," "fluttering feeling in stomach") were sampled as were such self-reported indicators of anxiety as "can't concentrate." Endler and Hunt submitted their data to sophisticated statistical analyses that provided separate estimates of the relative effects of hypothetical stimulus situations, response modes, and persons as determinants of test responses. The results indicated that the *interactions* of person, situation, and response mode were the most potent. Neither persons nor situations, taken alone, accounted for more than a trivial fraction of the test results. Thus anxiety reactions seem to depend not only on the individual, but also on the particular stimulus situation confronting him (for example, "receiving a police summons"), and on the specific response mode measured (for example, "heart beats faster," "get an uneasy feeling").

Endler and Hunt conclude that their findings demonstrate the individuality of personality so long stressed by Allport (2.1 and 2.2) and limit the value of responses on omnibus personality questionnaires. The validity of reported anxiety indicators can be increased by specifying the situation. But Endler and Hunt also make clear that it is not an issue of person *versus* situation. They suggest categorizing both situations and modes of response and then describing individuals in terms of the kinds of responses they tend to manifest in the various kinds of situations.

Jack Block (4.2) indicates why he thinks psychologists have failed to find evidence for the consistency of individual traits in a variety of situations; his theories are guided by the belief that "the idea of continuity and coherence in personality functioning must be affirmed." Mischel's paper (4.3) offers a quite different interpretation of the same findings. In his view the specificity of behavior is not artifactual but reflects accurately the discriminativeness of behavior and its dependence on environmental supports.

PSYCHODYNAMIC THEORIES (UNITS 5 AND 6)

In contrast to the concern of trait psychologists with quantification, large samples of subjects, and objective measurements, psychodynamic theorists attempt to study the whole individual in depth by using less formal techniques guided by clinical intuition. Like the trait theorists the psychodynamicist wants to go beyond observed behavior to hypothesized underlying dispositions. But the dispositions (for example, unconscious motives) inferred by the psychodynamicist tend to be more complexly and indirectly related to the behavioral signs from which they are inferred.

The two excerpts from Freud's writings (5.1 and 5.2) illustrate several important aspects of psychodynamic theory, which he developed almost single-handedly, and of psychoanalysis, which he invented. In the first selection Freud focuses on the second of his five stages of psychosexual development—oral, anal, phallic, latency, and genital. But he also deals with the broader questions of the transformations of instincts and the relationship of character traits to stages of psychosexual development. Freud theorizes that some of these early erotic impulses lose their importance when genital primacy is established, other impulses are preserved in the unconscious in a state of repression, and still others may be transformed into character traits. To substantiate his theoretical statements, Freud relies heavily on dream material and associations.

In the second selection, Freud deals with one of his most important concepts: the Oedipus complex. Freud considers this concept central to his proposed stages of childhood sexuality. The Oedipus complex is the focal point of the "phallic stage." This stage is the third and last stage of genital organization before the latency period and the final stage of genital maturity in Freud's scheme of psychosexual development. It is at this time that the superego is formed as a result of the process of identification.

These two short selections by Freud cannot even begin to convey the complexity, scope, and comprehensiveness of his total theorizing. Hopefully, the excerpts do convey some sense of Freud's conceptual style and the flavor of his clinically oriented theorizing. While Freud's approach to personality development drew heavily on psychosexual concepts, his modern followers have invoked more social concepts. Thus while Freud hypothesized such mechanisms as the Oedipus complex and castration dread, Erich Fromm (6.1) attributes important motivational properties to man's unbearable feelings of aloneness and insignificance. In a related contemporary vein Erik Erikson (6.2) views identity crisis as a social ingredient of human growth. The selections by Fromm and Erikson illustrate the expansion and development of fundamental Freudian concepts to include broad social and cultural forces and to construe personality development as a life-long process instead of as the product only of early childhood.

PSYCHODYNAMIC ASSESSMENT (UNIT 7)

The origins of psychodynamic assessment techniques were in the psychiatric clinic and in the intensive study of disturbed people. As in the trait approach, inferences are made about underlying dispositions, but both the evidence from which they are made and the rules by which the inferences are generated are *indirect* (as opposed to direct) and informal or intuitive (as opposed to standard and uniform). In Freud's view human behavior stems from motives that are outside man's awareness and that are rooted in the instincts of sex and aggression. Freud hypothesized persistent unconscious and irrational demands from within as the major determinants of behavior; man is in conflict with his environment until he internalizes the prohibitions of his culture. Freud saw man as hiding from his own unacceptable wishes and defensively camouflaging his deepest desires even from himself. Since the psychodynamic view sees human behavior as motivated by unconscious, irrational demands and as obscured by defenses, the individual's self-reports cannot be accepted at face value. Instead, Freud and his followers viewed a person's words and deeds and dreams as highly indirect, disguised, symbolic representations of unconscious underlying forces.

More recently psychodynamically oriented followers of Freud like Fromm (6.1) and Erikson (6.2 and 7.1) have proposed theories in which the role of instincts has been minimized and the role of the social milieu emphasized. These "neo-Freudian" conceptions of human nature have been less drive (or "id") oriented and more concerned with the "ego" aspects of personality functioning. Their greater concern with the social and interpersonal and their loosening of Freud's strict motivational determinism have resulted in their being considered more "humanistic" than the early psychodynamicists, though they have not abandoned the concept of intrapsychic dynamics.

Erikson's paper (7.1) is an eloquent explanation of informal clinical methods and the type of evidence used by psychodynamically oriented clinicians. Erikson artfully elaborates the intricate processes that guide his clinical interpretations. He illustrates his intuitive approach with detailed examples of how he tried to understand a patient's dream. His complex network of evidence emphasizes internal consistency by relating bits of data from the dream to other information about the patient including his responses to psychological tests such as the Rorschach and the Thematic Apperception Test.

While the clinician's intuitive methods may seem highly attractive, scientifically oriented psychologists cannot accept them on faith alone and seek empirical evidence on which to judge their worth. Therefore, many psychologists have tried to test the value of psychodynamic insights by means of the objective, quantitative, test-oriented methodology of trait psychology. In this vein Goldberg and Werts (7.2) consider the issue of the relationship between reliability and validity in clinical judgments. They adapt the method suggested by Campbell (3.4) to study clinicians' judgments, the sources clinicians use, and the traits they infer. They asked experienced clinical psychologists to rank groups of patients on four traits of the kind commonly employed in clinical settings. The rankings were based on tests which included information commonly available to clinicians carrying out psychological evaluations and which sampled four different types of clinical assessment procedures. Goldberg and Werts found that a clinician's judgment of a particular patient on a particular trait dimension did not agree with another clinician's judgment of the same patient on the same trait based on another data source. The authors discuss the implications of this failure in reliability for clinical judgments in general.

Chapman and Chapman (7.3) examine empirical evidence on the validity of the clinical inference procedures central to psychodynamic assessment techniques. The study which they conducted demonstrates an important systematic bias in observations of correlations between symptom statements and features of projective test protocols. The authors point out that some "signs" of male homosexuality derived from content analysis of the Rorschach test are commonly reported by clinicians even though the research literature indicates they are invalid. The two "signs" which research evidence suggests are valid, however, clinicians do not report observing. The authors demonstrate that the signs which have the strongest verbal associative connection to male homosexuality (for example, feminine clothing, rectum, and buttocks) are the ones that are most popular among practicing clinicians. In subsequent studies using naive undergraduates, the authors found further evidence for the prevalence of such systematic judgment biases.

SOCIAL BEHAVIOR THEORIES (UNIT 8)

In contrast to trait and psychodynamic theories, the social behavior (social learning) approach focuses on what the person does rather than on inferences about the internal conflicts and motives that he is hypothesized to have. The individual's behaviors are studied in relation to the specific conditions or events in the environment that seem to elicit, maintain, or modify them. Thus the focus is on human behavior and the conditions that seem to regulate it, rather than on inferences about global intrapsychic dispositions.

In Unit 8 there are articles by three influential psychologists who have developed behavioral approaches relevant to understanding personality. While these authors share many basic assumptions, their specific views of social learning differ substantially. Skinner (8.1) outlines the requirements of empirical analysis and shows how such concepts as "purpose," "incentive," and "goal" may be dealt with in the language of operant conditioning. These terms, according to Skinner, are inferences about the variables responsible for behavior. The consequences of a behavior determine whether it will occur again.

Expressions involving goals and purposes are shorthand references to the variables of which the behavior is a function. Skinner's name is often associated with research on operant conditioning in which pigeons are the subjects. His interest in complex human behavior and social concerns, however, is evident in his early novel, *Walden Two*, in which he presents his version of a Utopian society, and in much of his more recent writing.

Rotter, Chance, and Phares (8.2) are less insistent upon avoiding inferences regarding unobservables, but their approach is still highly focused upon behavior and learning. The construct of "subjective expectancy" is used to take into account the consequences a person expects for his behavior. Julian Rotter hypothesizes that behavior is a function of subjective expectancies and values, which in turn are a function of prior learning in similar situations. Elsewhere Rotter has distinguished between "specific" and "generalized expectancies." Specific expectancies can be modified readily by variations in the situation. Generalized expectancies, on the other hand, are assumed to be more consistent and stable across situations. An example of a generalized expectancy is Rotter's concept of "perceived locus of control": the degree to which people believe that they have control and feel personally responsible for what happens to them (that is, for the reinforcements they receive). Individual differences on this internal-external control dimension have been measured by a questionnaire that has yielded many correlates. The questionnaire was employed in several of the studies in Part II (17.3, 19.3, and 20.3). The notion of generalized expectancies as stable and consistent across situations makes them conceptually somewhat similar to traits, although their social learning antecedents are carefully specified.

Albert Bandura (8.3) develops the concept of modeling or "no trial learning" as a powerful means of transmitting and modifying behavioral repertoires. Bandura distinguishes between the learning (acquisition) and performance of responses. He notes that operant-conditioning methods (Skinner, 8.1) are suited to controlling existing responses (performance) but maintains that social responses are most likely learned (acquired) by humans in everyday life through observation of actual or symbolic models. Bandura summarizes and refutes Skinner's arguments against the use of modeling procedures in experiments and the theoretical applicability of the concept of model influence. He goes on to review an important study which compares the relative efficacy of real and symbolic modeling in the transmission of novel aggressive responses (Bandura, Ross, and Ross, 1963a). The findings of this study illustrate the acquisition of new responses through observation and the inhibitory and disinhibitory effects of modeling on the observer's subsequent behavior.

SOCIAL BEHAVIOR ASSESSMENT (UNIT 9)

Walter Mischel (9.1) underlines the close association of assessment and therapeutic behavior change in social learning (social behavior) approaches. In contrast to the use of behaviors as *signs* of dispositions in trait and psychodynamic (state) theories of personality, he focuses on the use of directly relevant behavior *samples* in assessment. The discussion again raises the recurrent issue of the specificity versus the consistency of behavior previously encountered in the context of trait approaches to assessment (Unit 4). Mischel emphasizes the distinction between contemporary social behavior theory and earlier behavior theories that tended to dwell on the study of lower organisms rather than on complex human behavior. Then Mischel (9.2) compares and contrasts a behavioral and psychodynamic approach to the same material, the case of "Pearson Brack," and further elaborates some of the distinctive features of behavioral assessment.

Kanfer and Saslow (9.3) contrast diagnostic classification (an assessment technique used by both trait and psychodynamic approaches) and behavioral analysis. They go into great detail regarding the various possible methods of data collection for a functional analysis of behavior. Their description shows that, contrary to some common stereotypes, the behavior analysis approach to assessment and therapy is highly individualized.

PHENOMENOLOGICAL THEORIES (UNIT 10)

Phenomenological theories are exceedingly diverse. Although phenomenological theorists differ on many points, they tend to be oriented to the "self" and are concerned with the person's subjective, internal experiences and personal concepts. Generally, they tend to reject motivational explanations such as those favored in psychodynamic theory. Instead, they emphasize the person's immediate experiences, current relationships, perceptions, and encounters. They also reject most of the assumptions of trait theorists. Instead, they view the person as an experiencing being—not a bundle of long-term dispositions. Many also emphasize man's positive strivings and tendencies toward growth and self-actualization.

Abraham Maslow (10.1) indicates just what the phenomenological approach is rejecting and what it proposes as an alternative. He sees the issue as one of two contrasting world views: one holistic, purposive, functional, and dynamic; the other atomistic, mechanical, taxonomic, static, and causal. He goes on to argue against the too simple notions of cause and effect which in his view characterize the writings of the behaviorists and argues for a reorganization of personality theory to account for the unity, the wholeness, of human personality.

Carl Rogers (10.2) illustrates the organismic quality of his conception of personality. Dealing in this instance with the problem of values, Rogers proposes that there is an organismic basis, shared with the rest of the animate world, for the achievement of a valuing process which enhances the self. According to his hypotheses these value directions are achieved by an openness to inner experiences and are common to those who are moving toward (or have achieved) this openness. Rogers supports his hypotheses with observations from his own clinical experience.

George Kelly (10.3) advocates the illumination of the person's own categories. He urges turning attention to the way each individual construes his experiences, rather than simply locating him on the dimensions of a personality theory. Kelly also argues against the use of the traditional construct of motivation in understanding human behavior. The excerpts quoted demonstrate Kelly's faith in man as an active, ever-changing creator of hypotheses and a player of multiple roles (rather than as a victim of his own impulses, defenses, and history). They also illustrate the techniques that Kelly feels enable the therapist to assist in the production of constructive alternatives.

PHENOMENOLOGICAL ASSESSMENT (UNIT 11)

There is no sharp conceptual break between phenomenological theories and assessment. In Unit 11.1 Kelly presents his ideas on methodology and urges that the phenomenological or humanistic approach not abandon technology, research, and experimentation. Rather, he contends that behavior is best explained by what man finds he can do with it. Psychology provides a structure for the continually changing referents of behavior, casting it into new perspectives and thereby aiding in the realization of the psychological freedom of man.

Sidney Jourard (11.2) begins by contrasting his humanistic image of man with the one that he feels emerges from traditional experimental psychology. He asserts that the humanistic psychologist's aim is not to render man predictable and controllable by somebody else but to liberate him. Jourard maintains that there are circumstances in which a person's behavior is totally free, totally self-determined, totally reflective of a true, inner self, unhampered by the impact of the situation. A humanistic methodology, he says, must strive to produce a situation in which a person will choose to reveal his experience to another person. In contrast, the typical psychological experiment, Jourard asserts, treats the subject as an object and puts him on the defensive to maintain a socially desirable image rather than to reveal himself. Aims and goals, according to Jourard, are what give behavior meaning and people will disclose these only to others whom they have reason to trust. Jourard proposes that self-disclosure can be optimized by permissive interpersonal conditions which permit a genuine dialogue between subject and experimenter. He stresses the importance of the interpersonal context of psychological research and indicates some of the variables which he believes affect what one person will disclose to another.

2 | Trait Theories

2.1 | DEFINITION OF PERSONALITY*

Gordon W. Allport

Since there is no such thing as a wrong definition of any term, if it is supported by usage, it is evident that no one, neither the theologian, the philosopher, the jurist, the sociologist, the man in the street, nor the psychologist, can monopolize "personality." For the psychologist, to be sure, some definitions seem to be more serviceable than others. Completely unsuitable are biosocial formulations in terms of social reputation or superficial charm (Flemming, 1933; Roback, 1931). The distinction between reputation (social effectiveness) and the true personality is one that will be observed rigidly throughout this . . . [article]. Omnibus definitions (Link, 1936) must likewise be rejected. More helpful are those conceptions that ascribe to personality a *solid organization* of dispositions and sentiments. Valuable likewise are definitions that refer to the *style of life*, to *modes of adaptation* to one's surroundings, to *progressive growth* and development and to *distinctiveness.*

Might we not merely say that, psychologically considered, personality is "what a man really is"? (Menninger, 1930) This terse expression states the essential biophysical position, and is acceptable enough in principle. Yet it is too brief and vague as it stands. The following amplification seems to serve the purpose better:

> Personality is the dynamic organization within the individual of those psychophysical systems that determine his unique adjustments to his environment. (Warren & Carmichael, 1930)

This formulation contains the seeds of the hierarchical, integrative, adjustive, and distinctive classes of definitions described above. In a sense, therefore, *it represents a synthesis of contemporary psychological usage.* But each portion of the definition is chosen for a particular reason, and these reasons must be made clear if the definition is to be accurately understood.

* SOURCE: Allport, G. W. *Personality: A psychological interpretation.* New York: Holt, Rinehart and Winston, 1937. Pp. 47–50, abridged, and pp. 339–342, abridged. Copyright 1937 by Holt, Rinehart and Winston, Inc. Copyright © 1965 by Gordon W. Allport. Reprinted by permission of Holt, Rinehart and Winston, Inc.

Dynamic Organization. To escape from the sterile enumerations of the omnibus definitions it is necessary to stress active organization. The crucial problem of psychology has always been mental organization (association). It is likewise the outstanding problem dealt with . . . [here]. Hence "organization" must appear in the definition. Yet this organization must be regarded as constantly evolving and changing, as motivational and as self-regulating; hence the qualification "dynamic." Organization must also imply at times the correlative process of *disorganization*, especially in those personalities that we are wont to regard as "abnormal."

Psychophysical Systems. Habits, specific and general attitudes, sentiments, and dispositions of other orders are all psychophysical systems. . . , these dispositions will be ordered within a theory of *traits*. The term "system" refers to traits or groups of traits in a latent or active condition. The term "psychophysical" reminds us that personality is neither exclusively mental nor exclusively neural. The organization entails the operation of both body and mind, inextricably fused into a personal unity.

Determine. This term is a natural consequence of the biophysical view. Personality *is* something and *does* something. It is not synonymous with behavior or activity; least of all is it merely the impression that this activity makes on others. It is what lies *behind* specific acts and *within* the individual. The systems that constitute personality are in every sense *determining tendencies*, and when aroused by suitable stimuli provoke those adjustive and expressive acts by which the personality comes to be known.

Unique. Strictly speaking every adjustment of every person is unique, in time and place, and in quality. In a sense, therefore, this criterion seems redundant. It becomes important, however, in our . . . discussions of the problem of *quantitative* variation among individuals in respect to the so-called "common" traits . . . and is therefore emphasized in the definition.

Adjustments to His Environment. This phrase has a functional and evolutionary significance. Personality is a mode of survival. "Adjustments," however, must be interpreted broadly enough to include maladjustments, and "environment" to include the behavioral environment (meaningful to the individual) as well as the surrounding geographical environment.

Above all, adjustment must not be considered as merely reactive adaptation such as plants and animals are capable of. The adjustments of men contain a great amount of spontaneous, creative behavior toward the environment. Adjustment to the physical world as well as to the imagined or ideal world—both being factors in the "behavioral environment"—involves *mastery* as well as passive adaptation.

RÉSUMÉ OF THE DOCTRINE OF TRAITS

In everyday life, no one, not even a psychologist, doubts that underlying the conduct of a mature person there are characteristic dispositions or traits. His enthusiasms, interests, and styles of expression are far too self-consistent and plainly patterned to be accounted for in terms of specific habits or identical elements. Nor can the stability and consistency of behavior be explained away by invoking nominalistic theories; stability and consistency are not due to the biosocial arrangement of unrelated activities into categories with verbal tags. Traits are not creations in the mind of the observer, nor are they verbal fictions; they are here accepted as biophysical facts, actual psychophysical dispositions related—though no one yet knows how—to persistent neural systems of stress and determination.

Traits are not, like the faculties of old, abstractions derived from a theory of mind-in-general. There is no essential resemblance between impersonal faculties, as Memory, Will, and Sagacity on the one hand, and the focalized sub-structures of a particular mind (interests, sentiments, general attitudes) on the other. Faculties are universal, traits personal; faculties are independent, traits inter-dependent; faculties are a priori, traits must be ascertained empirically in the individual case.

The doctrine of traits differs also from the theory of factors or any other system of common dimensions into which every individual is fitted categorically. Conceptualized nomothetic units (factors, instincts, needs, and the like) stress what is universal in men, not what is organized into integral, personal systems. The doctrine of traits emphasizes concrete individuality.

Traits are not directly observable; they are inferred (as any kind of determining tendency is inferred). Without such an inference the stability and consistency of personal behavior could not possibly be explained. Any specific action is a product of innumerable determinants, not only of traits but of momentary pressures and specialized influences. But it is the repeated occurrence of actions having the *same significance* (equivalence of response), following upon a definable range of stimuli having the same personal significance (equivalence of stimuli), that makes necessary the postulation of traits as states of Being. Traits are not at all times active, but they are persistent even when latent, and are distinguished by low thresholds of arousal.

It is one thing to admit traits as the most acceptable unit for investigation in the psychology of personality, but another to determine authoritatively the precise character of these traits in a given life. In order to avoid projection of his own nature and many other sources of error, the psychological investigator must use all the empirical tools of his science to make his inferences valid. Traits cannot be conjured into existence; they must be discovered.

In naming the traits that are discovered, there are many pitfalls, the chief one being the confusion of personality with character through the use of eulogistic and dyslogistic terms. Whenever this occurs the existential pattern of personality becomes hopelessly entangled with social judgments of merit and demerit. It is possible, though difficult, to achieve a psychological vocabulary of noncensorial trait-names. Most of these terms antedate psychology by centuries; they were invented because they were needed. Simply because it is difficult to employ them circumspectly, the investigator is not on that account justified in dispensing with them altogether and attempting to put mathematical or artificial symbols in their place. Regrettable though it may seem, the attributes of human personality can be depicted only with the aid of common speech, for it alone possesses the requisite flexibility, subtlety, and established intelligibility.

For the purposes of comparison and measurement certain segments of behavior (by virtue of the similarity of human equipment and the common exigencies of the cultural and physical environments) may be considered as distributed in a general population. These *common* traits as conceptualized by the investigator may, in a rough and approximate way, be scaled on a linear continuum. The "normality" of distribution obtained for such traits is a complex product of chance-biological variation, cultural conformity, and artifact. However carefully conceived and scaled, a common trait is at best an abstraction, for in its concrete form, in each particular life, it operates always in a unique fashion. *Individual* traits cannot be scaled at all in a general population, and for that reason they have been hitherto neglected by all excepting clinical investigators.

Some traits are clearly motivational, especially those sub-classes ordinarily known as interests, ambitions, complexes, and sentiments. Other traits are less dynamic in their operation, having an ability to steer (to stylize) behavior rather than to initiate it. But often the traits that are at first directive acquire driving power, and those that are at one time driving become merely directive.

Traits are not wholly independent of one another; nor are any other neuropsychic systems. They frequently exist in clusters, the arousal of one portion tending to spread to all regions in readiness for communication. Throughout this elaborate interplay, different foci of organization can be detected, a fact that justifies the conception of a *manifold* of traits even where they clearly overlap.

As this segregation among traits is only relative, so too is their self-consistency. In fact, the usefulness of any trait to its possessor depends to a great extent upon its flexibility. Even while it stabilizes conduct and economizes effort, the trait must not be rigid in its operation; for effective adjustment and mastery require variation. The range of situations that arouses traits must be expected to change according to circumstances. Also in any personality one must expect to find some contradiction and conflict among traits, as novelists and clinicians never tire of telling.

Variable though they are, still in every mature personality certain *central* traits can normally be identified. So too can *secondary* traits, though these are less distinctive, less prominent, and more circumscribed in their operation. Whenever a disposition is so little generalized that it is aroused by only a narrow range of stimulus situations, it is more properly called an *attitude* than a trait. Somewhat rarely a personality is dominated by one outstanding *cardinal* trait, to which other dispositions serve as merely subsidiary, congruent foci.

As is the case with all other forms of mental organization, the structure of true (individual) traits is a question of degree. But however much they may vary in respect to their consistency, scope, and independence, they have—according to . . . [Allport's] . . . theory . . .—certain essential characteristics. They are always biophysical in nature, concrete and personal in their organization, contemporaneous in their effect, capable of functional autonomy, but not structurally independent of one another; they are generalized (to the extent that the effective stimuli are equivalent, and to the extent that the resultant responses are equivalent). They are *modi vivendi*, ultimately deriving their significance from the role they play in advancing adaptation within, and mastery of, the personal environment.

REFERENCES

Flemming, E. G. The pleasing personality of high-school girls as related to other traits and measures. *Journal of Educational Sociology*, 1933, 6, 401–409.

Link, H. C. *The return to religion.* New York: Macmillan, 1936. P. 89.

Menninger, K. *The human mind.* New York and London: Knopf, 1930. P. 21.

Roback, A. A. *Personality, the crux of social intercourse.* Cambridge, Mass.: Sci.-art Publishers, 1931. Chapter 1.

Warren, H. C., & Carmichael, L. *Elements of human psychology.* New York: Houghton Mifflin, 1930.

2.2 | TRAITS REVISITED*

Gordon W. Allport

Years ago I ventured to present a paper before the Ninth International Congress at New Haven (G. W. Allport, 1931). It was entitled "What Is a Trait of Personality?" For me to return to the same topic on this honorific occasion is partly a sentimental indulgence, but partly too it is a self-imposed task to discover whether during the past 36 years I have learned anything new about this central problem in personality theory.

In my earlier paper I made eight bold assertions. A trait, I said,

1. Has more than nominal existence.
2. Is more generalized than a habit.
3. Is dynamic, or at least determinative, in behavior.
4. May be established empirically.
5. Is only relatively independent of other traits.
6. Is not synonymous with moral or social judgment.
7. May be viewed either in the light of the personality which contains it, or in the light of its distribution in the population at large.

To these criteria I added one more:

8. Acts, and even habits, that are inconsistent with a trait are not proof of the nonexistence of the trait.

* SOURCE: Allport, G. W. Traits revisited. *American Psychologist*, 1966, *21*, 1–10, abridged. Copyright 1966 by the American Psychological Association and reprinted by permission.

While these propositions still seem to me defensible they were originally framed in an age of psychological innocence. They now need reexamination in the light of subsequent criticism and research.

CRITICISM OF THE CONCEPT OF TRAIT

Some critics have challenged the whole concept of trait. Carr and Kingsbury (1938) point out the danger of reification. Our initial observation of behavior is only in terms of adverbs of action: John behaves aggressively. Then an adjective creeps in: John has an aggressive disposition. Soon a heavy substantive arrives, like William James' cow on the doormat: John has a trait of aggression. The result is the fallacy of misplaced concreteness.

The general positivist cleanup starting in the 1930s went even further. It swept out (or tried to sweep out) all entities, regarding them as question-begging redundancies. Thus Skinner (1953) writes:

> When we say that a man eats *because* he is hungry, smokes a great deal *because* he has the tobacco habit, fights *because* of the instinct of pugnacity, behaves brilliantly *because* of his intelligence, or plays the piano well *because* of his musical ability, we seem to be referring to causes. But on analysis these phrases prove to be merely redundant descriptions [p. 31].

It is clear that this line of attack is an assault not only upon the concept of trait, but upon all intervening variables whether they be conceived in terms of expectancies, attitudes, motives, capacities, sentiments, or traits. The resulting postulate of the "empty organism" is by now familiar to us all, and is the scientific credo of some. Carried to its logical extreme this reasoning would scrap the concept of personality itself—an eventuality that seems merely absurd to me.

More serious, to my mind, is the argument against what Block and Bennett (1955) called "traitology" arising from many studies of the variability of a person's behavior as it changes from situation to situation. Every parent knows that an offspring may be a hellion at home and an angel when he goes visiting. A businessman may be hardheaded in the office and a mere marshmallow in the hands of his pretty daughter.

Years ago the famous experiment by La Piere (1934) demonstrated that an innkeeper's prejudice seems to come and go according to the situation confronting him.

In recent months Hunt (1965) has listed various theories of personality that to his mind require revision in the light of recent evidence. Among them he questions the belief that personality traits are the major sources of behavior variance. He, like Miller (1963), advocates that we shift attention from traits to interactions among people, and look for consistency in behavior chiefly in situationally defined roles. Helson (1964) regards trait as the residual effect of previous stimulation, and thus subordinates it to the organism's present adaptation level.

Scepticism is likewise reflected in many investigations of "person perception." To try to discover the traits residing within a personality is regarded as either naive or impossible. Studies, therefore, concentrate only on the *process* of perceiving or judging, and reject the problem of validating the perception and judgment.

Studies too numerous to list have ascribed chief variance in behavior to situational factors, leaving only a mild residue to be accounted for in terms of idiosyncratic attitudes and traits. A prime example is Stouffer's study of *The American Soldier* (Stouffer et al., 1949). Differing opinions and preferences are ascribed so far as possible to the GI's age, marital status, educational level, location of residence, length of service, and the like. What remains is ascribed to "attitude." By this procedure personality becomes an appendage to demography (see G. W. Allport, 1950). It is not the integrated structure within the skin that determines behavior, but membership in a group, the person's assigned roles —in short, the prevailing situation. It is especially the sociologists and anthropologists who have this preference for explanations in terms of the "outside structure" rather than the "inside structure" (cf. F. H. Allport, 1955, Ch. 21).

I have mentioned only a few of the many varieties of situationism that flourish today. While not denying any of the evidence adduced I would point to their common error of interpretation. If a child is a hellion at home, an angel outside, he obviously has two contradictory tendencies in his nature, or perhaps a deeper genotype that would explain the opposing phenotypes. If in studies of person perception the process turns out to be complex and subtle, still there would be no perception at all unless there were something out there to perceive and to judge. If, as in Stouffer's studies, soldiers' opinions vary with their marital status or length of service, these opinions are still their own. The fact that my age, sex, social status help form my outlook on life does not change the fact that the outlook is a functioning part of me. Demography deals with distal forces— personality study with proximal forces. The fact that the innkeeper's behavior varies according to whether he is, or is not, physically confronted with Chinese applicants for hospitality tells nothing about his attitude structure, except that it is complex, and that several attitudes may converge into a given act of behavior.

Nor does it solve the problem to explain the variance in terms of statistical interaction effects. Whatever tendencies exist reside in a person, for a person is the sole possessor of the energy that leads to action. Admittedly different situations elicit differing tendencies from my repertoire. I do not perspire except in the heat, nor shiver except in the cold; but the outside temperature is not the mechanism of perspiring or shivering. My capacities and my tendencies lie within.

To the situationist I concede that our theory of traits cannot be so simpleminded as it once was. We are now challenged to untangle the complex web of tendencies that constitute a person, however contradictory they may seem to be when activated differentially in various situations.

ON THE OTHER HAND

In spite of gunfire from positivism and situationism, traits are still very much alive. Gibson (1941) has pointed out that the "concept of set or attitude is nearly universal in psychological thinking." And in an important but neglected paper—perhaps the last he ever wrote—McDougall (1937) argued that *tendencies* are the "indispensable postulates of all psychology." The concept of *trait* falls into this genre. As Walker (1964) says trait, however else defined, always connotes an enduring tendency of some sort. It is the structural counterpart of such functional concepts as "expectancy," and "goal-directedness."

After facing all the difficulties of situational and mood variations, also many of the methodological hazards such as response set, halo, and social desirability, Vernon (1964) concludes, "We could go a long way towards predicting behavior if we could assess these stable features in which people differ from one another [p. 181]." The powerful contributions of Thurstone, Guilford, Cattell, and Eysenck, based on factor analysis, agree that the search for traits should provide eventually a satisfactory taxonomy of personality and of its hierarchical structure. The witness of these and other thoughtful writers helps us withstand the pessimistic attacks of positivism and situationism.

It is clear that I am using "trait" as a generic term, to cover all the "permanent possibilities for action" of a generalized order. Traits are cortical, subcortical, or postural dispositions having the capacity to gate or guide specific phasic reactions. It is only the phasic aspect that is visible; the tonic is carried somehow in the still mysterious realm of neurodynamic structure. Traits, as I am here using the term, include long-range sets and attitudes, as well as such variables as "perceptual response dispositions," "personal constructs," and "cognitive styles."

Unlike McClelland (1951) I myself would regard traits (i.e., some traits) as motivatonal (others being merely stylistic). I would also insist that traits may be studied at two levels: (*a*) dimensionally, that is as an aspect of the psychology of individual differences, and (*b*) individually, in terms of *personal dispositions*. (Cf. G. W. Allport, 1961, Ch. 15.) It is the latter approach that brings us closest to the person we are studying.

As for factors, I regard them as a mixed blessing. In the investigations I shall soon report, factorial analysis, I find, has proved both helpful and unhelpful. My principal question is whether the factorial unit is idiomatic enough to reflect the structure of personality as the clinician, the counselor, or the man in the street apprehends it. Or are factorial dimensions screened so extensively and so widely attenuated—through item selection, correlation, axis manipulation, homogenization, and alphabetical labeling—that they impose an artifact of method upon the personal neural network as it exists in nature?

REFERENCES

Allport, F. H. *Theories of perception and the concept of structure.* New York: Wiley, 1955.
Allport, G. W. What is a trait of personality? *Journal of Abnormal and Social Psychology,* 1931, 25, 368–372.
Allport, G. W. Review of S. A. Stouffer et al., *The American soldier. Journal of Abnormal and Social Psychology,* 1950, 45, 168–172.
Allport, G. W. *Pattern and growth in personality.* New York: Holt, Rinehart and Winston, 1961.

Block, J., & Bennett, Lillian. The assessment of communication. *Human Relations,* 1955, *8* 317–325.

Carr, H. A., & Kingsbury, F. A. The concept of trait. *Psychological Review*, 1938, *45*, 497–524.

Gibson, J. J. A critical review of the concept of set in contemporary experimental psychology. *Psychological Bulletin*, 1941, *38*, 781–817.

Helson, H. *Adaptation-level theory.* New York: Harper & Row, 1964.

Hunt, J. McV. Traditional personality theory in the light of recent evidence. *American Scientist*, 1965, *53*, 80–96.

La Piere, R. Attitudes vs. actions. *Social Forces*, 1934, 230–237.

McClelland, D. C. *Personality.* New York: Holt, Rinehart and Winston, 1951.

McDougall, W. Tendencies as indispensable postulates of all psychology. In *Proceedings of the XI International Congress on Psychology: 1937.* Paris: Alcan, 1938. Pp. 157–170.

Miller, D. R. The study of social relationships: Situation identity, and social interaction. In S. Koch (Ed.), *Psychology: A study of a science.* Vol. 5. *The process areas, the person, and some applied fields: Their place in psychology and the social sciences.* New York: McGraw-Hill, 1963. Pp. 639–737.

Skinner, B. F. *Science and human behavior.* New York: Macmillan, 1953.

Stouffer, S. A., et al. *The American soldier.* Princeton, N.J.: Princeton University Press, 1949. 2 vols.

Vernon, P. E. *Personality assessment: A critical survey.* London: Methuen, 1964.

Walker, E. L. Psychological complexity as a basis for a theory of motivation and choice. In D. Levin (Ed.), *Nebraska symposium on motivation: 1964.* Lincoln, Neb.: University of Nebraska Press, 1964.

2.3 | ON PERSONALITY*

J. P. Guilford

The definition of personality adopted for use . . . starts logically from an axiom to which everyone seems agreed: each and every personality is unique. This statement includes identical twins, for it is possible to find differences even in pairs of such individuals. A person cannot be unique without differing from others. He is, of course, similar in some

* SOURCE: Guilford, J. P. *Personality.* New York: McGraw-Hill, 1959. Pp. 5–6, abridged. Copyright 1959 by McGraw-Hill Book Company. Reprinted by permission of McGraw-Hill Book Company.

respects. But considering his whole pattern of characteristics, he is different from all others. It is in individual differences, then, that we find the logical key to personality, and we shall find later that it is also a most useful, operational key. *An individual's personality,* then, *is his unique pattern of traits.*

TRAITS

This definition of personality is essentially in the integrative class. However, it has the advantage of not attempting to say what kinds of things are integrated. Instead, it uses the general term "trait," which must now be defined. We shall do so by indirect steps.

The definition of personality emphasizes individual differences. This means that we can best know personalities by comparing them with one another. There are no absolute standards for personalities; there are only other personalities from which our frames of reference must be derived. Comparisons of personalities must therefore be made.

It is humanly impossible for us to compare one "person-as-a-whole" with another "person-as-a-whole." The act of comparison is an analytical process. In fact, the act of observation of a single person is an analytical process, as is the act of observing anything. Things, including persons, are known by their properties. An object is round, or sharp, or hard, or all of these things. A person is observed to react promptly, or vigorously, or accurately, or in all of these ways. Properties are abstractions that come by way of analysis from totalities. Our abstraction of a property from a totality does not destroy the totality; it remains the same unitary object it was before. No one can therefore truthfully claim that his abstractions, however numerous, have exhausted the object or will ever completely account for it. But this is not sufficient reason for refusing to analyze. We can extend our observations and thus approach complete coverage of the totality if we have the patience to do so.

Comparisons of individuals are thus commonly made in terms of one aspect at a time, or at least in a limited number of aspects. Persons A and B differ in aspects c, d, e, f, j, and so on; persons X and Y differ in aspects d, f, g, j, m, and t, and so on. More often, our comparisons are between a person Q and the norms (typical qualities) for the population of which Q is a member.

The aspects or properties that we have just been considering are *traits. A trait is any distinguishable, relatively enduring way in which one individual differs from others.* "Trait" is thus a very broad, general term. A trait of personality may be as inclusive as a general attitude of self-confidence or as narrow as a specific habit, such as a conditioned muscular contraction in response to a sound. A trait may be a characteristic indicated by behavior, as in the two examples just given, or of physical make-up. The former is a behavior trait, the latter a somatic trait.

2.4 | EXTRAVERSION-INTROVERSION*

Carl G. Jung

Extraversion means an outward-turning of the libido (*q.v.*). With this concept I denote a manifest relatedness of subject to object in the sense of a positive movement of subjective interest towards the object. Everyone in the state of extraversion thinks, feels, and acts in relation to the object, and moreover in a direct and clearly observable fashion, so that no doubt can exist about his positive dependence upon the object. In a sense, therefore, extraversion is an outgoing transference of interest from the subject to the object. If it is an intellectual extraversion, the subject thinks himself into the object; if a feeling extraversion, then the subject feels himself into the object. The state of extraversion means a strong, if not exclusive, determination by the object. One should speak of an *active* extraversion when deliberately willed, and of a *passive* extraversion when the object compels it, *i.e.* attracts the interest of the subject of its own accord, even against the latter's intention. Should the state of extraversion become habitual, the *extraverted type* (*v.* Type) appears.

Introversion means a turning inwards of the libido (*q.v.*), whereby a negative relation of subject to object is expressed. Interest does not move towards the object, but recedes towards the subject. Everyone whose attitude is introverted thinks, feels, and acts in a way that clearly demonstrates that the subject is the chief factor of motivation while the object at most receives only a secondary value. Introversion may possess either a a more intellectual or more emotional character, just as it can be characterized by either intuition or sensation. Introversion is *active*, when the subject *wills* a certain seclusion in face of the object; it is *passive* when the subject is unable to restore again to the object the libido which is streaming back from it. When introversion is habitual, one speaks of an *introverted type* (*v.* Type).

* SOURCE: Jung, C. G. *Psychological types.* New York: Harcourt Brace & Co., Inc., 1924, pp. 542–543 and p. 567. Reprinted by permission.

2.5 | A DIMENSIONAL SYSTEM OF DIAGNOSIS*

H. J. Eysenck

We must now turn to . . . [the application of factor analysis] in the wider field of the psychotic and neurotic disorders in general, and to a discussion of the main changes in our thinking which are required when we give up the psychiatric notion of the classical syndromes as *disease entities* and accept instead the factor-analytic notion of *dimensions of personality*. An example may illustrate the difference, as well as the relation between the two notions. The concept of *hysteria* as a disease entity, analogous to tuberculosis . . . implies: (i) a single "cause" responsible for the symptoms observed, (ii) a homogeneity of all persons so diagnosed which sets them off qualitatively from all persons not so diagnosed, and (iii) a specific cure applicable to this "disease." The concept of hysteria in dimensional terms is illustrated in Fig. 1; this Figure summarizes research data. . . . According to this diagram, normal and abnormal subjects are distributed with respect to behaviour and test performance over a two-dimensional continuum or factor space. One of the two continua or factors is called "neuroticism," the other "extraversion-introversion." A person who is high on neuroticism and high on extraversion will show a distinct tendency to be labelled "hysteric" or "psychopath" by an examining psychiatrist, while a person who is high on neuroticism and high on introversion will more likely be labelled "anxiety state" or "reactive depressive." The group of introverted neurotic symptoms has been labelled *dysthymia* by the writer . . . A person high on neuroticism and intermediate with respect to extraversion-introversion is most likely to be labelled "mixed neurosis." An operational definition would, of course, be required of the dimensions involved. . . .

The differences between this model and the psychiatric one will be obvious. Instead of a variable number of disease entities, differing from psychiatrist to psychiatrist, and diagnosed only with low reliability, we have two dimensions along which every person can be ranged and given a numerical score. *Continuity* is thus substituted for *discontinuity*, and *measurement* for *discrete classification*. The large number of neurotics which on the existing scheme of classification turn out to combine features from several diagnostic categories, or have to be lumped together as "mixed" in their symptomatology, are accommodated as easily in the dimensional scheme as are the "typical" but rare hysterics and dysthymics. Lastly, the scheme implies testable relations between hysterics and psychopaths, on the one hand, and normal extraverts on the other; or between anxi-

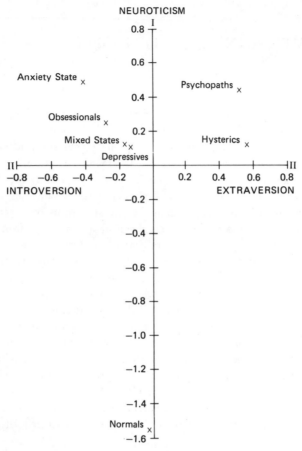

Figure 1 | POSITION OF ONE NORMAL AND SIX NEUROTIC GROUPS IN TWO-DIMENSIONAL FRAMEWORK DETERMINED BY CANONICAL VARIATE ANALYSIS OF OBJECTIVE TEST PERFORMANCES.

ety states and reactive depressives, on the one hand, and normal introverts on the other. Shifts from one diagnosis to another, which should not occur on the hypothesis of discrete disease entities, are easily accommodated in the dimensional scheme if the facts demonstrate shifts along one dimension or the other in the course of time, or as the consequence of specific experimental or therapeutic manipulation. Indeed . . . personality theories can be elaborated which predict such shifts on the basis of drug administration, brain operation, and other variables. The advantages of the dimensional system are considerable, and it may be noted that few psychiatrists are in fact willing to defend the old "disease entity" conception except in terms of its historical usefulness. Its early demise will be of considerable help in clearing the field and disabusing the minds of research workers of outmoded and erroneous notions.

2.6 | PERSONALITY DIMENSIONS*

H. J. Eysenck and S. Rachman

Assuming, then, for the moment that the concept of personality may have some scientific value, we may go on to search for the main dimensions of personality in the hope that these may be related to different types of neurotic behaviour. . . . We may also hope that the discovery of these main dimensions of personality will help us in the problem of *nosology*, or classification of neurotic disorders. Classification is an absolutely fundamental part of the scientific study of human personality; a satisfactory typology is as necessary in psychology as was Mendeleyeff's Table of the Elements in physics. This has, of course, always been recognized by psychologists, and almost everyone is acquainted with the famous typological classification into melancholics, cholerics, sanguines, and phlegmatics dating back to Galen and even earlier. As this system still has much to teach us, we will present it here as Figure 1; it immediately confronts us with one of the main problems of

* SOURCE: Eysenck, H. J., and Rachman, S. *The causes and cures of neurosis.* San Diego, Calif.: Robert R. Knapp, 1965. Pp. 15–20, abridged. Reprinted by permission.

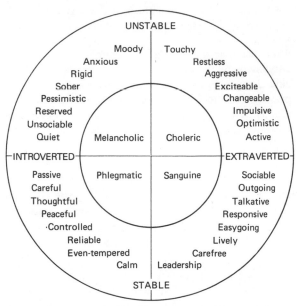

Figure 1 | THE INNER RING SHOWS THE "FOUR TEMPERAMENTS" OF HIPPOCRATES AND GALEN; THE OUTER RING SHOWS THE RESULTS OF MODERN FACTOR ANALYTIC STUDIES OF THE INTERCORRELATIONS BETWEEN TRAITS BY GUILFORD, CATTELL, EYSENCK, AND OTHERS.

classification. The first of these may be phrased in terms of the question: "Categorical or dimensional?" The famous German philosopher, Immanuel Kant, to whom this system owed much of its popularity during the last two hundred years, was quite specific in maintaining the categorical point of view, i.e., the notion that every person could be assigned to a particular category; he was a melancholic, or a phlegmatic, or a sanguine, or a choleric, but any mixtures of admixtures were inadmissible. This notion of categories is, of course similar to the psychiatric notion of disease entities and their corresponding diagnoses; hysteria, anxiety state, paranoia, obsessional illness, and so on are often treated as categorical entities in this sense.

Opposed to this notion, we have the view that any particular position in this two-dimensional framework is due to a combination of quantitative variations along the two continua labelled "introversion-extraversion" and "stable-unstable." Wundt (1903), who is the most notable proponent of Galen's system in modern times, favoured the dimensional view; he labelled the one axis "slow-quick" instead of introversion-extraversion, and the other "strong-weak" instead of unstable and stable.

It may be interesting to quote Wundt's very modern-sounding discussion:—

> The ancient differentiation into four temperaments . . . arose from acute psychological observation of individual differences between people . . . The fourfold division can be justified if we agree to postulate two principles in the individual reactivity of the affects: one of them refers to the *strength*, the other to the *speed of change* of a person's feelings. Cholerics and melancholics are inclined to strong affects, while sanguinists and phlegmatics are characterized by weak ones. A high rate of change is found in sanguinists and cholerics, a slow rate in melancholics and phlegmatics.
>
> It is well-known that the strong temperaments . . . are predestined towards the *Unluststimmungen*, while the weak ones show a happier ability to enjoy life . . . The two quickly changeable temperaments . . . are more susceptible to the impressions of the present; their mobility makes them respond to each new idea. The two slower temperaments, on the other hand, are more concerned with the future; failing to respond to each chance impression, they take time to pursue their own ideas. (pp. 637–638).

There is no reason to believe that the notion of the *typology* presupposes a categorical system; both Jung and Kretschmer, who were probably the best-known typologists of the inter-war period, postulated a dimensional rather than a categorical system. The widespread notion that typologies implied discontinuities, bimodal distributions, and the like does not accurately represent the writings and views of modern typologists (Eysenck, 1960).

Most writers on the subject of personality come down in favour of either the categorical or the dimensional point of view, without basing themselves on any experimental demonstration. It is, however, not impossible to devise experimental and statistical means for verifying the one and falsifying the other hypothesis. Eysenck (1950) has tried to do this in terms of the method of *criterion analysis*, which relies on separate factor analyses of intercorrelations between tests administered to two or more criterion groups (say, normals and psychotics), and a comparison of the factors emerging with the criterion column derived by biserial correlation between the tests and the criterion. The results of this method have, in every instance, supported the doctrine of continuity, and failed to support the doctrine of categorization, even when the latter seemed most firmly entrenched, as in the case of psychosis (Eysenck, 1952).

Assuming for the moment, therefore, the doctrine of dimensionality, we are required to build up, on an experimental and statistical basis, a quantitative system of personality description (Eysenck, Eysenck and Claridge, 1960). The most widely used tool for this purpose is, of course, factor analysis, and the main results of the application of this tool are shown in Figure 1. The outer ring in this Figure shows the results of a large number of factor analytic studies of questionnaires and ratings (Eysenck, 1960)....

Terms such as extraversion and introversion are used in our discussion in a sense strictly derived from empirical studies such as mentioned above; they should not be taken as having the same meaning here as they do in Jung's discussion. Jung, who is often erroneously credited with originating these terms which had been in use on the continent of Europe for several hundred years before he wrote his famous book on psychological types, has put forward a very complicated scheme of personality description; there would be no point in criticizing his scheme here. We merely wish to point out that our own use of these terms must stand and fall by empirical confirmation, and owes more to the work of factor analysts and early experimentalists like Heymans and Wiersma, than to Jung and his followers (Eysenck, 1960). A brief description of typical extreme extraverts and introverts may be useful at this point, to show the reader precisely what we mean by these terms.

The typical extravert is sociable, likes parties, has many friends, needs to have people to talk to, and does not like reading or studying by himself. He craves excitement, takes chances, often sticks his neck out, acts on the spur of the moment, and is generally an impulsive individual. He is fond of practical jokes, always has a ready answer, and generally likes change; he is carefree, easygoing, optimistic, and "likes to laugh and be merry." He prefers to keep moving and doing things, tends to be aggressive and loses his temper quickly; altogether his feelings are not kept under tight control, and he is not always a reliable person.

The typical introvert is a quiet, retiring sort of person, introspective, fond of books rather than people; he is reserved and distant except to intimate friends. He tends to plan ahead, "looks before he leaps," and mistrusts the impulse of the moment. He does not like excitement, takes matters of everyday life with proper seriousness, and likes a well-ordered mode of life. He keeps his feelings under close control, seldom behaves in an aggressive manner, and does not lose his temper easily. He is reliable, somewhat pessimistic and places great value on ethical standards.

These descriptions, of course, sound almost like caricatures because they describe, as it were, the "perfect" extravert and the "perfect" introvert; needless to say, few people closely resemble these extremes, and the majority of people undoubtedly are somewhat in the middle. This does not necessarily detract from the importance of these typological concepts, just as little as the fact that 50 per cent of the total population have IQs of between 90 and 110 detracts from the importance of intelligence as a concept in psychology.

It is perhaps less necessary to give a detailed description of the typology implicit in the second major dimension of personality shown in Figure 1. We have there labelled the one end "unstable"; this has often in the past been called a factor of *emotionality* or of *neuroticism*, and these terms adequately designate its meaning. At the one end we have people whose emotions are labile, strong, and easily aroused; they are moody, touchy, anxious, restless, and so forth. At the other extreme we have the people whose emotions are stable, less easily aroused, people who are calm, even-tempered, carefree, and reliable. Neurotics, needless to say, would be expected to have characteristics typical of the unstable type, normal persons typical of the stable type.

REFERENCES

Eysenck, H. J. Criterion analysis—an application of the hypothetico-deductive method to factor analysis. *Psychological Review*, 1950, *57*, 38–53.

Eysenck, H. J. *The scientific study of personality.* London: Routledge, 1952.

Eysenck, H. J. *The structure of human personality.* New York: Macmillan, 1960.

Eysenck, S. B. G., Eysenck, H. J., & Claridge, G. Dimensions of personality, psychiatric syndromes and mathematical models. *Journal of Mental Science*, 1960, *106*, 581–589.

Wundt, W. *Grundzuge der Physiologischen Psychologie.* Leipzig: W. Engelmann, 5th Ed., 1903.

3 | Trait Approaches to Assessment—I

3.1 | A PERSONALITY SCALE OF MANIFEST ANXIETY*

Janet A. Taylor

A series of recent studies (Lucas, 1952; Peck, 1950; Spence & Taylor, 1951; Taylor, 1951; Taylor & Spence, 1952; Wenar, 1950; Wesley, 1950) has shown that performance in a number of experimental situations ranging from simple conditioning and reaction time to a "therapy" situation involving experimentally induced stress, is related to the level of anxiety as revealed on a test of manifest anxiety. Most of these investigations were concerned with the role of drive or motivation in performance, drive level being varied by means of selection of subjects on the basis of extreme scores made on an anxiety scale rather than by experimental manipulation (e.g., electric shock, stress-producing instructions, etc.). The use of the anxiety scale in this connection was based on two assumptions: first, that variation in drive level of the individual is related to the level of internal anxiety or emotionality, and second, that the intensity of this anxiety could be ascertained by a paper and pencil test consisting of items describing what have been called overt or manifest symptoms of this state.

Since the scale has proved to be such a useful device in the selection of subjects for experimental purposes, a description of the construction of the test and the normative data that have been accumulated in connection with it may be of interest to other investigators in the field of human motivation.

* SOURCE: Taylor, J. A. A personality scale of manifest anxiety. *Journal of Abnormal and Social Psychology*, 1953, 48, 285–290. Copyright 1953 by the American Psychological Association and reprinted by permission.

DEVELOPMENT OF THE SCALE

The manifest anxiety scale was originally constructed by Taylor (1951) for use in a study of eyelid conditioning. Approximately 200 items from the Minnesota Multiphasic Personality Inventory were submitted to five clinicians, along with a definition of manifest anxiety that followed Cameron's (1947) description of chronic anxiety reactions. The judges were asked to designate the items indicative of manifest anxiety according to the definition. Sixty-five items on which there was 80 per cent agreement or better were selected for the anxiety scale. These 65 statements, supplemented by 135 additional "buffer" items uniformly classified by the judges as nonindicative of anxiety, were administered in group form to 352 students in a course in introductory psychology. The measures ranged from a low anxiety score of one to a high score of 36, with a median of approximately 14. The form of the distribution was slightly skewed in the direction of high anxiety.

Subsequently, the scale went through several modifications.[1] At present it consists of 50 of the original 65 items that showed a high correlation with the total anxiety scores in the original group tested. Furthermore, the buffer items have been changed so that the total test, which has been lengthened from 200 to 225 items, includes most of the items from the L, K, and F scales of the MMPI and 41 items that represent a rigidity scale developed by Wesley (1950). The 50 anxiety items are reproduced in Table 1, along with the responses to these items considered as "anxious" and the ordinal numbers of the statements as they appear in the present form of the test.

NORMATIVE DATA. Under the innocuous title of *Biographical Inventory*, the test in its present form has been administered to a total of 1,971 students in introductory psychology at the State University of Iowa during five successive semesters from September, 1948 to June, 1951. The distribution for this sample is presented in Fig. 1. As can be seen by inspection, the distribution shows a slight positive skew, as did the original scale. The fiftieth percentile falls at about 13, the eightieth at about 21, and the twentieth at about 7. The mean of the distribution is 14.56.

SEX DIFFERENCES. A comparison of the scores of males and females in this total sample revealed that the mean score of the women was somewhat higher. The difference between the two means however was not statistically significant. For this reason, both sexes have been included in a single distribution.

DIFFERENT POPULATIONS. Scores on the scale are also available for samples drawn from somewhat different populations. Distributions for 683 airmen tested at the beginning of basic training at Lackland Air Force Base and for 201 Northwestern University night-school students of introductory psychology show essentially the same form as the group reported above, while the quartiles are in close agreement.

[1] Hedlund, J. L., Farber, I. E., & Bechtoldt, H. P. Normative characteristics of the Manifest Anxiety Scale. Unpublished paper. The statistical analysis, along with most of the data collected with the scale, was carried out under the direction of H. P. Bechtoldt at the State University of Iowa.

Table 1 | ITEMS INCLUDED ON THE MANIFEST ANXIETY SCALE AND RESPONSES SCORED AS "ANXIOUS" ITEMS ARE NUMBERED AS THEY APPEAR IN THE COMPLETE BIOGRAPHICAL INVENTORY

4. I do not tire quickly. (False)
5. I am troubled by attacks of nausea.[a] (True)
7. I believe I am no more nervous than most others.[a] (False)
11. I have very few headaches. (False)
13. I work under a great deal of tension.[a] (True)
14. I cannot keep my mind on one thing. (True)
16. I worry over money and business. (True)
18. I frequently notice my hand shakes when I try to do something. (True)
24. I blush no more often than others.[a] (False)
25. I have diarrhea once a month or more.[a] (True)
26. I worry quite a bit over possible misfortunes.[a] (True)
27. I practically never blush. (False)
33. I am often afraid that I am going to blush. (True)
35. I have nightmares every few nights. (True)
36. My hands and feet are usually warm enough. (False)
37. I sweat very easily even on cool days. (True)
38. Sometimes when embarrassed, I break out in a sweat which annoys me greatly.[a] (True)
41. I hardly ever notice my heart pounding and I am seldom short of breath.[a] (False)
43. I feel hungry almost all the time. (True)
44. I am very seldom troubled by constipation.[a] (False)
48. I have a great deal of stomach trouble. (True)
51. I have had periods in which I lost sleep over worry.[a] (True)
54. My sleep is fitful and disturbed.[a] (True)
56. I dream frequently about things that are best kept to myself.[a] (True)
66. I am easily embarrassed. (True)

67. I am more sensitive than most other people.[a] (True)
77. I frequently find myself worrying about something.[a] (True)
82. I wish I could be as happy as others seem to be.[a] (True)
83. I am usually calm and not easily upset. (False)
86. I cry easily. (True)
87. I feel anxiety about something or someone almost all the time.[a] (True)
94. I am happy most of the time. (False)
99. It makes me nervous to have to wait. (True)
100. I have periods of such great restlessness that I cannot sit long in a chair.[a] (True)
103. Sometimes I become so excited that I find it hard to get to sleep. (True)
107. I have sometimes felt that difficulties were piling up so high that I could not overcome them.[a] (True)
112. I must admit that I have at times been worried beyond reason over something that really did not matter.[a] (True)
117. I have very few fears compared to my friends.[a] (False)
123. I have been afraid of things or people that I know could not hurt me. (True)
136. I certainly feel useless at times. (True)
138. I find it hard to keep my mind on a task or job. (True)
145. I am unusually self-conscious.[a] (True)
152. I am inclined to take things hard.[a] (True)
153. I am a high-strung person.[a] (True)
163. Life is a strain for me much of the time.[a] (True)
164. At times I think I am no good at all. (True)
168. I am certainly lacking in self-confidence.[a] (True)
183. I sometimes feel that I am about to go to pieces.[a] (True)
187. I shrink from facing a crisis or difficulty.[a] (True)
190. I am entirely self-confident.[a] (False)

[a] Statements rewritten for subsequent revision.

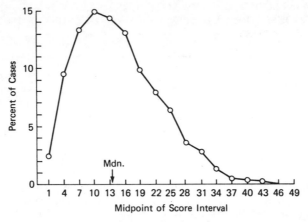

Figure 1 | FREQUENCY POLYGON SHOWING PER CENT OF THE 1,971 UNIVERSITY STUDENTS RECEIVING THE INDICATED SCORES ON THE MANIFEST ANXIETY SCALE.

CONSISTENCY OF SCORES.   In order to determine the stability of the anxiety scores over time, groups of individuals have been retested on the scale after various intervals. In one instance, the results of retesting 59 students in introductory psychology after a lapse of three weeks yielded a Pearson product-moment coefficient of .89. In a second test-retest study,[2] the scale was given to 163 students in an advanced undergraduate psychology course who had previously taken the test as introductory students. For 113 of these cases 5 months had elapsed since the first testing, while an interval of 9–17 months had intervened for the remaining 50. The test-retest coefficient was found to be .82 over 5 months and .81 for the longer period. Furthermore, no systematic change, upwards or downwards, was found in these distributions, i.e., the means of each of the three sets of scores remained essentially the same after retesting. Thus, for all groups tested, both the relative position of the individual in the group and his absolute score tended to remain constant over relatively long periods of time.

RELATIONSHIP OF THE BIOGRAPHICAL INVENTORY TO THE MMPI. Since it might be desired to obtain anxiety scores for individuals who have been given the complete MMPI rather than the Biographical Inventory, it is necessary to consider the effects of the different sets of filler items on the 50 anxiety statements. There is some evidence[3] to suggest that the distribution of anxiety scores given in the form of the MMPI will differ significantly from that obtained from the Biographical Inventory. The Biographical Inventory was administered to 282 freshmen males, and approximately 18 weeks later the group MMPI was given to the same students. The correlation between the two sets of measures, obtained by determining the scores on the 50 anxiety items

[2] See footnote 1.
[3] See footnote 1.

on each test, was .68. This, it will be noted, is a slightly lower figure than that obtained by test-retest on the Inventory after a comparable length of time. In addition, the forms of the distributions were statistically different, as indicated by a chi-square test of homogeneity. Since the initial scores of this group, obtained from the Biographical Inventory, were similar to those found with other groups, the discrepancy of the results between the Inventory and the MMPI suggests that the radical change in filler items may exert a definite influence on the anxiety scores. Before anxiety scores obtained from the MMPI can be evaluated it would appear to be necessary to have more normative data concerning the scale scores obtained from this form.

REVISION OF THE SCALE

A further revision of the scale is now being carried out by the writer. This variation represents an attempt to simplify the vocabulary and sentence structure of some of the anxiety items that appear to be difficult to comprehend, especially for a noncollege population. Toward this end, the 50 anxiety items were first submitted to 15 judges who were instructed to sort them into four piles according to comprehensibility, the first position representing the simplest to understand and the fourth the most difficult. It was found that 28 of the items had a mean scale value of 2.00 or more. These 28 items were selected for revision and rewritten in at least two alternate forms.[4] Each set of alternatives was then ranked by a different set of 18 judges, first for ease of understanding and then for faithfulness of meaning to the original statement. For most of the items, the alternative judged to be simplest was also chosen as being closest in meaning to the original item and was therefore selected for the new scale. For those items in which a discrepancy occurred, faithfulness of meaning was chosen over simplicity. However, in every case, the new statement selected for inclusion on the scale was judged simpler than the original. These 28 rewritten items are shown in Table 2.

RELATIONSHIP BETWEEN THE OLD AND NEW VERSIONS OF THE SCALE.   To demonstrate the relationship between the old and new versions of the test, both forms were administered to students in introductory psychology at Northwestern University College. A sample was selected from the college population for this purpose since it was thought that this group would show the least confusion in interpreting the original versions of the difficult items and, therefore, better demonstrate the comparability of the two forms than less verbally sophisticated individuals. Scores obtained from 59 students showed a Pearson product-moment correlation of .85 between the old and new versions, the latter being administered three weeks after the initial testing. This figure is quite comparable to the test-retest coefficient found for the previous form of the scale after a similar time interval. Considering only the 28 rewritten items, the correlation becomes .80.

[4] In rewriting the items, the Thorndike (1941) word count was consulted. These counts primarily determined substitution of words within an item whenever this was done.

Table 2 | THE 28 ITEMS REWRITTEN FOR THE REVISED FORM OF THE MANIFEST ANXIETY SCALE AND RESPONSES SCORED AS "ANXIOUS"

(Items are numbered as they appear in the Biographical Inventory.)

---

5. I am often sick to my stomach. (True)

7. I am about as nervous as other people. (False)

13. I work under a great deal of strain. (True)

24. I blush as often as others. (False)

25. I have diarrhea ("the runs") once a month or more. (True)

26. I worry quite a bit over possible troubles. (True)

38. When embarrassed I often break out in a sweat which is very annoying. (True)

41. I do not often notice my heart pounding and I am seldom short of breath. (False)

44. Often my bowels don't move for several days at a time. (True)

51. At times I lose sleep over worry. (True)

54. My sleep is restless and disturbed. (True)

56. I often dream about things I don't like to tell other people. (True)

67. My feelings are hurt easier than most people. (True)

77. I often find myself worrying about something. (True)

82. I wish I could be as happy as others. (True)

87. I feel anxious about something or someone almost all of the time. (True)

100. At times I am so restless that I cannot sit in a chair for very long. (True)

107. I have often felt that I faced so many difficulties I could not overcome them. (True)

112. At times I have been worried beyond reason about something that really did not matter. (True)

117. I do not have as many fears as my friends. (False)

145. I am more self-conscious than most people. (True)

152. I am the kind of person who takes things hard. (True)

153. I am a very nervous person. (True)

163. Life is often a strain for me. (True)

168. I am not at all confident of myself. (True)

183. At times I feel that I am going to crack up. (True)

187. I don't like to face a difficulty or make an important decision. (True)

190. I am very confident of myself. (False)

While the correlation coefficient shows the high degree of relationship between the old and revised forms, the question still remains as to whether rewriting the 28 items has reduced the difficulty level of these statements so as to minimize confusion and misinterpretation. In an attempt to determine this, the scores of the 59 students given both versions were analyzed into two components: that for the 28 difficult items and that for the 22 items left intact. For each form, scores on the 28 items were correlated with the remaining 22. It was reasoned that if the original forms of the 28 items were confusing, then the rewritten items, if attempts to simplify were successful, would show a higher correlation with the 22 items left intact than would the original statements. The actual correlations obtained in this manner were .81 for the old version and .83 for the new. Although the difference between the coefficients was in the desired direction, a *t* test indicated that it was statistically insignificant. However, a significant difference in correlations might be obtained with subjects of lesser educational attainment since misinterpretation of the 28 original items would be more likely to occur with such a group.

NORMATIVE CHARACTERISTIC OF THE NEW SCALE.   To determine further characteristics of the distribution of scores on the new version, 229 students in introductory psychology were given only the revised form of the scale (Ahana, 1952). It was found that the shape of the distribution and the values of the quartiles did not differ significantly from those obtained with the previous form.

Retest scores are also available for 179 individuals from the sample described above. A product-moment correlation of .88 was found after an intertest interval of four weeks. However, while the position of the individuals in the group tended to remain the same, a downward shift in the absolute scores of the entire distribution was noted from the test to retest. The difference between means (14.94 vs. 12.92) was significant at the .01 level of confidence, as indicated by a *t* test.

RELATIONSHIP OF THE ANXIETY SCALE TO OTHER MEASURES

The anxiety scale was developed for, and has been used exclusively as, a device for selecting experimental subjects, without regard to the relationship of the scores to more common clinical definitions (e.g., clinical observation). While defining degree of anxiety in terms of the anxiety-scale scores is a perfectly legitimate operational procedure, determining the relationship between this definition and clinical judgments might extend the applicability of both the scale and the experimental results found in the studies utilizing the scale.

In order to determine the relationship between the scale and clinical judgments, it would be necessary to have ratings made by trained observers for a large, randomly selected group of individuals and to correlate these with the anxiety-scale scores. Such an investigation has not yet been carried out. However, some indirect evidence on this point is provided by the anxiety scores of patients undergoing psychiatric treatment.[5] The anxiety scale used with these pateints is essentially the same as the unrevised Biographical Inventory except that it is being administered in an individual form.

Anxiety scores are available for 103 neurotic and psychotic individuals, drawn from both an in- and outpatient population. As can be seen from Fig. 2, the distribution of scores is highly skewed toward the low anxiety end of the scale. The median score is approximately 34, a score equivalent to the 98.8 percentile of the normal subjects shown in Fig. 1. Thus the distributions of scores for the patient and the normal group are markedly different.

On the assumption that psychiatric patients will tend to exhibit more manifest anxiety symptoms (as determined by direct observation) than do normal individuals, this difference between the two groups appears to indicate that there is some relationship between the anxiety-scale scores and clinical observation of manifest anxiety.

---

[5] These data are obtained from a study currently being conducted by the writer and K. W. Spence investigating the role of anxiety in neurotic and psychotic disorders by means of an eyelid conditioning technique.

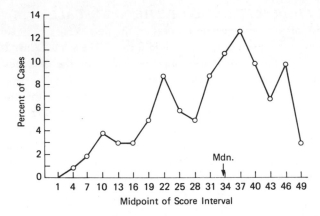

Figure 2 | GRAPH OF THE FREQUENCY DISTRIBUTION OF MANIFEST ANXIETY SCORES RECEIVED BY 103 PSYCHIATRIC PATIENTS.

SUMMARY

A manifest anxiety scale, consisting of items drawn from the Minnesota Multiphasic Personality Inventory judged by clinicians to be indicative of manifest anxiety, was developed as a device for selecting subjects for experiments in human motivation.

After statistical analysis the original 65-item scale was reduced to the 50 most discriminating statements. These items, supplemented by 225 statements nonindicative of anxiety, are given under the title of the Biographical Inventory. Normative data and test-retest correlations found with scale scores taken from the Biographical Inventory are presented.

A further revision of the scale was undertaken in which certain items were rewritten in an attempt to simplify their vocabulary and sentence structure. Characteristics of the scores obtained from this revised version were found to be similar to those of the previous form.

In an attempt to determine the relationship between the anxiety-scale scores and manifest anxiety as defined and observed by the clinician, the anxiety scores for groups of normal individuals and psychiatric patients were compared.

REFERENCES

Ahana, Ellen. A study on the reliability and internal consistency of a manifest anxiety scale. Unpublished master's thesis, Northwestern University, 1952.

Cameron, N. *The psychology of behavior disorders: a bio-social interpretation.* Boston: Houghton Mifflin, 1947.

Lucas, J. D. The interactive effects of anxiety, failure, and intraserial duplication. *Amer. J. Psychol.*, 1952, 65, 59–66.

Peck, Ruth. The influence of anxiety upon effectiveness of counseling. Unpublished doctor's dissertation, State University of Iowa, 1950.

Spence, K. W., & Taylor, Janet. Anxiety and strength of the UCS as determiners of the amount of eyelid conditioning. *J. exp. Psychol.*, 1951, *42*, 183–188.

Taylor, Janet A. The relationship of anxiety to the conditioned eyelid response. *J. exp. Psychol.*, 1951, *41*, 81–92.

Taylor, Janet A., & Spence, K. W. The relationship of anxiety to performance in serial learning. *J. exp. Psychol.*, 1952, *44*, 61–64.

Thorndike, E. L., & Lorge, I. *Teacher's word book of 20,000 words.* New York: Teachers College, 1941.

Wenar, C. Reaction time as a function of manifest anxiety and stimulus intensity. Unpublished doctor's dissertation, State University of Iowa, 1950.

Wesley, Elizabeth L. Perseverative behavior in a concept formation task. Unpublished doctor's dissertation, State University of Iowa, 1950.

3.2 | A UNIVERSAL CONCEPTION OF PERSONALITY STRUCTURE?* [1]

Frank T. Passini and Warren T. Norman

Previous analyses of peer-nomination data obtained using scales drawn from the Cattell Personality Sphere set have yielded a recurrent, highly stable five-factor structure. These results, reported by Tupes and Christal (1958, 1961) and by Norman (1963), were based on samples of subjects who had been exposed to one another in a variety of interpersonal situations over periods of time varying from as long as 3 years in some of the later studies to as short as 3 days in some of the earlier ones.

The interpretations given for these results and the implications drawn from them hinged on at least one basic assumption—*that the structure obtained reflected the*

* SOURCE: Passini, F. T., and Norman, W. T. A universal conception of personality structure? *Journal of Personality and Social Psychology*, 1966, 4, 44–49. Copyright 1966 by the American Psychological Association and reprinted by permission.

[1] This study was supported in part by Research Grant MH-07195-02, from the National Institute of Mental Health, United States Public Health Service, Warren T. Norman, project director.

organization of these attributes in the ratees. In particular it was assumed and argued by Norman (1963, p. 581) that these results were not, to any appreciable extent, simply a function of the method of data collection and analysis nor of the perceptual-cognitive organization *of the raters.*

The possibility that the data might have been based on random nominations was precluded both by variances on each of the several scales in excess of that which could be attributed to such a random process and by the very articulated character of the correlational matrices which yielded the recurrent factor structures. Nor, it was argued, could any explanation based on a single general determinant as "prestige," "likability," or whatever, have accounted for such a differentiated pattern of correlations of such a multifactor orthogonal structure.

The possibility that these results reflected primarily characteristics of the raters' (rather than of the ratees') psychological makeup also seemed unlikely. First, the instructions focused attention of the raters on attributes of the ratees. Second, scores for each ratee on each scale resulted from combining the independent judgments of several raters, thereby ruling out substantial contributions based on unique dyadic relationships or prior interactions. And finally, the fact that the data themselves required a five-dimensional, orthogonal structure to account for their communality made it "hard to imagine what sorts of alternative mechanisms [i.e., other than reasonably veridical perceptions of the ratees' attributes] could have produced the degree of differentiated consensus necessary to generate these results [Norman, 1963, p. 581]."

Nonetheless it was at least somewhat astonishing that such a clearly articulated, multidimensional structure could evolve on the basis of but 3 days of interpersonal interaction and observation. And it was no less amazing that longer periods of contact, extending to upwards of 3 years, resulted only in the most minor variations in this total structure. Indeed, in one of the early studies by Fiske (1949), even ratings by professional psychologists of persons they had observed intensively, if only briefly, yielded essentially the same factor structure, and this despite a number of procedural differences in data collection and analysis.

But if the structures obtained in these analyses reflected veridical judgments of the status of the ratees and the perceived complexity of these structures by the raters, then why did additional amounts of intimate interpersonal interaction or greater sophistication of the raters not result in more differentiated factor structures? And even more critically, the question of how brief and superficial a set of contacts was sufficient to produce this structure had been left unanswered. In particular, if this structure could be obtained from groups of subjects (raters and ratees) with virtually no opportunity for prior interaction or observation, then the inference that the previously obtained results veridically reflected attributes of the ratees would certainly be questionable.

The present study was thus undertaken to test whether subjects with virtually no opportunity to observe and interact with one another would produce mutual peer nominations on the scales used in the prior studies that would yield the structure recurrently obtained in the previous analyses. More explicitly, it was hypothesized that the same five-factor structure which had emerged in the previous studies would not be obtained when subjects were given no opportunity for prior interaction.

METHOD

SUBJECTS.   The subjects for this study were 84 University of Michigan undergraduates who were enrolled in an introductory experimental psychology course. The subjects were grouped on the basis of the lack of prior acquaintance and homogeneously by sex. The minimum number of individuals used in any one rating group was six and the largest was nine. These constraints yielded a total sample composed of 21 males and 63 females.

PROCEDURE.   The peer-nomination rating scales used in this study were identical with those used by Norman (1963). Each rating group was administered the scales with the same instructions used in the previous studies with but two exceptions. The first exception was the addition of a short introduction which was designed to explain briefly the task and the pedagogical value of the study since it was being conducted as an integral part of the course during the first regular class meeting of each section. Second, in view of the fact that we were asking subjects to rate their fellow students on personality scales when their contact had been limited to no more than being in the same room for less than 15 minutes without opportunity for verbal communication, the instructions used by Norman were modified by inserting the phrase "you would imagine" in the appropriate spots. The task was made plausible to the subjects by telling them that these data were needed to establish a base line for comparing results obtained from other samples of subjects who were better acquainted with one another. The experimenter ensured that there had been no prior contact among any members of the rating groups, and no verbal communication among the subjects was allowed until the ratings had been completed. It may be worth noting that at the University of Michigan, with its large undergraduate population, it was not at all difficult to find sections of introductory courses in which none of the students had ever seen one another before.

The administrative instructions required each rater to nominate one third of his group on Pole A and one third on Pole B of each scale, excluding himself (or herself) in each instance. Abbreviated descriptions of the rating scales used together with suggested names for the factors they represent and scoring procedures utilized are described in a previous report (Norman, 1963). In brief, the implementation of this study followed as closely as possible that used in the prior investigations to achieve maximum comparability.

The rating-scale scores were intercorrelated, squared multiple correlation estimates of communalities were obtained, and a factor analysis was carried out analytically using a principle axis method of factoring and a normalized varimax rotation procedure. The computer program was set to extract 100% of the common factor variance, but no specification of the number of factors to be extracted was given. For analysis the data from both the male and female groups were pooled and analyzed as one sample.

RESULTS

Table 1 presents the abbreviated factor matrix for Sample P based on this study together with the communality value for each scale. At the bottom of the table the per-

Table 1 | ABBREVIATED FACTOR MATRICES FROM THE PRESENT STUDY AND THE NORMAN (1963) STUDY[a]

SCALE	IP	IC	ID	IIP	IIC	IID	IIIP	IIIC	IIID	IVP	IVC	IVD	VP	VC	VD	bP^2	bC^2	bD^2
1	**80**	**90**	**90**													73	81	82
2	**67**	**78**	**79**													68	62	65
3	**67**	**79**	**79**				−32									81	79	73
4	**85**	**86**	**90**				−42									83	77	83
5	−30			**67**	**80**	**85**				37	32	30				53	72	78
6		33	−37	**65**	**64**	**72**					49	40				56	70	73
7	46			**70**	**80**	**79**										60	80	80
8				**67**	**74**	**73**										68	76	65
9		−33	−45	57	32	57	**72**	**66**	**43**		−35	−31			34	55	70	60
10				57	44	55	**61**	**86**	**42**						41	78	89	74
11		−30	−53	36		39	**55**	**68**	**37**							76	79	80
12			−31			45	**63**	**74**	**33**						45	73	72	57
13				51	56					**50**	**61**	**58**				56	70	58
14										**77**	**82**	**81**				65	73	70
15										**61**	**71**	**71**				47	60	60
16						30	−33			**58**	**65**	**65**				58	55	54
17	54			36				39					**71**	**75**	**60**	56	73	48
18						32	32	47	41	30			**69**	**74**	**84**	66	78	73
19								53					**20**	**46**	**56**	64	60	61
20													**72**	**68**	**70**	53	52	56
Percentage of variance	26	23	29	25	22	27	17	22	07	17	18	18	15	15	19			

[a] Sample P is from the present study. Samples C and D are from Norman (1963). Decimal points omitted for factor loadings and communalities. All values rounded to two significant digits. Loadings for a priori salients in boldface type. Principal axes solutions with normalized varimax rotations. Non-a-priori loadings <.30 omitted.

centage of common factor variance attributable to each factor is presented. The bold-face type indicates the loadings of a priori salients on that factor. To facilitate comparison, Table 1 also presents abbreviated versions of the factor matrices for two samples, C and D, from the previous study (Norman, 1963). In all matrices presented in Table 1 only loadings of .30 or greater for non-a-priori salients are entered.

It is apparent from these data that the factor structure that emerges when subjects are rating complete strangers is highly similar to that obtained from raters who had had considerable prior contact with one another. If we first consider the loadings on the a priori salients, it can be seen that although they tend to be lower in Sample P than in C they are still quite highly similar. The similarity is even greater between Sample P and Sample D. Turning our attention to the non-a-priori salients with loadings greater than .30, Sample P has two more such occurrences than does Sample C but three less than Sample D. Furthermore, it should be noted that of the 14 non-a-priori salients loading in Sample P, 5 of these are shared in common with both of the other two samples and 3 more are shared with one of the others.

If we consider now the communalities for Sample P, we see that, although they tend to be somewhat lower than those for Sample C, they are quite comparable to those for Sample D. Looking at the relative percentages of common variance accounted for by each factor there is again in Sample P no evidence for a large general factor and a fair degree of comparability across studies, except perhaps for Factor III in Sample D.

There is, however, one feature in which the present study is not directly comparable to the other two; that is, the sample in the present study was composed largely of female subjects. In order to see if this sex difference was a significant variable it was decided to compare these results with the relevant portion of the Tupes and Christal (1961) analysis of the Cattell study of 240 college females. Table 2 presents an abbreviated factor matrix for the first five factors from those data, with only those scales being presented which correspond to the scales used in the present study. From a comparison of Table 2 with Table 1 we see that again the factor structures are highly similar, with Sample P having one fewer aberrant loading than occurs in the Cattell data. The one thing which happened in the present study which was not evidenced in any of the other analyses was that the common factor variance for Scale 19 (polished, refined versus crude, boorish) distributed in a most peculiar fashion over all five factors.

DISCUSSION

In their 1958 report, Tupes and Christal conclude, "The results of these analyses clearly indicate that differences in samples, situations, and *length of acquaintanceship* [italics added] seem to have little effect on the factor structure underlying ratings of personality traits." The results of the present study go considerably beyond this. They indicate that this structure can be obtained in the *virtual absence of prior acquaintanceship*, and in a situation in which only the most superficial and restricted sort of observation of one another is permitted.

Table 2 | ABBREVIATED FACTOR MATRIX FROM THE TUPES AND CHRISTAL ANALYSIS OF CATTELL'S FEMALE DATA[a]

NORMAN SCALE	CATTELL SCALE	FACTOR					h^{2b}
		I	II	III	IV	V	
1	14	**81**					88
2	28	**71**					68
3	16	**69**		—48			85
4	29	**69**		—31			81
5	10		**80**				79
6	20		**80**				74
7	13		**84**				88
8	1	36	**62**				76
9	18			**74**			72
10	4		42	**59**		48	79
11	25		60	**33**		34	81
12	15			**70**		45	85
13	6				**69**	39	79
14	24				**81**		79
15	11	—45	38		**54**		78
16	12		42		**51**		64
17	27					**28**	56
18	8					**85**	89
19	19			32		**49**	86
20	34			—53	—40	**18**	70

[a] Decimal points omitted for factor loadings and communalities. All values rounded to two significant digits. Loadings for a priori salients in boldface type. Principle axes solutions with normalized varimax rotations. Non-a-priori loadings <.30 omitted.

[b] Communalities based on 12 rotated factors. Scales 17 and 19 loaded .62 and .54, respectively, on a sixth factor but no scale loaded as high as .30 on any of the remaining 6 factors.

In brief, the facts appear to be these. First, the raters in the present study could not possibly have had direct knowledge of the relative status of the ratees on such attributes as sociable-reclusive, cooperative-negativistic, responsible-undependable, etc. Second, when asked to rate these virtual strangers on such variables, they complied, managing somehow to arrive at the required number of choices on each scale. Third, when scored and analyzed, these nominations reflected a degree of interrater agreement on each scale and a structured pattern of interscale relationships that was highly similar to those obtained from groups of intimate acquaintances in previous studies.

Thus, all that was available to the raters was whatever they carried in their heads concerning the way and the degree to which personality traits are organized in people generally plus whatever observations they could make of the appearance and behavior of the others in their group in this highly restricted situation. How then are we to account for these results? To this question we can at present offer only a conjecture, but one which to us has some plausibility and which is, at least in part, testable.

Suppose that in the course of observing and interacting with other persons one normally develops what Cronbach (1958) termed an "implicit personality theory." That is, by whatever combination of mechanisms, people eventually and normally build up, however implicitly, a notion of the relative frequencies of joint occurrences of various personality attributes and behavioral dispositions in other persons. Let us assume further that, despite idiosyncratic differences that exist in these conceptual systems, they contain a certain core set of syndromes that is more or less common to most people of similar background. That is, we are assuming that a sizable proportion of persons tend to believe in common and for whatever reasons that certain clusters of attributes occur jointly in other persons with probability greater than .5 and that attributes in one such cluster are believed to occur more or less independently of those which form other clusters. And if we assume finally that certain phenotypic aspects of dress, demeanor, physical size, movement, and the like are incorporated into these syndromal stereotypes, we have at least a potential basis for an explanation of the results of the present study.

That is, if we accept the position that each rater brings to the situation an implicit personality theory which in certain aspects is similar to that of the other persons in the group and if observable features of the dress and manner of the participants are sufficient to provide an entree to one or more components of each of these common attribute clusters, then the interrater agreement and factorial structure obtained in the present study begins to seem a little less incredible.

If, however, these easily observable characteristics are but tenuously related to the central attributes of the several syndromes, then relations between self-appraisals on these core attributes and peer ratings on them should be lower for strangers than for persons more intimately acquainted with one another. Fortunately, some data relevant to this latter implication were available for comparison.

From a study by Norman and Bradford (1964), a heteromethod-heterotrait matrix based on these same scales for a sample of 182 fraternity men who had lived together with one another for a year or more was available. Using the criteria for "discriminant validity" proposed by Campbell and Fiske (1959), the data from the present study yielded a "validity diagonal" (self-ratings versus peer ratings) whose entries were exceeded in magnitude in 37.5% of the monomethod-heterotrait and heteromethod-heterotrait comparisons, while the "validities" for the subjects who were well known to one another were exceeded in only 10% of these comparisons.[2]

Thus for subjects with a history of interpersonal acquaintanceship, there exists a greater degree of correspondence between peer ratings of status on these attributes and self-ratings on these same scales than exists for relative strangers.

It would appear, then, that persons who have only the most superficial informa-

---

[2] Comparisons were made in terms of median values for blocks of a priori salients for each factor in each study. If the "validities" had been exceeded for 50% of the interblock comparisons, a chance level of heteromethod-monotrait relationship (i.e., "validity") would have been indicated.

tion about one another can draw upon their more-or-less comparable prior experiences and whatever easily observable cues are available to them to yield peer-rating structures that are highly similar to those obtained from subjects who are intimately acquainted with one another. But only in the latter sorts of groups will the peer ratings agree to any marked extent with self-appraisals.

At least three major questions, however, have been left totally unanswered by these analyses. To what degree can the set of cues available in the peer-rating situation be impoverished and yet have the ratings yield the recurrent five-factor structure for these scales? What is the basis upon which raters arrive at nearly consensual judgments of the status of near-strangers on these scales? By what means do peer ratings and self-ratings on these scales move from near unrelatedness to at least moderate alignment with increased acquaintanceship and how long does such movement take? Further research aimed at obtaining answers to these questions is sorely needed.

SUMMARY

The question was posed and tested whether Ss with no prior acquaintanceship nor any opportunity to interact with one another could, on the basis of only brief and superficial observations of physical appearance and manner, produce mutual nominations on a set of personality scales which would generate a factor structure similar to that obtained recurrently in prior studies which had employed samples of intimate associates. 84 university students who were unknown to one another made nominations on the same scales and under the same instructions used in the previous studies. The factor structure obtained from these data was highly similar to that found in the prior analyses. Self-ratings on these scales, however, were found to be virtually unrelated to the corresponding peer-nomination measures for this sample, whereas a moderately high degree of convergence had been found for a sample of close acquaintances in another study. A tentative explanation hinging on Cronbach's notion of an implicit personality theory was posed, and several additional studies prompted by these results were suggested.

REFERENCES

Campbell, D. T., & Fiske, D. W. Convergent and discriminant validation by the multitrait-multimethod matrix. *Psychological Bulletin*, 1959, 56, 81–105.

Cronbach, L. J. Proposals leading to analytic treatment of social perception scores. In R. Tagiuri & L. Petrullo (Eds.), *Person perception and interpersonal behavior.* Stanford, Calif.: Stanford University Press, 1958. Pp. 351–379.

Fiske, D. W. Factorial structures of personality ratings from different sources. *Journal of Abnormal and Social Psychology*, 1949, 44, 329–344.

Norman, W. T. Toward an adequate taxonomy of personality attributes: Replicated factor structure in peer nomination personality ratings. *Journal of Abnormal and Social Psychology*, 1963, 66, 574–583.

Norman, W. T., & Bradford, E. F. Heteromethod factor analyses of personality variables. Paper read at the Psychometric Society, Niagara Falls, Ontario, October 10, 1964.

Tupes, E. C., & Christal, R. E. Stability of personality trait rating factors obtained under diverse conditions, *USAF WADC Technical Note*, 1958, No. 58-61.

Tupes, E. C., & Christal, R. E. Recurrent personality factors based on trait ratings. *USAF ASD Technical Report*, 1961, No. 61-67.

3.3 | STUDENT ACCEPTANCE OF GENERALIZED PERSONALITY INTERPRETATIONS*

Roger E. Ulrich, Thomas J. Stachnik, and N. Ransdell Stainton

Previous investigators (Carter, 1963) have been concerned with how individuals react to personality interpretations which are based on information obtained from personality tests. Since "virtually every psychological trait can be observed to some degree in everyone" (Forer, 1949), it is possible that such interpretations may be given in terms so general that they could apply to almost anyone. The following study was conducted in an attempt to discover the degree of acceptance of vague, generalized personality interpretations, presumably derived from personality tests, and to determine whether the "prestige" of the person making the interpretation is related to acceptance.

PROCEDURE

Two experiments were performed involving 136 students from three educational psychology classes plus 79 other Ss. In the first experiment ($N = 57$), the instructor of the class administered both the Bell Adjustment Inventory and the House-Tree-Person (HTP) test. The students were told by the instructor that he would score and interpret each of their tests and return the interpretations to them at a later date. About a week later each student was given an interpretation with his or her name on it. All interpretations returned were identical, but the statements were arranged in a different order. The students were then asked to read and think about the interpretations carefully and to rate them as follows:

A. Rate the interpretation of your personality according to the following scale: I feel that the interpretation was:
    Excellent Good Average Poor Very Poor
B. Please make any additional comments about the test interpretation that you feel would be appropriate.

* SOURCE: Ulrich, R. E., Stachnik, T. J. and Stainton, N. R. Student acceptance of generalized personality interpretation. *Psychological Reports*, 1963, *13*, 831–834. Copyright 1963 by Southern Universities Press and reprinted by permission.

In the second experiment members of two classes (total $N = 79$) were given instructions for administering the tests to one other person, e.g., a roommate, neighbor, etc. Both the tests and the personality interpretations were the same as those used in Exp. I. The students were not to reveal to their Ss that they were part of an experiment. They were simply to state that they were studying personality testing and needed an S for practice. Ss were to be given the tests, and several days later they were to be given the interpretation. Ss were then to be instructed to rate the interpretation. The method of rating was similar to that of the first experiment.

The following interpretation, adapted from Forer (1949, p. 120), was used in both experiments.

You have a strong need for other people to like you and for them to admire you. You have a tendency to be critical of yourself. You have a great deal of unused capacity which you have not turned to your advantage. While you have some personality weaknesses, you are generally able to compensate for them. Your sexual adjustment has presented some problems for you. Disciplined and controlled on the outside, you tend to be worrisome and insecure inside. At times you have serious doubts as to whether you have made the right decision or done the right thing. You prefer a certain amount of change and variety and become dissatisfied when hemmed in by restrictions and limitations. You pride yourself as being an independent thinker and do not accept others' opinions without satisfactory proof. You had found it unwise to be too frank in revealing yourself to others. At times you are extroverted, affable, sociable, while at other times you are introverted, wary, and reserved. Some of your aspirations tend to be pretty unrealistic.

RESULTS

It is evident from the data that Ss for the most part accepted the interpretations. Table 1 shows the students' ratings of the test interpretation for the first experiment. Fifty-three of the 57 students rated the interpretation as good or excellent. Row 2 gives the students' ratings of the test interpretations for the second experiment. Fifty-nine of the 79 students rated the interpretation as good or excellent in spite of the fact that these interpretations were given by admittedly inexperienced students! Chi-square tests significant at the .001 level indicate that in both experiments the ratings given the interpretations were higher than chance expectancy.

Table 1 | RATINGS OF PERSONALITY INTERPRETATIONS

TOTAL	EXCELLENT	GOOD	AVERAGE	POOR	VERY POOR
Psychologist's Interpretations					
57	27	26	3	1	0
Student's Interpretations					
79	29	30	15	5	0

Other data obtained were the comments of Ss concerning the validity as well as the helpfulness of the interpretation. Several examples were chosen which are indicative of the opinions and reactions of the majority of Ss. The following statements were taken directly from the students' papers.

1. I feel that you have done a fine job with the material which you had to work with. I agree with almost all your statements and think they answer the problems I may have.
2. On the nose! Very good. I wish you had said more, but what you did mention was all true without a doubt. I wish you could go further into this personality sometime.
3. The results have brought out several points which have worried me because I was not sure if I had imagined these to be personality traits of mine. Tests like this could be valuable to an individual in helping him to solve some of his own problems.
4. I believe this interpretation applies to me individually, as there are too many facets which fit me too well to be a generalization.
5. The interpretation is surprisingly accurate and specific in description. I shall take note of many of the things said.
6. I feel that the interpretation does apply to me individually. For the first time things that I have been vaguely aware of have been put into concise and constructive statements which I would like to use as a plan for improving myself.
7. It appears to me that the results of this test are unbelievably close to the truth. For a short test of this type, I was expecting large generalizations for results, but this was not the case; and I give all the credit to the examiner whose conclusions were well calculated.

The first three statements were written by the group of Ss who were given the test and interpretation by a professional psychologist. The last four statements were written by those Ss given the test and interpretation by students. These results indicate not only that Ss were "taken in" by the interpretation, but also that Ss were very likely to praise highly the examiner on his conclusions.

DISCUSSION

The principal finding is that the majority of the people tested accepted a personality interpretation stated in general terms as an accurate description of their own personalities without being aware that the same interpretation could be applied to almost anyone.

A previous study (Forer, 1949) demonstrated the same phenomenon and suggested that the probability of acceptance of the interpretation was increased when it was made by a prestigeful person, i.e., a psychologist. However, in the present study the interpretations made by inexperienced students were as readily accepted as those made by a professional psychologist. The mean ratings given the student and psychologist interpretations were 4.05 and 4.38, respectively ($t = .21$, n.s.). This in part indicates the awe with which personality tests *per se* are viewed by the naive student or others of comparable test sophistication.

Furthermore, the fact that some of the students did praise the interpretation demonstrates that individuals accepting a general interpretation as an accurate description of their personality are very likely to praise the examiner. It has been noted that approval can serve as a reinforcement (Skinner, 1953), thereby increasing the probability that the approved behavior will recur. It thus follows that in a counseling setting such reinforcement might cause the examiner to continue to make this type of vague, general interpretation. When the counselor has given a test and is interpreting its results, general statements used by him are perhaps reinforced by statements of praise similar to those observed in the present experiment, although neither the client nor the counselor is capable of verbalizing the contingency which has caused such a situation to occur.

REFERENCES

Carter, N. Need correlates of gullibility. *Journal of Abnormal and Social Psychology*, 1963, *66*, 84–87.

Forer, B. R. The fallacy of personal validation: A classroom demonstration of gullibility. *Journal of Abnormal and Social Psychology*, 1949, *44*, 118–123.

Skinner, B. F. *Science and human behavior.* New York: Macmillan, 1953.

3.4 | RECOMMENDATIONS FOR APA TEST STANDARDS REGARDING CONSTRUCT, TRAIT, OR DISCRIMINANT VALIDITY*

Donald T. Campbell

SUGGESTED ADDITIONS TO THE RECOMMENDED EVIDENCES OF VALIDITY

Upon the basis of psychology's experience, more exhaustively assembled and discussed elsewhere . . . the following additions to the *Technical Recommendations* in the category of construct validity are suggested:

1. *Correlation with intelligence tests.* A new test, no matter what its content, should be correlated with an intelligence test of as similar format as possible (e.g., a

* SOURCE: Campbell, D. T. Recommendations for APA test standards regarding construct, trait, or discriminant validity. *American Psychologist*, 1960, *15*, 546–553, abridged and edited. Copyright 1960 by the American Psychological Association and reprinted by permission.

group intelligence test for a group personality test, etc.). If correlations are reported with independent trait-appropriate or criterion measures, it should be demonstrated that the new test correlates better with these measures than does the intelligence test.

This requirement is already somewhat recognized. Some test manuals for empathy and for personality traits report low correlations with intelligence as evidence favorable to validity. One major challenge to the validity of the F Scale, for example, is its high correlation with intelligence and the fact that its correlations with ethnocentrism, social class, conformity, and leadership are correlations previously demonstrated for test intelligence (e.g., Christie, 1954).

2. *Correlations with social desirability.* A new test of the voluntary self-descriptive sort should be correlated with some measure of the very general response tendency of describing oneself in a favorable light no matter what the trait-specific content of the items. If correlations are reported with trait-appropriate or criterion measures, then it should be demonstrated that the new test predicts these measures better than does the general social desirability factor. In lieu of this, construction features designed to eliminate the social desirability factor should be specified, as in the forced choice pairing of items previously equated on social desirability. Edwards (1957) reviews the evidence necessitating this requirement.

3. *Correlations with measures of acquiescence and other response sets.* Tests of the voluntary self-description type employing responses with multiple levels of endorsement (e.g., L-D-I, A-a-?-d-D, etc.) should report correlations with external measures of acquiescence response set and other likely response sets. For check lists, the correlation with general frequency of checking items independent of content should be reported. It should be demonstrated that the tests predict trait-appropriate or criterion measures better than do the response set scores. In lieu of this, it should be demonstrated that the test construction and scoring procedures are such as to prevent response sets from being confounded with trait-specific content in the total score, as through the use of items worded in opposite directions in equal numbers, etc. Cronbach (1946, 1950) and others (e.g., Chapman & Bock, 1958) have illustrated the extent to which extant tests have in fact produced scores predominantly a function of such trait-irrelevant sources of variance. (This is not to rule out the deliberate utilization of response-set variance, where the intent to do so is made explicit.)

4. *Self-description and stereotype keys for interpersonal perceptual accuracy tests.* Measures of empathy, interpersonal perception, social competence, and the like should compare the results of efforts to replicate the scores of particular social targets with the use of self-descriptions and stereotype scores as predictors; or such scores should be based upon competence in differentiating among social targets rather than upon the absolute discrepancy in predictions for a single social target. Gage, Leavitt, and Stone (1956) and Cronbach (1958) have described how misleading scores can be without such checks. Similarly, *Q* type correlations offered as validity data should be accompanied by control correlations based upon random matches, as in the manner of Corsini (1956) and Silverman (1959).

5. *Validity correlations higher than those for self-ratings.* Advocates of personality tests implicitly or explicitly claim that their scores are better measures (in some situa-

tions at least) than much quicker and more direct approaches such as simple self-ratings. While correlations with self-rating may in some circumstances be validating, it should also be demonstrated that the test scores predict independent trait-appropriate or criterion measures better than do self-ratings. The available evidence (as sampled, for example, by Campbell and Fiske, 1959) shows that this may only rarely be the case.

6. *Multitrait-multimethod matrix.* The demonstration of discriminant validity and the examination of the strength of method factors require a validational setting containing not only two or more methods of measuring a given trait, but also the measurement of two or more traits. This requirement is implicit in several of the points above and has been present in the range of validational evidence used in our field from the beginning (e.g., Symonds, 1931). It is frequently convenient to examine such evidence through a multitrait-multimethod matrix. Particularly does this seem desirable whare the test publisher offers a multiple-score test or a set of tests in a uniform battery. Achievement and ability tests need this fully as much as do personality tests. A detailed argument for this requirement is presented elsewhere (Campbell & Fiske, 1959).

REFERENCES

Campbell, D. T., & Fiske, D. W. Convergent and discriminant validation by the multitrait-multimethod matrix. *Psychological Bulletin*, 1959, 56, 81–105.

Chapman, L. J., & Bock, R. D. Components of variance due to acquiescence and content in the F Scale measure of authoritarianism. *Psychological Bulletin*, 1958, 55, 328–333.

Christie, R. Authoritarianism reexamined. In R. Christie & M. Jahoda (Eds.), *Studies in the scope and the method of the authoritarian personality.* New York: Free Press, 1954. Pp. 123–196.

Corsini, R. J. Understanding and similarity in marriage. *Journal of Abnormal and Social Psychology*, 1956, 52, 327–332.

Cronbach, L. J. Response sets and test validity. *Educational and Psychological Measurement*, 1946, 6, 475–494.

Cronbach, L. J. Further evidence on response sets and test design. *Educational and Psychological Measurement*, 1950, 10, 3–31.

Cronbach, L. J. Proposals leading to analytic treatment of social perception scores. In R. Tagiuri & L. Petrullo (Eds.), *Person perception and interpersonal behavior.* Stanford, Calif.: Stanford University Press, 1958. Pp. 353–379.

Edwards, A. L. *The social desirability variable in personality assessment and research.* New York: Holt, Rinehart and Winston, 1957.

Gage, N. L., Leavitt, G. S., & Stone, G. C. The intermediary key in the analysis of interpersonal perception. *Psychological Bulletin*, 1956, 53, 258–266.

Silverman, L. H. A Q-sort study of the validity of evaluations made from projective techniques. *Psychological Monographs,* 1959, 73 (7, Whole No. 477).

Symonds, P. M. *Diagnosing personality and conduct.* New York: Appleton, 1931.

4 | Trait Approaches to Assessment—II

4.1 | GENERALIZABILITY OF CONTRIBUTIONS FROM SOURCES OF VARIANCE IN THE S-R INVENTORIES OF ANXIOUSNESS*, [1]

Norman S. Endler and J. McV. Hunt

For nearly half a century, anxiety has been a focal matter in psychological theorizing. Anxiety began to take on focal status in the twenty-fifth of Freud's (1917) introductory lectures, even though in the fourth of his new introductory lectures (Freud, 1932) he relinquished his theory of its origin in frustration or "undischarged libidinal excitation" in favor of a theory in which he saw anxiety originating from punishment of the infant in the form of castration threats. Anxiety got full focal status in the theory of acquired drive (see Hull, 1943; Miller & Dollard, 1941). Nevertheless, the conceptual nature of anxiety has been confused. It has been viewed sometimes as a reaction to situations in which the person has encountered pain (Freud, 1932; Hull, 1943; Miller & Dollard, 1941). It has been viewed sometimes as a state of the organism which varies from occasion to occasion (Cattell & Scheier, 1961; Spielberger, 1966a). It has been viewed also as a chronic characteristic of persons which is relatively constant across both situations and occasions, and this view has been implicit for most of those who have constructed instruments for assessing individual differences in anxiousness as a trait (see Cattell, 1957; Hathaway & Meehl, 1951; Mandler & Sarason, 1952;

* SOURCE: Endler, N. S., and Hunt, J. McV. Sources of behavioral variance as measured by the S-R inventory of anxiousness. *Psychological Bulletin*, 1966, 65, 336–346. Copyright 1966 by the American Psychological Association and reprinted by permission.

[1] This study was supported in part by grants from the United States Public Health Service Nos. MH-08987 and MH-K6-18567, and in part by grants from York University, Toronto, from the Canada Council, and from the Research Board of the University of Illinois. The assistance of Kelly Hsia and Cheryl Schlafer with respect to some of the statistical analyses is gratefully acknowledged. We also wish to thank the many students who participated in this study, and the teachers, professors, and administrators of the participating institutions for their cooperation and assistance.

Taylor, 1953). Moreover, the distinction between situationally evoked reactions or states of anxiety and a common trait of anxiousness has been a special case in the debate over whether variability in behavior is more a matter of situational determinants, commonly held by those social psychological theorists (e.g., Cottrell, 1942a, 1942b; Dewey & Humber, 1951) who have taken their lead from George Herbert Mead (1934), or more a matter of personality traits, commonly held by both clinicians and personalogists (e.g., Cattell, 1946, 1950; Cattell & Scheier, 1961).

It was this issue of the relative importance of individual differences and of situations which originally led to the idea of constructing S-R Inventories of Traits (see Endler, Hunt, & Rosenstein, 1962). These S-R Inventories are distinctive because they separate explicitly described *situations* from the *modes of response* which serve as indicators of the reaction, state, or trait in the format. They thereby permit investigators to sample separately the situations, the modes of response, and the subjects, and they also permit them to partition the total variance in the responses or reports of responses among these main sources and their interactions.

On the basis of the results from the original form of the S-R Inventory of Anxiousness, Endler and Hunt (1966) found that neither individual differences nor situations contributed substantially, as main sources, more than about 4 to 6 per cent of the total variance (components sum) in the reported modes of response indicating anxiety. The modes of response themselves contributed of the order of 25 per cent of the variance. Nearly a third of the variance came from the simple interactions (subjects with situations: about 10 per cent; subjects with modes of response: about 11 per cent; and situations with modes of response: about 7 or 8 per cent). These findings helped to explain the traditionally low (.20 to .25) validity coefficients for omnibus inventories of anxiety. They suggested that validity coefficients might well be raised substantially by specifying the particular situations in which the response indicators of anxiety are reported by subjects on inventories and in which the subjects are to be observed. They also suggested that personality diagnosis and description might generally be improved by specifying the kinds of responses that persons make in various kinds of situations.

The results from which these fairly radical suggestions derive were based upon but the original, single form of the S-R Inventory of Anxiousness (Form O). This form contains a sample of 11 situations and a sample of 14 modes of response. The results reported came from but three samples of college students. In view of these limitations in sampling, the generalizability of the results for even the single trait of anxiousness may be questioned.

The purpose of the investigation reported here has been to determine to what extent the proportion of variance for subjects holds for still other samples of subjects, to what extent the proportion of variance from situations holds for other samples of situations, and to what extent the proportion of variance from modes of response holds for other samples of modes of response indicating anxiousness. This investigation, in contrast to the previous ones, moreover, compares the results from men and women separately in order to determine if consistent sex differences exist with respect to the sizes of the proportions of variance contributed by the three main sources and their interactions.

METHOD

The strategy of this investigation has been to construct five new forms of the S-R Inventory of Anxiousness, and to administer the original form and each of these new forms to each of several groups of men and women, or of adolescent boys and girls. In certain forms of the Inventory, the range of threat in the situations was deliberately exaggerated from situations which are typically innocuous ("You are just sitting down to dinner," or "You are undressing for bed") to others highly threatening (e.g., "You are getting up to give a speech before a large group"; "You receive a summons from the police"; "You are driving down the road when you meet two racing cars approaching you abreast") in order to determine how much of this would increase the proportion of variance contributed by situations. Moreover, a list of 125 situations was constructed to constitute a finite population, and several approximations of random samples were selected from this list to test the generality of the original findings. A similar procedure has been employed in sampling modes of response, even though it is not as easy to vary any dimension of anxiousness by choice of response indicators. Individual differences have been extended by sampling subjects of differing age and mental health. For each form of the Inventory with each sample of subjects, we have partitioned the variance derived from a three-way analysis of variance from the various main sources and their interactions by means of the variance components method reported by Gleser, Cronbach, and Rajaratnam (1965), Endler and Jobst (1964), and by Endler (1966). The variances for each source from all of the 43 samples of subjects and for all forms across their respective samples of subjects are presented for comparison in summary fashion as medians, semi-interquartile ranges, and ranges.

THE FORMS OF THE S-R INVENTORY OF ANXIOUSNESS.   The original form of the S-R Inventory of Anxiousness (Form O, consisting of 11 situations and 14 modes of response, totaling 154 items) has been used along with five other quite different forms in the present study. The format for each form provided a page for each of the situations, with the situations described at the top (e.g., "You are about to take the final examination for a course in which your status is doubtful"), and with the modes of response listed below. The subjects reported their various responses on rating scales of five steps which ranged in likelihood or intensity from none to very much. A low score (of one) always indicated the absence of or a very low level of that particular response-indicator of anxiousness; a high score (of five) always indicated the presence of and an intense reaction for that particular response-indicator of anxiousness.

The five new forms were: Form 1-X-62 consisting of 18 situations and 10 modes of response (180 items), Form UI-64-A, Form EY-L-64-A, and Form UI-66-A, each containing 14 situations and 10 modes of response (140 items), and Form SA-66 containing 12 situations and 10 modes of response (120 items).

SELECTION OF SITUATIONS.   In the case of Form O, the choice of the 11 situations was based on an intuitive attempt to select a variety of situations that would be familiar, through either first-hand or vicarious experience, to most college students and which would include both social and nonsocial situations varying from ones regarded typically as innocuous ("You are starting on a long automobile trip") to others typically regarded as very threatening ("You are on a ledge high upon a mountain side") and with most of them regarded as potentially quite threatening.

Since the factor analysis of situations in Form O (Endler, Hunt, & Rosenstein, 1962) had uncovered three kinds of situations (interpersonal danger, inanimate danger, and ambiguous danger), the 18 situations selected for Form 1-X-62 were arbitrarily chosen from a master list of 125 composed from suggestions by ourselves and our colleagues with about equal representation of each kind. The 14 situations in Form UI-64-A were deliberately selected from the master list, now extended to 200 in order to extend the range of danger. At the innocuous end, we added such situations as "sitting down to eat at your favorite restaurant" and "getting ready to go to bed." At the threatening end, we added such situations as "failing examinations," "being approached by cars racing abreast," and "receiving a police summons." This deliberate extension of the range of danger was done, as already noted, to determine the limits of proportion of variance that might come from situations as a single main-source. For the other three forms, the selection moved toward a random sampling of situations from the finite population of the master list of 200. In each case, however, the selection included representatives of each of the three kinds (interpersonal, inanimate, and ambiguous danger). Moreover, for Form EY-L-64-A and Form SA-66 the selection and descriptions of the situations were modified to be appropriate for use with young adolescents. All the others were used with samplings of adults and college students.

SELECTION OF MODES OF RESPONSE. For the original Form O, the 14 modes of response indicating anxiety or fear were chosen to represent both positive and negative reactions to situations because feelings of keen anticipatory excitement are commonly reported from the same situations that evoke excited withdrawal, because Hunt, Cole, and Reis (1958) had found some of their subjects reporting hope where others reported fear, and because both approach and withdrawal reactions incorporating various levels of excitement have been emphasized by Olds (1955) and by Schneirla (1959, 1964). We presumed that excited approach is the obverse of anxiousness. In this original Form O, moreover, the indicator responses were also chosen to sample the subjects' reported perceptions of their physiological reactions (the traditional expressive indicators of emotion) because these would be most amenable to validation via recording of the physiological reactions. Finally, the indicator responses were also chosen to include from the MMPI (Hathaway & Meehl, 1951) some of the items most useful diagnostically in the Taylor Anxiety Scale (Taylor, 1953).

Because the factor analyses of the 14 modes of response in Form O had discovered three kinds (distress, exhilaration, and autonomic reactions), the 10 modes of responses selected for Form 1-X-62, Form UI-64-A, Form EY-L-64-A, and Form UI-66-A always included the three scales with the highest loadings on each of these factor-kinds. Form SA-66 used eight modes from Form O plus two new ones ("hands trembling" and "get fluttering feeling in stomach").

Thus far, we have not yet constructed a master list of modes of response indicating anxiousness or fear. Moreover, we have found ourselves hard put to think of many beyond those already included among the 14 in Form O. Thus, the samples of situations in the various forms have been greatly varied, while the samples of response-indicators have consisted primarily of subsamples of the 14 originally employed in Form O plus the two new ones in Form SA-66.

Table 1 presents a synoptic description of the several forms of the S-R Inventory of Anxiousness with the numbers of situations and the numbers of modes of response in each and with the numbers of samples of men and women who responded for each form.[2]

SUBJECTS.   A total of 43 samples of subjects (22 of males and 21 females) have served in the work reported here. More than one sample of subjects have responded to each form of the Inventory. Except for Form UI-66-A, more than one sample of both males and females have responded to each form, with six samples of each having responded to Form EY-L-64-A and seven samples to the original form, Form O (see Table 1).

The various samples of subjects have been selected to represent not only a wide variation in collegiate populations, but also in ages from adolescence to middle age, and in social classes from upper middle to upper lower, and in mental health from typical samplings of high school and college students to adolescent patients of a mental health clinic. The college students have come from both private and public colleges and universities. They represent a geographical distribution ranging from institutions in the eastern, midwestern, and western portions of the United States and from one province (Ontario) in Canada. These samples also represent adults attending evening colleges in Toronto, adolescents attending both junior and senior high schools, and patients of the East York Mental Health Clinic. An attempt was made to give the original form of the S-R Inven-

[2] A table (Table A) containing all of the situations and modes of response for each and all of the various forms of the S-R Inventory of Anxiousness has been deposited with the NAPS.

Table 1 | SYNOPTIC DESCRIPTION OF THE VARIOUS FORMS OF THE S-R INVENTORY OF ANXIOUSNESS WITH NUMBER OF SITUATIONS, MODES OF RESPONSE, AND NUMBER OF SAMPLES ANALYZED[a]

FORM OF THE S-R INVENTORY	0	1-X-62	UI-64-A	EY-L-64-A	SA-66	UI-66-A
Number of situations	11	18	14	14	12	14
Number of modes of response	14	10	10	10	10	10
Number of male samples	7	3	3	6	2	1
Number of female samples	7	2	3	6	2	1

[a] See footnote 2 for ADI reference for the availability of the situations and modes of response in each of the forms.

Table 2 | NAME, SIZE OF SAMPLE, AND FORM OF S-R INVENTORY OF ANXIOUSNESS ADMINISTERED

NAME OF SAMPLE	FORM OF S-R	NUMBER OF MALES	NUMBER OF FEMALES
Penn State University	O	93	76
Penn State University	O	206	99
Penn State University	O	—	98
Dartmouth College	O	125	—
York University (Toronto)	O	30	23
York University (Toronto)	O	103	46
Forest Hill Collegiate (High School)	O	41	34
University of Illinois	O	53	55
York University	1-X-62	62	49
Atkinson College (evening, adult)	1-X-62	74	77
Atkinson College (evening, adult)	1-X-62	74	—
University of Illinois	UI-64-A	31	37
University of Colorado	UI-64-A	29	41
York University	UI-64-A	81	68
East York Collegiate (High School)	EY-L-64-A	140	95
Westwood Junior High	EY-L-64-A	55	59
St. Clair Junior High	EY-L-64-A	45	51
Oak Park Junior High	EY-L-64-A	58	61
Cosburn Junior High	EY-L-64-A	57	59
East York Mental Health Clinic	EY-L-64-A	49	33
St. Andrews Junior High	SA-66	75	68
St. Andrews Junior High	SA-66	72	74
University of Illinois	UI-66-A	46	71

tory of Anxiousness (Form O) to a sample of 31 psychotic patients of the Toronto Psychiatric Hospital, but interviewers had to fill out the inventory, and the cooperation of the patients was highly uncertain. The results from this sample have not been included among the results reported here. Table 2 presents the name of the institution from which each sample of subjects came, the size of the various samples, and the form of the S-R Inventory administered to each.

RESULTS

CONSISTENCY AMONG PROPORTIONS OF VARIANCE FROM EACH SOURCE. Table 3 presents the medians, semi-interquartile ranges (Q),[3] and the ranges of the variance components and of the percentages of the total variance (compo-

[3] The semi-interquartile range, Q, is the measure of variation most often used in connection with the median, $Q = (Q_3 - Q_1)/2$, where Q_3 and Q_1 are the third and first quartiles (i.e., the 75th and 25th percentiles), respectively. The semi-interquartile range represents one-half of the range of the middle 50 per cent of the observations. In general, the relationship between Q and the median is analogous to the relationship between the mean and the standard deviation. See Edwards (1967, pp. 13–14).

Table 3 | MEDIANS, SEMI-INTERQUARTILE RANGES (Q), AND RANGES OF VARI-ANCE COMPONENTS AND PERCENTAGE OF TOTAL VARIANCE FOR EACH COMPO-NENT SOURCE FOR REPORTED RESPONSE-INDICATORS TO SITUATIONS ON THE VARIOUS FORMS OF THE S-R INVENTORY OF ANXIOUSNESS

	PART A—MALES ($N = 22$ SAMPLES)					
	Median		Q^a		*Range*	
SOURCE	CHI-SQUARE COMPONENT	PCT.	CHI-SQUARE COMPONENT	PCT.	CHI-SQUARE COMPONENTS	PCTS.
Subject (S)	.095	4.44	.024	1.66	.021- .231	0.74- 9.73
Situation (Sit)	.083	3.95	.015	0.77	.049- .369	2.24- 13.66
Mode of Response (M-R)	.594	24.76	.166	4.97	.344-1.084	14.62- 40.13
S x Sit	.193	9.14	.025	1.16	.101- .527	3.74- 22.19
S x M-R	.225	10.34	.039	1.87	.128- .381	4.92- 16.12
Sit x M-R	.157	7.51	.071	2.25	.067- .297	4.05- 12.77
Residual	.746	37.06	.108	3.61	.585-1.082	22.46- 45.92
Total variation (Components sum)	2.285	100.00	.338	0.01	1.607-2.972	99.99-100.00
	PART B—FEMALES ($N = 21$ SAMPLES)					
Subject (S)	.096	4.56	.027	1.15	.047- .183	1.62- 7.58
Situation (Sit)	.182	7.78	.048	1.34	.082- .575	3.14- 19.86
Mode of Response (M-R)	.627	26.61	.348	4.32	.400-1.185	16.53- 45.45
S x Sit	.226	9.31	.033	1.88	.133- .289	4.61- 13.05
S x M-R	.245	11.06	.040	1.80	.172- .370	6.76- 15.20
Sit x M-R	.180	6.95	.071	2.04	.100- .333	4.68- 12.51
Residual	.731	34.33	.146	3.06	.622-1.106	22.93- 41.42
Total variation (Components sum)	2.607	100.00	.336	0.00	1.898-3.012	99.99-100.01

[a] Q is the semi-interquartile range: $Q = (Q_3 - Q_1)/2$.

nents sum) from each component source for the reported response-indicators of anxious-ness for all of the samples responding to each and all of the forms of the S-R Inventory.[4]

An inspection of Table 3 shows that, at least in general, the proportions of total variance reported by Endler and Hunt (1966) from three samples of college students on the original form of the S-R Inventory of Anxiousness are corroborated. Except in the

---

[4] The estimated variance components and percentages of total variation contributed by each component source for each sample of subjects have been deposited as Tables B-I with the American Documentation Institute. The original analysis of variance tables can readily be derived from the variance components' tables plus the data regarding number of situations, modes, and subjects presented in Tables 1 and 2 of this paper.

case of modes of response, the interaction between situations and modes of response and the residual, the semi-interquartile ranges (Qs), are below 2 per cent. The median proportions from subjects and situations are both below 5 per cent for males,[5] but a sex difference appears wherein the median proportion of total variance from situations for females (7.78 per cent) is nearly twice that for males (3.95 per cent). The median proportion of the total variance contributed by the modes of response is about a quarter for both females and males. Again, the median proportions of variance from each of the three two-way interactions is larger than that from either subjects or situations, except in the case of females for whom the interaction between situations and modes of response (6.95 per cent) is slightly less than that for situations (7.78 per cent). Again, slightly more than a third of the total variance derives from the three-way interaction and error (Residual).

Yet an inspection of the ranges in the proportions of variance from the various sources shows some instability across the samples of subjects and the samples of situations and of modes of response in the several forms of the S-R Inventory of Anxiousness. This instability is largest for modes of response, among the main sources, and for the residual.

EFFECTS OF VARYING THE SAMPLES OF SUBJECTS.   Although some variation among the proportions of total variance contributed by each of the main sources and their interactions does occur, what is important is how small variations are. Despite variations in the ages of subjects in the various samples and in the social classes from whence they came, and despite efforts to extend the variation of threat in the samples of situations, the proportion of total variance contributed by individual differences among subjects across situations never reaches as much as 10 per cent. Despite efforts to extend the variation of threat in the samples of situations, the proportion of total variance contributed by situations never reaches 15 per cent for men and never reaches 20 per cent for women. Moreover, the proportions of variance contributed by each of the three two-way interactions are nearly always higher than either of these two main sources, and typically the proportion of total variance from one of these two-way interactions is of the order of the combined proportion from these two main sources (not counting modes of response, the contribution of which is regularly large).

Sex differences. Nevertheless, some sex differences emerge which should be considered. The one most evident from Table 3 is that for the proportion of total variance

[5] An exception of this statement must be made for the sample of 31 male psychotic patients for which individual differences among subjects contributed 14.56 per cent. The other sources contributed as follows: situations, 2.63 per cent; modes of response, 12.14 per cent; subjects × situations, 12.14 per cent; subjects × modes of response, 14.94 per cent; situations × modes of response, 1.88 per cent; and the residual of 39.59 per cent of the total variance. In the case of the 26 psychotic women, the contributions to the total variance were subjects, 6.58 per cent; situations, 5.77 per cent; modes of response, 15.30 per cent; subjects × situations, 16.67 per cent; subjects × modes of response, 18.08 per cent; situations × modes of response, 2.55 per cent; and the residual, 35.05 per cent. Contact with these patients was so poor, however, that we have no assurance that their reports were discriminating with any consistency among either situations or modes of response.

contributed by situations. This is nearly twice as large for women (7.78 per cent) as for men (3.95 per cent). Other sex differences emerge when the range of threat or danger·in the sample of situations is extended, but these can best be mentioned below.

Age differences. Some evidence of age trends·in the proportions of variance contributed by the various sources can also be seen in Table 4. Especially marked is an increase in the proportion of total variance contributed by modes of response with age. This increase is especially marked between junior high school and high school, is absent between high school and college, but continues between college-aged students and adults attending night school. Another downward trend with age appears for the proportion contributed by the interaction between subjects and modes of response, and a very slight downward trend with age appears also for the proportion contributed by subjects. These trends may result from an increasing appreciation of the social desirability of the various modes of response and an increasing tendency to expect certain modes of response in certain kinds of situations. These trends appear to be somewhat steeper for females than for males, perhaps indicating that appreciation of social desirability plays a larger role for girls than for boys.

Social class. The factor of social class is considered in Table 5. This table considers only the findings from samples of students in high schools and junior high schools. The characteristics of the neighborhoods of the various schools provide a basis for assessing at least the modal social class of the individuals sampled. Forest Hill Collegiate (high school), for instance, is predominantly lower-upper class with a sprinkling of upper-middle class (for the criteria of social class, see Warner, Meeker, & Ells, 1949). St. Andrews Junior High School represents predominantly the upper-middle class. The East York Mental Health Clinic, East York Collegiate (high school), and the other four junior high schools (Westwood, St. Clair, Oak Park, and Cosburn) represent chiefly the upper-lower class. Again no one form of the Inventory went to all these groups (see Table 2), so the apparent trends are confounded with differing samples of situations and slightly differing samples of modes of response.

If one considers only the differences in the percentages for the upper-middle and the upper-lower classes, omitting the Forest Hill sample which was given Form O only, the percentage of total variance from subjects is greater for the upper-middle than for the upper-lower class. A similar but much less marked difference appears for the percentages of variance from situations. On the other hand, the differences in percentages of variance from modes of response are opposite in direction, substantially larger for both upper-lower class boys and girls than for upper-middle class boys and girls. This difference appears to result from less reticence about needing to urinate and having loose bowels among adolescents of the upper-lower class than among those of the upper-middle class. This still tentative finding also calls for further investigation.

While consistency in the proportions of total variance contributed by the various main sources and their interactions is the major finding, samples of subjects differing in age and in social class yield some variations in these proportions, and further investigation of the effects of age and social class is indicated. Combining these various samples into a single large sample and partitioning the variance might well raise to some degree the

Table 4 | A COMPARISON OF SAMPLES OF SUBJECTS FROM PREDOMINANTLY ADULT, COLLEGE, HIGH SCHOOL, AND JUNIOR HIGH SCHOOL AGE LEVELS IN TERMS OF MEDIANS AND RANGES OF PERCENTAGES OF TOTAL VARIATION FROM EACH COMPONENT SOURCE[a]

PART A—MALES

Source	Adult (N = 2)		College (N = 11)	
	MEDIAN	RANGE	MEDIAN	RANGE
Subject (S)	3.53	3.4- 3.7	4.93	0.7- 7.6
Situation (Sit)	3.14	2.9- 3.4	4.45	2.2-13.7
Mode of Response (M-R)	32.72	30.9-34.6	25.46	21.7-40.1
S x Sit	8.05	7.0- 9.1	9.65	3.7-12.7
S x M-R	7.05	6.8- 7.4	10.79	4.9-12.1
Sit x M-R	12.30	11.8-12.8	8.08	4.1-12.5
Residual	33.21	32.0-34.4	36.40	22.5-42.1

Source	High school (N = 2)		Junior high school (N = 6)	
Subject (S)	4.18	2.8- 5.6	5.30	3.8- 9.7
Situation (Sit)	4.34	3.8- 4.9	3.76	2.7- 5.8
Mode of Response (M-R)	26.09	20.9-32.9	20.04	14.6-24.7
S x Sit	9.90	7.5-12.3	9.20	7.7-22.2
S x M-R	10.81	7.9-13.7	12.35	8.9-16.1
Sit x M-R	7.74	4.1-11.4	5.07	4.5- 7.7
Residual	36.14	32.7-39.6	36.68	35.8-38.8

PART B—FEMALES

Source	Adult (N = 1)		College (N = 11)	
	MEDIAN	RANGE	MEDIAN	RANGE
Subject (S)	2.55	—	3.61	1.6- 6.9
Situation (Sit)	8.97	—	7.78	3.1-19.9
Mode of Response (M-R)	28.64	—	26.61	21.4-45.5
S x Sit	9.35	—	9.15	4.6-13.1
S x M-R	6.76	—	10.73	5.0-14.3
Sit x M-R	10.14	—	6.97	4.7-12.5
Residual	33.60	—	33.14	22.9-36.3

Source	High school (N = 2)		Junior high school (N = 6)	
Subject (S)	4.09	3.5- .47	5.03	2.4- 7.6
Situation (Sit)	8.34	7.5- 9.1	7.70	6.3- 9.7
Mode of Response (M-R)	27.36	23.4-31.3	24.96	16.5-32.7
S x Sit	9.66	7.7-11.7	9.15	6.3-12.0
S x M-R	11.57	7.9-15.3	9.52	7.0-11.9
Sit x M-R	8.34	5.9-10.8	6.79	6.1- 8.3
Residual	31.14	29.7-31.6	36.97	35.8-40.3

[a] Median of total variation source is always 100 per cent. N refers to the number of samples in all cases. Where $N = 1$, the median is equal to the percentages for that particular sample, and there obviously is no range.

Table 5 | A COMPARISON OF SAMPLES OF SUBJECTS FROM PREDOMINANTLY LOWER-UPPER TO UPPER-MIDDLE; UPPER-MIDDLE AND UPPER-LOWER SOCIAL CLASSES IN TERMS OF MEDIANS AND RANGES OF PERCENTAGES OF TOTAL VARIATION FROM EACH COMPONENT SOURCE[a]

| | PART A—MALES | | | | | |
| | Lower-Upper, etc. (N = 1) | | Upper-Middle (N = 2) | | Upper-Lower (N = 6) | |
Source	MEDIAN	RANGE	MEDIAN	RANGE	MEDIAN	RANGE
Subject (S)	5.57	—	9.19	8.7- 9.7	3.84	2.8- 6.5
Situation (Sit)	3.81	—	4.76	3.7- 5.8	3.76	2.7- 4.9
Mode of Response (M-R)	20.87	—	15.53	14.6-16.4	24.70	16.9-32.9
S x Sit	12.34	—	17.24	12.3-22.2	9.09	7.5- 9.4
S x M-R	13.73	—	10.79	8.9-12.7	11.06	7.9-16.1
Sit x M-R	4.05	—	5.07	4.7- 5.4	7.51	4.5-11.4
Residual	39.62	—	37.43	36.1-38.7	40.95	32.7-45.9

| | PART B—FEMALES | | | | | |
| | (N = 1) | | (N = 2) | | (N = 6) | |
Source	MEDIAN	RANGE	MEDIAN	RANGE	MEDIAN	RANGE
Subject (S)	4.72	—	6.67	5.8- 7.6	3.99	2.4- 6.5
Situation (Sit)	7.53	—	8.19	8.1- 8.3	7.26	3.8- 9.7
Mode of Response (M-R)	23.43	—	16.70	16.5-16.9	28.70	23.1-32.7
S x Sit	11.66	—	11.76	11.5-12.0	8.16	6.3-10.6
S x M-R	15.26	—	11.51	11.1-11.9	7.99	7.0-11.1
Sit x M-R	5.86	—	6.09	6.0- 6.1	7.39	5.0-10.8
Residual	31.55	—	39.10	37.9-40.3	36.68	29.7-41.4

[a] Median of total variation source is always 100 per cent. N refers to the number of samples in all cases. Where N = 1, the median is equal to the percentages for that particular sample and there is obviously no range.

proportion of variance contributed by individual differences among subjects across situations and modes of response. This remains to be done. Yet, inasmuch as the mean and standard deviation for the sample of clinic patients differs little from the means and standard deviations of the various samples of adolescents, any increase in the contribution from subjects brought about from combining samples can hardly be expected to be large.

EFFECTS OF EXTENDING THE RANGE OF THREAT IN SAMPLES OF SITUATIONS. Extending the range of danger or threat in the sampling of situations increases somewhat the proportion of total variance contributed by this source and increases also the proportion contributed by the interaction between situations and modes of response. Table 6 presents the medians and ranges of percentages of total variation from each component source for the sampling of situations in each form of the S-R Inventory of Anxiousness, excepting UI-66-A which was administered to only single samples of men and of women.[6] The situations in the original Form O and all the others,

[6] Form UI-66-A was administered to only one male and one female sample. For these samples the percentages for the component sources in the case of males were 4.93 for subjects, 3.30 for situations, 35.05 for M-R, 7.23 for subjects × situations, 11.05 for subjects × M-R 0.08 for situations × M-R, and 30.36 for residual; and in the case of females, 2.74 for subjects, 3.14 for situations, 45.45 for M-R, 8.06 for subjects × situations, 6.99 for subjects × M-R, 9.76 for situations × M-R, and 23.87 for residual.

Table 6 | MEDIANS AND RANGES OF PERCENTAGES OF TOTAL VARIATION FOR EACH COMPONENT SOURCE FOR EACH FORM OF THE S-R INVENTORY OF ANXIOUSNESS[a]

PART A—MALES

Source	Form O (N = 7)		Form 1-X-62 (N = 3)		Form UI-64-A (N = 3)	
	MEDIAN	RANGE	MEDIAN	RANGE	MEDIAN	RANGE
Subjects (S)	6.45	4.7- 7.6	3.40	2.0- 3.7	1.74	0.7- 4.2
Situation (Sit)	4.24	3.5- 5.1	2.88	2.2- 3.4	10.71	10.1-13.7
Mode of Response (M-R)	23.83	20.9-25.5	31.84	30.9-34.6	37.10	35.0-40.1
S x Sit	10.21	9.7-12.7	9.01	7.0- 9.1	5.33	3.7- 5.7
S x M-R	11.59	8.0-13.7	7.35	6.8- 9.6	9.04	4.9-10.8
Sit x M-R	5.50	4.1- 8.5	12.49	11.8-12.8	10.00	8.6-11.0
Residual	38.31	36.4-42.1	32.85	32.0-34.4	24.21	22.5-30.8

Source	Form EY-L-64-A (N = 6)		Form SA-66 (N = 2)			
Subjects (S)	3.84	2.8- 6.5	9.19	8.7- 9.7		
Situation (Sit)	3.76	2.7- 4.9	4.76	3.7- 5.8		
Mode of Response (M-R)	24.70	16.9-32.9	15.53	14.6-16.4		
S x Sit	9.09	7.5- 9.4	17.24	12.3-22.2		
S x M-R	11.06	7.9-16.1	10.79	8.9-12.7		
Sit x M-R	7.51	4.5-11.4	5.07	4.7- 5.4		
Residual	40.95	32.7-45.9	37.43	36.1-38.7		

PART B—FEMALES

Source	Form O (N = 7)		Form 1-X-62 (N = 2)		Form UI-64-A (N = 3)	
	MEDIAN	RANGE	MEDIAN	RANGE	MEDIAN	RANGE
Subjects (S)	4.98	3.6- 6.9	3.02	2.6- 3.5	1.62	1.6- 1.8
Situation (Sit)	7.53	5.8- 8.3	7.34	5.7- 9.0	14.03	13.1-19.9
Mode of Response (M-R)	23.43	21.4-26.6	30.22	28.6-31.8	38.45	34.5-38.9
S x Sit	11.41	9.0-13.1	9.25	9.2- 9.4	4.70	4.6- 5.6
S x M-R	11.51	10.7-15.3	6.70	6.7- 6.8	5.58	5.0- 7.4
Sit x M-R	5.86	4.7- 7.0	11.33	10.1-12.5	11.06	10.6-11.3
Residual	34.33	31.6-36.3	32.07	30.5-33.6	23.01	22.9-24.1

Source	Form EY-L-64-A (N = 6)		Form SA-66 (N = 2)	
Subjects (S)	3.99	2.4- 6.5	6.67	5.8- 7.6
Situation (Sit)	7.26	3.8- 9.7	8.19	8.1- 8.3
Mode of Response (M-R)	28.70	23.1-32.7	16.70	16.5-16.9
S x Sit	8.16	6.3-10.6	11.76	11.5-12.0
S x M-R	7.99	7.0-11.1	11.51	11.1-11.9
Sit x M-R	7.39	5.0-10.8	6.09	6.0- 6.1
Residual	36.68	29.7-41.4	39.10	37.9-40.3

[a] Median of total variation is always 100 per cent. N refers in all cases to the number of samples of subjects. Form UI-64-A is excluded from this table because there is only one sample for each sex.

except UI-64-A, contained at least a moderate degree of danger or threat and ranged considerably. The sampling of situations in UI-64-A was deliberately exaggerated in range of threat by including such innocuous items as "You are sitting down to read the evening paper," and "You are going to bed after a long day." At the other extreme, this sampling also included such extremes of threat as "You are driving down the road when you meet two racing cars approaching you abreast," and "You are reading about the situation in Cuba and a new threat of nuclear war." The sampling of situations in UI-64-A was bimodal. Such increasing of the range of threat had several effects upon the proportions of total variance. First of all, it served to increase the proportion from situations from a maximum of 5.1 per cent in males to a median of 10.71 per cent, and from a maximum of 9.7 per cent in females to a median of 13.1 per cent. Even so, the maximum proportion from situations never exceeds 13.7 per cent for males or 19.9 per cent for females. It served also to increase the proportion of total variance from modes of response for both males and females. The effects of increasing the range of threat on the two-way interactions are (a) to decrease the contribution from the interaction between subjects and situations, (b) to decrease the contribution from the interaction between subjects and modes of response (and to do it substantially more for females than for males), and (c) to increase the contribution from the interaction between situations and modes of response. Despite these alterations of the proportions deriving from increasing the range of threat, the proportion of the variance contributed by the three two-way interactions remains higher than that from the main sources of subjects and situations combined. Thus, even maximizing the range of threat fails to alter in any fundamental fashion the relationships among the proportions found with Form O for the three samples of college students.

DISCUSSION

These findings have a number of theoretical implications, which are relevant to the conceptual distinction between *state* and *trait* for anxiety. They are relevant to the issue of whether individual differences across situations are more or less important than situations in determining the reports of response-indicators of anxiousness. They are relevant to the measurement of anxiety. And, finally, if these findings hold true for such other common traits as hostility and honesty, they have something to say about personality description in general.

STATE ANXIETY VS. TRAIT ANXIETY. Cattel and Scheier (1958, 1961) distinguished chronic (trait) anxiety, defined as a relatively permanent characteristic of persons, from momentary (state) anxiety, defined as a state which varies from day to day and from moment to moment. The former they measured by means of a score-persons matrix (R-technique), the latter by means of a score-occasions matrix (P-technique). While they found evidence for this distinction between momentary states and individual differences in chronic anxiety levels, the instruments by means of which these factors were assessed failed to tie the anxiety indicators to specific situations.

Indicators of anxiety are required for responses or reactions to situations, for states, or for chronic levels. These indicators may be physiological or behavioral, and the behavioral may include the subject's report of feelings, actions, and physiological responses as is the case with the S-R Inventories of Anxiousness. Considerable ordinality exists among the indicators of anxiousness. Loose bowels and a compulsion to urinate, for instance, indicate more anxiety than sweaty palms and feelings of uneasiness. In the findings of this investigation, this ordinality provides the reason for the high proportion of variance (a quarter of the total or more) contributed regularly by modes of response. Highly threatening situations are more likely to evoke these response-indicators of high-level anxiety than less threatening ones, and this is shown by the fact that increasing the range of threat or danger in the sampling of situations (Table 6, Form UI-64-A) clearly increases the contribution to the total variance from the interaction between situations and modes of response.

Despite such evidence of relatively consistent S-R relationships, their contribution is limited (at least in the reports of our many subjects) to about 10 per cent of the total variance. On the other hand, our findings provide clear evidence of the idiosyncratic organization of anxiousness; they demonstrate again that individuality in personality which Allport (1937, 1962) so long stressed. The evidence derives from the fact that over a fifth of the total variance derives regularly from the two two-way interactions in which subjects participate (subjects by situations, and subjects by modes of response). In addition, there is the proportion of variance contributed by the three-way interaction among subject, situations, and modes of response which we have thus far failed to assess.[7] In the light of such findings and considerations, either occasion scores, without knowledge of the evocative situations, or trait scores can give but relatively little of the total information about the anxiousness of persons.

Trait anxiety does exist, however, and it may have at least three bases. It may be a chronic manifestation of the indicators of anxiety across situations evoked by conflicts or situations which people carry around in their minds. It may be a tendency to manifest the indicators of anxiety in a large proportion of situations. It may be manifest as a tendency to show especially strong response-indicators to a relatively few situations. Omnibus questionnaires about anxiousness do yield measures of trait anxiety. Unfortunately, from the fact that individual differences among subjects across situations contribute only about 5 per cent of the total variance, such measures of trait anxiety cannot be expected to predict anxious behavior very accurately. Among omnibus inventories, the S-R Inventory of Anxiousness is as good as any. In fact, total scores for subjects derived from it show higher correlations with the scores for the same subjects from the Cattell (1957) IPAT Anxiety Scale, the Mandler-Sarason (1952) Test Anxiety Questionnaire, and the Taylor (1953) Manifest Anxiety Scale than scores from any of these instruments show with each other (see Endler, Hunt, & Rosenstein, 1962, p. 17). Even so, from the statistical principle that the percentage of variance in common between two variables can be estimated by squaring the coefficient of correlation between measures of them, it is clear that the validity coefficients for such omnibus measures of anxiety can be expected to rise consistently no higher than those customarily found. They range between .2 and .25. Similarly, this finding that individual differences among subjects across situations contributes only about 5 per cent of the total variance in the response indicators of anxiety helps to explain why the effects of psychometrically assessed extremes of differences among individuals in anxiety typically yield small effects on conditioning (see Bitterman & Holtzman, 1952; Farber & Spence, 1953; Spence & Taylor, 1951; Taylor, 1951; Taylor & Spence, 1954) and on such relatively more complex learning as rote memorizing of a series of nonsense syllables (Farber & Spence, 1953; Montague, 1953; Spielberger, 1966b; Taylor & Spence, 1952). These studies have tended to show that anxiety facilitates conditioning of such simple responses as the eye blink and the galvanic skin response and that anxiety hampers the more complex memorizing of a series of nonsense syllables, but the differences between even extreme groups, based on their scores on omnibus measures of trait anxiety, have regularly been small and barely significant from a statistical standpoint. On the other hand, when Beam (1955) compared the

---

[7] Since the original (1962) studies, we have become aware of the need for and possibilities of administering several samplings of situations to each sampling of subjects. This avoids confounding the effect of a sampling of situations with a sampling of subjects and permits separation of the contribution of the triple interaction from the error. We have made one attempt to do this (see Endler & Hunt, 1968b). We have also compared the contributions from the various component sources for hostility with those for anxiety (see Endler & Hunt, 1968a).

conditioning of the galvanic skin response in a group of students under the situational stress of being about to appear in a play on opening night or about to have their doctoral orals with that of a presumably equivalent group well-removed in time from such situational stress, the differences in both the rate and the degree of conditioning were tremendous and very highly significant ($p < .001$). Moreover, when, in the same study, Beam compared the number of repetitions required by a group of students to memorize a series of nonsense syllables while under these forms of situational stress with the number of repetitions required by the same students to memorize an equivalent list at another occasion well removed in time from these stressful situations, the group averaged 1.5 as many repetitions under the situational stress as they did in the relatively stressless situation. Some of these students required six times as many repetitions to achieve the criterion under the situational stress than they did without it. From such considerations, it would appear that the differences in anxiety indicators obtainable within given individuals in contrasting situations is clearly much larger and more dependable than that between extreme groups obtained psychometrically with omnibus measures of anxiety.

THE ISSUE OF SUBJECTS VS. SITUATIONS.   The finding that neither individual differences across situations or situations per se contribute heavily to the total variance lends confirmation to the conclusion drawn by Endler & Hunt (1966) that this issue of the relative importance of subjects and situations is but a pseudo-issue.[8] The fact that these two main sources combined typically contribute no more to the total variance in the response-indicators of anxiousness than does either of the two-way interactions in which subjects participate strongly suggests that anxiety is idiosyncratically organized in each individual and that the issue of the relative importance of subjects and situations disappears.

TOWARD MORE VALID MEASUREMENT OF ANXIOUSNESS.   The fact that the contributions of the two-way interactions to the total variance loom so large suggests that improving the validity of measures of anxiousness demands specifying the situations concerning which subjects are asked to report their response-indicators and limiting the validating observations of their behavior to those specified situations. When the situations are so specified, validity coefficients ranging between .6 and .8 appear (see D'Zurilla, 1964; Hoy, 1966; and Paul, 1966). Thus, the suggested importance of specifying situa-

---

[8] In the original study, we missed this point and stressed the relative importance of situations over individual differences (Endler, Hunt, & Rosensten, 1962). We missed this point because I (Hunt) erroneously overruled my ex-student collaborators, albeit on what we took for expert advice, on how appropriately to partition the variance among the sources. So long as one merely compares the main sources, situations do appear to contribute several times as much of the variance as individual differences. This appeared to support the contention of the social psychologists over that of the personologists. But once the components method of partitioning the total variance (Gleser, Cronbach, & Rajaratnam, 1965; Endler, 1966) was employed, it became clearly evident that the variance contributed by each of the interactions is substantially larger than that from either of the main sources: individual differences or situations.

tions is corroborated. Doing it increases validity coefficients from the range of .2 to .25, typically found for omnibus measures of individual differences in anxiety, to a range from .6 to .8.

IMPLICATIONS FOR PERSONALITY DESCRIPTION.   If such findings hold for such other common traits as hostility and honesty, they have implications for personality description in general. First, they imply that attempting to devise better instruments with which to measure individual differences in traits across situations is doomed to the failure epitomized by validity coefficients ranging from .2 to .25. Second, they imply that it may be possible to save some of the loss of validity for personality description in general, where specifying particular situations may be unfeasible. These findings, as did those of Endler, Hunt, and Rosenstein (1962), suggest that it should be feasible to move in a fruitful direction by categorizing both situations and the response-indicators of the traits in question. Tucker's (1964) three-mode factor analysis constitutes one promising approach once the storage limitations of computers are sufficiently overcome to permit handling of sufficiently large samples of situations and modes of response. Until such a time, situations can be categorized by factor-analyzing situation-scores across individuals and modes of response somewhat after the fashion of Cattell's (1950) P-technique. In turn, modes of response can be categorized by factor-analyzing mode scores across individuals and situations. Once the situations and the modes of response are each categorized, it should become feasible to describe individuals in terms of the kinds of responses they are likely to make in the various kinds of situations.

SUMMARY

Six different forms of the S-R Inventory of Anxiousness, with differing samples of situations and of modes of response, were administered to 22 samples of male and to 21 samples of female subjects who varied in age, in social class, and in mental health. This was done to test the generalizability of the proportions of total variance from the several main sources and their interactions found by Endler and Hunt (1966) with but one form of the inventory used with three samples of college students.

Of the main sources of total variance, individual differences contribute typically only 4–5 per cent of the total variance, situations only about 4 per cent for males and about 8 per cent for females, but, because a certain ordinality exists among the reported modes of response indicating anxiety, these modes of response contribute about a quarter of the total variance. Each of the two-way interactions contributes typically about 10 per cent, and the triple interaction coupled with error contributes about a third of the total variance.

Some indications of age trends and of social-class differences in the proportions of variance from the several sources exist. Even though these are relatively small, they deserve further study. Deliberately increasing the range of threat in the sampling of situations increases the proportion of variance from situations to a maximum of 13.7 per cent for males and of 19.9 per cent for females; it also increases somewhat the proportion from the interaction of situations with modes of response.

These findings have implications for the theory of anxiety. They imply that the issue of the relative importance of individual differences and of situations is but a pseudo-issue. The fact that individual differences across situations and across modes of response contribute only about 5 per cent of the total variance in the reported indicators of anxiousness dooms omnibus inventories of anxiety to validity coefficients of the customary order of .2 to .25. On the other hand, the validity of reported anxiety indicators can be raised to coefficients ranging from .6 to .8 by specifying the situation. These findings also suggest that personality description in general might be improved considerably by categorizing both situations and modes of response and then by describing individuals in terms of the kinds of responses they tend to manifest in the various kinds of situations.

REFERENCES

Allport, G. W. *Personality.* New York: Holt, 1937.

Allport, G. W. The general and unique in psychological science. *J. Pers.,* 1962, *30*, 405–422.

Beam, J. C. Serial learning and conditioning under real-life stress. *J. abnorm. soc. Psychol.,* 1955, *51*, 543–551.

Bitterman, M. E., & Holtzman, W. H. Conditioning and extinction of the galvanic skin response as a function of anxiety. *J. abnorm. soc. Psychol.,* 1952, *47*, 615–623.

Cattell, R. B. *The description and measurement of personality.* New York: Harcourt, 1946.

Cattell, R. B. *Personality: A Systematic theoretical and factual study.* New York: McGraw-Hill, 1950.

Cattell, R. B. *Handbook for the I.P.A.T. Anxiety Scale.* Champaign, Ill.: Institute for Personality and Ability Testing, 1957.

Cattell, R. B., & Scheier, I. H. The nature of anxiety: A review of 13 multivariate analyses comparing 814 variables. *Psychol. Rep.,* Monograph Supplement, 1958, *5*, 351–388.

Cattell, R. B., & Scheier, I. H. *The meaning and measurement of neuroticism and anxiety.* New York: Ronald, 1961.

Cottrell, L. S., Jr. The adjustment of the individual to his age and sex roles. *Amer. sociol. Rev.,* 1942, *7*, 618–625. (a)

Cottrell, L. S., Jr. The analysis of situational fields. *Amer. sociol. Rev.,* 1942, *7*, 370–382. (b)

Dewey, R., & Humber, W. J. *The development of human behavior.* New York: Macmillan, 1951.

D'Zurilla, T. J. Effects of behavioral influence techniques applied in group discussions on subsequent verbal participation. Unpublished doctoral dissertation, University of Illinois, 1964.

Edwards, A. L. *Statistical methods.* (2nd ed.) New York: Holt, Rinehart and Winston, 1967.

Endler, N. S. Estimating variance components from mean squares for random and mixed effects analysis of variance models. *Percept. Mot. Skills,* 1966, *22*, 559–570.

Endler, N. S., & Hunt, J. McV. Sources of behavioral variance as measured by the S-R Inventory of Anxiousness. *Psychol. Bull.,* 1966, *65*, 6, 338–346.

Endler, N. S., & Hunt, J. McV. S-R Inventories of Hostility and comparisons of the proportions of variance from persons, responses, and situations for hostility and anxiousness. *J. Pers. soc. Psychol.,* 1968, *9*, 309–315. (a)

Endler, N. S. & Hunt, J. McV. Triple-interaction variance in the S-R Inventory of Anxiousness. *Percept. mot. Skills*, 1968, 27, (3). (b)

Endler, N. S., & Hunt, J. McV., & Rosenstein, A. J. An S-R Inventory of Anxiousness. *Psychol. Monogr.*, 1962, 76, No. 17 (Whole No. 536), 1–33.

Endler, N. S., & Jobst, W. J. Components of variance derived from mean squares for random, mixed, and fixed effects analysis of variance models. Technical Report: Project No. MH-08987–USPHS. Urbana, Ill.: University of Illinois, Psychological Development Laboratory, Oct., 1964, mimeographed.

Farber, I. E., & Spence, K. W. Complex learning and conditioning as a function of anxiety. *J. exp. Psychol.*, 1953, 45, 120–125.

Freud, S. *Introductory lectures of psychoanalysis* (1917). (2nd ed.; trans. by Joan Riviere.) London: G. Allen, 1940.

Freud, S. *New introductory lectures on psychoanalysis* (1932). (Trans. by W. J. H. Sprott.) New York: Norton, 1933.

Gleser, G. C., Cronbach, L. J., & Rajaratnam, N. Generalizability of sources influenced by multiple sources of variance. *Psychometrika*, 1965, 30, 395–418.

Hathaway, S. R., & Meehl, P. E. *An atlas for the clinical use of the MMPI*. Minneapolis: University of Minnesota Press, 1951.

Hoy, Elizabeth. The influence of incongruity on reported anxiety. Unpublished master's thesis, York University, 1966.

Hull, C. L. *Principles of behavior*. New York: Appleton, 1943.

Hunt, J. McV., Cole, Marie-Louise Wakeman, & Reis, Eva E. S. Situational cues distinguishing anger, fear, and sorrow. *Amer. J. Psychol.*, 1958, 71, 138–151.

Mandler, G., & Sarason, S. B. A study of anxiety and learning. *J. abnorm. soc. Psychol.*, 1952, 47, 166–173.

Mead, G. H. *Mind, self, and society*. Chicago: University of Chicago Press, 1934.

Miller, N. E., & Dollard, J. *Social learning and imitation*. New Haven, Conn.: Yale University Press, 1941.

Montague, E. K. The role of anxiety in serial rote learning. *J. exp. Psychol.*, 1953, 45, 91–96.

Olds, J. Physiological mechanisms of reward. In M. R. Jones (Ed.), *Nebraska symposium on motivation: 1955*. Lincoln, Neb.: University of Nebraska Press, 1955.

Paul, G. L. *Insight versus desensitization in psychotherapy: An experiment in anxiety reduction*. Stanford, Calif.: Stanford University Press, 1966.

Schneirla, T. C. An evolutionary and developmental theory of biphasic processes underlying approach and withdrawal. In M. R. Jones (Ed.), *Nebraska symposium on motivation: 1959*. Lincoln, Neb.: University of Nebraska Press, 1959.

Schneirla, T. C. Aspects of stimulation and organization in approach/withdrawal processes underlying vertebrate behavioral development. In D. H. Lehrman, R. Hinde, & Evelyn Shaw (Eds.), *Advances in the study of behavior*. New York: Academic Press, Inc., 1964.

Spence, K. W., & Taylor, Janet A. Anxiety and strength of the UCS as determiners of the amount of eyelid conditioning. *J. exp. Psychol.*, 1951, 42, 183–188.

Spielberger, C. D. Theory and research on anxiety. In C. D. Spielberger (Ed.), *Anxiety and behavior*. New York: Academic Press, Inc., 1966. Pp. 3–20. (a)

Spielberger, C. D. The effects of anxiety on complex learning and academic achievement. In C. D. Spielberger (Ed.), *Anxiety and behavior*. New York: Academic Press, Inc., 1966. Pp. 361–398. (b)

Taylor, Janet A. The relationship of anxiety to the conditioned eyelid response. *J. exp. Psychol.*, 1951, 41, 81–92.

Taylor, Janet A. A personality scale of manifest anxiety. *J. abnorm. soc. Psychol.*, 1953, 48, 285–290.

Taylor, Janet A., & Spence, K. W. The relationship of anxiety level to performance on serial learning. *J. exp. Psychol.*, 1952, 44, 61–64.

Taylor, Janet A., & Spence, K. W. Conditioning level in the behavior disorders. *J. abnorm. soc. Psychol.*, 1954, 49, 497–502.

Tucker, L. R. The extension of factor analysis to three-dimension matrices. In N. Frederiksen (Ed.), *Contributions to mathematical psychology.* New York: Holt, Rinehart and Winston, 1964.

Warner, W. L., Meeker, Marchia, & Ells, K. *Social class in America: A manual for the measurement of social status.* Chicago: Science Research Associates, 1949.

4.2 | SOME REASONS FOR THE APPARENT INCONSISTENCY OF PERSONALITY*

Jack Block

The study of personality seeks regularities in behavior and this search is usually made operational by evaluations of the correlations among different, theoretically related behaviors. To date, the empirical evidence for personality consistency has not been inspiriting. As a principle or aspiration of a science aimed at human understanding, the idea of continuity and coherence in personality functioning must be affirmed. Whereupon the question becomes: Why have psychologists, in their many research efforts, been unable to display the presumed harmonies in individual behavior?

The present note collects and lists some of the reasons for this state of affairs. The problem is viewed as arising both from deficiencies in the way psychologists operationalize their concepts and from deficiencies in the way they conceptualize their operations; and it is in these terms that our discussion will proceed. There are some psychometric reasons, as well, for the apparent inconsistency observed in behaviors, having to do with such matters as attenuation effects and the vexing influence of "method variance," but these statistical concerns have been dealt with elsewhere (Block, 1963, 1964; Humphreys, 1960); so the present argument can be entirely psychological.

* SOURCE: Block, J. Some reasons for the apparent inconsistency of personality. *Psychological Bulletin*, 1968, 70, 210–212. Copyright 1968 by the American Psychological Association and reprinted by permission.

To exemplify the several points to be made, the personality dimension of ego control will be used, although, of course, other personality constructs instead might have been employed. By ego control is meant something akin to excessive behavioral constraint or rigidity ("the overcontroller") at one end of the dimension and something like excessive behavioral reactivity or spontaneity ("the undercontroller") at the other end of the continuum. For further articulation of the ego-control concept, the reader may wish to consult other sources (e.g., Block, 1965; Block & Turula, 1963).

There is evidence for a common thread through a large variety of behaviors that can be accounted for by the concept of ego control. Undercontrollers in one situation are often undercontrollers in another context as well and the same is true of overcontrollers. But also, and often, an individual who is impulsive in one situation will appear constrained in another circumstance; such behavior apparently denies the usefulness of a generalizing personality variable. This last kind of datum, of apparent inconsistency, can not be questioned or explained away by psychometric manipulation; it is there and further instances can be multiplied at will. What can be questioned, however, is the implication immediately, frequently, and strongly drawn from such observations to the effect that a personality dimension—in the present instance, ego control—necessarily loses its cogency as a basis for conceptualizing behavior because of the inconsistencies observed. We can question this implication if, and only if, a higher form of lawfulness can be found in the behaviors pointed to as evidence for temperamental inconsistency. The apparent discordancies must be resolved within a framework provided by a theory, or, at least, a theory must have the promise of integrating these otherwise upsetting data.

There are at least four ways in which these superficially embarrassing behavioral inconsistencies may come about:

1. *The behaviors being contrasted and correlated may not all be significant or salient for the individual.* Thus, it is psychologically uneconomical and as a rule not necessary to deliberate excessively before deciding whether to walk down the right aisle or the left aisle of a theatre. The decision problem confronting the individual in this particular situation is essentially unimportant. Consequently, an individual may make his theatre-lobby decision in a rather cavalier or "impulsive" way. Or he may give reign to a slight position preference which, because it is consistent, may suggest a "rigidity" or highly controlled patterning in his behavior. It is specious to contrast such peripheral behaviors of an individual with the way in which he copes with centrally involving situations such as friendship formation or aggression imposition, and yet, unwittingly, the comparison is often made. When correlation is sought between behaviors formulated in salient situations on the one hand and behaviors formulated in uninvolving situations on the other, then behavior will appear more whimsical than congruent. If we are to seek consistency, it must be sought among behaviors that are at comparable levels in the hierarchy of behaviors.

2. *Formulations of personality which are context blind or do not attempt to take environmental factors into account will encounter many behaviors that will appear inconsistent.* Thus, a generally spontaneous child may in certain circumstances behave in a highly constricted way. This vacillation and apparent inconsistency readily becomes understandable when it is realized that these certain circumstances are always *unfamiliar*

ones for the child. Behavior often appears capricious because the nature of the stimulus situation in which the individual finds himself is not comprehended or attended to by the observer and his theory. Explicit theoretical conceptualization of environmental factors is a fruitful way of integrating and assimilating behaviors which from a context-blind view-point appear inconsistent. It is still a way that is almost untried.

3. *The behaviors being related may not be mediated by the same underlying varia-bles.* Thus, in a basketball game two players may each demonstrate a wide variety of shots and sequencing of shots at the basket. The one player may have spent solitary, obsessive years before a hoop, planfully developing precisely the repertoire and combina-tions he is now manifesting. The second player, in the heat of athletic endeavor, may in spontaneous and impromptu fashion manifest a fully equivalent variety of basket-making attempts (and with no less accuracy if he is a good athlete). These phenotypically equivalent behaviors are in the first player mediated by controlled, deliberate develop-ment of a differentiated behavioral repertoire; in the second player, behavioral variety is mediated by his kinesthetic spontaneity. In a rather different situation, where prior culti-vation of ability is not available as a resource, the first player may now appear rigid and behaviorally impoverished; the second player can continue to be spontaneous. These two individuals, behaviorally equivalent in the first situation, are quite different in the second situation; and this difference suggests an inconsistency of behavior. If the mediating variables underlying a given action are not analyzed or considered, behavior can appear paradoxical when closer assessment will reveal a lawful basis for the discrepancy.

4. *When an individual has reached certain personal limits, previous behavioral consistencies may break down.* Thus, an acutely paranoid individual will manifest both extremely overcontrolled behaviors and extremely undercontrolled behaviors more or less conjointly. Etiologically, this contrary behavioral state appears to come about when the preparanoid individual finds his former ability to consistently contain his excessive impulses is becoming exceeded in certain directions of expression, with a resultant absence of control in these special areas. The former, often quite striking coherence the preparanoid personality manifests has been disrupted because the *bounds* or *limits* within which the coherence can be maintained have been transcended. Such extremist behaviors are especially likely to be judged psychopathological. Indeed, one of the explanations why psychiatrists and clinical psychologists often argue against the existence of an internally consistent ego apparatus is that they in their practice so often encounter those relatively few individuals in whom personal limits have been reached and therefore personal con-sonance shattered. More generally, psychologists have not given the notion of bounds or limits sufficient attention and application. Relationships tend to be posited unequivocally, without recognizing the bounds within which the relationship can be expected to hold and beyond which the relationship fails and is replaced by other relationships.

The foregoing remarks and recognitions are not new but their implications are often neglected by the busy psychologist concerned more with the action of research than with contemplative conceptualization. But both are required. If we are to respond to our empirical disappointments in the pursuit of personality consistency, that response should comprehend the reasons for former failure rather than perpetuate and proliferate a fundamentally unpsychological approach to the understanding of personality.

SUMMARY

The empirical literature on consistency of personality is replete with instances of the absence of "expected" relationships. Some conceptual reasons are listed that may account for these apparent inconsistencies. These reasons include: (a) the mixing of behaviors of different levels of salience, (b) the failure to recognize the effect of environmental factors, (c) the comparison of behaviors mediated by different underlying variables, and (d) the failure to specify or to recognize the bounds within which the posited relationship may be expected to exist. Clearer and closer conceptualization with regard to these issues can set the stage for improved empirical demonstrations of personality consistency.

REFERENCES

Block, J. The equivalence of measures and the correction for attenuation. *Psychological Bulletin*, 1963, *60*, 152–156.

Block, J. Recognizing attenuation effects in the strategy of research. *Psychological Bulletin*, 1964, *62*, 214–216.

Block, J. *The challenge of response sets.* New York: Appleton, 1965.

Block, J., & Turula, E. Identification, ego control, and adjustment. *Child Development*, 1963, *34*, 945–953.

Humphreys, L. G. Note on the multitrait-multimethod matrix. *Psychological Bulletin*, 1960, *57*, 86–88.

4.3 | CONTINUITY AND CHANGE IN PERSONALITY[*][1]

Walter Mischel

The question of continuity and change in personality has enduring importance, and the position that one takes on this topic profoundly influences one's approach to most other issues in personality psychology. Almost no psychologist, myself included, would argue with the basic and widely shared assumption that continuity does exist in personality

* SOURCE: Mischel, W. Continuity and change in personality. *American Psychologist*, 1969, *24*, 1012–1018. Copyright 1969 by the American Psychological Association and reprinted by permission.

[1] This article is based on a paper presented at the symposium "Behavioral Continuity and Change with Development," held at the meeting of the Society for Research in Child Development, Santa Monica, California, March 27, 1969. Preparation of this paper was facilitated by Grant M-6830, from the National Institutes of Health, United States Public Health Service.

development (e.g., Kagan, 1969). Indeed, few other phenomena seem to be so intuitively self-evident. The experience of subjective continuity in ourselves—of basic oneness and durability in the self—is perhaps the most compelling and fundamental feature of personality. This experience of continuity seems to be an intrinsic feature of the mind, and the loss of a sense of felt consistency may be a chief characteristic of personality disorganization.

Clinically, it seems remarkable how each of us generally manages to reconcile his seemingly diverse behaviors into one self-consistent whole. A man may steal on one occasion, lie on another, donate generously to charity on a third, cheat on a fourth, and still construe himself readily as "basically honest and moral." Just like the personality theorist who studies them, our subjects also are skilled at transforming their seemingly discrepant behavior into a constructed continuity, making unified wholes out of almost anything.

It might be interesting to fantasize a situation in which the personality theorist and his subjects sat down together to examine each subject's data on behavioral consistency cross-situationally or over time. Actually it might not even be a bad idea for psychologists to enact such a fantasy. In inspecting these data the theorist would look for genotypic unities that he is sure must be there; his subject would look for genotypic unities and be even more convinced that they exist and would proceed to find his own, often emerging with unities unknown to the theorist. But the consistency data on the IBM sheets, even if they reached statistical significance, probably would account for only a trivial portion of the variance, as Hunt (1965) has pointed out. A correlation of .30 leaves us understanding less than 10% of the relevant variance. And even correlations of that magnitude are not very common and have come to be considered good in research on the consistency of any noncognitive dimension of personality.

How does one reconcile our shared perception of continuity with the equally impressive evidence that on virtually all of our dispositional measures of personality substantial changes occur in the characteristics of the individual longitudinally over time and, even more dramatically, across seemingly similar settings cross-sectionally? I had the occasion to broadly review the voluminous evidence available on this topic of consistency and specificity (Mischel, 1968). In my appraisal, the overall evidence from many sources (clinical, experimental, developmental, correlational) shows the human mind to function like an extraordinarily effective reducing valve that creates and maintains the perception of continuity even in the face of perpetual observed changes in actual behavior. Often this cognitive construction of continuity, while not arbitrary, is only very tenuously related to the phenomena that are construed.

To understand continuity properly it is necessary to be more specific and to talk about types of variations and the conditions that regulate them. In this regard it may be useful to distinguish between consistency in various types of human activity.

There is a great deal of evidence that our cognitive constructions about ourselves and the world—our personal theories about ourselves and those around us (both in our roles as persons and as psychologists)—often are extremely stable and highly resistant to change. Data from many sources converge to document this point. Studies of the self-concept, of impression formation in person perception and in clinical judgment, of cognitive sets guiding selective attention—all these phenomena and many more document the consistency and tenacious continuity of many human construction systems (Mischel, 1968). Often these construction systems are built quickly and on the basis of little information (e.g., Bruner, Olver, & Greenfield, 1966). But, once established, these theories, whether generated by our subjects or ourselves, become exceedingly difficult to disconfirm.

An impressive degree of continuity also has been shown for another aspect of cognition: These are the features of problem solving called cognitive styles. Significant continuity often has been demonstrated on many cognitive style dimensions (e.g., Kagan, 1969; Witkin, Goodenough, & Karp, 1967). The current prolific cognitive style explorations on this topic provide excellent evidence of developmental continuity. In this case the research also reveals a welcome continuity in our professional developmental history. Research into consistent individual differences in cognition has had deep roots and a long and distinguished history in experimental psychology. Simple cognitive measures like reaction time and response speed and duration have intrigued psychologists since the earliest laboratory work on mental measurement began more than 70 years ago. Individual differences on specific measures of problem solving, such as speed of reaction time and weight judgments, began to be explored in 1890 by James McKeen Cattell and others. Their studies of responses on specific cognitive and ability measures in the early laboratories were neglected when the development of practical intelligence testing started in this century. At that time, Binet and Henri shifted attention to the measurement of generalized intelligence by studying individual differences in more complex global tasks. Now it is refreshing to witness the reawakened interest in such enduringly important topics as reaction time and "conceptual tempo" and it is good to see sophisticated consistency evidence for it (Kagan, 1969). The generality and stability of behaviors assessed by these cognitive measures often have been found to be among the best available in personality research.

Some puzzling problems may arise, however, from the correlations found between some of the most promising new cognitive style measures and the traditional measures of generalized intelligence such as the performance IQ on the WISC. That is, correlations between measures of generalized intelligence and cognitive style such as Witkin's field dependence raise the question of the degree to which the consistency of cognitive styles may be due to their associations with intellectual abilities. The obtained generality and stability, as well as the external personality correlates, of at least some cognitive style measures thus may rest in part on their sizable correlations with indexes of more generalized intelligence and achievement behavior, as has been found in other studies (e.g., Crandall & Sinkeldam, 1964; Elliott, 1961). To illustrate, the Witkin measures of cognitive style are strongly related to performance IQ ability indexes. Indeed the relationship between the Witkin Embedded Figures Test and the Wechsler Intelligence Block Design subtest is so strong that Witkin (1965) has indicated he is willing to use Block Design scores when available as a substitute for other field-dependence measures. When such cognitive styles as field independence and such coping patterns as "intellectualization" are substantially correlated with IQ then the stability reported for them and their correlates (e.g., by Schimek, 1968) may partly reflect the stability of the IQ.

This issue might also constitute a problem in interpreting such cognitive styles as

Kagan's conceptual tempo. To the extent that conceptual tempo involves reaction time, and fast reaction time is a determinant of generalized performance IQ, one would have to be alert to their interrelations, as has been pointed out by Campbell and Fiske (1959). It will be interesting to continue to explore exactly how conceptual tempo and other cognitive styles based on performance indexes such as response speed and accuracy take us beyond generalized ability measurement and into the domain of personality traits. Ultimately research on cognitive styles surely will provide a clearer analysis of intellective behavior. The implications of cognitive styles for the concept of general intelligence (as well as the reverse relation) should then become more explicit than they are now. In the course of these explorations the meaning of intercorrelations among diverse cognitive style measures—such as conceptual tempo, field dependence-independence, leveling-sharpening, and so on—will become clearer. At the same time our understanding of the interactions among cognitive and noncognitive personality dimensions hopefully will improve.

When we turn away from cognitive and intellective dimensions to the domain of personality and interpersonal behavior, consistency evidence is generally much harder to establish, at least whenever we use conventional tactics and the correlation coefficient (e.g., Maccoby, 1969). On the basis of past literature on this topic, one should no longer be surprised when consistency correlations for social behavior patterns turn out to be quite low. Theoretically, in my view, one should not expect social behavior to be consistent unless the relevant social learning and cognitive conditions are arranged to maintain the behavior cross-situationally. On theoretical as well as on empirical grounds, much of the time there is no reason to expect great consistency in the social behaviors comprising most of our personality dimensions.

It is not possible to even begin to cite here the extensive evidence that I believe supports this point, namely, that noncognitive global personality dispositions are much less global than traditional psychodynamic and trait positions have assumed them to be (Mischel, 1968). A great deal of behavioral specificity has been found regularly on character traits such as rigidity, social conformity, aggression, on attitudes to authority, and on virtually any other nonintellective personality dimension (Mischel, 1968; Peterson, 1968; Vernon, 1964). Some of the data on delay of gratification with young children, emerging from our current studies at Stanford, are illustrative. In an ongoing longitudinal study on this problem we have obtained evidence that delay of gratification has some developmental consistency and increases with age, up to a point.[2] Much more impressive in my view, however, is our finding that within any child there exists tremendous variability on this dimension. Now we are studying how long preschool children will actually sit still alone in a chair waiting for a preferred but delayed outcome before they signal to terminate the waiting period and settle for a less preferred but immediately available gratification. We are finding that the same 3½-year-old child who on one occasion may terminate his waiting in less than half a minute may be capable of waiting by himself up to an hour on another occasion a few weeks earlier or later, *if* cognitive and attentional

[2] W. Mischel, E. B. Ebbesen, & A. Raskoff. In progress research report, Stanford University, entitled "Determinants of Delay of Gratification and Waiting Behavior in Preschool Children."

conditions are appropriately arranged. Our conclusion is that some significant predictions of length of voluntary delay of gratification certainly can be made from individual differences data; but the most powerful predictions by far come from knowledge of the cognitive and incentive conditions that prevail in the particular situation of interest.

These results are not at all atypical. A tribute to the interaction of person and environment is usually offered at the front of every elementary textbook in the form of Kurt Lewin's famous equation: Behavior is a function of person and environment. In spite of such lip service to the stimulus, most of our personality theories and methods still take no serious account of conditions in the regulation of behavior. Literally thousands of tests exist to measure dispositions, and virtually none is available to measure the psychological environment in which development and change occurs.

Evidence on observed instability and inconsistency in behavior often has been interpreted to reflect the imperfections of our tests and tools and the resulting unreliability and errors of our measurements, as due to the fallibility of the human clinical judge and his ratings, and as due to many other methodological problems. Undoubtedly all these sources contribute real problems. Some of these have been excellently conceptualized by Emmerich (1969). His emphasis on the need for considering rate and mean changes over age if one is to achieve a proper understanding of continuity, growth, and psychological differentiation is especially important. Likewise, his call for longitudinal, multimeasure, and multivariate studies needs to be heeded most seriously.

I am more and more convinced, however, hopefully by data as well as on theoretical grounds, that the observed inconsistency so regularly found in studies of noncognitive personality dimensions often reflects the state of nature and not merely the noise of measurement. Of course, that does not imply a capriciously haphazard world—only one in which personality consistencies seem greater than they are and in which behavioral complexities seem simpler than they are. This would, if true, be extremely functional. After all, if people tried to be radical behaviorists and to describe each other in operational terms they would soon run out of breath and expire. It is essential for the mind to be a reducing valve—if it were not it might literally blow itself!

Perhaps the most widely accepted argument for consistency in the face of seeming diversity is the one mentioned so often, the distinction between the phenotypic and the genotypic. Thus most theorizing on continuity seems to have been guided by a model that assumes a set of genotypic personality dispositions that endure, although their overt response forms may change. This model, of course, is the one shared by traditional trait and dynamic dispositional theories of personality. The model was well summarized in the example of how a child at age 12 may substitute excessive obedience to a parent for his earlier phobic reaction as a way of reducing anxiety over parental rejection (Kagan, 1969). At the level of physical analogy Kagan spoke of how the litre of water in the closed system is converted to steam and recondensed to liquid.

This type of hydraulic Freudian-derived personality model, while widely shared by personality theorists, is of course not the only one available and not the only one necessary to deal with phenomena of continuity and change. Indeed, in the opinion of many clinical psychologists the hydraulic phenotypic-genotypic model applied to personality dynamics, psychotherapy, and symptom substitution has turned out to be a conceptual trap leading to some tragic pragmatic mistakes in clinical treatment and diagnosis for the last 50 years (e.g., Mischel, 1968; Peterson, 1968). I am referring, of course, to the unjustified belief that seemingly diverse personality problems must constitute symptoms of an underlying generalized core disorder rather than being relatively discrete problems often under the control of relatively independent causes and maintaining conditions.

The analysis of diverse behaviors as if they were symptomatic surface manifestations of more unitary underlying dispositional forces also is prevalent in our theories of personality development (e.g., Kagan, 1969; Maddi, 1968). But while diverse behaviors often may be in the service of the same motive or disposition, often they are not. In accord with the genotype-phenotype distinction, if a child shows attachment and dependency in some contexts but not in others one would begin a search to separate phenotypes from genotypes. But it is also possible that seeming inconsistencies, rather than serving one underlying motive, actually may be under the control of relatively separate causal variables. The two behavior patterns may not reflect a phenotype in the service of a genotype but rather may reflect discrimination learning in the service of the total organism. Likewise, while a child's fears sometimes may be in the service of an underlying motive, most research on the topic would lead me to predict it is more likely that the fear would involve an organized response system with its own behavioral life, being evoked and maintained by its own set of regulating conditions (e.g., Bandura, 1969; Paul, 1967).

When we observe a woman who seems hostile and fiercely independent some of the time but passive, dependent, and feminine on other occasions, our reducing valve usually makes us choose between the two syndromes. We decide that one pattern is in the service of the other, or that both are in the service of a third motive. She must be a really castrating lady with a facade of passivity—or perhaps she is a warm, passive-dependent woman with a surface defense of aggressiveness. But perhaps nature is bigger than our concepts and it is possible for the lady to be a hostile, fiercely independent, passive, dependent, feminine, aggressive, warm, castrating person all-in-one. Of course which of these she is at any particular moment would not be random and capricious—it would depend on who she is with, when, how, and much, much more. But each of these aspects of her self may be a quite genuine and real aspect of her total being. (Perhaps we need more adjectives and hyphens in our personality descriptions. That is what is meant, I think, by "moderator variables.")

I am skeptical about the utility of the genotype-phenotype distinction at the present level of behavioral analysis in personality psychology because I fear it grossly oversimplifies the complexity of organized behavior and its often nonlinear causes. The genotype-phenotype oversimplification may mask the complex relations between the behavior and the organism that generates it, the other behaviors available to the organism, the history of the behavior, and the current evoking and maintaining conditions that regulate its occurrence and its generalization.

The question of the nature of the similarity or dissimilarity among the diverse responses emitted by a person is one of the thorniest in psychology. Even when one response pattern is not in the service of another the two of course may still interact. No matter how seemingly separated the various branches of behavior may be, one can always construe some common origins for them and some current interactions. At the very least, all behavior from an organism, no matter how diverse, still has unity because it is all generated from the same source—from the same one person. At the other extreme, incidentally, few response patterns are ever phenotypically or physically identical: Their similarity always has to be grouped on some higher-order dimension of meaning. To make sense of bits of raw behavior one always has to group them into larger common categories. The interesting theoretical issue is just what the bases of these groupings should be. Dispositional theories try to categorize behaviors in terms of the hypothesized historical psychic forces that diverse behaviors supposedly serve; but it is also possible to categorize the behaviors in terms of the unifying evoking and maintaining conditions that they jointly share.

Moreover, few potent response patterns can occur without exerting radical consequences for the other alternatives available to the person. Thus an extremely "fast-tempo" child may be so active that, in addition to fatiguing his parents, he may as Kagan (1969) found, smile less. Perhaps that happens because he is too busy to smile. My comment about how fast-tempo children may be too busy to smile is not really facetious. One of the intriguing features of any strong response syndrome is that it soon prevents all kinds of other intrinsically incompatible behaviors. If a child darts about a lot and is fast there are all sorts of other things he automatically cannot do. His speed in living, his pace, not only automatically influences his other possible behavior, it also soon starts to shape his environment. I now expect my fast-tempo children to be fast tempo, and currently it takes almost no cues from them to convince me I am right about them.

It would have been relatively simple to assess and predict personality if it had turned out to consist mainly of stable highly generalized response patterns that occur regularly in relation to many diverse stimulus constellations. The degree and subtlety of discrimination shown in human behavior, however, is at least as impressive as is the variety and extensiveness of stimulus generalization. What people do in any situation may be altered radically even by seemingly minor variations in prior experiences or slight modifications in stimulus attributes or in the specific characteristics of the evoking situation. From my theoretical perspective this state of affairs—namely, the enormously subtle discriminations that people continuously make, and consequently the flexibility of behavior—is not a cause of gloom. Instead, the relative specificity of behavior, and its dependence on environmental supports, is the expected result of complex discrimination learning and subtle cognitive differentiation. When the eliciting and evoking conditions that maintain behavior change—as they generally do across settings—then behavior surely will change also. While the continuous interplay of person and condition may have been a surprise for faculty and trait psychology it should come as no upset for us now. If one pays more than verbal tribute to the dependency of behavior on conditions, and to the modification of behavior when situations change, then the so-called negative results of dispositional research on behavioral continuity appear attributable largely to the limitations of the assumptions that have guided the research. From the viewpoint of social behavior theory the findings of behavioral specificity, rather than primarily reflecting measurement errors, are actually congruent with results from experimental research on the determinants and modification of social behavior (Mischel, 1968). When response consequences and valences change so do actions; but when maintaining conditions remain stable so does behavior.

The last decade has seen an exciting growth of research on cognitive styles and many researchers have begun to study the person as an information-processing and problem-solving organism. Generally, however, these processes have been viewed in dimensional and dispositional terms and quickly translated back to fit the consistency assumptions of traditional global trait and psychodynamic theory. Individual differences on dimensions such as conceptual tempo, field dependence, leveling-sharpening, and so on, have been isolated with some promising results. Less progress has been made in applying the concepts and language of information processing and cognitive styles to forming a better theoretical conception of personality structure itself. It has become fashionable to speak of the organism as creating plans, generating rules, and, depending on his needs and situations, devising strategies. These tactics yield payoffs and consequences, and in light of these the person modifies his plans accordingly. But when contingencies change stably, what happens? For example, what happens when the mother-dependent child finds that his preschool peers now consistently have little patience for his whining, attention-getting bids, and instead respect independence and self-confidence? Generally the child's behavior changes in accord with the new contingencies, and if the contingencies shift so does the behavior—if the contingencies remain stable so does the new syndrome that the child now displays. Then what has happened to the child's dependency trait?

One might argue that the basic genotype remained but its manifestation phenotypically has altered. But is this just a "symptom" change leaving unaffected the psyche that generated it and the life space in which it unfolds? A vigorous "No!" to this question comes from much research on behavior change in the last few years (e.g., Bijou, 1965; Fairweather, 1967; Mischel, 1966; Patterson, Ray, & Shaw, 1969).

What would happen conceptually if we treated the organism as truly active and dynamic rather than as the carrier of a stable dispositional reservoir of motives and traits? Might one then more easily think of changes in the developing organism not as phenotypic overlays that mask genotypic unities but as genuinely new strategies in which many of the person's old plans are discarded and replaced by more appropriate ones in the course of development? (Perhaps Gordon Allport's idea of functional autonomy needs to be rethought.) Can the person even become involved in plans to change what he *is* as well as what he does? George Kelly and the existentialists in their search for human nature noted that existence precedes essence. According to that position, to find out what I *am* I need to know what I *do*. And if my actions change do they leave me (the "real me") behind? Or perhaps they just leave some of my discarded psychological genotypes behind?

A search for a personality psychology that has conceptual room for major variability and changes within the individual's dispositions can easily be misinterpreted as undermining the concept of personality itself. That would be an unfortunate misconstruction. Instead, we do need to recognize that discontinuities—real ones and not merely superficial or trivial veneer changes—are part of the genuine phenomena of personality. If one accepts that proposition, an adequate conceptualization of personality will have to go beyond the conventional definition of stable and broad enduring individual differences in behavioral dispositions. We may have to tolerate more dissonance than we like in our personality theory. To be more than nominally dynamic our personality theories will have to have as much room for human discrimination as for generalization, as much place for personality change as for stability, and as much concern for man's self-regulation as for his victimization by either enduring intrapsychic forces or by momentary environmental constraints.

REFERENCES

Bandura, A. *Principles of behavior modification.* New York: Holt, Rinehart and Winston, 1969.

Bijou, S. W. Experimental studies of child behavior, normal and deviant. In L. Krasner & L. P. Ullmann (Eds.), *Research in behavior modification.* New York: Holt, Rinehart and Winston, 1965.

Bruner, J. S., Olver, R. R., & Greenfield, P. M. *Studies in cognitive growth.* New York: Wiley, 1966.

Campbell, D., & Fiske, D. Convergent and discriminant validation by the multitrait-multimethod matrix. *Psychological Bulletin*, 1959, *56*, 81–105.

Crandall, V. J., & Sinkeldam, C. Children's dependent and achievement behaviors in social situations and their perceptual field dependence. *Journal of Personality*, 1964, *32*, 1–22.

Elliott, R. Interrelationships among measures of field dependence, ability, and personality traits. *Journal of Abnormal and Social Psychology*, 1961, *63*, 27–36.

Emmerich, W. Models of continuity and change. Paper presented at the meeting of the Society for Research in Child Development, March 27, 1969, Santa Monica, California.

Fairweather, G. W. *Methods in experimental social innovation.* New York: Wiley, 1967.

Hunt, J. McV. Traditional personality theory in the light of recent evidence. *American Scientist*, 1965, *53*, 80–96.

Kagan, J. Continuity in development. Paper presented at the meeting of the Society for Research in Child Development, March 27, 1969, Santa Monica, California.

Maccoby, E. E. Tracing individuality within age-related change. Paper presented at the meeting of the Society for Research in Child Development, March 27, 1969, Santa Monica, California.

Maddi, S. R. *Personality theories: A comparative analysis.* Homewood, Ill.: Dorsey Press, 1968.

Mischel, W. A social learning view of sex differences in behavior. In E. E. Maccoby (Ed.), *The development of sex differences.* Stanford, Calif.: Stanford University Press, 1966.

Mischel, W. *Personality and assessment.* New York: Wiley, 1968.

Patterson, G. R., Ray, R. S., & Shaw, D. A. Direct intervention in families of deviant children. *Oregon Research Institute Bulletin*, 1969, *8*(9), 1–62.

Paul, G. L. Insight versus desensitization in psychotherapy two years after termination. *Journal of Consulting Psychology*, 1967, *31*, 333–348.

Peterson, D. *The clinical study of social behavior.* New York: Appleton, 1968.

Schimek, J. G. Cognitive style and defenses: A longitudinal study of intellectualization and field independence. *Journal of Abnormal Psychology*, 1968, 73, 575–580.

Vernon, P. S. *Personality assessment: A critical survey.* New York: Wiley, 1964.

Witkin, H. Psychological differentiation and forms of pathology. *Journal of Abnormal Psychology*, 1965, 70, 317–336.

Witkin, H. A., Goodenough, D. R., & Karp, S. A. Stability of cognitive style from childhood to young adulthood. *Journal of Personality and Social Psychology*, 1967, 7, 291–300.

5 | Psychodynamic Theories—I

5.1 | ON TRANSFORMATIONS OF INSTINCT AS EXEMPLIFIED IN ANAL EROTISM*

Sigmund Freud

Some years ago, observations made during psycho-analysis led me to suspect that the constant co-existence in any one of the three character-traits of *orderliness, parsimony* and *obstinacy* indicated an intensification of the anal-erotic components in his sexual constitution, and that these modes of reaction, which were favoured by his ego, had been established during the course of his development through the assimilation of his anal erotism [Freud, 1908a].

In that publication my main object was to make known the fact of this established relation; I was little concerned about its theoretical significance. Since then there has been a general consensus of opinion that each one of the three qualities, avarice, pedantry and obstinacy, springs from anal-erotic sources—or, to express it more cautiously and more completely—draws powerful contributions from those sources. The cases in which these defects of character were combined and which in consequence bore a special stamp (the "anal character") were merely extreme instances, which were bound to betray the particular connection that interests us here even to an unobservant eye.

As a result of numerous impressions, and in particular of one specially cogent analytical observation, I came to the conclusion a few years later that in the development of the libido in man the phase of genital primacy must be preceded by a "pregenital organization" in which sadism and anal erotism play the leading parts [Freud, 1913].

From that moment we had to face the problem of the later history of the anal-erotic instinctual impulses. What becomes of them when, owing to the establishment of a definitive genital organization, they have lost their importance in sexual life? Do they

* SOURCE: Freud, S. On transformations of instinct as exemplified in anal erotism. In J. Strachey (Ed.), *The standard edition of the complete psychological works of Sigmund Freud*, Vol. XVII. London: The Hogarth Press Ltd., and the Institute of Psycho-Analysis, 1955. Pp. 127–133. Reprinted by permission of Sigmund Freud Copyrights, Ltd., The Institute of Psycho-Analysis, the Hogarth Press Ltd., and Basic Books.

preserve their original nature, but in a state of repression? Are they sublimated or assimilated by transformation into character-traits? Or do they find a place within the new organization of sexuality characterized by genital primacy? Or, since none of these vicissitudes of anal erotism is likely to be the only one, to what extent and in what way does each of them share in deciding its fate? For the organic sources of anal erotism cannot of course be buried as a result of the emergence of the genital organization.

One would think that there could be no lack of material from which to provide an answer, since the processes of development and transformation in question must have taken place in everyone undergoing analysis. Yet the material is so obscure, the abundance of ever-recurring impressions so confusing, that even now I am unable to solve the problem fully and can do no more than make some contributions to its solution. In making them I need not refrain from mentioning, where the context allows it, other instinctual transformations besides anal-erotic ones. Finally, it scarcely requires to be emphasized that the developmental events here described—just as the others found in psycho-analysis—have been inferred from the regressions into which they had been forced by neurotic processes.

As a starting-point for this discussion we may take the fact that it appears as if in the products of the unconscious—spontaneous ideas, phantasies and symptoms—the concepts *faeces* (money, gift) [Freud, 1908a], *baby* and *penis* are ill-distinguished from one another and are easily interchangeable. We realize, of course, that to express oneself in this way is incorrectly to apply to the sphere of the unconscious terms which belong properly to other regions of mental life, and that we have been led astray by the advantages offered by an analogy. To put the matter in a form less open to objection, these elements in the unconscious are often treated as if they were equivalent and could replace one another freely.

This is most easily seen in the relation between "baby" and "penis." It cannot be without significance that in the symbolic language of dreams, as well as of everyday life, both may be replaced by the same symbol; both baby and penis are called a "little one," ["*das Kleine*"] [Freud, 1900]. It is a well-known fact that symbolic speech often ignores difference of sex. The "little one," which originally meant the male genital organ, may thus have acquired a secondary application to the female genitals.

If we penetrate deeply enough into the neurosis of a woman, we not infrequently meet with the repressed wish to possess a penis like a man. We call this wish "envy for a penis" and include it in the castration complex. Chance mishaps in the life of such a woman, mishaps which are themselves frequently the result of a very masculine disposition, have re-activated this infantile wish and, through the backward flow of libido, made it the chief vehicle of her neurotic symptoms. In other women we find no evidence of this wish for a penis; it is replaced by the wish for a baby, the frustration of which in real life can lead to the outbreak of a neurosis. It looks as if such women had understood (although this could not possibly have acted as a motive) that nature has given babies to women as a substitute for the penis that has been denied them. With other women, again, we learn that both wishes were present in their childhood and that one replaced the other. At first they had wanted a penis like a man; then at a later, though still childish, stage there appeared instead the wish for a baby. The impression is forced upon us that this variety in our findings is caused by accidental factors during childhood (e.g. the presence or absence of brothers or the birth of a new baby at some favourable time of life), so that the wish for a penis and the wish for a baby would be fundamentally identical.

We can say what the ultimate outcome of the infantile wish for a penis is in women in whom the determinants of a neurosis in later life are absent: it changes into the wish for a *man*, and thus puts up with the man as an appendage to the penis. This transformation, therefore, turns an impulse which is hostile to the female sexual function into one which is favourable to it. Such women are in this way made capable of an erotic life based on the masculine type of object-love, which can exist alongside the feminine one proper, derived from narcissism. We already know [see Freud, 1914] that in other cases it is only a baby that makes the transition from narcissistic self-love to object-love possible. So that in this respect too a baby can be represented by the penis.

I have had occasional opportunities of being told women's dreams that had occurred after their first experience of intercourse. They revealed an unmistakable wish in the woman to keep for herself the penis which she had felt. Apart from their libidinal origin, then, these dreams indicated a temporary regression from man to penis as the object of her wish. One would certainly be inclined to trace back the wish for a man in a purely rationalistic way to the wish for a baby, since a woman is bound to understand sooner or later that there can be no baby without the co-operation of a man. It is, however, more likely that the wish for a man arises independently of the wish for a baby, and that when it arises—from understandable motives belonging entirely to ego-psychology—the original wish for a penis becomes attached to it as an unconscious libidinal reinforcement. The importance of the process described lies in the fact that a part of the young woman's narcissistic masculinity is thus changed into femininity, and so can no longer operate in a way harmful to the female sexual function.

Along another path, a part of the erotism of the pregenital phase, too, becomes available for use in the phase of genital primacy. The baby is regarded as "lumf" [Freud, 1909] (cf. the analysis of "Little Hans"), as something which becomes detached from the body by passing through the bowel. A certain amount of libidinal cathexis which originally attached to the contents of the bowel can thus be extended to the baby born through it. Linguistic evidence of this identity of baby and faeces is contained in the expression "to give someone a baby." For its faeces are the infant's first gift, a part of his body which he will give up only on persuasion by someone he loves, to whom indeed, he will make a spontaneous gift of it as a token of affection; for, as a rule, infants do not dirty strangers. (There are similar if less intense reactions with urine.) Defaecation affords the first occasion on which the child must decide between a narcissistic and an object-loving attitude. He either parts obediently with his faeces, "sacrifices" them to his love, or else retains them for purposes of auto-erotic satisfaction and later as a means of asserting his own will. If he makes the latter choice we are in the presence of defiance (obstinacy) which, accordingly, springs from a narcissistic clinging to anal erotism.

It is probable that the first meaning which a child's interest in faeces develops is that of "gift" rather than "gold" or "money." The child knows no money apart from what is given him—no money acquired and none inherited of his own. Since his faeces are his first gift, the child easily transfers his interest from that substance to the new one which he comes across as the most valuable gift in life. Those who question this derivation of gifts should consider their experience of psycho-analytic treatment, study the gifts they receive as doctors from their patients, and watch the storms of transference which a gift from them can rouse in their patients.

Thus the interest in faeces is continued partly as interest in money, partly as a wish for a baby, in which later an anal-erotic and a genital impulse ("envy for a penis") converge. But the penis has another anal-erotic significance apart from its relation to the interest in a baby. The relationship between the penis and the passage lined with mucous membrane which it fills and excites already has its prototype in the pregenital, anal-sadistic phase. The faecal mass, or as one patient called it, the faecal "stick," represents as it were the first penis, and the stimulated mucous membrane of the rectum represents that of the vagina. There are people whose anal erotism remains vigorous and unmodified up to the age preceding puberty (ten to twelve years); we learn from them that during the pregenital phase they had already developed in phantasy and in perverse play an organization analogous to the genital one, in which penis and vagina were represented by the faecal stick and the rectum. In other people— obsessional neurotics—we can observe the result of a regressive debasement of the genital organization. This is expressed in the fact that every phantasy originally conceived on the genital level is transposed to the anal level—the penis being replaced by the faecal mass and the vagina by the rectum.

As the interest in faeces recedes in a normal way, the organic analogy we have described here has the effect of transferring the interest on to the penis. When, later, in the course of the child's researches [Freud, 1908b] he discovers that babies are born from the bowel, they inherit the greater part of his anal erotism; they have, however, been preceded by the penis in this as well as in another sense.

I feel sure that by this time the manifold interrelations of the series—faeces, penis, baby—have become totally unintelligible; so I will try to remedy the defect by presenting them diagramatically, and in considering the diagram [Fig. 1] we can review the same material in a different order. Unfortunately, this technical device is not sufficiently pliable for our purpose, or possibly we have not yet learned to use it with effect. In any case I hope the reader will not expect too much from it.

Anal erotism finds a narcissistic application in the production of defiance, which constitutes an important reaction on the part of the ego against demands made by other people. Interest in faeces is carried over first to interest in gifts, and then to interest in money. In girls, the discovery of the penis gives rise to envy for it, which later changes into the wish for a man as the possessor of a penis. Even before this the wish for a penis has changed into the wish for a baby, or the latter wish has taken the place of the former one. An organic analogy between penis and baby (dotted line) is expressed by the existence of a symbol ("little one") common to both. A rational wish (double line) then leads from the wish for a baby to the wish for a man: we have already appreciated the importance of this instinctual transformation.

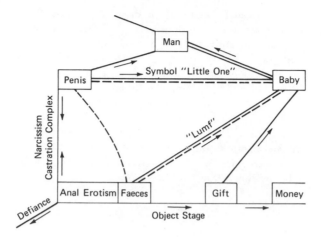

Another part of the nexus of relations can be observed much more clearly in the male. It arises when the boy's sexual researches lead him to the discovery of the absence of a penis in women. He concludes that the penis must be a detachable part of the body, something analogous to faeces, the first piece of bodily substance the child had to part with. Thus the old anal defiance enters into the composition of the castration complex. The organic analogy which enabled the intestinal contents to be the forerunner of the penis during the pregenital phase cannot come into account as a motive; but the boy's sexual researches lead him to a psychical substitute for it. When a baby appears on the scene he regards it as "lumf," in accordance with those researches, and he cathects it with powerful anal-erotic interest. When social experiences teach that a baby is to be regarded as a love-token, a gift, the wish for a baby receives a second contribution from the same source. Faeces, penis and baby are all three solid bodies; they all three, by forcible entry or expulsion, stimulate a membranous passage, i.e. the rectum and the vagina, the latter being as it were 'taken on lease' from the rectum, as Lou Andreas-Salomé [1916] aptly remarks. Infantile sexual researches can only lead to the conclusion that the baby follows the same route as the faecal mass. The function of the penis is not usually discovered by those researches. But it is interesting to note that after so many détours an organic correspondence reappears in the psychical sphere as an unconscious identity.

REFERENCES

Andreas-Salomé, L. " 'Anal' und 'Sexual,' " *Imago*, 1916, *4*, 249.

Freud, S. [1900] The interpretation of dreams. In Strachey, J. (Ed.), *The standard edition of the complete psychological works of Sigmund Freud*, Vol. IV–V. London: Hogarth Press, Ltd. and the Institute of Psycho-Analysis, 1955.

Freud, S. [1908a] Character and anal erotism. In Strachey, J. (Ed.), *The standard edition of the complete psychological works of Sigmund Freud*, Vol. IX. London: Hogarth Press, Ltd. and the Institute of Psycho-Analysis, 1955.

Freud, S. [1908b] On the sexual theories of children. In Strachey, J. (Ed.), *The standard edition of the complete psychological works of Sigmund Freud*, Vol. IX. London: Hogarth Press, Ltd. and the Institute of Psycho-Analysis, 1955.

Freud, S. [1909] Analysis of a phobia in a five-year-old boy. In Strachey, J. (Ed.), *The standard edition of the complete psychological works of Sigmund Freud*, Vol. X. London: Hogarth Press, Ltd. and the Institute of Psycho-Analysis, 1955.

Freud, S. [1913] The predisposition to obsessional neurosis. In Strachey, J. (Ed.), *The standard edition of the complete pyschological works of Sigmund Freud*, Vol. XII. London: Hogarth Press, Ltd. and the Institute of Psycho-Analysis, 1955.

Freud, S. [1914] On narcissism: An introduction. In Strachey, J. (Ed.), *The standard edition of the complete psychological works of Sigmund Freud*, Vol. XIV. London: Hogarth Press, Ltd. and the Institute of Psycho-Analysis, 1955.

5.2 | THE DISSOLUTION[1] OF THE OEDIPUS COMPLEX*

Sigmund Freud

To an ever-increasing extent the Oedipus complex reveals its importance as the central phenomenon of the sexual period of early childhood. After that, its dissolution takes place; it succumbs to repression, as we say, and is followed by the latency period. It has not yet become clear, however, what it is that brings about its destruction. Analyses seem to show that it is the experience of painful disappointments. The little girl likes to regard herself as what her father loves above all else; but the time comes when she has to endure a harsh punishment from him and she is cast out of her fool's paradise.

[1] [*"Untergang."* We learn from Ernest Jones (1957), p. 114, that Ferenczi, in a letter of March 24, 1924, objected to the strength of this word and suggested that it was chosen as a reaction to Rank's ideas on the importance of the "birth trauma." Freud, replying two days later, "admitted that the word in the title might have been emotionally influenced by his feelings about Rank's new ideas, but said that the paper itself was quite independent of the latter" (Jones, 1957). It must be pointed out, indeed that the phrase *"Untergang des Ödipuskomplexes"* had in fact been used twice by Freud in *The Ego and the Id* (1923a), which was written before the publication of Rank's hypothesis. . . . In the same passage he had in fact also used the still stronger word *"Zertrümmerung* (demolition)."]

* SOURCE: Freud, S. The dissolution of the Oedipus Complex. In J. Strachey (Ed.), *The standard edition of the complete psychological works of Sigmund Freud*, Vol. XIX. London: Hogarth Press Ltd., 1961. Pp. 173–179. Reprinted by permission of Sigmund Freud Copyrights Ltd., The Institute of Psycho-Analysis, Hogarth Press Ltd., and Basic Books.

The boy regards his mother as his own property; but he finds one day that she has transferred her love and solicitude to a new arrival. Reflection must deepen our sense of the importance of those influences, for it will emphasize the fact that distressing experiences of this sort which act in opposition to the content of the complex, are inevitable. Even when no special events occur, like those we have mentioned as examples, the absence of the satisfaction hoped for, the continued denial of the desired baby, must in the end lead the small lover to turn away from his hopeless longing. In this way the Oedipus complex would go to its destruction from its lack of success, from the effects of its internal impossibility.

Another view is that the Oedipus complex must collapse because the time has come for its disintegration, just as the milk-teeth fall out when the permanent ones begin to grow. Although the majority of human beings go through the Oedipus•complex as an individual experience, it is nevertheless a phenomenon which is determined and laid down by heredity and which is bound to pass away according to programme when the next pre-ordained phase of development sets in. This being so, it is of no great importance what the occasions are which allow this to happen, or, indeed, whether any such occasions can be discovered at all.[2]

The justice of both these views cannot be disputed. Moreover, they are compatible. There is room for the ontogenetic view side by side with the more far-reaching phylogenetic one. It is also true that even at birth the whole individual is destined to die, and perhaps his organic disposition may already contain the indication of what he is to die from. Nevertheless, it remains of interest to follow out how this innate programme is carried out and in what way accidental noxae exploit his disposition.

We have lately[3] been made more clearly aware than before that a child's sexual development advances to a certain phase at which the genital organ has already taken over the leading role. But this genital is the male one only, or, more correctly, the penis; the female genital has remained undiscovered. This phallic phase, which is contemporaneous with the Oedipus complex, does not develop further to the definitive genital organization, but is submerged, and is succeeded by the latency period. Its termination, however, takes place in a typical manner and in conjunction with events that are of regular recurrence.

When the (male) child's interest turns to his genitals he betrays the fact by manipulating them frequently; and he then finds that the adults do not approve of this behaviour. More or less plainly, more or less brutally, a threat is pronounced that this part of him which he values so highly will be taken away from him. Usually it is from women that the threat emanates; very often they seek to strengthen their authority by a reference to the father or the doctor, who, so they say, will carry out the puhishment. In a number of cases the women will themselves mitigate the threat in a symbolic manner by telling the child that what is to be removed is not his genital, which actually plays a passive part, but his hand, which is the active culprit. It happens particularly often that the little boy is threatened with castration, not because he plays with his

[2] [The ideas contained in this and the preceding paragraph had been expressed by Freud in very similar terms in Section IV of " 'A Child Is Being Beaten' " (1919) . . . , p. 188.]

[3] [See "The Infantile Genital Organization of the Libido" (Freud, 1923b), p. 141 . . .]

penis with his hand, but because he wets his bed every night and cannot be got to be clean. Those in charge of him behave as if this nocturnal incontinence was the result and the proof of his being unduly concerned with his penis, and they are probably right.[4] In any case, long-continued bed-wetting is to be equated with the emissions of adults. It is an expression of the same excitation of the genitals which has impelled the child to masturbate at this period.

Now it is my view that what brings about the destruction of the child's phallic genital organization is this threat of castration. Not immediately, it is true, and not without other influences being brought to bear as well. For to begin with the boy does not believe in the threat or obey it in the least. Psycho-analysis has recently attached importance to two experiences which all children go through and which, it is suggested, prepare them for the loss of highly valued parts of the body. These experiences are the withdrawal of the mother's breast—at first intermittently and later for good—and the daily demand on them to give up the contents of the bowel. But there is no evidence to show that, when the threat of castration takes place, those experiences have any effect.[5] It is not until a *fresh* experience comes his way that the child begins to reckon with the possibility of being castrated, and then only hesitatingly and unwillingly, and not without making efforts to depreciate the significance of something he has himself observed.

The observation which finally breaks down his unbelief is the sight of the female genitals. Sooner or later the child, who is so proud of his possession of a penis, has a view of the genital region of a little girl, and cannot help being convinced of the absence of a penis in a creature who is so like himself. With this, the loss of his own penis becomes imaginable, and the threat of castration takes its deferred effect.

We should not be as short-sighted as the person in charge of the child who threatens him with castration, and we must not overlook the fact that at this time masturbation by no means represents the whole of his sexual life. As can be clearly shown, he stands in the Oedipus attitude to his parents; his masturbation is only a genital discharge of the sexual excitation belonging to the complex, and throughout his later years will owe its importance to that relationship. The Oedipus complex offered the child two possibilities of satisfaction, an active and a passive one. He could put himself in his father's place in a masculine fashion and have intercourse with his mother as his father did, in which case he would soon have felt the latter as a hindrance; or he might want to take the place of his mother and be loved by his father, in which case his mother would become superfluous. The child may have had only very vague notions as to what constitutes a satisfying erotic intercourse; but certainly the penis must play a part in it, for the sensations in his own organ were evidence of that. So far he had had

---

[4] [Cf. the case history of "Dora" (Freud, 1905b) . . . , p. 74 and the second of the *Three Essays* (1905a . . . , p. 190.]

[5] [Cf. a footnote added, at about the time this paper was written, to the case history of "Little Hans" (Freud, 1909) . . . , p. 8 in which reference is made to papers by Andreas-Salomé (1916), A. Stärcke (1910) and Alexander (1922). A third experience of separation—that of birth—is also mentioned there, but, as in the present passage, Freud objects to the confusion with the castration complex. Cf. also a footnote to "The Infantile Genital Organization of the Libido" (Freud, 1923b), p. 144 . . .]

no occasion to doubt that women possessed a penis. But now his acceptance of the possibility of castration, his recognition that women were castrated, made an end of both possible ways of obtaining satisfaction from the Oedipus complex. For both of them entailed the loss of his penis—the masculine one as a resulting punishment and the feminine one as a precondition. If the satisfaction of love in the field of the Oedipus complex is to cost the child his penis, a conflict is bound to arise between his narcissistic interest in that part of his body and the libidinal cathexis of his parental objects. In this conflict the first of these forces normally triumphs: the child's ego turns away from the Oedipus complex.

I have described elsewhere how this turning away takes place.[6] The object-cathexes are given up and replaced by identifications. The authority of the father or the parents is introjected into the ego, and there it forms the nucleus of the super-ego, which takes over the severity of the father and perpetuates his prohibition against incest, and so secures the ego from the return of the libidinal object-cathexis. The libidinal trends belonging to the Oedipus complex are in part desexualized and sublimated (a thing which probably happens with every transformation into an identification) and in part inhibited in their aim and changed into impulses of affection. The whole process has, on the one hand, preserved the genital organ—has averted the danger of its loss—and, on the other, has paralysed it—has removed its function. This process ushers in the latency period, which now interrupts the child's sexual development.

I see no reason for denying the name of a "repression" to the ego's turning away from the Oedipus complex, although later repressions come about for the most part with the participation of the super-ego, which in this case is only just being formed. But the process we have described is more than a repression. It is equivalent, if it is ideally carried out, to a destruction and an abolition of the complex. We may plausibly assume that we have here come upon the borderline—never a very sharply drawn one—between the normal and the pathological. If the ego has in fact not achieved much more than a *repression* of the complex, the latter persists in an unconscious state in the id and will later manifest its pathogenic effect.

Analytic observation enables us to recognize or guess these connections between the phallic organization, the Oedipus complex, the threat of castration, the formation of the super-ego and the latency period. These connections justify the statement that the destruction of the Oedipus complex is brought about by the threat of castration. But this does not dispose of the problem; there is room for a theoretical speculation which may upset the results we have come to or put them in a new light. Before we start along this new path, however, we must turn to a question which has arisen in the course of this discussion and has so far been left on one side. The process which has been described refers, as has been expressly said, to male children only. How does the corresponding development take place in little girls?

At this point our material—for some incomprehensible reason[7]—becomes far more obscure and full of gaps. The female sex, too, develops an Oedipus complex, a super-

---

[6] [In Chapter III of *The Ego and the Id* . . . (Freud, 1923a), p. 29 ff. . . .]

[7] [Freud suggested some explanation for this in Section I of his paper on "Female Sexuality" (1931).]

ego and a latency period. May we also attribute a phallic organization and a castration complex to it? The answer is in the affirmative; but these things cannot be the same as they are in boys. Here the feminist demand for equal rights for the sexes does not take us far, for the morphological distinction is bound to find expression in differences of psychical development.[8] "Anatomy is Destiny," to vary a saying of Napoleon's. The little girl's clitoris behaves just like a penis to begin with; but, when she makes a comparison with a playfellow of the other sex, she perceives that she has "come off badly"[9] and she feels this as a wrong done to her and as a ground for inferiority. For a while still she consoles herself with the expectation that later on, when she grows older, she will acquire just as big an appendage as the boy's. Here the masculinity complex of women branches off. A female child, however, does not understand her lack of a penis as being a sex character; she explains it by assuming that at some earlier date she had possessed an equally large organ and had then lost it by castration. She seems not to extend this inference from herself to other, adult females, but, entirely on the lines of the phallic phase, to regard them as possessing large and complete—that is to say, male—genitals. The essential difference thus comes about that the girl accepts castration as an accomplished fact, whereas the boy fears the possibility of its occurrence.

The fear of castration being thus excluded in the little girl, a powerful motive also drops out for the setting-up of a super-ego and for the breaking-off of the infantile genital organization. In her, far more than in the boy, these changes seem to be the result of upbringing and of intimidation from outside which threatens her with a loss of love. The girl's Oedipus complex is much simpler than that of the small bearer of the penis; in my experience, it seldom goes beyond the taking of her mother's place and the adopting of a feminine attitude towards her father. Renunciation of the penis is not tolerated by the girl without some attempt at compensation. She slips—along the line of a symbolic equation, one might say—from the penis to a baby. Her Oedipus complex culminates in a desire, which is long retained, to receive a baby from her father as a gift—to bear him a child.[10] One has an impression that the Oedipus complex is then gradually given up because this wish is never fulfilled. The two wishes—to possess a penis and a child—remain strongly cathected in the unconscious and help to prepare the female creature for her later sexual role. The comparatively lesser strength of the sadistic contribution to her sexual instinct, which we may no doubt connect with the stunted growth of her penis, makes it easier in her case for the direct sexual trends to be transformed into aim-inhibited trends of an affectionate kind. It must be admitted, however, that in general our insight into these developmental processes in girls is unsatisfactory, incomplete and vague.[11]

[8] [See Freud's paper, written about eighteen months after this one, on "Some Psychical Consequences of the Anatomical Distinction between the Sexes" (1925), p. 248. . . . Much of what follows is elaborated there. The paraphrase of Napoleon's epigram had appeared already in the second paper on the psychology of love (1912), . . . p. 189.]

[9] [Literally, "come off too short."]

[10] [Cf. Freud's paper on "Transformations of Instinct" (1917), . . . p. 128 ff.]

[11] [Freud discussed this topic much more fully in his papers on the anatomical distinction between the sexes (1925) and on female sexuality (1931), in both of which he gave a very different account of the girl's Oedipus complex from the present one.]

I have no doubt that the chronological and causal relations described here between the Oedipus complex, sexual intimidation (the threat of castration), the formation of the super-ego and the beginning of the latency period are of a typical kind; but I do not wish to assert that this type is the only possible one. Variations in the chronological order and in the linking-up of these events are bound to have a very important bearing on the development of the individual.

REFERENCES

Alexander, F. [1922]. Kastrationskomplex und Charakter, *Int. Z. Psychoan.*, 8, 121.
    (Trans.: 'The Castration Complex in the Formation of Character,' *Int. J. Psycho-Anal.*, 4, (1923), 11.)

Andreas-Salomé, L. [1916]. Anal und Sexual, *Imago*, 4, 249.

Freud, S. [1905a]. *Drei Abhandlungen zur Sexualtheorie*, Vienna, G.S., 5, 3; G.W., 5, 29.
    (Trans.: *Three Essays on the Theory of Sexuality*, London, 1949; *Standard Ed.*, 7, 125.)

Freud, S. [1905b]. Bruchtück einer Hysterie-Analyse, G.S., 8, 3; G.W., 5, 163.
    (Trans.: Fragment of an Analysis of a Case of Hysteria, C.P., 3, 13; *Standard Ed.*, 7, 3.)

Freud, S. [1909]. Analyse der Phobie eines fünfjährigen Knaben, G.S., 8, 129; G.W., 7, 243.
    (Trans.: Analysis of a Phobia in a Five-Year-Old Boy, C.P., 3, 149; *Standard Ed.*, 10, 3.)

Freud, S. [1912]. Über die allgemeinste Erniedrigung des Liebeslebens, G.S., 5, 198; G.W., 8, 78.
    (Trans.: On the Universal Tendency to Debasement in the Sphere of Love, C.P., 4, 203; *Standard Ed.*, 11, 179.)

Freud, S. [1917]. Über Triebumsetzungen insbesondere der Analerotik, G.S., 5, 268; G.W., 10, 402.
    (Trans.: On Transformations of Instinct as Exemplified in Anal Erotism, C.P., 2, 164; *Standard Ed.*, 17, 127.)

Freud, S. [1919]. "Ein Kind wird geschlagen," G.S., 5, 344; G.W., 12, 197.
    (Trans.: "A Child Is Being Beaten," C.P., 2, 172; *Standard Ed.*, 17, 177.)

Freud, S. [1923a]. *Das Ich und das Es*, Vienna. G.S., 6, 353; G.W., 13, 237.
    (Trans.: *The Ego and the Id*, London, 1927; *Standard Ed.*, 19, 3.)

Freud, S. [1923b]. Die infantile Genitalorganisation, G.S., 5, 232; G.W., 13, 293.
    (Trans.: The Infantile Genital Organization, C.P., 2, 244; *Standard Ed.*, 19, 141.)

Freud, S. [1925]. Einige psychische Folgen des anatomischen Geschlechtsunterschieds, G.S., 11, 8; G.W., 14, 19.
    (Trans.: Some Psychical Consequences of the Anatomical Distinction between the Sexes, C.P., 5, 186; *Standard Ed.*, 19, 243.)

Freud, S. [1931]. Uber die weibliche Sexualität, G.S., 12, 120; G.W., 14, 517.
    (Trans.: Female Sexuality, C.P., 5, 252; *Standard Ed.*, 21, 223.)

Jones, E. *Sigmund Freud: Life and Work,* Vol. 3, London and New York.

Stärke, A. [1910] Der Kastrationskomplex, *Int. Z. (ärztle.) Psychoanal.*, 1, 9.

6 | Psychodynamic Theories—II

6.1 | MECHANISMS OF ESCAPE*

Erich Fromm

I come now to the main question: What is the root of both the masochistic perversion and masochistic character traits respectively? Furthermore, what is the common root of both the masochistic and the sadistic strivings?

The direction in which the answer lies has already been suggested in the beginning of this chapter. Both the masochistic and sadistic strivings tend to help the individual to escape his unbearable feeling of aloneness and powerlessness. Psychoanalytic and other empirical observations of masochistic persons give ample evidence (which I cannot quote here without transcending the scope of this . . . [work]) that they are filled with a terror of aloneness and insignificance. Frequently this feeling is not conscious; often it is covered by compensatory feelings of eminence and perfection. However, if one only penetrates deeply enough into the unconscious dynamics of such a person, one finds these feelings without fail. The individual finds himself "free" in the negative sense, that is, alone with his self and confronting an alienated, hostile world. In this situation, to quote a telling description of Dostoevski, in *The Brothers Karamasov*, he has "no more pressing need than the one to find somebody to whom he can surrender, as quickly as possible, that gift of freedom which he, the unfortunate creature, was born with." The frightened individual seeks for somebody or something to tie his self to; he cannot bear to be his own individual self any longer, and he tries frantically to get rid of it and to feel security again by the elimination of this burden: the self.

Masochism is one way toward this goal. The different forms which the masochistic strivings assume have one aim: *to get rid of the individual self, to lose oneself;* in other words, *to get rid of the burden of freedom.* This aim is obvious in those masochistic strivings in which the individual seeks to submit to a person or power which he feels as being overwhelmingly strong. (Incidentally, the conviction of superior strength of an-

* SOURCE: Fromm, E. *Escape from freedom.* New York: Rinehart & Co., Inc., 1941. Pp. 151–156, abridged. Copyright 1941, © 1969 by Erich Fromm. Reprinted by permission of Holt, Rinehart and Winston, Inc.

other person is always to be understood in relative terms. It can be based either upon the actual strength of the other person, or upon a conviction of one's own utter insignificance and powerlessness. In the latter event a mouse or a leaf can assume threatening features.) In other forms of masochistic strivings the essential aim is the same. In the masochistic feeling of smallness we find a tendency which serves to increase the original feeling of insignificance. How is this to be understood? Can we assume that by making a fear worse one is trying to remedy it? Indeed, this is what the masochistic person does. As long as I struggle between my desire to be independent and strong and my feeling of insignificance or powerlessness I am caught in a tormenting conflict. If I succeed in reducing my individual self to nothing, if I can overcome the awareness of my separateness as an individual, I may save myself from this conflict. To feel utterly small and helpless is one way toward this aim; to be overwhelmed by pain and agony another; to be overcome by the effects of intoxication still another. The phantasy of suicide is the last hope if all other means have not succeeded in bringing relief from the burden of aloneness.

Under certain conditions these masochistic strivings are relatively successful. If the individual finds cultural patterns that satisfy these masochistic strivings (like the submission under the "leader" in Fascist ideology), he gains some security by finding himself united with millions of others who share these feelings. Yet even in these cases, the masochistic "solution" is no more of a solution than neurotic manifestations ever are: the individual succeeds in eliminating the conspicuous suffering but not in removing the underlying conflict and the silent unhappiness. When the masochistic striving does not find a cultural pattern or when it quantitatively exceeds the average amount of masochism in the individual's social group, the masochistic solution does not even solve anything in relative terms. It springs from an unbearable situation, tends to overcome it, and leaves the individual caught in new suffering. If human behavior were always rational and purposeful, masochism would be as inexplicable as neurotic manifestations in general are. This, however, is what the study of emotional and mental disturbances has taught us: that human behavior can be motivated by strivings which are caused by anxiety or some other unbearable state of mind, that these strivings tend to overcome this emotional state and yet merely cover up its most visible manifestations, or not even these. Neurotic manifestations resemble the irrational behavior in a panic. Thus a man, trapped in a fire, stands at the window of his room and shouts for help, forgetting entirely that no one can hear him and that he could still escape by the staircase which will also be aflame in a few minutes. He shouts because he wants to be saved, and for the moment this behavior appears to be a step on the way to being saved—and yet it will end in complete catastrophe. In the same way the masochistic strivings are caused by the desire to get rid of the individual self with all its shortcomings, conflicts, risks, doubts, and unbearable aloneness, but they only succeed in removing the most noticeable pain or they even lead to greater suffering. The irrationality of masochism, as of all other neurotic manifestations, consists in the ultimate futility of the means adopted to solve an untenable emotional situation.

These considerations refer to an important difference between neurotic and rational activity. In the latter the *result* corresponds to the *motivation* of an activity—one acts in order to attain a certain result. In neurotic strivings one acts from a compulsion which has essentially a negative chacter: to escape an unbearable situation. The strivings tend in a direction which only fictitiously is a solution. Actually the result is contradictory to what the person wants to attain; the compulsion to get rid of an unbearable feeling was so strong that the person was unable to choose a line of action that could be a solution in any other but a fictitious sense.

The implication of this for masochism is that the individual is driven by an unbearable feeling of aloneness and insignificance. He then attempts to overcome it by getting rid of his self (as a psychological, not as a physiological entity); his way to achieve this is to belittle himself, to suffer, to make himself utterly insignificant. But pain and suffering are not what he wants; pain and suffering are the price he pays for an aim which he compulsively tries to attain. The price is dear. He has to pay more and more and, like a peon, he only gets into greater debts without ever getting what he has paid for: inner peace and tranquillity.

I have spoken of the masochistic perversion because it proves beyond doubt that suffering can be something sought for. However, in the masochistic perversion as little as in moral masochism suffering is not the real aim; in both cases it is the means to an aim: forgetting one's self. The difference between the perversion and masochistic character traits lies essentially in the following: In the perversion the trend to get rid of one's self is expressed through the medium of the body and linked up with sexual feelings. While in moral masochism, the masochistic trends get hold of the whole person and tend to destroy all the aims which the ego consciously tries to achieve, in the perversion the masochistic strivings are more or less restricted to the physical realm; moreover by their amalgamation with sex they participate in the release of tension occurring in the sexual sphere and thus find some direct release.

The annihilation of the individual self and the attempt to overcome thereby the unbearable feeling of powerlessness are only one side of the masochistic strivings. The other side is the attempt to become a part of a bigger and more powerful whole outside of oneself, to submerge and participate in it. This power can be a person, an institution, God, the nation, conscience, or a psychic compulsion. By becoming part of a power which is felt as unshakably strong, eternal, and glamorous, one participates in its strength and glory. One surrenders one's own self and renounces all strength and pride connected with it, one loses one's integrity as an individual and surrenders freedom; but one gains a new security and a new pride in the participation in the power in which one submerges. One gains also security against the torture of doubt. The masochistic person, whether his master is an authority outside of himself or whether he has internalized the master as conscience or a psychic compulsion, is saved from making decisions, saved from the final responsibility for the fate of his self, and thereby saved from the doubt of what decision to make. He is also saved from the doubt of what the meaning of his life is or who "he" is. These questions are answered by the relationship to the power to which he has attached himself. The meaning of his life and the identity of his self are determined by the greater whole into which the self has submerged.

6.2 | ON THE LIFE CYCLE*

Erik H. Erikson

Among the indispensable co-ordinates of identity is that of the life cycle, for we assume that not until adolescence does the individual develop the prerequisites in physiological growth, mental maturation, and social responsibility to experience and pass through the crisis of identity. We may, in fact, speak of the identity crisis as the psychosocial aspect of adolescing. Nor could this stage be passed without identity having found a form which will decisively determine later life.

Let us, once more, start out from Freud's far-reaching discovery that neurotic conflict is not very different in content from the "normative" conflicts which every child must live through in his childhood, and the residues of which every adult carries with him in the recesses of his personality. For man, in order to remain psychologically alive, constantly re-resolves these conflicts just as his body unceasingly combats the encroachment of physical deterioration. However, since I cannot accept the conclusion that just to be alive, or not to be sick, means to be healthy, or, as I would prefer to say in matters of personality, *vital*, I must have recourse to a few concepts which are not part of the official terminology of my field.

I shall present human growth from the point of view of the conflicts, inner and outer, which the vital personality weathers, re-emerging from each crisis with an increased sense of inner unity, with an increase of good judgment, and an increase in the capacity "to do well" according to his own standards and to the standards of those who are significant to him. The use of the words "to do well" of course points up the whole question of cultural relativity. Those who are significant to a man may think he is doing well when he "does some good" or when he "does well" in the sense of acquiring possessions; when he is doing well in the sense of learning new skills and new knowledge or when he is not much more than just getting along; when he learns to conform all around or to rebel significantly; when he is merely free from neurotic symptoms or manages to contain within his vitality all manner of profound conflict.

There are many formulations of what constitutes a "healthy" personality in an adult. But if we take up only one—in this case, Marie Jahoda's definition, according to which a healthy personality *actively masters* his environment, shows a certain *unity of personality,* and is able to *perceive* the world and himself *correctly* (Jahoda, 1950)—it is clear that all of these criteria are relative to the child's cognitive and social development. In fact, we may say that childhood is defined by their initial absence and by their gradual devel-

* SOURCE: Erikson, E. H. *Identity, youth and crisis.* New York: W. W. Norton & Co., Inc., 1968. Pp. 91–96, abridged. Copyright 1968. Reprinted by permission of W. W. Norton & Co., Inc., and Faber and Faber, Ltd.

opment in complex steps of increasing differentiation. How, then, does a vital personality grow or, as it were, accrue from the successive stages of the increasing capacity to adapt to life's necessities—with some vital enthusiasm to spare?

Whenever we try to understand growth, it is well to remember the *epigenetic principle* which is derived from the growth of organisms *in utero*. Somewhat generalized, this principle states that anything that grows has a ground plan, and that out of this ground plan the parts arise, each part having its time of special ascendancy, until all parts have arisen to form a functioning whole. This, obviously, is true for fetal development where each part of the organism has its critical time of ascendance or danger of defect. At birth the baby leaves the chemical exchange of the womb for the social exchange system of his society, where his gradually increasing capacities meet the opportunities and limitations of his culture. How the maturing organism continues to unfold, not by developing new organs but by means of a prescribed sequence of locomotor, sensory, and social capacities, is described in the child-development literature. As pointed out, psychoanalysis has given us an understanding of the more idiosyncratic experiences, and especially the inner conflicts, which constitute the manner in which an individual becomes a distinct personality. But here, too, it is important to realize that in the sequence of his most personal experiences the healthy child, given a reasonable amount of proper guidance, can be trusted to obey inner laws of development, laws which create a succession of potentialities for significant interaction with those persons who tend and respond to him and those institutions which are ready for him. While such interaction varies from culture to culture, it must remain within "the proper rate and the proper sequence" which governs all epigenesis. Personality, therefore, can be said to develop according to steps predetermined in the human organism's readiness to be driven toward, to be aware of, and to interact with a widening radius of significant individuals and institutions.

It is for this reason that, in the presentation of stages in the development of the personality, we employ an epigenetic diagram analogous to the one employed in *Childhood and Society* (Erikson, 1963) for an analysis of Freud's psychosexual stages. It is, in fact, an implicit purpose of this presentation to bridge the theory of infantile sexuality (without repeating it here in detail) and our knowledge of the child's physical and social growth.

The diagram is presented on p. 101. The double-lined squares signify both a sequence of stages and a gradual development of component parts; in other words, the diagram formalizes a progression through time of a differentiation of parts. This indicates (1) that each item of the vital personality to be discussed is systematically related to all others, and that they all depend on the proper development in the proper sequence of each item; and (2) that each item exists in some form before "its" decisive and critical time normally arrives.

If I say, for example, that a sense of basic trust is the first component of mental vitality to develop in life, a sense of autonomous will the second, and a sense of initiative the third, the diagram expresses a number of fundamental relations that exist among the three components, as well as a few fundamental facts for each.

Each comes to its ascendance, meets its crisis, and finds its lasting solution in ways to be described here, toward the end of the stages mentioned. All of them exist in the

	1	2	3	4	5	6	7	8
VIII								INTEGRITY vs. DESPAIR
VII							GENERATIVITY vs. STAGNATION	
VI					INTIMACY vs. ISOLATION			
V	Temporal Perspective vs. Time Confusion	Self-Certainty vs. Self-Consciousness	Role Experimentation vs. Role Fixation	Apprenticeship vs. Work Paralysis	IDENTITY vs. IDENTITY CONFUSION	Sexual Polarization vs. Bisexual Confusion	Leader- and Followership vs. Authority Confusion	Ideological Commitment vs. Confusion of Values
IV				INDUSTRY vs. INFERIORITY	Task Identification vs. Sense of Futility			
III			INITIATIVE vs. GUILT		Anticipation of Roles vs. Role Inhibition			
II		AUTONOMY vs. SHAME, DOUBT			Will to Be Oneself vs. Self-Doubt			
I	TRUST vs. MISTRUST				Mutual Recognition vs. Autistic Isolation			

beginning in some form, although we do not make a point of this fact, and we shall not confuse things by calling these components different names at earlier or later stages. A baby may show something like "autonomy" from the beginning, for example, in the particular way in which he angrily tries to wriggle his hand free when tightly held. However, under normal conditions, it is not until the second year that he begins to experience the whole critical alternative between being an autonomous creature and being a dependent one, and it is not until then that he is ready for a specifically new encounter with his environment. The environment, in turn, now feels called upon to convey to him its particular ideas and concepts of autonomy in ways decisively contributing to his personal character, his relative efficiency, and the strength of his vitality.

It is this encounter, together with the resulting crisis, which is to be described for each stage. Each stage becomes a crisis because incipient growth and awareness in a new part function go together with a shift in instinctual energy and yet also cause a specific vulnerability in that part. One of the most difficult questions to decide, therefore, is whether or not a child at a given stage is weak or strong. Perhaps it would be best to say that he is always vulnerable in some respects and completely oblivious and insensitive in others, but that at the same time he is unbelievably persistent in the same respects in which he is vulnerable. It must be added that the baby's weakness gives him power; out of his very dependence and weakness he makes signs to which his environment, if it is guided well by a responsiveness combining "instinctive" and traditional patterns, is peculiarly sensitive. A baby's presence exerts a consistent and persistent domination over the outer and inner lives of every member of a household. Because these members must reorient themselves to accommodate his presence, they must also grow as individuals and as a group. It is as true to say that babies control and bring up their families as it is to say the converse. A family can bring up a baby only by being brought up by him. His growth consists of a series of challenges to them to serve his newly developing potentialities for social interaction.

Each successive step, then, is a potential crisis because of a radical change in perspective. Crisis is used here in a developmental sense to connote not a threat of catastrophe, but a turning point, a crucial period of increased vulnerability and heightened potential, and therefore, the ontogenetic source of generational strength and maladjustment. The most radical change of all, from intrauterine to extrauterine life, comes at the very beginning of life. But in postnatal existence, too, such radical adjustments of perspective as lying relaxed, sitting firmly, and running fast must all be accomplished in their own good time. With them, the interpersonal perspective also changes rapidly and often radically, as is testified by the proximity in time of such opposites as "not letting mother out of sight" and "wanting to be independent." Thus, different capacities use different opportunities to become full-grown components of the ever-new configuration that is the growing personality.

REFERENCES

Jahoda, Marie, "Toward a Social Psychology of Mental Health," *Symposium on the Healthy Personality*, Supplement II: Problems of Infancy and Childhood, Transactions of Fourth Conference, March, 1950, M. J. E. Benn, (Ed.), New York: Josiah Macy, Jr. Foundation, 1950.

Erikson, Erik H., *Childhood and Society*, 2nd ed. New York: W. W. Norton, 1963, Part I.

7 | Psychodynamic Assessment

7.1 | THE NATURE OF CLINICAL EVIDENCE*

Erik H. Erikson

As I proceed with the task of describing how the clinical method in psychotherapy "actually works," I find that I tentatively place myself next to the historian, although with no intention of crowding him. The words "history taking" and "case history" as used in the clinical field are more than mere figures of speech. They may serve us as a first step in making objective that element of subjectivity which in essence characterizes all the clinical arts and sciences.

R. G. Collingwood defines as an historical process one "in which the past, so far as it is historically known, survives in the present." Thus being "itself a process of thought . . . it exists only in so far as the minds which are parts of it know themselves for parts of it." And again: "History is the life of mind itself which is not mind except so far as it *both lives in historical process and knows itself as so living*" (Collingwood, 1956).

It is not my task to argue the philosophy of history. The analogy between the clinician and the historian as defined by Collingwood to me centers in the case-historian's highly "self-conscious" function in the act of history-taking, and thus in the process of the case. Beyond this the analogy breaks down; it could remain relevant for our work only if the historian were also a kind of clinical statesman, correcting events as he records them, and recording as he directs. Such a conscious clinician-historian-statesman may well emerge generations hence from our joint work, although by then he may not use our terms or be aware of our dilemmas. Some of you may already see him seeking a foothold in such crises as economic "recessions," as he alternately interprets what he observes as cyclic, pathological or beneficial, and makes history as he thus interprets it.

Let me restate the psychotherapeutic encounter, then, as an historical one. A person has declared an emergency and has surrendered his self-regulation to a treatment procedure. Besides having become a subjective *patient*, he has accepted the role of a formal *client*. To some degree, he has had to interrupt his autonomous life-history as lived in the

* SOURCE: Erikson, E. H. The nature of clinical evidence. In *Daedalus*, On Evidence and Inference, Fall, 1958. Pp. 65–87, abridged. Reprinted by permission of *Daedalus*, Journal of the American Academy of Arts and Sciences, Boston, Mass.

unself-conscious balances of his private and his public life in order, for a while, to "favor" a part-aspect of himself and to observe it with the diagnostic help of a curative method: as he is "under observation," he becomes self-observant. As a patient he is inclined, and as a client encouraged, to historicize his own position by thinking back to the onset of the disturbance, and to ponder what world order (magic, scientific, ethical) was violated and must be restored before his "normal" place in history can be reassumed. He participates in becoming a *case*, a fact which he may live down socially, but which, nevertheless, may forever change his own opinion of himself.

The clinician, in turn, appointed to judge the bit of interrupted life put before him, and to introduce himself and his method into it, finds himself part of another man's most intimate life history. Luckily, he also remains the functionary of a healing profession with a systematic orientation, based on a coherent world image—be it the theory that man is surrounded by evil spirits, or under the temptation of the devil, or the victim of chemical poisons, or subject to inner conflicts, or the representative of destructive social forces. But in inviting his client to look at himself with the help of professional theories and techniques the clinician makes himself part of the client's life history, even as he asks the client to become a case history in the annals of healing.

In northern California I knew an old Shaman woman who laughed merrily at my conception of mental disease, and then sincerely—to the point of ceremonial tears—told me of her way of sucking the "pains" out of her patients. She was as convinced of her ability to cure and to understand as I was of mine. While occupying extreme opposites in the history of American psychiatry, we felt like colleagues. This feeling was based on some joint sense of the historical relativity of all psychotherapy: the relativity of the patient's outlook on his symptoms; of the role he assumes by dint of being a patient; of the kind of help which he seeks; and of the kinds of help he finds available. The old Shaman woman and I disagreed about the locus of emotional sickness, what it was, and what specific methods would cure it. Yet, when she related the origin of a child's illness to the familial tensions existing within her tribe, when she attributed the "pain" (which had gotten "under a child's skin") to his grandmother's sorcery (ambivalence) I knew she dealt with the same forces, and with the same kinds of conviction, as I did in my part of American culture and in my professional nook. This experience has been repeated in discussions with colleagues who, although not necessarily more "primitive," are oriented toward different psychiatric "persuasions."

To summarize: the disciplined psychotherapist today finds himself heir to medical methods and concepts, and allied with the procedures of the biological sciences. On the other hand, he recognizes his activities as a function of historical processes, and is forced to conclude that in some sense he is "making history" as he "takes" it.

It is in such apparent quicksand that we must seek the tracks of clinical evidence. No wonder that often the only clinical material which impresses some as being at all "scientific" is the evidence of the auxiliary methods of psychotherapy—neurological examination, chemical analysis, sociological study, psychological experiment, etc.—all of which derive their laws of evidence from a non-clinical field, and each of which, strictly speaking, puts the patient into non-therapeutic conditions of observation. Each of these methods may "objectify" *some* matters immensely, provide inestimable supportive evidence for *some* theories, and lead to independent methods of cure in *some* classes of patients. But it is not of the nature of the evidence provided in the psychotherapeutic encounter itself.

To introduce such evidence, I need a specimen. This will consist of my reporting to you what a patient *said* to me, how he *behaved* in doing so and what I, in turn, *thought* and *did*—a highly suspect method. And, indeed, we may well stand at the beginning of a period when consultation rooms (already airier and lighter than Freud's) will have, as it were, many more doors open in the direction of an enlightened community's resources, even as they now have research windows in the form of one-way screens, cameras, and recording equipment. For the kind of evidence to be highlighted here, however, it is still essential that, for longer periods or for shorter ones, these doors be closed, soundproof, and impenetrable.

I am not trying to ward off legitimate study of the setting from which our examples come. I know only too well that many of our interpretations seem to be of the variety of that given by one Jew to another in a Polish railroad station. "Where are you going?" asked the first. "To Minsk," said the other. "To Minsk!" exclaimed the first. "You say you go to Minsk so that I should believe you go to Pinsk! You are going to Minsk anyway— so why do you lie?" There is a widespread prejudice that the psychotherapist, point for point, uncovers what he claims the patient "really," and often unconsciously, had in mind, and that he has sufficient Pinsk-Minsk reversals in his technical arsenal to come out with the flat assertion that the evidence is on the side of his claim. It is for this very reason that I will try to demonstrate what method there may be in clinical judgment. I will select as my specimen the most subjective of all data, a dream report.

A young man in his early twenties comes to his therapeutic hour and reports that he has had the most disturbing dream of his life. The dream, he says, vividly recalls his state of panic at the time of the "mental breakdown" which caused him to enter treatment half a year earlier. He cannot let go of the dream; it seemed painfully real on awakening; and even in the hour of reporting the dream-state seems still vivid enough to threaten the patient's sense of reality. He is afraid that this is the end of his sanity.

The dream: *"There was a big face sitting in a buggy of the horse-and-buggy days. The face was completely empty, and there was horrible, slimy, snaky hair all around it. I am not sure it wasn't my mother."* The dream report itself, given with wordy plaintiveness, is as usual followed by a variety of incidental reports, protestations and exclamations, which at one point give way to a rather coherent account of the patient's relationship with his deceased grandfather, a country parson. Here the patient's mood changes to a deeply moved and moving admission of desperate nostalgia for cultural and personal values once observed and received.

Everything said in this hour is linked, of course, with the material of previous appointments. It must be understood that whatever answer can come of one episode will owe its clarity to the fact that it responds to previous questions and complements previous half-answers. Such *evidential continuity* can be only roughly sketched here; even to account for this one hour would take many hours. Let me briefly state, then, that I listened to the patient, who faced me in an easy chair, with only occasional interruptions for clarification, and that I gave him a résumé of what sense his dream had made to me only at the conclusion of the appointment. It so happened that this interpretation proved convincing to us both and, in the long run, strategic for the whole treatment which, incidentally, ended well.

As I turn to the task of indicating what inferences helped me to formulate one of the most probable of the many possible meanings of this dream report I must ask you to join me in what Freud has called "free-floating attention," an attention which turns inward to the observer's ruminations while remaining turned outward to the field of observation, and which, far from focusing on any one item too intentionally, rather waits to be impressed by recurring themes. These will first faintly but ever more insistently signal the nature of the patient's distress and its location. To find the zone, the position, and the danger I must avoid for the moment all temptations to go off on *one* tangent in order to prove it alone as relevant. It is rather the gradual establishment of strategic intersections on a number of tangents that eventually makes it possible to locate in the observed phenomena that central core which comprises the "evidence."

The patient's behavior and report confront me with a crisis, and it is my first task to perceive where the patient stands in the treatment procedure, and what I must do next. What a clinician must do first and last depends, of course, on the setting of his work. Mine is an open residential institution, working with severe neuroses, on the borderline of psychosis or psychopathy. In such a setting, our patients may display, in their most regressed moments, the milder forms of a disturbance in the sense of reality; in their daily behavior, they usually try to entertain, educate, and employ themselves in rational and useful ways; and in their best moments, they can be expected to be insightful and at times creative. The hospital thus can be said to take a number of risks, and to provide, on the other hand, special opportunities for the patient's abilities to work, to be active, and to share in social responsibilities. That a patient fits into this setting has been established in advance by several weeks of probationary evaluation. During this period the patient's history has been taken in psychiatric interviews with him and perhaps with members of his family; he has been given a physical examination by a physician and has been confronted with standardized tests by psychologists who perform their work "blindly," that is without knowledge of the patient's history; and finally, the results have been presented to the whole staff at a meeting, at the conclusion of which the patient is interviewed by the medical director, questioned by staff members, and assigned to "his therapist." Such preliminary screening has provided the therapist with an over-all diagnosis which defines a certain range of expectable mental states, indicating the patient's special danger points and his special prospects for improvement. Needless to say, not even the best preparation can quite predict what depths and heights may be reached once the therapeutic process gets under way.

A dream report of the kind just mentioned, in a setting of this kind, thus will first of all impress the clinical observer as a diagnostic sign. This is an "anxiety dream." An anxiety dream may happen to anybody, and a mild perseverance of the dream state into the day is not pathological as such. But this patient's dream appears to be only the visual center of a severe affective disturbance: no doubt if such a state were to persist it could precipitate him into a generalized panic such as brought him to our clinic in the first place. The original test report had put the liability of the patient's state into these words: "The tests indicate borderline psychotic features in an inhibited, obsessive-compulsive character. However, the patient seems to be able to take spontaneously adequate distance from these borderline tendencies. He seems, at present, to be struggling to strengthen a rather precarious control over aggressive impulses, and probably feels a good deal of anxiety." The course of the treatment has confirmed this and other test results. The report of this horrible dream which intrudes itself on the patient's waking life now takes its place beside the data of the tests, and the range and spectrum of the patient's moods and states as observed in the treatment, and shows him on the lowest level attained since admission, i.e. relatively closest to an *inability* "to take adequate distance from his borderline tendencies."

The first "prediction" to be made is whether this dream is the sign of an impending collapse, or, on the contrary, a potentially beneficial clinical crisis. The first would mean that the patient is slipping away from me and that I must think, as it were, of the emergency net; the second, that he is reaching out for me with an important message which I must try to understand and answer. I decided for the latter alternative. Although the patient acted as if he were close to a breakdown, I had the impression that, in fact, there was a challenge in all this, and a rather angry one. I can explain this only by presenting a number of inferences of a kind made very rapidly in a clinician's mind, but demonstrable only through an analysis of the patient's verbal and behavioral communications and of my own intellectual and affective reactions.

The experienced dream interpreter often finds himself "reading" a dream report as a practitioner of medicine scans an X-ray picture: especially in the cases of wordy or reticent patients or of lengthy case reports, a dream often lays bare the stark inner facts. At this point one may ask: But can *two* clinicians look at the same dream and see the same "stark inner facts"? This is a legitimate question, which I shall try to answer below.

Let us first pay attention to the dream images. The main item is a large face without identifying features. There are no spoken words, and there is no motion. There are no people in the dream. Most apparent then, are omissions. I say this on the basis of an inventory of dream configurations, which I published in a review of "the first dream subjected to exhaustive analysis" by Freud (Erikson, 1954). Such a methodological step is elementary, but clinical workers often fail to make explicit, even to themselves, what inventories of evidential signs they regularly but unwittingly scan. In my article I suggested a list of configurations against which the student can check the individual dream production for present and absent dream configurations. It must suffice here to indicate that the dream being discussed is characterized by a significant omission of important items present in most dreams: motion, action, people, spoken words. All we have instead is a motionless image of a faceless face, which may or may not represent the patient's mother.

The patient's precarious state and the urgency with which he looked at me when telling me his dream induced me to ignore for the moment the reference to his mother. His facial and tonal expression rather reminded me of a series of critical moments during his treatment when he was obviously not quite sure that I was "all there" and apprehensive that I might disapprove of him and disappear in anger. This focused my attention on a question which the clinician must sooner or later consider when faced with any of his patient's productions, namely, his own place in them.

While the psychotherapist should not force his way into his patient's dream images, sometimes he does well to raise discreetly the masks of the various dream persons to see whether he can find his own face or person or role represented. Here the mask is an empty face, with plenty of horrible hair. My often unruly white hair surrounding a reddish face easily enters my patients' imaginative productions, either as the feature of a benevolent Santa Claus or that of a threatening ogre. At that particular time, I had to consider another autobiographic item. In the third month of therapy, I had "abandoned" the patient to have an emergency operation (which he, to use clinical shorthand, had ascribed to his evil eye, that is to his as yet unverbalized anger). At the time of this dream report I still was on occasion mildly uncomfortable—a matter which can never be hidden from such patients. A sensitive patient will, of course, be in conflict between his sympathy, which makes him want me to take care of myself, and his rightful claim that I should take care of him—for he feels that only the therapist's total presence can provide him with sufficient identity to weather his crises. I concluded that the empty face had something to do with a certain tenuousness in our relation, and that one message of the dream might be something like this: "If I never know whether and when you think of yourself rather than attending to me, or when you will absent yourself, maybe die, how can I have or gain what I need most—a coherent personality, an identity, a face?"

Such an indirect message, however, even if understood as referring to the immediate present and to the therapeutic situation itself, always proves to be "overdetermined," that is, to consist of a condensed code transmitting a number of other messages, from other life situations, seemingly removed from the therapy. This we call "transference."

Among those who are acquainted with this kind of material, some would as a matter of course connect the patient's implied fear of "losing a face" with his remark that he was not sure the face was not his mother's—a double negation easily understood as an affirmation. However, just because the inference of a "mother transference" is at present an almost stereotyped requirement, I should like to approach the whole matter by way of two methodological detours.

Clinical work is always research in progress, and this patient's dream happened to fit especially well into my research at the time. I should say, in passing, that this can be a mixed blessing for the therapeutic contract. A research-minded clinician—and a literary one, as well—must always take care lest his patients become footnotes to his favorite thesis or topic. I was studying in Pittsburgh and in Stockbridge the "identity crises" of a number of young people, college as well as seminary students, workmen and artists. My work was to delineate further a syndrome called *Identity-Diffusion*, a term which describes the inability of young people in the late 'teens and early twenties to establish their station and vocation in life, and the tendency of some to develop apparently malignant symptoms and regressions. Such research must re-open rather than close questions of finalistic diagnosis. Perhaps there are certain stages in the life cycle when even seemingly malignant disturbances are more profitably treated as aggravated life crises rather than as diseases subject to routine psychiatric diagnosis. Here the clinician must be guided by the proposition that if he can hope to save only a small sub-group, or, indeed, only one patient, he must disregard existing statistical verdicts. For one new case, understood in new ways, will soon prove to be "typical" for a class of patients.

But any new diagnostic impression immediately calls for new psychosocial considerations. What we have described as a therapeutic need in one patient, namely, to gain identity by claiming the total presence of his therapist, is analogous with the need of young people anywhere for ideological affirmation. This need is aggravated in certain critical periods of history, when young people may try to find various forms of "confirmation" in groups that range from idealistic youth movements to criminal gangs.

The young man in question was one among a small group of our patients who came from theological seminaries. He had developed his symptoms when attending a Protestant seminary in the Middle West where he was training for missionary work in Asia. He had not found the expected transformation in prayer, a matter which both for reasons of honesty and of inner need, he had taken more seriously than many successful believers. To him the wish to gaze through the glass darkly and to come "face to face" was a desperate need not easily satisfied in some modern seminaries. I need not remind you of the many references in The Bible to God's "making his face to shine upon" man, or God's face being turned away or being distant. The therapeutic theme inferred from the patient's report of an anxiety dream in which a face was horribly unrecognizable thus also seemed to echo relevantly this patient's religious scruples at the time of the appearance of psychiatric symptoms—the common denominator being a wish to break through to a provider of identity.

This detour has led us from the immediate clinical situation to the vocational crisis immediately preceding the patient's breakdown. The "buggy" in the dream will lead us a step further back into the patient's adolescent identity crisis. The horse and buggy is, of course, an historical symbol of culture change. Depending on one's ideology, it is a derisive term connoting hopelessly old-fashioned ways, or it is a symbol of nostalgia for the good old days. Here we come to a trend in the family's history most decisive for the patient's identity crisis. They came from Minnesota where the mother's father had been a rural clergyman of character, strength, and communal esteem. Such grandfathers represent to many men of today a world as yet more homogeneous in its feudal values, masterly and cruel with a good conscience, self-restrained and pious without loss of self-esteem. When the patient's parents had moved from the north country to then still smog-covered Pittsburgh, his mother especially had found it impossible to overcome an intense nostalgia for the rural ways of her youth. She had, in fact, imbued the boy with this nostalgia for a rural existence and had demonstrated marked disappointment when the patient, at the beginning of his identity crisis (maybe in order to cut through the family's cultural conflict) had temporarily threatened to become a hot-rodder and a hep-cat—roles which were beneath the family's "class." The horse and buggy obviously is in greatest ideological as well as technological contrast to the modern means of locomotor acceleration, and, thus, a symbol of changing times, of identity diffusion, and of cultural regression. Here the horrible motionlessness of the dream may reveal itself as an important configurational item, meaning something like being stuck in a world of competitive change and motion. And even as I inferred in my thoughts that the face sitting in the buggy must *also* represent the deceased grandfather's, also framed by white hair, the patient spontaneously embarked on that above-mentioned series of memories concerning the past when his grandfather had taken him by the hand to acquaint him with the technology of an old farm in Minnesota. Here the patient's vocabulary became poetic, his description vivid, and he seemed to be breaking through to a genuinely positive emotional experience. Yet his tearfulness remained strangely perverse, almost strangled by anger, as if he were saying: "One must not promise a child such certainty, and then let him down."

I should point out here that as clinicians we consider a patient's "associations" our best leads to the meaning of an item brought up in a clinical encounter. By associated evidence we mean everything which comes to the patient's mind during a clinical session. Here, except in cases of stark disorganization of thought, we must assume that what we call the synthesizing function of the ego will, sometimes with but mostly without conscious knowledge, tend to associate what "belongs together" and condense seemingly separate items into strong images and affects, be the various items ever so remote in history, separate in space, and contradictory in logical terms. Once the therapist has convinced himself of a certain combination in the patient of character, intelligence, and a wish to get well, he can rely on the patient's capacity to produce during a series of therapeutic encounters a sequence of themes, thoughts, and affects which seek their own concordance and provide their own cross-references. It is, of course, this basic synthesizing trend in clinical material itself which permits the clinician to observe with free-floating attention, to refrain from undue interference, and to expect sooner or later a confluence of the patient's search for curative clarification and his own endeavor to recognize meaning and relevance. This expectation is in no way disproved by the fact that much of a clinician's work consists of the recognition and removal of the patient's inner and often unconscious resistances to his own wish to see clearly and to get well. We shall return to this point.

We add to our previous inferences the assumption that the face in the dream is a condensed representation of my face as that of his "doctor" who is not so well himself, and the face of his grandfather, who is now dead and whom as a rebellious youth the patient had defied—in fact, shortly before his death. The immediate clinical situation, then, and the patient's childhood history are found to have a common denominator in the idea that the patient wishes to base his future sanity on a man of wisdom and firm identity while, in both instances, the patient seems to fear that his anger may have destroyed, or may yet destroy, this resource. We have every reason to suspect that some of his insistence on finding security in prayer, and yet his failure to find it, belongs in the same context.

The theme of the horse and buggy as a rural symbol served to establish a possible connection between the nostalgic mother and her dead father; and we now finally turn our attention to the fact that the patient, half-denying what he was half-suggesting, had said, "I am not sure it wasn't my mother." Here the most repetitious complaint of the whole course of therapy must be reviewed. While the grandfather's had been, all in all, the most consistently reassuring countenance in the patient's life, the mother's pretty, soft, and loving face had since earliest childhood been marred in the patient's memory and imagination by moments when she seemed absorbed and distorted by strong and painful emotions. The tests, given before any history-taking, had picked out the following theme: "The mother-figure appears in the Thematic Apperception Tests as one who seeks to control her son by her protectiveness of him, and by 'self-pity' and demonstrations of her frailty at any aggressive act on his part. She is, in the stories, 'frightened' at any show of rebelliousness, and content only when the son is passive and compliant. There appears to be considerable aggression, probably partly conscious, toward this figure." And indeed, it was with anger as well as with horror that the patient would repeatedly describe the mother of his memory as utterly exasperated, and this at those times when he had been too rough, too careless, too stubborn, or too persistent.

We are not concerned here with accusing this actual mother of having behaved this way; we can only be sure that she appeared this way in certain retrospective moods of the patient. Such memories are typical for a class of patients, and the question whether this is so because they have in common a type of mother or a typical reaction to their mothers, or both, occupies the thinking of clinicians. At any rate many of these patients are deeply, if often unconsciously, convinced that they have caused a basic disturbance in their mothers—a disturbance, which, of course, is one of the prime causes rather than an effect of the small child's anxiety and anger. No doubt, in our time, when corporal punishment and severe scolding have become less fashionable, parents resort to the seemingly less cruel means of presenting themselves as deeply hurt by the child's willfulness. The "violated" mother thus has become more prominent in the arsenal of guilt images, and in some cases proves to be a hindrance to the conclusion of adolescence—as if one had to go away back and away down to make an essential restitution before adulthood could be approached. It is in keeping with this trend that the patients under discussion here, young people who in late adolescence face a breakdown of "borderline" proportions, all prove partially regressed to the earliest task in life, namely, that of acquiring a sense of basic trust strong enough to balance that sense of basic mistrust to which new-born man, most dependent of all young animals, and endowed with fewer inborn instinctive regulations, is subject in his infancy. We all relive earlier and earliest stages of our existence in dreams, in artistic experience, and in religious devotion, only to emerge refreshed and invigorated. These patients, however, experience such "partial regression" in a lonely, sudden, and intense fashion, and most of all with a sense of irreversible doom. This, too, is in this dream.

Tracing one main theme of the dream retrospectively, we have recognized it in four periods of the patient's life: the present treatment—and the patient's fear that by some act of horrible anger (on his part or on mine or both) he might lose me and thus his chance to regain his identity through trust in me; his immediately preceding religious education—and his abortive attempt at finding through prayer that "presence" which would cure his inner void; his earlier youth—and his hope to gain strength, peace, and identity by identifying himself with his grandfather; and, finally, early childhood—and his desperate wish to keep alive in himself the charitable face of his mother in order to overcome fear, guilt, and anger over her emotions. Such redundancy points to a central theme which, once found, gives added meaning to all the associated material. The theme is: "Whenever I begin to have faith in somebody's strength and love, some angry and sickly emotions pervade the relationship, and I end up mistrusting, empty, and a victim of anger and despair."

You may be getting a bit tired of the clinician's habit of speaking for the patient, of putting into his mouth inferences which, so it would seem, he could get out of it, for the asking. Perhaps so, but the clinician has no right to test his reconstructions until his trial formulations have combined to a comprehensive interpretation which feels right, and which promises, when appropriately verbalized, to feel right to the patient. When this point is reached, the clinician usually finds himself compelled to speak.

We have not yet exhausted the categories of thought which must precede such intervention. I have not explicitly stated what my "persuasion," what specifically Freudian concepts of dream life would make me look for in this dream. If according to Freud a successful dream is an attempt at representing a wish as fulfilled, the attempted and miscarried fulfillment in this dream is that of finding a face with a lasting identity. If an anxiety dream startling the dreamer out of his sleep is a symptom of a derailed wish-fulfillment, the central theme just formulated indicates at least one inner disturbance which caused the miscarriage of trust. This becomes even clearer when we come to the mandatory question as to what was the remnant of the previous day which had upset the sleeping patient sufficiently to cause this dream. Why did the patient have this dream on the preceding night, of all nights?

You will not expect me to give an account of the previous day's appointment as well. Suffice it to say that the patient had confessed to increased well-being in work and in love and had expressed enhanced trust in, and even something akin to affection for me. This, paradoxically, his unconscious had not been able to tolerate. The paradox resolves itself if we consider that cure means the loss of the right to rely on therapy; for the cured patient, to speak with Saint Francis, would not so much seek to be loved as to love, and not so much to be consoled as to console, to the limit of his capacity. The dream shocks the patient out of his dangerous increase in self-confidence (and confidence in me) by reminding him of unwise trust and premature graduations in the past. The dream report communicates, protesting somewhat too loudly, that the patient is still sick. We must come to the conclusion that his dream was sicker than the patient was, although his treatment was by no means near conclusion.

A most comprehensive omission in all this material points to what is as yet to come: there is no father in these familial associations. The patient's father images became dominant in a later period of the treatment. You may also have missed a sexual interpretation of the dream. Did not Freud explain the Medusa, the angry face with snake-hair and an open mouth, as a symbol of the feminine void, and an expression of the masculine horror of femininity? It is true that some of the dream material which concerns the mother's emotions, could be easily traced to infantile observations and ruminations concerning "female trouble," pregnancy, and post-partum upsets. Facelessness, in this sense, can also mean inner void, and "castration." Does it, then, or does it not contradict Freudian symbolism, if I emphasize in this equally horrifying but entirely empty face, a representation of facelessness, of loss of face, of lack of identity? In the context of one interpretation, the dream image would be primarily symbolic of a sexual idea which is to be warded off, in the second a representation of a danger to the continuous existence of individual identity (and thus of the "ego"). Theoretical considerations would show that these interpretations can and must be systematically related to one another. In this case the controversy is superseded by the clinical consideration that a symbol is a symbol only when it can be demonstrated to be at work. Furthermore it would be futile to use sexual symbolism dogmatically when acute ego needs can be discerned as dominant in strongly concordant material. The sexual symbolism of this dream was taken up in due time, when it reappeared in another context, namely that of manhood and sexuality, and revealed the bisexual confusion inherent in all identity diffusion.

Controversies in regard to the therapeutic priority of particular interpretations can in principle be settled in discussions along the evidential lines sketched in this paper. However, since interpretation in this field must deal systematically with motivations which often are the more unconscious the more compelling they are, the whole area of evidential consensus is apt to be beclouded with age-old defensive attitudes of belief and disbelief. On the one hand, psychotherapists themselves are apt to solidify transient controversies in "schools" of thought which make dogmas out of theories and mark skepticism as resistance and unbelief, thus (unconsciously) using traditional methods of meeting the unknown where it is most personal. On the other hand, in the field of man's motivation, insights already firmly gained are forever subject to renewed repression and denial. It is in the very nature of man's intelligence that it can serve both the rational approaches to the facts of nature and also the rationalization and disguise of man's own nature. Therefore, in dealing with the *sense of evidence* in clinical matters, we must accept irrational belief as well as irrational disbelief as part of an inescapable dilemma which calls for a new kind of disciplined self-awareness.

So much for inferences concerning the meaning of the dream. It is not necessary in this presentation to insist that all of this and infinitely more can go through a clinician's head fast enough to make him react to the patient's behavior with whatever skillful determination is at his disposal. I may now confess that the initial invitation really requested me to tell you "how a *good* clinician works." I have replaced this embarrassing little word with dots until now when I can make it operational. It marks the good clinician that much can go on in him without clogging his communication at the moment of therapeutic intervention, when only the central theme may come to his awareness. On the other hand, he must also be able to call it all to explicit awareness when the circumstances permit the time to spell it out—for how else could such thinking be disciplined, shared and taught? Such sharing and teaching, however, if it is to transcend clinical impressionism, presupposes a communality of conceptual approaches. I cannot give you today more than a mere inkling that there is a systematic relationship between clinical observation on the one hand and, on the other, such conceptual points of view as Freud has introduced into psychiatry: a *structural* point of view denoting a kind of anatomy of the mind, a *dynamic* point of view denoting a kind of physiology of mental forces and of their transformations and, finally, a *genetic* point of view reconstructing the differentiation during distinct childhood stages of an inner organization and of certain energy transformations. But even as such propositions are tested on a wide front of inquiry (from the direct observation of children and perception experiments to "metapsychological" discussion), it stands to reason that clinical evidence is characterized by a human immediacy which transcends formulations ultimately derived from mechanistic patterns of thought.

To enlarge on this would lead me to the question of the collaboration of the clinician and the theoretician. Let me, instead, return to the problem of how, having perused all the above in his own mind, the clinician prepares for therapeutic intervention. For we have postulated that such intervention and the patient's reactions to it are an integral part of the evidence provided in the therapeutic encounter. Therapists of different persuasions differ as to what constitutes an interpretation: an impersonal and authoritative explanation, a warm and fatherly suggestion, an expansive sermon or a sparse encouragement to go on and see what comes up next. In each case, however, the tone of the interpretation will be influenced by the therapist's emotions, of which the patient is anxiously aware.

The preferred mode of interpretation (and this is the second prediction to be made in a clinical encounter) in our case necessarily included a relatively explicit statement of the therapist's emotional response to the dream report. Patients of the type of our young man, still smarting in his twenties under what he considered his mother's strange emotions in his infancy, can learn to delineate social reality and to tolerate emotional tension only if the therapist can juxtapose his own emotional reactions— hopefully more disciplined—to the patient's emotions. Therefore, as I reviewed with the patient in brief words most of what I have put before you, I was also able to tell him without anger, but not without some indignation, that my response to his account had included some feeling of anger. I explained that he had worried me, had made me feel pity, had touched me with his memories, and had burdened me with the proof, all at once, of the goodness of mothers, of the immortality of grandfathers, of my own perfection, and of God's grace. The demonstration that anger can be raised to the level of an educative and self-educative indignation is a not irrelevant by-product of many an interpretation.

The words used in an interpretation, however, are hard to remember and when reproduced often sound as arbitrary as any private language developed by two people in the course of an intimate association. Let me, therefore, state a generality instead. A good therapeutic interpretation, while often brief and simple in form, should be based on an implicit theme such as I have put before you, a theme common at the same time to a dominant trend in the patient's relation to the therapist, to a significant portion of his symptomatology, to an important period of his childhood, and to corresponding facets of his work and love-life. Although all of these trends may seem to be disparate enough further to bewilder the patient upon confrontation, clinical experience proves otherwise: they *are* (as I must repeat in conclusion) very closely related to each other in the patient's own struggling ego, for which the traumatic past is of course a present frontier, perceived as acute conflict. Such an interpretation, therefore, joins the patient's and the therapist's modes of problem-solving.

The intervention in this case, however, highlights one methodological point truly unique to clinical work, namely, the disposition of the clinician's "mixed" feelings, his emotions and opinions. The evidence is not "all in" if he does not succeed in using his own emotional responses during a clinical encounter as an evidential source and as a guide in intervention, instead of putting them aside with a spurious claim to unassailable objectivity. It is here that the requirement of the therapist's own psychoanalytic treatment as a didactic experience proves itself as essential, for the personal equation in the observer's emotional response is as important in psychotherapy as that of the senses in the laboratory. Repressed emotions easily hide themselves in the therapist's most stubborn blind spots.

What do we expect the patient to contribute to the closure of such evidence? What tells us that our interpretation was "right," and, therefore, made the evidence as conclusive as it can be in our kind of work? The simplest answer is that this particular patient was delighted when I told him of my thoughts and of my anger over his unnecessary attempts to burden me with a future which he could well learn to manage—a statement which was not meant to be a therapeutic "suggestion," a clinical slap on the back, but was based on what I knew of his inner resources as well as of the use he made of the opportunities offered in our clinical community. The patient left the hour —which he had begun with a sense of dire disaster—with a broad smile and obvious encouragement. In a most immediate way, this could be said to "clinch" the evidence; at least it shows that our predictions had not gone wildly astray.

I think I have outlined the rationale for my action and the patient's reaction. He had taken a chance with himself and with me, I thought. Under my protection and the hospital's he had hit bottom by chancing a repetition of his original breakdown. He had gone to the very border of unreality and had gleaned from it a highly condensed and seemingly anarchic image. I had shown him that the image, while experienced like a symptom, was in fact a kind of creation, or at any rate a condensed and highly meaningful communication and challenge, for which my particular clinical theory had made me receptive enough to be able to "talk back" without hesitation. A sense of mutuality and reality was thus restored, reinforced by the fact that while accepting his transferences as meaningful, I had refused to become drawn into them. I played neither mother, grandfather, nor God (this is the hardest), but had offered him my help as defined by my professional status in attempting to understand what was behind his helplessness. By relating the fact that his underlying anger aroused mine, and that I could say so without endangering either myself or him, I could show him that in his dream he had also confronted anger in the image of a Medusa—a Gorgon which, neither of us being a hero, we could yet slay together.

This, then, is an example which ends on a convincing note, leaving both the patient and the practitioner with the feeling that they are a pretty clever pair. If it were always required to clinch a piece of clinical evidence in this manner, we should have few convincing examples. To demonstrate other kinds, however, would take other hours.

Undoubtedly some may be inclined to interpret what I have reported in a different way. Against such a contingency, I can only claim (and hope to have demonstrated) that there is enough method in our work systematically to force favorite assumptions to become probable inferences by cross-checking them diagnostically, genetically, structurally, and in a number of other ways, all sufficiently systematized to allow for orderly discussion. Furthermore, in the long run, clinical evidence consists of a series of such encounters as I have outlined here, the series being characterized by a concomitantly progressive or regressive shift in all the areas mentioned.

Clinical training essentially consists of the charting of such series. In each step, our auxiliary methods must help us to work with reasonable precision and with the courage to revise our assumptions and our techniques systematically, if and when the clinical evidence should show that we overestimated or underestimated the patient or ourselves, the chances waiting for him in his environment, or the usefulness of our particular discipline.

In order to counteract such subjectivity and selectivity as I have put before you today, whole treatments are now being sound-filmed so that qualified secondary observers can follow the procedure. This may be important in some lines of research, and advantageous in training; yet, it is obvious that this process only puts a second observer in the position to decide, on the basis of his reactions and selections, whether or not he agrees with the judgments made by the original observer on the basis of his unrecorded and unrecordable reactions and selections; all the while, between the recording and the analysis of the data, history will be found to have marched on.

Neither will the nature of clinical evidence change in such new developments as *group-psychotherapy*, where a therapist faces a group of patients and they face one another as well as him, permitting a number of combinations and variations of the basic elements of a clinical encounter. Clinical evidence, finally, will be much enhanced but not changed in nature by a sharpened awareness (such as now emanates from *sociological studies*) of the psychotherapist's as well as the patient's position in society and history.

It is in this historical connection that we may return to the fate of the word "clinical." The individualistic character of my specimen and of our conceptual framework will be found to have their most explicit opposite in the practices and theories in the Communist part of the world, where different views are held regarding neuroses (they are taken to be a matter of nerves, subject to neurological treatment); regarding psychiatry proper; and finally, regarding the asocial and, in a sense, amoral aspects of some emotional disturbance. In the Far East, the word "clinical" is again assuming an entirely different historical connotation, insofar as it concerns mind at all: in Communist China the "thought analyst" faces individuals considered to be in need of reform. He encourages sincere confessions and self-analyses in order to realign thoughts with "the people's will." It will be interesting to learn more by comparison about the ideological implications of concepts of mental sickness, of social deviancy, and of psychological cure.

The ideological relativity implicit in clinical work may, to some, militate against its scientific value. I could not indicate in this paper what can be gleaned from clinical theory and application. I could only try to give an introduction to the clinician's basic view which asserts that you may learn about the nature of things as you find out what you can do *with* them, but that the true nature of man reveals itself only in the attempt to do something *for* him.

REFERENCES

Collingwood, R. G. *The idea of history.* New York: Oxford, 1956. Pp. 226–227.
Erikson, E. H. The dream specimen of psychoanalysis. *Journal of the American Psychoanalytic Association,* 1954, *2,* 5–56.

7.2 | THE RELIABILITY OF CLINICIANS' JUDGMENTS: A MULTITRAIT-MULTIMETHOD APPROACH*[1]

Lewis R. Goldberg and Charles E. Werts

Studies of the accuracy of inferences made by experienced clinical psychologists from personality test data have, in general, indicated (*a*) little validity for these inferences on an absolute basis (e.g., Goldberg, 1959; Holtzman & Sells, 1954; Kelly & Fiske, 1951), and (*b*) no relative validity for these inferences over rather simple actuarial procedures (e.g., Goldberg, 1965; Gough, 1962; Meehl, 1954; Oskamp, 1962). While early reactions to this literature included some denials of the conclusiveness of the available evidence (e.g., Holt, 1958; Hutt, 1956), later reactions have included some attempts to understand those aspects of the judgmental process which might logically lead to inferential errors (e.g., Cline & Richards, 1962; Hammond, Hursch, & Todd, 1964; Richards, 1963).

The bulk of the empirical studies of clinical judgments have focused on their valid-

* SOURCE: Goldberg, L. R., and Werts, C. E. The reliability of clinicians' judgments: A multitrait-multimethod approach. *Journal of Consulting Psychology,* 1966, 30, 199–206. Copyright 1966 by the American Psychological Association and reprinted by permission.

[1] The present report includes a reanalysis and summary by the first author of data originally collected by the second author (Werts, 1960). The authors wish to thank the four clinical judges for contributing their time so generously to this project; Daniel N. Weiner for providing the test protocols; and Dean Peabody, Leonard Rorer, Kenneth Howard, and Robert Nichols for their critical reading of a preliminary draft of this article. The preparation of this report was supported, in part, by Grant MH 04439 from the National Institutes of Health, United States Public Health Service.

ity, while relatively few studies have investigated the reliability of these judgments. General psychometric theory, however, posits a strong constraint imposed by the reliability of a measure on its potential validity. Extending the logic of test theory to include clinical psychologists as diagnostic instruments (e.g., Hunt, 1959), one might reasonably inquire whether clinical judgments typically are (*a*) relatively reliable, but often simply misaligned with reality, or (*b*) so lacking in reliability that their relationships with any stable external criterion would by necessity be severely attenuated.

Recently, the concept of reliability, itself, has been undergoing a searching reevaluation (e.g., Fiske, 1963). The classic dichotomy between internal consistency (homogeneity) and retest stability has been fused in the recent work of Cronbach and his associates (e.g., Cronbach & Gleser, 1964; Cronbach, Rajaratnam, & Gleser, 1963), while simultaneously being expanded in the writings of Cattell and his associates (e.g., Cattell, 1964; Cattell & Tsujioka, 1964). Both schools of thought, however, recognize *generalizability* as the common element in all definitions of reliability. Within the domain of clinical judgments, inferential reliability includes, as specific components, generalizability (*a*) over time, for the same judges using the same data (stability), (*b*) over judges, for the same data from the same occasion (consensus), and (*c*) over data sources, administered on the same occasion and interpreted by the same judge (convergence). Each of these three "reliabilities," in turn, might be expected to have significant interactions with the characteristics (traits) being evaluated, on the one hand, and the reference populations (targets), on the other. Clearly, then, investigation of the reliability of clinicians' judgments is complicated by covariation across at least five parameters (time, judges, data sources, traits, and targets), and no study of the reliability of clinical inferences is ever likely to provide definitive conclusions.

One type of solution to the general problem of simultaneously displaying covariation across a number of parameters has been offered by Campbell and Fiske (1959). While their multitrait-multimethod matrix was originally proposed as a means of estimating the convergent and discriminant validity of tests within the general model of construct validation (e.g., Campbell, 1960; Cronbach & Meehl, 1955), the suitability of this method for studying clinicians' judgments was quickly noted by Meehl:

> In order to place any confidence in either the theoretical constructs we employ in discussing patients, or in the instrument-interpreter combinations we use to assess them, studies of convergent and discriminative validity must be carried out. The Campbell-Fiske multitrait-multimethod matrix, or the multiperson-multimethod variant of it, should be useful for this purpose [1960; pp. 25–26].

Two clinical judgment studies using variants of the Campbell-Fiske methodology have been published. Howard (1962) had seven clinical psychologists rank-order 10 needs for each of 10 patients from Rorschach, Thematic Apperception Test (TAT), and Sentence Completion protocols. While Howard did not publish his correlation matrix, a chi-square analysis led him to conclude that the average intratest correlation between judges ($\bar{r} = .19$) indicated some significant, though very slight, consensus in these judgments. Intrajudge convergence between tests, however, averaged only .13, and the average of the interjudge agreement correlations between tests was only .05.

In a later study, Howard (1963) asked his seven clinicians to rate the same 10 patients on five traits, using the same three projective tests. Again, the correlation matrix was not reported, but an analysis of variance indicated that the average inter-judge agreement correlations between tests were not significant for any trait. On the other hand, intrajudge-intertest agreement (convergence) and intratest-interjudge agreement (consensus) were both significantly higher for less inferential traits (e.g., verbal fluency, productivity) than for more inferential traits (e.g., psychotherapy prognosis, adjustment).

While both of Howard's studies explored significant aspects of inferential reliability, certain methodological problems, applicable to *any* single study, demand further research in this domain. For example, since Howard utilized only one group of 10 patients, the generalizability of his findings to different target populations is still open to question. Moreover, clinicians might legitimately argue that the task of ranking 10 needs (e.g., "harmavoidance," "succorance," "blamavoidance") ipsatively for each patient (Howard, 1962) falls somewhat outside their usual clinical responsibilities, thereby questioning the generality of these findings to more commonly used traits. The present study included a larger sample of targets (replications across four different patient samples) as well as a set of traits more commonly employed in clinical settings.

Perhaps an even more important methodological issue arises from the relatively common practice of asking a judge to rate the same target, either on the same trait using different data sources, or on different traits using the same data source. In the former case, any idiosyncratic and non-test-specific habit of the target (e.g., use of particular words or phrases, general verbal fluency, etc.) should spuriously increase convergence. In the latter case, any general evaluative impression of the target (e.g., a "halo" effect) might systematically distort trait discrimination. The design of the present study insures that judges, traits, targets, and data sources are all completely unconfounded, and, therefore, these findings should provide an unusual comparison with other studies of inferential reliability.

PROCEDURE

Four experienced clinical psychologists independently ranked each of four sets of 10 neuropsychiatric patients on one of four traits, using one of four data sources. The intercorrelations among rankings were pooled across the four samples to form an average multitrait-multimethod judgmental matrix. The design, which is illustrated in Table 1, is explained in greater detail on page 120.

JUDGES.   The four judges used in this study were practicing clinical psychologists, all of whom had considerable postgraduate clinical experience and were familiar with the population of patients from which the experimental sample was drawn. The four judges received their PhD degrees, respectively, from the University of Iowa, Northwestern University, the University of Minnesota, and Stanford University.

Table 1 | EXPERIMENTAL DESIGN[a]

Sample	Traits	TESTS			
		MMPI	W-B	ROR	VOC
A	SA	J_1	J_4	J_2	J_3
	ES	J_2	J_1	J_3	J_4
	IQ	J_3	J_2	J_4	J_1
	D	J_4	J_3	J_1	J_2
B	SA	J_3	J_2	J_4	J_1
	ES	J_4	J_3	J_1	J_2
	IQ	J_1	J_4	J_2	J_3
	D	J_2	J_1	J_3	J_4
C	SA	J_2	J_1	J_3	J_4
	ES	J_3	J_2	J_4	J_1
	IQ	J_4	J_3	J_1	J_2
	D	J_1	J_4	J_2	J_3
D	SA	J_4	J_3	J_1	J_2
	ES	J_1	J_4	J_2	J_3
	IQ	J_2	J_1	J_3	J_4
	D	J_3	J_2	J_4	J_1

[a] This table should be read as follows: The 10 patients in Sample A were ranked on Social Adjustment by Judge 1 using the MMPI as a data source.

TRAITS. Four of the most frequently used constructs in the diagnostic reports of clinical psychologists—Social Adjustment (SA), Ego Strength (ES), Intelligence (IQ), and Dependency (D)—were utilized in this study. In order to ascertain how these concepts were actually being used by experienced clinical psychologists, no attempt was made to further define these constructs for the judges.

PATIENT SAMPLES. Of the several thousand outpatients who had been tested between the years 1947 and 1950 at the Veterans Administration Mental Hygiene Clinic at Fort Snelling, Minnesota, four groups of 10 each were carefully selected so as to (a) equate the four samples on all relevant traits while (b) maximizing trait variation within each sample. Each patient sample consisted of males who varied (a) in social adjustment, from relatively normal to grossly psychotic; (b) in intelligence, from dull-normal to superior (as measured by Wechsler-Bellevue scores); and (c) in vocational adjustment, from unemployed to presently employed in a well-paying and responsible position which had been held for many years.

DATA SOURCES. The four sources of data were intended to include information commonly available to clinical psychologists carrying out psychological evaluations (e.g., Sundberg, 1961) as well as to represent four rather different types of clinical assessment procedures. An intelligence test (the Wechsler-Bellevue), a projective test (the Rorschach), a structured personality inventory (the MMPI), and a vocational history were selected for study.

EXPERIMENTAL DESIGN. The experimental design of this study might best be visualized as a cube whose three dimensions are tests, judges, and traits. There were four such cubes utilized in this study, each containing a different set of 10 patients. Alternatively, the design may be thought of as a 4×4 Latin square, replicated four times. Each judge ranked four different sets of 10 protocols each, ranking each of the sets (*a*) on a different trait and (*b*) by means of a different data source. Thus, no judge ranked any set of protocols on more than one trait, and no judge ranked more than one trait from any single set of protocols.

Table 1 summarizes the experimental design for this study. Each judge first ranked, on *one* of the four traits, a packet of 40 test protocols. The 40 protocols, each from a different patient, were composed of four sets of 10, each set comprising a different data source (e.g., Judge 1 first received the 10 MMPIs from Sample C, the 10 Rorschachs from Sample A, the 10 Wechslers from Sample B, and the 10 Vocational Histories from Sample D, and he ranked each set on Dependency; he then received, in turn, the three other packets, each to be judged on a different trait).

STATISTICAL ANALYSIS. Within each of the four patient samples product-moment correlations were computed among all pairs of rankings. These correlations were converted to Zs, averaged across the four samples, and the averages then reconverted to correlation coefficients. The signs of the correlations for the trait of Dependency were reversed, so that all correlations reflect rankings in the socially desirable direction.

RESULTS

Table 2 presents the average multitrait-multimethod correlation matrix. The correlations between judgments of the *same trait* made from different data sources (e.g., the monotrait-heteromethod correlations) are presented in the triangles just below the main diagonal of the table. There are six such monotrait-heteromethod correlations available *for each trait:* (*a*) MMPI versus Rorschach, (*b*) MMPI versus Wechsler, (*c*) MMPI versus Vocational History, (*d*) Rorschach versus Wechsler, (*e*) Rorschach versus Vocational History, and (*f*) Wechsler versus Vocational History. These correlations indicate the extent to which the clinicians agreed in their judgments of the same patients on the

Table 2 | MULTITRAIT-MULTIMETHOD MATRIX FOR FOUR TRAITS JUDGED FROM FOUR DATA SOURCES

	SOCIAL ADJUSTMENT (SA)				EGO STRENGTH (ES)				INTELLIGENCE (IQ)				DEPENDENCY[a] (D)			
	MMPI	ROR	W-B	VOC	MMPI	ROR	W-B	VOC	MMPI	ROR	W-B	VOC	MMPI	ROR	W-B	VOC
SA MMPI																
SA ROR	.64															
SA W-B	.22	−.01														
SA VOC	.16	−.15	.01													
ES MMPI	.80	.08	.24	−.13												
ES ROR	.29	−.02	.07	−.23	.10											
ES W-B	.02	−.01	.66	.11	.06	−.02										
ES VOC	−.01	−.21	.57	.76	−.11	−.31	.23									
IQ MMPI	.13	.05	.15	−.38	.11	.03	.10	−.24								
IQ ROR	.37	.34	.21	−.19	.26	.39	.36	.06	.14							
IQ W-B	.09	.02	.54	.10	.11	.39	.77	−.03	.38	.43						
IQ VOC	.09	−.11	.49	.20	−.09	.30	.05	.14	−.12	.00	.59					
D MMPI	.54	−.09	.24	−.24	.64	.02	−.04	−.08	.20	−.29	−.07	−.05				
D ROR	.12	−.03	.45	.08	.15	.21	.33	.02	.11	.16	.49	.51	.08			
D W-B	.11	−.01	.08	−.01	.07	.10	.12	−.03	.20	.32	.35	.21	−.03	.09		
D VOC	.02	.16	.09	.47	−.25	−.14	.12	.65	.00	.12	.10	.14	.15	.03	−.14	

[a] Signs of the correlations for Dependency have been reversed.

same trait when the judgments were made from different data sources. Since there were four traits under study, there are 24 monotrait-heteromethod correlations. If the clinicians tended to agree in their judgments of the same trait evaluated by different data sources, the monotrait-heteromethod correlations would be high.

The circled values in Table 2 are the correlations between judgments of *different traits* made from the same data source (heterotrait-monomethod correlations). There are six such heterotrait-monomethod correlations *for each data source:* (*a*) Social Adjustment versus Ego Strength, (*b*) Social Adjustment versus Intelligence, (*c*) Social Adjustment versus Dependency, (*d*) Ego Strength versus Intelligence, (*e*) Ego Strength versus Dependency, and (*f*) Intelligence versus Dependency. Since there were four data sources, there are 24 such heterotrait-monomethod correlations presented in Table 2. The size of these correlations indicates the extent to which judgments from the same data sources tend to be correlated across different traits; these correlations reflect the effects of "method variance" (Campbell & Fiske, 1959).

The remaining values presented in Table 2 are the correlations between judgments of different traits made from different data sources (heterotrait-heteromethod correlations). There are 72 such values, reflecting the strength of association between traits, with method variance removed.

Inspection of the monotrait-heteromethod correlations in Table 2 reveals evidence of very low convergence. These correlations ranged from —.31 (Ego Strength: Rorschach versus Vocational History) to .64 (Social Adjustment: MMPI versus Rorschach). On the other hand, there is evidence of considerable method variance, the heterotrait-monomethod correlations ranging from —.03 (Rorschach: Social Adjustment versus Dependency) to .80 (MMPI: Social Adjustment versus Ego Strength).

A summary of these findings is presented in Table 3. The top half of Table 3 summarizes the evidence for interjudge convergence. The first column presents the average monotrait-heteromethod correlations for each trait (the average of the elements in each of the off-diagonal triangles in Table 2). These average correlations would be high if the clinicians were agreeing with each other. The second column presents the average heterotrait-heteromethod correlations (the average of the noncircled elements from the rectangles in Table 2). These values, which are free from method variance, should be considerably lower than those in the first column, if convergence is to be established. The third column presents the average heterotrait correlations (the average of *all* of the values from the heterotrait rectangles in Table 2). These values, inflated by some method variance, should ideally be low compared to the monotrait-heteromethod correlations if interjudge convergence—rather than method variance—was the predominant judgmental factor involved.

Of the four traits, only Intelligence yielded an average coefficient of convergence numerically higher ($\bar{r} = .25$) than the average heterotrait correlations ($\bar{r} = .16$). While this tiny a degree of convergence for a trait as significant as Intelligence seems incredible, the results for the other three traits were even worse! Social Adjustment yielded an average coefficient of convergence of .17, exactly equal to its average heterotrait correlation. The corresponding averages were a mere .03 for Dependency (against a heterotrait $\bar{r}$ of .14) and — .01 for Ego Strength (against a heterotrait $\bar{r}$ of .18). In general, the

Table 3 | SUMMARY OF THE MULTITRAIT-MULTIMETHOD MATRIX: AVERAGE CORRELATIONS

	MONOTRAIT-HETEROMETHOD	HETEROTRAIT-HETEROMETHOD	TOTAL HETEROTRAIT
Trait			
Social adjustment	.17	.07	.17
Ego strength	—.01	.07	.18
Intelligence	.25	.11	.16
Dependency	.03	.08	.14
Mean	.11	.08	.16
	HETEROTRAIT-MONOMETHOD	HETEROTRAIT-HETEROMETHOD	TOTAL HETEROMETHOD
Data source			
MMPI	.45	.03	.06
Rorschach	.15	.12	.10
Wechsler-Bellevue	.46	.16	.15
Vocational history	.43	.02	.03
Mean	.37	.08	.08

monotrait-heteromethod correlations averaged only .11, while the heterotrait correlations averaged .16!

The bottom half of Table 3 presents another summary of the correlations in Table 2, now rearranged by data sources. The first column lists the average heterotrait-monomethod correlations (the circle elements in Table 2), for each data source. Note that the average monomethod correlations (indexes of method variance) were *all* greater than the average heteromethod correlations. The average monomethod correlation for the MMPI was .45, against a heteromethod $\bar{r}$ of .06. For the Wechsler-Bellevue, the average monomethod correlation was .46, against a heteromethod $\bar{r}$ of .15, and for the Vocational History the corresponding values were .43, against .03. For the Rorschach, however, the monomethod correlations were small ($\bar{r} = .15$), against a heteromethod $\bar{r}$ of .10.

The findings reported in Table 3 indicate that for each of these four traits, the judgments of one experienced clinician working from one data source bear no relationship to the judgments of another clinician working from another data source. However, Table 3 indicates that clinicians' judgments do tend to covary when they are using the same data source but focusing on different traits. Are these enigmatic findings simply a function of the perceived difficulty of the judgmental task? If so, the judgments made by individual clinicians, if made on repeated occasions, should be quite unstable.

Table 4 presents some evidence relating to this possibility. One judge was asked to carry out the identical ranking procedures 2 months after his first attempt, and the rank correlations (rhos) for this judge are presented in Table 4. On the average, the test-retest reliability of this judge was .61, indicating considerable stability for his judgments and making less tenable the hypothesis that the task was perceived as an impossibly difficult one. For this judge, judgments of Ego Strength from either the MMPI or the

Table 4 | TEST-RETEST STABILITY COEFFICIENTS FOR ONE JUDGE[a]

TRAITS	MMPI	VOCATIONAL HISTORY	RORSCHACH	WECHSLER-BELLEVUE
Social adjustment	.88**	.58*	.46	.09
Ego strength	1.00**	.93**	.78**	.69*
Dependency	.78**	.77**	.53	—.12
Intelligence	.10	.54	.72*	1.00**

[a] Each coefficient represents a rank-correlation (rho) between the original rankings and those carried out 2 months later.
* $p < .05$.
** $p < .01$.

Vocational History and judgments of Intelligence from the Wechsler-Bellevue were remarkably stable. On the other hand, his judgments of either Social Adjustment or Dependency from the Wechsler and Intelligence from the MMPI were extremely unstable.

While the present study focused primarily on the convergence of clinical judgments, some data are available which bear on their validity. Since the clinicians were asked to judge Intelligence from all four data sources, it was possible to relate these judgments to Intelligence as measured by the Wechsler-Bellevue. Table 5 presents the results of this analysis. Of the 12 rank correlations listed in Table 5 not involving the Wechsler, only 5 were positive and significantly above zero, and 3 of these 5 came from one judge. It appears as if one judge was able to do this task quite accurately, while the other three judges were not. Since in any particular setting the "best" judge is typically not known, the accuracy of the average judge becomes important. For this task, however, the average judge's inferences, while positive, did not differ significantly from zero.

Table 5 | RANK CORRELATIONS BETWEEN INTELLIGENCE RANKINGS AND WECHSLER-BELLEVUE IQs

TEST	JUDGE				AVERAGE
	1	2	3	4	
MMPI	.21	—.71*	.60*	.88**	.24
Vocational history	.26	.50	.12	.84**	.43
Rorschach	.33	.66*	.07	.69*	.44
Wechsler-Bellevue	1.00**	1.00**	1.00**	1.00**	1.00**

* $p < .05$.
** $p < .01$.

DISCUSSION

In a classic study of the reliability of clinical judgments, Little and Shneidman (1959) reported the results of a comprehensive analysis of diverse kinds of inferences about 12 subjects made by expert clinicians from each of five kinds of data sources—Rorschach, TAT, MMPI, Make-a-Picture-Story (MAPS), and Anamnesis. From their findings, these investigators extrapolated that:

> For the tests used, agreement on diagnoses will be only slightly better than chance, judgments of maladjustment will be skewed toward the pathological, agreement with psychiatrists as to personality dynamics will be modest, and the clinician's reliability in all these areas will leave much to be desired [Little & Shneidman, 1959, p. 27].

The findings from the present study confirm Little and Shneidman's predictions. These results, averaged across four samples of patients, clearly indicate that an experienced clinician's judgments from one data source do *not* correlate with another clinician's judgments from another data source, even though both clinicians are diagnosing the very same patient on—ostensibly—the very same trait! Moreover, this finding occurs regardless of whether the trait being rated is a highly global one (e.g., Social Adjustment, Ego Strength) or a more specific one (e.g., Dependency). These findings become all the more striking when one realizes that each of the four patient samples utilized in this study was selected to span as great a range of the traits as possible, thus eliminating the possibility that a lack of convergence could stem from a restriction of trait range. Moreover, the ranking procedure used in this study insured that the results were not an artifact of coarse grouping of trait ratings.

In contrast to Howard's (1962) study, the present study utilized traits commonly employed in the diagnostic reports of psychologists working in clinics and hospitals. On a priori grounds, one might reasonably expect that clinicians' judgments should show their maximum convergence for the traits used in this study, and that other traits would fare even worse. Considering the findings from this study, however, it is difficult to imagine how any other results could look worse.

The finding that judgments made from the same data source tend to be correlated, even across diverse traits, is by now a widely substantiated one (e.g., Campbell & Fiske, 1959). The present study provides additional evidence of the magnitude of monomethod-heterotrait agreement among judgments and demonstrates how instrument-bound clinical judgments can become.

The experimental design of the present study (in which judges, traits, and methods are each unconfounded), while not presented as a standard for all studies of inferential reliability, should serve as a model for a significant control condition in the more typical experimental design. While it is, of course, important to ascertain the degree of consensus among judges viewing the same set of patients from the same data source, high correlations among judges in such studies may have little bearing on the inferential reliability of the *trait* being rated. And, as pointed out earlier, when the same judges rate the same subjects using more than one data source, the possibility of an artifactual consensus through accidental contaminating cues cannot easily be discounted.

Finally, it might be argued that the lack of convergence demonstrated in the present study simply serves to illustrate the differing "levels" (e.g., Leary, 1957) tapped by each data source. While one conceivably might want to argue that Dependency as inferred from the Rorschach was at a "deeper" level than Dependency inferred from the MMPI, the tenuousness of such reasoning becomes apparent when one tries to interpret the findings for Intelligence in the same manner. On the other hand, one might argue that judgments of Dependency should not be made from an intelligence test, nor judgments of Intelligence from the MMPI. While it is not uncommon for such multitrait-monomethod judgments to be made in clinical practice, the present study should certainly serve to question the wisdom of this activity.

SUMMARY

Four experienced clinical psychologists independently ranked each of 4 equated samples of 10 patients on 1 of 4 traits (Social Adjustment, Ego Strength, Intelligence, and Dependency), using 1 of 4 data sources (MMPI, Rorschach, Wechsler, and a Vocational History). A 4×4 Latin square design insured that the usual sources of judgmental confounding were absent from this study. The findings indicate quite clearly that the judgments of 1 clinician working from 1 data source bear no systematic relationship to those of another clinician working from another data source, even though both judges are ranking the same patients on the same trait. On the other hand, judgments of diverse traits from the same data source do tend to be related.

REFERENCES

Campbell, D. T. Recommendations for APA test standards regarding construct, trait, or discriminant validity. *American Psychologist*, 1960, *15*, 546–553.

Campbell, D. T., & Fiske, D. W. Convergent and discriminant validation by the multitrait-multimethod matrix. *Psychological Bulletin*, 1959, *56*, 81–105.

Cattell, R. B. Validity and reliability: A proposed more basic set of concepts. *Journal of Educational Psychology*, 1964, *55*, 1–22.

Cattell, R. B., & Tsujioka, B. The importance of factor-trueness and validity, vs. homogeneity and orthogonality, in test scales. *Educational and Psychological Measurement*, 1964, *24*, 3–30.

Cline, V. B., & Richards, J. M., Jr. Components of accuracy of interpersonal perception scores and the clinical and statistical prediction controversy. *Psychological Record*, 1962, *12*, 373–381.

Cronbach, L. J., & Gleser, G. C. The signal-noise ratio in the comparison of reliability coefficients. *Educational and Psychological Measurement*, 1964, *24*, 467–480.

Cronbach, L. J., & Meehl, P. E. Construct validity in psychological tests. *Psychological Bulletin*, 1955, *52*, 281–302.

Cronbach, L. J., Rajaratnam, N., & Gleser, G. C. Theory of generalizability: A liberalization of reliability theory. *British Journal of Statistical Psychology*, 1963, *16*, 137–163.

Fiske, D. W. Homogeneity and variation in measuring personality. *American Psychologist*, 1963, *18*, 643–652.

Goldberg, L. R. The effectiveness of clinicians' judgments: The diagnosis of organic brain damage from the Bender-Gestalt Test. *Journal of Consulting Psychology*, 1959, *23*, 25–33.

Goldberg, L. R. Diagnosticians vs. diagnostic signs: The diagnosis of psychosis vs. neurosis from the MMPI. *Psychological Monographs*, 1965, 79(9, Whole No. 602).

Gough, H. G. Clinical vs. statistical prediction in psychology. In L. Postman (Ed.), *Psychology in the making*. New York: Knopf, 1962. Pp. 526–584.

Hammond, K. R., Hursch, C. J., & Todd, F. J. Analyzing the components of clinical inference. *Psychological Review*, 1964, *71*, 438–456.

Holt, R. R. Clinical and statistical prediction: A reformulation and some new data. *Journal of Abnormal and Social Psychology*, 1958, *56*, 1–12.

Holtzman, W. H., & Sells, S. B. Prediction of flying success by critical analysis of test protocols. *Journal of Abnormal and Social Psychology*, 1954, *49*, 485–490.

Howard, K. I. The convergent and discriminant validation of ipsative ratings from three projective instruments. *Journal of Clinical Psychology*, 1962, *18*, 183–188.

Howard, K. I. Ratings of projective test protocols as a function of degree of inference. *Educational and Psychological Measurement*, 1963, *23*, 267–275.

Hunt, W. A. An actuarial approach to clinical judgment. In B. M. Bass & I. A. Berg (Eds.), *Objective approaches to personality assessment*. Princeton, N.J.: Van Nostrand, 1959. Pp. 169–189.

Hutt, M. L. Actuarial and clinical approaches to psychodiagnosis. *Psychological Reports*, 1956, *2*, 413–419.

Kelly, E. L., & Fiske, D. W. *The prediction of performance in clinical psychology*. Ann Arbor, Mich.: University of Michigan Press, 1951.

Leary, T. *Interpersonal diagnosis of personality*. New York: Ronald, 1957.

Little, K. B., & Shneidman, E. S. Congruencies among interpretations of psychological test and anamnestic data. *Psychological Monographs*, 1959, 73(6, Whole No. 476).

Meehl, P. E. *Clinical vs. statistical prediction: A theoretical analysis and a review of the evidence*. Minneapolis: University of Minnesota Press, 1954.

Meehl, P. E. The cognitive activity of the clinician. *American Psychologist*, 1960, *15*, 19–27.

Oskamp, S. The relationship of clinical experience and training methods to several criteria of clinical prediction. *Psychological Monographs*, 1962, 76(28, Whole No. 547).

Richards, J. M., Jr. Reconceptualization of the clinical and statistical prediction controversy in terms of components of accuracy of interpersonal perception scores. *Psychological Reports*, 1963, *12*, 443–448.

Sundberg, N. D. The practice of psychological testing in clinical services in the United States. *American Psychologist*, 1961, *16*, 79–83.

Werts, C. E., Jr. Multidimensional analysis of psychological constructs. Unpublished PhD dissertation, University of Minnesota, 1960.

7.3 | ILLUSORY CORRELATION AS AN OBSTACLE TO THE USE OF VALID PSYCHODIAGNOSTIC SIGNS*, [1]

Loren J. Chapman and Jean P. Chapman

The psychodiagnostician who uses psychological tests relies usually on his clinical experience for interpreting test responses. He accumulates observations of the different responses that occur as correlates of various personality characteristics of patients. He later uses this information to infer, at least tentatively, the presence of similar characteristics in patients giving similar responses. To do this, the diagnostician must assume, of course, that he is able to observe and remember which characteristics of test performance occur as correlates of each characteristic of personality. The inference of characteristics of personality from the occurrence of isolated characteristics of performance, instead of interpretation in terms of more complex patterns of test performance, is often termed the "sign" approach. This frequently deprecated, yet widely used, approach to projective test interpretation is the focus of the present study.

A large body of research literature demonstrates that many diagnostic test signs lack the psychological meanings that clinical observers have claimed for them. It is not surprising, then, that other studies have demonstrated that psychodiagnosticians are usually less able than they believe to make valid statements about patients on the basis of tests. Little and Shneidman (1959) made this point very clearly. In an especially well-controlled study, they found that eminent clinicians performed only slightly above chance.

The enormous discrepancy between the reports of clinical observers and the research evidence concerning the meanings of test responses has long been a puzzle. The conflict of evidence has been especially disquieting because clinicians usually show substantial consensus as to specific meanings of various test responses although these same meanings may have been discredited by research evidence.

The present writers (Chapman & Chapman, 1967) have recently suggested a possible resolution of this enigma by demonstrating a source of massive systematic error in observations of correlations between symptom statements and features of projective test protocols. The projective test studied was the Draw-a-Person Test, which has been largely discredited as a measure of personality by the research evidence (Swensen,

* SOURCE: Chapman, L. J., and Chapman, J. P. Illusory correlation as an obstacle to the use of valid psychodiagnostic signs. *Journal of Abnormal Psychology*, 1969, 74, 271–280. Copyright 1969 by the American Psychological Association and reprinted by permission.

[1] This study was supported by Research Grant MH-07987 from the National Institute of Mental Health, United States Public Health Service. The authors are indebted to Fred Cosentino for his assistance in the gathering and analysis of the data, and to Richard McFall for his critique of the manuscript.

1957). Naive undergraduates viewed a series of 45 Draw-a-Person Test drawings paired with contrived symptom statements about the alleged patients who drew them. In these contrived materials there was no correlation between the occurrence of any symptom statement and any drawing characteristic. The undergraduate Ss "rediscovered" the same correlations between drawing characteristics and symptoms that a group of clinicians most often reported observing in their clinical practice. These relationships are called "illusory correlations" because the naive Ss reported observing them, although they were actually absent in the experimental materials. Moreover, the popularity of the various illusory correlations corresponded to strength of rated, verbal associative connection between symptom and drawing characteristic. These findings suggest that the popular meanings of many test signs, as reported by clinicians, are illusory correlations based on verbal associative connection of the test sign to the symptom, rather than on valid observations.

Not all tests, however, are as completely lacking in validity as the Draw-a-Person Test. Performance on most psychodiagnostic tests has some correlation with personality characteristics. In light of the research evidence indicating that clinicians are only moderately successful in the interpretation of psychodiagnostic test performance, one must wonder whether clinicians' observations of valid signs, when such signs are present, is impeded by their proclivity to observe, instead, associatively based illusory correlations. This question is the central interest of the present paper.

To investigate this issue, it was first necessary to choose a symptom and a test for which both valid and invalid signs have been reported by clinical observers. Male homosexuality and Rorschach content analysis were chosen because they appear to fulfill these criteria. Wheeler (1949) offered 20 Rorschach signs of male homosexuality. Clinicians commonly report several of these signs as substantiated by their own clinical experience, but research evidence strongly supports only two of the signs. Three studies by different investigators (Davids, Joelson, & McArthur, 1956; Hooker, 1958; Wheeler, 1949) have reported statistically interpretable evidence on the validity of all 20 Wheeler-Rorschach content signs, and these studies show some agreement. Table 1 presents the z values for those Wheeler signs that distinguished homosexual and heterosexual groups in one or more of the three studies at the .05 level using a one-tailed test. For Wheeler's study, the z values were computed by the present writers from Wheeler's published data, using the formula for the critical ratio between uncorrelated proportions. Hooker obtained her

Table 1 | CRITICAL RATIO (z) VALUES FOR WHEELER SIGNS THAT DISTINGUISHED MALE HOMOSEXUALS FROM HETEROSEXUALS IN THREE STUDIES

STUDY	z VALUE					
	Sign 7	Sign 8	Sign 10	Sign 17	Sign 19	Sign 20
Wheeler	1.64			1.79		
Davids, Joelson, & McArthur	1.70	2.17	1.65		1.80	
Hooker		1.94				1.90

values using the comparable formula for correlated proportions, after matching pairs of Ss by total number of responses. Davids et al. did not indicate which formula they used.

As seen in Table 1, Wheeler Signs 7 and 8 were both found to distinguish homosexual from heterosexual groups in two of the three studies. Wheeler Sign 7 is a response on Card IV of "human or animal—contorted, monstrous, or threatening," and Wheeler Sign 8 is a response on Card V, W or Center D, of a "human, or humanized animal." Wheeler's example of "humans" is "woman dressed as a bat" which indicates that the humans are animalized humans. Signs 10, 17, 19, and 20 were each found to distinguish the groups in one study but were tested and not found valid in the other two studies. A finding by chance alone of a significant difference for one sign out of 20 is not unexpected. Therefore, for purposes of this study, Signs 7 and 8 were considered the only clinically valid signs. This conclusion tends to be supported by Reitzell (1949) who reported Signs 7, 8, and 16 as the most discriminating of the 20 Wheeler signs. Unfortunately, her data cannot be analyzed statistically because she reported them in terms of number of responses of each type given by homosexual and nonhomosexual groups, rather than the number of Ss in each group who gave each sign.

The hypotheses of this study are:

1. The "popularity" of signs among practicing clinicians has little relationship to the objective clinical validity of the signs, as indicated by research evidence.
2. The most popular signs among practicing clinicians are the ones that have the strongest verbal associative connection to male homosexuality.
3. Naive observers, when presented with contrived Rorschach responses arbitrarily paired with statements of symptoms of the patient who gave each response, erroneously report observing that these same associatively based invalid signs occur as correlates of homosexuality.
4. The naive observers report these associatively based illusory correlations even when the materials are contrived so that other (clinically) valid correlations are present.

PART I

EXPERIMENT 1: CLINICAL OBSERVATIONS BY PRACTICING PSYCHO-DIAGNOSTICIANS.   It was first necessary to learn the kinds of Rorschach content that psychodiagnosticians believe they have observed most often in the protocols of male homosexuals. A questionnaire was prepared for circulation among practicing clinicians. The questionnaire was anonymous, but it asked the clinician to list his academic degrees and the years he obtained them, as well as the number of years of his psychodiagnostic experience.

INSTRUCTIONS.   Although the more traditional clinical use of the Rorschach is the interpretation of Rorschach determinants, many practicing clinicians in recent years have observed that the content of Rorschach responses is also related to the patient's emotional problems. Some of these observed relationships have been discussed in published reports, while others have not. We wish to ask about your observations concerning the content of Rorschach responses by two kinds of patients.

1. Have you seen the Rorschach protocols of a number of men who have problems concerning homosexual impulses, either overt or covert?
2. What kinds of Rorschach content have you observed to be prominent in the Rorschach protocols of men with problems concerning homosexual impulses?
3. If possible, would you list some examples of the kinds of responses made by such men.

Altogether 76 copies of this questionnaire were sent to clinicians at internship training centers, academic psychology departments, and other leading clinical installations. Each of 11 recipients received several copies with the request that he circulate them to his colleagues.

RESULTS. Questionnaires were returned by 42 clinicians 32 of whom said that they had seen the Rorschach protocols of a number of men with homosexual problems and were willing to list the kinds of Rorschach content they had observed. Of these 32 clinicians, 22 reported having the PhD degree and 10 the master's degree. They reported 2–29-yr. psychodiagnostic experience, with a mean of 9.1.

The clinicians' most frequent responses are listed in Table 2. Only two clinicians listed one of the two valid Wheeler signs. Both of these were Wheeler Sign 7. Most of the clinicians listed one or more of five invalid Wheeler signs. Two of these five signs have, as previously discussed, each received support in only one of three studies, and the other three were supported by none of them.

In order to test the hypothesis that the popularity of the invalid signs of homosexuality is based on high-strength, verbal associative connection with homosexuality, ratings of strength of associative connection were obtained. The following rating item, used for "anality," illustrates the format that was used.

Table 2 | THE FIVE WHEELER-RORSCHACH CONTENT SIGNS OF MALE HOMO-SEXUALITY MOST FREQUENTLY REPORTED BY THE CLINICIANS

WHEELER SIGN	PERCENTAGE OF CLINICIANS RE-PORTING THE SIGN
16 Human or animal anal content	44
20 Feminine clothing	38
4 Humans with sex confused	28[a]
5 Humans with sex uncertain	16[a]
19 Male or female genitalia	38

[a] The percentages listed here are for the clinicians' reports of this content regardless of the card on which they observed it. Wheeler limited Signs 4 and 5 to Card III, but few of the clinicians specified a card. Wheeler described sexual confusion on Card I as Sign 2, but did not describe sexual uncertainty on that card despite the conceptual similarity of these two classes of percepts.

The tendency for "homosexuality" to call to mind "rectum" and "buttocks" is
a. Very strong.
b. Strong.
c. Moderate.
d. Slight.
e. Very slight.
f. No tendency at all.

Rating items were used for both of the two unpopular valid signs as well as for the five popular invalid signs that are listed in Table 2. The wordings of the signs were in some cases rephrased, as in the example above, to facilitate understanding by the raters. These wordings are listed in Table 3. Because of their conceptual similarity, "sexual uncertainty" and "sexual confusion" were represented in the ratings by a single item of "part man—part woman." In addition, there was one item each for "food" and "maps," which were used as filler items in the studies that follow.

The eight items concerned with homosexuality were intermixed with 80 other items in the same format, most of which were not concerned with sexual material. The questionnaire was given to a group of 34 undergraduate students who did not participate in the other studies reported in this paper.

The six associative ratings from a to f were assigned values from 6 to 1 and a mean was computed for each item. Table 3 reports the mean rated associative strength between homosexuality and each of the eight categories.

As seen in Table 3, the popular invalid signs have a much stronger associative connection to homosexuality than either the unpopular clinically valid signs or the two categories of filler items. There is no overlap between the mean rated strength of the popular invalid signs and that of the other signs and categories of filler items. The rated associative strength to homosexuality of the lowest rated popular invalid sign (feminine

Table 3 | MEAN RATED STRENGTH OF ASSOCIATIVE CONNECTION BETWEEN HOMOSEXUALITY AND CONTENT AREAS

CONTENT AREA	MEAN RATED STRENGTH
Popular invalid signs	
Rectum and buttocks	4.38
Part man—part woman	3.53
Feminine clothing	3.12
Sexual organs	4.47
Unpopular valid signs	
Part animal—part human	1.93
Monsters	1.68
Filler items	
Food	1.09
Maps	1.09

clothing) was compared with that of the highest rated unpopular valid sign (part animal —part human). The difference was significant as indicated by a two-tailed t test ($t =$ 3.52, $p < .001$). These data suggest that whether or not a clinician reports a given category of percepts as a correlate of homosexuality is determined primarily by the strength of its verbal associative connection to the symptom, rather than by objective reality. This inference is congruent with earlier findings (Chapman & Chapman, 1967) concerning the Draw-a-Person Test.

PART II

Laboratory studies were designed to determine whether naive observers, presented with contrived statements of patients' symptoms and their Rorschach responses, would make the same errors of observation that the clinicians appear to have made in their observational reports. The demonstration in the laboratory of these systematic errors of observation based on verbal associative connection would lend strong additional support to the contention that the clinicians' reports reflect illusory correlation based on associative connection.

SUBJECTS. The Ss in the laboratory studies were tested under 13 conditions which, for convenience of exposition, were divided into three experiments (Experiments II, III, and IV). All Ss were students in an introductory psychology course. The number of Ss in Conditions 1–13 were 60, 43, 53, 37, 39, 52, 49, 59, 54, 61, 60, 60, and 66, respectively. No S served in more than one condition. All Ss were asked on a questionnaire if they had any familiarity or experience with principles of Rorschach interpretation. The occasional S who indicated any such familiarity was not included in the sample.

EXPERIMENT II {CONDITIONS 1–5}: ILLUSORY CORRELATION IN THE ABSENCE OF VALID RELATIONSHIPS. Experiment II was designed to determine if the invalid signs that were found to be popular with the clinicians would also be reported by naive observers when no valid relationship is present between any category of percepts and the symptom of male homosexuality. This study contained five conditions, each of which was designed to explain, on the basis of illusory correlation, the popularity of the report of one of the five popular invalid signs listed in Table 2.

METHOD. Clinical materials were fabricated to be shown to naive observers. The materials consisted of 30 Rorschach cards, on each of which one percept (or response) was paired with two statements of the emotional problems of the purported patient who was alleged to have given the response. The cards were covered with transparent plastic. Rorschach percepts were indicated by circling an area of the card and pasting on it a typed statement of the verbalization. For example, for one of the 30 Rorschach responses, the center area of Card V—or area D-7 (Beck, 1961)—was circled and labeled "Bugs Bunny." In a corner of the card appeared the statement:

The man who said this

1. has sexual feelings toward other men.
2. feels sad and depressed much of the time.

The 30 percepts were chosen so that six fell into each of five categories, which were:

A. One popular invalid sign
B. Wheeler Sign 7: Human or animal—contorted, monstrous, or threatening on Card IV (a clinically valid sign)
C. Wheeler Sign 8: Humanized animal or an animalized human on Card V (a clinically valid sign)
D. Geographic features (a filler category)
E. Food (a filler category)

There were five conditions in Experiment II, which differed only as to which invalid sign was used. In all other respects, both the procedure and materials in all five conditions were identical. The invalid signs for the five conditions were: Condition 1—human or animal with anal content; Condition 2—feminine clothing; Condition 3—humans on Cards I or III with sex confused; Condition 4—humans on Cards I or III with sex uncertain; and Condition 5—male or female genitalia.

The percepts used for each category are listed below. Locations of percepts are indicated using Beck's system. The percepts chosen for the seven Wheeler signs were Wheeler's (1949) examples, and others modeled after his examples.

Wheeler Sign 7. Human or animal, contorted, monstrous or threatening. All were on Card IV, W: (*a*) a horrid beast, (*b*) Frankenstein, (*c*) a headless monster about to step on me, (*d*) man looking back through legs, (*e*) a giant with shrunken arms, and (*f*) a deformed man doing a back bend.

Wheeler Sign 8. Humanized animal or animalized human, on Card V. Four were W responses: (*a*) woman with butterfly wings, (*b*) an alligator in a fur coat, (*c*) man dressed like a bat, (*d*) a pigeon wearing mittens. Two were D-7: (*e*) a dog wearing clothes, and (*f*) Bugs Bunny.

Human or animal anal content. (*a*) Card I, Dd-22, rectum, (*b*) Card VII (inverted), Dd-25, anus, (*c*) Card IV, W, anal opening of man bending over, (*d*) Card VI, W (without D-3), horse's rear end, (*e*) Card IX, both D-1, woman's buttocks, and (*f*) Card II, D-4, anal opening.

Feminine clothing. (*a*) Card III, D-10, woman's high-heeled shoe, (*b*) Card II, D-2, woman's hat, (*c*) Card X, D-9, fur stole, (*d*) Card VIII, D-5, woman's laced corset, (*e*) Card III, D-7, woman's bra, and (*f*) Card VI, D-1 (inverted), woman's fur cape.

Sexual confusion. Three of these percepts were on Card I, D-4: (*a*) it looks like a woman but with broad shoulders, (*b*) upper part is male and the bottom is female, (*c*) this has shoulders like a man but breasts and hips like a woman. Three were on Card III,

D-9: (*d*) looks like a man below the waist but like a woman above, (*e*) a man but with breasts, (*f*) a woman, here are her breasts, but has the feet of a man.

Sexual uncertainty. Three of these percepts were on Card I, D-4: (*a*) I guess this is a man or maybe it's a woman, (*b*) a person can't tell if it's a man or a woman, (*c*) a human, could be masculine or feminine. Three were on Card III, D-9: (*d*) a person, might be male or it might be female, (*e*) could either be a man or a woman, and (*f*) two people, but I can't tell what sex they are.

Male or female genitalia. (*a*) Card I, Dd-22, testicles, (*b*) Card II, D-3, female genital organ, (*c*) Card III, Dd-26, penis, (*d*) Card X, D-11, male genitalia, (*e*) Card VI, D-2, penis, and (*f*) Card III, D-8, vagina.

Geographic features. (*a*) Card VII (inverted), D-2, map of North and South America, (*b*) Card VII, D-3, map of Spain, (*c*) Card X, D-9, map of California, (*d*) Card II (inverted), D-2, map of South America, (*e*) Card X, D-13, New Zealand, and (*f*) Card VI (inverted, Dd-25, map of California.

Food. (*a*) Card VII, D-4, a loaf of rye bread split in half, (*b*) Card IX, D-6, raspberry sherbet, (*c*) Card VIII, D-7, jello, (*d*) Card VI, D-6, asparagus tips, (*e*) Card X, D-2, scrambled eggs, and (*f*) Card III, D-1, bowl of fruit.

The two statements of emotional problems or symptoms listed on the cards were drawn from a pool of four such statements. These were:

1. He has sexual feelings towards other men.
2. He believes other people are plotting against him.
3. He feels sad and depressed much of the time.
4. He has strong feelings of inferiority.

The statements of symptoms and Rorschach percepts were paired on the 30 cards so that each of the four symptom statements appeared 15 times. Each symptom statement was paired with three of the six percepts from each of the five categories of percepts. Thus there was no relationship between the occurrence of any one of the four symptoms and any one of the five categories of response.

The prediction was that despite this lack of true correlation in the experimental materials, *S*s who viewed the series of 30 cards in each of the five conditions would believe that they observed that the symptom statement, "He has sexual feelings toward other men," had appeared more often with the associatively based invalid sign than with any of the other four categories of content.

The testing was done in groups of 30 or fewer. The *S*s were given some brief introductory information as to the nature of the Rorschach. They were told that Rorschach responses indicate personality functioning. However, they were given no information about categories of either content or determinants. They were then told:

> I am going to show you a series of inkblots, one at a time. On each inkblot you will find a typed statement of what one patient saw on this blot and also what his two chief emotional problems are. Each of these 30 cards represents a different patient. You will see what 30 different patients said they saw on a card. Now let me

tell you what I want you to do. Please carefully study each inkblot and the statement of what the patient said that he saw in it. Also study the statement of the patient's two severe emotional problems. When everyone has looked at all of the cards, I'm going to give you a questionnaire in which I will ask you about the kinds of things seen by patients with each kind of problem.

The cards were circulated in a prearranged pattern so that each S saw each of the 30 cards for 60 sec. After S had seen the 30 cards, he was given a questionnaire which presented four items (one for each of the four symptom statements) in the following format.

Some of the things in the inkblots were seen by men who have the following problem:

He has sexual feelings toward other men.

Did you notice any general kind of thing that was seen most often by men with this problem? Yes _____ No _____. If your answer is yes, name that kind of thing, and give one example of that kind of thing.

Kind of thing _____
Example _____

Two forms of the questionnaire were used with different orders of the four items.

RESULTS.   Since the responses to the homosexual item were of primary interest in the present paper, the analysis of the results focused on this item. Table 4 shows the correlates reported for homosexuality by Ss in each of the five conditions. As seen there, very few Ss indicated that they could find no relationship between the percepts and the symptoms. In each condition, Ss, as predicted, reported that they observed the hypothesized illusory correlate as accompanying homosexual problems more often than any other category of percept. Chi-square analysis indicated that the distributions of responses among the five categories departed from chance ($p < .01$) for each condition except Condition 4, in which the hypothesized illusory correlate was sexual uncertainty.

The frequent report of the invalid Wheeler signs as illusory correlates of homosexuality cannot be attributed to a higher frequency of report for all symptom statements. The mean percentage report of the five signs for the other three symptoms were as follows: anality, 4%; feminine clothing, 13%; sexual confusion, 9%; sexual uncertainty, 8%; and genitalia, 10%. In none of the five conditions was the illusory correlate of homosexuality the most frequently reported correlate of any one of the other three symptoms.

One may conclude from the data of Table 4 that the observation of popular invalid signs of male homosexuality were reproduced in the laboratory as illusory correlates. On the other hand, the clinically valid signs of homosexuality were not reported as illusory correlates of that symptom any more often than were the two filler categories.

Table 4 | PERCENTAGE OF NAIVE OBSERVERS REPORTING EACH OF FIVE CATE-
GORIES OF PERCEPT AS MOST OFTEN ACCOMPANYING THE PROBLEM OF HOMO-
SEXUALITY FOR EACH OF THE FIVE CONDITIONS IN EXPERIMENT II

CORRELATE REPORTED	CONDITION				
	1 *Anality*	2 *Feminine clothing*	3 *Sexual confusion*	4 *Sexual uncertainty*	5 *Genitalia*
Predicted illusory correlate	58	40	45	24	51
Clinical valid signs					
Human or animal, monstrous	8	14	13	10	3
Part animal—part human	3	14	6	8	0
Filler categories					
Geographic features	12	5	13	16	13
Food	8	16	15	18	13
Other correlates	0	0	2	10	8
No correlate reported	10	12	6	13	13

EXPERIMENT III {CONDITIONS 6–11}: ILLUSORY CORRELATION IN THE PRESENCE OF VALID RELATIONSHIPS. Experiment III was under-taken to determine if the associatively based illusory correlates are reported by naive observers even if the clinically valid signs have contrived validity in the experimental task materials. To build in contrived validity, the clinically valid Wheeler Signs 7 and 8 were paired with the symptom statement of homosexuality more often than with the other classes of percepts.

METHOD. Only two of the five popular invalid signs were chosen to be used in Experiment III. They were anality and sexual confusion.

The task materials were almost identical to those used in Experiment II. The instructions and answer sheets were unchanged. The percepts, as well as the pool of symptom statements were the same as those previously used in Conditions 2 and 4 in which anality and sexual confusion were used as popular invalid signs. As in the earlier conditions, each *S* saw 30 cards, six presenting a percept of a popular invalid sign, six for each of the two clinically valid signs (Wheeler Signs 7 and 8), and six for each of the two filler categories (geography and food). The task materials differed from Experiment II only in the percentage of clinically valid percepts that were accompanied by the symptom statement of homosexuality. Three degrees of contrived validity were investi-gated: one in which the symptom statement of homosexuality occurred with two-thirds of the percepts of each of the two valid signs, one in which it occurred with five-sixths of them, and one in which it occurred with all of them. After being rounded off to the nearest percentage point the values of the three degrees of contrived validity were 67%, 83%, and 100%, respectively. The combination of three degrees of contrived validity with each of two popular invalid signs yielded six conditions altogether. In Conditions 6,

7, and 8, the popular invalid sign was sexual confusion, with contrived validity for Signs 7 and 8 of 67%, 83%, and 100%, respectively. In Conditions 9, 10, and 11, the popular invalid sign was anality with the same three degrees of contrived validity for Signs 7 and 8. As in Experiment II, 50% of each of the other three categories of percepts were accompanied by the symptom statement of homosexuality, as well as by the other three symptom statements.

RESULTS.   Table 5 shows the percentage of *S*s in each condition who reported the co-occurrence with homosexuality of each of the five categories of percepts. The most striking feature of these data is the degree to which the illusory correlates based on associative connection are impervious to the contrary influence of valid correlations. In all six conditions, the clinically popular invalid sign was the most frequently reported correlate of the symptom statement.

Table 5 | PERCENTAGE OF *S*s IN EXPERIMENT III REPORTING THE OBSERVATION OF EACH CATEGORY OF PERCEPT AS A CORRELATE OF HOMOSEXUALITY

CATEGORY	PERCENTAGE CONTRIVED VALIDITY FOR SIGNS 7 AND 8		
	67%	*83%*	*100%*
CONDITIONS 6, 7, AND 8			
Invalid signs			
Sexual confusion	50	41	46
Valid signs			
Human or animal—monstrous	12	27	20
Part animal—part human	10	6	14
Filler categories			
Geographic features	2	12	5
Food	8	0	2
Other correlates	10	6	8
No correlate reported	10	8	5
CONDITIONS 9, 10, AND 11			
Invalid signs			
Anality	54	34	55
Valid signs			
Human or animal—monstrous	16	16	15
Part animal—part human	13	23	13
Filler categories			
Geographic features	6	13	5
Food	2	3	2
Other correlates	0	3	2
No correlate reported	9	7	8

For each of the six conditions, the report of the homosexual symptom statement was distributed among the various categories of percepts significantly different from chance, as shown by chi-square analyses ($p < .01$ in every case). The number of Ss who chose the invalid sign as a correlate was compared with the number who chose one or the other of the two valid signs. A goodness-of-fit chi-square was used with the expected values being one-third of the Ss for the invalid sign, and two-thirds of the Ss for the two valid signs combined. In five of the six comparisons the difference was significant ($p < .01$ in each case). The one nonsignificant difference was for anality when the clinically valid signs had 83% contrived validity. The difference for this condition fell short of significance ($\chi^2 = 3.03$, $df = 1$, $p < .10$). These findings indicate that the invalid signs were reported as correlates of homosexuality more often than were the valid signs, which had objectively true correlations with the symptom.

Another way to view these data is in terms of a comparison of the number of Ss who reported the popular invalid signs, and the number who reported the valid signs, as correlates of homosexuality at each of the four levels of contrived validity of the two valid signs. (The four levels are the 50% co-occurrence of the clinically valid sign with the symptom statement—from Experiment II—plus the 67%, 83%, and 100% levels of contrived validity of Experiment III.) When the popular invalid sign was sexual confusion, these four conditions did not differ on frequency of report of the invalid sign ($\chi^2 = .84$, $df = 3$, $.80 < p < .90$). They also did not differ on number of Ss reporting one or the other of the two valid signs ($\chi^2 = 4.92$, $df = 3$, $.10 < p < .20$). When the popular invalid sign was anality, the four conditions of contrived validity differed in both the number of Ss reporting the popular invalid sign ($\chi^2 = 8.47$, $df = 3$, $p < .05$) and in the number reporting one or the other of the two valid signs ($\chi^2 = 13.05$, $df = 3$, $p < .01$). Inspection of the data for the three anality conditions indicates that Ss achieved highest accuracy by both criteria in the 83% validity condition. These findings indicate that increasing the contrived validity had a small effect in reducing the report of one popular invalid sign as a correlate of homosexuality, but not the other. The validity was accurately perceived to a slight degree.

Further analyses were performed to seek evidence on the accuracy of perception of the contrived validity. For the three conditions for which sexual confusion was the popular invalid sign, more Ss chose the valid sign than the filler items for the 100% validity condition ($\chi^2 = 9.38$, $df = 1$, $p < .01$) but this difference did not emerge on either the 67% or 83% validity conditions. For the three conditions for which anality was the popular invalid sign, Ss reported the valid signs more often than the filler categories for all three levels of contrived validity ($p < .05$ in all three cases). These findings again show that the contrived validity was to some degree accurately perceived, despite the fact that its presence did little to reduce the frequency of report of the illusory correlates.

EXPERIMENT IV: ACCURACY OF REPORT IN THE ABSENCE OF POPULAR INVALID SIGNS—CONDITION 12.

The most striking findings of Experiment III were the frequency of report of the illusory correlates, and the low accuracy of Ss observational reports of the valid signs. These findings might lead one to wonder if the infrequent detection of valid signs on these tasks is due to the distracting influence of illusory correlates or whether the valid signs are inherently difficult to discover. Further, one might wonder whether associatively based illusory correlation occurs only when the detection of valid signs is very difficult.

In defense of the tasks used in Experiment III, one might point out that they surely present the observer with a less difficult job of information processing than does conventional clinical practice. In clinical practice, the symptoms are more numerous and more ambiguous, and many percepts are given by each patient. Also, the clinician encounters the patients over a long period of time, so that retrospective falsification of observations should occur more often. Nevertheless, it is of interest to determine if accuracy is higher on a task that is comparable to those of Experiment III, but in which associatively based popular invalid correlates are absent. The first part of Experiment IV (Condition 12) was designed to give evidence on this question.

METHOD.   The stimulus materials were almost identical to those of the two 83% validity conditions (Conditions 7 and 10) of Experiment III. The symptom statement of homosexuality accompanied 83% of the percepts of the two clinically valid signs (Signs 7 and 8) and 50% of the other categories of percepts. The only change from Conditions 7 and 10 was that in Condition 12, nonsexual body parts were substituted for a popular invalid sign. The percepts for the category of nonsexual body parts were: (*a*) Card II, D-4, hands, (*b*) Card VII, D-1, gray hair, (*c*) Card IX, Dd-31, nose, (*d*) Card I, Dds-30, eyes, (*e*) Card II, D-2, foot, and (*f*) Card VI, Dd-25, toe. Thus, each S saw five classes of percepts: nonsexual body parts, humanized animals, monsters, food, and geographical features. The mode of administration of the task was identical to that of Experiment III.

RESULTS.   Table 6 shows the percentage of Ss who reported each category of percept as a correlate of homosexuality. The distribution of Ss among the five categories differed from chance ($\chi^2 = 26.23$, $df = 4$, $p < .001$). As seen in Table 6, the two clinically valid signs were the most frequently reported categories, and 65% of the Ss reported one or the other of them. This value is almost double the percentage reported in the comparable conditions of Experiment III, and the rise in accuracy was significant ($\chi^2 = 11.6$, $df = 1$, $p < .001$).

CONDITION 13.   The second part of Experiment IV was designed to eliminate one possible source of doubt concerning the meaning of the findings in Condition 12. One might speculate that the greater accuracy in Condition 12 than in Conditions 7 and 10 is not attributable to accurate observation of the valid correlates, but to illusory correlation. Table 3 showed that the clinically valid signs have a slightly stronger verbal associative connection to homosexuality than do the two filler categories. This associative connection might produce illusory correlation when stronger verbal associates are absent.

Table 6 | PERCENTAGE OF *S*s REPORTING EACH CATEGORY OF PERCEPT AS A CORRELATE OF HOMOSEXUALITY IN THE TWO CONDITIONS OF EXPERIMENT IV

CATEGORY	PERCENTAGE OF *S*s REPORTING EACH CATEGORY OF PERCEPT	
	Condition 12[a]	Condition 13[b]
Clinically valid signs		
Part animal—part human	27	17
Human or animal—monstrous	38	18
Filler categories		
Body parts	15	23
Food	3	24
Geographic features	8	9
Other correlates	2	4
No correlate reported	7	4

[a] Eighty-three percent contrived validity for Signs 7 and 8, 50% for the other three categories.
[b] Fifty percent contrived validity for all five categories.

METHOD.   In Condition 13 the percepts were identical to those used in Condition 12, but each class of percept appeared equally often with each symptom statement. If the increased accuracy of report of valid correlates in Condition 12 was an artifact of illusory correlation, it should remain in this condition. If the increased accuracy of report reflected increased accuracy of observation, it should disappear.

RESULTS.   The results appear in Table 6. The distribution of people reporting the five categories of percepts did not differ from chance ($\chi^2 = 5.17$, $df = 4$, $p > .05$), and the two clinically valid signs were reported at almost exactly the mean frequencies of the other three categories of correlates. This finding demonstrates that the increased accuracy of report in Condition 12 was due to increased accuracy of observation, and was not attributable to illusory correlation.

DISCUSSION

There was a marked congruence between the reports of the clinicians as to their observations in clinical practice and the reports of the naive observers in the contrived experimental situations. Almost none of the 32 practicing psychodiagnosticians reported observing either of the two signs of male homosexuality that research findings indicate are clinically valid. Instead, they tended to agree with one another in reporting several signs that appear invalid in published research, but which have a high strength verbal associative connection to the symptom of homosexuality.

The naive observers presented with contrived clinical materials reported similar erroneous observations. They reported the associatively based signs as illusory correlates of homosexuality both when there were no valid relationships present and when the two clinically valid signs had a contrived validity in the task materials.

One of the most striking findings of these studies is the persistence of illusory correlation in the face of contradictory reality. Even in the two conditions in which all of the percepts of the two valid signs were paired with homosexuality, these two valid signs were reported as correlates of the symptom less often than the associatively based invalid signs. In addition, the low accuracy of report of the valid signs cannot be attributed entirely to there being too much information for the observer to process. Instead, the low accuracy is, to a considerable degree, a result of Ss' susceptibility to the illusory correlation. Experiment IV showed that, when the percepts that have a high associative connection to the symptom were not presented, the observers almost doubled their accuracy of report of valid correlates. The illusory correlates blind the observer to the presence of valid correlates of the symptom.

Associatively based illusory correlation is a powerful bias in the observational report of correlations between classes of events. Yet its influence is so unapparent that many practicing psychodiagnosticians have overlooked it, and have substituted illusory correlates for valid correlates in their diagnostic practice. One possible solution to this problem might be to demonstrate to graduate students, as part of their training, their own propensities toward illusory correlation.

SUMMARY

Practicing psychodiagnosticians ($N = 32$), when surveyed, failed to report observing Wheeler-Rorschach Signs 7 and 8 as accompanying male homosexuality although research evidence indicates that these are valid signs. They instead reported observing Wheeler Signs 4, 5, 16, 19, and 20, which research literature indicates are invalid. These popular invalid signs were found to have much stronger rated, verbal associative connections to male homosexuality than the unpopular valid signs. Six hundred and ninety-three undergraduates (divided among 13 conditions) viewed 30 Rorschach cards on each of which was arbitrarily designated a patient's response and his two symptoms. The Ss "rediscovered" the same invalid Rorschach content signs of homosexuality as the clinicians reported observing in their clinical practice, although these relationships were absent in the experimental materials. They did so regardless of the degree to which the clinically valid signs were valid in the contrived task materials.

REFERENCES

Beck, S. *Rorschach's test.* Vol. 1. *Basic processes.* (3rd ed.) New York: Grune & Stratton, 1961.

Chapman, L. J., & Chapman, J. P. The genesis of popular but erroneous psychodiagnostic observations. *Journal of Abnormal Psychology*, 1967, 72, 193–204.

Davids, A., Joelson, M., & McArthur, C. Rorschach and TAT indices of homosexuality in overt homosexuals, neurotics, and normal males. *Journal of Abnormal and Social Psychology*, 1956, *53*, 161–172.

Hooker, E. Male homosexuality in the Rorschach. *Journal of Projective Techniques*, 1958, *22*, 33–54.

Little, K. B., & Shneidman, E. S. Congruencies among interpretations of psychological test and anamnestic data. *Psychological Monographs*, 1959, *73*(6, Whole No. 476).

Reitzell, J. M. A comparative study of hysterics, homosexuals and alcoholics using content analysis of Rorschach responses. *Rorschach Research Exchange*, 1949, *13*, 127–141.

Swensen, C. H. Empirical evaluations of human figure drawings. *Psychological Bulletin*, 1957, *54*, 431–466.

Wheeler, W. M. An analysis of Rorschach indices of male homosexuality. *Rorschach Research Exchange*, 1949, *13*, 97–126.

8 | Social Behavior Theories

8.1 | GOALS, PURPOSES, AND OTHER FINAL CAUSES*

B. F. Skinner

It is not correct to say that operant reinforcement "strengthens the response which precedes it." The response has already occurred and cannot be changed. What is changed is the future probability of responses in the same *class*. It is the operant as a class of behavior, rather than the response as a particular instance, which is conditioned. There is, therefore, no violation of the fundamental principle of science which rules out "final causes." But this principle is violated when it is asserted that behavior is under the control of an "incentive" or "goal" which the organism has not yet achieved or a "purpose" which it has not yet fulfilled. Statements which use such words as "incentive" or "purpose" are usually reducible to statements about operant conditioning, and only a slight change is required to bring them within the framework of a natural science. Instead of saying that a man behaves because of the consequences which *are* to follow his behavior, we simply say that he behaves because of the consequences which *have* followed similar behavior in the past. This is of course, the Law of Effect or operant conditioning.

It is sometimes argued that a response is not fully described until its purpose is referred to as a current property. But what is meant by "describe"? If we observe someone walking down the street, we may report this event in the language of physical science. If we then add that "his purpose is to mail a letter," have we said anything which was not included in our first report? Evidently so, since a man may walk down the street "for many purposes" and in the same physical way in each case. But the distinction which needs to be made is not between instances of behavior; it is between the variables of which behavior is a function. Purpose is not a property of the behavior itself; it is a way of referring to controlling variables. If we make our report after we have seen our subject mail his letter and turn back, we attribute "purpose" to him from the event which

* SOURCE: Skinner, B. F. *Science and human behavior.* New York: The Free Press, 1953. Pp. 87–90, abridged. Copyright 1953 by the Macmillan Company. Reprinted by permission of the Macmillan Company.

brought the behavior of walking down the street to an end. This event "gives meaning" to his performance, not by amplifying a description of the behavior as such, but by indicating an independent variable of which it may have been a function. We cannot see his "purpose" before seeing that he mails a letter, unless we have observed similar behavior and similar consequences before. Where we have done this, we use the term simply to predict that he will mail a letter upon this occasion.

Nor can our subject see his own purpose without reference to similar events. If we ask him why he is going down the street or what his purpose is and he says, "I am going to mail a letter," we have not learned anything new about his behavior but only about some of its possible causes. The subject himself, of course, may be in an advantageous position in describing these variables because he has had an extended contact with his own behavior for many years. But his statement is not therefore in a different class from similar statements made by others who have observed his behavior upon fewer occasions. . . . he is simply making a plausible prediction in terms of his experiences with himself. Moreover, he may be wrong. He may report that he is "going to mail a letter," and he may indeed carry an unmailed letter in his hand and may mail it at the end of the street, but we may still be able to show that his behavior is primarily determined by the fact that upon past occasions he has encountered someone who is important to him upon just such a walk. He may not be "aware of this purpose" in the sense of being able to say that his behavior is strong for this reason.

The fact that operant behavior seems to be "directed toward the future" is misleading. Consider, for example, the case of "looking for something." In what sense is the "something" which has not yet been found relevant to the behavior? Suppose we condition a pigeon to peck a spot on the wall of a box and then, when the operant is well established, remove the spot. The bird now goes to the usual place along the wall. It raises its head, cocks its eye in the usual direction, and may even emit a weak peck in the usual place. Before extinction is very far advanced, it returns to the same place again and again in similar behavior. Must we say that the pigeon is "looking for the spot"? Must we take the "looked for" spot into account in explaining the behavior?

It is not difficult to interpret this example in terms of operant reinforcement. Since visual stimulation from the spot has usually preceded the receipt of food, the spot has become a conditioned reinforcer. It strengthens the behavior of looking in given directions from different positions. Although we have undertaken to condition only the pecking response, we have in fact strengthened many different kinds of precurrent behavior which bring the bird into positions from which it sees the spot and pecks it. These responses continue to appear, even though we have removed the spot, until extinction occurs. The spot which is "being looked for" is the spot which has occurred in the past as the immediate reinforcement of the behavior of looking. In general, looking for something consists of emitting responses which in the past have produced "something" as a consequence.

The same interpretation applies to human behavior. When we see a man moving about a room opening drawers, looking under magazines, and so on, we may describe his behavior in fully objective terms: "Now he is in a certain part of the room; he has grasped a book between the thumb and forefinger of his right hand; he is lifting the book and bending his head so that any object under the book can be seen." We may also "interpret" his behavior or "read a meaning into it" by saying that "he is looking for something" or, more specifically, that "he is looking for his glasses." What we have added is not a further description of his behavior but an inference about some of the variables responsible for it. There is no *current* goal, incentive, purpose, or meaning to be taken into account. This is so even if we ask him what he is doing and he says, "I am looking for my glasses." This is not a further description of his behavior but of the variables of which his behavior is a function; it is equivalent to "I have lost my glasses," "I shall stop what I am doing when I find my glasses," or "When I have done this in the past, I have found my glasses." These translations may seem unnecessarily roundabout, but only because expressions involving goals and purposes are abbreviations.

Very often we attribute purpose to behavior as another way of describing its biological adaptability. This issue has already been discussed, but one point may be added. In both operant conditioning and the evolutionary selection of behavioral characteristics, consequences alter future probability. Reflexes and other innate patterns of behavior evolve because they increase the chances of survival of the *species*. Operants grow strong because they are followed by important consequences in the life of the *individual*. Both processes raise the question of purpose for the same reason, and in both the appeal to a final cause may be rejected in the same way. A spider does not possess the elaborate behavioral repertoire with which it constructs a web because that web will enable it to capture the food it needs to survive. It possesses this behavior because similar behavior on the part of spiders in the past has enabled *them* to capture the food *they* needed to survive. A series of events have been relevant to the behavior of web-making in its earlier evolutionary history. We are wrong in saying that we observe the "purpose" of the web when we observe similar events in the life of the individual.

8.2 | AN INTRODUCTION TO SOCIAL LEARNING THEORY*

Julian B. Rotter, June E. Chance, and E. Jerry Phares

BASIC CONCEPTS

In SLT [social learning theory (of personality)], four basic concepts are utilized in the prediction of behavior. These concepts are behavior potential, expectancy, reinforcement value, and the psychological situation. In addition, somewhat broader concepts are utilized for problems involving more general behavioral predictions, that is, those dealing with behavior over a period of time and those including many specific situations. These broader conceptualizations will be discussed later. This section is primarily concerned with definition and measurement of basic concepts relevant to more specific situations or to testing experimental hypotheses in laboratory settings.

BEHAVIOR POTENTIAL.   Behavior potential may be defined as the potentiality of any behavior's occurring in any given situation or situations as calculated in relation to any single reinforcement or set of reinforcements.

Behavior potential is a relative concept. That is, one calculates the potentiality of any behavior's occurring in relation to the other alternatives open to the individual. Thus, it is possible to say only that in a specific situation the potentiality for occurrence of behavior x is greater than that for behavior z.

The SLT concept of behavior is quite broad. Indeed, behavior may be that which is directly observed but also that which is indirect or implicit. This notion includes a broad spectrum of possibilities—swearing, running, crying, fighting, smiling, choosing, and so on, are all included. These are all observable behaviors, but implicit behaviors that can only be measured indirectly, such as rationalizing, repressing, considering alternatives, planning, and reclassifying, would also be included. The objective study of cognitive activity is a difficult but important aspect of social learning theory. Principles governing the occurrence of such cognitive activities are not considered different from those that might apply to any observable behavior.

EXPECTANCY.   Expectancy may be defined as the probability held by the individual that a particular reinforcement will occur as a function of a specific behavior on his

* SOURCE: Rotter, J. B., Chance, J. E., and Phares, E. J., (Eds.), *Applications of a social learning theory of personality.* New York: Holt, Rinehart and Winston, Inc., 1972. Pp. 11–15, abridged. Copyright © 1972 by Holt, Rinehart and Winston, Inc. Reprinted by permission of Holt, Rinehart and Winston, Inc.

part in a specific situation or situations. Expectancy is systematically independent of the value or importance of the reinforcement.

While simple cognitions also may be regarded as having some of the characteristics of expectancies, the term expectancy will be used to refer to the expectancy for behavior-reinforcement sequences (Rotter, 1960, 1967). Historically, expectancy has often been described as either an objective or subjective concept. Lewin (1951), for example, stressed the subjective nature of expectancy. Brunswik (1951), however, emphasized objective probability—a probability determined primarily by objectively describable past events.

In SLT the concept of expectancy is defined as a subjective probability, but this definition does not imply inaccessibility to objective measurement. People's probability statements, and other behaviors relating to the probability of occurrence of an event, often differ systematically from their actuarial experience with the event in the past. A variety of other factors operate in specific instances to influence one's probability estimates. Such factors may include the nature or the categorization of a situation, patterning and sequential considerations, uniqueness of events, generalization, and the perception of causality.

REINFORCEMENT VALUE. The reinforcement value of any one of a group of potential external reinforcements may be ideally defined as the degree of the person's preference for that reinforcement to occur if the possibilities of occurrence of all alternatives were equal.

Again, reinforcement value is a relative term. Measurement of reinforcement value occurs in a choice situation. That is, reinforcement value refers to a preference, and preference indicates that one favors something over something else. Such preferences show consistency and reliability within our culture and also, generally speaking, can be shown to be systematically independent of expectancy. These and other considerations will be discussed in greater detail later.

THE PSYCHOLOGICAL SITUATION. Behavior does not occur in a vacuum. A person is continuously reacting to aspects of his external and internal environment. Since he reacts selectively to many kinds of stimulation, internal and external simultaneously, in a way consistent with his unique experience and because the different aspects of his environment mutually affect each other, we choose to speak of the psychological situation rather than the stimulus. Methods of determining generality or determining the dimensions of similarity among situations have been described by Rotter (1955).

Several writers have pointed out the difficulty of identifying situations independently of behavior. That is, how can one describe a situation, as one might a physical stimulus, independently of the particular S's response? However, the problem is not really so different from that of describing stimuli along dimensions of color, although it is perhaps vastly more complicated in social situations. In the case of color stimuli, ultimately the criterion is a response made by an observer, sometimes aided by an intermediate instrument. The response is one that is at the level of sensory discrimination and thus leads to high observer agreement. In the case of social situations, the level of discrimination is common sense based on an understanding of a culture rather than a reading from an instrument. As such, reliability of discrimination may be limited but still be sufficiently high to make practical predictions possible. Specific situations can be identified as school situations, employment situations, girl friend situations, and so on. For the purpose of generality, various kinds of psychological constructs can be devised to arrive at broader classes of situations having similar meaning to S. The utility of such classes would have to be empirically determined, depending on the S's response. The objective referents for these situations, which provide the basis for prediction, however, can be independent of the specific S. That is, they can be reliably identified by cultural, common sense terms.

BASIC FORMULAS. The preceding variables and their relations may be conveniently stated in the formulas that follow. It should be remembered, however, that these formulas do not at this time imply any precise mathematical relations. Indeed, although the relation between expectancy and reinforcement value is probably a multiplicative one, there is little systematic data at this point that would allow one to evolve any precise mathematical statement.

The basic formula is stated thus:

$$BP_{x, s_1, R_a} = f(E_{x, R_a s_1} \, \& \, RV_{a, s_1}) \tag{1}$$

Formula (1) says, The potential for behavior *x* to occur, in situation 1 in relation to reinforcement *a*, is a function of the expectancy of the occurrence of reinforcement *a*, following behavior *x* in situation 1, and the value of reinforcement *a* in situation 1.

Formula (1) is obviously limited, inasmuch as it deals only with the potential for a given behavior to occur in relation to a single reinforcement. As noted earlier, description at the level of personality constructs usually demands a broader, more generalized concept of behavior, reflected in the following formula:

$$BP_{(x-n), s_{(1-n)}, R_{(a-n)}} = f[E_{(x-n), s_{(1-n)}, R_{(a-n)}} \, \& \, RV_{(a-n), s_{(1-n)}}] \tag{2}$$

Formula (2) says, The potentiality of functionally related behaviors *x* to *n* to occur, in specified situations 1 to *n* in relation to potential reinforcements *a* to *n*, is a function of the expectancies of these behaviors leading to these reinforcements in these situations and the values of these reinforcements in these situations. To enhance communication by reducing verbal complexity, three terms—need potential, freedom of movement, and need value—have been introduced. A formula incorporating these latter terms is:

$$NP = f(FM \, \& \, NV) \tag{3}$$

Thus, need potential is a function of freedom of movement and need value. In broader predictive or clinical situations, formula (3) would more likely be used, while formula (2) would be more appropriate in testing more specific, experimental hypotheses.

The fourth variable, situation, is left implicit in formula (3). SLT is highly committed to the importance of the psychological situation. It is emphasized that behavior varies as the situation does. But obviously, there is also transituational generality in behavior. If there were not, there would be no point in discussing personality as a construct or as a field of study. However, along with generality there is also situational specificity. While it may be true that person A is generally more aggressive than person B, nonetheless, there can arise many occasions on which person B behaves more aggressively than does person A. Predictions based solely on internal characteristics of the individual are not sufficient to account for the complexities of human behavior.

REFERENCES

Brunswik, E. The probability point of view. In M. H. Marx (Ed.), *Psychological theory.* New York: Macmillan, 1951.

Lewin, K. The nature of field theory. In M. H. Marx (Ed.), *Psychological theory.* New York: Macmillan, 1951.

Rotter, J. B. The role of the psychological situation in determining the direction of human behavior. In M. R. Jones (Ed.), *Nebraska symposium on motivation.* Lincoln, Neb.: University of Nebraska Press, 1955. Pp. 245–269.

Rotter, J. B. Some implications of a social learning theory for the prediction of goal directed behavior from testing procedures. *Psychological Review*, 1960, 67, 301–316.

Rotter, J. B. Beliefs, social attitudes and behavior: A social learning analysis. In Jessor, R., & Feshback, S. (Eds.), *Cognition, personality and clinical psychology.* San Francisco: Jossey-Bass, Inc., 1967.

8.3 | ON MODELING*

Albert Bandura

Most theories of behavior assume that, in order for learning to occur, the subject must perform a response and experience prompt response-contingent reinforcing consequences. This conceptualization of the learning process presents two important theoretical problems.

First, it requires the subject to perform some approximation of the response before he can learn it. In cases in which a behavioral pattern contains a highly unique combination of elements selected from an almost infinite number of alternatives, the probability

* SOURCE: Bandura, A. Behavioral modifications through modeling procedures. In L. Krasner and L. P. Ullmann (Eds.), *Research in behavior modification.* New York: Holt, Rinehart and Winston, Inc., 1966. Pp. 310–340, abridged and edited. Copyright © 1965 by Holt, Rinehart and Winston, Inc. Reprinted by permission of Holt, Rinehart and Winston, Inc.

of occurrence of the desired response, or even one that has some remote resemblance to it, will be zero. Nor is the successive-approximations shaping procedure likely to be of much aid in altering this probability value. It is highly doubtful, for example, that an experimenter could get a mynah bird to sing a chorus of "Sweet Adeline" during his lifetime by differential reinforcement of the birds squeaks and squawks. Nevertheless, a recent appearance of a gifted mynah bird on television demonstrated how a young housewife who had employed modeling procedures succeeded, not only in training her feathered friend to sing this sentimental ballad with considerable fidelity, but also developed in the bird an extensive verbal repertoire.

Second, traditional behavior theories assume that the subject somehow suspends learning until the occurrence of reinforcing consequences following the termination of the response. Thus, if an experimenter were to inform a child that Columbus discovered America in 1492, the acquisition of this knowledge is presumably delayed and made contingent on the occurrence of a rewarding payoff. While consequent reinforcing events can alter significantly the future probability of occurrence of preceding responses, these events can hardly serve as a necessary precondition for their acquisition.

. . . I shall present some research supporting a theory of *no-trial learning*, a process of response acquisition that is highly prevalent among Homo sapiens, exceedingly efficient and, in cases where errors are dangerous or costly, becomes an indispensable means of transmitting and modifying behavioral repertoires. For example, one does not employ trial-and-error or operant conditioning methods in training children to swim, adolescents to drive an automobile, or in getting adults to acquire vocational skills. Indeed, if training proceeded in this manner, very few persons would ever survive the process of socialization. It is evident from informal observation that the behavior of models is utilized extensively to accelerate the acquisition process, and to prevent one-trial extinction of the organism in situations where an error may produce fatal consequences.

In assessing the relative efficacy of modeling and operant conditioning procedures in promoting behavioral change, it is important to distinguish learning from performance. Operant conditioning is an exceedingly reliable and efficient method for strengthening and maintaining responses that already exist in the behavioral repertoire of an organism. Through careful management of incentives, the frequency, amplitude, latency, and the discriminative patterning of responses can be readily modified. Most of the psychotherapeutic applications of this principle have, in fact, been concerned with problems of performance rather than of learning. By selecting an adequate reinforcer and arranging the appropriate response-reinforcement contingencies, a therapist can induce a mute catatonic, who possesses a language repertoire, to emit linguistic responses; schizophrenics who have previously acquired adequate eating repertoires can be impelled to feed themselves within specified time schedules, and college students who command an abundant supply of personal pronouns can be subtly prompted to emit these verbal responses at a relatively high rate.

While operant conditioning methods are well suited for controlling existing responses, they are often exceedingly laborious and inefficient for developing new behavioral repertoires. The fact that a patient and persistent experimenter may eventually develop a novel response in an organism through the method of successive approximations, *provided he carefully arranges a benign environment in which errors will not produce fatal consequences*, is no proof that this is the manner in which social responses are typically acquired in everyday life. Let me illustrate this point by referring to Bachrach's (1963) case of Rodent E. Lee, a southern cousin of Barnabus, the Barnard rat (Pierrol & Sherman, 1958, reported in Lundin, 1961, pp. 178–184). Through a long series of training sessions, based on differential reinforcement, the rat ultimately learned a relatively complicated chain of responses in which he climbed a circular stairway to a second landing, lowered a draw bridge to cross the miniature room, rode a cable car down an inclined plane, climbed a second set of stairs to a third story, struck two piano keys on a miniature Steinway, crawled through a wire tunnel, and after entering an elevator, the winded rodent pulled a chain that lowered the elevator to the ground floor where he received a well-earned delectable pellet, immediately after striking a bar.

Let us expand this rodent colonial mansion to human proportions, enlist a resurrected Rodent E. Lee as the performing subject, and substitute a bottle of bonded bourbon for the pellets. In getting him to master this sequential task, would one embark on a similar training program requiring Rodent E. Lee to engage in a lengthy series of random trial-and-error behavior, in which correct responses are reinforced positively, while inappropriate or incorrectly sequenced responses are left unrewarded? I seriously doubt that anyone would so choose to accomplish the training objective. Obviously, the simplest and most commonly employed procedure would be to provide the General with either a skilled model who demonstrated the correct responses in their appropriate sequence, or a symbolic model presented pictorially or through verbal descriptions. It is a safe prediction that the General would exhibit the entire novel repertoire on the first trial without having had to engage in tedious and haphazard trial-and-error experimentation.

Much social learning is fostered by exposure to real-life models who perform, intentionally or unwittingly, patterns of behavior that may be imitated by others. Once a learner has developed an adequate verbal repertoire, however, increasing reliance is placed on the use of verbally or pictorially present symbolic models. A psychological trainee, for example, can learn the complex repertoire necessary for administering an intelligence test simply by matching the responses described in the instructional manual. Since, however, an actual performance is apt to provide substantially more relevant cues with greater clarity than can be conveyed by a verbal description, a combination of verbal and demonstrational procedures is usually most effective in transmitting new patterns of behavior.

RELATIVE EFFICACY OF OPERANT CONDITIONING AND MODELING PROCEDURES

The relative superiority of modeling procedures over operant conditioning techniques in promoting behavioral change is most apparent in learning situations in which there is no reliable eliciting stimulus for the desired responses apart from the discriminative cues provided by social models as they exhibit the behavior. If a child had no occasion to hear the word "successive approximations," for example, it is doubtful whether this verbal response could ever be shaped by differential reinforcement of the child's random vocalizations. Even in cases where some stimulus is known to be capable of eliciting an approximation to the desired behavior, the process of learning can be considerably shortened and accelerated by the provision of models. This is particularly true when the presence of strong dominant repertoires limit the opportunity for reinforcing the desired subordinate responses because of their infrequent occurrence. [An experiment designed to test the validity of Piaget's stage theory of moral development provides a laboratory illustration of the latter point (Bandura & McDonald, 1963): see Unit 15.1.] . . .

If the proverbial Martian were to review earth-man's psychological literature he would undoubtedly be quite puzzled by the fact that researchers interested in the learning process have focused their attention almost exclusively on the slower and more laborious trial-and-error procedures, to the relative neglect of more prevalent and economical processes and methods.

Skinner has, of course, recognized the utility of "echoic" procedures for "short-circuiting of the process of progressive approximation" in the development of verbal operants (Skinner, 1957). This is not surprising, since operant conditioning procedures alone would be totally ineffective in shaping linguistic responses. As illustrated . . . , verbalizing models are not only helpful, but actually indispensable in promoting language learning. Had Skinner extended the application of modeling procedures to other classes of responses, the amount of attention devoted by current researchers to experimental analyses of imitative or observational learning would probably be more commensurate with the obviously important contribution of modeling variables to social learning in everyday life.

In a recent article, Skinner (1963) expressed some reservations about the use of modeling procedures in learning experiments because they circumvent the operant analysis of behavior. It is true that modeling techniques typically produce rapid acquisition of patterned responses and, therefore, throw relatively little light on the behavioral processes that characterize the slower operant conditioning procedure. This outcome, however, can hardly be considered a regrettable state of affairs. Indeed, the fact that organisms can readily acquire through observation complex operants without undergoing hazardous consequences and needless experimentation has contributed more to man's longevity than all the remarkable advances in medical science.

Skinner's arguments against the utilization of models in social learning are somewhat puzzling. It is highly debatable, for example, that modeling procedures that teach a person how to operate a machine are not concerned with problems of response acquisition:

> Verbal instruction may be defended when the resulting behavior is not the primary object of interest; for example, the experimenter may show a subject how to operate a piece of equipment rather than shape his behavior through reinforcement so long as he is not concerned with the acquisition of the response but with what happens to it later. Verbal communication is not, however, a substitute for the arrangement and manipulation of variables. (Skinner, 1963, p. 510)

On the contrary, modeling procedures are most efficacious in transmitting new response patterns, whereas operant conditioning methods as applied to human behavior are typically concerned with the management and control of previously learned responses.

The argument that verbally presented models may have limited applicability because they are ineffective with nonverbal organisms ("The scope of the verbal substitute can be estimated by considering how a nonverbal organism, human or otherwise, could be similarly 'instructed'" [Skinner, 1963]), simply highlights the inadvisability of relying too heavily on infrahuman organisms for establishing principles of human behavior. The social training of children at a preverbal developmental level is partly achieved through the use of nonverbal demonstrations of the desired responses. It would be interesting, for example, to record the total time required to train a young child to tie his shoelaces by means of operant conditioning without the aid of response-guidance modeling procedures. As verbal repertoires are gradually extended through social imitation, behavioral demonstrations are frequently replaced by their verbal equivalents. It is often implicitly assumed, for reasons that are not entirely clear, that human behavioral processes do not constitute genuine or important phenomena unless they have been reproduced in animals. This reasoning would lead one to conclude that verbal communication in humans is of limited significance because no experimenter has ever succeeded in teaching a pigeon or a rodent to articulate in any known human language system.

The preceding discussion has emphasized the indispensability of models, particularly in situations fraught with potentially perilous consequences, and in developing highly novel responses as illustrated by language learning. It might be argued that in the latter case a successive regression of learners would eventuate in a single individual with no model for imitation and, consequently, our lonesome survivor could never develop linguistic responses. The initial occurrence of a given verbal operant, however, poses no problems for language learning since any vocal response can be selected arbitrarily to symbolize a particular object or event. A person who studies human behavior, for example, could be labeled arbitrarily a "zoogrozyconologist." The language learning problem arises, however, when a cultural agent is assigned the delightful task of teaching a second person the word "zoogrozyconologist" without the aid of a verbalizing model.

Most behavioral innovations are struck upon by individuals more or less without design, and the patterns that generate rewarding consequences are rapidly adopted by other group members and transmitted to succeeding generations. Similarly, individuals who have attempted provisionally, or performed unwittingly, responses that generate aversive consequences, by their examples progressively limit the range of trial-and-error behavior exhibited by contemporary and future generations. Once certain behavioral repertoires have thus become an enduring part of a culture, its members are spared the travail of trial-and-error discovery. It would be difficult to imagine a culture in which its language, mores, vocational and avocational patterns, familial customs, and its educational, social, and political practices were shaped in each new member through a process of operant conditioning, without the response guidance of models who exhibit the accumulated cultural repertoires in their own behavior.

THREE EFFECTS OF MODELING INFLUENCES

Exposure to the behavior of models may have three rather different effects that may be reflected in the topography, frequency, or magnitude of the observers' subsequent behavior (Bandura, 1962, 1963a; Bandura & Walters, 1963). In the first place, the observer may acquire new responses that did not exist in his behavioral repertoire. In demonstrating this *modeling effect* experimentally, the model exhibits responses that the observer has not yet learned to make, and he must reproduce them in substantially identical form (Bandura, Ross, & Ross, 1961, 1963a). The component responses that enter into the development of more complex novel patterns are usually present in the observers' behavioral repertoires as products either of maturation or of prior social learning. Consequently, learning is most frequently reflected in the unique combination of response components, or the evocation of previously learned responses by new stimuli.

Exposure to models may also strengthen or weaken inhibitory responses in the observer. These *inhibitory* and *disinhibitory effects* are evident when the frequency of imitative and nonmatching responses increases or decreases, often as a function of rewarding or punishing response consequences to the model (Bandura, 1963b; Bandura, Ross, & Ross, 1963b; Walter, Leat, & Mezei, 1963). The observable changes produced by vicarious reinforcing events may reflect several different processes. Reinforcers administered to a model undoubtedly serve a discriminative function, signifying the probable reinforcement contingencies associated with the modeled classes of responses. In addition, rewarding consequences may result in vicarious extinction of inhibitory responses. Conversely, observed aversive outcomes tend to establish conditioned emotional responses (Bandura & Rosenthal, 1964; Berger, 1962) that help to support avoidant and inhibitory repertoires.

Finally, the behavior of models may elicit previously learned responses that match precisely or bear some resemblance to those exhibited by the model. This *response facilitation effect* can be distinguished from disinhibition when the behavior in question is not likely to have incurred punishment and, therefore, any increase in responsivity is not attributable to the reduction of inhibitory responses.

These three effects of the observation of models are clearly illustrated in a study that was designed to investigate the social transmission of novel aggressive responses (Bandura, Ross, & Ross, 1961). Nursery school children were assigned to one of four treatment conditions, or to a control group. One group of children observed an aggressive model who exhibited relatively unique forms of physical and verbal aggression toward a large inflated plastic doll; a second group viewed the same model behave in a very subdued and inhibited manner, while children in the control group had no exposure to the models.

It might be expected, on the basis of saliency and similarity of cues, that the more remote the model is from reality the weaker his modeling influence. This investigation was therefore later extended (Bandura, Ross, & Ross, 1963a) in order to compare the relative efficacy of real life, and pictorially presented symbolic models who differed on the reality-fictional stimulus dimension. Children in the human film-aggression group viewed a movie showing the adults who had served as models in the earlier experiment

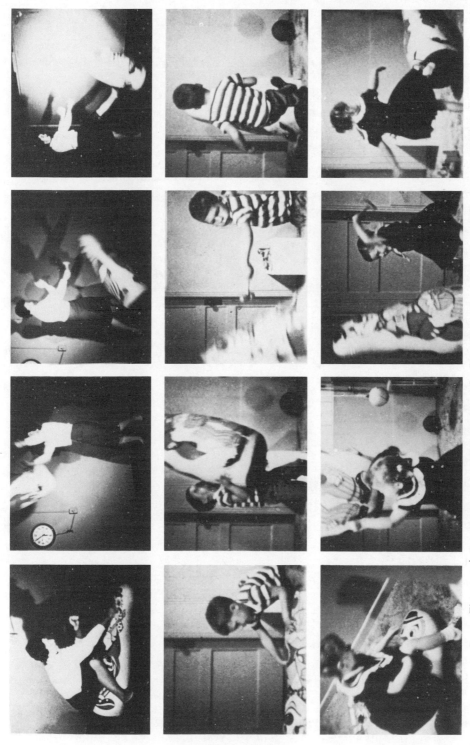

Figure 1 | PHOTOGRAPHS OF CHILDREN REPRODUCING THE BEHAVIOR EXHIBITED BY AN AGGRESSIVE MODEL. (REPRODUCED FROM BANDURA, ROSS, & ROSS, 1963A, P. 8. COPYRIGHT BY AMERICAN PSYCHOLOGICAL ASSOCIATION AND REPRODUCED BY PERMISSION.)

performing the same novel aggressive acts; children in the cartoon-aggressive group were presented a movie in which the model costumed as a cartoon cat exhibited the aggressive behavior toward the plastic doll.

During the acquisition period, the children simply watched the model's behavior but could not perform the responses he exhibited; consequently, any learning that occurred was purely on an observational or covert basis. This same no-trial learning procedure was employed in all of the experiments in the program of research discussed in this chapter.

After exposure to their respective models, all children, including those in the control group, were mildly frustrated and then tested for the amount of imitative and non-matching aggressive behavior.

Children who observed the aggressive models displayed a great number of precisely imitative physical and verbal responses, whereas such behavior rarely occurred in either the nonaggressive-model group or the control group. Illustrations of this modeling effect are provided in Figure 1 [Bandura, Ross & Ross 1963a], which depicts a boy and a girl reproducing the behavior of the female model whom they had observed in the film condition. These new repertoires were developed through a 10-minute exposure. Had the investigator attempted to shape these responses gradually by differential reinforcement, particularly the linguistic patterns that included relatively unique combinations of verbal elements such as "Pow, sock him in the nose," "He sure is a tough fella," "He keeps

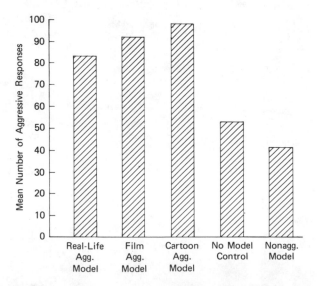

Figure 2 | MEAN FREQUENCY OF AGGRESSIVE RESPONSES PERFORMED BY CONTROL CHILDREN AND BY THOSE WHO HAD BEEN EXPOSED TO AGGRESSIVE AND IN-HIBITED MODELS. (COPYRIGHT © 1967, NATIONAL ASSOCIATION FOR THE EDUCA-TION OF YOUNG CHILDREN, AND REPRINTED WITH PERMISSION FROM: THE ROLE OF MODELING PROCESSES IN PERSONALITY DEVELOPMENT, BY A. BANDURA. IN *THE YOUNG CHILD: REVIEWS OF RESEARCH*, VOL. II. EDITED BY W. W. HARTUP & N. L. SMOTHERGILL.)

coming back for more," the research assistants would undoubtedly still be toiling in the laboratory.

The behavior of the models not only effectively shaped the form of the children's aggressive responses, but it also produced substantial disinhibitory effects. Children who had observed the aggressive models exhibited approximately twice as much aggression as did subjects in either the nonaggressive-model group or the control group. By contrast, children who witnessed the subdued nonaggressive models displayed the inhibited behavior characteristic of their model and expressed significantly less aggression than the control children (Figure 2) [Bandura, 1963a].

While the nonhuman cartoon character produced somewhat weaker modeling effects, nevertheless it was equally influential in reducing inhibitions over aggression. The finding that film-mediated human models can be as effective as real-life models in transmitting and disinhibiting responses suggests that televised models may play an important role in shaping and modifying social response patterns.

The results of these experiments also provide some evidence for facilitation effects. In one of the four physically imitative acts, for example, the model pummelled the doll with a mallet. Relative to children in the nonaggressive-model and control groups, subjects who had observed the aggressive models displayed significantly more behavior in which they pounded a peg board with the mallet (Bandura, 1962). Since this type of play activity is socially sanctioned, the heightened responsivity reflects primarily the operation of a facilitative or enchancement effect, rather than a disinhibitory process.

REFERENCES

Bachrach, A. J. Psychotherapy as a response chain. Paper presented at V. A. Hospital, Palo Alto, March 1963.

Bandura, A. Social learning through imitation. In M. R. Jones (Ed.), *Nebraska symposium on motivation: 1962.* Lincoln, Neb.: University of Nebraska Press, 1962, 211–215.

Bandura, A. The role of imitation in personality development. *Journal of Nursery Education,* 1963, *18,* 207–215. (a)

Bandura, A. Behavior theory and identificatory learning. *American Journal of Orthopsychiatry,* 1963, *33,* 591–601. (b)

Bandura, A., & McDonald, F. J. Influence of social reinforcement and the behavior of models in shaping children's moral judgments. *Journal of Abnormal and Social Psychology,* 1963, 67, 274–281.

Bandura, A., & Rosenthal, T. L. Vicarious classical conditioning as a function of arousal level. Unpublished manuscript, Stanford University, 1964.

Bandura, A., Ross, Dorothea, & Ross, Sheila A. Transmission of aggression through imitation of aggressive models. *Journal of Abnormal and Social Psychology,* 1961, 63, 575–582.

Bandura, A., Ross, Dorothea, & Ross, Sheila A. Imitation of film-mediated aggressive models. *Journal of Abnormal and Social Psychology,* 1963, 66, 3–11. (a)

Bandura, A., Ross, Dorothea, & Ross, Sheila A. Vicarious reinforcement and imitative learning. *Journal of Abnormal and Social Psychology,* 1963, 67, 601–607. (b)

Bandura, A., & Walters, R. H. *Social learning and personality development.* New York: Holt, Rinehart and Winston, 1963.

Berger, S. M. Conditioning through vicarious instigation. *Psychological Review*, 1962, 69, 450–466.

Lundin, R. W. *Personality: an experimental approach.* New York: Macmillan, 1961.

Pierrol, R., & Sherman, G. *Barnabus, the Barnard rat demonstration.* New York: Barnard College, 1958.

Skinner, B. F. *Verbal behavior.* New York: Appleton, 1957.

Skinner, B. F. Operant behavior. *American Psychologist*, 1963, 18, 503–515.

Walters, R. H., Leat, M., & Mezei, L. Inhibition and disinhibition of responses through empathetic learning. *Canadian Journal of Psychology*, 1963, 17, 235–243.

9 | Social Behavior Assessment

9.1 | IMPLICATIONS OF BEHAVIOR THEORY FOR PERSONALITY ASSESSMENT*

Walter Mischel

The two main forms of traditional personality theories that have influenced personality assessment have been trait theories and dynamic or state theories. While there are enormous variations among these trait and state theories I would like to comment here on their main common characteristics and to contrast them broadly with a social behavior approach to assessment.

Trait-state theories focus on personality as a theoretical construct and try to infer the unobservable internal predispositions, attributes, and motives of the individual. Social behavior theory—in which I include a host of behaviorally-oriented current social learning models—on the other hand, focuses on direct samples of behavior itself. Adherence to one or the other approach—the trait-state as opposed to the behavioral—immediately dictates major differences in our choice of virtually the entire strategy for assessment, therapy, and research.

Trait-state theories view test data primarily as cues to infer broad underlying dispositions in the person; in social behavior theory the individual's responses themselves are of main interest. While trait and dynamic state theories employ data as highly indirect and generalized *signs* or *symptoms*, in behavior theory test data serve as more direct and specific *samples* of behavior in specific situations. Assessors guided by trait-state theory infer the subject's personality from the signs revealed in his test behavior. To predict behavior in a new situation one estimates how the inferred personality attributes will interact with the conditions in the criterion situation.

In the social behavior approach, however, assessment and prediction involve the experimental analysis of the stimulus conditions that control the behavior of interest

---

* SOURCE: Mischel, W. Implications of behavior theory for personality assessment. Paper presented at the Western Psychological Association, March, 1968, San Diego, California, abridged and edited. Reprinted by permission of Walter Mischel.

which itself is sampled in the test situation. Thus, if a boy's mother complains that he is extremely overdemanding the boy would be observed with his mother, both when she behaves as she usually does and when her reactions are deliberately modified. This tactic is best illustrated in functional analyses of behavior (as described in Mischel, 1968). The behavior assessor introduces into the test situation, either directly or symbolically, the conditions of interest, and instead of seeking to tap signs of durable internal states, he systematically varies these stimulus conditions and observes their effects on behavior. Similarly, in the assessment of intellectual performance, rather than employing fixed, standardized test conditions as the subject works on problems, the assessor may purposefully vary the testing conditions to assess how such variables as praise, failure, or changes in the clarity, complexity, or arrangement with which the test materials are presented influence the child's problem-solving. His interest is in how learning conditions change the individual's performance, and not in estimates of the subject's performance level in comparison to other persons. When a client complains of feeling distressed, or anxious, or depressed one tries to establish referents for these feelings so that, if desired, the conditions affecting them can be changed.

The emphasis on behavior should not obscure the fact that behavior often is subtle and covert and complex and not merely an overt motor act. In social behavior analyses internal states, of course, are studiable through their observable referents, such as indices of emotional arousal or reports about subjective experiences, and may provide important information. Unfortunately, these referents, being harder to get, often have been ignored in favor of less interesting responses like bar-pressing or plunger-pulling, and not always because these are necessarily more appropriate for the particular problem. The principles that emerge from studies of the variables that control behavior in turn become the bases for developing a theory, not about traits and states, but about the manner in which behavior develops and changes in response to stimulus changes.

Behavior theory applied to human behavior must focus on molar and interpersonal response patterns in relation to complex social stimuli. For example, the subtle verbal and emotional behavior displayed by other persons, his expressions of anguish or delight, his fears and hopes—rather than a colored signal light, may constitute the events of interest. These molar units of analysis contrast with the sound clicks and muscle twitches often associated with stereotypes about S-R analyses in the animal laboratory. Anyone who wants to understand what his client is saying cannot avoid dealing directly with issues of meaning.

The traditional psychometric interest has been to assess how well a subject compares to others in a standard situation. Assessment in the behavioral model is not primarily concerned with the *degree* of performance deficit or with the *amount* of inappropriate behavior, but rather investigates the conditions that produce and maintain specific deficits or inappropriate patterns. The goal of performance assessment in the behavioral model is to identify the exact manipulations needed to change and improve the problematic behavior by bringing it increasingly closer to the defined therapeutic objectives. Assessment then becomes part of a series of experiments in which relevant stimulus conditions are introduced and varied directly or verbally and symbolically so that their effects on behavior can be evaluated. These evaluations can be obtained by asking the client, by role play, by *in vivo* sampling, and by direct observation.

Trait and state theories, in contrast to behavior theory, do not require close similarity between test behavior and criterion behavior, and typically the test behavior elicited has no direct relation to criterion behavior. For example, according to traditional trait-state assessments one might try to predict whether a Peace Corps volunteer will succeed by analyzing what he says to an inkblot; or his drawings may be read as a sign of interpersonal adjustment, and his doodles may be construed as signs of his achievement motive. In the trait-state approach prediction is based on inferences linking these test signs to internal states and then relating these states to performance on an external criterion. In contrast, behavioral assessments would try to arrange *samples* of relevant behavior—for instance, if the Peace Corps candidate is to teach in Nigeria one might want to know about his teaching skills especially with Black youngsters and especially under conditions that simulate those in the field.

While the relationship between sampled assessment behavior and criterion behavior thus is *direct* in the behavioral model it is typically *indirect* in trait-state assessments, reflecting the fundamental difference in the causal explanatory chain conceptualized by the two positions. Trait-state theories posit basic underlying causes in the form of predispositions or psychodynamics—broad motives, needs, complexes, basic attitudes, and so on—which supposedly generate numerous diverse manifestations, much as a physical disease produces a host of symptoms. In assessment, therefore, these underlying predisposing causes are inferred from their symptomatic behavioral manifestations. According to social behavior theory, in contrast, behavior is controlled by stimulus conditions and assessment therefore is aimed at a functional analysis which relates behavior to the conditions that covary with it. Of course a person's history changes the meaning of current stimuli. Often what he has done before is the best index of what he will do again in similar situations. Thus to predict the likelihood of future psychiatric hospitalization, for example, the person's past history in this regard is one of the best predictors.

Traditionally a chief purpose of personality psychology has been to identify the individual's position on one or more dimensions (e.g., introversion) by comparing him with norms based on other persons tested under comparable standardized conditions. In accord with trait theory it had been assumed that an individual's position on these continua would be relatively stable across testing situations and over lengthy time periods if the test instrument was sufficiently reliable. Consequently, the main assessment emphasis was on the development of *reliable* instruments administered under standard conditions to tap accurately the presumably stable, enduring underlying traits possessed by the person. If this could be done effectively it would be most useful. However, voluminous research in the last decade repeatedly shows that performances on all tests are affected by a variety of stimulus conditions, can be modified by numerous environmental manipulations, and provide little support for the existence of stable, broad unchangeable personality traits.

A great deal of behavioral specificity has been found regularly on character traits like "rigidity" or social conformity, or on virtually any other nonintellective personality dimension (Vernon, 1964; Mischel, 1968). Results of this kind present a fundamental problem for all approaches to personality that assume the existence of relatively situation-free broad dispositional syndromes. Considering the fact that specificity tends to be high among the subcomponents of traits like dependency or self-control or attitudes toward authority it should not be surprising that inferences about these dispositions, either by the clinician or by the statistician, have had little utility for assessment.

The interpretation of all data on behavioral consistency depends of course on the criteria chosen to evaluate them. Consistency coefficients averaging from about .30 to .40, for example, like those found by Hartshorne and May forty years ago can be construed either as evidence for the relative specificity of the particular behaviors, or as support for the presence of some generality (Burton, 1963). In correlational research one has to distinguish clearly between "statistically significant" associations and equivalence. When the sample of subjects is large a correlation of .30 or even .20 easily may reach significance and suggests an association that is not likely on the basis of chance. The same coefficient, however, accounts for less than 10 percent of the relevant variance. While this may provide the researcher with a "significant" finding it involves an error term that the conscientious practitioner cannot afford.

Dispositions, of course, can be inferred only from behavioral measurements and these involve "errors of measurement." Gradually, however, even psychometricians are acknowledging that behavioral fluctuations reflect more than imperfections in our measuring instruments (Loevinger, 1957). The modest and often zero intercorrelations obtained between different measures used as referents for behaviors such as dependency or aggression emphasize the importance of considering more specific antecedents and more specific contingencies in the analysis of these syndromes. In light of the empirical data the utility of describing behavior with molar trait units (e.g., dependency) is being questioned increasingly (e.g., Brim, 1960; Hartup, 1963)—and indeed has to be challenged.

Behavioral assessments focus on specific behavioral samples rather than on behavioral signs of broad underlying global dispositions. That seems justified not only for practical reasons of parsimony but also for theoretical reasons. In this perspective one turns to the analysis of the relations between behavior and the conditions that influence it. One therefore emphasizes as precisely and specifically as possible what the person *does*—including what he does inside his head—rather than inferences about what he *has*. What people do, of course, includes much more than motor acts. Unlike rats and other lower organisms who have been psychology's favorite subjects, humans do exceedingly complex and varied things. They organize and disorganize societies, create works of art, talk, and write theories about these phenomena as well as about each other and themselves. An adequate psychology ultimately must be able to deal with such complex human behaviors and not merely with travels through a maze. The hope of behavior theory—and its challenge—is to apply to man the rigor of precise analyses. It will be a herculean task to analyze man's transactions with the social environment, without simultaneously violating him through oversimplification and thus losing him in the process.

REFERENCES

Brim, O. G., Jr. Personality development as role-learning. In I. Iscoe, & H. Stevenson (Eds.), *Personality development in children.* Austin, Tex.: University of Texas Press, 1960. Pp. 127–159.

Burton, R. V. Generality of honesty reconsidered. *Psychological Review*, 1963, 70, 481–499.

Hartup, W. W. Dependence and independence. In H. W. Stevenson et al. (Eds.), *Child psychology (Sixty-second Yearbook of the National Society for the Study of Education).* Chicago: University of Chicago Press, 1963. Pp. 333–363.

Loevinger, J. Objective tests as instruments of psychological theory. *Psychological Reports Monographs*, No. 9, Southern University Press, 1957.

Mischel, W. *Personality and assessment.* New York: Wiley, 1968.

Vernon, P. E. *Personality assessment: A critical survey.* New York: Wiley, 1964.

9.2 | THE CASE OF PEARSON BRACK*

Walter Mischel

Some of the main differences between the psychodynamic assessment of causes and the approach of social behavior theory are best illustrated by comparing their analyses of a clinical problem. The well-known case of "Pearson Brack," an American airman in the Second World War, serves as a clear example (Grinker & Spiegel, 1945, pp. 197–207).

Pearson Brack was a B-25 bombardier in the Tunisian theater of operations when his problems began. On his tenth and eleventh bombing missions he had fainted when his airplane reached an altitude of 10,000 feet. Afterward, trying to recall what had happened, Brack remembered only that he had felt cold and sleepy and then had awakened, finding himself leaning on his bomb sight. Just before the two missions on which Brack had fainted he had experienced a narrow escape from death; during his ninth mission his airplane was almost destroyed and he was injured seriously. While nearing an important bombing target, and under very heavy flak and fighter resistance, Brack's plane had suddenly jolted and rolled over, and then began to fall in a seemingly endless dive. The pilot did regain control, barely in time to avoid crashing to the ground, and successfully brought the plane back into the flight formation to complete

---

* SOURCE: Mischel, W. *Personality and assessment.* New York: John Wiley & Sons, Inc., 1968, Pp. 262–272. Copyright © 1968 by John Wiley & Sons, Inc. Reprinted by permission.

the mission. During the plane's fall, however, Brack was hurled violently against the bomb sight. He sustained a heavy blow on the left side of his chest and his injuries were so severe that he immediately began to cough up blood. Nevertheless, he managed to release his bombs on the target. Upon his return, Brack was hospitalized for four weeks, and then seemed to be healed and was returned to full duty. It was on the next two missions, the tenth and eleventh, that he fainted. The two fainting episodes again brought Brack to the attention of the flight surgeon. As a first step, the medical board that reviewed his case considered and ruled out any residual organic damage as the possible cause of his fainting at high altitudes. After excluding an organic etiology the case was interpreted from a psychodynamic viewpoint. The psychiatrist hypothesized that the fainting was symptomatic of deep underlying anxiety, related to Brack's brittle personality structure. He viewed Brack's fainting as a surface manifestation of basic fear and anxiety, and of dynamics that could be understood and treated only in the light of the analysis of childhood traumas and identifications. He therefore proceeded, in accord with psychodynamic theory, to search for signs of latent or repressed pervasive anxiety and for their hypothetical distant historical sources.

When interviewed Brack clearly recognized that he could not fly above about 9000 feet. But he rejected the idea that his troubles resulted from basic underlying, long-standing anxieties, and he asked for specific help that might make it possible for him to rejoin his crew in combat flying. The psychiatrist, however, interpreted Brack's overt behavior as a defensive facade (Grinker & Spiegel, 1945, p. 198):

> Although he did not directly show hostility when told that his troubles might be due to fear, he constantly rejected this idea, laughing and joking at such a possibility. He stated that he had never been afraid of anything. He described himself as one of the best bombardiers in his outfit, and talked about his activities in combat with a great deal of pride and jocularity. He attempted to produce the impression of the typical carefree, aggressive combat crew member. There was something about his attitude, however, which was not wholly convincing. The effect was theatrical and overplayed.

Brack's refusal to accept the psychiatrist's interpretation about the "underlying anxieties" supposedly responsible for his problem led to further assessments apparently designed to convince him (p. 198):

> Because it was impossible to establish any insight into his underlying anxieties in psychotherapeutic interviews, a pentothal interview was undertaken overseas. He was told that he was in his plane with his crew going to the target.

The pentothal interview, however, produced no direct evidence of anxiety. He talked about the ninth mission in great detail, speaking with various crew members as if he were actually in the plane again, but he remained entirely calm and unemotional and "showed no anxiety whatsoever" (p. 198). Because "no anxiety could be realized either in interviews or under pentothal" (p. 199), the psychiatrist next took the rare (and excellent) step of accompanying Brack on a practice flight so that he could watch his reactions while in the air. Brack's behavior en route to the field, and during the early stages of the flight, was described as showing "more than his usual amount of jocularity and aggressive humor" (p. 199). He seemed to be "in good humor and cheerful." A few times Brack teased the psychiatrist (who presumably had spent little time in combat) about the possibility that distant unidentified planes might really turn out to be German fighter planes. The psychiatrist, however, grimly noted that "the joke was unrealistic since German aircraft had never penetrated to this area" (p. 199). Indeed, he interpreted Brack's total behavior as a sign of "a frightened individual whistling past the graveyard" (p. 199).

When the plane reached an altitude of about 10,000 feet, Brack began to pale, tremble, and breathe rapidly; fainting was barely avoided by having him breathe slowly and deeply. As soon as the pilot brought the plane down to an altitude of 8500 feet, Brack recovered and again became fully alert and calm.

It should be noted that, from the viewpoint of social behavior theory, a fairly clear causal relationship now seemed to be established. When Brack's plane ascended to an altitude of 10,000 feet he became ill; when he remained below that altitude he felt well. This relationship occurred not only on the practice flight but also on the tenth and eleventh mission when his fainting problem had first begun. Although post hoc speculations about etiology are never satisfying, it is plausible that Brack's severe injury on the ninth mission may have occurred when his plane was at the cruising altitude of about 10,000 feet. The contiguity between altitude cues at that height and Brack's painful, nearly fatal, traumatic experience may have made the former conditioned stimuli capable of eliciting an intense arousal reaction that led to fainting. Although the etiology cannot be certain the treatment implications seem clear for social behavior theory: render the traumatic cues neutral by desensitizing Brack to them through slow, graded exposure under conditions that prevent arousal and that, instead, insure incompatible responses such as relaxation.

Thus, from the perspective of social behavior theory, the relevant causes of Brack's problem are the current conditions that actually control its occurrence, in this case altitude cues previously associated with a trauma. From the perspective of psychodynamic theory, however, the causes are his underlying, inferred characterological anxiety and its supposed childhood antecedents. Consequently the psychiatrist ignored the evident correlation between the altitude and the problem and instead continued his search for hypothesized "roots" in the form of repressed underlying anxieties.

Brack fully recognized, of course, that he collapsed and could not function in planes at high altitudes. He firmly rejected, however, the belief that unconscious anxieties rooted in his basic character development and early childhood were the causes responsible for this problem. He felt, instead, that his trouble was somehow related to his painful injury and traumatic experiences on the ninth mission. The psychiatrist, however, kept pressing for Brack to admit his underlying fears, and the two men became embroiled in a prolonged semantic dispute. This controversy seemed to center on such words as "afraid" and "nervous" which the psychiatrist wanted Brack to call himself. In this phase the psychiatrist reported repeatedly that the patient still completely resisted any interpretation about his underlying deep fears; Brack insisted that the after-effects of his painful injury and trauma in the plane made him faint on planes. In subsequent interviews, the psychiatrist, for example, "pointed out to the patient that the tremor he exhibited in the air was very similar to the tremor of nervousness" (p. 200). Brack, however, "took the attitude that the therapist, if the latter wanted to, had a right to think that he was scared but that he, the patient, could never be convinced that this was the source of his trouble."

The semantic dispute between the bombardier and his psychiatrist about Brack's true subjective internal state continued and had serious consequences (p. 200):

> Since it was manifestly impossible to establish any insight in a patient with such strong resistance and so much organic fixation, it was felt that the best method of procedure would be to have the patient return to combat and to ask his Flight Surgeon to observe him carefully for signs of anxiety and to work out the anxiety with him on the spot.

On his next mission Brack efficiently executed his duties over a very rough target and, although he did not faint when the altitude exceeded 9000 feet, he returned exhausted and soaked with perspiration. The flight surgeon feared that Brack might still be suffering from the effects of his pulmonary injury and so referred him to the hospital. The chief medical officer interpreted his cardiogram as possibly showing recent posterior wall damage. He informed Brack that he had a contusion of the heart, ordering six months of rest from the date of the injury. When Brack next saw his therapist he told him that (p. 200):

> ... he guessed there was something wrong with him after all, because the doctor in the hospital had found it. He was more cheerful than ever, although somewhat more calm and less talkative than when first seen. Because there was now so much organic fixation, psychotherapy did not appear likely to be successful and it was determined to return the patient to the United States for further observation and treatment.

After his return to the United States Brack felt increasingly nervous and depressed. He complained of anxiety dreams of falling in an airplane. He was admitted to a convalescent hospital where, remarkably, he found himself facing the same psychiatrist who also had been transferred to the United States. Brack interpreted his own nervous and depressed feelings as due to not having completed his job overseas. He had left his friends behind in combat while he was returned to his family and safety in the midst of war. The psychiatrist, however, in accord with his theoretical convictions, pressed for analogies between Brack's current problems and his childhood, exploring in pentothal interviews his early life memories and his feelings about his alcoholic father. For example, Brack was asked why he felt depressed (p. 203):

> He answered that he felt it was probably because he had failed to complete his job overseas. He was then asked if possibly he did not also feel bad because his behavior had been evasive and he had escaped facing his responsibilities in the same way as his father escaped similar responsibilities. He said, "No, I don't drink." He was told

that his way of escaping was not through drinking but through failing to face his real feelings. He was then reminded that overseas he had failed to face up to his own anxiety and fear of flying. He answered that he did not know at that time he was afraid. He was asked if he knew it now, and he said he was not sure.

While the persistence and directness with which the psychiatrist seemed to seek validating evidence for his own theoretical hypotheses may seem extreme, it is not necessarily atypical. Indeed the case of Brack has been used in a major neodynamic text on abnormal behavior (White, 1964) as one of the main illustrations. It is not surprising therefore that after reviewing literature on psychodynamic therapy Bandura (1967) concludes that clients' "insights" after traditional psychotherapy can be predicted better from knowledge of their therapists' belief systems than from information about the clients' actual past history. He takes the view that insight into the supposedly "basic" intrapsychic causes of behavior "may primarily represent a conversion to the therapist's point of view rather than a process of self-discovery" (Bandura, 1967, p. 78). Considering the data on the constraining effects of trait hypotheses upon observation . . . this interpretation seems especially plausible.

The struggle between patient and psychiatrist continued. Brack sought direct help, suggesting, for example, that he might "get over his uneasiness in planes by repeatedly exposing himself to flights" (p. 204). Predictably, his intuitively sound suggestion for extinction treatment was interpreted as "markedly evasive," and "because of his continued difficulty in clearly recognizing the source of his anxiety, it was determined to give him another pentothal interview" (p. 204).

Gradually, over the course of many sessions, Brack's "resistance" was indeed slowly worn down, and at last he began to offer the expected self-revelations. For example:

> "I guess I have been trying to fool myself about a lot of things. I am really worried about a lot of things and I don't like to admit it." (p. 205)

These confessions were promptly reinforced by the therapist (p. 205):

> He was then told that his confidence and general feeling of security had been shattered by his flying experiences when he had the fall and injury, and that this was only natural, but that he would get over it. He was told that he could never really get better as long as he would not recognize how he really felt, but that, now that he knew what was the matter with him, he would start on the road to recovery.

At this point Brack again asked for direct help to overcome his flying problems, possibly by returning to flying itself. According to the therapist's dynamic interpretations, the "basic" cause of Brack's fainting in the plane, and of his nervousness and depression when removed from his duties, was the result of an inadequate identification with his father. Until that was handled he could not fly (p. 205):

> The patient's maturity, achieved through identification with his grandfather and based on a rejection of his own father, was at best tenuous. It did not appear to represent an actual maturity but rather an imitation of maturity. The attempt to

achieve an ego-ideal by imitation, rather than through a real identification, was characteristic of this man. It was the essence of his behavior as a combat crew member, which was characterized by evasive aggressiveness, jocularity and sang-froid. These reactions, actually felt by some combat crew members, were only imitated by the patient while in combat to cover up his actual fright—the whistling in the dark technique.

Although throughout the many months of arguing Brack had kept asking for a chance to be helped to overcome his flying problem (p. 206):

> In view of his fragile maturity, his long-standing insecurity and the actual psychological trauma incurred during his fall, it was considered that a return to a flying assignment at this time would not be wise.

At this point the case description ended. . . .

The case of Brack highlights some of the chief differences between the current social behavior approach and traditional psychodynamic assessments. Social behavior theory searches for causes in the conditions that demonstrably control the defined behaviors of interest; traditional dynamic theories infer hypothetical causes, such as deficient "ego ideals," from behavioral "signs" and tie these to post hoc historical reconstructions on the basis of the clinician's theory. It is generally impossible, of course, to accurately reconstruct unique historical circumstances many years after they occurred even if one hunts for them diligently. Indeed, it is notoriously difficult to obtain even a partially accurate reconstruction of personal events long after they have taken place, since even such close eyewitnesses as parents simply forget the bulk of what happened (Mednick & Shaffer, 1963; Pyles, Stolz, & MacFarlane, 1935; Robbins, 1963; Wenar, 1961; Wenar & Coulter, 1962).

The research on clinical inferences . . . makes it untenable to prefer the clinician's judgments about the hypothetical causes of behavior to the client's own constructions and interpretations about himself. Psychodynamic assessments further assume that persons are victims of enduring unconscious and irrational forces that prevent them from properly evaluating themselves. In fact, there in no convincing evidence that unconscious processes play an important role in learning, discrimination, and performance (e.g., Eriksen, 1960, 1966). As we have seen . . . , awareness appears to be a critical ingredient in most learning situations. In the context of prediction, we have also seen that the person's predictions about his own behavior, and his self-reports, generally are more accurate than the clinician's predictions about him. . . . In light of these considerations it seems unjustified to retain the psychodynamic belief that persons with problems cannot reach appropriate decisions about their desired goals without the benefit of interpretations about their unconscious processes from clinical "experts."

Social behavior assessments look for the client's definition of his own problems and then offer courses of action to help him achieve his own goals, leaving the choices to him whenever possible and as soon as possible. In Brack's case, for example, social behavior theory probably would have led to a treatment program of counterconditioning and gradual extinction not dissimilar to the one he requested spontaneously. Brack's goals—to be helped to fly again and to overcome the aftermath of his injury—would be accepted as reasonable, rather than as the defensive facade of a brittle and immature individual from whom "unconscious anxieties" had to be extracted, in spite of himself. Social behavior assessments and treatments are intended to remove problems and to help people develop more constructive behavior—but not to remake the people in a new mold. Elimination of a problem—such as fainting at high altitudes—is not intended to reconstruct the whole person but only to help him with specified goals. If professionals in other fields substituted their own omnibus goals for the client's particular self-described problems as freely as psychodynamicists routinely do, they surely would be brought to court as defendants rather than as expert witnesses. In social behavior assessments the client is viewed as an active collaborator, who may require specific guidance and information about action alternatives and contingencies—just as clients expect from all other professionals. However, it is the client who, as long as he is legally responsible for himself, has ultimate responsibility for his own choices. In the behavior-change programs described by Bijou (1965) and his colleagues, for example, parents are taught principles about the conditions that affect their relations to their children, and are shown concretely how to implement them. Whether or not they choose to use them is, at every step, entirely up to them.

Finally, social behavior therapies, like other forms of planned change, do not and should not intend to achieve highly generalized total personality reorganizations except in the unlikely event that this is the client's explicit goal. The aim of behavior assessments is to design treatments for specified objectives rather than to produce overall conversions.

REFERENCES

Bandura, A. Behavioral psychotherapy. *Scientific American*, 1967, *216*, 78–86.

Bijou, S. W. Experimental studies of child behavior, normal and deviant. In L. Krasner & L. P. Ullmann (Eds.), *Research in behavior modification.* New York: Holt, Rinehart and Winston, 1965. Pp. 56–81.

Eriksen, C. W. Discrimination and learning without awareness: A methodological survey and evaluation. *Psychological Review*, 1960, *67*, 279–300.

Eriksen, C. W. Cognitive responses to internally cued anxiety. In C. D. Spielberger (Ed.), *Anxiety and behavior.* New York: Academic Press, 1966, 327–360.

Grinker, R. R., & Spiegel, J. P. *Men under stress.* Philadelphia: Blakiston, 1945.

Mednick, S. A., & Shaffer, J. B. Mothers' retrospective reports in child-rearing research. *American Journal of Orthopsychiatry*, 1963, *33*, 457–461.

Pyles, M. K., Stolz, H. R., & MacFarlane, J. W. The accuracy of mothers' reports on birth and developmental data. *Child Development*, 1935, *6*, 165–176.

Robbins, L. C. The accuracy of parental recall of aspects of child development and of child rearing practices. *Journal of Abnormal and Social Psychology*, 1963, *66*, 261–270.

Wenar, C. The reliability of mothers' histories. *Child Development*, 1961, *32*, 491–500.

Wenar, C., & Coulter, J. B. A reliability study of developmental histories. *Child Development*, 1962, *33*, 453–462.

White, R. W. *The abnormal personality.* New York: Ronald Press, 1964.

9.3 | BEHAVIORAL ANALYSIS: AN ALTERNATIVE TO DIAGNOSTIC CLASSIFICATION*[1]

Frederick H. Kanfer and George Saslow

During the past decade attacks on conventional psychiatric diagnosis have been so widespread that many clinicians now use diagnostic labels sparingly and apologetically. The continued adherence to the nosological terms of the traditional classificatory scheme suggests some utility of the present categorization of behavior disorders, despite its apparently low reliability (Ash, 1949; Rotter, 1954); its limited prognostic value (Freedman, 1958; Windle, 1952); and its multiple feebly related assumptive supports. In a recent study of this problem, the symptom patterns of carefully diagnosed paranoid schizophrenics were compared. Katz et al. (1964) found considerable divergence among patients with the same diagnosis and concluded that "diagnostic systems which are more circumscribed in their intent, for example, based on manifest behavior alone, rather than systems which attempt to comprehend etiology, symptom patterns and prognosis, may be more directly applicable to current problems in psychiatric research" (p. 202).

We propose here to examine some sources of dissatisfaction with the present approach to diagnosis, to describe a framework for a behavioral analysis of individual patients which implies both suggestions for treatment and outcome criteria for the single case, and to indicate the conditions for collecting the data for such an analysis.

PROBLEMS IN CURRENT DIAGNOSTIC SYSTEMS

Numerous criticisms deal with the internal consistency, the explicitness, the precision, and the reliability of psychiatric classifications. It seems to us that the more important fault lies in our lack of sufficient knowledge to categorize behavior along those pertinent dimensions which permit prediction of responses to social stresses, life crises, or psychiatric treatment. This limitation obviates anything but a crude and tentative approximation to a taxonomy of effective individual behavior.

Zigler and Phillips (1961), in discussing the requirement for an adequate system of classification, suggest that an etiologically-oriented closed system of diagnosis is premature. Instead, they believe that an empirical attack is needed, using "symptoms broadly defined as meaningful and discernible behaviors, as the basis of the classifica-

* SOURCE: Kanfer, F. H., and Saslow, G. Behavioral analysis: An alternative to the diagnostic classification. *Archives of General Psychiatry*, 1965, *12*, 529–538. Copyright 1965. Reprinted by permission of the American Medical Association.

[1] This paper was written in conjunction with Research Grant MH 06921-03 from the National Institutes of Mental Health, United States Public Health Service.

tory system" (p. 616). But symptoms as a class of responses are defined after all only by their nuisance value to the patient's social environment or to himself as a social being. They are also notoriously unreliable in predicting the patient's particular etiological history or his response to treatment. An alternate approach lies in an attempt to identify classes of dependent variables in human behavior which would allow inferences about the particular controlling factors, the social stimuli, the physiological stimuli, and the reinforcing stimuli, of which they are a function. In the present early stage of the art of psychological prognostication, it appears most reasonable to develop a program of analysis which is closely related to subsequent treatment. A classification scheme which implies a program for behavioral change is one which has not only utility but the potential for experimental validation.

The task of assessment and prognosis can therefore be reduced to efforts which answer the following three questions: (a) which specific behavior patterns require change in their frequency of occurrence, their intensity, their duration or in the conditions under which they occur, (b) what are the best practical means which can produce the desired changes in this individual (manipulation of the environment, of the behavior, or the self-attitudes of the patient), and (c) what factors are currently maintaining it and what are the conditions under which this behavior was acquired. The investigation of the history of the problematic behavior is mainly of academic interest, except as it contributes information about the probable efficacy of a specific treatment method.

EXPECTATIONS OF CURRENT DIAGNOSTIC SYSTEMS.   In traditional medicine, a diagnostic statement about a patient has often been viewed as an essential prerequisite to treatment because a diagnosis suggests that the physician has some knowledge of the origin and future course of the illness. Further, in medicine diagnosis frequently brings together the accumulated knowledge about the pathological process which leads to the manifestation of the symptoms, and the experiences which others have had in the past in treating patients with such a disease process. Modern medicine recognizes that any particular disease need not have a single cause or even a small number of antecedent conditions. Nevertheless, the diagnostic label attempts to define at least the necessary conditions which are most relevant in considering a treatment program. Some diagnostic classification system is also invaluable as a basis for many social decisions involving entire populations. For example, planning for treatment facilities, research efforts and educational programs take into account the distribution frequencies of specified syndromes in the general population.

Ledley and Lusted (1959) give an excellent conception of the traditional model in medicine by their analysis of the reasoning underlying it. The authors differentiate between a disease complex and a symptom complex. While the former describes known pathological processes and their correlated signs, the latter represents particular signs present in a particular patient. The bridge between disease and symptom complexes is provided by available medical knowledge and the final diagnosis is tantamount to labeling the disease complex. However, the current gaps in medical knowledge necessitate the use of probability statements when relating disease to symptoms, admitting that there is some possibility for error in the diagnosis. Once the diagnosis is established, decisions about treatment still depend on many other factors including social, moral, and economic conditions. Ledley and Lusted (1959) thus separate the clinical diagnosis into a two-step process. A statistical procedure is suggested to facilitate the primary or diagnostic labeling process. However, the choice of treatment depends not only on the diagnosis proper. Treatment decisions are also influenced by the moral, ethical, social, and economic conditions of the individual patient, his family, and the society in which he lives. The proper assignment of the weight to be given to each of these values must in the last analysis be left to the physician's judgment (Ledley and Lusted, 1959).

The Ledley and Lusted model presumes available methods for the observation of relevant behavior (the symptom complex), and some scientific knowledge relating it to known antecedents or correlates (the disease process). Contemporary theories of behavior pathology do not yet provide adequate guidelines for the observer to suggest what is to be observed. In fact, Szasz (1960) has expressed the view that the medical model may be totally inadequate because psychiatry should be concerned with problems of living and not with diseases of the brain or other biological organs. Szasz (1960) argues that "mental illness is a myth, whose function it is to disguise and thus render more potable the bitter pill of moral conflict in human relations" (p. 118).

The attack against use of the medical model in psychiatry comes from many quarters. Scheflen (1958) describes a model of somatic psychiatry which is very similar to the traditional medical model of disease. A pathological process results in onset of an illness; the symptoms are correlated with a pathological state and represent our evidence of "mental disease." Treatment consists of removal of the pathogen, and the state of health is restored. Scheflen suggests that this traditional medical model is used in psychiatry not on the basis of its adequacy but because of its emotional appeal.

The limitations of the somatic model have been discussed even in some areas of medicine for which the model seems most appropriate. For example, in the nomenclature for diagnosis of disease of the heart and blood vessels, the criteria committee of the New York Heart Association (1953) suggests the use of multiple criteria for cardiovascular diseases, including a statement of the patient's functional capacity. The committee suggests that the functional capacity be ". . . estimated by appraising the patient's ability to perform physical activity" (p. 80), and decided largely by inference from his history. Further, ". . . (it) should not be influenced by the character of the structural lesion or by an opinion as to treatment or prognosis" (p. 81). This approach makes it clear that a comprehensive assessment of a patient, regardless of the physical disease which he suffers, must also take into account his social effectiveness and the particular ways in which physiological, anatomical, and psychological factors interact to produce a particular behavior pattern in an individual patient.

MULTIPLE DIAGNOSIS.   A widely used practical solution and circumvention of the difficulty inherent in the application of the medical model to psychiatric diagnosis is offered by Noyes and Kolb (1963). They suggest that the clinician construct a diagnostic formulation consisting of three parts: (1) A *genetic* diagnosis incorporating the constitutional, somatic, and historical-traumatic factors representing the primary sources or determinants of the mental illness; (2) A *dynamic* diagnosis which describes the mechanisms and techniques unconsciously used by the individual to manage anxiety, enhance self-esteem, i.e., that traces the psychopathological processes; and (3) A *clinical* diagnosis which conveys useful connotations concerning the reaction syndrome, the probable course of the disorder, and the methods of treatment which will most probably prove beneficial. Noyes' and Kolb's multiple criteria (Noyes & Kolb, 1963) can be arranged along three simpler dimensions of diagnosis which may have some practical value to the clinician: (1) etiological, (2) behavioral, and (3) predictive. The kind of information which is conveyed by each type of diagnostic label is somewhat different and specifically adapted to the purpose for which the diagnosis is used. The triple-label approach attempts to counter the criticism aimed at use of any single classificatory system. Confusion in a single system is due in part to the fact that a diagnostic formulation intended to describe current behavior, for example, may be found useless in an attempt to predict the response to specific treatment, or to postdict the patient's personal history and development, or to permit collection of frequency data on hospital populations.

CLASSIFICATION BY ETIOLOGY.

The Kraepelinian system and portions of the 1952 APA classification emphasize etiological factors. They share the assumption that common etiological factors lead to similar symptoms and respond to similar treatment. This dimension of diagnosis is considerably more fruitful when dealing with behavior disorders which are mainly under control of some biological condition. When a patient is known to suffer from excessive intake of alcohol his hallucinatory behavior, lack of motor coordination, poor judgment, and other behavioral evidence of disorganization can often be related directly to some antecedent condition such as the toxic effect of alcohol on the central nervous system, liver, etc. For these cases, classification by etiology also has some implications for prognosis and treatment. Acute hallucinations and other disorganized behavior due to alcohol usually clear up when the alcohol level in the blood stream falls. Similar examples can be drawn from any class of behavior disorders in which a change in behavior is associated primarily or exclusively with a single, *particular* antecedent factor. Under these conditions this factor can be called a pathogen and the situation closely approximates the condition described by the traditional medical model.

Utilization of this dimension as a basis for psychiatric diagnosis, however, has many problems apart from the rarity with which a specified condition can be shown to have a direct "causal" relationship to a pathogen. Among the current areas of ignorance in the fields of psychology and psychiatry, the etiology of most common disturbances probably takes first place. No specific family environment, no dramatic traumatic experience, or known constitutional abnormality has yet been found which results in the same pattern of disordered behavior. While current research efforts have aimed at investigating family patterns of schizophrenic patients, and several studies suggest a relationship between the mother's behavior and a schizophrenic process in the child (Jackson,

1960), it is not at all clear why the presence of these same factors in other families fails to yield a similar incidence of schizophrenia. Further, patients may exhibit behavior diagnosed as schizophrenic when there is not evidence of the postulated mother-child relationship.

In a recent paper Meehl (1962) postulates schizophrenia as a neurological disease, with learned content and a dispositional basis. With this array of interactive etiological factors, it is clear that the etiological dimension for classification would at best result in an extremely cumbersome system, at worst in a useless one.

CLASSIFICATION BY SYMPTOMS. A clinical diagnosis often is a summarizing statement about the way in which a person behaves. On the assumption that a variety of behaviors are correlated and consistent in any given individual, it becomes more economical to assign the individual to a class of persons than to list and categorize all of his behaviors. The utility of such a system rests heavily on the availability of empirical evidence concerning correlations among various behaviors (response-response relationships), and the further assumption that the frequency of occurrence of such behaviors is relatively independent of specific stimulus conditions and of specific reinforcement. There are two major limitations to such a system. The first is that diagnosis by symptoms, as we have indicated in an earlier section, is often misleading because it implies common etiological factors. Freedman (1958) suggests that schizophrenia is not a disease entity in the sense that it has a unique etiology, pathogenesis, etc., but that it represents the evocation of a final common pathway in the same sense as do headache, epilepsy, sore throat, or indeed any other symptom complex. It is further suggested that the term "schizophrenia has outlived its usefulness and should be discarded" (p. 5). Opler (1957, 1963) has further shown the importance of cultural factors in the divergence of symptoms observed in patients collectively labeled as schizophrenic.

Descriptive classification is not always this deceptive, however. Assessment of intellectual performance sometimes results in a diagnostic statement which has predictive value for the patient's behavior in school or on a job. To date, there seem to be very few general statements about individual characteristics which have as much predictive utility as the IQ.

A second limitation is that the current approach to diagnosis by symptoms tends to center on a group of behaviors which is often irrelevant with regard to the patient's total life pattern. These behaviors may be of interest only because they are popularly associated with deviancy and disorder. For example, occasional mild delusions interfere little or not at all with the social or occupational effectiveness of many ambulatory patients. Nevertheless, admission of their occurrence is often sufficient for a diagnosis of psychosis. Refinement of such an approach beyond current usage appears possible, as shown for example by Lorr et al. (1963) but this does not remove the above limitations.

Utilization of a symptom-descriptive approach frequently focuses attention on by-products of larger behavior patterns, and results in attempted treatment of behaviors (symptoms) which may be simple consequences of other important aspects of the patient's life. Emphasis on the patient's subjective complaints, moods and feelings tends to encourage use of a syndrome-oriented classification. It also results frequently in efforts to change the feelings, anxieties, and moods (or at least the patient's report about them), rather than to investigate the life conditions, interpersonal reactions, and environmental factors which produce and maintain these habitual response patterns.

CLASSIFICATION BY PROGNOSIS.   To date, the least effort has been devoted to construction of a classification system which assigns patients to the same category on the basis of their similar response to specific treatments. The proper question raised for such a classification system consists of the manner in which a patient will react to treatments, regardless of his current behavior, or his past history. The numerous studies attempting to establish prognostic signs from projective personality tests or somatic tests represent efforts to categorize the patients on this dimension.

Windle (1952) has called attention to the low degree of predictability afforded by personality (projective) test scores, and has pointed out the difficulties encountered in evaluating research in this area due to the inadequate description of the population sampled and of the improvement criteria. In a later review Fulkerson and Barry (1961) came to the similar conclusion that psychological test performance is a poor predictor of outcome in mental illness. They suggest that demographic variables such as severity, duration, acuteness of onset, degree of precipitating stress, etc., appear to have stronger relationships to outcome than test data. The lack of reliable relationships between diagnostic categories, test data, demographic variables, or other measures taken on the patient on the one hand, and duration of illness, response to specific treatment, or degree of recovery, on the other hand, precludes the construction of a simple empiric framework for a diagnostic-prognostic classification system based only on an array of symptoms.

None of the currently used dimensions for diagnosis is directly related to methods of modification of a patient's behavior, attitudes, response patterns, and interpersonal actions. Since the etiological model clearly stresses causative factors, it is much more compatible with a personality theory which strongly emphasizes genetic-developmental factors. The classification by symptoms facilitates social-administrative decisions about patients by providing some basis for judging the degree of deviation from social and ethical norms. Such a classification is compatible with a personality theory founded on the normal curve hypothesis and concerned with characterization by comparison with a fictitious average. The prognostic-predictive approach appears to have the most direct practical applicability. If continued research were to support certain early findings, it would be indeed comforting to be able to predict outcome of mental illness from a patient's premorbid social competence score (Zigler & Phillips, 1961), or from the patient's score on an ego-strength scale (Barron, 1953), or from many of the other signs and single variables which have been shown to have some predictive powers. It is unfortunate that these powers are frequently dissipated in cross validation. As Fulkerson and Barry (1961) have indicated, single predictors have not yet shown much success.

A FUNCTIONAL (BEHAVIORAL-ANALYTIC) APPROACH

The growing literature on behavior modification procedures derived from learning theory (Bandura, 1961; Ferster, 1965; Kanfer, 1961; Krasner, 1962; Wolpe, 1958) suggests that an effective diagnostic procedure would be one in which the eventual therapeutic methods can be directly related to the information obtained from a continuing assessment of the patient's current behaviors and their controlling stimuli. Ferster (1965) has said ". . . a functional analysis of behavior has the advantage that it specifies the causes of behavior in the form of explicit environmental events which can be objectively identified and which are potentially manipulable" (p. 3). Such a diagnostic undertaking makes the assumption that a description of the problematic behavior, its controlling factors, and the means by which it can be changed are the most appropriate "explanations." It further makes the assumption that a diagnostic evaluation is never complete. It implies that additional information about the circumstances of the patient's life pattern, relationships among his behaviors, and controlling stimuli in his social milieu and his private experience is obtained continuously until it proves sufficient to effect a noticeable change in the patient's behavior, thus resolving "the problem." In a functional approach it is necessary to continue evaluation of the patient's life pattern and its controlling factors, concurrent with attempted manipulation of these variables by reinforcement, direct intervention, or other means until the resultant change in the patient's behavior permits restoration of more efficient life experiences.

The present approach shares with some psychological theories the assumption that psychotherapy is *not* an effort aimed at removal of intrapsychic conflicts, nor at a change in the personality structure by therapeutic interactions of intense nonverbal nature, (e.g., transference, self-actualization, etc.). We adopt the assumption instead that the job of psychological treatment involves the utilization of a variety of methods to devise a program which controls the patient's environment, his behavior, and the consequences of his behavior in such a way that the presenting problem is resolved. We hypothesize that the essential ingredients of a psychotherapeutic endeavor usually involve two separate stages: (1) a change in the perceptual discriminations of a patient, i.e. in his approach to perceiving, classifying, and organizing sensory events, including perception of himself, and (2) changes in the response patterns which he has established in relation to social objects and to himself over the years (Kanfer, 1961). In addition, the clinician's task may involve direct intervention in the patient's environmental circumstances, modification of the behavior of other people significant in his life, and control of reinforcing stimuli which are available either through self-administration, or by contingency upon the behavior of others. These latter procedures complement the verbal interactions of traditional psychotherapy. They require that the clinician, at the invitation of the patient or his family, participate more fully in planning the total life pattern of the patient outside the clinician's office.

It is necessary to indicate what the theoretical view here presented does *not* espouse in order to understand the differences from other procedures. It does *not* rest upon the assumption that (*a*) insight is a sine qua non of psychotherapy, (*b*) changes in thoughts or ideas inevitably lead to ultimate changes in actions, (*c*) verbal therapeutic sessions serve as replications of and equivalents for actual life situations, and (*d*) a symptom can be removed only by uprooting its cause or origin. In the absence of these assumptions it becomes unnecessary to conceptualize behavior disorder in etiological terms, in psychodynamic terms, or in terms of a specifiable disease process. While psychotherapy by verbal means may be sufficient in some instances, the combination of behavior modification in life situations as well as in verbal interactions serves to extend the armamentarium of the therapist. Therefore verbal psychotherapy is seen as an *adjunct* in the implementation of therapeutic behavior changes in the patient's total life pattern, not as an end in itself, nor as the sole vehicle for increasing psychological effectiveness.

In embracing this view of behavior modification, there is a further commitment to a constant interplay between assessment and therapeutic strategies. An initial diagnostic formulation seeks to ascertain the major variables which can be directly controlled or modified during treatment. During successive treatment stages additional information is collected about the patient's behavior repertoire, his reinforcement history, the pertinent controlling stimuli in his social and physical environment, and the sociological limitations within which both patient and therapist have to operate. Therefore, the initial formulation will constantly be enlarged or changed, resulting either in confirmation of the previous therapeutic strategy or in its change.

A GUIDE TO A FUNCTIONAL ANALYSIS OF INDIVIDUAL BEHAVIOR. In order to help the clinician in the collection and organization of information for a behavioral analysis, we have constructed an outline which aims to provide a working model of the patient's behavior at a relatively low level of abstraction. A series of questions are so organized as to yield immediate implications for treatment. This outline has been found useful both in clinical practice and in teaching. Following is a brief summary of the categories in the outline.

1. Analysis of a Problem Situation:[2] The patient's major complaints are categorized into classes of behavioral excesses and deficits. For each excess or deficit the dimensions of frequency, intensity, duration, appropriateness of form, and stimulus conditions are described. In content, the response classes represent the major targets of the therapeutic intervention. As an additional indispensable feature, the behavioral assets of the patient are listed for utilization in a therapy program.

---

[2] For each patient a detailed analysis is required. For example, a list of behavioral excesses may include specific aggressive acts, hallucinatory behaviors, crying, submission to others in social situations, etc. It is recognized that some behaviors can be viewed as excesses or deficits depending on the vantage point from which the imbalance is observed. For instance, excessive withdrawal and deficient social responsiveness, or excessive social autonomy (nonconformity) and deficient self-inhibitory behavior may be complementary. The particular view taken is of consequence because of its impact on a treatment plan. Regarding certain behavior as excessively aggressive, to be reduced by constraints, clearly differs from regarding the same behavior as a deficit in self-control, subject to increase by training and treatment.

2. Clarification of the Problem Situation: Here we consider the people and circumstances which tend to maintain the problem behaviors, and the consequences of these behaviors to the patient and to others in his environment. Attention is given also to the consequences of changes in these behaviors which may result from psychiatric intervention.

3. Motivational Analysis: Since reinforcing stimuli are idiosyncratic and depend for their effect on a number of unique parameters for each person, a hierarchy of particular persons, events, and objects which serve as reinforcers is established for each patient. Included in this hierarchy are those reinforcing events which facilitate approach behaviors as well as those which, because of their aversiveness, prompt avoidance responses. This information has as its purpose to lay plans for utilization of various reinforcers in prescription of a specific behavior therapy program for the patient, and to permit utilization of appropriate reinforcing behaviors by the therapist and significant others in the patient's social environment.

4. Developmental Analysis: Questions are asked about the patient's biological equipment, his sociocultural experiences, and his characteristic behavioral development. They are phrased in such a way as (a) to evoke descriptions of his habitual behavior at various chronological stages of his life, (b) to relate specific new stimulus conditions to noticeable changes from his habitual behavior, and (c) to relate such altered behavior and other residuals of biological and sociocultural events to the present problem.

5. Analysis of Self-Control: This section examines both the methods and the degree of self-control exercised by the patient in his daily life. Persons, events, or institutions which have successfully reinforced self-controlling behaviors are considered. The deficits or excesses of self-control are evaluated in relation to their importance as therapeutic targets and to their utilization in a therapeutic program.

6. Analysis of Social Relationships: Examination of the patient's social network is carried out to evaluate the significance of people in the patient's environment who have some influence over the problematic behaviors, or who in turn are influenced by the patient for his own satisfactions. These interpersonal relationships are reviewed in order to plan the potential participation of significant others in a treatment program, based on the principles of behavior modification. The review also helps the therapist to consider the range of actual social relationships in which the patient needs to function.

7. Analysis of the Social-Cultural-Physical Environment: In this section we add to the preceding analysis of the patient's behavior as an individual, consideration of the norms in his natural environment. Agreements and discrepancies between the patient's idiosyncratic life patterns and the norms in his environment are defined so that the importance of these factors can be decided in formlating treatment goals which allow as explicitly for the patient's needs as for the pressures of his social environment.

The preceding outline has as its purpose to achieve definition of a patient's problem in a manner which suggests specific treatment operations, or that none are feasible, and specific behaviors as targets for modification. Therefore, the formulation is *action oriented*. It can be used as a guide for the initial collection of information, as a device for organizing available data, or as a design for treatment.

The formulation of a treatment plan follows from this type of analysis because knowledge of the reinforcing conditions suggests the motivational controls at the disposal of the clinician for the modification of the patient's behavior. The analysis of specific problem behaviors also provides a series of goals for psychotherapy or other treatment, and for the evaluation of treatment progress. Knowledge of the patient's biological, social, and cultural conditions should help to determine what resources can be used, and what limitations must be considered in a treatment plan.

The various categories attempt to call attention to important variables affecting the patient's *current* behavior. Therefore, they aim to elicit descriptions of low-level abstraction. Answers to these specific questions are best phrased by describing classes of events reported by the patient, observed by others, or by critical incidents described by an informant. The analysis does not exclude description of the patient's habitual verbal-symbolic behaviors. However, in using verbal behaviors as the basis for this analysis, one should be cautious not to "explain" verbal processes in terms of postulated internal mechanisms without adequate supportive evidence, nor should inference be made about nonobserved processes or events without corroborative evidence. The analysis includes many items which are not known or not applicable for a given patient. Lack of information on some items does not necessarily indicate incompleteness of the analysis. These lacks must be noted nevertheless because they often contribute to the better understanding of what the patient needs to learn to become an autonomous person. Just as important is an inventory of his existing socially effective behavioral repertoire which can be put in the service of any treatment procedure.

This analysis is consistent with our earlier formulations of the principles of comprehensive medicine (Guze, Matarazzo, & Saslow, 1953; Saslow, 1952) which emphasized the joint operation of biological, social, and psychological factors in psychiatric disorders. The language and orientation of the proposed approach are rooted in contemporary learning theory. The conceptual framework is consonant with the view that the course of psychiatric disorders can be modified by systematic application of scientific principles from the fields of psychology and medicine to the patient's habitual mode of living.

This approach is not a substitute for assignment of the patient to traditional diagnostic categories. Such labeling may be desirable for statistical, administrative, or research purposes. But the current analysis is intended to replace other diagnostic formulations purporting to serve as a basis for making decisions about specific therapeutic interventions.

METHODS OF DATA COLLECTION
FOR A FUNCTIONAL ANALYSIS

Traditional diagnostic approaches have utilized as the main sources of information the patient's verbal report, his nonverbal behavior during an interview, and his performance on psychological tests. These observations are sufficient if one regards behavior problems only as a property of the patient's particular pattern of associations or his personality structure. A mental disorder would be expected to reveal itself by stylistic characteristics in the patient's behavior repertoire. However, if one views behavior disorders as sets of response patterns which are learned under particular conditions and maintained by definable environmental and internal stimuli, an assessment of the patient's behavior output is insufficient unless it also describes the conditions under which it occurs. This view requires an expansion of the clinician's sources of observations to include the stimulation fields in which the patient lives, and the variations of patient behavior as a function of exposure to these various stimulational variables. Therefore, the resourceful clinician need not limit himself to test findings, interview observations in the clinician's office, or referral histories alone in the formulation of the specific case. Nor need he regard himself as hopelessly handicapped when the patient has little observational or communicative skill in verbally reconstructing his life experiences for the clinician. Regardless of the patient's communicative skills the data must consist of a description of the patient's behavior *in relationship* to varying environmental conditions.

A behavioral analysis excludes no data relating to a patient's past or present experiences as irrelevant. However, the relative merit of any information (as, e.g., growing up in a broken home or having had homosexual experiences) lies in its relation to the independent variables which can be identified as controlling the current problematic behavior. The observation that a patient has hallucinated on occasions may be important only if it has bearing on his present problem. If looked upon in isolation, a report about hallucinations may be misleading, resulting in emphasis on classification rather than treatment.

In the *psychiatric interview* a behavioral-analytic approach opposes acceptance of the content of the verbal self-report as equivalent to actual events or experiences. However, verbal reports provide information concerning the patient's verbal construction of his environment and of his person, his recall of past experiences, and his fantasies about them. While these self-descriptions do not represent data about events which actually occur internally, they do represent current behaviors of the patient and indicate the verbal chains and repertoires which the patient has built up. Therefore, the verbal behavior may be useful for description of a patient's thinking processes. To make the most of such an approach, variations on traditional interview procedures may be obtained by such techniques as role playing, discussion, and interpretation of current life events, or controlled free association. Since there is little experimental evidence of specific relationships between the patient's verbal statements and his nonverbal behavioral acts, the verbal report alone remains insufficient for a complete analysis and for prediction of his daily behavior. Further, it is well known that a person responds to environmental conditions and to internal cues which he cannot describe adequately. Therefore, any verbal report may miss or mask the most important aspects of a behavioral analysis, i.e., the description of the relationship between antecedent conditions and subsequent behavior.

In addition to the use of the clinician's own person as a controlled stimulus object in interview situations, *observations of interaction with significant others* can be used for the analysis of variations in frequency of various behaviors as a function of the person with whom the patient interacts. For example, use of prescribed standard roles for nurses and attendants, utilization of members of the patient's family or his friends, may be made to obtain data relevant to the patient's habitual interpersonal response pattern. Such observations are especially useful if in a later interview the patient is asked to describe and discuss the observed sessions. Confrontations with tape recordings for comparisons between the patient's report and the actual session as witnessed by the observer may provide information about the patient's perception of himself and others as well as his habitual behavior toward peers, authority figures, and other significant people in his life.

Except in working with children or family units, insufficient use has been made of material obtained from *other informants* in interviews about the patient. These reports can aid the observer to recognize behavioral domains in which the patient's report deviates from or agrees with the descriptions provided by others. Such information is also useful for contrasting the patient's reports about his presumptive effects on another person with the stated effects by that person. If a patient's interpersonal problems extend to areas in which social contacts are not clearly defined, contributions by informants other than the patient are essential.

It must be noted that verbal reports by other informants may be no more congruent with actual events than the patient's own reports and need to be equally related to the informant's own credibility. If such crucial figures as parents, spouses, employers can be so interviewed, they also provide the clinician with some information about those people with whom the patient must interact repeatedly and with whom interpersonal problems may have developed.

Some observation of the patient's daily *work behavior* represents an excellent source of information, if it can be made available. Observation of the patient by the clinician or his staff may be preferable to descriptions by peers or supervisors. Work observations are especially important for patients whose complaints include difficulties in their daily work activity or who describe work situations as contributing factors to their problem. While freer use of this technique may be hampered by cultural attitudes toward psychiatric treatment in the marginally adjusted, such observations may be freely accessible in hospital situations or in sheltered work situations. With use of behavior rating scales or other simple measurement devices, brief samples of patient behaviors in work situations can be obtained by minimally trained observers.

The patient himself may be asked to provide samples of his own behavior by using tape recorders for the recording of segments of interactions in his family, at work, or in other situations during his everyday life. A television monitoring system for the patient's behavior is an excellent technique from a theoretical viewpoint but it is extremely cumbersome and expensive. Use of recordings for diagnostic and therapeutic purposes has been reported by some investigators (Bach, 1963; Cameron, 1964; Slack, 1960). Playback of the recordings and a recording of the patient's reactions to the playback can be used further in interviews to clarify the patient's behavior toward others and his reaction to himself as a social stimulus.

Psychological tests represent problems to be solved under specified interactional conditions. Between the highly standardized intelligence tests and the unstructured and ambiguous projective tests lies a dimension of structure along which more and more responsibility for providing appropriate responses falls on the patient. By comparison with interview procedures, most psychological tests provide a relatively greater standardization of stimulus conditions. But, in addition to the specific answers given on intelligence tests or on projective tests these tests also provide a behavioral sample of the patient's reaction to a problem situation in a relatively stressful interpersonal setting. Therefore, psychological tests can provide not only quantitative scores but they can also be treated as a miniature life experience, yielding information about the patient's interpersonal behavior and variations in his behavior as a function of the nature of the stimulus conditions.

In this section we have mentioned only some of the numerous life situations which can be evaluated in order to provide information about the patient. Criteria for their use lies in economy, accessibility to the clinician, and relevance to the patient's problem. While it is more convenient to gather data from a patient in an office, it may be necessary for the clinician to have first-hand information about the actual conditions under which the patient lives and works. Such familiarity may be obtained either by utilization of informants or by the clinician's entry into the home, the job situation, or the social environment in which the patient lives. Under all these conditions the clinician is effective only if it is possible for him to maintain a nonparticipating, objective, and observational role with no untoward consequences for the patient or the treatment relationship.

The methods of data collecting for a functional analysis described here differ from traditional psychiatric approaches only in that they require inclusion of the physical and social stimulus field in which the patient actually operates. Only a full appraisal of the patient's living and working conditions and his way of life allow a description of the actual problems which the patient faces and the specification of steps to be taken for altering the problematic situation.

SUMMARY

Current psychiatric classification falls short of providing a satisfactory basis for the understanding and treatment of maladaptive behavior. Diagnostic schemas now in use are based on etiology, symptom description, or prognosis. While each of these approaches has a limited utility, no unified schema is available which permits prediction of response to treatment or future course of the disorder from the assignment of the patient to a specific category.

This paper suggests a behavior-analytic approach which is based on contemporary learning theory, as an alternative to assignment of the patient to a conventional diagnostic category. It includes the summary of an outline which can serve as a guide for the collection of information and formulation of the problem, including the biological, social, and behavioral conditions which are determining the patient's behavior. The outline aims toward integration of information about a patient for formulation of an action plan which would modify the patient's problematic behavior. Emphasis is given to the particular variables affecting the *individual* patient rather than determination of the similarity of the patient's history or his symptoms to known pathological groups.

The last section of the paper deals with methods useful for collection of information necessary to complete such a behavior analysis.

REFERENCES

Ash, P.: Reliability of Psychiatric Diagnosis, *J Abnorm Soc Psychol* 44:272–277, 1949.
Bach, G.: In Alexander, S.: Fight Promoter for Battle of Sexes, *Life* 54:102–108 (May 17) 1963.

Bandura, A.: Psychotherapy as Learning Process, *Psychol Bull* 58:143–159, 1961.

Barron, F.: Ego-Strength Scale Which Predicts Response to Psychotherapy, *J Consult Psychol* 17:235–241, 1953.

Cameron, D. E., et al: Automation of Psychotherapy, *Compr Psychiat* 5:1–14, 1964.

Ferster, C. R.: Classification of Behavioral Pathology in Ullmann, L. P. and Krasner, L. (eds.): *Behavior Modification Research*, New York: Holt, Rinehart and Winston, 1965.

Freedman, D. A.: Various Etiologies of Schizophrenic Syndrome, *Dis Nerv Syst* 19:1–6. 1958.

Fulkerson, S. E., and Barry, J. R.: Methodology and Research on Prognostic Use of Psychological Tests, *Psychol Bull* 58:177–204, 1961.

Guze, S. B.; Matarazzo, J. D.; and Saslow, G.: Formulation of Principles of Comprehensive Medicine with Special Reference to Learning Theory, *J Clin Psychol* 9:127–136, 1953.

Jackson, D. D. A.: *Etiology of Schizophrenia*, New York: Basic Books, 1960.

Kanfer, F. H.: Comments on Learning in Psychotherapy, *Psychol Rep* 9:681–699, 1961.

Katz, M. M.; Cole, J. O.; and Lowery, H. A.: Nonspecificity of Diagnosis of Paranoid Schizophrenia, *Arch Gen Psychiat* 11:197–202, 1964.

Krasner, L.: Therapist as Social Reinforcement Machine, in Strupp, H., and Luborsky, L. (eds.): *Research in Psychotherapy*, Washington, D.C.: American Psychological Association, 1962.

Ledley, R. S., and Lusted, L. B.: Reasoning Foundations of Medical Diagnosis, *Science* 130:9–21, 1959.

Lorr, M.; Klett, C. J.; and McNair, D. M.: *Syndromes of Psychosis,* New York: Macmillan, 1963.

Meehl, P. E.: Schizotaxia, Schizotypy, Schizophrenia, *Amer Psychol* 17:827–838, 1962.

New York Heart Association: *Nomenclature and Criteria for Diagnosis of Diseases of the Heart and Blood Vessels*, New York: New York Heart Association, 1953.

Noyes, A. P., and Kolb, L. C.: *Modern Clinical Psychiatry,* Philadelphia: Saunders, 1963.

Opler, M. K.: Schizophrenia and Culture, *Sci Amer* 197:103–112, 1957.

Opler, M. K.: Need for New Diagnostic Categories in Psychiatry, *J Nat Med Assoc* 55:133–137, 1963.

Rotter, J. B.: *Social Learning and Clinical Psychology*, Englewood Cliffs, N.J.: Prentice-Hall, 1954.

Saslow, G.: On Concept of Comprehensive Medicine, *Bull Menninger Clin* 16:57–65, 1952.

Scheflen, A. E.: Analysis of Thought Model Which Persists in Psychiatry, *Psychosom Med* 20:235–241, 1958.

Slack, C. W.: Experimenter-Subject Psychotherapy—A New Method of Introducing Intensive Office Treatment for Unreachable Cases, *Ment Hyg* 44:238–256, 1960.

Szasz, T. S.: Myth of Mental Illness, *Amer Psychol* 15:113–118, 1960.

Windle, C.: Psychological Tests in Psychopathological Prognosis, *Psychol Bull* 49:451–482, 1952.

Wolpe, J.: *Psychotherapy in Reciprocal Inhibition*, Stanford, Calif.: Stanford University Press, 1958.

Zigler, E., and Phillips, L.: Psychiatric Diagnosis: Critique, *J Abnorm Soc Psychol* 63:607–618, 1961.

10 | Phenomenological Theories

10.1 | DYNAMICS OF PERSONALITY ORGANIZATION*

Abraham H. Maslow

THE GENERAL-DYNAMIC POINT OF VIEW

The general point of view to which one must come in the study of personality and which is being propounded in this paper is holistic rather than atomistic, functional rather than taxonomic, dynamic rather than static, dynamic rather than causal, purposive rather than simple-mechanical. In spite of the fact that these opposing factors are ordinarily looked upon as a series of separable dichotomies they are not so considered by the writer. For him they tend strongly to coalesce into two unitary but contrasting world views. This seems to be true for some other writers as well, for the one who thinks dynamically finds it easier and more natural to think also holistically rather than atomistically, purposively rather than mechanically, and so on. This point of view we shall call the general-dynamic point of view.

Opposed to this interpretation is found an organized and unitary viewpoint which is simultaneously atomistic, taxonomic, static, causal and simple-mechanical. The atomistic thinker finds it much more natural to think also statically rather than dynamically, mechanically rather than purposively, etc. This general point of view I shall call arbitrarily general-atomistic. I have no doubt that it is possible to demonstrate not only that these partial views *tend* to go together but that they *must* logically go together.

In the field of psychology this general-atomistic point of view received its most consistent and detailed expression in the writings of the behaviorists. The opposite outlook, the general-dynamic, has been put forward most eloquently in the writings of the Gestalt psychologists, and, in a less systematic way, by Alfred Adler. It is not my inten-

* SOURCE: Pp. 519–524, abridged. In Maslow, A. H. Dynamics of personality organization. *Psychological Review*, 1943, *50*, 514–539. Copyright 1943 by the American Psychological Association and reprinted by permission.

tion here to attempt a detailed critique of behaviorism. I wish only to add a few remarks on the causality concept, an aspect of the general-dynamic theory which seems to me to be centrally important and which psychological writers have slurred or neglected altogether.

This concept lies at the very heart of the general-atomistic point of view and is a natural, even necessary, consequence of it. If one sees the world as a collection of intrinsically independent entities, there remains to be solved the obvious phenomenological fact that these entities nevertheless have to do with each other. The first attempt to solve this problem gives rise to the notion of the simple billiard ball kind of causality in which one separate thing does something to another separate thing, but in which the entities involved continue to retain their essential identity. Such a view is easy enough to maintain and actually seemed absolute so long as the old physics gave us our world theory. But the advance in physics and chemistry made modification necessary. For instance, the usually more sophisticated phrasing today is in terms of "multiple causation." It is recognized that the interrelationships holding within the world are too complex, too intricate to describe in the same way as we do the clicking of billiard balls on a table. But the answer is most often simply a complexifying of the original notion rather than a basic restructuring of it. Instead of one cause, there are many, but they are conceived to act in the same way—separately and independent of each other. The billiard ball is now hit not by one other ball, but by ten simultaneously, and we simply have to use a somewhat more complicated arithmetic to understand what happens. The essential procedures are still addition of separate entities into an "and-sum" to use Wertheimer's phrase. No change is felt to be necessary in the fundamental envisagement of the complex happenings. No matter how complex the phenomenon may be, there is no essentially new thing happening. In this way the notion of cause is stretched more and more to fit new needs until sometimes it seems to have no relation but a historical one to the old concept. Actually, however, different though they may seem, they remain in essence the same since they continue to reflect the same world view.

It is particularly with personality data that the causality theory falls down most completely. We have already been able to demonstrate that within any personality syndrome, relationship other than causal exists. That is to say, if we had to use causal vocabulary we should have to say that every part of the syndrome is both a cause and an effect of every other part as well as of any grouping of these other parts, and furthermore we should have to say that each part is both a cause and effect of the whole of which it is a part. Such an absurd conclusion is the only one which is possible if we use only the causality concept. Even if we attempt to meet the situation by introducing the new concept of a "circular or reversible causality," we could not completely describe the relations within the syndrome nor the relations of the part to the whole.

Nor is this the only shortcoming of causality vocabulary with which we must deal. There is also the difficult problem of the description of the interaction or interrelation between a syndrome as a whole and all the forces bearing upon it from the "outside." The syndrome of self-esteem, for instance, has been shown to tend to change as a whole.

That is to say, effective external influences do not affect single parts of the syndrome, but rather influence the syndrome as a whole. If we try to change Johnny's stammering and address ourselves specifically to this and only this, the chances are very great that we shall find either (1) that we have changed nothing at all, or else (2) that we have changed not Johnny's stammering alone but rather Johnny's self-esteem in general, or even Johnny-as-a-whole-individual. External influences usually tend to change the whole human being, not just a bit or a part of him.

There are yet other peculiarities in this situation which defy description by the ordinary causal vocabulary. Thus there is a phenomenon which is very difficult to describe. The nearest I can come to expressing it is to say that it is as if the organism (or any other syndrome) "swallows the cause and creates the effect." When an effective sitmulus, a traumatic experience let us say, impinges upon the personality, there are certain consequences of this experience. But these consequences practically never bear a one to one or a straight line relationship to the original "causal" experience. What actually happens is that the experience, if it is effective, changes the whole personality. This personality, now different from what it was before, expresses itself differently and behaves differently than before. Let us suppose that this effect would be that his facial twitch gets a little worse. Has this 10 per cent increase of the tic been "caused" by the traumatic situation? If we say it has, then it can be shown that we must, if we wish to be consistent, say that every single effective stimulus that has ever impinged on the organism has also caused this 10 per cent increase in the facial tic. For every experience is taken into the organism, in the same sense that food is digested and by intussusception becomes the organism itself. Is the sandwich I ate an hour ago the "cause" of the words I now set down, or was it the coffee I drank, or what I ate yesterday, or was it the lesson in writing I got years ago, or the book I read a week ago?

It would certainly seem obvious that any important expression, such as writing a paper in which one is deeply interested, is not "caused" by anything in particular, but is an expression of, or a creation of the whole personality which in turn is an "effect" of almost everything that has ever happened to it. It should seem just as natural for the psychologist to think of the stimulus or cause as being taken in by the personality by means of a readjustment, as to think of it as hitting the organism and pushing it. The net result here would be, not a cause and effect remaining separate, but simply a new personality (new by however little).

Still another way of demonstrating the inadequacy for psychology of conventional cause-effect notions is to show that the organism is not a passive agent to which causes or stimuli *do* something, but that it is an active agent entering into a complex mutual relationship with the cause, doing something to it as well. For readers of the psychoanalytic literature this is a commonplace, and it is necessary only to remind the reader of the facts that we can be blind to stimuli, we can distort them, reconstruct or reshape them if they are distorted. We can seek them out or avoid them. We can sift them out and select from among them. Or finally, we can even create them if need be.

The causality concept rests on the assumption of an atomistic world with entities which remain discrete, even though they interact. The personality, however, is not separate from its expressions, effects, or the stimuli impinging upon it (causes) and so at least for psychological data it must be replaced by another conception.[1] This conception—general-dynamics—cannot be stated simply, since it involves fundamental reorganization of viewpoint, but must be expounded step by step.

---

[1] I am aware that more sophisticated scientists and philosophers have now replaced the causality notion with an interpretation in terms of "functional" relationships, *i.e.*, A is a function of B *or* if A, then B. By so doing, it seems to me that they have given up the nuclear aspects of the concept of cause, that is to say, of necessity, and of acting upon. Simple linear coefficients of correlations are examples of functional statements which are however often used as *contrasting* with cause-effect relationships. It serves no purpose to retain the word "cause" if it means the very opposite of what it used to mean. In any case, we are then left with the problems of necessary or intrinsic relationship, and of the ways in which change comes about. These problems must be solved, not abandoned or denied.

10.2 | TOWARD A MODERN APPROACH TO VALUES: THE VALUING PROCESS IN THE MATURE PERSON*

Carl R. Rogers

There is a great deal of concern today with the problem of values. Youth, in almost every country, is deeply uncertain of its value orientation; the values associated with various religions have lost much of their influence; sophisticated individuals in every culture seem unsure and troubled as to the goals they hold in esteem. The reasons are not far to seek. The world culture, in all its aspects, seems increasingly scientific and relativistic, and the rigid, absolute views on values which come to us from the past appear anachronistic. Even more important, perhaps, is the fact that the modern individual is assailed from every angle by divergent and contradictory value claims. It is no longer possible, as it was in the not too distant historical past, to settle comfortably into the value system of one's forebears or one's community and live out one's life without ever examining the nature and the assumptions of that system.

* SOURCE: Rogers, C. R. Toward a modern approach to values: The valuing process in the mature person. *Journal of Abnormal and Social Psychology*, 1964, 68, 160–167. Copyright 1964 by the American Psychological Association and reprinted by permission.

In this situation it is not surprising that value orientations from the past appear to be in a state of disintegration or collapse. Men question whether there are, or can be, any universal values. It is often felt that we may have lost, in our modern world, all possibility of any general or cross-cultural basis for values. One natural result of this uncertainty and confusion is that there is an increasing concern about, interest in, and a searching for, a sound or meaningful value approach which can hold its own in today's world.

I share this general concern. As with other issues the general problem faced by the culture is painfully and specifically evident in the cultural microcosm which is called the therapeutic relationship, which is my sphere of experience.

As a consequence of this experience I should like to attempt a modest theoretical approach to this whole problem. I have observed changes in the approach to values as the individual grows from infancy to adulthood. I observe further changes when, if he is fortunate, he continues to grow toward true psychological maturity. Many of these observations grow out of my experience as therapist, where I have had the mind stretching opportunity of seeing the ways in which individuals move toward a richer life. From these observations I believe I see some directional threads emerging which might offer a new concept of the valuing process, more tenable in the modern world. I have made a beginning by presenting some of these ideas partially in previous writings (Rogers, 1951, 1959); I would like now to voice them more clearly and more fully.

SOME DEFINITIONS

Charles Morris (1956, pp. 9–12) has made some useful distinctions in regard to values. There are "operative values," which are the behaviors of organisms in which they show preference for one object or objective rather than another. The lowly earthworm, selecting the smooth arm of a Y maze rather than the arm which is paved with sandpaper, is giving an indication of an operative value.

There are also "conceived values," the preference of an individual for a symbolized object. "Honesty is the best policy" is such a conceived value.

There is also the term "objective value," to refer to what is objectively preferable, whether or not it is sensed or conceived of as desirable. I will be concerned primarily with operative or conceptualized values.

INFANT'S WAY OF VALUING

Let me first speak about the infant. The living human being has, at the outset, a clear approach to values. We can infer from studying his behavior that he prefers those experiences which maintain, enhance, or actualize his organism, and rejects those which do not serve this end. Watch him for a bit:

> Hunger is negatively valued. His expression of this often comes through loud and clear.
> Food is positively valued. But when he is satisfied, food is negatively valued, and the same milk he responded to so eagerly is now spit out, or the breast which

seemed so satisfying is now rejected as he turns his head away from the nipple with an amusing facial expression of disgust and revulsion.

He values security, and the holding and caressing which seem to communicate security.

He values new experience for its own sake, and we observe this in his obvious pleasure in discovering his toes, in his searching movements, in his endless curiosity.

He shows a clear negative valuing of pain, bitter tastes, sudden loud sounds.

All of this is commonplace, but let us look at these facts in terms of what they tell us about the infant's approach to values. It is first of all a flexible, changing, valuing *process*, not a fixed system. He likes food and dislikes the same food. He values security and rest, and rejects it for new experience. What is going on seems best described as an organismic valuing process, in which each element, each moment of what he is experiencing is somehow weighed, and selected or rejected, depending on whether, at that moment, it tends to actualize the organism or not. This complicated weighing of experience is clearly an organismic, not a conscious or symbolic function. These are operative, not conceived values. But this process can nonetheless deal with complex value problems. I would remind you of the experiment in which young infants had spread in front of them a score or more of dishes of natural (that is, unflavored) foods. Over a period of time they clearly tended to value the foods which enhanced their own survival, growth, and development. If for a time a child gorged himself on starches, this would soon be balanced by a protein "binge." If at times he chose a diet deficient in some vitamin, he would later seek out foods rich in this very vitamin. The physiological wisdom of his body guided his behavioral movements, resulting in what we might think of as objectively sound value choices.

Another aspect of the infant's approach to values is that the source or locus of the evaluating process is clearly within himself. Unlike many of us, he *knows* what he likes and dislikes, and the origin of these value choices lies strictly within himself. He is the center of the valuing process, the evidence for his choices being supplied by his own senses. He is not at this point influenced by what his parents think he should prefer, or by what the church says, or by the opinion of the latest "expert" in the field, or by the persuasive talents of an advertising firm. It is from within his own experiencing that his organism is saying in nonverbal terms, "This is good for me." "That is bad for me." "I like this." "I strongly dislike that." He would laugh at our concern over values, if he could understand it.

CHANGE IN VALUING PROCESS

What happens to this efficient, soundly based valuing process? By what sequence of events do we exchange it for the more rigid, uncertain, inefficient approach to values which characterizes most of us as adults? Let me try to state briefly one of the major ways in which I think this happens.

The infant needs love, wants it, tends to behave in ways which will bring a repetition of this wanted experience. But this brings complications. He pulls baby sister's hair, and finds it satisfying to hear her wails and protests. He then hears that he is "a naughty, bad boy," and this may be reinforced by a slap on the hand. He is cut off from affection. As this experience is repeated, and many, many others like it, he gradually learns that what "feels good" is often "bad" in the eyes of significant others. Then the next step occurs, in which he comes to take the same attitude toward himself which these others have taken. Now, as he pulls his sister's hair, he solemnly intones, "Bad, bad boy." He is introjecting the value judgment of another, taking it in as his own. To that degree he loses touch with his own organismic valuing process. He has deserted the wisdom of his organism, giving up the locus of evaluation, and is trying to behave in terms of values set by another, in order to hold love.

Or take another example at an older level. A boy senses, though perhaps not consciously, that he is more loved and prized by his parents when he thinks of being a doctor than when he thinks of being an artist. Gradually he introjects the values attached to being a doctor. He comes to want, above all, to be a doctor. Then in college he is baffled by the fact that he repeatedly fails in chemistry, which is absolutely necessary to becoming a physician, in spite of the fact that the guidance counselor assures him he has the ability to pass the course. Only in counseling interviews does he begin to realize how completely he has lost touch with his organismic reactions, how out of touch he is with his own valuing process.

Perhaps these illustrations will indicate that in an attempt to gain or hold love, approval, esteem, the individual relinquishes the locus of evaluation which was his in infancy, and places it in others. He learns to have a basic *dis*trust for his own experiencing as a guide to his behavior. He learns from others a large number of conceived values, and adopts them as his own, even though they may be widely discrepant from what he is experiencing.

SOME INTROJECTED PATTERNS

It is in this fashion, I believe, that most of us accumulate the introjected value patterns by which we live. In the fantastically complex culture of today, the patterns we introject as desirable or undesirable come from a variety of sources and are often highly contradictory. Let me list a few of the introjections which are commonly held.

Sexual desires and behaviors are mostly bad. The sources of this construct are many—parents, church, teachers.

Disobedience is bad. Here parents and teachers combine with the military to emphasize this concept. To obey is good. To obey without question is even better.

Making money is the highest good. The sources of this conceived value are too numerous to mention.

Learning an accumulation of scholarly facts is highly desirable. Education is the source.

Communism is utterly bad. Here the government is a major source.

To love thy neighbor is the highest good. This concept comes from the church, perhaps from the parents.

Cooperation and teamwork are preferable to acting alone. Here companions are an important source.

Cheating is clever and desirable. The peer group again is the origin.

Coca-Colas, chewing gum, electric refrigerators, and automobiles are all utterly desirable. From Jamaica to Japan, from Copenhagen to Kowloon, the "Coca-Cola culture" has come to be regarded as the acme of desirability.

This is a small and diversified sample of the myriads of conceived values which individuals often introject, and hold as their own, without ever having considered their inner organismic reactions to these patterns and objects.

COMMON CHARACTERISTICS OF ADULT VALUING

I believe it will be clear from the foregoing that the usual adult—I feel I am speaking for most of us—has an approach to values which has these characteristics:

The majority of his values are introjected from other individuals or groups significant to him, but are regarded by him as his own.

The source or locus of evaluation on most matters lies outside of himself.

The criterion by which his values are set is the degree to which they will cause him to be loved, accepted, or esteemed.

These conceived preferences are either not related at all, or not clearly related, to his own process of experiencing.

Often there is a wide and unrecognized discrepancy between the evidence supplied by his own experience, and these conceived values.

Because these conceptions are not open to testing in experience, he must hold them in a rigid and unchanging fashion. The alternative would be a collapse of his values. Hence his values are "right."

Because they are untestable, there is no ready way of solving contradictions. If he has taken in from the community the conception that money is the *summum bonum* and from the church the conception that love of one's neighbor is the highest value, he has no way of discovering which has more value for *him*. Hence a common aspect of modern life is living with absolutely contradictory values. We calmly discuss the possibility of dropping a hydrogen bomb on Russia, but find tears in our eyes when we see headlines about the suffering of one small child.

Because he has relinquished the locus of evaluation to others, and has lost touch with his own valuing process, he feels profoundly insecure and easily threatened in his values. If some of these concepts were destroyed, what would take their place? This threatening possibility makes him hold his value conceptions more rigidly or more confusedly, or both.

FUNDAMENTAL DISCREPANCY

I believe that this picture of the individual, with values mostly introjected, held as fixed concepts, rarely examined or tested, is the picture of most of us. By taking over the conceptions of others as our own, we lose contact with the potential wisdom of our own functioning, and lose confidence in ourselves. Since these value constructs are often sharply at variance with what is going on in our own experiencing, we have in a very basic way divorced ourselves from ourselves, and this accounts for much of modern strain and insecurity. This fundamental discrepancy between the individual's concept and what he is actually experiencing, between the intellectual structure of his values and the valuing process going on unrecognized within—this is a part of the fundamental estrangement of modern man from himself.

RESTORING CONTACT WITH EXPERIENCE

Some individuals are fortunate in going beyond the picture I have just given, developing further in the direction of psychological maturity. We see this happen in psychotherapy where we endeavor to provide a climate favorable to the growth of the person. We also see it happen in life, whenever life provides a therapeutic climate for the individual. Let me concentrate on this further maturing of a value approach as I have seen it in therapy.

As the client senses and realizes that he is prized as a person[1] he can slowly begin to value the different aspects of himself. Most importantly, he can begin, with much difficulty at first, to sense and to feel what is going on within him, what he is feeling, what he is experiencing, how he is reacting. He uses his experiencing as a direct referent to which he can turn in forming accurate conceptualizations and as a guide to his beahvior. Gendlin (1961, 1962) has elaborated the way in which this occurs. As his experiencing becomes more and more open to him, as he is able to live more freely in the process of his feelings, then significant changes begin to occur in his approach to values. It begins to assume many of the characteristics it had in infancy.

INTROJECTED VALUES IN RELATION TO EXPERIENCING

Perhaps I can indicate this by reviewing a few of the brief examples of introjected values which I have given, and suggesting what happens to them as the individual comes closer to what is going on within him.

The individual in therapy looks back and realizes, "But I *enjoyed* pulling my sister's hair—and that doesn't make me a bad person."

The student failing chemistry realizes, as he gets close to his own experiencing, "I don't like chemistry; I don't value being a doctor, even though my parents do; and I am not a failure for having these feelings."

The adult recognizes that sexual desires and behavior may be richly satisfying and permanently enriching in their consequences, or shallow and temporary and less than satisfying. He goes by his own experiencing, which does not always coincide with social norms.

---

[1] The therapeutic relationship is not devoid of values. When it is most effective it is, I believe, marked by one primary value, namely, that this person (the client) has *worth*.

He recognizes freely that this communist book or person expresses attitudes and goals which he shares as well as ideas and values which he does not share.

He realizes that at times he experiences cooperation as meaningful and valuable to him, and that at other times he wishes to be alone and act alone.

VALUING IN THE MATURE PERSON

The valuing process which seems to develop in this more mature person is in some ways very much like that in the infant, and in some ways quite different. It is fluid, flexible, based on this particular moment, and the degree to which this moment is experienced as enhancing and actualizing. Values are not held rigidly, but are continually changing. The painting which last year seemed meaningful now appears uninteresting, the way of working with individuals which was formerly experienced as good now seems inadequate, the belief which then seemed true is now experienced as only partly true, or perhaps false.

Another characteristic of the way this person values experience is that it is highly differentiated, or as the semanticists would say, extensional. The examples in the preceding section indicate that what were previously rather solid monolithic introjected values now become differentiated, tied to a particular time and experience.

Another characteristic of the mature individual's approach is that the locus of evaluation is again established firmly within the person. It is his own experience which provides the value information or feedback. This does not mean that he is not open to all the evidence he can obtain from other sources. But it means that this is taken for what it is—outside evidence—and is not as significant as his own reactions. Thus he may be told by a friend that a new book is very disappointing. He reads two unfavorable reviews of the book. Thus his tentative hypothesis is that he will not value the book. Yet if he reads the book his valuing will be based upon the reactions it stirs in *him*, not on what he has been told by others.

There is also involved in this valuing process a letting oneself down into the immediacy of what one is experiencing, endeavoring to sense and to clarify all its complex meanings. I think of a client who, toward the close of therapy, when puzzled about an issue, would put his head in his hands and say, "Now what *is* it that I'm feeling? I want to get next to it. I want to learn what it is." Then he would wait, quietly and patiently, trying to listen to himself, until he could discern the exact flavor of the feelings he was experiencing. He, like others, was trying to get close to himself.

In getting close to what is going on within himself, the process is much more complex than it is in the infant. In the mature person it has much more scope and sweep. For there is involved in the present moment of experiencing the memory traces of all the relevant learnings from the past. This moment has not only its immediate sensory impact, but it has meaning growing out of similar experiences in the past (Gendlin, 1962). It has both the new and the old in it. So when I experience a painting or a person, my experiencing contains within it the learnings I have accumulated from past meetings with paintings or persons, as well as the new impact of this particular encounter. Likewise the moment of experiencing contains, for the mature adult, hypotheses about consequences. "It is not pleasant to express forthrightly my negative feelings to this person, but past experience indicates that in a continuing relationship it will be helpful in the long run." Past and future are both in this moment and enter into the valuing.

I find that in the person I am speaking of (and here again we see a similarity to the infant), the criterion of the valuing process is the degree to which the object of the experience actualizes the individual himself. Does it make him a richer, more complete, more fully developed person? This may sound as though it were a selfish or unsocial criterion, but it does not prove to be so, since deep and helpful relationships with others are experienced as actualizing.

Like the infant, too, the psychologically mature adult trusts and uses the wisdom of his organism, with the difference that he is able to do so knowingly. He realizes that if he can trust all of himself, his feelings and his intuitions may be wiser than his mind, that as a total person he can be more sensitive and accurate than his thoughts alone. Hence he is not afraid to say, "I feel that this experience [or this thing, or this direction] is good. Later I will probably know *why* I feel it is good." He trusts the totality of himself, having moved toward becoming what Lancelot Whyte (1950) regards as "the unitary man."

It should be evident from what I have been saying that this valuing process in the mature individual is not an easy or simple thing. The process is complex, the choices often very perplexing and difficult, and there is no guarantee that the choice which is made will in fact prove to be self-actualizing. But because whatever evidence exists is available to the individual, and because he is open to his experiencing, errors are correctable. If this chosen course of action is not self-enhancing this will be sensed and he can make an adjustment or revision. He thrives on a maximum feedback interchange, and thus, like the gyroscopic compass on a ship, can continually correct his course toward his true goal of self-fulfillment.

SOME PROPOSITIONS REGARDING THE VALUING PROCESS

Let me sharpen the meaning of what I have been saying by stating two propositions which contain the essential elements of this viewpoint. While it may not be possible to devise empirical tests of each proposition in its entirety, yet each is to some degree capable of being tested through the methods of psychological science. I would also state that though the following propositions are stated firmly in order to give them clarity, I am actually advancing them as decidedly tentative hypotheses.

Hypothesis I. There is an organismic base for an organized valuing process within the human individual.

It is hypothesized that this base is something the human being shares with the rest of the animate world. It is part of the functioning life process of any healthy organism. It is the capacity for receiving feedback information which enables the organism continually to adjust its behavior and reactions so as to achieve the maximum possible self-enchancement.

Hypothesis II. This valuing process in the human being is effective in achieving self-enhancement to the degree that the individual is open to the experiencing which is going on within himself.

I have tried to give two examples of individuals who are close to their own experiencing: the tiny infant who has not yet learned to deny in his awareness the processes going on within; and the psychologically mature person who has relearned the advantages of this open state.

There is a corollary to this second proposition which might be put in the following terms. One way of assisting the individual to move toward openness to experience is through a relationship in which he is prized as a separate person, in which the experiencing going on within him is empathically understood and valued, and in which he is given the freedom to experience his own feelings and those of others without being threatened in doing so.

This corollary obviously grows out of therapeutic experience. It is a brief statement of the essential qualities in the therapeutic relationship. There are already some empirical studies, of which the one by Barrett-Lennard (1962) is a good example, which give support to such a statement.

PROPOSITIONS REGARDING THE OUTCOMES OF THE VALUING PROCESS

I come now to the nub of any theory of values or valuing. What are its consequences? I should like to move into this new ground by stating bluntly two propositions as to the qualities of behavior which emerge from this valuing process. I shall then give some of the evidence from my experience as a therapist in support of these propositions.

Hypothesis III. In persons who are moving toward greater openness to their experiencing, there is an organismic commonality of value directions.

Hypothesis IV. These common value directions are of such kinds as to enhance the development of the individual himself, of others in his community, and to make for the survival and evolution of his species.

It has been a striking fact of my experience that in therapy, where individuals are valued, where there is greater freedom to feel and to be, certain value directions seem to emerge. These are not chaotic directions but instead exhibit a surprising commonality. This commonality is not dependent on the personality of the therapist, for I have seen these trends emerge in the clients of therapists sharply different in personality. This commonality does not seem to be due to the influences of any one culture, for I have found evidence of these directions in cultures as divergent as those of the United States, Holland, France, and Japan. I like to think that this commonality of value directions is due to the fact that we all belong to the same species—that just as a human infant tends, individually, to select a diet similar to that selected by other human infants, so a client in therapy tends, individually, to choose value directions similar to those chosen by other clients. As a species there may be certain elements of experience which tend to make for inner development and which would be chosen by all individuals if they were genuinely free to choose.

Let me indicate a few of these value directions as I see them in my clients as they move in the direction of personal growth and maturity.

They tend to move away from façades. Pretense, defensiveness, putting up a front, tend to be negatively valued.

They tend to move away from "oughts." The compelling feeling of "I ought to do or be thus and so" is negatively valued. The client moves away from being what he "ought to be," no matter who has set that imperative.

They tend to move away from meeting the expectations of others. Pleasing others, as a goal in itself, is negatively valued.

Being real is positively valued. The client tends to move toward being himself, being his real feelings, being what he is. This seems to be a very deep preference.

Self-direction is positively valued. The client discovers an increasing pride and confidence in making his own choices, guiding his own life.

One's self, one's own feelings come to be positively valued. From a point where he looks upon himself with contempt and despair, the client comes to value himself and his reactions as being of worth.

Being a process is positively valued. From desiring some fixed goal, clients come to prefer the excitement of being a process of potentialities being born.

Sensitivity to others and acceptance of others is positively valued. The client comes to appreciate others for what they are, just as he has come to appreciate himself for what he is.

Deep relationships are positively valued. To achieve a close, intimate, real, fully communicative relationship with another person seems to meet a deep need in every individual, and is very highly valued.

Perhaps more than all else, the client comes to value an openness to all of his inner and outer experience. To be open to and sensitive to his own *inner* reactions and feelings, the reactions and feelings of others, and the realities of the objective world—this is a direction which he clearly prefers. This openness becomes the client's most valued resource.

These then are some of the preferred directions which I have observed in individuals moving toward personal maturity. Though I am sure that the list I have given is inadequate and perhaps to some degree inaccurate, it holds for me exciting possibilities. Let me try to explain why.

I find it significant that when individuals are prized as persons, the values they select do not run the full gamut of possibilities. I do not find, in such a climate of freedom, that one person comes to value fraud and murder and thievery, while another values a life of self-sacrifice, and another values only money. Instead there seems to be a deep and underlying thread of commonality. I believe that when the human being is inwardly free to choose whatever he deeply values, he tends to value those objects, experiences, and goals which make for his own survival, growth, and development, and for the survival and development of others. I hypothesize that it is *characteristic* of the human organism to prefer such actualizing and socialized goals when he is exposed to a growth promoting climate.

A corollary of what I have been saying is that in *any* culture, given a climate of respect and freedom in which he is valued as a person, the mature individual would tend to choose and prefer these same value directions. This is a significant hypothesis which could be tested. It means that though the individual of whom I am speaking would not have a consistent or even a stable system of conceived values, the valuing process within him would lead to emerging value directions which would be constant across cultures and across time.

Another implication I see is that individuals who exhibit the fluid valuing process I have tried to describe, whose value directions are generally those I have listed, would be highly effective in the ongoing process of human evolution. If the human species is to survive at all on this globe, the human being must become more readily adaptive to new problems and situations, must be able to select that which is valuable for development and survival out of new and complex situations, must be accurate in his appreciation of reality if he is to make such selections. The psychologically mature person as I have described him has, I believe, the qualities which would cause him to value those experiences which would make for the survival and enhancement of the human race. He would be a worthy participant and guide in the process of human evolution.

Finally, it appears that we have returned to the issue of universality of values, but by a different route. Instead of universal values "out there," or a universal value system imposed by some group—philosophers, rulers, priests, or psychologists—we have the possibility of universal human value directions *emerging* from the experiencing of the human organism. Evidence from therapy indicates that both personal and social values emerge as natural, and experienced, when the individual is close to his own organismic valuing process. The suggestion is that though modern man no longer trusts religion or science or philosophy nor any system of beliefs to *give* him values, he may find an organismic valuing base within himself which, if he can learn again to be in touch with it, will prove to be an organized, adaptive, and social approach to the perplexing value issues which face all of us.

SUMMARY

A description is given of the change in the value orientation of the individual from infancy to average adulthood, and from this adult status to a greater degree of psychological maturity attained through psychotherapy or fortunate life circumstances. On the basis of these observations, the theory is advanced that there is an organismic basis for the valuing process within the human individual; that this valuing process is effective to the degree that the individual is open to his experiencing; that in persons relatively open to their experiencing there is an important commonality or universality of value directions; that these directions make for the constructive enhancement of the individual and his community, and for the survival and evolution of his species.

REFERENCES

Barrett-Lennard, G. T. Dimensions of therapist response as causal factors in therapeutic change. *Psychol. Monogr.*, 1962, 76, (43, Whole No. 562).

Gendlin, E. T. Experiencing: A variable in the process of therapeutic change. *Amer. J. Psychother.*, 1961, *15*, 233–245.

Gendlin, E. T. *Experiencing and the creation of meaning.* New York: Free Press, 1962.

Morris, C. W. *Varieties of human value.* Chicago: University of Chicago Press, 1956.

Rogers, C. R. *Client-centered therapy.* Boston: Houghton Mifflin, 1951.

Rogers, C. R. A theory of therapy, personality and interpersonal relationships. In S. Koch (Ed.), *Psychology: A study of a science.* Vol. 3. *Formulations of the person and the social context.* New York: McGraw-Hill, 1959. Pp. 185–256.

Whyte, L. L. *The next development in man.* New York: Mentor Books, 1950.

10.3 | MAN'S CONSTRUCTION OF HIS ALTERNATIVES*

George A. Kelly

...Absolutism is coming under [much] attack. It has been pointed out, for example, that the subject-predicate form of our Indo-European languages has led us to confound objects with what is said about them. Thus every time we open our mouths to say something we break forth with a dogmatism. Each sentence, instead of sounding like a proposal of an idea to be examined in the light of personal experience, echoes through the room like the disembodied rumblings of an oracle. Even as we try to describe a theory of personal constructions of events, one that stands in contrast to theories that claim to spring from events directly, we are caught up in the assumptions and structure of the very language upon which we depend for communication. In view of this fact, we can think of no better way of disclaiming the assumptions of our language than by introducing this paper with the paradoxical statement that we are proposing half-truths only.

* SOURCE: Kelly, G. A. Man's construction of his alternatives. In G. Lindzey (Ed.), *Assessment of human motives.* New York: Rinehart & Co., 1958. Pp. 35–61, abridged. Copyright © 1958 by Gardner Lindzey. Reprinted by permission of Holt, Rinehart and Winston, Inc.

. . . Because the topic of motivation falls into this disputed area where modern man has had such a difficult time reconciling rationality with irrationality, we propose to start our serious discussion at this particular point. We should like to deal with those matters which are called rational—and therefore by quirk of our language structure assumed actually to be rational—together with those matters which are called irrational —for the same reason—both in the very same psychological terms . . .

For centuries Western man has roamed his world impaling every object he has met on the horns of the dilemmas he chose to fashion out of his language. In fact, an individual, if he was very bright and had a vocabulary well stocked with psychological terms, could do a pretty substantial job of impaling himself. Recently so many people have learned to do it in so many ingenious ways that apparently half the world will have to be trained in psychotherapy in order to keep the other half off its own hooks. Yet, even so, it may be that what most of the psychotherapists are doing is lifting people off one set of hooks and hanging them on other more comfortable, more socially acceptable, hooks.

Let us see if we can make this point a little clearer. For example, on occasion I may say of myself—in fact, on occasion I *do* say of myself—"I am an introvert." "I," the subject, "am an introvert," the predicate. The language form of the statement clearly places the onus of being an introvert on the subject—on me. What I actually am, the words say, is an introvert.

The listener, being the more or less credulous person to whom I make the statement, says to himself, "So George Kelly is an introvert—I always suspected he was." Or he may say, "Him an introvert? He's no introvert," a response which implies scarcely less credulity on the part of my listener. Yet the proper interpretation of my statement is that *I construe* myself to be an introvert, or, if I am merely being coy or devious, I am inveigling *my listener into construing* me in terms of introversion. The point that gets lost in the shuffle of words is the psychological fact that I have identified myself in terms of a personal construct—"introversion." If my listener is uncritical enough to be taken in by this quirk of language, he may waste a lot of time either in believing that he must construe me as an introvert or in disputing the point.

In clinical interviewing, and particularly in psychotherapeutic interviewing, when the clinician is unable to deal with such a statement as a personal construction, rather than as fact or fallacy, the hour is likely to come to a close with both parties annoyed with each other and both dreading their next appointment. But more than this, if I say of myself that I am an introvert, I am likely to be caught in my own subject-predicate trap. Even the inner self—my self—becomes burdened with the onus of acutally being an introvert or of finding some way to be rid of the introversion that has climbed on my back. What has happened is that I named myself with a name and, having done so, too quickly forgot who invented the name and what he had on his mind at the time. From now on I try frantically to cope with what I have called myself. Moreover, my family and friends are often quite willing to join in the struggle.

. . . May not introversion turn out to be a construct which is altogether irrelevant? If it is not relevant is it any more meaningful to say that I am not an introvert than to say that I am? Yet classical logic fails to make any distinctions between its negatives and its irrelevancies, while modern psychology ought to make it increasingly clear to each of us that no proposition has more than a limited range of relevance, beyond which it makes no sense either to affirm or deny. So we now ought to visualize propositions which are not universal in their range of application but useful only within a restricted range of convenience. For each proposition, then, we see three alternatives, not two: It can be affirmed, it can be denied, or it can be declared irrelevant in the context to which it is applied. Thus we argue, not for the inclusion of the long excluded middle—something between the "Yes" and the "No"—but for a third possibility that is beyond the meaningful range of yes and no.

. . .—the word is beholden to the person who utters it, or more properly speaking, to the *construction* system, that complex of personal constructs of which it is a part.

This concern with personal meaning should prove no less valuable to the scientist than it has to the psychotherapist. It stems from the notion that, when a person uses a word, he is expressing, in part, his own construction of events. One comes to understand the communication, therefore, not by assuming the magical existence of the word's counterpart in reality and then invoking that counterpart by incantation; nor does he understand it by scrounging through a pile of accumulated facts to see if one of them will own up to the word; rather, he understands the communication by examining the personal construction system within which the word arose and within which it came to have intimate meaning for the individual who attempted to communicate.

. . . Or if we deal with a realm which so many believe is essentially irrational in nature, are we not capitulating ourselves to irrationality? And if we attempt to think rationally about the behavior of an individual who is acting irrationally, are we not closing our eyes to an irrationality that actually exists? Are we not hiding behind a safe intellectualism? All of these questions rise out of the long-accepted assumptions of a subject-predicate mode of thought that tries to make reality responsible for the words that are used to construe it. Because of the currency of this kind of interpretation we run the risk we mentioned a few moments ago—the risk of being bracketed with either the classic rationalists or the modern intuitionists.

Actually we are neither. Our position is that of a psychology of personal constructs (Kelly, 1955), a psychologist's system for construing persons who themselves construe in all kinds of other ways. Thus I, Person A, employ Construct A′, a component construct within my own construction system, to understand Construct B′, a component construct with Person B's construction system. His B′ is not a truth revealed to him by nature. Nor is my A′ revealed to me by his human nature. Construct A′ is my responsibility, just as B′ is his. In each instance the validity of the construct rests, among other things, upon its prophetic effectiveness, not upon any claim to external origin, either divine or natural.

. . . After months or, in some cases, years of psychotherapy with the same client, it did often prove to be possible to predict his behavior in terms of motives. This, of course, was gratifying; but predictive efficiency is not the only criterion of a good construction, for one's understanding of a client should also point the way to resolving his difficulties. It was precisely at this point that motivational constructs failed to be of practical service, just as they had failed to be of service in helping children and teachers get along with each other. Always the psychotherapeutic solution turned out to be a reconstruing process, not a mere labeling of the client's motives. To be sure, there were clients who never reduced their reconstructions to precise verbal terms, yet still were able to extricate themselves from vexing circumstances. And there were clients who got along best under conditions of support and reassurance with a minimum of verbal structuring on the part of the therapist. But even in these cases, the solutions were not worked out in terms of anything that could properly be called motives, and the evidence always pointed to some kind of reconstruing process that enabled the client to make his choice between new sets of alternatives not previously open to him in a psychological sense.

. . . A half century ago William McDougall published his little volume, *Physiological Psychology* (1905). In the opening pages he called his contemporary psychologists' attention to the fact that the concept of *energy* had been invented by physicists in order to account for movement of objects, and that some psychologists had blandly assumed that they too would have to find a place for it in their systems. While McDougall was to go on in his lifetime to formulate a theoretical system based on instinctual drives and thus, it seems to us, failed to heed his own warning, what he said about the construct of energy still provides us with a springboard for expounding a quite different theoretical position.

The physical world presented itself to preclassical man as a world of solid objects. He saw matter as an essentially inert substance, rather than as a complex of related motion. His axes of reference were spatial dimensions—length, breadth, depth—rather than temporal dimensions. The flow of time was something he could do very little about, and he was inclined to take a passive attitude toward it. Even mass, a dimension which lent itself to more dynamic interpretations, was likely to be construed in terms of size equivalents.

Classical man, as he emerged upon the scene, gradually became aware of motion as something that had eluded his predecessors. But for him motion was still superimposed upon nature's rocks and hills. Inert matter was still the phenomenon, motion was only the epiphenomenon. Action, vitality, and energy were the breath of life that had to be breathed into the inertness of nature's realities. In Classical Greece this thought was magnificently expressed in new forms of architecture and sculpture that made the marble quarried from the Greek islands reach for the open sky, or ripple like a soft garment in the warm Aegean breeze. But motion, though an intrinsic feature of the Greek idiom, was always something superimposed, something added. It belonged to the world of the ideal and not to the hard world of reality.

THE CONSTRUCT OF MOTIVATION IMPLIES THAT
MAN IS ESSENTIALLY INERT

Today our modern psychology approaches its study of man from the same vantage point. He is viewed as something static in his natural state, hence something upon which motion, life, and action have to be superimposed. In substance he is still perceived as like the marble out of which the Greeks carved their statues of flowing motion and ethereal grace. He comes alive, according to most of the psychology of our day, only through the application of special enlivening forces. We call these forces by such names as "motives," "incentives," "needs," and "drives." Thus, just as the physicists had to erect the construct of energy to fill the gap left by their premature assumption of a basically static universe, so psychology has had to burden itself with a construct made necessary by its inadequate assumption about the basic nature of man.

We now arrive at the same point in our theoretical reasoning at which we arrived some years earlier in appraising our clinical experience. In each instance we find that efforts to assess human motives run into practical difficulty because they assume inherently static properties in human nature. It seems appropriate, therefore, at this juncture to re-examine our implied assumptions about human nature. If we then decide to base our thinking upon new assumptions we can next turn to the array of new constructs that may be erected for the proper elaboration of the fresh theoretical position.

IN THIS THEORY THE CONSTRUCT OF MOTIVATION
IS REDUNDANT IN EXPLAINING MAN'S ACTIVITY

There are several ways in which we can approach our problem. We could, for example, suggest to ourselves, as we once suggested to certain unperceptive classroom teachers, that we examine what a person does when he is not being motivated. Does he turn into some kind of inert substance? If not—and he won't—should we not follow up our observation with a basic assumption that any person is motivated, motivated for no other reason than that he is alive? Life itself could be defined as a form of process or movement. Thus, in designating man as our object of psychological inquiry, we should be taking it for granted that movement is an essential property of his being, not something that has to be accounted for separately. We should be talking about a form of movement—man—not something that has to be motivated.

Pursuant to this line of reasoning, motivation ceases to be a special topic of psychology. Nor, on the other hand, can it be said that motivation constitutes the whole of psychological substance, although from the standpoint of another theoretical system it might be proper to characterize our position so. *Within our system*, however, the term "motivation" can appear only as a redundancy.

How can we further characterize this stand with respect to motivation? Perhaps this will help: Motivational theories can be divided into two types, push theories and pull theories. Under push theories we find such terms as drive, motive, or even stimulus. Pull theories use such constructs as purpose, value, or need. In terms of a well-known metaphor, these are the pitchfork theories on the one hand and the carrot theories on the other. But our theory is neither of these. Since we prefer to look to the nature of the animal himself, ours is probably best called a jackass theory.

Thus far our reasoning has led us to a point of view from which the construct of "human motives" appears redundant—redundant, that is, as far as accounting for human action is concerned. But traditional motivational theory is not quite so easily dismissed. There is another issue that now comes to the fore. It is the question of what directions human actions can be expected to take.

THE CONSTRUCT OF MOTIVATION IS NOT NEEDED TO EXPLAIN DIRECTIONALITY OF MOVEMENT

We must recognize that the construct of "motive" has been traditionally used for two purposes; to account for the fact that the person is active rather than inert, and also for the fact that he chooses to move in some directions rather than in others. It is not surprising that, in the past, a single construct has been used to cover both issues; for if we take the view that the human organism is set in motion only by the impact of special forces, it is reasonable to assume also that those forces must give it direction as well as impetus. But now, if we accept the view that the organism is already in motion simply by virtue of its being alive, then we have to ask ourselves if we do not still require the services of "motives" to explain the directionality of the movement. Our answer to this question is "No." Let us see why.

Here, as before, we turn first to our experiences as a clinician to find the earliest inklings of a new theoretical position. Specifically, we turn to experiences in psychotherapy.

Clinical experience: When a psychologist undertakes psychotherapy with a client he can approach his task from any one of a number of viewpoints. He can, as many do, devote most of his attention to a kind of running criticism of the mistakes the client makes, his fallacies, his irrationalities, his misperceptions, his resistances, his primitive mechanisms. Or, as others do, he can keep measuring his client; so much progress today, so much loss yesterday, gains in this respect, relapses in that. If he prefers, he can keep his attention upon his own role, or the relation between himself and his client, with the thought that it is not actually given to him ever to know how the client's mind works, nor is it his responsibility to make sure that it works correctly, but only that he should provide the kind of warm and responsive human setting in which the client can best solve his own problems.

Any one of these approaches may prove helpful to the client. But there is still another approach that, from our personal experience, can prove most helpful to the client and to the psychotherapist. Instead of assuming, on the one hand, that the therapist is obliged to bring the client's thinking into line, or, on the other, that the client will mysteriously bring his own thinking into line once he has been given the proper setting, we can take the stand that client and therapist are conjoining in an exploratory venture. The therapist assumes neither the position of judge nor that of the sympathetic bystander. He is sincere about this; he is willing to learn along with his client. He is the client's fellow researcher who seeks first to understand, then to examine, and finally to assist the client in subjecting alternatives to experimental test and revision.

The psychologist who goes at psychotherapy this way says to himself, "I am about to have the rare opportunity of examining the inner workings of that most intricate creation in all of nature, a human personality. While many scholars have written about the complexity of this human personality, I am now about to see for myself how one particular personality functions. Moreover, I am about to have an experienced colleague join me in this venture, the very person whose personality is to be examined. He will help me as best he can, but there will be times when he cannot help, when he will be as puzzled and confused as I am."

. . . We began to be as skeptical of motives as direction-finding devices as we were skeptical of them as action-producing forces. Over and over again, it appeared that our clients were making their choices, not in terms of the alternatives we saw open to them, but in terms of the alternatives they saw open to them. It was their network of constructions that made up the daily mazes that they ran, not the pure realities that appeared to us to surround them. To try to explain a temper tantrum or an accute schizophrenic episode in terms of motives only was to miss the whole point of the client's system of personal dilemmas. . . . The child's temper tantrum is, for him, one of the few remaining choices left to him. So for the psychotic; with his pathways structured the way they are in his mind, he has simply chosen from a particular limited set of alternatives. How else can he behave? His other alternatives are even less acceptable.

. . . The criteria by which a person chooses between the alternatives, in terms of which he has structured his world, are themselves cast in terms of constructions. Not only do men construe their alternatives, but they construe also criteria for choosing between them. For us psychologists who try to understand what is going on in the minds of our clients it is not as simple as saying that the client will persist in rewarding behavior, or even that he will vacillate between immediate and remote rewards. We have to know what this person construes to be a reward, or, still better, we can bypass such motivational terms as "reward," which ought to be redefined for each new client and on each new occasion, and abstract from human behavior some psychological principle that will transcend the tedious varieties of personalized motives.

If we succeed in this achievement we may be able to escape that common pitfall of so-called objective thinking, the tendency to reify our constructs and treat them as if they were not constructs at all, but actually all the things that they were originally only intended to construe. Such a formulation may even make it safer for us to write operational definitions for purposes of research, without becoming lost in the subject-predicate fallacy. In clinical language it may enable us to avoid concretistic thinking—the so-called brain-injured type of thinking—which is what we call operationalism when we happen to find it in a client who is frantically holding on to his mental faculties.

. . . If man, as the psychologist is to see him, exists primarily in the dimensions of time, and only secondarily in the dimensions of space, then the terms which we erect for understanding him ought to take primary account of this view. If we want to know why man does what he does, then the terms of our whys should extend themselves in time rather than in space; they should be events rather than things; they should be mileposts rather than destinations. Clearly, man lives in the present. He stands firmly astride the chasm that separates the past from the future. He is the only connecting link between these two universes. He, and he only, can bring them into harmony with each other. To be sure, there are other forms of existence that have belonged to the past and, presumably, will also belong to the future. A rock that has rested firm for ages may well exist in the future also, but it does not link the past with the future. In its mute way it links only past with past. It does not anticipate; it does not reach out both ways to snatch handfuls from each of the two worlds in order to bring them together and subject them to the same stern laws. Only man does that.

If this is the picture of man, as the psychologist envisions him—man, a form of movement; man, always quick enough, as long as he is alive, to stay astride the darting present—then we cannot expect to explain him either entirely in terms of the past or entirely in terms of the future. We can explain him, psychologically, only as a link between the two. Let us, therefore, formulate our basic postulate for a psychological theory in the light of this conjunctive vision of man. We can say it this way: *A person's processes are psychologically channelized by the ways in which he anticipates events.*

THE NATURE OF PERSONAL CONSTRUCTS

Taking this proposition as a point of departure, we can quickly begin to sketch a theoretical structure for psychology that will, undoubtedly, turn out to be novel in many unexpected ways. We can say next that man develops his way of anticipating events by construing, by scratching out his channels of thought. Thus he builds his own maze. His runways are the constructs he forms, each a two-way street, each essentially a pair of alternatives between which he can choose.

Another person, attempting to enter this labyrinth, soon gets lost. Even a therapist has to be led patiently back and forth through the system, sometimes for months on end, before he can find his way without the client's help, or tell to what overt behavior each passageway will lead. Many of the runways are conveniently posted with word signs, but most of them are dark, cryptically labeled, or without any word signs at all. Some are rarely traveled. Some the client is reluctant to disclose to his guest. Often therapists lose patience and prematurely start trying to blast shortcuts in which both they and their clients soon become trapped. But worst of all, there are therapists who refuse to believe that they are in the strangely structured world of man; they insist only that the meanderings in which they are led are merely the play of whimsical motives upon their blind and helpless client.

Our figure of speech should not be taken too literally. The labyrinth is conceived as a network of constructs, each of which is essentially an abstraction and, as such, can be picked up and laid down over many different events in order to bring them into focus and clothe them with personal meaning. Moreover, the constructs are subject to continual revision, although the complex interdependent relation between constructs in the system often makes it precarious for the person to revise one construct without taking into account the disruptive effect upon major segments of the system.

In our efforts to communicate the notion of a personal construct system we repeatedly run into difficulty because listeners identify personal constructs with the classic view of a concept. Concepts have long been known as units of logic and are treated as if they existed independently of any particular person's psychological processes. But when we use the notion of "construct" we have nothing of this sort in mind; we are talking about a psychological process in a living person. Such a construct has, for us, no existence independent of the person whose thinking it characterizes. The question of whether it is logical or not has no bearing on its existence, for it is wholly a psychological rather than a logical affair. Furthermore, since it is a psychological affair, it has no necessary allegiance to the verbal forms in which classical concepts have been traditionally cast. The personal construct we talk about bears no essential relation to grammatical structure, syntax, words, language, or even communication; nor does it imply consciousness. It is simply a psychologically construed unit for understanding human processes.

We must confess that we often run into another kind of difficulty. In an effort to understand what we are talking about, a listener often asks if the personal construct is an intellectual affair. We find that willy-nilly, we invite this kind of question because of our use of such terms as thought and thinking. Moreover, we are speaking in the terms of a language system whose words stand for traditional divisions of mental life, such as "intellectual."

Let us answer this way. A construct owes no special allegiance to the intellect, as against the will or the emotions. In fact, we do not find it either necessary or desirable to make that classic trichotomous division of mental life. After all, there is so much that is "emotional" in those behaviors commonly called "intellectual," and there is so much "intellectualized" contamination in typical "emotional" upheavals that the distinction becomes merely a burdensome nuisance. For some time now we have been quite happy to chuck all these notions of intellect, will, and emotion; so far, we cannot say we have experienced any serious loss.

Now we are at the point in our discourse where we hope our listeners are ready to assume, either from conviction or for the sake of argument, that man, from a psychological viewpoint, makes of himself a bridge between past and future in a manner that is unique among creatures, that, again from a psychological viewpoint, his processes are channelized by the personal constructs he erects in order to perform this function, and, finally, that he organizes his constructs into a personal system that is no more conscious than it is unconscious and no more intellectual than it is emotional. This personal construct system provides him with both freedom of decision and limitation of action—freedom, because it permits him to deal with the meanings of events rather than forces him to be helplessly pushed about by them, and limitation, because he can never make choices outside the world of alternatives he has erected for himself.

THE CHOICE COROLLARY

We have left to the last the question of what determines man's behavioral choices between his self-construed alternatives. Each choice that he makes has implications for his future. Each turn of the road he chooses to travel brings him to a fresh vantage point from which he can judge the validity of his past choices and elaborate his present pattern of alternatives for choices yet to be made. Always the future beckons him and always he reaches out in tremulous anticipation to touch it. He lives in anticipation; we mean this literally; *he lives in anticipation!* His behavior is governed, not simply by *what* he anticipates—whether good or bad, pleasant or unpleasant, self-vindicating or self-confounding—but by *where* he believes his choices will place him in respect to the remaining turns in the road. If he chooses this fork in the road, will it lead to a better vantage point from which to see the road beyond or will it be the one that abruptly brings him face-to-face with a blank wall?

What we are saying about the criteria of man's choices is *not* a second theoretical assumption, added to our basic postulate to take the place of the traditional beliefs in separate motives, but is a natural outgrowth of that postulate—a corollary to it. Let us state it so. *A person chooses for himself that alternative in a dichotomized construct through which he anticipates the greater possibility for extension and definition of his system.*

Such a corollary appears to us to be implicit in our postulate that a person's processes are psychologically channelized by the ways in which he anticipates events. For the sake of simplification we have skipped over the formal statement of some of the intervening corollaries of personal construct theory: the corollary that deals with construing, the corollary that deals with the construct system, and the corollary that deals with the dichotomous nature of constructs. But we have probably covered these intervening ideas well enough in the course of our exposition.

What we are saying in this crucial *Choice Corollary* gives us the final ground for dismissing motivation as a necessary psychological construct. It is that if a person's processes are channelized by the ways in which he anticipates events he will make his choices in such a way that he apparently defines or extends his sytem of channels, for this must necessarily be his comprehensive way of anticipating events.

At the risk of being tedious, let us recapitulate again. We shall be brief. Perhaps we can condense the argument into three sentences. First we saw no need for a closet full of motives to explain the fact that man was active rather than inert; there was no sense in assuming that he was inert in the first place. And now we see no need to invoke a concept of motives to explain the directions that his actions take; the fact that he lives in anticipation automatically takes care of that. Result: no catalogue of motives to clutter up our system and, we hope, a much more coherent psychological theory about living man.

. . . Is this a dynamic theory? This is the kind of question our clinical colleagues are likely to ask. We are tempted to give a flat "No" to that question. No, this is not what is ordinarily called a dynamic theory; it intentionally parts company with psychoanalysis, for example—respectfully, but nonetheless intentionally. However, if what is meant by a "dynamic theory" is a theory that envisions man as active rather than inert, then this is an all-out dynamic theory. It is so dynamic that it does not need any special system of dynamics to keep it running! What must be made clear, or our whole discourse falls flat on its face, is that we do not envision the behavior of man in terms of the external forces bearing upon him; that is a view we are quite ready to leave to the dialectic materialists and to some of their unwitting allies who keep chattering about scientific determinism and other subject-predicate forms of nonsense.

Is this rationalism revisited? We anticipated this question at the beginning of our discussion. We are tempted to answer now by claiming that it is one of the few genuine departures from rationalism, perhaps the first in the field of psychology. But here is a tricky question, because it is not often clear whether one is referring to extrapsychological rationalism or to an essential-psychological rationalism that is often imperfect when judged by classical standards and often branded as "irrationality," or whether the question refers simply to any verbalized structure applied to the behavior of man in an effort to understand him.

Certainly ours is not an extrapsychological rationalism. Instead, it frankly attempts to deal with the essential rationalism that is actually demonstrated in the thinking of man. In doing so it deals with what is sometimes called the world of the irrational and non-rational.

But, in another sense, our interpretation, in its own right and quite apart from its subject matter, is a psychologist's rationale designed to help him understand how man comes to believe and act the way he does. Such a rationale approaches its task the way it does, not because it believes that logic has to be as it is because there is no other way for it to be, not because it believes that man behaves the way he does because there is no other way for him to react to external determining forces, nor even because the rationale's own construction of man provides him with no alternatives, but, rather, because we have the hunch that the way to understand all things, even the ramblings of a regressed schizophrenic client, is to construe them so that they will be made predictable. To some persons this approach spells rationalism, pure and simple, probably because they are firmly convinced that the nether world of man's motives is so hopelessly irrational that anyone who tries to understand that world sensibly must surely be avoiding contact with man as he really is.

Finally, there is the most important question of all; how does the system work? That is a topic to be postponed to another time and occasion. Of course, we think it does work. We use it in psychotherapy and in psychodiagnostic planning for psychotherapy. We also find a place for it in dealing with many of the affairs of everyday life. But there is no place here for the recitation of such details. We hope only that, so far as we have gone, we have been reasonably clear, and a mite provocative, for only by being both clear and provocative can we give our listeners something they can set their teeth into.

REFERENCES

Kelly, G. A. *The psychology of personal constructs.* 2 vols. New York: Norton, 1955.
McDougall, W. *Physiological psychology.* London: Dent, 1905.

11 | Phenomenological Assessment

11.1 | HUMANISTIC METHODOLOGY IN PSYCHOLOGICAL RESEARCH*

George A. Kelly

Yet it must be said that much that passes for humanism today is more backward-wishing than forward-seeking, more antitechnological than instrumental. If looking backward will serve to disengage us from the strictures of today's intellectualisms, well and good. But if it renders us insensitive to living man, his immobilizing circumstances and his untried potentialities it will turn us down the path of scholasticism rather than of renaissance.

. . . It would, in my opinion, be a serious mistake for psychologists who hope to raise man from the position of an unwitting subject in an experiment to a posture of greater dignity, to abandon technology. The spirit of man is not enlarged by withholding his tools. Just, as I have recalled, it took the technology of gunpowder and the printing press to turn humanism into something more than classicism, so now it requires an appropriate technology for humanistic psychology to realize its objectives. A man without instruments may look dignified enough to those who do not stand in his shoes, but he most certainly will be incapable of making the most of his potentialities.

. . . But I must remember that the psychologist who makes it possible for me to accomplish a difficult leap has done me no disservice unless I am endangered by my own impulses. He has shown me how to realize one of my hidden potentialities. That is humanism. What I am still convinced I cannot do I am scarcely free to attempt, but what

* SOURCE: Kelly, G. A. Humanistic methodology in psychological research. In B. A. Maher (Ed.), *Clinical psychology and personality*. New York: John Wiley & Sons, Inc., 1969. Pp. 133–146, abridged. Copyright © 1969 by John Wiley & Sons, Inc. Reprinted by permission of John Wiley & Sons, Inc.

I have been shown can be done adds a new dimension to my freedom and makes it all the more real. Of course, I must admit that if I am continually prodded by the applied psychologists to make jumps I would prefer to avoid I am likely to become irritable.

. . . This is crucial: humanistic psychology needs a technology through which to express its humane intentions. Humanity needs to be implemented, not merely characterized and eulogized. It is only when the subject, rather than the experimenter, becomes the model of the psychologist's man, or psychology's technology is mistaken for its theory, or theory encapsulates the reality it seeks to envision that humanistic ends are necessarily frustrated. It is not that man is what Skinner makes of him, but rather that what Skinner can do man can do—and more. Skinner's subjects are not the model of man; Skinner is.

. . . Since the model of man in humanistic research is the experimenter rather than the subject, it follows that the humanistic psychologist will make the most of what those whom he has enlisted to help him have to say (Kelly, 1965). Too often it turns out that the experiment the psychologist thinks he is performing is not the one in which his subject is engaged. If the two experimenters are to collaborate each needs some idea of what the other is doing. What is frequently regarded merely as the subject's "behavior" may be for him no less of a venture, and have no less extensive implications, than the "experimenter's" efforts. This can be particularly true when students from elementary classes in psychology are required to serve as subjects in dissertation research in order to get satisfactory marks. For many students this provides an intriguing opportunity for some venturesome experimentation with psychologists. In any case, what is confirmed or disconfirmed by a student's experience, even when imperfectly articulated or reluctantly confided, is likely to be vastly more relevant to the outcomes—or the interpretations that should be placed upon the outcomes—than the hypotheses the "experimenter" has secretly perpetrated.

At the very least humanistic research means that each person who participates should at some point be apprised of what the "experimenter" thinks he is doing, and what he considers evidence of what. It is of equal importance to ask what the "subject" thinks is being done, and what he considers evidence of what. Since this can change during the course of the experiment it is appropriate to ask "subjects" what their perception of the experimental design was at each important juncture in the procedure.[1]

This is not merely a concession to scientific ethics; it can make a great deal of difference in what conclusions are drawn. It is therefore an essential step for any researcher who is intellectually curious enough to want to know what is going on in his own laboratory. To look only at "behaviors" is to lose sight of man, and to dismiss as "too unreliable" what men have to say about what they believed was at stake is to remain willfully ignorant of the experimentation that was actually performed.

But this candor in the exchange between experimenter and subject is only a minimum requisite of humanistically oriented research. An all-out pursuit of humanistic

---

[1] I recall the insistence of one of my teachers, Christian Ruckmick—a Titchenerian—that the subjects in my dissertation research be called "Observers." It has taken me a long time to realize how perceptive he was.

objectives draws much more into its orbit. Even the design of the experiment, including both the intended intervention and the control of other suspected interventions, can take shape from collaboration among those who participate. Moreover, the subject's convictions and doubts about what must govern his efforts to cope with the experimental circumstances are themselves implicit hypotheses in the existential undertaking, regardless of what the experimenter hypothesizes. They ought therefore to be built systematically into the assumptive structure the research is designed to test. The null hypothesis may not be the most ubiquitous alternative in competition with an experimenter's hunch; it often turns out that his subjects' hypotheses are.

. . . This is not to say that the humanistic psychologist need be unconcerned with precision in his research, though the scope of his outlook may often make him appear that way. If precise measurement will reveal faint cues to what is going on it should not be befogged by the global phraseologies of existentialism and phenomenology. The object of precision is to provide greater sensitivity to psychological processes not easily perceived, not to build impregnability into one's findings by adding decimal places.

. . . I think it is safe to say that when any experimental conclusion, regardless of the statistical level at which it appears to be supported, violates one's sense of experiential reality it should be regarded with more than usual skepticism. This is not the same as saying that subjective judgment is better than objective judgment, but rather, in the best humanistic tradition, they will confirm each other. What man knows best is established by what he fully experiences, not exclusively by what he is compelled to concede.

. . . There is much to be said for a research strategy that insists on the psychologist having a first-hand clinical understanding of what he proposes to investigate before he sits down to write formal hypotheses about it. Certainly much time and expense could be saved if investigators would take the trouble to make the objects of their inquiries palpable before they start talking about intervening variables and mediational processes. Once the psychologist has seen "hostility," for example, with his own eyes, heard its sounds from both victim and obsessed, felt its pangs, restrained its impulses, lifted its myriad masks, struggled with its lingering consequences, and sensed its infinite variations he is in a far better position to undertake the disciplined task of formalizing the test of its properties.

. . . It is incredible that humanistic psychology should allow itself to stand opposed to the study of behavior, as suggested by some of our colleagues. Quite to the contrary, exploration by means of man's behavior is what once set humanism apart from scholasticism. But what now separates humanism from the behaviorism that arose in the early decades of this century—and lingered beyond its time—is that behavior is more to be used than explained. Indeed what best explains behavior is what it does, just as what best explains man is what he does. So the humanist asks what behavior can do.

The behaviorist worries about what made human acts inevitable in the scheme of material things. But I cannot imagine a lively humanist so preoccupied with a guilt-laden inquisition into why behavior had to happen in the otherwise rational life of man. But he may well inquire into the unfortunate undertakings that have brought man so close to the brink of disaster, both in his personal life and in his societal life. He might do so, not so much seeking what to blame them on—for the responsibility must ultimately be borne by man rather than by his circumstances—as seeking the constructions men have erected to channel their efforts so.

. . . Because of the present uncertainty of its stand on experimental research I fear there is a real danger of the recent humanistic psychology movement fizzling out. In their outright opposition to so much that is considered synonymous with "scientific research" and "experimental psychology," humanists may convince themselves and others that they oppose research in general and experimentation in particular. Nothing could be more incongruous than for humanistic psychology to become frozen in this posture. What could be more vital to psychology than to recognize that experimentation is even more characteristically human than it is scientific?

More than any of the other themes which guide psychologists, humanism invites their audacity and encourages their willingness to attempt what others believe to be preposterous. It would rather be absurd than subservient. In this respect it is allied to existentialism. The humanistic researcher looks for what man can do that he has never done before, rather than for conclusive explanations for what man has been doing all the time—and which, unfortunately, he may continue to do indefinitely should he allow himself to believe that he is what circumstances have made of him, or that he is destined to "be himself" and himself only.

Man's actions are best understood in an expanding context of all that is seen to be possible for him, rather than within the boundaries of his presumed nature, his reflexes, his brain, his complexes, his chronological age, his intelligence, or his culture. This, of course, means that, as unsuspected potentialities materialize, we shall probably have to keep changing the coordinates in terms of which we plot his life processes. But it does suggest, at the same time, that psychology can become a vital part of the on-going human enterprise. . . .

. . . Behavior plays a crucial role, and behavior is best explained by what man finds he can do with it. More and more his ventures tell him what that may be. Thus, to the ever-alert humanist, the frame of reference within which the explanation of behavior takes shape is continually changing, and, in doing so, throws man's acts into new psychological and sociological perspectives.

To provide an enabling structure for the progressively shifting referents of behavior is to realize the psychological freedom of man. Such a structure is more substantial to human freedom than tearing down the ghettos in which men without hope congregate or insulating timid souls from the manipulative efforts of applied psychologists. I hope it is clear that this humanistic version of freedom is far removed from that which, too often, men have been able to envision for themselves only in civil chaos, in undisciplined liberty, in hallucinatory indulgence, or in a polite disengagement of man from man (Kelly, 1966).

The antecedents of behavior do not determine what it must be, but, like humanism's antecedent classicism, offer us a breath-catching glimpse of what man's capacity for behavior exploration might accomplish beyond those trackless seas that are too much accepted as the outer boundaries of our psychological world. Yet there is danger that humanistic psychology, in looking back over its shoulder, may, as behaviorism did, lose track of where it is going.

REFERENCES

Kelly, G. A. The strategy of psychological research. *Bulletin of the British Psychological Society*, April, 1965, 1–15.

Kelly, G. A. A psychology of the optimal man. In Mahrer, A. (Ed.), *Goals of psychotherapy*. New York: Appleton, 1966.

11.2 | EXPERIMENTER-SUBJECT DIALOGUE: A PARADIGM FOR A HUMANISTIC SCIENCE OF PSYCHOLOGY*

Sidney M. Jourard

The image of man that emerges from traditional experimental psychology is of a "determined" being, subject to the controlling influences of assorted variables. This is not at all an image of man with which we can gladly identify. Indeed, one of the aims of a humanistic science of psychology is to liberate man from the constraining or inciting pressures of "determiners." A humanistic psychologist, like his less humanistic colleague, is concerned to identify factors that affect man's experience and action, but his aim is not to render man predictable to, and controllable by, somebody else. Rather, his aim is to understand how determining variables function, in order that man might be liberated from their impact as he pursues his own free projects.

In pursuing the project of developing a humanistic research methodology for psychology, the hypothesis occurred to me that the aspect which human subjects show to psychological experimenters may be an artifact of the typical relationship established by the researchers with their subjects. If people show only certain of their possibilities to investigators who relate to human subjects in a prescribed, impersonal way, it is possible that if a different and mutually revealing kind of relationship between experimenters

* SOURCE: Jourard, S. M. Experimenter-subject dialogue: a paradigm for a humanistic science of psychology. In J. Bugental (Ed.), *Challenges of humanistic psychology*. New York: McGraw-Hill, 1967. Pp. 109–116. Copyright © 1967 by McGraw-Hill, Inc. Reprinted by permission of McGraw-Hill Book Co.

and subjects were established, different facets of the latters' beings would be disclosed. Perhaps a more valid image of man might emerge if research done in the past were repeated in the context of mutual knowledge and trust.

I have begun to explore the possibility of replicating typical psychological experiments, first in the impersonal way their designers conducted the studies, and then in the context of greater openness and mutual knowing between the psychologist and his subjects. Some of my students likewise are exploring in this vein. The remarks that follow give a more detailed consideration of the rationale for such replication and an introduction to some preliminary findings. At this stage, we are only beginning a project that may take many years and many collaborators to bring to fruition.

TWO KINDS OF ENCOUNTERS

Ultimately, we come to know something or somebody if that being *shows itself* to us. If we are dealing with stones, animals, stars, or viruses, the problem of knowing calls first for making contact with the object of study and then for devising means of getting it to disclose its mysteries. Natural scientists have shown incredible ingenuity in this task. They have devised gadgets which reveal previously inaccessible aspects of the being of all kinds of phenomena: Xrays, telescopes and microscopes, transducers, and recorders of light, sound, and movement. This equipment has enabled scientists to find answers to questions they pose about the being of things, objects, and processes in the world.

To know the being of *man* is a different problem. Existentialists have said that man is the being whose being is *in question*, i.e., not fixed. Man chooses his projects and thereby produces his own being. He chooses his ways to be in the world, and upon how he has chosen to be will depend the aspects of his being that he will show to anyone who happens to be looking. One choice open to him is whether he will show himself at all or choose to hide in a cave. Another option is whether he will aim to reveal his experience, his "being-for-himself," to another person or seek to conceal and misrepresent it.

If a man chooses to be fully known, he will show himself freely to another man, in all possible ways. His behavior, which is the "outside" of his being-for-himself (his experience), is unintelligible, however, unless he provides the observer with the key. Behavior is actually a code—or, better, a cipher—analogous to Etruscan writing or Egyptian hieroglyphics. It is the embodiment of a meaning assigned to it by the one who behaves. The observer can guess at this meaning, but the key rests with the behaver himself. The behavior carries out his intentions, his goals, and his projects. It is the goal of the action which gives it meaning. Yet it is precisely aims and goals that people seek most strongly to conceal from others, fearing that if the intentions were known, the other person might interfere. Machiavelli knew this when he advised his Prince to conceal his ultimate aims from his subjects. They were to be kept mystified. People will disclose their aims and the ways they construe the world only to those whom they have reason to trust. Without the trust and goodwill, a person will conceal or misrepresent his experience, hoping thus to mystify the other and to get him to misconstrue the action that is visible.

ENCOUNTERS THAT MYSTIFY.   Suppose a young man is attracted to a pretty girl. At first, she is indifferent to his display of manly charms. He then tries to change her experience of him, in the hope that she will ultimately change her behavior toward him. What he does before her is the expression of his intent: "I want her to tumble for me." But he does not say this to her directly. If he did, it might frighten her away. Instead, he pretends he has no such wishes. He tries to appear as the kind of young man in whose physical presence she will want to stay. Once he wins her attention, he may start the next stage of his secret project. He will speak of jazz and Bach, philosophy and baseball. Then, he may remark about her lovely complexion and hair. His hand, apparently by accident, brushes against her shoulder, and she does not pull away. He suggests they go somewhere for a drink. There, he invites her to tell him about herself, and he seems to listen to every word with rapt attention.

Viewed from an abstract perspective, this encounter between the boy and the girl may seem a mystifying one. He tries to mislead her as to his intentions. He is "on the make," and he tries to manipulate her experience and action so that she will behave in the service of *his* goals, not her own. When a person is thus on the make, he will show aspects of himself that aim at persuading or influencing the other. The other person has been reduced from the status of a person to the status of an object, a manipulandum, something to be used if it is useful and neutralized or changed if it not.

There is another kind of encounter that people may undertake in order to fulfill different aims. This is *dialogue*.

ENCOUNTERS THAT REVEAL.   In genuine dialogue (Buber, 1958), each experiences the other as a person, as the origin and source of his intentional acts. Each participant aims to show his being to the other *as it is for him.* Transparency (Jourard, 1964), not mystification, is one of the goals. It matters little whether the dialogue is nonverbal or verbal or whether it occurs between a philosopher and his pupil, a therapist and his patient, a parent and child, or two friends. The aim is to show oneself in willful honesty before the other and to respond to the other with an expression of one's experience as the other has affected it. Dialogue is like mutual unveiling, where each seeks to be experienced and confirmed by the other as the one he is for himself. Such dialogue is most likely to occur when the two people each believe the other is trustworthy and of goodwill. The threat that motivates people to conceal their intentions and experience in manipulative encounters is absent in dialogue. The aims that make the action of each intelligible to the other will be fully revealed.

Now, I would like to examine the relationship between an experimenter and his subject in the light of these analyses of the two kinds of encounters.

EXPERIMENTER-SUBJECT RELATIONSHIP: MANIPULATION OR DIALOGUE?

The usual encounter between a psychological researcher and his subject has more in common with the example of the young man on the make than it has with dialogue.

The experimenter wants something from the subject, but he wants to keep him partly mystified as to what it is. Moreover, he does not want to fr.ghten the subject away, so the psychological researcher often cloaks his intentions with camouflage. If he "tips his hand," he may influence the subject and bias the findings. He tells the subject as little as he can when the latter appears in the laboratory.

Actually, in some ways a research psychologist tries to impersonate a machine by depersonalizing himself. He tries to be invisible or to be "constant." He seldom tries to find out from his subject just how that person experiences him, the researcher, either perceptually or in his fantasy.

FAILURE OF THE IMPERSONAL MODEL.   Increasingly, workers are finding that this effort to eliminate bias is failing. Rosenthal (1963) and Orne (1962), among others, are showing that when a psychologist is with a human subject he functions not unlike a subtle propagandist or attitude and action manipulator. They have shown that the data gotten from subjects (that is, the subjects' disclosures encoded in words or in nonverbal behavior) can be likened to expressions of compliance on the part of the subjects to confirm the psychologist's hypotheses about people of that sort. In fact, it seems to me that human subjects, to the extent that they are free, will please a researcher and confirm just about any of his hypotheses; witness the many confirmations of radically conflicting hypotheses. A person truly can choose a being, in the laboratory, that will uphold or refute his *experience* (fantasy or perceptual) of what the researcher wants him to show.

We researchers may be victims of the same myopia that has long afflicted physicians, preventing them from realizing that many diseases are actually *iatrogenic*—outcomes of the doctor-patient relationship. Laing and Esterson (1964) have shown, for example, that schizophrenia—its symptoms as recorded in textbooks—is (at least in part and perhaps fully) a function of the disconfirming attitudes of relatives and physicians toward the patient's experience of his world, as well as a way of being which is evoked by the mental hospital milieu itself. It is known that instances of invalidism have occurred because a doctor implied to a patient, "Your heart is not as healthy as it might be."

In research, we have recognized the "social-desirability" variable (Edwards, 1957). It has been investigated, and techniques have been proposed to bypass it or to make allowances for it. We have recognized subjects' tendencies to misrepresent their experiences in order to produce some desired image of themselves in the mind of the investigator. So we have invented tests and traps to catch their conscious and unconscious deceptions, e.g., the "Lie" and K scales on the MMPI (Minnesota Multiphasic Personality Inventory). We have utilized projective tests in the hope that a person will unwittingly reveal hidden aspects of himself. What we may not have realized is that a subject in a research project is no fool. He knows that many times his future career may depend upon how he appears through test and experimental findings. So he has a vested interest in such misrepresentation. It is very sane for him to protect himself. He has no guarantee, at least in his experience, that his responses will help the psychologist to help *him* (the subject) fulfill himself more fully. Our commitments as experimenters and as testers and the settings in which we work sometimes make it insane for a person to uncloak himself.

THE DYADIC EFFECT.   Research in self-disclosure (Jourard, 1964) has amply shown that what a person will disclose to another is a function of many variables, including the subject matter to be disclosed, the characteristics of the person, the setting in which disclosure is to take place, and—more important—the characteristics of the audience person. The most powerful "determiner" of self-disclosure appears to be the willingness of the audience person to disclose *himself* to the subject to the same extent that he expects the subject to confide his own experiences. I have termed this the *dyadic effect.* It asserts, as a general principle, that "disclosure begets disclosure." Now this is not, by any means, the only condition under which a man might reveal his experience to another. He will often disclose himself unilaterally, without reciprocation, when he believes that it serves his interests to do so. This is what happens, for example, in much psychotherapeutic inverviewing. The patient discloses much more about himself than the therapist does, on the implicit promise that if he does so, his lot will be improved.

It is necessary to ask whether the relationship between the experimenter and his subject is such that a dyadic effect can occur. Is it anything like dialogue? Do the laboratory setting and the typical relationship between an investigator and his human subject provide the conditions for the fullest, most authentic disclosure of self by the latter, whether in words, in writing, or by means of action of unequivocal, revealed meaning?

In most psychological investigations, the psychologist is a stranger to the subject. It is hoped that the subject is naive, unself-conscious, and willing to disclose himself, verbally or behaviorally and only through his responses, which are to be recorded on objective machines. Perhaps some people enter a laboratory in that spirit. Probably some infants and children are ready and willing to trust and to show themselves in that manner. However, I am convinced that the people who serve in psychological studies quickly become sophisticated and learn to play their parts. They are often taught what their part is by older, more experienced subjects who have served in many studies. This is also what happens to newcomers to a prison or mental hospital. The "old pros" show the ropes to the novices. I have ample reason to suspect that many subjects rattle off their performances before a researcher in a cynical way, giving him much "data" to carry off with him, away from people, to the calculating room. There the psychologist conducts complex analyses of variance and writes up his findings as part of his dialogue with his colleagues. But the people he is arguing about, the subjects, may be out in the pubs telling their cronies about how they "put one over."

Not only do we not provide human subjects with a setting and a relationship within which authentic self-disclosure can take place, but we also limit their vocabulary. Thus we limit our subjects' disclosures. We note only their GSR (galvanic skin response) reading or their questionnaire responses or the marks they leave on an event recorder. We ignore as irrelevant all the other possible means by which a person could show us what the laboratory conditions and the experiment have meant to him. We appear not to be interested in grounding our psychology on his experience. Rather, we want only to account for variance in the one kind of message we got from him and his fellow subjects. This message is just a response: serialized, fragmented, quantified. We assume that such responses have the same experiential meanings for each of the subjects or assume that whatever meanings the responses have for them are irrelevant. This is, I think, a mistake.

We can do something about this and, moreover, do it in the spirit of experimental inquiry. We can begin to change the status of the subject from that of an anonymous *object* of our study to that of a *person*, a *collaborator* in our enterprise. We can let him tell the story of his experience in our studies in a variety of idioms. We can let him show what our stimuli have meant to him through his manipulations of our gadgetry, through his responses to questionnaires, with drawings, and with words. We can invite him to reveal his being. We can prepare ourselves so that he will want to produce a multifaceted record of his experiencing in our laboratories. We can show him how we have recorded his responses and tell him what we think they mean. We can ask him to examine and then authenticate or revise our recorded version of the meaning of his experience for him. We can let him cross-examine us to get to know and trust us, to find out what we are up to, and to decide whether he wishes to take part. Heaven knows what we might find. We might well emerge with richer images of man.

PRELIMINARY DIALOGUE-BASED REPLICATIONS

My students and I have made a beginning in reperforming experiments in the kind of relationship climate I have been describing. However, I would like to see such studies done by more workers to see which "classes of response" and which "psychological functions" are affected by the interpersonal context of dialogue and which are not.

Here is a progress report on what we have done so far toward discovering whether the dialogic quality of the relationship between reseacher and subject makes a difference.

One of my students, W. R. Rivenbark (1963–1964), varied the way in which he conducted interviews with subjects. Under one set of conditions, he responded to the subjects' self-disclosures with disclosures of his own which reported true experiences of his that were comparable to those of his subjects. Subjects interviewed under these conditions—as opposed to the conditions under which the interviewer was technically competent but impersonal and anonymous—reported that they liked the interviewer and the interview more and that they saw the interviewer as more human and more trust-worthy, and they indicated that they would like to be interviewed by him again.

Rivenbark also conducted a simple word-association test, presenting words from the list given by Rapaport (1946) in his *Diagnostic Psychological Testing*. His procedure was as follows: He gave some general, impersonal instructions to his subjects, letting them know what he expected from them. Then, he gave them one-half of the words from the list. Next, he gave them an opportunity to disclose themselves to him in writing, in response to questions, or in mutually revealing dialogue. After this, he administered the rest of the words and secured the subjects' responses. Finally, he made a rating of the degree to which he judged that good rapport and willingness to be open existed in his relationship with each person. He did not ask the subjects to do this. Then, he studied the reaction times of the subjects in response to the stimulus words. There were no differences in mean reaction time or in the kind of responses given between groups differentiated in terms of the way they disclosed themselves to the experimenter, that is, in writing, in response to spoken questions, or in dialogue. Rivenbark did find, however, that there was a significant correlation (rho of .68) between his ratings of "goodness of rapport" and the mean *increase* in reaction time between the first administration of stimulus words and the last.

We have no idea just now of what this finding means in terms of psychodynamics. It does show that either the experimenter's or the subject's experience of the relationship between them—in this case, the experimenter's—was related to differences in the objective outcome of the experiment. True, there is much wrong, from a methodological viewpoint, with this study, but it is a beginning at the kind of replication discussed above.

SUBJECT'S ATTITUDES ABOUT CONFIDING.   Rivenbark conducted still another exploratory study, this time directed toward people's views as to how trustworthy psychologists and their tools are. He prepared a list of fifteen possible confidants to whom, or settings within which, one might reveal intimate and personal data about himself. He asked twenty-five male and thirty female college students to rank these confidants or settings according to how willing they would be to confide fully under such circumstances. His findings, expressed as median ranks, are shown in Table 1.

Significantly, the research psychologist was ranked ninth. Anonymous research questionnaires were ranked fifth by women and seventh by men. This investigation may be thought of as similar to the work of public relations firms engaged to determine the

Table 1 | STUDENTS' READINESS TO CONFIDE IN DIFFERENT SETTINGS[a]

SETTING	MALE RANK	FEMALE RANK
Tell a radio or TV audience	15	15
Tell a stranger on a bus or train	14	14
Tell at a cocktail party with friends and strangers present	13	12
Write on an application for a job or club membership	12	13
Write in an autobiography for publication	11	11
Tell in a bull session with friends	10	10
Tell an interviewer for scientific purposes	9	9
Write in a letter to a friend	8	8
Write in an anonymous questionnaire for scientific purposes	7	5
Tell a priest or minister	6	6
Tell a psychotherapist	5	2
Write in a secret diary	4	7
Tell closest parent	3	4
Tell best same-sex friend	2	3
Tell best opposite-sex friend or spouse	1	1

[a] Taken from Rivenbark, 1963–1964.

"public image" of their clients. Though I dislike the term "image" in this context, I feel justified, on the basis of these data, in urging all research psychologists to seek to earn an authentically higher rank as prospective recipients of the disclosures of their subjects.

IMPORTANCE OF RESPONSIVENESS. Another student, W. J. Powell, Jr. (1964), did a doctoral dissertation which was more carefully controlled than Rivenbark's exploratory study. He conducted interviews with college students, asking them to make themselves as fully known to him, the interviewer, as they cared to. He carefully controlled all extraneous variables and compared the increase in self-disclosure (using an operant-conditioning design) that occurred when, on the one hand, he responded to the students' disclosures with authentic disclosures of his own (in contrast to "reflecting" the feeling or content of their disclosures) and when, on the other hand, he responded with expressions of approval and support. He found that "approving, supporting" responses did not increase the students' disclosures at all. Reflection and restatement of their disclosures resulted in an increase in disclosure of negative self-statements, but did not affect positive, self-enhancing expressions. Self-disclosure from the researcher was associated with significant increases in the subjects' disclosures of both positive and negative self-references.

Another student, Miss Lee Reifel (1965–1966), conducted an interview with a girl whom she had never met, in the context of a game we invented, called "Invitations." The questions or topics for disclosure were typed on cards, and the rules were that the subject could ask the interviewer any question that she was willing to answer herself, and vice versa. In this interview, the girl became incredibly involved and revealed literally all she had to reveal. Miss Reifel disclosed much about herself, too. By the end of the interview, which lasted several hours, they knew each other very well indeed. In another interview, Miss Reifel began by using the cards as a guide, to "get acquainted" with a female student. However, for the first half of the session, she confined herself to asking questions only. The girl was to answer if she chose, but Miss Reifel would not explain or disclose more. Then Miss Reifel changed the rules and began to disclose herself truthfully regarding each question before she asked it of the student. The transformation in terms of openness and extent of self-disclosure on the part of the girl was remarkable.

TOWARD GREATER EXPERIMENTAL VALIDITY

We are continuing with this kind of research, still in the spirit of exploration. There are many technical problems to solve in a replication project of the sort we have begun. We shall need to learn better how to rate or measure the degree to which mutually self-revealing dialogue is being attained in any given relationship between a researcher and his subject. But we begin with a simple either-or discrimination between the impersonal researcher and the one who engages in a mutually revealing conversation before the experiment. More refined measures can be evolved with experience.

It would be helpful, in attempting replications in dialogue of representative experiments, if experimenters were trained to be more versatile in interacting with human beings. Perhaps we could insist that they be nice people, capable of entering into close, confiding relationships with a broad range of people. To be "nice" does not mean to be softheaded or unreliable in one's calculation of results. Training in experimental design, physiology, and statistics is no guarantee that one is qualified to interact in a confirming and evocative way with another person. I believe we can no longer afford to ignore the effect of the experimenter on the experience and behavior of the subject. We can no longer afford to divert nice, tenderhearted humanitarians into clinical work and leave the research for hard-nosed, hardhearted, impersonal folk. If an experimental psychologist is unpleasant and threatening in the eyes of others, it might be better to confine him to the calculating room or else let him contact human subjects only when the design for the experiment calls for an impersonal investigator. If a person has gone into psychology to get away from people, let him design experiments, build equipment, analyze data, run computers, and so on. We need all the versatility we can get in psychology.

At least, however, when we want to find out how people behave and disclose themselves under more permissive interpersonal conditions, let the one who encounters the subjects be someone who, by training and by commitment, is able to enter into dialogue. How strange that good animal psychologists view their animal subjects like individual persons, worthy of respect, while experimental psychologists frequently treat their human subjects as if they were anonymous animal objects! It is already known that "gentled," tame animals show different behavioral and physiological characteristics from those shown by nongentled or "wild" ones ("wild" means, here, defensive and hostile in the presence of humans). Yet many of our subjects are assumed to be tame and trusting when, in fact, they are wild. Genuine dialogue may prove to be the appropriate context for research in *human* (free) beings. When the experimenter-subject relationship varies, we might expect the subjects' responses to stimuli to vary. It is appropriate to consider the question: What will man prove to be like when he is studied by an investigator who consents to be studied by the subject?

If we do no more than study the effects of various modes of experimenter-subject relationship on the outcome of psychological experiments, and if we do this systematically, while including dialogue as one of the relationship modes, we shall have enriched our psychological knowledge considerably. Just as important, we may have taken a step toward reconciling the conflict between humanistic and nonhumanistic orientations to our discipline.

REFERENCES

Buber, M. *I and thou.* New York: Scribner, 1958.
Edwards, A. L. *The social desirability variable in personality assessment and research.* New York: Holt, Rinehart and Winston, 1957.
Jourard, S. M. *The transparent self: Self-disclosure and well-being.* Princeton, N.J.: Van Nostrand, 1964.
Laing, R. D., & Esterson, A. *Sanity, madness and the family.* Vol. 1. *Families of schizophrenics.* London: Tavistock, 1964.

Orne, M. T. On the social psychology of the psychological experiment: With particular reference to demand characteristics and their implications. *American Psychologist*, 1962, *17*, 776–783.

Powell, W. J., Jr. A comparison of the reinforcing effects of three types of experimenter response on two classes of verbal behavior in an experimental interview. Unpublished doctoral dissertation, University of Florida, 1964.

Rapaport, D., et al. *Diagnostic psychological testing.* Vol. 2. Chicago: Year Book Medical Publishers, 1946.

Reifel, Lee. Unpublished research, Department of Psychology, University of Florida, 1965–1966.

Rivenbark, W. R. Unpublished research, Department of Psychology, University of Florida, 1963–1964.

Rosenthal, R. On the social psychology of the psychological experiment. *American Scientist*, 1963, *51*, 268–283.

II | PERSONALITY DEVELOPMENT AND BASIC PROCESSES

12 | Introduction to Part II

Harriet N. Mischel

In Part II basic personality processes are considered in research papers from some of the main areas currently studied by personality psychologists. The topics here include: learning and motivation; the process of sex typing and its influence on personality development; the conceptualization and determinants of imitative behavior; the phenomena of frustration, aggression, and anxiety; the nature of psychological defense; self-control; and the formation of self-concepts and their relation to behavior.

The readings in this part reflect the increasing integration of the area of personality with behavioral and cognitive psychology. The phenomena of personality are being conceptualized to a large extent in terms of basic learning, cognitive, and perceptual principles. Researchers are turning from a search for global dispositions associated with classical trait and psychodynamic theories to the analysis of interactions between personality variables (individual differences) and conditions (situations) and their effects on behavior.

LEARNING AND MOTIVATION (UNIT 13)

The articles in Unit 13 deal with the process or mechanisms of social learning and motivation. The role of awareness in human learning is of both theoretical and practical importance. The study by DeNike (13.1) illustrates the care which must be taken when one attempts to ascertain the temporal relationship between awareness and performance. His results indicate that awareness of the relevant rules and contingencies for reinforcement greatly facilitates learning. His subjects showed no appreciable improvement in a word-naming task until they guessed correctly that social reinforcement from the experimenter depended on their saying human nouns. DeNike is quick to point out, however, that these findings do not distinguish between the ways in which awareness might best be conceptualized—whether as mediating behavior, as correlated with behavior, or as irrelevant to behavior.

Mischel and Staub (13.2) investigate the effect of children's expectancy on their choice to delay gratification. Their results show that generalized expectancy influences behavior most strongly when situationally determined expectancies (cues) are weakest. They administered a measure of generalized expectancy (see Unit 8.2) for success in ability areas to their subjects. Three weeks later the subjects worked on a series of problems. One group of subjects experienced success, a second, failure, and a third was given no information. Next they had to make many choices between a noncontingent but less preferred reward and a more desirable reward whose attainment was contingent upon their successful performance on a task similar to the one on which they had previously either succeeded, failed, or received no information. On this choice, subjects who had succeeded chose much more often to work for the contingent preferred reward than did those who failed. The effects of success and failure in the specific situation superseded the individual differences in generalized expectancy for success in determining the children's delay behavior. But in the no-information condition, generalized expectancy was a highly significant determinant of the children's choice to work for contingent rewards. The authors conclude that such behavioral referents of "ego strength" as the ability to delay gratification are actually largely determined by the subject's specific and generalized expectations that he can satisfy the requirements for obtaining the delayed gratifications.

Weiner (13.3) suggests that achievement striving may function as a moderating variable in a learning situation by influencing how a person reacts to performance feedback. Students who were classified as low in achievement motivation tended to resume interrupted tasks after an interpolated success experience but not after failure, while students classified as high in achievement motivation resumed the interrupted tasks following failure but not following success. The studies by Mischel and Staub and by Weiner illustrate the possibility of studying both the effects of what the subject brings into the experiment, his expectancies and motivations, and the effects of the experimental situation on the subject's behavior.

SEX TYPING AND PERSONALITY DEVELOPMENT (UNIT 14)

Psychological sex differences and the sex-typing processes through which they develop are crucial aspects of personality. Greenstein (14.1) and Rosenberg and Sutton-Smith (14.2) report findings which indicate that there is much greater complexity in real life sex typing than sex-role stereotypes would lead us to expect. Greenstein reports that in father-son pairs rated as having a close relationship the sons showed more overt homosexuality. This suggests that, contrary to the predictions of classical psychodynamic theory, a close relationship with the father may not lead to greater masculinity in the son. Rosenberg and Sutton-Smith present results which indicate that the shaping of interests is a two-way relationship with genuine interaction and mutual influence between parent and child.

Broverman *et al*. (14.3) explore the relationship between stereotypically sex-typed interests and personality traits and adjustment. They found some dramatic bias. Stereotypically masculine traits are seen by clinicians as indices of good adjustment, while stereotypically feminine traits are seen as indications of poor mental health. The authors also raise some questions about the biasing effects of using stereotyped traits and about clinical judgments in general.

IDENTIFICATION AND OBSERVATIONAL
LEARNING (UNIT 15)

Some theorists have assumed that the moral development of children occurs in a predetermined sequence of age-related stages. Bandura and McDonald (15.1) challenge the age specificity of children's moral judgments and their presumed imperviousness to specific social stimulus events. Bandura and McDonald show that the behavior of models and the use of social reinforcement can change children's moral judgments. They conclude that moral judgment stages are reversible and that the developmental stage sequence proposed by Piaget is neither predetermined nor invariant. The Bandura and McDonald study demonstrates the effectiveness of modeling or observational learning. Children can learn new behaviors as a result of observing adults who exhibit these behaviors and can even generalize (that is, respond to new stimulus situations) in a manner consistent with the model.

The study by Grusec and Mischel (15.2) specifies the effect of a model's social characteristics on the extent to which his behaviors are learned by others. This study separates the effects of model characteristics on acquisition (learning) from those on the performance of the learned responses. (Recall that this is one of the important distinctions in recent social learning theories, see Unit 8.3.) The study shows that the model's characteristics of future control and rewardingness affect not merely the later performance of the modeled behavior by the children. These qualities also affect the actual learning of this behavior at the time it is being modeled.

Baron (15.3) studies adult subjects in his investigation of model characteristics which affect imitative behavior. His results suggest that variations in level of attraction toward the model on the part of observers produce specific (rather than generalized) effects on imitative behavior. The model's attractiveness may facilitate or interfere with imitation, depending on the specific conditions of the situation. In the condition in which the model was unsuccessful in performing the experimental task (that is, was low in competence), attraction actually interfered with imitation, whereas when the model displayed a high level of competence the model's attractiveness facilitated imitative behavior.

FRUSTRATION AND AGGRESSION (UNIT 16)

The nature and management of aggression is a research topic with obviously important social implications. The studies included in Unit 16 help to clarify some of the conditions that encourage and sustain violence. Mallick and McCandless (16.1) examine the popular assumption that aggressive acting-out behavior reduces or serves as a catharsis for aggression and hostility. Instead of supporting this notion their findings suggest that aggressive expression by children, with or without previous frustration, does not reduce their subsequent aggression but under some circumstances actually may increase it. However, offering a reasonable positive interpretation of the frustrating situation to the child seemed to have a beneficial effect. The authors are surprised to find that although girls give more favorable like-dislike ratings of their frustraters than boys, they behave just as aggressively in the permissive situation of anonymity.

Hartmann (16.2) employs male adolescent delinquents as subjects in an experimental design which permits separate assessments of the effects of anger instigation, of observing aggressive responses, and of observing the pain reactions of the victim. The results show that regardless of the observer's arousal level, witnessing aggressive responses results in greater subsequent interpersonal aggression. Moreover, anger-aroused subjects who saw a film which focused on a victim's pain responses, later displayed more aggressive behavior than did those who saw a film which focused upon the aggressive behavior of the agent. There is also a general tendency for delinquents with longer and more serious criminal records to give more aggressive responses in the experimental situation.

Rule and Hewitt (16.3) investigate the results of anger arousal on physiological changes (cardiac response) as well as on overt aggression. Their intriguing results suggest that heart rate does not reflect emotional tension level except under circumstances in which responses can be initiated to cope with the arousal. They subjected three groups to situations which were designed to be highly, moderately, and minimally thwarting. These differences were not reflected in differential heart-rate elevation until the subjects were told they could retaliate, at which time the group which had had a difficult learning task and had received derogatory comments from a peer (high thwart) showed the greatest elevation in heart rate.

ANXIETY (UNIT 17)

While anxiety is no longer viewed as the primary and almost exclusive root of personality development and of personality disorders, it continues to be a topic of central interest to personality researchers. The articles in Unit 17 illustrate a new approach to the study of anxiety and its effects; in this approach the individual, the stimulus conditions, and the response mode measured are all considered in interaction. The study by Spielberger (17.1) shows that the effects of anxiety on complex performance (college grades) is moderated by intelligence. Students who ranked high in self-reported anxiety had lower grade averages than did students who reported low anxiety. However, at extreme ends of the ability range (measured by tests of scholastic aptitude) anxiety level did not influence grades. At both the extremely low level of scholastic aptitude and the extremely high level, college performance depended primarily on ability regardless of anxiety level. This finding is congruent with much other research in the area which indicates that self-report measures of trait anxiety and other nonquestionnaire behaviors are moderated by a variety of other subject variables. For example, age, sex, and aspects of the situation such as the type of behavior being examined, the instructions, and the experimenter, all may affect the relationship between anxiety and performance.

Houston (17.3) examines how subjects' stress reactions are affected by their general beliefs concerning their control over life events and their experimentally manipulated control over a particular stress situation. Self-reported anxiety was much greater when the subject he could not act to avoid the stress (electric shock). Physiological arousal (heart rate) was greatest when subjects thought they could avoid shock by performing a difficult task. Thus, the effect of the subject's control on his response to threat depends on the specific conditions of the control which he may exercise. Houston found that the relationship between general beliefs regarding control and anxiety in stressful situations depends on the measure of anxiety used.

Bandura and Menlove (17.4) focus on the treatment of anxiety as evidenced by avoidance behavior. Their study investigates anxiety as a real-life phenomenon (children's fear of dogs). Unlike the other papers in this section, their measure of anxiety involves neither physiological nor self-report responses. Instead, they use a series of performance tasks in which children were required to engage in increasingly close interactions with a previously feared dog. The results support the researchers' hypothesis that modeled approach responses serve to neutralize (extinguish) mediating arousal reactions which motivate and control avoidance behavior (see Unit 8) and show that observation of a model's fearless behavior is an important technique for treating phobias.

DEFENSE (UNIT 18)

The notion of defense is deeply rooted in Freudian theory. "Defense mechanisms" refer to attempts to cope with stress and anxiety-arousing cues. According to psychodynamic theory these efforts are at least partly unconscious. A chief function of the unconscious mind, as construed by Freud and his early followers, was to screen and monitor memories and perceptual inputs. The term "repression" refers to the relegation or return of unacceptable (that is, anxiety-arousing) material to the unconscious region of the mind. Psychodynamic theory asserts that this process occurs without the person's awareness. Symptoms, jokes, dreams, and "slips of the tongue" are often offered as examples of the disguised and distorted forms in which repressed materials may return (see Freud, 5.1 and 5.2).

The concept of repression has been the subject of extensive empirical research for many years. Anxiety-producing (or ego-threatening) experiences seem to produce a disruption in memory. The crux of the issue is whether reduced recall following ego threat is best explained by the mechanism of response competition (response interference) or by repression. Holmes (18.2) reviews the highlights of the controversy. Holmes contends that the mechanism of interference through response competition accounts for the data and that a concept of represssion is not needed, and he provides experimental data to support that view. Although he concludes that the recall deficit thought by some to be a function of repression is in fact a function of interference, he acknowledges that the possibility of a mechanism of repression is not ruled out.

While sometimes the reaction to anxiety-arousing cues is cognitive avoidance, there are instances in which the reaction is a sharpening or focusing of attention. Vigilance or sensitization to anxiety-provoking memories or perceptual material seems related to the intellectual ruminations described by psychodynamic theorists in their postulation of the defense mechanism of intellectualization, defensive worrying, and "repetition compulsion" (Freud). Dulany (18.1) reports a careful investigation of some of the conditions under which perceptual defense and perceptual vigilance may be learned. He points out that in order to understand the exact significance of a particular threatening stimulus for a particular individual one has to create the relevant learning history in the experiment.

In his experiment Dulany uses avoidance-learning procedures to change the comparative recognizability of material presented below the threshold for clear awareness. Dulany concludes that his results show that the learning of perceptual defense and vigilance occurred in accord with a behavior theory analysis of the learning process. When recognition of the critical stimulus was punished and nonrecognition was instrumental for the avoidance of shock (analogous to anxiety reduction), defense was learned. Conversely, subjects became increasingly vigilant when recognition of the threatening stimulus was anxiety reducing (that is, resulted in shock avoidance), and competing responses (recognition of other figures) were punished. Dulany found that his subjects were unable to verbalize the rules regulating the occurrence of shock and concludes that learning took place without awareness in his study. But the objection may be raised that the interrogation Dulany used may not have been sufficiently sensitive to detect awareness (cf. 13.1). In any case Dulany's over-all results point to the possibility of producing diverse phenomena of "defense" by controlling learning conditions without hypothesizing special unconscious areas and unique mechanisms.

SELF-CONTROL (UNIT 19)

Self-control refers in general to the ways in which the individual may influence his own behavior and modify it to reach particular objectives. One hallmark of self-control is the choice to delay available gratification for the sake of other goals; such a choice requires a person to impose frustrations on himself. Learning to wait for desired outcomes and to behave in light of expected future consequences is an essential step in socialization, and the concept of voluntary postponement of immediate gratification for the sake of more distant long-term gains is fundamental for many conceptualizations of complex human behavior.

The importance of self-control has been widely recognized by personality theorists from Freud to the present and continues to attract much research interest. In one group of recent studies, for example, Mischel and his co-workers have explored some of the psychological processes occurring during the delay period itself. Mischel, Ebbesen, and Zeiss (19.1) investigate the role of cognitive distractions during the delay period. The over-all results indicate that distractions, either cognitive or overt, which transform the aversive delay period into a more positive or interesting experience, greatly facilitate delay. The finding that attentional and cognitive mechanisms which enhanced the salience of the rewards served to shorten the length of voluntary delay contradicts predictions based on earlier theoretical views that voluntary delay behavior should be easier when the delayed object is psychologically more salient.

Meichenbaum and Goodman (19.2) also focus on the attentional and cognitive mechanisms of delay. They trained children to talk to themselves and specifically to use private speech for orienting, organizing, regulating, and self-rewarding functions. In this manner they were able to help the children to achieve greater self-control. For example, children assigned to a remedial class because of impulsive behavior and/or low scores on one of various school-administered intelligence tests were trained to talk to themselves in an attempt to increase self-control. The goals of the training procedure were to teach the child a cognitive style (or learning set) by which he could determine the demands of a task, cognitively rehearse, guide his performance by means of self-instruction and, when appropriate, reinforce himself. The results indicate that the children receiving this instruction improved on a variety of psychometric tests used to differentiate impulsive from nonimpulsive children. They maintained this improvement on a follow-up assessment one month later. Interestingly, there was no parallel improvement in the children's classroom behavior, indicating the specificity of self-control training. In their second study Meichenbaum and Goodman examine the contributions of the different components of the cognitive treatment procedure. They found that specific training in self instructions, in addition to modeling, was necessary in order for the children to reduce their errors on the psychometric tasks.

The final paper in Unit 19 deals with perceived locus of control as a personality dimension on which individual differences can be measured. This generalized expectancy construct is part of Rotter's social learning theory (8.2). The questionnaire devised to measure a person's position on this dimension, the I-E scale, has yielded many correlates, for example, with intelligence and with reactions to failure (see also the paper by Houston, 17.3). Phares, Wilson, and Klyver (19.3) seek to show how situational variables can interact with the dispositional variable of perceived locus of control. Internal and External subjects, as defined by Rotter's scale, were failed on tasks which they believed to measure their intellectual function. Half of the subjects took the tests under distractive conditions (that is, the experimenters read to each other or discussed various topics with each other in a clearly audible manner). The other half had no such distractions while they were taking the test. In the distractive condition there were no differences in statements of blame between subjects scoring high on internal locus of control and those scoring high on external locus of control. In the nondistractive condition, however, Internals were significantly less prone to use blaming behavior than were Externals, as the authors had predicted.

SELF-CONCEPTS (UNIT 20)

Gergen (20.1) questions the accuracy of the pervasive notion of personal consistency that we have about ourselves and about others. After surveying some of the empirical evidence available, Gergen concludes that the assumption of a unified, consistent self-concept is unwarranted. He suggests that instead of a single self-concept, the construct should be revised in the direction of a process of self-conception and a theory of multiple selves, and he explores the relevant theoretical issues.

Self-esteem is a central aspect of the self-concept. The paper by Gelfand (20.2) defines self-esteem in terms of the value an individual places on himself. She reasons that this value depends on past success and failure experiences and reports a study in which she attempted to alter self-esteem through success or failure experiences. As expected, she found that, at least momentarily, success increased self-esteem and failure decreased it. Gelfand also explored experimentally the relationship between self-esteem and other aspects of behavior, such as dependency, conformity, and susceptibility to influence. She found that people low in initial self-esteem were more easily influenced to conform in a verbal conditioning situation than were those high in self-esteem. Regardless of their initial level of self-esteem, people who experienced failure became more susceptible in an experimental manipulation to subsequent attempts to influence their behavior than those who had experienced success. Finally, children exposed to experiences inconsistent with their initial (and presumably customary) self-evaluations were the most responsive to social influence. Thus, high-esteem children who experienced failure were more influenced on a verbal conditioning task than were those children whose experiences were consistent with their initial self-esteem ratings. This finding seems particularly interesting in view of Gergen's statements (20.1) about the function of the consistency notion of self-concept.

The final paper in Unit 20 links the constructs of self-esteem and self-control. The high self-esteem person is conceptualized not only as valuing himself but as perceiving himself as competent, whereas the person low in self-esteem is likely to see himself as unable to deal effectively with his environment. The experiment by Fitch (20.3) was designed primarily to see if people attribute causality for performance in a way which enhances self-esteem or in a way which is consistent with customary self-esteem. The results indicated that both high and low self-esteem subjects attributed significantly more causality to internal sources for success outcomes than for failure outcomes, supporting the notion that causal attributions are made in ways that enhance self-esteem. Fitch also reports results on the role of consistency in causal attribution. Taken collectively the papers in Unit 20 point to the complex interaction of personality variables and situational determinants in the phenomena of self-esteem.

13 | Learning and Motivation

13.1 | THE TEMPORAL RELATIONSHIP BETWEEN AWARENESS AND PERFORMANCE IN VERBAL CONDITIONING*,[1]

L. Douglas DeNike

In verbal-conditioning experiments, Ss seemingly unaware of the principle by which reinforcement was administered have nonetheless shown systematic changes in their verbal behavior in response to reinforcement. Such changes have been widely accepted as evidence of learning without awareness (see reviews by Greenspoon, 1962; Krasner, 1958; Salzinger, 1959). However, in verbal-conditioning studies reporting learning without awareness, insensitive methods for assessing awareness have typically been employed (Spielberger, 1965). In recent experiments in which awareness was evaluated more thoroughly, the findings have strongly suggested that performance gains in verbal conditioning are consciously mediated (e.g., Dulany, 1961, 1962; Levin, 1961; Spielberger, 1962; Tatz, 1960).

The results of these recent experiments, which support a cognitive interpretation, have included the following: (a) Performance gains were limited chiefly to aware Ss, i.e., to Ss who verbalized hypotheses which, if used as the basis for response selection, would lead to an increased output of the reinforced response class. (b) Performance gains were limited to specific responses for which a given S was aware of a response-reinforcement contingency; e.g., Ss reinforced for constructing sentences beginning with the pronouns "I" and "we," who were aware of the reinforcement contingency

* SOURCE: DeNike, L. D. The temporal relationship between awareness and performance in verbal conditioning. *Journal of Experimental Psychology*, 1964, 68, 521–529. Copyright 1964 by the American Psychological Association and reprinted by permission.

[1] This paper was based on a dissertation submitted to the Psychology Department of Duke University in partial fulfillment of the requirements for the PhD degree. The writer expresses deep appreciation to Charles D. Spielberger, now at Vanderbilt University, for his dedicated supervision. The writer is also indebted to K. D. Kroupa, I. H. Bernstein, A. R. Dennison, and R. G. Ratliff for their assistance in the study. This research was supported in part by a grant (MH-7446) from the National Institute of Mental Health, United States Public Health Service, to the dissertation supervisor.

for only one of these pronouns, showed conditioning effects only for that pronoun. (*c*) Initial performance gains for aware *S*s tended to occur on the particular trial block identified by *S* as that on which he first became aware. (*d*) Instructions which provided information about the presence and/or significance of the reinforcement facilitated awareness, and enhanced the performance gains of aware *S*s.

However, since awareness is usually assessed through questioning *after* the conditioning trials, it is possible that *S*s who then verbalize correct or correlated hypotheses may have conditioned without awareness, and subsequently rationalized their performance by claiming that they developed their hypotheses during conditioning. Thus it would seem that the clarification of the temporal sequence of events in verbal conditioning is crucial to the differentiation between alternative theoretical accounts of this phenomenon. If awareness is a *consequence* of performance gains (Postman & Sassenrath, 1961), or is *suggested* to *S*s by questioning (Krasner, 1962), performance gains should begin prior to the time at which *S*s develop awareness. But if performance gains are mediated by awareness, acquisition of the reinforced response class should occur only for aware *S*s, and only for trials subsequent to their developing correct or correlated hypotheses.

The principal goal of the present study was to examine the temporal relationship between awareness and performance by having *S*s write down their "thoughts about the experiment" after each trial block during conditioning. In order to evaluate the comparability of this procedure to customary methods for assessing awareness, a post-conditioning interview was also employed.

METHOD

SUBJECTS.   The *S*s were 82 female undergraduate students enrolled in the introductory psychology course at Duke University, who volunteered for an experiment on "verbal behavior." Each *S* received credit toward a course requirement for participating. None of the *S*s were previously known to the *E*s, nor had any of them previously participated in a verbal-conditioning experiment.

CONDITIONING TASK AND APPARATUS.   The conditioning task, adapted from Greenspoon (1955), required *S*s to say words. Human nouns (i.e., nouns denoting a person or persons, such as ARCHITECT, GIRL, PROTESTANTS, SPANIARD, UNCLE) constituted the critical response class to be reinforced. The definition of the critical response class approximated the usage of Matarazzo, Saslow, and Pareis (1960) who found that "human responses" could be reliably scored and readily conditioned. The conditioning procedures were carried out in a small room containing two chairs, a tape recorder, and a 3 × 5 ft. table bisected across its width by a screen approximately 15 in. in height. The *S* and *E* sat at opposite ends of the table. The height of the screen which separated them enabled each to see the other's face, but not the other's writing activity. A 15-w. red light, mounted on a 3 × 3 in. metal box, stood on the table on *S*'s side of the screen. The switch which operated the light, and the tape recorder, were located on *E*'s side of the screen.

CONDITIONING PROCEDURE.   The *E*, a male graduate student, initially engaged *S* in a few moments of casual conversation to establish rapport. Following this, *S* was seated, and *E* read these instructions:

We are doing a study on verbal behavior and how people use words. Your job today will be very simple. I want you to say words—any words at all will do, for instance, PIANO, COWS, BARBER, HOUSES, PEOPLE—and there is no time limit, but they must be words; no sentences and no numbers. We will be making a tape recording of the words. As you are no doubt aware, subjects' *thoughts* about an experiment in which they're participating are important to take into account, in order to better understand what they did in the experiment. So I'd like you to write out, briefly but clearly, any thoughts that come to you that have any relation to the experiment. We're not interested in just *any* thoughts you might have—you need not dwell on personal matters—but we would like to get any thoughts that you have about the experiment. After you say a group of words, this light will go on. (The *E* operated the switch which turned on the red light.) That's your signal to pause and write down the thoughts that you then have in the space provided on the recording sheet in front of you. Don't feel hurried while you're doing this; take the time necessary to express yourself fully so that it will be clear to us later. Now, have you got something to write with? (The *E* paused and allowed the *S* to produce her own writing implement if she had one; otherwise, he provided a sharpened pencil.) When you have finished writing down your thoughts for any particular pause, say "Okay." Then after you see the light go out, go right back to saying words. (The *E* turned off the red light.) Don't state your thoughts aloud to me. If, between one pause and the next one, no thoughts occur to you, write the word "None" in the space provided for that pause, and then say "Okay." Now, that's quite a mouthful of instructions you've been given; is everything clear? (The *E* smiled, paused, and, in response to questions, repeated appropriate parts of the instructions in a deliberate manner. Questions concerning the overall purpose of the experiment were answered with the assurance that it would be explained afterward. When *S* had no further questions, the tape recorder was turned on and *E* sat down.) All right,———(*S*'s first name), you can start saying words when you are ready.

Each *S* was required to say a total of 300 response words and each word was recorded by *E* as either a human noun or other word. After each trial block of 25 words, the red light was turned on and the tape recorder was stopped while *S* was writing. The first two trial blocks provided a measure of *S*'s operant rate for saying human nouns. In the first operant trial block, *E* reinforced *S*'s third response word by saying "Mmm-hmm." This practice was found by Matarazzo et al. (1960) to lessen *S*'s surprise and/or confusion when systematic reinforcement was introduced later. The *E* remained silent for the other operant trials.

After the operant trials, each *S* was assigned to the Experimental or the Control group. The first 60 *S*'s were assigned on a random basis which provided that 3 *S*s were assigned to the Experimental group for each *S* assigned to the Control group. The last 22 *S*s were assigned in the same 3 to 1 ratio, but their operant rates were taken into account so that the mean operant rates for the two groups would be approximately equated. Beginning with the third trial block, *S*s in the Experimental group ($N = 61$) were reinforced with "Mmm-hmm" for each human noun response. The Ss in the Control group ($N = 21$) were reinforced with "Mmm-hmm" according to a predetermined random schedule for 10% of their response words. The 10% rate of reinforcement for control Ss approximateed the mean operant rate for "human responses" found by Matarazzo et al. (1960).

POSTCONDITIONING INTERVIEW. Upon completion of the conditioning task each S was directed to a nearby room, where she was interviewed according to a detailed schedule of questions[2] by a second E who had no knowledge of the group to which S had been assigned nor of her performance on the conditioning task. The questions, adapted from those used in previous studies (DeNike & Spielberger, 1963; Spielberger & DeNike, 1962), were designed to detect Ss' hypotheses about the relation of the reinforcement to their verbal responses, and the extent to which Ss wanted the reinforcement and tried to get it. Upon completion of the interview, each S was asked what she had heard about the experiment prior to participation. No S indicated any significant prior knowledge of the procedures. The interviewer then briefly explained the procedures and their rationale, and cautioned S not to talk about the experiment.

RESULTS

INCIDENCE OF AWARENESS

Definition of awareness The Ss' awareness was determined by examining the "thoughts about the experiment" (notes) which they had written during the conditioning trials. A statement in S's notes that E had responded to the words S said was taken as a reference to the reinforcement whether or not S used the word "Mmm-hmm." The Ss who recorded in their notes a correct response-reinforcement hypothesis (one which would have yielded essentially 100% reinforcement if acted upon consistently) were rated as *aware.* For example, one S wrote, "The words I said which denoted a human being were responded to by an affirmative murmur from the experimenter." Another wrote, "Oh, for heaven's sake, why didn't you say you wanted names of people. I thought you were clearing your throat." The Ss who did not record correct hypotheses in their notes were classified as *unaware.*

Reliability of awareness ratings For the Experiment group four judges independently rated each S's notes for awareness. Two raters were considered to be in *agreement* with respect to a particular S if they both classified her as aware, or if both classified her as unaware. For each possible pair of raters, the percentage of Ss in the Experimental group on whom the two raters agreed was calculated; these percentages of agreement

[2] The interview schedule has been deposited with the American Documentation Institute. Order Document No. 8107 from ADI Auxiliary Publications Project, Photoduplication Service, Library of Congress, Washington, D.C. 20540.

between pairs of raters varied from 90.1% to 95.1%. The notes of the 2 Ss for whom there was no consensus (unanimity or a 3 to 1 majority) among the four raters were submitted to a fifth rater. By this process, 21 Ss were judged aware, and 40 unaware. Since the percentages of agreement between pairs of raters were relatively high and since there was unanimity or a 3 to 1 majority among the raters for 59 of 61 Ss in the Experimental group (96.7%), it was concluded that the reliability (objectivity) of the awareness ratings was satisfactory.

EFFECTS OF AWARENESS ON CONDITIONING

Reliability of scoring of response words   Performance on the conditioning task was measured by the number of human nouns given during each trial block as recorded by E. In order to assess the reliability of E's tallies of human nouns, the operant trial-block performance of 10 Ss was independently tallied by the writer from the tape recordings. Only responses given during the operant trials were tallied so that the scoring would not be based by E's "Mmm-hmm." The mean percent agreement between E and the writer for the 10 Ss was 96.8%. The product-moment correlation for the total number of human nouns scored for each S by E and the writer was .97. Thus the findings of the present study confirm the report of Matarazzo et al. (1960) that "human responses" can be reliably scored.

Conditioning performance of aware, unaware, and control Ss   Prior to the analysis of the conditioning data, the number of human nouns given by each S in the two operant trial blocks was averaged to determine S's operant rate. Since the mean operant rates for the Experimental and Control groups did not significantly differ when statistically evaluated, $CR = 0.15$, it was concluded that the two goups were adequately matched with respect to the number of human nouns emitted prior to the introduction of reinforcement.

In order to assess the influence of awareness on performance, the Experimental group was divided into Aware and Unaware groups. The mean numbers of human nouns given by aware, unaware, and control Ss for the operant trial blocks (averaged) and the 10 subsequent reinforced trial blocks are presented in Fig. 1. The Aware, Unaware, and Control groups were quite comparable with respect to their mean operant rates, as may be noted in Fig. 1. When the performance data for the operant trials of these three groups were subjected to analysis of variance (simple randomized design, Lindquist, 1953), it was found that there were no significant differences among the three groups in mean operant rate.

It may be noted in Fig. 1 that output of human noun responses in the Aware group increased over trials, whereas the other two groups did not show any performance gains. An analysis of variance of the conditioning data, including the operant trials, resulted in a significant Groups × Trials interaction, $F(20, 790) = 3.74$, $p < .001$, indicating that the slopes of the curves in Fig. 1 differed. The test for linear trend

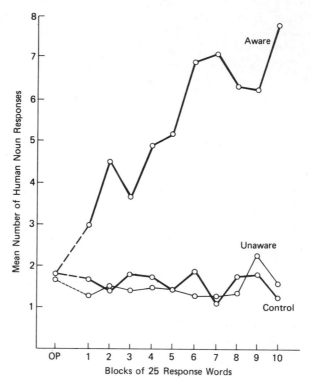

Figure 1 | PERFORMANCE OF AWARE $(N = 21)$, UNAWARE $(N = 40)$, AND CONTROL $(N = 21)$ Ss ON THE CONDITIONING TASK.

(Winer, 1962, pp. 71–73) was highly significant for the Aware group, $F (1, 200) =$ 28.46, $p < .001$, but not for the Unaware group, $F (1, 390) = .65$, nor for the Control group, $F (1, 200) = .13$. When the Unaware group was compared with the Control group by analysis of variance, no significant effects were found (all Fs less than unity). Thus, the performance of unaware Ss as a group was undistinguishable from that of randomly reinforced controls, and only Ss who verbalized a correct response-reinforcement contingency in their notes tended as a group to acquire the reinforced response class.

PERFORMANCE OF AWARE Ss BEFORE AND AFTER VERBALIZATION OF AWARENESS

Some investigators (e.g., Philbrick & Postman, 1955; Postman & Sassenrath, 1961) have reported slight but statistically significant performance gains prior to verbalization of the contingency of reinforcement in Ss who eventually developed correct hypotheses. In order to test for this kind of learning without awareness, the performance of 15 of the aware Ss[3] was examined as a function of the trial block on which each verbalized awareness, i.e., wrote her correct hypothesis in her notes. The mean number of human nouns for these Ss for the operant and reinforced trial blocks are presented as the "raw data" curves in Fig. 2. The conditioning data in Fig. 2 were arrayed so that the trial blocks on which each S first recorded her correct hypothesis were aligned, and designated the "zero" trial block. The trial blocks prior to and subsequent to the "zero" block were labeled, respectively, with negative and positive integers, after the practice of Philbrick and Postman (1955). Since Ss recorded correct hypotheses at different times, the number of data entries on which the points of the "raw data" curves in Fig. 2 were based varied from 9 to 15.

It will be observed in Fig. 2 that performance for the preverbalization trial blocks did not rise above the operant level, while performance on the "zero" trial block and later trial blocks was consistently above that level. In order to evaluate these data, the preverbalization trial blocks (—4 to —1) and postverbalization trial blocks (+1 to

---

[3] These Ss recorded a correct hypothesis between the second reinforced trial block and the final trial block. Five Ss who recorded a correct hypothesis immediately after the first reinforced trial block were excluded from this analysis since they had no clearly specifiable preawareness trials. Similarly, one S who recorded the contingency on the final trial block was excluded because she had no clearly specifiable postawareness trials.

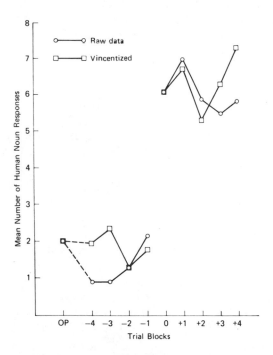

Figure 2 | PERFORMANCE ON THE CONDITIONING TASK FOR THE AWARE Ss WHO WROTE CORRECT HYPOTHESES BETWEEN THE SECOND REINFORCED TRIAL BLOCK AND THE FINAL TRIAL BLOCK.

+4) were Vincentized (Munn, 1950) so that each S's performance contributed to each data point. It may be noted that the curves for the Vincentized data, which are also presented in Fig. 2, are similar to the "raw data" curves. The Vincentized data were subjected to three separate tests of linear trend: (a) over all trial blocks including the "zero" block; (b) over the preverbalization trials (the operant and four preverbalization trial blocks); and (c) over the postverbalization trials (the four postverbalization trial blocks only). The overall trend of the data was highly significant, F $(1, 126) = 22.69$, $p <$ .001, indicating that there was a pronounced tendency for performance to increase over all trials. However, neither the pre- nor the postverbalization trend Fs exceeded unity. Thus, there was no tendency for performance to increase *during* the preverbalization trial blocks, nor *during* the postverbalization blocks.

On the assumptions that aware Ss (a) developed their correct hypotheses during the "zero" trial block, and (b) began promptly to select their responses on the basis of these hypotheses, it would be expected that performance gains would begin on the "zero" trial block. In order to test this expectation, the performance data for trial blocks "—1" and "zero" were compared. It was found that performance on the "zero" trial block was significantly above performance on the "—1" block for both the raw data, t $(14) = 2.73$, $p < .05$, and the Vincentized data, t $(14) = 3.08$, $p < .01$.

Thus, it would appear that performance gains first occurred at the trial block on which Ss recorded their correct hypotheses; and that performance for aware Ss was essentially unchanging within the preverbalization, and within the postverbalization, blocks. Hence, there was no evidence of conditioning prior to verbalization of a correct response-reinforcement contingency.

DISCUSSION

In the present study, only Ss who were aware of a correct response-reinforcement contingency showed performance gains. Moreover, the performance increments of aware Ss first occurred on the trial block for which they wrote their correct hypothesis in their notes; there were no performance gains for these Ss prior to the "zero" trial block. The performance of the systematically reinforced Ss who were unaware of a correct contingency did not differ from that of the randomly reinforced control group. These findings were consistent with the results of other verbal-conditioning experiments in which awareness was carefully assessed, in (a) demonstrating relationships between verbal reports and performance, and (b) failing to adduce evidence for learning without awareness. The results support the hypothesis that a cognitive learning process mediates performance gains in verbal conditioning.

Learning theories which posit the direct and automatic strengthening of response tendencies by reinforcement would not explain the complete absence of performance gains for the unaware Ss in the present study, nor the absence of performance gains for the aware Ss on the preverbalization trials. Such theories would predict gradual increments in performance over trials for all Ss. However, a modified theory of automatic strengthening such as that espoused by Postman and Sassenrath (1961) might be invoked to account for the present results. On the hypothesis that *"verbalization of a principle may be considered at the same time a result of past improvement and a condition of further improvement* [Postman & Sassenrath, 1961, p. 124]," it might be speculated that the aware Ss in the present study showed initial performance gains without awareness in the early trials of their "zero" blocks, and consequently became aware of the response-reinforcement contingency. However, the specificity of the hypothetical automatic reinforcement effect to the "zero" blocks of aware Ss in the present study would appear incompatible with theories ascribing general transsituational efficacy to verbal reinforcing stimuli.

Although learning without awareness was not found in this study, it might be argued that the instructions to write "thoughts about the experiment" induced vigilance or self-consciousness in Ss which inhibited the automatic and unconscious influence of reinforcement. Indeed, it is conceivable that Ss' mere knowledge that their behavior was being studied sufficed to vitiate learning-without-awareness effects. Thus, it could still be maintained that in real-life situations reinforcement operates to strengthen automatically the responses it follows, despite the absence of evidence for learning without awareness in better-designed laboratory studies of verbal conditioning. Empirical validation of this line of reasoning, however, is lacking at present and is apparently most difficult to obtain (Azrin, Holz, Ulrich, & Goldiamond, 1961).

COMPARISON OF NOTE-WRITING AND INTERVIEW METHODS FOR ASSESSING AWARENESS

In previous investigations of verbal conditioning, interpretations of interview or questionnaire data in terms of mediating cognitive processes have been challenged on the grounds that such verbal reports, gathered by questioning Ss after the conditioning task, may have been unduly influenced by E's suggestion of hypotheses and by Ss' retrospective distortions. The note-writing procedures employed to assess awareness during the conditioning trials in the present study were clearly less susceptible to such hypothetical biasing factors than were the postconditioning interviews used in most previous verbal-conditioning experiments. Furthermore, awareness ratings made on the basis of Ss' notes agreed with those independently made on the basis of the postconditioning interview for 58 of the 61 Ss in the Experimental group. Thus, it would appear that note-writing and interview techniques yield essentially comparable results in distinguishing between aware and unaware Ss, and that the biasing effects introduced by interviewing Ss after the conditioning period are not large. Additional evidence of the validity of postconditioning interview data as indexes of mediating states is reported in DeNike (1963).

Although aware Ss indicated in the interview that they became aware on the average about one trial block before that on which they recorded their correct hypotheses, no performance gains were found prior to the trial block on which these Ss wrote correct hypotheses in their notes. Thus, it would appear that during the 25 words of their "zero" trial blocks, aware Ss could develop enough confidence in their hypotheses both to begin acting on them and to record them. The finding of a temporal relationship between awareness and performance was generally consistent with the findings of previous verbal-conditioning studies (Spielberger, 1962; Spielberger & Levin, 1962) in which Ss initially showed performance gains on the trial block which they specified during a postconditioning interview as that on which they became aware.

STATUS OF AWARENESS

Since the methods employed in the present study permitted the temporal relationship between awareness and performance gains to be evaluated, and since no performance gains were found prior to awareness, the conclusion that Ss' awareness importantly influenced their subsequent performance appears warranted. The results suggest that the effects of awareness (assessed through ongoing recording of Ss' "thoughts about the experiment") on behavior can be empirically established for at least some experimental contexts. But as Farber (1963) has noted, "This does not mean that the reports obtained need be regarded as the manifest proof of an autonomous cognitive machinery guiding our every action [p. 195]." Whether Ss' awareness under particular conditions should best be conceptualized as mediating behavior, as merely correlated with behavior, or as irrelevant to behavior would appear to be determinable only through appropriate research. It is hoped that the present results may help to stimulate such inquiry by affirming the viewpoint that awareness constitutes a legitimate subject for empirical investigation.

SUMMARY

Differential predictions concerning the role of awareness in verbal conditioning were tested through an experimental analysis of the temporal relationship between awareness and the inception of performance gains. Female college students were reinforced for "human noun" responses in a word-naming task and Ss' awareness of this response-reinforcement contingency was assessed through ratings of "thoughts about the experiment" which each S recorded during the conditioning trials. Performance gains were found only for aware Ss. Furthermore, increments in performance first occurred on the trial block on which aware Ss first recorded their correct hypotheses (verbalized awareness). The results were interpreted as supporting the hypothesis that performance gains in verbal conditioning are consciously mediated.

REFERENCES

Azrin, N. H., Holz, W., Ulrich, R., & Goldiamond, I. The control of the content of conversation through reinforcement. *J. exp. Anal. Behav.*, 1961, *4*, 25–30.

DeNike, L. D. *Awareness in verbal conditioning: The assessment of awareness from verbal reports written by subjects during conditioning.* (Doctoral dissertation, Duke University) Ann Arbor, Mich.: University Microfilms, 1963, No. 64–8560.

DeNike, L. D., & Spielberger, C. D. Induced mediating states in verbal conditioning. *J. verbal Learn. verbal Behav.*, 1963, *1*, 339–345.

Dulany, D. E. Hypotheses and habits in verbal "operant conditioning." *J. abnorm. soc. Psychol.*, 1961, *63*, 251–263.

Dulany, D. E. The place of hypotheses and intentions: An analysis of verbal control in verbal conditioning. *J. Pers.*, 1962, *30* (Suppl.), 102–129.

Farber, I. E. The things people say to themselves. *Amer. Psychologist*, 1963, *18*, 185–197.

Greenspoon, J. The reinforcing effect of two spoken sounds on the frequency of two responses. *Amer. J. Psychol.*, 1955, *68*, 409–416.

Greenspoon, J. Verbal conditioning and clinical psychology. In A. J. Bachrach (Ed.), *Experimental foundations of clinical psychology.* New York: Basic Books, 1962. Pp. 510–553.

Krasner, L. Studies of the conditioning of verbal behavior. *Psychol. Bull.*, 1958, *55*, 148–170.

Krasner, L. Verbal conditioning and awareness. Paper read at American Psychological Association meetings, St. Louis, September 1962.

Levin, S. M. The effects of awareness on verbal conditioning. *J. exp. Psychol.*, 1961, *61*, 67–75.

Lindquist, E. F. *Design and analysis of experiments in psychology and education.* Boston: Houghton Mifflin, 1953.

Matarazzo, J. D., Saslow, G., & Pareis, E. N. Verbal conditioning of two response classes: Some methodological considerations. *J. abnorm. soc. Psychol.*, 1960, *61*, 190–206.

Munn, N. L. *Handbook of psychological research on the rat: An introduction to animal psychology.* Boston: Houghton Mifflin, 1950.

Philbrick, E. B., & Postman, L. A further analysis of "learning without awareness." *Amer. J. Psychol.*, 1955, *68*, 417–424.

Postman, L., & Sassenrath, J. M. The automatic action of verbal rewards and punishments. *J. gen. Psychol.*, 1961, *65*, 109–136.

Salzinger, K. Experimental manipulation of verbal behavior: A review. *J. gen. Psychol.*, 1959, *61*, 65–94.

Spielberger, C. D. The role of awareness in verbal conditioning. *J. Pers.*, 1962, *30* (Suppl.) 73–101.

Spielberger, C. D. Theoretical and epistemological issues in verbal conditioning. In S. Rosenberg (Ed.), *Directions in psycholinguistics.* New York: Macmillan, 1965.

Spielberger, C. D., & DeNike, L. D. Operant conditioning of plural nouns: A failure to replicate the Greenspoon effect. *Psychol. Rep.*, 1962, *11*, 355–366.

Spielberger, C. D., & Levin, S. M. What is learned in verbal conditioning? *J. verbal Learn. verbal Behav.*, 1962, *1*, 125–132.

Tatz, S. J. Symbolic activity in "learning without awareness." *Amer. J. Psychol.*, 1960, *73*, 239–247.

Winer, B. J. *Statistical principles in experimental design.* New York: McGraw-Hill, 1962.

13.2 | EFFECTS OF EXPECTANCY ON WORKING AND WAITING FOR LARGER REWARDS*[1]

Walter Mischel and Ervin Staub

Although there has been extensive speculation about the antecedents of delay of gratification (e.g., Freud, 1959), and widespread recognition of the importance of this aspect of self-control, experimental investigations in this area have been relatively scarce (e.g., Block & Martin, 1955; Livson & Mussen, 1957; Mahrer, 1956). This study is part of a program investigating the antecedents of choices in which immediate gratification is deferred for the sake of larger, more valued but nonimmediate outcomes. The paradigm confronts subjects with choices between immediately available, less valued rewards and delayed, more valued rewards. The antecedents and correlates of such choices were found to be associated with other indices traditionally subsumed under the "ego-strength" construct (e.g., Mischel, 1961a, 1961b, 1961c; Mischel & Gilligan, 1964). The task now is to further isolate the variables governing this behavior.

The conceptualization of this choice behavior is based on a social learning theory (especially Rotter, 1954) in which each choice is a function of the expectancy that it will lead to particular reinforcement in a given situation and of the value of the reinforcement. The expectancy that the delayed reward will be forthcoming is a main determinant of the choice to defer immediate gratification for the sake of a larger delayed reward. Support for this comes from studies by Mahrer (1956) and by Mischel (1963), which showed that preferences for delayed rewards are affected by the individual's experimentally manipulated promise-keeping history, and the length of the delay interval (Mischel & Metzner, 1962).

Previous work studied choice conflicts between smaller, immediately available rewards as opposed to larger rewards which could not be attained without a delay period, but in most life situations the contingencies for attaining larger rewards involve more than simple waiting. The present investigation deals with contingent choices when the smaller reward is immediately available but the larger reward is contingent on instrumental activity, both with and without additional delay. It was reasoned that when attainment of the more valuable reward is contingent on satisfactory performance on a task, the individual's expectancy for success will be a main determinant of his choice. Moreover, when attainment of the more valuable reward is contingent on both successful per-

* SOURCE: Mischel, W., & Staub, E. Effects of expectancy on working and waiting for larger rewards. *Journal of Personality and Social Psychology*, 1965, 2, 625–633. Copyright 1965 by the American Psychological Association and reprinted by permission.

[1] This study was supported by Research Grant M-06830 from the National Institutes of Health, United States Public Health Service. Grateful acknowledgement is made to the administrative officials and teachers of the Palo Alto Unified School System who cooperated in this study.

formance and an additional delay period, the individual's expectancy for success, as well as his expectancy that the reward will be obtained in spite of the delay period, both enter as choice determinants.

Consider the components of expectancy itself. According to social learning theory, expectancy is a function of specific situational expectancies and of generalized expectancies prior to the specific situation, based on the individual's previous reinforcement history in similar situations (Rotter, 1954). Most studies on the generalization of expectancies conducted within social learning theory focus on how verbal expectancy *statements* are affected by success and failure on related tasks (e.g., Jessor, 1954; Mischel, 1958a).[2] The present experiment examined the interaction of generalized and situational expectancies and their effects on subsequent choice behavior.

A measure of generalized expectancy for success was administered to eighth-grade boys. Three weeks later, these subjects worked on problems and obtained one of three kinds of information about their performance. In one treatment subjects obtained success, in a second failure, and in a third no information. Following this, the children chose between less valuable, noncontingent, immediately available rewards and more valuable but contingent rewards. There were five variations in the contingencies for the more valuable rewards and each subject chose under all variations. Namely, the contingency was: (*a*) successful performance on a task similar to one of the treatment tasks, (*b*) same as *a* but with an additional delay period, (*c*) successful performance on a task dissimilar to one of the treatment tasks, (*d*) same as *c* but with an additional delay period, (*e*) only a delay period.

It was anticipated that subjects would discriminate between choice conditions as a function of the particular contingencies on which reward attainment depends. Contingent rewards should be chosen most when the probability for attaining them is greatest. Therefore, when the contingency for attaining more valuable rewards includes successful performance (work) as well as a delay period, they will be chosen less than when there is only one contingency (either working or waiting).

Second, rewards contingent on success on a task similar to one on which the person previously succeeded will be chosen more frequently than those requiring success on a task similar to one on which he previously failed.

This study also explored the extent to which obtained success and failure on tasks affect choice preferences when attainment of the larger reward is contingent on success on tasks dissimilar to the treatment tasks and when it is *not* contingent on the subject's own performance. The extent of such generalization is an empirical question, and no directional hypotheses were formulated. The question here was: does success or failure on tasks affect, or generalize to, choice preferences for larger rewards dependent on contingencies dissimilar to those on which success or failure was obtained, and on contingencies independent of the individual's own performance (i.e., delay only)? Further, if such generalization effects occur, are they related to generalized expectancies?

Finally, it was reasoned that when situational expectancies are minimal the effects of

[2] There have been important exceptions (e.g., Feather, 1959, 1961) but these were conducted in a motive-expectancy-value model (e.g., Feather, 1963) and not in social learning theory.

generalized expectancies will be strong and the converse. Thus, when the person succeeds or fails on tasks similar to those involved in the contingency for attaining the more valuable reward, specific situational expectancy is large and generalized expectancy should have little effect on choice. However, in the absence of information directly relevant to the contingencies on which the more valued reward depends, generalized expectancies for success should affect choices, with more contingent large rewards chosen by subjects with high generalized expectancies for success.

METHOD

SUBJECTS.　　The data came from 89 eighth-grade boys from the physical education class of a public school in the Palo Alto, California, area.

OVERALL PROCEDURE.　　A measure of generalized expectancies for success was administered to all subjects. Three weeks later these subjects worked on problems and obtained either success, failure, or no information. After these treatments, the children chose between immediately available, noncontingent smaller rewards or contingent larger rewards, with five kinds of requirements for attaining the larger reward.

MEASUREMENT OF GENERALIZED EXPECTANCIES FOR SUCCESS. This assessment was conducted in large groups in two consecutive hours by the same male experimenter. The subjects were told that a series of problems had been administered to many junior high school students. They were asked to estimate, as accurately as possible, by writing the appropriate numbers: "how many students at your grade level out of one hundred in your school" and "how many students at your grade level out of one hundred all over the country" would "have better results than you" on two different problems, described as requiring, respectively, "verbal reasoning" and "general information."

ASSIGNMENT TO TREATMENTS AND DESIGN.　　Assignment of subjects to treatment groups was independent of generalized expectancy scores. To avoid possible differences between classrooms, all subjects were drawn by prior arrangement from a large physical education class divided randomly into six subgroups, with 13–25 children in each. The experimental procedures were administered to each subgroup in small classrooms in random sequence. Two subgroups received no information and within four subgroups half the subjects received the failure and half the success manipulations, with an odd-even seating procedure used to select which subjects obtained failure and which success. An approximately equal number of subjects were exposed to each treatment.

　　Note that the six subgroups served only as testing units and do not correspond with the cells of the design. After completion of all experimental procedures (described below), but before scoring the dependent data, subjects in each treatment were subdivided into those with high and low generalized expectancies. The four expectancy statements obtained from each subject were summed and the mean for each subject was computed. The median of this distribution of mean expectancy scores was 79.5 and subjects were dichotomized into those with "high" as opposed to "low" generalized expectancies on the basis of their position above or below the median. This provided the six groups of the design shown in Table 1: success, failure, and no information with high and low generalized expectancy groups in each treatment, and a range of 13–17 subjects in each group. To equalize the number of subjects in each group, 11 subjects were randomly eliminated, reducing each cell to the size of the smallest ($N = 13$ per cell). The total mean for all subjects with "high" generalized expectancies for success was 88.46 ($N = 39$) and for those with "low" generalized expectancies it was 45.21 ($N = 39$). The adequacy of the sampling procedures was supported by the fact that the mean generalized expectancy scores of subjects classified as high did not differ significantly between treatments. Likewise, the mean generalized expectancy scores of subjects classified as low were not significantly different between treatments. The overall design thus contained five sets of dependent measures (described below) for six groups.

EXPERIMENTAL TREATMENTS. The experimental session was conducted by a new male experimenter described as coming from a different university and working on another project, so as to minimize the connection with the first session. All subjects were told that they would be tested on several abilities in order to compare their performance with other boys at their grade level. They were urged to do as well as possible and given four sets of problems. Three problems were adaptations from the Digit Span, Similarities, and Coding subtests of the Wechsler Intelligence Scale for Children. The fourth was called a "Verbal Reasoning" test and consisted of groups of words which had to be rearranged to relate meaningfully to neighboring words.

Subjects in the no-information condition were given only the above instructions and then performed the tasks without obtaining information about their performance. Subjects in the success or failure groups received false results after their performance on each problem.

In order to make the manipulated scores seem more plausible, subjects were told that sometimes boys who usually do well in many school subjects do not do as well on these tests and similarly that boys who may not be doing so well on some of their school work may perform well on these special ability tests. To increase the ambiguity of the scoring procedure and the plausibility of the false information, the time allowed for each test was too short to permit completion.

At the completion of each problem, worksheets were collected and in the success and failure groups the "score" was returned to the subject on a slip of paper with a letter grade and a percentile score. In the success group children received a "B" on the first problem and an "A" on each of the remaining three, with percentile scores ranging from 80 on the first problem to 90 on the last. The percentiles indicated their standing relative to other students at their grade level. In the failure group, subjects received a "D" on the first problem and an "F" on each of the remaining three problems with percentile scores indicating that their performance was below 80–90% of the students at their grade level. Communication about grades was not permitted.

DEPENDENT MEASURES. After completing the problems, subjects in all groups were told that the experimenter wanted to:

find out how children and adults of different ages choose when they are offered choices between different objects. This does not have anything to do with abilities, but please consider carefully each choice you make so that you will really choose what you prefer.

All subjects were given a series of 25 choices, each between an immediately obtainable smaller or less valuable reward as opposed to a larger or more valuable reward. The more valued rewards could be obtained only under one of five conditions (Table 1). There were five choices in each condition and each subject chose under all conditions.

In four conditions attainment of the larger reward was contingent upon successful performance on a task. In two of these the task was described with the same general label as one of the tasks (verbal reasoning) on which success, failure, or no information had been obtained earlier. These are the *"contingent similar"* conditions (1 and 2 in Table 1), and in one of them (2) attainment of the larger reward was also dependent upon a waiting period ("contingent similar delay" condition). In the next two conditions the larger reward was contingent upon successful performance on a task described with a new label (general information) that had not been included in the series on which subjects had performed earlier. These are the *"contingent dissimilar"* conditions (3 and 4 in Table 1). Again, in one of these (4) the larger reward was also dependent upon a waiting period. Thus in Conditions 1–4 attainment of larger rewards was contingent upon successful performance on tasks similar and dissimilar to the initial tasks, with and without an additional delay period. In the fifth condition, the more valuable reward was not contingent upon any task performance and depended only on willingness to wait ("noncontingent delay"). The same set of five choice pairs was used in each of these five conditions, resulting in a total of 25 choices.

In each of the five conditions, subjects were presented with the following five objects as smaller, immediate rewards: $1.00; two *Mad* magazines; small bag of peanuts; one hit tune record; plastic checker set. These were paired, respectively, against the following five corresponding larger rewards: $1.50; three *Mad* magazines; large can of mixed nuts; three hit tune records; wooden checker set. The delay conditions always involved a delay of 3 weeks before the larger reward could be obtained. For example, the contingent similar delay condition refers to solving a problem requiring verbal reasoning plus waiting 3 weeks in order to obtain the larger reward, whereas the noncontingent delay condition merely required 3 weeks of waiting before the larger reward could be obtained.

The 25 choices were presented in the same random sequence, in the group administration procedure described previously (Mischel & Gilligan, 1964). Children were provided individual booklets containing on each page a brief description of a given set of paired objects and the associated contingency. After the experimenter had displayed both rewards and explained the contingency, the children were instructed to record their choice, and to turn the page in preparation for the next set of items. The subjects were also advised to choose carefully and realistically because in *one* of the choices they would actually receive the item they selected, either on the same day or after the prescribed contingency, depending upon their recorded preference. After the choices, subjects worked on one more problem on which they obtained high grades. This was exclusively for "therapeutic" purposes

Table 1 | EXPERIMENTAL DESIGN AND MEAN CHOICES OF LARGE REWARDS BY ALL GROUPS IN ALL CHOICE CONDITIONS[a]

Treatment and general expectancy	CHOICE CONDITIONS (CONTINGENCIES)				
	Large rewards contingent on task				Large rewards non-contingent on task
	SIMILAR TO A		DISSIMILAR TO A		
	Without delay (1)	Plus delay (2)	Without delay (3)	Plus delay (4)	Delay only (5)
Success on A					
High	3.39	2.69	2.92	2.92	4.08
Low	3.27	3.00	3.69	2.92	3.38
Failure on A					
High	2.31	1.54	3.00	3.08	4.08
Low	2.08	1.38	2.77	2.23	2.46
No information on A					
High	3.77	2.85	3.54	2.85	3.54
Low	2.08	1.54	2.15	2.15	3.23

[a] "A" refers to treatment tasks.

and was included because the explanation of the procedure and the purpose of the experiment was postponed until all data were collected. All children were instructed not to talk about the experiment.

RESULTS

OVERALL ANALYSIS. As a first step, an overall analysis of variance was performed for the effects of generalized expectancy, treatments, and choice conditions on choices in all conditions (Lindquist, 1953, Type III). The results (Table 2) show a significant effect of generalized expectancy ($p < .05$) and significant effect of choice conditions ($p < .001$). Although none of the two-way interactions reached significance, the triple interaction was significant ($p < .05$). The effect of treatments ($F = 2.82$, $df = 2/72$) tended to approach but did not reach acceptable significance (an F of 3.13 is required for $p < .05$).

A selected comparison between the combined task contingent choice conditions (1–4) and the noncontingent choice condition (5) showed that larger rewards were chosen less frequently when they were dependent on successful task performance than when they required only waiting ($t = 23.94$, $df = 77$, $p < .001$). A selected comparison between task contingent conditions without delay (1 and 3 combined) and task contingent conditions plus delay (2 and 4 combined) showed that the addition of a delay period reduced the number of large reward choices ($t = 14.54$, $df = 77$, $p < .001$).

EFFECTS OF SUCCESS AND FAILURE. A main aim was to investigate the effects of success and failure on an initial task upon subsequent choices in which the larger reward is contingent upon successful performance on a *similar* task. This required comparison of the success and failure groups in the contingent similar task conditions (1 and 2 combined). Further, a comparison was made of the number of large reward choices of the success and failure groups in the contingent *dissimilar* task condition (3 and 4 combined). The question here was: Did success and failure treatments affect choice preferences when the larger reward was contingent on the successful performance of tasks dissimilar to those on which success or failure was initially obtained? An analysis of variance (Lindquist, 1953, Type III) was performed to examine the effect of success and failure treatments, generalized expectancy, and task similarity-dissimilarity on the number of task contingent large reward choices (Conditions 1–4). The results, summarized in Table 3, show significant effects of success and failure treatments ($p < .05$). The effects of similar versus dissimilar contingent choice conditions, the interaction between choice conditions and treatments, and the three-way interaction were all significant. The effect of generalized expectancy was not significant.

The effects of success and failure treatments were consistent with the hypothesis. Following success as compared to failure, all subjects (irrespective of generalized expectancy) chose significantly more large rewards when the contingencies were similar ($t = 3.52$, $df = 50$, $p < .001$), but not when they were dissimilar ($t < 1$). Hence the significant double interaction in Table 3.

Table 2 | OVERALL ANALYSIS OF VARIANCE OF LARGE REWARD CHOICES IN ALL GROUPS AND ALL CHOICE CONDITIONS

SOURCE	*df*	*MS*	*F*
Between subjects	77		
General expectancy (B)	1	29.36	4.68*
Treatment (C)	2	17.70	2.82
B × C	2	10.35	1.65
Error (b)	72	6.28	
Within subjects	312		
Choice condition (A)	4	17.39	13.69**
A × B	4	1.10	.87
A × C	8	1.88	1.48
A × B × C	8	2.71	2.13*
Error (w)	288	1.27	
Total	389		

* $p < .05$.
** $p < .001$.

Table 3 | ANALYSIS OF VARIANCE OF LARGE CONTINGENT REWARD CHOICES (CONDITIONS 1–4) FOR THE SUCCESS AND FAILURE GROUPS

SOURCE	df	MS	F
Between subjects	51		
General expectancy (B)	1	.50	
Treatment (C)	1	66.24	6.33*
B × C	1	9.22	
Error (b)	48	10.47	
Within subjects	52		
Choice condition (A)	1	25.01	7.15*
A × B	1	.40	
A × C	1	21.24	6.07*
A × B × C	1	27.79	7.79**
Error (w)	48	3.50	
Total	103		

* $p < .05$.
** $p < .01$.

This double interaction (Treatment × Choice Condition) was even stronger for subjects with low than with high generalized expectancies. Hence there was a significant triple interaction (Table 3). Separate comparisons for subjects with high and low generalized expectancy in similar and dissimilar contingent conditions following success and failure are in Table 4. Both subjects with high and low generalized expectancy chose more larger rewards on similar contingent choices following success than failure. Although this mean difference was highly significant for low generalized expectancy subjects ($t = 3.40$, $p < .01$), it just reaches acceptable significance for those with high generalized expectancy ($t = 1.84$, $p < .05$, one-tailed test).[3] Comparison of the success and failure groups on *dissimilar* contingencies showed no differences ($t < 1$) in the choices of children with high generalized expectancy but for those with low generalized expectancy there was a nonsignificant trend ($t = 1.63$, $df = 24$, $p < .15$, two-tailed test) for more large reward choices following success.

COMPARISONS OF CONTINGENT CHOICES BY SUBJECTS WITH HIGH AND LOW GENERALIZED EXPECTANCIES IN SUCCESS AND FAILURE VERSUS NO-INFORMATION TREATMENT.

Table 4 compares the mean choices of subjects with high and low generalized expectancy separately in the success, failure, and no-information groups on similar and dissimilar contingent choice conditions. The results for success versus failure already have been presented. Comparing subjects with low generalized expectancy in the success and the no-information groups showed that after success they chose more contingent rewards on similar contingencies ($p < .01$)

[3] All t tests in this paper are two-tailed except for tests of the explicitly predicted differences on contingent similar choices following success as opposed to failure which are one-tailed.

Table 4 | COMPARISON OF PAIRS OF MEANS FOR ALL TREATMENTS: LARGE REWARD CHOICES IN CONTINGENT SIMILAR AND DISSIMILAR CONDITIONS BY SUBJECTS WITH HIGH AND LOW GENERALIZED EXPECTANCIES[a]

GENERAL EXPECTANCY	TREATMENT COMPARISONS					
	Success (I) versus failure (II)		*Success (I) versus no information (III)*		*Failure (II) versus no information (III)*	
	CONTIN-GENT SIMILAR	CONTIN-GENT DISSIMILAR	CONTIN-GENT SIMILAR	CONTIN-GENT DISSIMILAR	CONTIN-GENT SIMILAR	CONTIN-GENT DISSIMILAR
High						
t	1.84*	< 1	< 1	< 1	2.36*	< 1
Direction	I > II				III > II	
Low						
t	I > II	1.63	2.69**	1.96	< 1	< 1
Direction	3.40***	I > II	I > III	I > III		

[a] t tests comparing success with failure on contingent similar are one-tailed (explicitly hypothesized differences); all other t tests are two-tailed; $df = 24$ for each test.

* $p < .05$.

** $p < .02$.

*** $p < .01$.

and likewise on dissimilar contingencies, although the latter difference approaches but falls short of acceptable significance with a two-tailed test ($t = 1.96$, $df = 24$, $p < .10$). In contrast, these comparisons did not reach or approach significance for subjects with high generalized expectancy (both t values < 1).

Comparing subjects with high generalized expectancies for success in the failure and no-information groups showed that after failure they chose fewer contingent rewards on similar but not on dissimilar contingencies. For subjects with low generalized expectancies for success, choices were not significantly different following failure and no information.

In sum, in the absence of information about performance, subjects with high generalized expectancies behaved like those who obtained success, whereas subjects with low generalized expectancies behaved like those with similarly low expectancies who obtained failure. For subjects with high generalized expectancies, failure (compared to no information) significantly reduced large reward choices only on similar contingencies. For those with low generalized expectancies, success (compared to no information) significantly increased large reward choices on similar contingencies with a strong trend also on dissimilar contingencies.

EFFECTS OF GENERALIZED EXPECTANCY. Recall that a significant effect of generalized expectancy was found in the initial overall analysis of variance (Table 2). The three-way interaction in the overall analysis of variance indicated, however, that generalized expectancies did not affect all experimental groups equally in all choice conditions and the analysis of variance for success and failure groups only on task contingent choices showed no significant effects of generalized expectancies although there were interactions.

It was anticipated that in the no-information group subjects with high as opposed to low generalized expectancies would choose more task contingent large rewards (Conditions 1–4 in Table 1). This prediction was supported ($t = 2.45$, $df = 24$, $p < .03$). Comparable t tests in the success and failure groups did not reach significance ($t < 1$).

NONCONTINGENT (DELAY ONLY) CHOICES. The effect of generalized expectancies and treatments was also examined when the larger reward required delay but was not contingent on performance (Condition 5 in Table 1). It was not predicted that generalized expectancies for success would affect choices in this condition but the data indicated differences as a function of generalized expectancies (see Table 1). Analysis of variance for all treatment groups on choices in this condition showed a significant effect of generalized expectancies ($F = 8.72$, $df = 1/72$, $p < .01$). Treatment effect and interactions were not significant ($F < 2$). Subjects with high generalized expectancies for success waited for larger rewards more than those with low expectancies in all treatments (see means in Table 1 for Choice Condition 5). However, t tests showed that this mean difference was significant in the failure group ($t = 2.60$, $df = 24$, $p < .02$) while it did not approach significance in the success group ($t = .92$, $df = 24$, ns) and was negligible in the no-information group ($t = .48$). That is, following failure, subjects with high generalized expectancies for success chose to wait for larger rewards which were independent of performance more than those with low generalized expectancies. Following success and no information, generalized expectancies did not affect choices in this condition.

DISCUSSION

The highly significant effects of choice conditions clearly demonstrated the importance of the specific contingencies for attainment of larger or more valued rewards as determinants of waiting and working for them. Larger rewards whose attainment required only waiting were chosen more frequently than those that required successful work. Moreover, when larger rewards were contingent on waiting as well as successful work they were chosen less frequently than when they required only successful work. The findings show that accurate predictions about this aspect of self-control require detailed analysis of the specific contingencies for attainment of the more valuable outcome. The results suggest that behaviors frequently used as indices of "ego strength" and treated as if they were referents for relatively stable, general, and situation-free traits may largely be determined by situational contingencies.

Multiple contingencies (successful work plus additional delay) presumably reduced the subjective probability for attaining contingent rewards. It is also possible that the combined contingencies altered the reward value of the contingent larger rewards, by making their attainment more aversive rather than less probable. The present study was not designed to differentiate between these possibilities and illustrates only that individuals discriminate between contingencies in these choices, with additional risk contingencies decreasing willingness to work and wait for larger rewards. Likewise, the fact that "delay only" resulted in the greatest number of large reward choices should not lead to generalizations beyond the sample and tasks used. In some circumstances or cultures it is likely that contingencies involving successful work (even with a high risk of failure) would be more preferred than those requiring only a waiting period. This seems especially plausible when trust in the "promise-maker" is minimal or when waiting is a highly noxious activity (Mischel, 1958b). Obviously there are great individual differences with respect to this. Note, for example, that following both success and failure, children with low generalized expectancy for success chose slightly (not significantly) more larger rewards when the contingency required success on a task dissimilar to the initial task but without additional delay than when it required delay only (Table 1).

The results demonstrate that generalized expectancies for success, presumably based on previous reinforcement in similar earlier situations, are determinants of choices when there is no information in the situation relevant to success probability. In the absence of such information, subjects with low generalized expectancies behave like those with similarly low expectancies who actually obtained failure, whereas subjects with high generalized expectancies behave like those who succeeded.

However, when specific expectancies about outcomes within the situation are relatively clear, as in the success and failure treatments, they tend to minimize the effects of generalized expectancy, particularly when the contingencies are highly similar to those on which situational success or failure was obtained. There are major individual differences in the extent to which subjects discriminate between similar and dissimilar contingencies and specific contingencies interact both with treatment and with generalized expectancy. Treatment effects on dissimilar contingencies were minimal in this study, with trends only for subjects who had low generalized expectancies. This is consistent with the discussed data on specific contingencies and subjects' discriminations between contingencies, as well as the interactions with generalized expectancy.

It is also of interest that subjects' direct estimates of generalized expectancy for success, rather than indirect inferences about motivational states, provided useful measures which predicted delay of gratification behavior. The usefulness of such direct self-estimates from subjects supports earlier findings about the utility of self-predictions in a very different assessment context (Mischel, 1965).

Generalized expectancies produced an unpredicted significant effect in the noncontingent (delay only) choice condition. In this condition subjects with high generalized expectancy for success waited for larger rewards more than those with low expectancies. This difference was significant after the failure treatment but not after success or no information. It seems plausible that generalized expectancy, as measured in this study, was also correlated with expectancies that the promised reward will be forthcoming, even when this is independent of the person's own performance and contingent primarily on the promise-maker. However, since there were no significant differences between subjects with high and low generalized expectancies in willingness to wait for larger reward in the no-information and success groups, and since the difference was significant only in the failure group, it appears more reasonable that "confirmed failure" for subjects with low generalized expectancies decreased their discriminations about specific contingencies and generalized to choice situations in which attainment of a larger reward was independent of their own performance.

Extrapolating to life situations, in the absence of new information about outcomes relevant to the contingencies on which rewards depend, individuals with low generalized expectancies for success behave as if they cannot fulfill the contingency. That is, they behave like individuals who already failed on tasks similar to those on which reward is contingent. Following actual failure on tasks similar to those on which reward is contingent, they are less willing to wait for larger rewards than subjects with high generalized expectancies for success, even when the reward is not contingent on their own work and requires only waiting. However, when given information indicating that they can probably fulfill the relevant contingencies (success treatment) their willingness to work and wait for larger rewards increases and indeed they behave like subjects with high generalized expectancies for success. The implications for increasing an individual's willingness to work and wait for larger rewards are clear: increase the probability that he can fulfill the necessary specific contingencies. While this is hardly surprising, it needs to be taken seriously in therapeutic programs designed to enhance ego strength and suggests that specific training to increase the expectancy for success with respect to working and waiting for more valued outcomes is a potent means of strengthening this aspect of self-control.

SUMMARY

This study investigated the effects of situational and generalized expectancies for success on choices of immediate, less valuable, noncontingent rewards as opposed to more valuable contingent rewards. Measures of generalized expectancy for success were administered to eighth-grade boys who later worked on a series of problems and obtained either success, failure, or no information for performance. Thereafter, each S chose between less valuable, noncontingent rewards and more valuable rewards whose attainment was contingent on successful solutions of problems varying in their similarity-dissimilarity to the original problems and/or an additional delay period. As predicted, contingent rewards were chosen more after success than failure and Ss discriminated between specific contingencies. The effects of situational success and failure tended to minimize the effects of generalized expectancies. Moreover, in the no-information condition children with high generalized expectancies for success chose more contingent rewards than those with low expectancies and behaved like subjects in the success condition. Children with low generalized expectancies who received no information about their performance behaved like those with similarly low generalized expectancies who had obtained failure. Following failure, generalized expectancies for success affected willingness to wait for larger rewards even when their attainment was independent of performance.

REFERENCES

Block, J., & Martin, B. Prediction of behavior of children under frustration. *Journal of Abnormal and Social Psychology*, 1955, *51*, 281–285.

Feather, N. T. Success probability and choice behavior. *Journal of Experimental Psychology*, 1959, *58*, 257–266.

Feather, N. T. The relationship of persistence at a task to expectation of success and achievement related motives. *Journal of Abnormal and Social Psychology*, 1961, *63*, 552–561.

Feather, N. T. Mowrer's revised two-factor theory and the motive-expectancy-value model. *Psychological Review*, 1963, *70*, 500–515.

Freud, A. Formulations regarding the two principles of mental functioning. (Orig. publ. 1911) In, *Collected papers*. Vol. 4. New York: Basic Books, 1959. Pp. 13–21.

Jessor, R. The generalization of expectancies. *Journal of Abnormal and Social Psychology*, 1954, *49*, 196–200.

Lindquist, E. F. *Design and analysis of experiments in psychology and education.* Boston: Houghton Mifflin, 1953.

Livson, N., & Mussen, P. H. The relation of ego control to overt aggression and dependency. *Journal of Abnormal and Social Psychology*, 1957, *55*, 66–71.

Mahrer, A. R. The role of expectancy in delayed reinforcement. *Journal of Experimental Psychology*, 1956, *52*, 101–106.

Mischel, Harriet. Trust and delay of gratification. Unpublished doctoral dissertation, Harvard University, 1963.

Mischel, W. The effect of the commitment situation on the generalization of expectancies. *Journal of Personality*, 1958, *26*, 508–516. (a)

Mischel, W. Preference for delayed reinforcement: An experimental study of a cultural observation. *Journal of Abnormal and Social Psychology*, 1958, *56*, 57–61. (b)

Mischel, W. Delay of gratification, need for achievement, and acquiescence in another culture. *Journal of Abnormal and Social Psychology*, 1961, *62*, 543–552. (a)

Mischel, W. Father-absence and delay of gratification: Cross-cultural comparisons. *Journal of Abnormal and Social Psychology*, 1961, *63*, 116–124. (b)

Mischel, W. Preference for delayed reinforcement and social responsibility. *Journal of Abnormal and Social Psychology*, 1961, *62*, 1–7. (c)

Mischel, W. Predicting the success of Peace Corps volunteers in Nigeria. *Journal of Personality and Social Psychology*, 1965, *1*, 510–517.

Mischel, W., & Gilligan, Carol. Delay of gratification, motivation for the prohibited gratification, and responses to temptation. *Journal of Abnormal and Social Psychology*, 1964, *69*, 411–417.

Mischel, W., & Metzner, R. Preference for delayed reward as a function of age, intelligence, and length of delay interval. *Journal of Abnormal and Social Psychology*, 1962, *64*, 425–431.

Rotter, J. B. *Social learning and clinical psychology.* Englewood Cliffs, N.J.: Prentice-Hall, 1954.

13.3 | NEED ACHIEVEMENT AND THE RESUMPTION OF INCOMPLETED TASKS*[1]

Bernard Weiner

Theoretical conceptions of motivation proposed by Freud (1938) and Lewin (1935) have assumed that a wish or intention, once aroused, persists until the goal is attained. These theorists also postulated that the attainment of related goals may have substitute value, that is, may result in a decrement in the strength of the persisting tendency to strive for the original goal.

The starting point for the experimental investigation of substitution was Ovsiankina's (1928) demonstration that there is a strong tendency to resume tasks interrupted before completion. Lissner (1933) showed that there is a decrease in the strength of the tendency to resume previously interrupted tasks following the attainment of related goals; he also demonstrated that the decrease in the tendency to resume is a positive function of the degree of difficulty of the substitute action. Mahler (1933) found that the degree of reality of the substitute activity is also an important determinant of substitute value, and Henle (1944) demonstrated that substitute value is a positive function of the valence of the substitute task. In these studies the behavioral criterion for substitute value was a decrease in the amount of spontaneous resumption of previously interrupted tasks.

Other investigators have suggested that the attainment of goals similar to a desired goal will lead to an increase rather than a decrease in the resultant tendency to strive for that goal. Murray (1954) found a greater frequency of aggressive responses toward significant authority figures as a patient progressed through psychotherapy. He employed Miller's (1944) approach-avoidance conflict model to explain these results. Murray suggested that during therapy sessions hostile responses directed toward individuals similar to a disliked authority figure were not punished. This was represented conceptually as a lowering of the avoidance gradient, which resulted in a subsequent increase in the number of aggressive responses made toward the originally feared authority figure.

The apparent contradiction between these studies suggests that the enhancing or decremental effect of goal attainment may be related to the relative strength of the approach and avoidance tendencies to strive for the original goal. It is postulated that in situations where greater approach than avoidance motivation is aroused, attainment

* SOURCE: Weiner, B. Need achievement and the resumption of incompleted tasks. *Journal of Personality and Social Psychology*, 1965, *1*, 165–168. Copyright 1965 by the American Psychological Association and reprinted by permission.

[1] This research was part of a project on Personality Dynamics financed by a grant from the Ford Foundation.

The author wishes to thank J. W. Atkinson and S. Karabenick for their suggestions in conducting this research.

of goals similar to a desired goal will lead to a decrease in the resultant motivation to approach the original goal. Thus goal attainment will have substitute value. However, where the stimulus situation elicits greater avoidance than approach motivation, attainment of goals similar to a desired goal will increase the tendency to strive for the original goal. In this situation goal attainment will have instigating rather than substitutive properties.

Previous research (Atkinson, 1957) has indicated that individuals classified as high in need for achievement (n Ach) have a greater tendency to approach than avoid achievement-oriented activities, while individuals classified as low in n Ach are likely to be anxious about failure and avoid problem-solving tasks. It is hypothesized therefore that in situations where achievement motivation is aroused, individuals high in n Ach will not spontaneously resume previously interrupted tasks following success experiences (goal attainment), but will exhibit resumption following interpolated failures. Conversely, individuals classified as low in n Ach will tend to resume previously interrupted tasks following interpolated success experiences, but not following interpolated failures.

PROCEDURE

Subjects were 30 male undergraduates at the University of Michigan. All were enrolled in the introductory psychology course and were required to participate in psychological experiments.

Subjects participated in two experimental sessions. During the first hour they were administered a Thematic Apperception Test (TAT), Picture Series 2, 33, 52, 24 (Atkinson, 1958). This was scored for n Ach according to the method of content analysis developed by McClelland, Atkinson, Clark, and Lowell (1953). Interscorer reliability for n Ach was $r = .88$.[2]

During the second hour subjects found three booklets placed on their desks. Two of these were identical "Zeigarnik" booklets. The booklets contained 20 different simple puzzle tasks, for example, connecting dots, anagrams, etc. There were two forms of every puzzle, a long and a short form. Long puzzles ordinarily cannot be completed within the allotted time period, while short puzzles can be completed. Four random sequences of puzzles were selected so each booklet contained 10 tasks of the long form and 10 of the short form.

The third booklet on the subjects' desks contained a series of geometrical designs. The task required tracing over the design without lifting the pencil from the paper or retracing a line. There were two different booklet forms, one containing 10 soluble puzzles (success condition) and one containing 3 soluble and 7 insoluble puzzles (failure condition).

Subjects were first given the Zeigarnik booklet. Seventy-five seconds were allowed for each task. The condition of administration was ego involving (Atkinson, 1953). Subjects then were given the "tracing" booklet. Before starting this task they were told:

2 The author wishes to thank Howard Eggeth for his assistance in the reliability check.

You may find some of these puzzles difficult. Previous norms indicate that the average college student can complete only about half of the puzzles, or 5 of the 10.

Subjects were allowed to work on the puzzles for 10 minutes. At the end of this time the experimenter had subjects count the number of correctly completed puzzles and write that number on their booklet.

The experimenter then said:

There is one further task to do this hour, but I need a few minutes to organize the material. In the past individuals have requested to look again at the first test booklet, so I had the secretary make some extra copies and I have put them on your desks. While I put together this material you may do anything you like with the extra copy.

Five minutes were allowed for spontaneous resumption of the tasks.

RESULTS

Twenty-five subjects arrived for both experimental hours. All subjects in the success condition correctly completed at least nine of the designs, while subjects in the failure condition completed no more than three of the designs.

Results indicate that subjects high (above the median) in n Ach more frequently resumed interrupted tasks following interpolated failure as opposed to interpolated success experiences ($p = .045$, one-tailed, Fisher exact test). Subjects low in n Ach more frequently resumed tasks following success rather than failure experiences ($p = .07$, one-tailed, Fisher exact test; see Table 1). There is a significant Conditions $\times$ n Ach interaction ($\chi^2 = 6.00$, $p < .025$).

Table 1 | RELATION OF TASK RESUMPTION TO ACHIEVEMENT MOTIVATION AND SUCCESS OR FAILURE CONDITION

CONDITION	MOTIVE CLASSIFICATION			
	High		*Low*	
	RESUME		RESUME	
	Yes	No	Yes	No
Success	0	7	7	1
Failure	3	2	2	3

DISCUSSION

Prior studies frequently reveal interaction effects between individual differences in anxiety and n Ach and various experimental conditions. Atkinson (1953) found subjects classified as high in n Ach recall more incompleted tasks than subjects low in n Ach when the conditions are ego involving, but not when the conditions are relaxed. Lucas (1952) found that following continual failure experiences subjects classified as high in anxiety suffered decrements in level of performance, while subjects low in anxiety improved their level of performance. Child and Whiting (1950) found that subjects with histories of success reported they more frequently "relax" following attainment of a difficult goal, while individuals with histories of failure who expected to encounter frustration reported they more frequently strive for new goals following goal attainment. The above investigations used recall, level of performance, and instigation of new activities as dependent variables. This study replicates and extends these results, employing task resumption as the dependent variable.

As indicated by Atkinson (1953) the subjects used by Lewin and his associates were frequently "volunteers." Research cited by Atkinson (1953) indicates volunteer subjects are more likely to be highly motivated to achieve success. It is expected that under these conditions attainment of goals related to a desired goal will have substitute value.

Murray (1954), on the other hand, was working with clinical patients. It is likely that for these individuals the fear of making an aggressive response toward a significant authority figure exceeded their aggressive approach tendency. It is expected that under these conditions attainment of goals related to a desired goal will increase the tendency to strive for the original goal.

These interactions indicate that behavioral models proposed to account for these data will have to include both individual difference components and determinants which capture the differential reactions which these individuals exhibit under success and failure conditions. As Atkinson (1960) and Child (1954) have indicated, the drive model used by Spence and his associates (Spence, 1958) has not been able to account for the increment in performance which subjects low in anxiety exhibit under stressful (failure) situations. The model for achievement-oriented behavior proposed by Atkinson (1957) can handle data which reveal an increment in performance under ego-involving situations for individuals low in anxiety, but it does not account for the increment in the tendency to approach achievement-related goals which high-anxiety individuals exhibit following success experiences. A model which can adequately account for the interaction effects reviewed above remains to be formulated.

SUMMARY

Ss classified according to strength of achievement motivation were given 20 tasks and were interrupted at ½ the tasks before completion. ½ the Ss were then given interpolated success experiences, and ½ were given interpolated failures. Ss classified as high in n Achievement spontaneously tended to resume the interrupted tasks following failure but not following success; Ss classified as low in n Achievement tended to resume the tasks following interpolated success but not after failure. The results support previous findings in the area. The behavioral models as presently formulated cannot account for these interactions.

REFERENCES

Atkinson, J. W. The achievement motive and recall of interrupted and completed tasks. *Journal of Experimental Psychology*, 1953, *46*, 381–390.

Atkinson, J. W. Motivational determinants of risk-taking behavior. *Psychological Review*, 1957, *64*, 359–372.

Atkinson, J. W. (Ed.) *Motives in fantasy, action, and society.* Princeton, N.J.: Van Nostrand, 1958.

Atkinson, J. W. Personality dynamics. *Annual Review of Psychology*, 1960, *11*, 255–290.

Child, I. L. Personality. *Annual Review of Psychology*, 1954, *5*, 149–170.

Child, I. L., & Whiting, J. W. M. Effects of goal attainment: Relaxation versus renewed striving. *Journal of Abnormal and Social Psychology*, 1950, *45*, 667–681.

Freud, S. *The basic writings of Sigmund Freud.* New York: Random House, 1938.

Henle, Mary. The influence of valence on substitution. *Journal of Psychology*, 1944, *17*, 11–19.

Lewin, K. *A dynamic theory of personality.* New York: McGraw-Hill, 1935.

Lissner, K. Die Entspannung von Bedürfuissen durch Ersatzhandlungen. *Psychologische Forschung*, 1933, *18*, 218–250.

Lucas, J. D. The interactive effects of anxiety, failure and interserial duplication. *American Journal of Psychology*, 1952, *55*, 59–66.

McClelland, D. C., Atkinson, J. W., Clark, R. A., & Lowell, E. L. *The achievement motive.* New York: Appleton, 1953.

Mahler, W. Ersatzhandlungen verschiedener Realitätsgrades. *Psychologische Forschung*, 1933, *18*, 27–89.

Miller, N. E. Experimental studies of conflict. In J. McV. Hunt (Ed.), *Personality and the behavior disorders.* Vol. 1. New York: Ronald, 1944. Pp. 431–465.

Murray, E. J. A case study in a behavioral analysis of psychotherapy. *Journal of Abnormal and Social Psychology*, 1954, *49*, 305–310.

Ovsiankina, Marie. Wiederaufnahme unterbrochener Handlungen. *Psychologische Forschung*, 1928, *11*, 302–379.

Spence, K. W. A theory of emotionally based drive (*D*) and its relation to performance in simple learning situations. *American Psychologist*, 1958, *13*, 131–141.

14 | Sex Typing and Personality Development

14.1 | FATHER CHARACTERISTICS AND SEX TYPING*[1]

Jules M. Greenstein

The development of sex-typical or sex-atypical behavior has usually been attributed to some process of identification or imitation learning. In the male child, it is often assumed that both the development of culturally normative sex-appropriate social behavior (masculinity) and the development of sex-appropriate biological behavior (heterosexuality) are contingent upon some characteristics of the child's father. One prominent variant of Freudian identification theory labeled defensive identification by Mowrer (1950) and aggressive identification by Bronfenbrenner (1960) emphasizes the fear-evoking aspects of the father's role as the agent which leads the male child to identify with the aggressor. Another version of identification theory, the developmental identification hypothesis attributes appropriate sex typing in males to the nurturant and hence secondary reinforcing aspects of the father's behavior (Mowrer, 1950). A third approach, the social power theory (Parsons, 1955), considers identification to be a function of the relative power of the father as a controller of resources.

Common to all identification theories are the following assumptions: the male child initially identifies with the mother; through a modeling process, certain specified role characteristics of the father, such as his relative power or nurturance, facilitate or inhibit a shift in identification to the father; and the resulting father identification pro-

* SOURCE: Greenstein, J. M. Father characteristics and sex typing. *Journal of Personality and Social Psychology*, 1966, 3, 271–277. Copyright 1966 by the American Psychological Association and reprinted by permission.

[1] This paper is based on a dissertation submitted to the Graduate School of Rutgers—the State University in partial fulfillment of the requirements for the PhD degree. The author wishes to express his appreciation to Nelson G. Hanawalt, under whose supervision the investigation was conducted, and to the staff of the New Jersey State Diagnostic Center for their participation in the research.

motes appropriate sex typing such as masculine interests and attitudes and heterosexuality. Bronfenbrenner (1958) has pointed out that many studies of sex-role identification have left it unclear whether the identification refers to the learning process, the real or perceived similarity to a parent, or to an end product such as masculinity or heterosexuality. Nevertheless, considerable data have been collected which suggest that one or another aspect of the end product, sex typing, is related to such model characteristics as father nurturance, father power, or some combination of these consistent with major identification theory models (Bandura, Ross, & Ross, 1963; Mussen, 1961; Mussen & Distler, 1959, 1960; Payne & Mussen, 1956; Sears, 1953).

The role of the father is so central to identification theories of sex typing that a corollary assumption is often made that where the father is absent, the male child remains mother-identified and may be likely to develop feminine sex-social characteristics and latent, or even overt, homosexual tendencies (Fenichel, 1945, p. 95). Studies of the effects of father absence (Bach, 1946; Leichty, 1960; Lynn & Sawrey, 1959; Sears, Pintler, & Sears, 1946) have suggested the development of inappropriate sex typing, but these studies have been limited to young children or to the effects of very short periods of father absence. The effects of prolonged father absence on sex typing in the adolescent or adult have not been systematically determined. Practical problems in securing data have also limited research aimed at testing hypotheses as to the effects of various father characteristics on sex typing. Such father characteristics as closeness or relative dominance in the family have been measured only indirectly by the mother's report (Sears, 1953; Sears, Maccoby, & Levin, 1957) or by the child's perception of the father (Mussen, 1961; Mussen & Distler, 1959, 1960). Measures of sex typing have been limited to choice of role in doll play or to responses to a masculinity-femininity inventory and have not been extended to the dimension of homosexuality-heterosexuality.

The present paper reports the results of an investigation which attempted to overcome the limitations of prior research by trying to: assess the effects of prolonged father absence on male adolescents; measure degree of father-closeness and relative decision-making dominance by direct observation rather than by indirect report; and evaluate the effects of absence, closeness, and dominance on the latent and overt homosexuality dimensions of sex typing as well as on the more conventional masculinity-femininity measures.

METHOD

SUBJECTS. The subjects were 75 delinquent boys ranging in age from 13 to 18 residing temporarily at the New Jersey State Diagnostic Center. Criteria for inclusion in the father-absent (FA) group required that the subject had spent at least 3 years of life prior to age 12 in a home where no male adult resided. Inclusion in the father-present (FP) group required that the subject had spent his entire life in a home consisting of both natural parents or substitute parents acquired during the first year of life. Sampling was on the basis of consecutive admissions meeting the criteria.

FA group. The FA group consisted of 25 subjects with a mean age of 15.5, mean IQ of 98.0, and median length of father absence of 8.2 years. All had lost their fathers as a result of desertion, separation, or divorce.

FP group. The FP group consisted of 50 subjects with a mean age of 15.3 and a mean IQ of 96.6. There were no significant differences between the FP and FA groups in age, IQ, or birth order. Although the FP group may have been higher in socioeconomic status because of the presence of a male breadwinner, both groups were from the lower income levels and the mothers were of identical educational levels.

RATINGS OF FATHER CHARACTERISTICS.   Both parents of each subject in the FP group were interviewed frequently by a psychiatric social worker who rated the father on 6-point rating scales for dominance and closeness.

Father-dominance rating. In forming their ratings of relative decision-making dominance, the interviewing social workers were instructed to consider:

> Who appears to take charge in asking questions, making demands, or relating events?
> Who seems to dominate when mother and father have minor disagreements?
> Who seems to be more confident in making minor decisions, signing permits, etc.?
> Who takes the initiative in starting and terminating conversations?
> Does one tend to silence or belittle the other in his or her presence?
> What does each parent say about the other?
> Does one appear to be frightened of the other?

In order to remain as close as possible to the meaning of dominance at the level of clinical observation, these questions were to be used as guidelines in forming a single global rating of father dominance on a 6-point scale ranging from "Father is very clearly and strongly the dominant partner; mother has very little say in things" to "Mother is very clearly and strongly the dominant partner; father has very little say in things."

Father-closeness rating. A similar procedure was used for rating father closeness. The interviewing social workers were instructed to consider:

> What does the father say about the son?
> How familiar is he with those events in the son's life that a father should know about?
> How concerned is he with his son's adjustment?
> Does he spontaneously go out of his way to make things easier for his son?
> Does he show ease or discomfort in talking to his son?
> Do they have things to talk about or does the father devote his time to giving one-way sermons?
> Does the father really seem to want to gain insight into his son's behavior?

The final rating was again on a 6-point scale ranging from "Father is obviously very warm towards, involved with, and emotionally close to his son" to "Father is obviously cold towards, uninvolved with, and emotionally distant from his son."

Reliability of ratings. Since only the social worker routinely assigned to each subject had direct contact with the parents, no direct measure of rating reliability was obtainable. An effort was made to secure an indirect estimate of rating reliability by the investigator's interviewing each subject and questioning him about his parents, their characteristics, and his relationship to them. From the manner in which the parents were described, ratings of dominance and closeness were obtained which were then correlated with the social worker ratings. Although this procedure confounded reliability and validity of the ratings, it allowed for an estimate of the probable lower ranges of interrater reliability. The magnitude of the obtained correlations of $r = .59$ for dominance and $r = .68$ for closeness suggests that interrater reliability would have been considerably higher if it were obtainable and that the social workers' ratings could be treated as reasonably objective.

MEASURES OF SEX TYPING.   Three related, though logically distinct, aspects of sex typing were chosen: homosexual tendencies, fantasy identification, and masculinity-femininity. A variety of measures were chosen to tap both overt and covert aspects of these dimensions, selection being based on objectivity and reliability of scoring, past evidence of construct validity, and pertinence to the dimension measured.

Overt homosexuality. Part of the routine examination at the Diagnostic Center is a psychiatric interview conducted under sodium amytal medication. During this interview, questions regarding the subjects' past behavior are asked which permit the measurement of frequency of overt homosexual experiences. Since simple division of the sample into homosexual and nonhomosexual groups would require better knowledge of what constitutes a normal degree of homosexuality than is presently available, a simple ordinal scale of overt homosexual tendencies was constructed. The classifications used and number of subjects in the combined FA and FP groups falling into each class were as follows:

1.   Frequent homosexual experiences since puberty ($n = 15$).
2.   Several homosexual experiences since puberty ($n = 11$).
3.   One homosexual experience since puberty ($n = 8$).
4.   Nonhomosexual but sexually deviant experiences ($n = 10$).[2]
5.   No deviant experiences reported ($n = 31$).

Wheeler Rorschach Indices. The Rorschach indices of homosexuality originally derived by Wheeler (1949) have gained construct validity as a measure of latent homosexual tendencies in studies by Davids, Joelson, and McArthur (1956), Hooker (1958), and Aronson (1952). In slightly revised form to improve reliability by considering only the subject's first two responses to each Rorschach card and by scoring each sign only once, the Wheeler Indices were used

[2] All subjects in this category were referred for molesting young girls, sexually exposing themselves, or both.

as a measure of covert homosexual tendencies. The interrater scoring reliability between the investigator's scoring and that of an independent rater was found to be $r = .86$.

VC Figure Preference Test. The Masculine Preference score of the VC Figure Preference Test (Webster, 1957) is a factorially derived measure of preference for male over female sex symbols which are embedded in disguised form in a test of artistic preference. Since one of the frequently reported characteristics of male homosexuals is a revulsion for female organs or an attraction towards the male, the Figure Preference Test was used as a second measure of latent homosexuality.

TAT hero choice. As the measure of fantasy identification, eight TAT cards depicting either a male and female figure together or a single figure of ambiguous sex were presented to the subjects. Stories were written in response to the usual instructions and were scored on a 5-point scale according to the degree to which the subject chose a male or female as the central character. Since adopting the point of view of a female in one's fantasy productions is implied in the construct feminine identification, the TAT Female Hero Choice measure was considered most appropriate for tapping this aspect of sex typing. An r of .93 was obtained between the investigator's scoring and that of an independent rater.

Masculinity-femininity. The three M-F scales of the Vassar College Attitude Inventory (Sanford, Webster, & Freedman, 1957) were used as measures of the masculinity-femininity dimension. These scales provide independent measures of three clusters of items which are usually not separated in conventional M-F inventories. The three scales have been labeled by Bereiter (1960) "Feminine Interests" (MF-I), "Feminine Passivity" (MF-II), and "Feminine Sensitivity" (MF-III).

RESULTS

DIFFERENCES BETWEEN FA AND FP GROUPS.   In most instances comparisons of FA and FP groups were possible by straightforward use of t tests for independent samples. Scores on the Wheeler Rorschach Indices were sharply skewed and significance of the differences between groups was tested by means of the nonparametric Mann-Whitney U test. Data on frequency of overt homosexual experiences presented in Table 1 were analyzed by treating the absence or presence of the father as a dichotomized variable; that is, as a set of ranks in which all subjects were tied within either of the two ranks. Kendall's rank-correlation coefficient tau, corrected for ties in both variables (Kendall, 1948), was computed and its significance from zero tested. This permitted a more powerful test of the association between father absence and overt homosexuality than the more conventional chi-square test, since the latter is insensitive to order within the variables and would have required combining categories because of the small expected frequencies.

The obtained tau of .15 for the data in Table 1 is not great enough to warrant rejection of the hypothesis of no association between father absence and overt homosexuality ($p < .17$).

Table 2 presents the means obtained on test measures of homosexual tendencies, feminine fantasy identification, and masculinity-femininity. In each instance, a high score

Table 1 | FREQUENCY OF HOMOSEXUAL EXPERIENCE IN FA AND FP GROUPS

TYPE OF EXPERIENCE	FATHER ABSENT ($N = 25$) N	FATHER PRESENT ($N = 50$) N
Frequent homosexual experiences	7	8
Several homosexual experiences	4	7
One homosexual experience	3	5
Nonhomosexual but deviant experience	2	8
Nonhomosexual, nondeviant experience	9	22

Table 2 | COMPARISON OF FA AND FP GROUPS ON TEST MEASURES OF SEX TYPING

TEST	FATHER ABSENT ($N = 25$) M	FATHER PRESENT ($N = 50$) M	t
Homosexual tendencies			
Figure Preference Test	25.16	25.48	−0.18
Wheeler Rorschach Indices[a]	2.16	2.18	−0.11
Fantasy identification			
TAT Female Hero Choice	20.50	20.56	−0.23
Masculinity-femininity			
Feminine interests	5.68	5.42	0.60
Feminine passivity	19.84	19.92	−0.07
Feminine sensitivity	18.00	17.24	0.89

[a] Means are presented only for comparison; significance was tested by the Mann-Whitney U test.

is in the direction of deviant sex typing. None of the differences approach significance and there is no consistent pattern favoring either group.

Since there was considerable variation within the FA group in length of father absence, an effort was made to determine whether this source of variation may have concealed differences between the groups. Length of father absence within the FA group was correlated with each of the measures of sex typing. Presumably, a longer period of father absence should result in a greater deviation in sex typing according to identification theories, particularly since in the sample studied a shorter period of father absence usually meant the presence of a father during some fraction of the Oedipal period. The rank correlations obtained, however, ranged from .16 to −.17 and none approached significance.

FATHER DOMINANCE AND SEX TYPING. Since ratings for father dominance and father closeness were skewed and at no better than an ordinal level of measurement, the procedure of computing Kendall's tau and testing its two-tailed significance was preferred to the procedure of dichotomizing the FP group and thereby losing information about degrees of dominance and closeness.

The Kendall rank correlations obtained between father dominance and the sex-typing measures ranged from .12 to — .15. Since none approached significance, the hypothesis of a negative association between father dominance and deviation in sex typing was not confirmed.

FATHER CLOSENESS AND SEX TYPING. The only significant findings were obtained when father closeness was correlated with the measures of deviation in sex typing. Here, however, the significant findings are in a direction *converse* to that predicted by the developmental identification theory. Reference to Table 3 shows that the greater the degree of father closeness, the greater the frequency of overt homosexual experiences. When the measures of latent homosexual tendencies are considered, the correlations are in the same direction and approach statistical significance ($p < .09$, two-tailed). Father closeness does not appear to affect the masculinity-femininity dimension, and only in fantasy identification is there any slight measure of support for the developmental identification hypothesis. Here, the association between father distance and feminine identification in TAT productions is too small, however, to warrant rejection of the hypothesis of no association ($p < .12$, two-tailed).

DISCUSSION

Contrary to the expectations based upon current identification theories, this investigation failed to find significant differences between father-absent and father-present boys in any of the dimensions usually related to sex typing. The expectation that sex typing might be related to the power distribution within the family was also unconfirmed. The

Table 3 | RANK CORRELATIONS BETWEEN FATHER CLOSENESS AND SEX TYPING MEASURES

MEASURE	TAU
Homosexual tendencies	
Overt homosexuality	.27***
Figure Preference Test	.19**
Wheeler Rorschach Indices	.18**
Fantasy identification	
TAT Female Hero Choice	—.17*
Masculinity-femininity	—.05
Feminine interests	—.09
Feminine passivity	—.05
Feminine sensitivity	

  * $p = .12$.
 ** $p = .09$.
*** $p = .03$.

finding that father closeness is associated with overt homosexuality rather than its converse seems to contradict the developmental identification hypothesis and deserves further analysis. Surprisingly, of the three subjects whose fathers were rated as "obviously very warm towards, involved with, and emotionally close to his son," two had engaged in frequent homosexual acts and one of these confessed to being a homosexual prostitute. None of the four boys whose fathers were considered "obviously cold towards, uninvolved with, and emotionally distant from his son" reported any homosexual experiences at all when questioned under sodium amytal.

A possible explanation of these data may emerge if the acquisition of heterosexuality were attributed to some process other than identification with the father. It is possible, for example, that learning by differential reinforcement rather than by modeling may be more decisive in the acquisition of sex-appropriate behavior. Such a possibility seems most apparent when heterosexuality is considered, since unlike the parents' sex-typical social behavior their specifically sexual behavior is usually unobserved by the child and therefore not subject to imitation learning. If this hypothesis were true, homosexuality would be relatively independent of those father characteristics which presumably facilitate identification with the father.

A theory of sex typing which does not require identification as a mediating process has been outlined by Colley (1959). According to this theory, the acquisition of appropriate sex typing is contingent upon what the child learns of the expectations which the significant adults and others in his life have for him. Thus, a moderate amount of seductive behavior towards the male child by the mother is considered to be important as a means of encouraging the development of heterosexual approach behavior. Similarly, a certain optimum of hostile and rivalrous behavior on the part of the father is important in discouraging homosexual approach behavior. This theory has the advantage over derivatives of Freudian identification theory in not requiring different determinants of the acquisition process in males and females. It also circumvents the thorny problem faced by all identification theories of explaining how it is possible for a fatherless boy to develop appropriate sex typing at all. Colley points out that:

> Even in a father's absence, an appropriately identified mother will respond to a boy "as if" he were a male and will expect him to treat her as a male would treat a female. When she and her son are together in the presence of other males she will expect of him some competition, hostility, and lack of sexuality in his relations with the other males regardless of their ages. Her interpretive approval or disapproval of his play with other male children . . . also serve to let him know what she expects of male with male interactions [pp. 173–174].

Not only does the Colley differential expectation theory permit an alternative explanation for the absence of differences in sex typing between the FA and FP boys, it also suggests a possible explanation of the significant association between father closeness and homosexual tendencies. It may have been that those fathers rated as closest to their sons were also the most seductive towards their sons. A high degree of implicit sexualization of the father-son relationship would, according to the differential expectation theory, predispose the child towards sexual approach behavior with males.

A review of the case histories of the subjects used in this study gives considerable credence to the possibility that judgments of seductiveness may have been confounded with, or included as a major component of, ratings of father closeness. One of the fathers rated closest to his son spoke with great delight about how he enjoyed washing his son and ministering to him when the boy was small. On one visit to the institution, he is reported to have hugged and kissed his son, calling him "my darling." Another of the fathers rated as closest spoke at length of how important it was to him that his son love him. In both instances the child became involved in frequent homosexual acts, although in neither case was the child considered to be particularly effeminate.

An explanation in terms of direct reinforcement rather than modeling as the process by which homosexual tendencies may be acquired offered itself repeatedly as individual case histories were reviewed. The only subject who was willing to characterize himself as a homosexual and who anticipated a future life within a homosexual subculture did not have a father; yet he attributed his own homosexuality and transvestism to his mother's dressing him in girl's clothing during his early childhood and curtailing his efforts at male behavior. Almost identical cases of the mother's direct reinforcement of sex-atypical behavior have been reported by Litin, Giffin, and Johnson (1956).

Of course, no conclusions may be drawn from the anecdotal reports upon which these speculations are based. A differential reinforcement theory of sex typing stands as much in need of experimental confirmation as do identification theories. Nevertheless, the present data suggest extreme caution in treating sex typing solely from the point of view of identification or modeling theory.

SUMMARY

In an attempt to test two identification theories of sex typing, frequency of overt homosexuality and test measures of latent homosexuality, feminine identification, and masculinity-femininity were obtained from 25 father-absent and 50 father-present male adolescent delinquents. The fathers of the father-present Ss were rated for degree of dominance and closeness to their sons. Results indicated no significant differences between the father-absent and father-present Ss and no significant correlations between father dominance and the sex-typing measures. Contrary to the developmental identification hypothesis, a small but significant correlation was found between degree of father closeness and frequency of overt homosexuality. Results were considered to be more consistent with a differential reinforcement theory of sex typing than with identification theory.

REFERENCES

Aronson, M. L. A study of the Freudian theory of paranoia by means of the Rorschach test. *Journal of Projective Techniques*, 1952, *16*, 397–411.

Bach, G. R. Father-fantasies and father-typing in father-separated children. *Child Development*, 1946, *17*, 63–80.

Bandura, A., Ross, Dorothea, & Ross, Sheila A. A comparative test of the status envy, social power, and secondary reinforcement theories of identificatory learning. *Journal of Abnormal and Social Psychology*, 1963, 67, 527–534.

Bereiter, C. A factor analytic study of the VC Attitude Inventory scales. Unpublished manuscript, Mary Conover Mellon Foundation, Poughkeepsie, New York, 1960.

Bronfenbrenner, U. The study of identification through interpersonal perception. In R. Tagiuri & L. Petrullo (Eds.), *Person perception and interpersonal behavior.* Stanford, Calif.: Stanford University Press, 1958. Pp. 110–130.

Bronfenbrenner, U. Freudian theories of identification and their derivatives. *Child Development*, 1960, *31*, 15–40.

Colley, T. The nature and origins of psychological sexual identity. *Psychological Review*, 1959, 66, 165–177.

Davids, A., Joelson, M., & McArthur, C. Rorschach and TAT indices of homosexuality in overt homosexuals, neurotics, and normal males. *Journal of Abnormal and Social Psychology*, 1956, 53, 161–172.

Fenichel, O. *The psychoanalytic theory of neurosis.* New York: Norton, 1945.

Hooker, E. Male homosexuality in the Rorschach. *Journal of Projective Techniques*, 1958, *22*, 33–54.

Kendall, M. G. *Rank correlation methods.* London: Griffin, 1948.

Leichty, M. M. The effect of father-absence during early childhood upon the Oedipal situation as reflected in young adults. *Merrill-Palmer Quarterly*, 1960, 6, 212–217.

Litin, E. M., Giffin, M. E., & Johnson, A. M. Parental influences in unusual sexual behavior in children. *Psychoanalytic Quarterly*, 1956, *25*, 37–55.

Lynn, D. B., & Sawrey, W. L. The effects of father absence on Norwegian boys and girls. *Journal of Abnormal and Social Psychology*, 1959, 59, 258–262.

Mowrer, O. H. *Learning theory and personality dynamics.* New York: Ronald, 1950.

Mussen, P. H. Some antecedents and consequents of masculine sex-typing in adolescent boys. *Psychological Monographs*, 1961, *75*(2, Whole No. 506).

Mussen, P. H., & Distler, L. Masculinity, identification, and father-son relationships. *Journal of Abnormal and Social Psychology*, 1959, 59, 350–356.

Mussen, P. H., & Distler, L. Child-rearing antecedents of masculine identification in kindergarten boys. *Child Development*, 1960, *31*, 89–100.

Parsons, T. Family structure and the socialization of the child. In T. Parsons & R. F. Bales (Eds.), *Family, socialization, and interaction process.* New York: Free Press, 1955. Pp. 35–131.

Payne, D. E., & Mussen, P. H. Parent-child relations and father identification among adolescent boys. *Journal of Abnormal and Social Psychology*, 1956, *52*, 358–362.

Sanford, N., Webster, H., & Freedman, M. *VC Attitude Inventory.* Poughkeepsie, N.Y.: Vassar College, Mary Conover Mellon Foundation, 1957.

Sears, Pauline S. Child-rearing factors related to playing of sex-typed roles. *American Psychologist*, 1953, *8*, 431. (Abstract)

Sears, R. R., Maccoby, Eleanor E., & Levin, H. *Patterns of child rearing.* New York: Harper & Row, 1957.

Sears, R R., Pintler, M. H., & Sears, Pauline. Effect of father-separation on preschool children's doll play aggression. *Child Development*, 1946, *17*, 219–243.

Webster, H. *VC Figure Preference Test.* Poughkeepsie, N.Y.: Vassar College, Mary Conover Mellon Foundation, 1957.

Wheeler, W. M. An analysis of Rorschach indices of homosexuality. *Rorschach Research Exchange*, 1949, *13*, 97–126.

14.2 | FAMILY INTERACTION EFFECTS ON MASCULINITY-FEMININITY*[1]

B. G. Rosenberg and B. Sutton-Smith

It is traditionally assumed that sex roles are learned through the child's identification with the like-sex parent (Kagan, 1964). Accumulating research, however, points to the fact that children also have effects upon each other's sex roles, and perhaps even have effects upon the sex roles of their parents (Bell, 1964; Sampson, 1966; Warren, 1966). In earlier studies, the present authors have attempted to identify some of the behavioral outcomes of the constant interaction between siblings (Rosenberg, 1966; Rosenberg & Sutton-Smith, 1964a, 1964b, 1966, 1967; Rosenberg, Sutton-Smith, & Griffiths, 1965; Rosenberg, Sutton-Smith, & Landy, 1966; Sutton-Smith, Roberts, & Rosenberg, 1964; Sutton-Smith & Rosenberg, 1965, 1966a, 1966b, 1968). Unfortunately, when sibling positions are used as status variables and differences shown in a variety of dependent variables, there is always the possibility that the outcomes are not actually determined by the interaction between the siblings, but are due to the differential parental treatment of the siblings. What is required is a design in which parent and sibling variables are controlled at the same time (Rosenberg et al., 1966). The present paper which is concerned with sex-role characteristics, takes both parental and sibling variables into account. The dependent variables are the subject's, his sibling's, and his parents' responses to a masculinity-femininity inventory; the independent variables are several types of the two-child family. This approach to actual siblings and actual parents and the investigation of the covariation of their masculinity-femininity responses with the distinctive family structures of which they are members provides the possibility of investigating whether or not sex-role attributes are indeed influenced by these interactional structures and not simply by identification with the same-sex parent.

METHOD

The sample was composed of 160 college sophomore females, their actual siblings (males and females) and their native mothers and fathers. The Gough (1952) Scale of Psychological Femininity (Fe) was administered directly to the female subjects, while the scale was mailed to the subject's own sibling, mother, and father. All subjects were

* SOURCE: Rosenberg, B. G., & Sutton-Smith, B. Family interaction effects on masculinity-femininity. *Journal of Personality and Social Psychology*, 1968, 8, 117–120. Copyright 1968 by the American Psychological Association and reprinted by permission.

[1] This study was supported by Grant MH 07994-04 from the National Institute of Mental Health.

members of two-child families. Analysis of variance, multiple t tests, and correlational techniques were employed in the analyses. Analysis involved correlations within all members of the quadrad of the two-child families, for example, mother-first daughter, mother-second daughter, father-first daughter, father-second daughter, daughter-daughter, and mother-father. Thus, for each of the several quadrads investigated, there are correlations of the femininity scores of all members of each family and comparisons of mean Fe scores for all members.

RESULTS[2]

Table 1 presents the mean Fe scores for all subjects with summaries for birth order and like- versus opposite-sex dyads. As expected, girls ($\overline{X} = 22.41$) are higher on Fe than boys ($\overline{X} = 15.90$; $t = 63$, $df = 138$, $p < .001$); mothers ($\overline{X} = 24.42$) are higher on Fe than daughters ($\overline{X} = 23.09$, $t = 3.45$, $df = 138$, $p < .01$); and fathers ($\overline{X} = 17.46$) are higher on Fe than sons ($\overline{X} = 15.90$, $t = 3.18$, $df = 138$, $p < .01$). Simple analysis of variance performed on these data yielded directional findings for subject ($F = 2.07$, $df = 3/156$, $p < .10$), and father ($F = 1.50$, $df = 3/156$, $p < .20$), and significance for sibling ($F = 49.00$, $df = 3/156$, $p < .001$). These findings were sufficiently suggestive that a complex analysis of variance was conducted to examine the interaction of ordinal position (A) and sibling sex status (B) on the subject's Fe scores. The results of the analysis indicated that sibling sex status (i.e., sex of sibling) is the significant source of variance ($F = 4.66$, $df = 1/156$, $p < .05$), not ordinal position or the interaction. Apparently, sex of sibling does make a difference in the subject's Fe scores. As can be seen, members of like-sex (all-girl) dyads achieve significantly higher Fe scores ($\overline{X} = 23.61$) than members of opposite-sex (a boy and a girl) dyads ($\overline{X} = 22.41$), with a girl with a sister significantly higher on Fe than a girl with a brother.

[2] The authors are indebted to Judith Griffiths and Frank Landy for their assistance in the statistical analysis.

Table 1 | MEAN FE SCORES FOR FEMALES, THEIR SIBLINGS, MOTHERS, AND FATHERS IN THE TWO-CHILD FAMILIES

	SELF	SIBLING	MOTHER	FATHER
Girl with a younger sister (F1F$_{60}$)[a]	23.93	22.92	24.77	16.73
Girl with a younger brother (F1M$_{40}$)	22.35	15.52	24.45	17.40
Girl with an older sister (FF2$_{30}$)	22.97	23.43	24.40	16.20
Girl with an older brother (MF2$_{30}$)	22.50	16.40	23.70	17.50
1st born$_{100}$	23.30	19.96	24.64	17.00
2nd born$_{60}$	22.73	19.92	24.05	16.87
Like-sex siblings$_{90}$	23.61	23.08	24.64	16.55
Opposite-sex siblings$_{70}$	22.41	15.90	24.13	17.46

[a] The number (e.g., F1F$_{60}$) refers to 60 subjects, their 60 siblings, 60 mothers, and 60 fathers in that category.

A complex analysis of variance performed on sibling's Fe scores was highly significant ($F = 49.05$, $df = 1/156$, $p < .001$) as was expected. A third analysis of variance of mother's Fe scores did not obtain significance.

Finally, a similar analysis performed on father's Fe scores indicated that sibling sex status is the significant source of variance ($F = 3.97$, $df = 1/156$, $p < .05$), suggesting fathers differentially respond to the sex of the children. A father with a girl and a boy is significantly higher on Fe scores ($\overline{X} = 17.46$) than a father with two girls ($\overline{X} = 16.55$). Birth order, alone, is not a significant source of variance in any of the above analyses.

A content analysis of individual items revealed that this finding is true for the more subtle Fe items on the Gough Scale (e.g., "sometimes I have the same dream over and over," "a windstorm terrifies me") as well as for the more obvious items (e.g., "I would like the work of a building contractor," "I think I would like the work of a dress designer"). In brief, the results of this analysis consistently differentiate fathers of opposite-sex dyads from fathers of like-sex dyads in their willingness to admit to anxiety, discomfort, sensitivity, emotional disturbances, and so on, admissions about those behaviors which are traditionally viewed as feminine.

The correlations of Fe scores of each member of the quadrad by sex composition of the children is presented in Table 2. As can be seen, the magnitudes of the coefficients obtained are not striking. The patterns of correlations for the girl-girl dyad as compared with the girl-boy dyad are, however, quite distinctive. In the girl-girl dyad, the girls' scores correlate with each other, and their sibling's scores correlate with the mothers', so that we have, in effect, some mutuality in the females in this family structure, but the father scores on this inventory make him the isolate. By contrast, in the girl-boy family, the scores of the mother, father, and boy intercorrelate amongst each other, and the girl is the isolate, except that her Fe does correlate with that of her mother.

Table 2 | INTERCORRELATIONS WITHIN THE FAMILY OF FE SCORES

	SELF-SIBLING	SELF-MOTHER	SELF-FATHER	SIBLING-MOTHER	SIBLING-FATHER	MOTHER-FATHER
$F1F_{60}$	.26**	−.06	.10	.14	.11	.13
$F1M_{40}$	−.04	.37**	−.02	.25*	.31**	.12
$FF2_{30}$	.33**	−.02	.20	.27	−.23	−.18
$MF2_{30}$	.13	.01	.04	.30*	.24	.40**
1st born$_{100}$	.27***	.12	.03	.16*	.04	.12
2nd born$_{80}$	.23*	.00	.10	.26**	−.19*	.11
Like sex$_{90}$	.28***	−.04	.14	.18*	−.01	.04
Opposite sex$_{70}$	.03	.23**	.00	.25**	.28**	.23**

* $p < .10$.
** $p < .05$.
*** $p < .01$.

DISCUSSION

It seems clear that there are interrelationships within the family structure that reflect themselves in the measure of psychological femininity. The results show that sibling's status is related to sex-role preference, a finding already well established (Brim, 1958; Rosenberg & Sutton-Smith, 1964a). The results also give support to those who have suggested that the father plays a more critical role in the development of the children's sex role preferences than does the mother (Brodbeck, 1954; Bronfenbrenner, 1961; Gray, 1959; Johnson, 1963; Parsons & Bales, 1955; Rothbart & Maccoby, 1966; Sears, 1951). In the present data, the father's scores vary systematically as a function of the sex of the child; the mother's do not. Of greater interest to the present investigators, however, is the manner in which the sex-role preferences vary with the distinctive structure of the two types of family here presented, the girl-girl family and the girl-boy family.

In the girl-girl family, it was noted that the father's scores do not correlate with those of other members of his family and are less feminine than those of the father in the girl-boy family. This discovery parallels an earlier finding with preadolescent children that a boy with two sisters expresses more masculinity on a sex role inventory than a boy with one sister (Rosenberg & Sutton-Smith, 1964a). Both the boys in that study and the fathers in this appear to be responding to a majority of females by stronger masculine self-representation. The cogency of this interpretation is supported by the finding that in the boy-girl family, where neither boy nor father are outnumbered, both show more feminine scores, together with correlations between their own and the mother's scores. These interrelationships together with the content analysis of the boy and father inventory responses support the view that in the boy-girl family both boy and father are more accepting of feminine elements in their own sex-role preferences. This finding is also in accord with an earlier study in which boys from such opposite-sex families were shown to be more interested in expressive-creative occupations than boys from single-sex families (Sutton-Smith et al., 1964). We have, therefore, the situation that in the girl-girl family the father responds to his relative isolation (defined in terms of our correlational measures) by emphasizing his masculinity, and in the boy-girl family the girl responds to her relative isolation, by identifying more strongly with the mother. Each isolate appears to counter the importance of the opposite sex in these two families by increasing their own sex-appropriate responses.

This apparently counteractive response to isolation can be interpreted in clinical terms as a reaction on the part of both isolates to a sense of sex role inadequacy by a compensatory heightening of their own sex-role characteristics. Or it can be interpreted in structural or normative terms as an attempt to reestablish a sex-role balance in a family in danger of skewing too strongly towards one or the other sex-role polarity (Parsons & Bales, 1955). It is sufficient for the present investigators to reemphasize that the understanding of sex-role learning clearly requires taking into consideration the various sources of influence examined in this study. Sex-role learning involves sibling-sibling and child-parent effects as well as parent-child effects. The general character of the varying possible constellations and the compensatory or structural balances which may take place within them cannot be known until there are a significant number of studies which concurrently take into account a multiplicity of effects as in the present case.

SUMMARY

The present study compares the responses of 160 college females from girl-girl and girl-boy 2-child families with the responses of their actual siblings, mothers, and fathers on the Gough Scale of Psychological Femininity. Major interaction effects result from the sex of the sibling and from the effects of sibling sex on the father's Fe score. In the girl-girl family, the scores of the females intercorrelate, but the father is a relative isolate and has lowered femininity scores. In the girl-boy family, the scores of the boy, mother, and father intercorrelate, but the girl is a relative isolate, and heightens her identification with the mother. The complexity of these interaction effects is contrasted with traditional sex-role theory which suggests that sex-role characteristics are acquired only from the same-sex parent.

REFERENCES

Bell, R. Q. The problem of direction of effects in studies of parents and children. Paper presented at the conference on research methodology in parent-child interaction, Upstate Medical Center, Syracuse, October 1964.

Brim, O. G. Family structure and sex role learning by children: A further analysis of Helen Koch's data. *Sociometry*, 1958, *21*, 1–16.

Brodbeck, A. J. Learning and identification: IV. Oedipal motivation as a determinant of conscious development. *Journal of Genetic Psychology*, 1954, *84*, 219–227.

Bronfenbrenner, U. Some familial antecedents of responsibility and leadership in adolescents. In L. Petrullo and B. M. Bass (Eds.), *Leadership and interpersonal behavior.* New York: Holt, Rinehart and Winston, Inc., 1961.

Gough, H. Identifying psychological femininity. *Educational and Psychological Measurement*, 1952, *12*, 427–439.

Gray, S. W. Perceived similarity to parents and adjustment. *Child Development*, 1959, *30*, 91–107.

Johnson, M. Sex role learning in the nuclear family. *Child Development*, 1963, *34*, 319–333.

Kagan, J. Acquisition and significance of sex-typing and sex role identity. In M. L. Hoffman & L. W. Hoffman (Eds.), *Review of child development research.* New York: Russell Sage, 1964. Pp. 137–168.

Parsons, T., & Bales, R. F. *Family, socialization and interaction process.* New York: Free Press, 1955.

Rosenberg, B. G. Family interaction and sex role identification. *American Journal of Orthopsychiatry*, 1966, *36*, 355–356.

Rosenberg, B. G., & Sutton-Smith, B. Ordinal position and sex role identification. *Genetic Psychology Monographs*, 1964, *70*, 297–328. (a)

Rosenberg, B. G., & Sutton-Smith, B. The relationship of ordinal position and sibling sex status to cognitive abilities. *Psychonomic Science*, 1964, *1*, 81–82. (b)

Rosenberg, B. G., & Sutton-Smith, B. Sibling associations, family size, and cognitive abilities. *Journal of Genetic Psychology*, 1966, *107*, 271–279.

Rosenberg, B. G., & Sutton-Smith, B. Intra-family effects on sex role identity. Paper presented at the meeting of the Society for Research in Child Development, New York, April 1967.

Rosenberg, B. G., Sutton-Smith, B., & Griffiths, J. Sibling differences in empathic style. *Perceptual and Motor Skills*, 1965, *21*, 811–814.

Rosenberg, B. G., Sutton-Smith, B., & Landy, F. The interaction of father-absence and sibling-presence effects on cognitive ability. Paper presented at the meeting of the Midwestern Psychological Association, Chicago, May 1966.

Rothbart, M. K., & Maccoby, E. Parents' differential reactions to sons and daughters. *Journal of Personality and Social Psychology*, 1966, *4*, 237–243.

Sampson, E. E. The study of ordinal position: Antecedents and outcomes. In B. Maher (Ed.), *Progress in experimental personality research.* Vol. 2. New York: Academic Press, 1965.

Sears, P. S. Doll play aggression in normal young children: Influence of sex, age, sibling status, father's absence. *Psychological Monographs*, 1951, *65* (6, Whole No. 323).

Sutton-Smith, B., Roberts, J. R., & Rosenberg, B. B. Sibling associations and role involvement. *Merrill-Palmer Quarterly*, 1964, *10*, 25–38.

Sutton-Smith, B., & Rosenberg, B. G. Age changes in the effects of ordinal position on sex role identification. *Journal of Genetic Psychology*, 1965, *107*, 61–73.

Sutton-Smith, B., & Rosenberg, B. G. The dramatic sibling. *Perceptual and Motor Skills*, 1966, *22*, 993–994. (a)

Sutton-Smith, B., & Rosenberg, B. G. A factor analysis of power styles in the family. Paper presented at the meeting of the American Psychological Association, New York, September 1966. (b)

Sutton-Smith, B., & Rosenberg, B. G. Sibling consensus on power tactics. *Journal of Genetic Psychology*, 1968, *112*, 63–72.

Warren, J. R. Birth order and social behavior. *Psychological Bulletin*, 1966, *65*, 38–49.

14.3 | SEX-ROLE STEREOTYPES AND CLINICAL JUDGMENTS OF MENTAL HEALTH*

Inge K. Broverman, Donald M. Broverman,
Frank E. Clarkson, Paul S. Rosenkrantz,
and Susan R. Vogel

Evidence of the existence of sex-role stereotypes, that is, highly consensual norms and beliefs about the differing characteristics of men and women, is abundantly present in the literature (Anastasi & Foley, 1949; Fernberger, 1948; Komarovsky, 1950; McKee & Sherriffs, 1957; Rosenkrantz, Vogel, Bee, Broverman, & Broverman, 1968; Seward,

* SOURCE: Broverman, I. K., Broverman, D. M., Clarkson, F. E., Rosenkrantz, P. S., & Vogel, S. R. Sex-role stereotypes and clinical judgments of mental health. *Journal of Consulting and Clinical Psychology*, 1970, *34*, 1–7. Copyright by the American Psychological Association and reprinted by permission.

1946; Seward & Larson, 1968; Wylie, 1961). Similarly, the differential valuations of behaviors and characteristics stereotypically ascribed to men and women are well established (Kitay, 1940; Lynn, 1959; McKee & Sherriffs, 1959; Rosenkrantz et al., 1968; White, 1950), that is, stereotypically masculine traits are more often perceived as socially desirable than are attributes which are stereotypically feminine. The literature also indicates that the social desirabilities of behaviors are positively related to the clinical ratings of these same behaviors in terms of "normality-abnormality" (Cowen, 1961), "adjustment" (Wiener, Blumberg, Segman, & Cooper, 1959), and "health-sickness" (Kogan, Quinn, Ax, & Ripley, 1957).

Given the relationships existing between masculine versus feminine characteristics and social desirability, on the one hand, and between mental health and social desirability on the other, it seems reasonable to expect that clinicians will maintain parallel distinctions in their concepts of what, behaviorally, is healthy or pathological when considering men versus women. More specifically, particular behaviors and characteristics may be thought indicative of pathology in members of one sex, but not pathological in members of the opposite sex.

The present paper, then, tests the hypothesis that clinical judgments about the traits characterizing healthy, mature individuals will differ as a function of the sex of the person judged. Furthermore, these differences in clinical judgments are expected to parallel the stereotypic sex-role differences previously reported (Rosenkrantz et al., 1968).

Finally, the present paper hypothesizes that behavioral attributes which are regarded as healthy for an adult, sex unspecified, and thus presumably viewed from an ideal, absolute standpoint, will more often be considered by clinicians as healthy or appropriate for men than for women. This hypothesis derives from the assumption that abstract notions of health will tend to be more influenced by the greater social value of masculine stereotypic characteristics than by the lesser valued feminine stereotypic characteristics.

The authors are suggesting, then, that a double standard of health exists wherein ideal concepts of health for a mature adult, sex unspecified, are meant primarily for men, less so for women.

METHOD

SUBJECTS.   Seventy-nine clinically-trained psychologists, psychiatrists, or social workers (46 men, 33 women) served as *S*s. Of these, 31 men and 18 women had PhD or MD degrees. The *S*s were all actively functioning in clinical settings. The ages varied between 23 and 55 years and experience ranged from internship to extensive professional experience.

INSTRUMENT.   The authors have developed a Stereotype Questionnaire which is described in detail elsewhere (Rosenkrantz et al., 1968). Briefly, the questionnaire consists of 122 bipolar items each of which describes, with an adjective or a short phrase, a particular behavior trait or characteristic such as:

Very aggressive   Not at all aggressive
Doesn't hide emotions at all   Always hides emotions

One pole of each item can be characterized as typically masculine, the other as typically feminine (Rosenkrantz et al., 1968). On 41 items, 70% or better agreement occurred as to which pole characterizes men or women, respectively, in both a sample of college men and in a sample of college women (Rosenkrantz et al., 1968). These items have been classified as "stereotypic."

The questionnaire used in the present study differs slightly from the original questionnaire. Seven original items seemed to reflect adolescent concerns with sex, for example, "very proud of sexual ability . . . not at all concerned with sexual ability." These items were replaced by seven more general items. Since three of the discarded items were stereotypic, the present questionnaire contains only 38 stereotypic items. These items are shown in Table 1.

Finally, in a prior study, judgments have been obtained from samples of Ss as to which pole of each item represents the more socially desirable behavior or trait for an adult individual in general, regardless of sex. On 27 of the 38 stereotypic items, the masculine pole is more socially desirable, (male-valued items), and on the remaining 11 stereotypic items, the feminine pole is the more socially desirable one (female-valued items).

INSTRUCTIONS.   The clinicians were given the 122-item questionnaire with one of three sets of instructions, "male," "female," or "adult." Seventeen men and 10 women were given the "male" instructions which stated "think of normal, adult men and then indicate on each item the pole to which a mature, healthy, socially competent adult man would be closer." The Ss were asked to look at the opposing poles of each item in terms of directions rather than extremes of behavior. Another 14 men and 12 women were given "female" instructions, that is, they were asked to describe a "mature, healthy, socially competent adult woman." Finally, 15 men and 11 women were given "adult" instructions. These Ss were asked to describe a "healthy, mature, socially competent adult person" (sex unspecified). Responses to these "adult" instructions may be considered indicative of "ideal" health patterns, without respect to sex.

SCORES.   Although Ss responded to all 122 items, only the stereotypic items which reflect highly consensual, clear distinctions between men and women, as perceived by lay people were analyzed. The questionnaires were scored by counting the number of Ss that marked each pole of each stereotypic item, within each set of instructions. Since some Ss occasionally left an item blank, the proportion of Ss marking each pole was computed for each item. Two types of scores were developed: "agreement" scores and "health" scores.

The agreement scores consisted of the proportion of Ss on that pole of each item which was marked by the majority of the Ss. Three agreement scores for each

Table 1 | MALE-VALUED AND FEMALE-VALUED STEREOTYPIC ITEMS

FEMININE POLE	MASCULINE POLE
Male-valued items	
Not at all aggressive	Very aggressive
Not at all independent	Very independent
Very emotional	Not at all emotional
Does not hide emotions at all	Almost always hides emotions
Very subjective	Very objective
Very easily influenced	Not at all easily influenced
Very submissive	Very dominant
Dislikes math and science very much	Likes math and science very much
Very excitable in a minor crisis	Not at all excitable in a minor crisis
Very passive	Very active
Not at all competitive	Very competitive
Very illogical	Very logical
Very home oriented	Very worldly
Not at all skilled in business	Very skilled in business
Very sneaky	Very direct
Does not know the way of the world	Knows the way of the world
Feelings easily hurt	Feelings not easily hurt
Not at all adventurous	Very adventurous
Has difficulty making decisions	Can make decisions easily
Cries very easily	Never cries
Almost never acts as a leader	Almost always acts as a leader
Not at all self-confident	Very self-confident
Very uncomfortable about being aggressive	Not at all uncomfortable about being aggressive
Not at all ambitious	Very ambitious
Unable to separate feelings from ideas	Easily able to separate feelings from ideas
Very dependent	Not at all dependent
Very conceited about appearance	Never conceited about appearance
Female-valued items	
Very talkative	Not at all talkative
Very tactful	Very blunt
Very gentle	Very rough
Very aware of feelings of others	Not at all aware of feelings of others
Very religious	Not at all religious
Very interested in own appearance	Not at all interested in own appearance
Very neat in habits	Very sloppy in habits
Very quiet	Very loud
Very strong need for security	Very little need for security
Enjoys art and literature very much	Does not enjoy art and literature at all
Easily expresses tender feelings	Does not express tender feelings at all

item were computed; namely, a "masculinity agreement score" based on *S*s receiving the "male" instructions, a "feminity agreement score," and an "adult agreement score" derived from the *S*s receiving the "female" and "adult" instructions, respectively.

The health scores are based on the assumption that the pole which the majority of the clinicians consider to be healthy for an adult, independent of sex, reflects an ideal standard of health. Hence, the proportion of Ss with either male or female instructions who marked that pole of an item which was most often designated as healthy for an adult was taken as a "health" score. Thus, two health scores were computed for each of the stereotypic items: a "masculinity health score" from Ss with "male" instructions, and a "femininity health score" from Ss with "female" instructions.

RESULTS

SEX DIFFERENCES IN SUBJECT RESPONSES.   The masculinity, femininity, and adult health and agreement scores of the male clinicians were first compared to the comparable scores of the female clinicians via *t* tests. None of these *t* tests were significant (the probability levels ranged from .25 to .90). Since the male and female Ss did not differ significantly in any way, all further analyses were performed with the samples of men and women combined.

AGREEMENT SCORES.   The means and sigmas of the adult, masculinity, and femininity agreement scores across the 38 stereotypic items are shown in Table 2. For each of these three scores, the average proportion of Ss agreeing as to which pole reflects the more healthy behavior or trait is significantly greater than the .50 agreement one would expect by chance. Thus, the average masculinity agreement score is .831 ($z = 3.15$, $p < .001$), the average femininity agreement score is .763 ($z = 2.68$, $p < .005$), and the average adult agreement score is .866 ($z = 3.73$, $p < .001$). These means indicate that on the stereotypic items clinicians strongly agree on the behaviors and attributes which characterize a healthy man, a healthy woman, or a healthy adult independent of sex, respectively.

RELATIONSHIP BETWEEN CLINICAL JUDGMENTS OF HEALTH AND STUDENT JUDGMENTS OF SOCIAL DESIRABILITY.   Other studies indicate that social desirability is related to clinical judgments of mental health (Cowen, 1961; Kogan et al., 1957; Wiener et al., 1959). The relation between social desirability

Table 2 | MEANS AND STANDARD DEVIATIONS FOR ADULT, MASCULINITY, AND FEMININITY AGREEMENT SCORES ON 38 STEREOTYPIC ITEMS

AGREEMENT SCORE	*M*	*SD*	DEVIATION FROM CHANCE	
			Z	*p*
Adult	.866	.116	3.73	< .001
Masculinity	.831	.122	3.15	< .001
Feminity	.763	.164	2.68	< .005

and clinical judgment was tested in the present data by comparing the previously established socially desirable poles of the stereotypic items (Rosenkrantz et al., 1968) to the poles of those items which the clinicians judged to be the healthier and more mature for an *adult*. Table 3 shows that the relationship is, as predicted, highly significant ($\chi^2 = 23.64$, $p < .001$). The present data, then, confirm the previously reported relationships that social desirability, as perceived by nonprofessional Ss, is strongly related to professional concepts of mental health.

The four items on which there is disagreement between health and social desirability ratings are: to be emotional; not to hide emotions; to be religious; to have a very strong need for security. The first two items are considered to be healthy for adults by clinicians but not by students; the second two items have the reverse pattern of ratings.

SEX-ROLE STEREOTYPE AND MASCULINITY VERSUS FEMININITY HEALTH SCORES.

On 27 of the 38 stereotypic items, the male pole is perceived as more socially desirable by a sample of college students (male-valued items); while on 11 items, the feminine pole is seen as more socially desirable (female-valued items). A hypothesis of this paper is that the masculinity health scores will tend to be greater than the femininity health scores on the male-valued items, while the femininity health scores will tend to be greater than the masculinity health scores on the female-valued items. In other words, the relationship of the clinicians' judgments of health for men and women are expected to parallel the relationship between stereotypic sex-role behaviors and social desirability. The data support the hypothesis. Thus, on 25 of the 27 male-valued items, the masculinity health score exceeds the femininity health score; while 7 of the 11 female-valued items have higher femininity health scores than masculinity health scores. On four of the female-valued items, the masculinity health score exceeds the femininity health score. The chi-square derived from these data is 10.73 ($df = 1$, $p < .001$). This result indicates that clinicians tend to consider socially desirable masculine characteristics more often as healthy for men than for women. On the other hand, only about half of the socially desirable feminine characteristics are considered more often as healthy for women rather than for men.

On the face of it, the finding that clinicians tend to ascribe male-valued stereotypic traits more often to healthy men than to healthy women may seem trite. However, an

Table 3 | CHI-SQUARE ANALYSIS OF SOCIAL DESIRABILITY VERSUS ADULT HEALTH SCORES ON 38 STEREOTYPIC ITEMS[a]

ITEM	POLE ELECTED BY MAJORITY OF CLINICIANS FOR HEALTHY ADULTS
Socially desirable pole	34
Socially undesirable pole	4

[a] $\chi^2 = 23.64$, $p < .001$.

examination of the content of these items suggests that this trite-seeming phenomenon conceals a powerful, negative assessment of women. For instance, among these items, clinicians are more likely to suggest that healthy women differ from healthy men by being more submissive, less independent, less adventurous, more easily influenced, less aggressive, less competitive, more excitable in minor crises, having their feelings more easily hurt, being more emotional, more conceited about their appearance, less objective, and disliking math and science. This constellation seems a most unusual way of describing any mature, healthy individual.

MEAN DIFFERENCES BETWEEN MASCULINITY HEALTH SCORES AND FEMININITY HEALTH SCORES. The above chi-square analysis reports a significant pattern of differences between masculine and feminine health scores in relationship to the stereotypic items. It is possible, however, that the differences, while in a consistent, predictable direction, actually are trivial in magnitude. A *t* test, performed between the means of the masculinity and femininity health scores, yielded a *t* of 2.16 ($p < .05$), indicating that the mean masculinity health score (.827) differed significantly from the mean femininity health score (.747). Thus, despite massive agreement about the health dimension per se, men and women appear to be located at significantly different points along this well-defined dimension of health.

CONCEPTS OF THE HEALTHY ADULT VERSUS CONCEPTS OF HEALTHY MEN AND HEALTHY WOMEN. Another hypothesis of this paper is that the concepts of health for a sex-unspecified adult, and for a man, will not differ, but that the concepts of health for women will differ significantly from those of the adult.

This hypothesis was tested by performing *t* tests between the adult agreement scores versus the masculinity and femininity health scores. Table 4 indicates, as predicted, that the adult and masculine concepts of health do not differ significantly ($t = 1.38$, $p > .10$), whereas, a significant difference does exist between the concepts of health for adults versus females ($t = 3.33, p < .01$).

Table 4 | RELATION OF ADULT HEALTH SCORES TO MASCULINITY HEALTH SCORES AND TO FEMININITY HEALTH SCORES ON 38 STEREOTYPIC ITEMS

HEALTH SCORE	M	SD
Masculinity	.827	.130
		$t = 1.38*$
Adult	.866	.115
		$t = 3.33**$
Femininity	.747	.187

* $df = 74, p > .05$.
** $df = 74, p < .01$.

These results, then, confirm the hypothesis that a double standard of health exists for men and women, that is, the general standard of health is actually applied only to men, while healthy women are perceived as significantly less healthy by adult standards.

DISCUSSION

The results of the present study indicate that high agreement exists among clinicians as to the attributes characterizing healthy adult men, healthy adult women, and healthy adults, sex unspecified. This agreement, furthermore, holds for both men and women clinicians. The results of this study also support the hypotheses that (a) clinicians have different concepts of health for men and women and (b) these differences parallel the sex-role stereotypes prevalant in our society.

Although no control for the theoretical orientation of the clinicians was attempted, it is unlikely that a particular theoretical orientation was disproportionately represented in the sample. A counterindication is that the clinicians' concepts of health for a mature adult are strongly related to the concepts of social desirability held by college students. This positive relationship between social desirability and concepts of health replicates findings by a number of other investigators (Cowen, 1961; Kogan et al., 1957; Wiener et al., 1959).

The clinicians' concepts of a healthy, mature man do not differ significantly from their concepts of a healthy adult. However, the clinicians' concepts of a mature healthy woman do differ significantly from their adult health concepts. Clinicians are significantly less likely to attribute traits which characterize healthy adults to a woman than they are likely to attribute these traits to a healthy man.

Speculation about the reasons for and the effects of this double standard of health and its ramifications seems appropriate. In the first place, men and women do differ biologically, and these biological differences appear to be reflected behaviorally, with each sex being more effective in certain behaviors (Broverman, Klaiber, Kobayashi, & Vogel, 1968). However, we know of no evidence indicating that these biologically-based behaviors are the basis of the attributes stereotypically attributed to men and to women. Even if biological factors did contribute to the formation of the sex-role stereotypes, enormous overlap undoubtedly exists between the sexes with respect to such traits as logical ability, objectivity, independence, etc., that is, a great many women undoubtedly possess these characteristics to a greater degree than do many men. In addition, variation in these traits within each sex is certainly great. In view of the within-sex variability, and the overlap between sexes, it seems inappropriate to apply different standards of health to men compared to women on purely biological grounds.

More likely, the double standard of health for men and women stems from the clinicians' acceptance of an "adjustment" notion of health, for example, health consists of a good adjustment to one's environment. In our society, men and women are systematically trained, practically from birth on, to fulfill different social roles. An adjustment notion of health, plus the existence of differential norms of male and female behavior in our society, automatically lead to a double standard of health. Thus, for a woman to be healthy, from an adjustment viewpoint, she must adjust to and accept the behavioral norms for her sex, even though these behaviors are generally less socially desirable and considered to be less healthy for the generalized competent, mature adult.

By way of analogy, one could argue that a black person who conformed to the "pre-civil rights" southern Negro stereotype, that is, a docile, unambitious, childlike, etc., person, was well adjusted to his environment and, therefore, a healthy and mature adult. Our recent history testifies to the bankruptcy of this concept. Alternative definitions of mental health and maturity are implied by concepts of innate drives toward self-actualization, toward mastery of the environment, and toward fulfillment of one's potential (Allport, 1955; Bühler, 1959; Erikson, 1950; Maslow, 1954; Rogers, 1951). Such innate drives, in both blacks and women, are certainly in conflict with becoming adjusted to a social environment with associated restrictive stereotypes. Acceptance of an adjustment notion of health, then, places women in the conflictual position of having to decide whether to exhibit those positive characteristics considered desirable for men and adults, and thus have their "femininity" questioned, that is, be deviant in terms of being a woman; or to behave in the prescribed feminine manner, accept second-class adult status, and possibly live a lie to boot.

Another problem with the adjustment notion of health lies in the conflict between the overt laws and ethics existing in our society versus the covert but real customs and mores which significantly shape an individual's behavior. Thus, while American society continually emphasizes equality of opportunity and freedom of choice, social pressures toward conformity to the sex-role stereotypes tend to restrict the actual career choices open to women, and, to a lesser extent, men. A girl who wants to become an engineer or business executive, or a boy who aspires to a career as a ballet dancer or a nurse, will at least encounter raised eyebrows. More likely, considerable obstacles will be put in the path of each by parents, teachers, and counselors.

We are not suggesting that it is the clinicians who pose this dilemma for women. Rather, we see the judgments of our sample of clinicians as merely reflecting the sex-role stereotypes, and the differing valuations of these stereotypes, prevalent in our society. It is the attitudes of our society that create the difficulty. However, the present study does provide evidence that clinicians do accept these sex-role stereotypes, at least implicitly, and, by so doing, help to perpetuate the stereotypes. Therapists should be concerned about whether the influence of the sex-role stereotypes on their professional activities acts to reinforce social and intrapsychic conflict. Clinicians undoubtedly exert an influence on social standards and attitudes beyond that of other groups. This influence arises not only from their effect on many individuals through conventional clinical functioning, but also out of their role as "expert" which leads to consultation to governmental and private agencies of all kinds, as well as guidance of the general public.

It may be worthwhile for clinicians to critically examine their attitudes concerning sex-role stereotypes, as well as their position with respect to an adjustment notion of health. The cause of mental health may be better served if both men and women are encouraged toward maximum realization of individual potential, rather than to an adjustment to existing restrictive sex roles.

SUMMARY

A sex-role Stereotype Questionnaire consisting of 122 bipolar items was given to actively functioning clinicians with one of three sets of instructions: To describe a healthy, mature, socially competent (a) adult, sex unspecified, (b) a man, or (c) a woman. It was hypothesized that clinical judgments about the characteristics of healthy individuals would differ as a function of sex of person judged, and furthermore, that these differences in clinical judgments would parallel stereotypic sex-role differences. A second hypothesis predicted that behaviors and characteristics judged healthy for an adult, sex unspecified, which are presumed to reflect an ideal standard of health, will resemble behaviors judged healthy for men, but differ from behaviors judged healthy for women. Both hypotheses were confirmed. Possible reasons for and the effects of this double standard of health are discussed.

REFERENCES

Allport, G. W. *Becoming.* Princeton: Yale University Press, 1955.

Anastasi, A., & Foley, J. P., Jr. *Differential psychology.* New York: Macmillan, 1949.

Broverman, D. M., Klaiber, E. L., Kobayashi, Y., & Vogel, W. Roles of activation and inhibition in sex differences in cognitive abilities. *Psychological Review*, 1968, 75, 23–50.

Bühler, C. Theoretical observations about life's basic tendencies. *American Journal of Psychotherapy*, 1959, 13, 561–581.

Cowen, E. L. The social desirability of trait descriptive terms: Preliminary norms and sex differences. *Journal of Social Psychology*, 1961, 53, 225–233.

Erikson, E. H. *Childhood and society.* New York: Norton, 1950.

Fernberger, S. W. Persistence of stereotypes concerning sex differences. *Journal of Abnormal and Social Psychology*, 1948, 43, 97–101.

Kitay, P. M. A comparison of the sexes in their attitudes and beliefs about women. *Sociometry*, 1940, 34, 399–407.

Kogan, W. S., Quinn, R., Ax, A. F., & Ripley, H. S. Some methodological problems in the quantification of clinical assessment by Q array. *Journal of Consulting Psychology*, 1957, 21, 57–62.

Komarovsky, M. Functional analysis of sex roles. *American Sociological Review*, 1950, 15, 508–516.

Lynn, D. B. A note on sex differences in the development of masculine and feminine identification. *Psychological Review*, 1959, 66, 126–135.

Maslow, A. H. *Motivation and personality.* New York: Harper & Row, 1954.

McKee, J. P., & Sherriffs, A. C. The differential evaluation of males and females. *Journal of Personality*, 1957, 25, 356–371.

McKee, J. P., & Sherriffs, A. C. Men's and women's beliefs, ideals, and self-concepts. *American Journal of Sociology*, 1959, 64, 356–363.

Rogers, C. R. *Client-centered therapy; Its current practice, implications, and theory.* Boston: Houghton Mifflin, 1951.

Rosenkrantz, P., Vogel, S., Bee, H., Broverman, I., & Broverman, D. Sex-role stereotypes and self-concepts in college students. *Journal of Consulting and Clinical Psychology*, 1968, 32, 287–295.

Seward, G. H. *Sex and the social order.* New York: McGraw-Hill, 1946.

Seward, G. H., & Larson, W. R. Adolescent concepts of social sex roles in the United States and the two Germanies. *Human Development,* 1968, *11,* 217–248.

White, L., Jr. *Educating our daughters.* New York: Harper & Row, 1950.

Wiener, M., Blumberg, A., Segman, S., & Cooper, A. A judgment of adjustment by psychologists, psychiatric social workers, and college students, and its relationship to social desirability. *Journal of Abnormal Social Psychology,* 1959, *59,* 315–321.

Wylie, R. *The self concept.* Lincoln, Neb.: University of Nebraska Press, 1961.

15 | Identification and Observational Learning

15.1 | INFLUENCE OF SOCIAL REINFORCEMENT
AND THE BEHAVIOR OF MODELS IN
SHAPING CHILDREN'S MORAL JUDGMENTS*[1]

Albert Bandura and Frederick J. McDonald

Most of the literature and theorizing in the area of developmental psychology has been guided by various forms of stage theories (Erikson, 1950; Freud, 1949; Gesell & Ilg, 1943; Piaget, 1948, 1954; Sullivan, 1953). Although there appears to be relatively little agreement among these theories concerning the number and the content of stages considered to be necessary to account for the course of personality development, they all share in common the assumption that social behavior can be categorized in terms of a predetermined sequence of stages with varying degrees of continuity or discontinuity between successive developmental periods. Typically, the emergence of these presumably age-specific modes of behavior is attributed to ontogenetic factors rather than to specific social stimulus events which are likely to be favored in a social learning theory of the developmental process.

The stage and social learning approaches differ not only in the relative emphasis placed upon time schedules or reinforcement schedules in explaining the occurrence of changes in social behavior, but also in the assumptions made concerning the regularity

* SOURCE: Bandura, A., & McDonald, F. J. Influence of social reinforcement and the behavior of models in shaping children's moral judgments. *Journal of Abnormal and Social Psychology*, 1963, 67, 274–281. Copyright 1963 by the American Psychological Association and reprinted by permission.

[1] This investigation was supported in part by Research Grant M-5162 from the National Institutes of Health, United States Public Health Service.

The authors wish to express their appreciation to Florence Mote, Charles Carver, and Nathan Kroman for their aid in arranging the research facilities, and to Peter Gumpert for his assistance with the statistical analyses. We also wish to express our gratitude to the many students who served as experimenters and as models in this project.

and invariance of response sequences, and the nature of response variability. Stage theories, for example, generally stress intraindividual variability over time, and minimize interindividual variability in behavior due to sex, intellectual, socioeconomic, ethnic, and cultural differences. To the extent that children representing such diverse backgrounds experience differential contingencies and schedules of reinforcement, as well as exposure to social models who differ widely in the behavior they exhibit, considerable interindividual behavioral variability would be expected. Similarly, the sequence of developmental changes is considered in social learning theory to be primarily a function of changes in reinforcement contingencies and other learning variables rather than an unfolding of genetically programed response predispositions.

Despite the considerable attention devoted to theoretical analyses of the learning process, a comprehensive theory of *social learning* has been relatively slow in developing. By and large, current principles of learning have been based upon investigations involving simple fractional responses which are neither social nor developmental in nature, and often with animals as subjects. Although recent years have witnessed a widespread application of learning principles to developmental psychology, the experimentation has been primarily confined to operant or instrumental conditioning of responses that are modeled on the fractional responses elicited in experimentation with infrahuman organisms (for example, manipulating plungers, pressing bars, levers, buttons, etc.). Moreover, a good deal of this research has been designed to reduce complex social learning to available simple learning principles, rather than to extend the range of principles and procedures in order to account more adequately for complex social phenomena.

It is generally assumed that social responses are acquired through the method of successive approximations by means of differential reinforcement (Skinner, 1953). The effectiveness of reinforcement procedures in shaping and maintaining behavior in both animals and humans is well documented by research. It is doubtful, however, if many social responses would ever be acquired if social training proceeded solely by this method. This is particularly true of behavior for which there is no reliable eliciting stimulus apart from the cues provided by others as they performed the behavior. If a child had no occasion to hear speech, for example, or in the case of a deaf-blind person (Keller, 1927), no opportunity to match laryngeal muscular responses of a verbalizing model, it would probably be exceedingly difficult or impossible to teach a person appropriate linguistic responses.

Even in cases where some stimulus is known to be capable of eliciting an approximation to the desired behavior, the process of learning can be considerably shortened by the provision of social models (Bandura & Huston, 1961; Bandura, Ross, & Ross, 1961, 1963). Thus, in both instances, imitation of modeling behavior is an essential aspect of social learning.

In the experiment reported in this paper a social learning theory combining the principles of instrumental conditioning and imitation was applied to a developmental problem that has been approached from a stage point of view.

According to Piaget (1948), one can distinguish two clear-cut stages of moral judgment demarcated from each other at approximately 7 years of age. In the first stage, defined as *objective responsibility*, children judge the gravity of a deviant act in terms of the amount of material damages, and disregard the intentionality of the action. By contrast, during the second or *subjective responsibility* state, children judge conduct in terms of its intent rather than its material consequences. While these stages are predetermined (for example, Piaget reports that young children are relatively incapable of adopting a subjective orientation and he was unable to find a single case of objective morality in older children), the factors responsible for the transition from one stage to the other are not entirely clear. Presumably, the principal antecedent of objective judgmental behavior is the "natural spontaneous and unconscious egocentrism" of child thought reinforced to some extent by adult authoritarianism, which produces submissiveness and preoccupation with external consequences. As the child matures, however, he gains increasing autonomy, his relationships become based upon mutual reciprocity and cooperation giving rise to the emergence of subjective morality.

The purpose of the present investigation was to demonstrate that moral judgment responses are less age-specific than implied by Piaget, and that children's moral orientations can be altered and even reversed by the manipulation of response-reinforcement contingencies and by the provision of appropriate social models.

In this experiment children who exhibited predominantly objective and subjective moral orientations were assigned at random to one of three experimental conditions. One group of children observed adult models who expressed moral judgments counter to the group's orientation and the children were positively reinforced for adopting the models' evaluative responses. A second group observed the models but the children received no reinforcement for matching the models' behavior. The third group had no exposure to the models but each child was reinforced whenever he expressed moral judgments that ran counter to his dominant evaluative tendencies. Thus the experimental design permitted a test of the relative efficacy of social reinforcement, the behavior of models, and these two factors combined in shaping children's moral judgments.

It was predicted, for reasons given in the preceding sections, that the combined use of models and social reinforcement would be the most powerful condition for altering the children's behavior and that the provision of models alone would be of intermediate effectiveness. Since the presence of a strong dominant response limits the opportunity for reinforcement of an alternative response which is clearly subordinate, it was expected that social reinforcement alone would be the least effective of the three treatment methods.

METHOD

SUBJECTS.　　A total of 78 boys and 87 girls ranging in age from 5 to 11 years served as subjects in various phases of the study. They were drawn from two sources, a Jewish religious school and an elementary public school serving predominantly middle-class communities. The research was conducted on week ends in the religious school and on weekdays in the public school facility. Female students from Stanford University served in the roles of experimenters and models.

STIMULUS ITEMS.   Following the procedure employed by Piaget (1948), the children were presented with pairs of stories each of which described a well-intentioned act which resulted in considerable material damage, contrasted with a selfishly or maliciously motivated act producing minor consequences. The children were asked to judge, "Who did the naughtier thing?" and to provide a reason for their choice. An illustrative stimulus item, taken from Piaget, is given below:

1. John was in his room when his mother called him to dinner. John goes down, and opens the door to the dining room. But behind the door was a chair, and on the chair was a tray with fifteen cups on it. John did not know the cups were behind the door. He opens the door, the door hits the tray, bang go the fifteen cups, and they all get broken.

2. One day when Henry's mother was out, Henry tried to get some cookies out of the cupboard. He climbed up on a chair, but the cookie jar was still too high, and he couldn't reach it. But while he was trying to get the cookie jar, he knocked over a cup. The cup fell down and broke.

Six of the story items employed in the present experiment were identical with those developed by Piaget except for minor modifications in wording or content to make the story situations more appropriate for American children. In addition, a set of 36 new paired items was devised to provide a sufficient number of stories so as to obtain a fairly reliable estimate of children's moral judgments at three different phases of the experiment, i.e., base operant test, experimental treatment, and posttest. In each of these story situations which were modeled after Piaget's items, intentionality was contrasted with serious consequences. These items were carefully pretested on a sample of 30 children in order to clarify any ambiguities, to gauge the children's interpretations of the seriousness of the depicted consequences, and to remove any irrelevant cues which might lead the children to judge the depicted actions in terms other than intentions or consequences.

Except for the assignment of the six Piaget items to both the operant test and the posttest set, for reasons which will be explained later, the remaining stories were distributed randomly into three different groups.

DESIGN AND PROCEDURE.   A summary of the overall experimental design is presented in Table 1.

Operant level of objective and subjective responses. In the first phase of the experiment, the children were individually administered 12 pairs of stories to furnish measures of the operant levels of objective and subjective moral judgments at the various age levels. These data provided both a check on Piaget's normative findings and the basis for forming the experimental treatment groups.

Experimental treatments. On the basis of operant test performances, 48 children who were decidedly subjective in their moral orientation (Mean percentage of subjective responses = 80), and 36 who gave high base rates of objective responses (Mean percentage of objective responses = 83) were selected from the total sample to participate in the second and third phases of the experiment. The children in each of the two classes of moral orientation were equally divided between boys and girls. They were also further categorized into younger and older children and then

Table 1 | SUMMARY OF THE EXPERIMENTAL DESIGN

EXPERIMENTAL GROUPS	STEP 1 ASSESSMENT OF OPERANT LEVEL OF OBJECTIVE AND SUBJECTIVE MORAL RESPONSES	STEP 2 EXPERIMENTAL TREATMENTS	STEP 3 POSTTREATMENT MEASUREMENT OF SUBJECTIVE AND OBJECTIVE MORAL RESPONSES WITH MODELS AND REINFORCEMENT ABSENT
Subjective moral orientation			
I $(N = 16)$	Step 1	Model emits objective responses and positively reinforced; child reinforced for objective responses.	Step 3
II $(N = 16)$	Step 1	Model emits objective responses and positively reinforced; child not reinforced for objective responses.	Step 3
III $(N = 16)$	Step 1	No model present; child reinforced for objective responses.	Step 3
Objective moral orientation			
IV $(N = 12)$	Step 1	Model emits subjective responses and positively reinforced; child reinforced for subjective responses.	Step 3
V $(N = 12)$	Step 1	Model emits subjective responses and positively reinforced; child not reinforced for subjective responses.	Step 3
VI $(N = 12)$	Step 1	No model present; child reinforced for subjective responses.	Step 3

assigned at random to one of three experimental treatment conditions. Thus the experimental groups were balanced with respect to age and sex of child.

In the *model and child reinforced condition*, both the model and the child were administered alternately 12 different sets of story items with the model receiving the first story, the child the second one, and so on. To each of the 12 items, the model consistently expressed judgmental responses in opposition to the child's moral orientation (for example, objective responses with subjective children, and vice versa), and the experimenter reinforced the model's behavior with verbal approval responses such as "Very good," "That's fine," and "That's good." The child was similarly reinforced whenever he adapted the model's class of moral judgments in response to his own set of items. To control for any intermodel variability in length or content of evaluative responses, the subjective and objective answers for the models' test items were prepared in advance.

The procedure for children in the *model reinforced, child not reinforced condition*, was identical with the treatment described above with the exception that the children received no reinforcement for matching the moral judgment responses of their respective models.

In the *model absent, child reinforced condition*, no model was present; the experimenter simply administered the 24 story items to the child and reinforced him with verbal approval whenever he produced an evaluative response that ran counter to his dominant orientation.

The time elapsing between the operant testing and the experimental phase of the study ranged from 1 to 3 weeks with the majority of the children receiving the experimental treatment after a 2-week period.

A total of nine experimenter-model pairs participated in the treatment phase of the experiment. To control for possible differences in experimenter or model influences across conditions or sex groups, each pair was assigned groups of subjects in triplets, i.e., boys and girls taken from each of the three treatment conditions.

Students who served as the experimenters' assistants brought the children individually from their classrooms to the experimental session and introduced them to their experimenters. The experimenter explained that she would like to have the child judge a second set of stories similar to the ones he had completed on a previous occasion. In the conditions involving the presence of models, the experimenter further explained that she was collecting normative data on a large sample of people, including both children and adults, and to expedite matters she invited the adult subjects to appear at the school so that the items could be administered to both groups simultaneously. To add to the credibility of the situation, the experimenter read to the model the same instructions the child had received in the operant test session, as though the model was a naive subject. The experimenter then read the story situations to the model and the child who were seated facing the experimenter, delivered the social reinforcement whenever appropriate, and recorded the responses.

It was found in the preliminary pretesting of the stories that they were sufficiently structured with respect to the intentionality-consequences dichotomy so that children's identification of the naughtier story character was virtually a perfect predictor that the children would provide the corresponding subjective or objective reasons for their choices. Since there is some evidence that reinforcement given immediately is considerably more effective than when delayed (Mahrer, 1956), the reinforcement value of the experimenter's approval would have been considerably reduced if administered following the children's explanations, not only because of the delay involved but also because many responses, some relevant others irrelevant, occur during the intervening period, thus making it difficult to specify the behavior being reinforced. For this reason, the experimenters reinforced the children immediately following correct choice responses, and again after they gave the appropriate explanations.

The measure of learning was the percentage of objective judgmental response produced by the subjective children and the percentage of subjective responses performed by the objectively oriented subjects.

Posttest. Following the completion of the treatment procedure, the child reported to another room in the building. Here a second experimenter presented the child with 12 additional stories to obtain further information about the generality and stability of changes in judgmental responses when models and social reinforcement were absent. The experimenter simply read the stories to the child and recorded his verbal responses without comment.

In view of Piaget's contention that moral judgments are age-specific and considerably resistant to out-of-phase changes, it was decided to repeat, in the posttest, the Piaget items included in the set of operant test stories. If the interpolated social influence experience succeeded in altering children's evaluative responses, such findings would throw considerable doubt on the validity of a developmental stage theory of morality.

Different sets of experimenters conducted each of the three phases of the study, with a total of 10 experimenters participating in the posttesting. The utilization of different rooms and different sets of experimenters provided a more stringent test of generalization effects than if the same experimenters had been used throughout the investigation.

The experiment was concluded with a brief interview designed to assess the child's awareness of the behavior exhibited by the model, the social reinforcers administered by the experimenter, and the response-reinforcement contingency in the experimental situation.

RESULTS

Since the data disclosed no significant differences in operant levels or in responsivity to the social influence procedures for children drawn from the two different school settings, the data were combined in the statistical analyses.

JUDGMENTAL RESPONSES AS A FUNCTION OF AGE.

The mean percentage of subjective moral judgment responses for boys and girls at 1-year intervals are presented in Figure 1. The normative data based on the present sample of children show that subjectivity is positively associated with age ($F = 4.84$, $p < .01$), but unrelated to sex

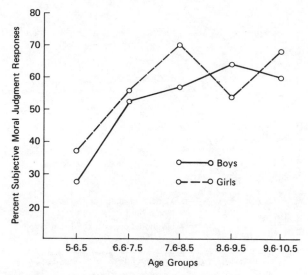

Figure 1 | MEAN PERCENTAGE OF SUBJECTIVE MORAL JUDGMENT RESPONSES PRODUCED BY BOYS AND GIRLS AT DIFFERENT AGE LEVELS.

differences at any age level. It is evident from these findings, however, that objective and subjective judgments exist together rather than as successive developmental stages. Most young children were capable of exercising subjective judgements, and a large majority of the older children exhibited varying degrees of objective morality.

INFLUENCE OF REINFORCEMENT AND MODELING CUES.   Figure 2 presents the curves for the acquisition and the generalization of objective moral judgment responses by subjective children in each of the three experimental conditions.

Results of the analysis of variance performed on these data are summarized in Table 2. The main effects of experimental conditions and phases, as well as their inter-action effects, are highly significant sources of variance. Further comparisons of pairs of means by the *t* test reveal that subjective children who were exposed to objective models, and those who were positively reinforced for matching their models' moral judgments, not only modified their moral orientations toward objectivity, but also remained objectively oriented in their post-experimental judgmental behavior (Table 3).

The provision of models alone, however, was as effective in altering the children's moral judgments as was the experimental condition combining modeling cues with social reinforcement. As predicted, the experimental conditions utilizing modeling procedures proved to be considerably more powerful than was operant conditioning alone, which produced a slight increase in objective judgmental responses but not of statistically significant magnitude (Table 3).

Some additional evidence for the efficacy of the behavior of models in accelerating

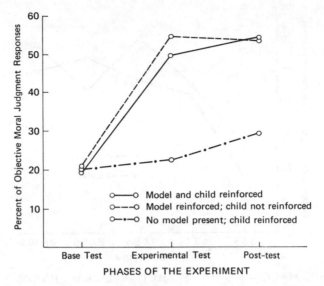

Figure 2 | MEAN PERCENTAGE OF OBJECTIVE MORAL JUDGMENT RESPONSES PRO-
DUCED BY SUBJECTIVE CHILDREN ON EACH OF THE THREE TEST PERIODS FOR
EACH OF THREE EXPERIMENTAL CONDITIONS.

the acquisition process is provided in the finding that only 9% of the children who were
exposed to the objective models failed to produce a single objective response; in contrast,
38% of the subjects in the operant conditioning group did not emit a single objective
response despite obtaining twice as many acquisition trials.

Table 2 | ANALYSIS OF VARIANCE OF OBJECTIVE MORAL JUDGMENT RESPONSES
PRODUCED BY SUBJECTIVE CHILDREN

SOURCE	df	MS	F
Conditions (C)	2	5,226.2	3.24*
Sex (S)	1	1,344.4	<1
C $\times$ S	2	3,671.4	2.28
Error (b)	42	1,612.1	
Phases (P)	2	9,505.8	
P $\times$ C	4	1,430.3	35.46**
P $\times$ S	2	203.8	5.34**
P $\times$ C $\times$ S	4	747.6	<1
Error (w)	84	268.1	2.79*

* $p < .05.$
** $p < .001.$

Table 3 | COMPARISON OF PAIRS OF MEANS ACROSS EXPERIMENTAL PHASES AND BETWEEN TREATMENT CONDITIONS

SCORES	BASE TEST VERSUS EXPERIMENTAL PHASE	BASE TEST VERSUS POSTTEST	EXPERIMENTAL PHASE VERSUS POSTTEST
	t	t	t
Within conditions			
Objective treatment			
Model and Reinforcement	5.31****	5.74****	<1
Model	5.84****	5.74****	<1
Reinforcement	<1	1.52	<1
Subjective treatment			
Model and Reinforcement	3.12***	3.09**	<1
Model	4.10***	2.69*	1.87
Reinforcement	2.04	<1	1.99

	MODEL + REINFORCE-MENT VERSUS MODEL	MODEL + REINFORCE-MENT VERSUS REINFORCE-MENT	MODEL VERSUS REIN-FORCEMENT
Between conditions			
Objective treatment			
Experimental phase	<1	2.81**	3.34***
Posttest	<1	2.68**	2.61**
Subjective treatment			
Experimental phase	<1	1.11	1.13
Posttest	<1	2.81**	2.15*

     * $p < .05$.
    ** $p < .02$.
   *** $p < .01$.
  **** $p < .001$.

The significant triple interaction effect shows that modeling combined with reinforcement exerted a greater influence on girls than on boys whereas, relative to girls, boys were more responsive to modeling cues when reinforcement was absent.

The acquisition and generalization data for objective children treated subjectively are presented graphically in Figure 3.

Analysis of variance of this set of scores reveals that the experimental treatments were highly influential in modifying the children's orientations from objective to subjective morality (Table 4). Although the differences between the three experimental groups did not reach statistical significance, evidently the two conditions utilizing modeling procedures were the principal contributors to the main treatment effect. Comparison of pairs

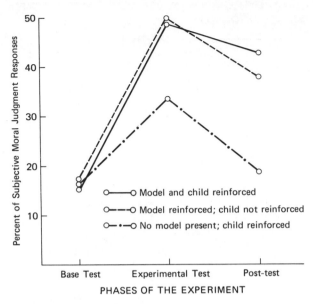

Figure 3 | MEAN PERCENTAGE OF SUBJECTIVE MORAL JUDGMENT RESPONSES PRODUCED BY OBJECTIVE CHILDREN ON EACH OF THE THREE TEST PERIODS FOR EACH OF THREE EXPERIMENTAL CONDITIONS.

of means across phases yielded no significant differences for the operant conditioning group. The modeling conditions, on the other hand, produced significant and relatively stable increases in subjective moral judgment responses (Table 3).

DISCUSSION

The results of the present study provide evidence that subjective morality increases gradually with age, but fail to substantiate Piaget's theory of demarcated sequential stages of moral development. Children at all age levels exhibited discriminative repertories of moral judgments in which both objective and subjective classes of responses exist concurrently. A recent study by Durkin (1961) provides some additional support for the specificity of children's moral judgment behavior.

The utility of Piaget's stage theory of morality is further limited by the finding that children's judgmental responses are readily modifiable, particularly through the utilization of adult modeling cues.

In most experimental demonstrations of modeling effects the model exhibits a given set of responses and the observer reproduces these responses in substantially identical form in similar or identical stimulus context (Bandura, 1962). The findings of the present study reveal, however, that a general class of behavior may be readily acquired through observation of social models and consequently, the observer responds to new stimulus sensations in a manner consistent with the model's predisposition even though

Table 4 | ANALYSIS OF VARIANCE OF SUBJECTIVE MORAL JUDGMENT RESPONSES PRODUCED BY OBJECTIVE CHILDREN

SOURCE	df	MS	F
Conditions (C)	2	1,869.2	1.76
Sex (S)	1	2,821.3	2.66
C × S	2	208.6	<1
Error (b)	30	1,059.9	
Experimental phases			
(P)	2	7,057.5	16.38**
P × C	4	422.1	<1
P × S	2	99.4	<1
P × C × S	4	132.9	<1
Error (w)	60	430.9	

** $p < .001$.

the subject had never observed the model respond to the same stimuli. These results illustrate the potency of modeling cues for shaping generalized patterns of social behavior.

The failure of operant conditioning procedures alone in altering moral judgment behavior is not at all surprising considering that the desired responses were much weaker than the competing dominant class of moral judgments. In many cases, particularly in the objective treatment condition, the subordinate responses occurred relatively infrequently; consequently there was little opportunity to influence them through reinforcement. In fact, the absence of a statistically significant conditions effect for children who experienced the subjective treatment largely resulted from several of the subjects in the operant conditioning group who happened to emit subjective responses on early trials and increased this behavior under reinforcement.

It is apparent, however, from both sets of data that operant conditioning procedures are particularly inefficient when there are strong dominant response tendencies and the desired alternative responses are only weakly developed or absent. In such cases, the provision of models who exhibit the desired behavior is an exceedingly effective procedure for eliciting from others appropriate matching responses early in the learning sequence and thus accelerating the acquisition process.

The results of the present study fail to confirm the hypothesis that a combination of reinforcement and modeling procedures constitutes a more powerful learning condition than modeling alone. Several factors might have accounted for the lack of differences between these two treatment conditions. In some cases the mere exposure to modeling cues produced rapid and complete changes in moral orientations and consequently the addition of reinforcement could not contribute any performance increments. This interpretation, however, does not fully account for the data since the majority of children were not performing at or near the ceiling level. Results from a series of experiments of social learning by means of imitation provide an alternative explanation (Bandura,

1962). These studies suggest that the process of response acquisition is based upon contiguity of sensory events and that reinforcement may function primarily as a performance related variable. In the present investigation the models' responses were highly consistent and sufficiently distinctive to insure observation and imitative learning. The experimenters' positive evaluative statements, however, may have served as relatively weak reinforcers. Had more highly desired incentives been employed as reinforcing agents, it is very likely that the addition of reinforcement would have significantly enhanced the children's reproduction of the modeled judgmental orientations.

SUMMARY

This experiment was designed to test the relative efficacy of social reinforcement and modeling procedures in modifying moral judgmental responses considered by Piaget to be age-specific. One group of children observed adult models who expressed moral judgments counter to the group's orientation, and the children were reinforced with approval for adopting the model's evaluative responses. A second group observed the models but received no reinforcement for matching their behavior. A third group of children had no exposure to models but were reinforced for moral judgments that ran counter to their dominant evaluative tendencies. Following the treatments, the children were tested for generalization effects. The experimental treatments produced substantial changes in the children's moral judgment responses. Conditions utilizing modeling cues proved to be more effective than the operant conditioning procedure.

REFERENCES

Bandura, A. Social learning through imitation. In M. R. Jones (Ed.), *Nebraska symposium on motivation: 1962.* Lincoln, Neb.: University of Nebraska Press, 1962. Pp. 211–269.

Bandura, A., & Huston, Aletha C. Identification as a process of incidental learning. *J. abnorm. soc. Psychol.*, 1961, *63*, 311–318.

Bandura, A., Ross, Dorothea, & Ross, Sheila A. Transmission of aggression through imitation of aggressive models. *J. abnorm. soc. Psychol.*, 1961, *63*, 575–582.

Bandura, A., Ross, Dorothea, & Ross, Sheila A. Imitation of film-mediated aggressive models. *J. abnorm. soc. Psychol.*, 1963, *66*, 3–11.

Durkin, Dolores. The specificity of children's moral judgments. *J. genet. Psychol.*, 1961, *98*, 3–13.

Erikson, E. H. *Childhood and society.* New York: Norton, 1950.

Freud, S. *An outline of psychoanalysis.* New York: Norton, 1949.

Gesell, A., & Ilg, F. L. *Infant and child in the culture of today.* New York: Harper & Row, 1943.

Keller, Helen. *The story of my life.* New York: Doubleday, 1927.

Mahrer, A. R. The role of expectancy in delayed reinforcement. *J. exp. Psychol.*, 1956, *52*, 101–106.

Piaget, J. *The moral judgment of the child.* New York: Free Press, 1948.

Piaget, J. *The construction of reality in the child.* New York: Basic Books, 1954.

Skinner, B. F. *Science and human behavior.* New York: Macmillan, 1953.

Sullivan, H. S. *The interpersonal theory of psychiatry.* New York: Norton, 1953.

15.2 | MODEL'S CHARACTERISTICS AS DETERMINANTS OF SOCIAL LEARNING*[1]

Joan Grusec and Walter Mischel

In a recent study Mischel and Grusec (1966) found that a model's social characteristics affect the extent to which preschool children rehearse and transmit aspects of his behavior. In that study the model exhibited *neutral* behavior which had no direct consequences for the child, and also behaved in ways that had direct negative consequences for him (*aversive* behavior). Subjects rehearsed the model's neutral and aversive behaviors most frequently when the model had been noncontingently rewarding in a prior interaction, and also had some control over their future resources. The children transmitted the model's aversive behaviors to an experimental confederate most frequently when the model had been highly rewarding, regardless of her potential control over the child's future. Neither rewardingness nor future control significantly affected the transmission of neutral behavior.

In this study, as in others in which the social characteristics of the model have been manipulated (e.g., Bandura & Huston, 1961; Bandura, Ross, & Ross, 1963a), it was not possible to determine whether these characteristics affected only the observer's willingness to *perform* modeled behaviors or whether they also affected the degree to which he learned those behaviors. The fact that the model's rewardingness and potential control differentially influenced the observer's rehearsal and transmission of the neutral and aversive behaviors suggests that differing expectancies about the outcome of performance may have been generated in these two parts of the experimental situation. But it is also possible that subjects more closely observed an adult who was rewarding and who they believed would be their new teacher than one who was nonrewarding and who they believed would never return. Such greater attentiveness might have increased the degree to which they learned the model's behaviors. Indeed, this would be predicted by certain power theories of identification. Maccoby (1959), for example, suggests that when an adult has control over resources which are important for the needs of a child the child will be motivated to attend more closely to, and engage in more role practice of, that adult's behavior. This occurs because knowledge of that behavior helps the child to guide his plans about future actions.

The purpose of the present study was to determine if the characteristics possessed by a model do affect the degree to which observers learn his behaviors. Presumably, the

* SOURCE: Grusec, J., & Mischel, W. Model's characteristics as determinants of social learning. *Journal of Personality and Social Psychology*, 1966, 4, 211–215. Copyright 1966 by the American Psychological Association and reprinted by permission.

[1] This study was supported by Research Grant MH 6830 from the United States Public Health Service. Thanks are due to Ruth Wallace who served as co-experimenter.

amount of learning would be mediated by differences in attention and, perhaps, in covert rehearsal. If the behavior of a model who controls resources is more closely observed and learned than that of a model who does not control resources, such differences should be revealed when the observer is directly reinforced in a posttest for reproduction of what he observed. That is, between-group differences in recall would suggest that the model's behavior had not been learned to the same degree.

To adequately assess the extent to which a model's behavior had been learned it would be necessary to eliminate any *overt* rehearsal of that behavior. The results obtained by Mischel and Grusec (1966) indicate that overt rehearsal would give this group additional practice at performing the model's behaviors. It would thus be difficult to determine whether any difference in the acquisition measure obtained for this group, and for one interacting with a model who did not control resources, was a function of differential attention paid to the model and covert rehearsal or to a difference in the amount of practice in performing his behaviors. Accordingly, the present study was designed to minimize the opportunity for overt rehearsal of the model's behavior in his presence. In addition, subjects were not allowed to stay in a stimulus situation which might have evoked the model's distinctive behaviors after the model finished displaying them.

In the present experiment nursery-school children interacted in a 15-minute play session with a model who was either high or low in both rewardingness and future control. Thereafter, in the context of a game, the model displayed both aversive and neutral behaviors with varying frequency. At the termination of the game an experimental confederate offered attractive incentives to all subjects contingent upon reproduction of as many of the model's behaviors as they could recall. This acquisition test was conducted in the model's absence and after her rewardingness and potential future control had been made equivalent for all subjects.

METHOD

SUBJECTS

The subjects were 28 children from the Stanford University nursery school, ranging in age from 38 months to 56 months, with a mean age of 46 months. Eight girls and six boys were randomly assigned to each of the two experimental groups, and the same two female experimenters were used with all children.

EXPERIMENTAL GROUPS

Subjects were assigned to one of the following two groups: the model was high in rewardingness and would have control over them in the future, and the model was low in rewardingness and would have no control over them in the future.[2]

[2] These two conditions were selected because they produced the most extreme effects in the Mischel and Grusec (1966) study.

High reward-high control. In this group the model and the subject played together with a number of very attractive toys (e.g., puzzles, battery-operated cars and planes, colorful blocks, dolls). During this play the model displayed warmth and affection and frequently praised the child. She thus attempted to establish herself as highly uncontingently rewarding and as having attractive resources at her disposal. In addition, the model described herself to the child as his new nursery-school teacher, thereby presenting herself as someone who would have future control over him.

Low reward-low control. In this group subjects were given unattractive toys to play with (e.g., a broken toy car, a much-used coloring book and crayons). The model did not play with the child, but informed him that she had some work to finish. She sat at a desk at the other side of the room from the child and busily worked at some papers. Any attention bids made by the child received minimal, although pleasant, responses. The model thus attempted to establish herself as low in rewardingness and as having few resources at her disposal. In addition, she described herself to the child as a visiting nursery-school teacher who was leaving in an hour to take the bus back to Milwaukee. She thereby presented herself as someone who would have no future control over him.

PROCEDURE

Establishment of the model's characteristics. Each child was brought individually to the experimental room by the experimenter's assistant who introduced the child and the model and then left, saying that she would return soon. The model described herself to the child as either his new nursery-school teacher (high control), or as a visiting teacher (low control) who was leaving that same day. A play session lasting 15 minutes followed in which the model displayed either high rewardingness or low rewardingness, as described above. At the end of the play session the model reminded the child of her role as his new teacher or as a visiting teacher.

Presentation of neutral and aversive behaviors. The model next announced to the child that she was going to show him how to play a special game, and went to uncover a toy cash register placed on a table in another corner of the experimental room. At the same time the experimental confederate entered the room and sat down, saying that she wanted to watch the game.

The model showed the child a large container of toys and told him to take one he liked. The toy he chose was put in a paper bag, and he was told he could take it home.

The model and the child sat down in front of the cash register and proceeded to play with it. This play involved making change, opening and closing the register drawer, and hitting the register keys. During the game all subjects were exposed to the following two kinds of behavior:

1. Neutral behaviors. (*a*) Hat—the model began the game by placing a hat on her head and commenting how pretty it was. At the end of the game she took off the hat. (*b*) Marching—the model hit a key on the register and then marched around the table saying, "March, march, march, march, march." This sequence was repeated three times.

2. Aversive behaviors. (*a*) Imposed delay—when the child first touched the

cash register, the model said that if one wants to play with anything badly enough one ought to be able to wait for it, and instructed him to sit still with his hands in his lap until she had finished counting. She then very slowly and methodically repeated the numbers "1, 2, 3" 15 times. (*b*) Criticism and removal of reward— the cash register was constructed so that, unknown to the subject, the model could make the drawer come all the way out when it was opened, giving the appearance that it was broken. When this happened, as the child "broke" the drawer, the model exclaimed sharply, "Oh my! Do you know what this makes you? It makes you a storewrecker, and when you're a storewrecker you lose your toy." She then removed the toy the child had previously received, saying sternly, "You try not to be a storewrecker again!"

The model performed the marching and the counting sequences at two different times in the course of playing with the cash register, while she put on and took off the hat only once, and made the drawer "break" only once. The marching was done in a way which would minimize the chance of overt rehearsal by the child. For example, immediately after the model marched, she instructed the child to sit very still while she counted. Obviously the child could not overtly rehearse the wearing of the hat since the model had the hat on her head. In the previous study (Mischel & Grusec, 1966) only one child had rehearsed the label "storewrecker," and only two of the six subjects in the high reward-high control group who had rehearsed the model's counting did so in her presence. (Rehearsal of the aversive behaviors had not occurred at all in the low reward-low control groups.) Thus it was assumed that overt rehearsal of the model's behaviors would be minimal in the present study. In fact, only one subject (in the high reward-high control condition) overtly rehearsed any of the model's behaviors, and this child rehearsed the model's counting.

Equating the model's characteristics. At the end of the game the model covered up the cash register, and the experimental confederate excused herself and left the room. The model then played for 5 minutes with all subjects as she had played with subjects in the high-reward condition before the game. In the course of this 5 minutes of play she returned the toy the child had lost when he "broke" the drawer. The intent of this procedure was to minimize differences between subjects in the degree to which they now viewed her as noncontingently rewarding.

After this play period the experimental confederate returned to the room and handed the model a note. The model told subjects in high-control conditions that the note stated she had received a telephone call which said she was needed elsewhere and so could not be their new teacher. Subjects in the low-control condition were told that the note said it was time for her to go. Thus, for all subjects, the model would have no control over them in the future. The model then said goodbye, put on her coat, and left the room.

ASSESSMENT OF LEARNING

The experimental confederate now remained alone in the room with the child and told him that she wanted to see how good he was at remembering all the things that had happened while he and the model had played store. She seated the subject in front of the cash register and gave him an attractive picture sticker or a cookie as an immediate reward for each aspect of the model's behavior during the game which he correctly recalled. In addition, she told him that as soon as he had recalled everything he would be allowed to leave and return to the nursery school.

Only the model's two aversive and two neutral behaviors were scored, although subjects were reinforced for recalling any relevant aspect of the model's behavior (e.g., "she pushed the keys"). If a subject mentioned that the model had marched or counted, he was asked to demonstrate this. He was scored as recalling the marching behavior if he either marched around the table or indicated verbally that the model had done so. Counting was scored as recalled if the child indicated that the model had said "1, 2, 3." If he said that the model put on the hat, he was scored as having recalled this. Extensive probes were used only in an attempt to elicit the label "storewrecker." If a subject mentioned that the drawer had come out of the cash register, the confederate asked "What happened?" If this probe was unsuccessful, she said, "What did [model] say you were?" If the subject did not mention that the drawer had broken, he was reminded that this had happened and then asked the two probe questions. Only use of the word "storewrecker" was scored as correct recall of the model's criticism.

As each item of the model's behavior was recalled the confederate asked, "What else did [model] do when you were playing store?" and "Can you remember anything else [model] did?" This continued until the child insisted that he could not remember anything else.

The experimental assistant and the model-experimenter, who watched the acquisition testing through a one-way mirror, each recorded independently everything the child recalled. There was 100% agreement in their recording.

RESULTS

Inspection of the data revealed no difference in the number of individual items of the model's behavior recalled for boys and girls. Thus the data from both sexes were combined for statistical analysis.

Table 1 shows the number of children who recalled each of the model's neutral behaviors (wearing the hat and marching) and the number who recalled each of the model's aversive behaviors (counting and calling the child a "storewrecker"). None of the differences between groups in number of children recalling any single item of behavior was statistically significant (all χ^2 values < 1.35, all p values $> .20$, $df = 1$ in each

Table 1 | NUMBER OF CHILDREN IN EACH GROUP RECALLING EACH OF THE MODEL'S BEHAVIORS AND MEAN TOTAL RECALL

GROUP	MODEL'S BEHAVIORS				
	Hat	*Marching*	*Counting*	*Criticism*	*Mean total recall*
High reward-high control	9	12	10	2	2.36
Low reward-low control	6	9	6	1	1.57

comparison). However, the mean number of total items of the model's behavior recalled by each child in the high reward-high control condition was 2.36 ($SD = .71$) while the mean number of items recalled by children in the low reward-low control condition was 1.57 ($SD = .88$). A comparison of these two means yielded a t of 2.34 ($p < .025$, $df = 26$, one-tailed). Thus the behavior of a model who is a controller of resources (high in rewardingness and future control) was recalled better than the behavior of a model who is not a controller of resources (low in rewardingness and future control).

DISCUSSION

Although the results were not impressively strong, they indicate that the learning of social behaviors is affected by the characteristics of the agent who initially exhibited them. Children who interacted with a model who was highly rewarding and who had control over their future resources were able to recall more of that model's behavior when given external incentives for doing so than were children who interacted with a model who was not rewarding and who had no future control over them.[3] These differences in recall presumably reflect differences in acquisition or learning of the model's behaviors. It seems likely that they were mediated by the amount of attention paid to the model in the two groups and perhaps also by the amount of covert practice of the modeled behavior in which the children engaged. The present results support theories of identification which stress the power of the model as a determinant of the degree to which his behaviors are acquired (e.g., Maccoby, 1959).

It was impossible to know from earlier studies that varied the model's social characteristics (Bandura & Huston, 1961; Bandura, Ross, & Ross, 1963a; Mischel & Grusec, 1966) whether these characteristics affected the degree to which observers actually *learned* the model's behaviors or whether they influenced only willingness to *perform* them. This is because previous investigations did not assess the observer's learning by offering attractive incentives to all subjects contingent on their reproducing the model's behavior. The only relevant earlier attempt to measure acquisition by this technique (Bandura, 1965) found no learning differences between groups who had witnessed models obtaining positive or negative consequences for their behavior. Obviously, however, acquisition differences could not have been the result of observed response consequences since these occurred *after* the model's behavior had been observed. The model's attributes, or the response consequences his behavior engenders, can affect the observer's attention and learning of the displayed behaviors only if they are presented *before* exposure to the modeled behaviors. The results of the present experiment suggest that

[3] It is of interest that so few children were able to recall the critical label storewrecker since Mischel and Grusec (1966) found that this label was frequently transmitted to an experimental confederate. In that study, however, all the events that had occurred during the game before the transmission phase were reviewed verbally by the model. It may have been this review which helped more children to remember and to use the critical label. The children in the present study were, on the average, 6 months younger than those in the first study, and the inability of all but three of the present subjects to remember a relatively difficult label may have been due to their age.

when this is done the model's attributes do influence the degree to which his behaviors are learned and not merely the observer's subsequent willingness to perform them.

The amount of imitation which occurs in a given situation is certainly more than a function of the amount of the model's behavior that the observer has learned. An explanation of imitative behavior involving only differences in acquisition would be insufficient to account for the finding that rewardingness and future control affect the rehearsal and transmission of a model's neutral and aversive behaviors differently (Mischel & Grusec, 1966). An adequate explanation of this result would have to consider apparently different determinants of rehearsal and transmission of the same behaviors—determinants which might involve differing expectancies about the outcomes of behavior rehearsed in the model's presence and of behavior transmitted to someone else. In addition, there is ample evidence that response consequences to the model at the *end* of a sequence of modeled behavior affect the degree to which an observer subsequently *performs* that model's behavior (Bandura, 1965; Bandura, Ross, & Ross, 1963b; Walters, Leat, & Mezei, 1963).

In summary, then, comprehensive accounts of the effects of a model's social characteristics on imitation of his behavior probably would have to deal with differences in amount learned about the model's behavior as well as differences in the observer's expectation about the outcome of performing the particular learned behavior. Presumably, differences in acquisition would be mediated by differential attention and covert rehearsal, while differences in performance would be mediated by expectancies about the consequences of particular performances in the eliciting situation.

SUMMARY

This study investigated the effect of a model's social characteristics on the extent to which his behaviors are learned by others. Preschool children interacted either with a highly rewarding adult model who would have control over their future resources "future control"), or with a nonrewarding model who would not have future control. Thereafter the model behaved in ways designed to be aversive to them (criticism and imposed delay of reward) and also displayed novel neutral behaviors. To test the extent to which Ss learned these behaviors an experimental confederate rewarded the children for every aspect of the model's behaviors which they could reproduce in the model's absence. Children who had initially interacted with a rewarding model who had future control were able to reproduce significantly more of her behaviors than those who had interacted with a model who was not rewarding and had no future control. Thus, the model's social characteristics may affect the observer's learning of modeled behavior, and not merely his willingness to perform them.

REFERENCES

Bandura, A. Influence of model's reinforcement contingencies on the acquisition of imitative responses. *Journal of Personality and Social Psychology*, 1965, *1*, 589–595.

Bandura, A., & Huston, A. C. Identification as a process of incidental learning. *Journal of Abnormal and Social Psychology*, 1961, *63*, 311–318.

Bandura, A., Ross, D., & Ross, S. A. A. A comparative test of the status envy, social power, and secondary reinforcement theories of identificatory learning. *Journal of Abnormal and Social Psychology*, 1963, *67*, 527–534. (a)

Bandura, A., Ross, D., & Ross, S. A. Vicarious reinforcement and imitative learning. *Journal of Abnormal and Social Psychology*, 1963, *67*, 601–607. (b)

Maccoby, E. E. Role-taking in childhood and its consequences for social learning. *Child Development*, 1959, *30*, 239–252.

Mischel, W., & Grusec, J. Determinants of the rehearsal and transmission of neutral and aversive behaviors. *Journal of Personality and Social Psychology*, 1966, *3*, 197–205.

Walters, R. H., Leat, M., & Mezei, L. Inhibition and disinhibition of responses through empathetic learning. *Canadian Journal of Psychology*, 1963, *17*, 235–243.

15.3 | ATTRACTION TOWARD THE MODEL AND MODEL'S COMPETENCE AS DETERMINANTS OF ADULT IMITATIVE BEHAVIOR*

Robert A. Baron[1]

Several recent experiments (e.g., Flanders, 1968) have investigated the acquisition of a tendency to match the behavior of another individual by adult human subjects. The results of these studies have suggested that several variables known to influence learning in nonsocial situations also affect the learning of imitation. Thus, adult imitative behavior has been shown to be a function of probability of reinforcement for imitation (e.g., Kanareff & Lanzetta, 1958), magnitude of reinforcement for imitation (e.g., Lanzetta & Kanareff, 1959), and gambling or problem-solving instructions to subjects (Kanareff & Lanzetta, 1960). In addition, the results of several other experiments have indicated that

* SOURCE: Baron, R. A. Attraction toward the model and model's competence as determinants of adult imitative behavior. *Journal of Personality and Social Psychology*, 1970, *14*, 345–351. Copyright 1970 by the American Psychological Association and reprinted by permission.

[1] The author wishes to express his appreciation to Beverly Beard and Lee Hursh for their aid in the collection of the data, and to Harold R. Keller and Milton E. Rosenbaum for their assistance in the preparation of this manuscript. Thanks are also due to Gerald L. Clore who kindly supplied copies of the Attitude Questionnaire and Interpersonal Judgment Scale.

acquisition of matching behavior is also influenced by variables which appear to be particularly relevant to behavior in social situations. Among these variables are the competence of the model (e.g., Rosenbaum & Tucker, 1962), amount of prior social agreement from the model (Chalmers, Horne, & Rosenbaum, 1963), and cooperative or competitive instructions to subjects (O'Connell, 1965). The present experiment was designed to investigate the effects of an additional variable of this type, that of level of attraction toward the model, on the learning of imitation by adult subjects.

In his recent review of the literature on imitation, Flanders (1968) has called attention to a lack of information regarding the effects on imitative behavior of variations in the affective relationship between the observer and the model. In addition, Bandura, Grusec, and Menlove (1967) have listed the nature of the relationship between the observer and the model as one of three classes of variables they consider to be of primary importance in influencing modeling processes. Thus, it seemed important to investigate level of attraction toward the model as a variable which might exert an important effect upon adult imitative behavior. Although no experiments known to the author have investigated the effects of this variable on the learning of imitation by adult subjects, several studies performed with children have reported findings relevant to this topic. These studies (e.g., Bandura & Huston, 1961; Grusec & Mischel, 1966; Mischel & Grusec, 1966) have investigated the effects on imitation of variations in level of model's nurturance or rewardingness, and have generally reported that children show more imitation of the behaviors of nurturant or highly rewarding models than nonnurturant or less rewarding models. Bandura et al. (1967, p. 449) have indicated that a high level of nurturance may increase children's attraction to the model. Thus, the results of these studies may be interpreted as suggesting that among children, imitation is facilitated by a high level of attraction toward the model. An additional study (Rosekrans, 1967) has reported that boys show more imitation and recall of the behaviors of models described as highly similar to themselves than models described as highly dissimilar to themselves. If high similarity is associated with high attraction toward the model, as Rosekrans has suggested (1967, p. 314), the results of this study may also be interpreted as suggesting that imitation is facilitated by a high level of attraction toward the model.

On the basis of the findings reported above, it was hypothesized that level of attraction toward the model would also exert a significant effect upon adult imitative behavior. Specifically, it was predicted that subjects would show a higher level of imitation and would also learn to match the behavior of the model more rapidly under conditions of high attraction than under low attraction.

Byrne and his co-workers (e.g., Byrne, 1961; Byrne & Nelson, 1965; Byrne & Rhamey, 1965) have demonstrated repeatedly that level of attraction toward a stranger is a positive linear function of the degree of apparent attitude similarity between subjects and a stranger. Thus, it was decided to attempt to manipulate attraction toward the model in the present experiment by varying the level of attitude similarity between observers and the model. It was expected that a high level of similarity would lead to a higher level of attraction toward the model than a low level of similarity.

Several previous investigations (e.g., Chalmers et al., 1963; Rosenbaum & Tucker,

1962) have demonstrated that model's competence exerts a significant effect upon adult imitative behavior. Specifically, these studies have reported that adult subjects learn to match the behavior of a competent (i.e., successful) model more rapidly than that of an incompetent (i.e., unsuccessful) model. In view of the relatively strong effect of model's competence obtained in these studies, it seemed important to investigate the possibility that this variable would interact with level of attraction toward the model in influencing adult imitative behavior. Thus, model's competence was included as a second variable in the present study. In the absence of previous experimental evidence concerning the joint effects of model's competence and attraction, no specific predictions regarding the occurrence or form of any possible interaction between these two variables were formulated. However, in accordance with the results of previous studies (e.g., Rosenbaum & Tucker, 1962) it was predicted that subjects would learn to match the behavior of a competent model more rapidly than that of an incompetent model.

METHOD

SUBJECTS. Forty-eight undergraduates (24 males, 24 females) enrolled in sections of elementary psychology at the University of South Carolina participated in the experiment. Students took part in the experiment in order to earn extra points toward their course grade.

DESIGN. A 2 $\times$ 2 factorial design based upon two levels of attraction (low, high) and two levels of model's competence (low, high) was employed. An equal number of males and females were assigned to each cell of this design.

APPARATUS. The apparatus consisted of two Lafayette Model 2000 Multi-choice stimulus display units, and a master control panel for these units. Each of these units contained five rows of seven lights each. However, only the top two rows were operative in the present experiment. In each of these rows, moving from left to right, the first light was white, the next four lights were yellow, the sixth light was red, and the seventh light was green. These lights were controlled by individual push-button switches on the master control panel. Each subject unit also contained four red push-button switches. Depression of these switches illuminated corresponding lights on the master control panel.

MANIPULATION OF ATTRACTION TOWARD THE MODEL. The procedures employed to manipulate level of attraction toward the model were based upon those devised by Byrne (1961). Thus, they will not be reported in detail here. Briefly, subjects came to the experiment in pairs, under the restriction that members of each pair could not be previously acquainted. They were conducted to separate rooms by the experimenter and seated at tables. The experimenter then returned to a third room from which she read instructions to the subjects over an intercom system. These instructions indicated that the experiment was concerned with the subjects' ability to make judgments about others on the basis of a limited amount of information. The experimenter explained that in order to study this problem, both subjects would fill out an attitude questionnaire (AQ) designed to measure their opinions on a wide variety of topics. After that, their questionnaires would be collected and exchanged so that they each received the AQ filled out by the other subject. They were then to read the answers given by their partner and make a series of judgments about him on a second questionnaire, the Interpersonal Judgment scale (IJS) which the experimenter would distribute at the same time that she exchanged the AQs. In reality, the AQs returned to the subjects were constructed by the experimenter. In the high attraction (HA) condition, the answers supposedly given by the subject's partner agreed with those originally given by the subjects on all 12 items of the AQ, while in the low attraction (LA) condition these answers disagreed with those given by subject on all 12 items. Agreement and disagreement were defined, after Byrne and Griffitt (1966), as answers differing from those given by subjects by one or three scale positions, respectively. The measure of attraction was the sum of the ratings made by subjects about their partner on the last two items of the IJS (e.g., Byrne & Nelson, 1965). These items required subjects to indicate how much they liked their partner, and how much they would like to work with him in another experiment, on 7-point scales.

While collecting the subject's completed IJS, the experimenter remarked that many subjects had requested permission to see the ratings made about them by their partner, and that since she had already collected the other subject's IJS, she would allow the subject to see these now. In reality the IJS given to the subjects had been filled out in advance by the experimenter. In the HA condition the ratings made about subjects by their partner were highly favorable, while in the LA condition these ratings were highly unfavorable. The actual ratings shown to the subjects were the same as those employed by Byrne and Rhamey (1965). These authors have demonstrated that favorable or unfavorable judgments about the subject ostensibly made by a stranger significantly influence attraction toward the stranger. Thus, these procedures were introduced in order to strengthen the manipulation of level of attraction toward the model.

IMITATION SITUATION. Upon completion of the procedures described above, the experimenter returned and seated each subject at a screened table within their individual rooms. These tables held the imitation apparatus, which had been hidden from the subjects' view up until this time. The experimenter then returned to the third experimental room which contained the master control panel for the imitation apparatus, and read the instructions for this part of the experiment. These instructions indicated that the second part of the sudy was concerned with gambling behavior and that in order to study this behavior, each subject would make a series of bets upon a number of imaginary horse races. Subjects were then told to consult a card on the side of the screen which surrounded the table at which they were sitting in order to determine whether they were Subject A or Subject B. In reality both subjects were informed that they were Subject B. The experimenter then explained that on each race, the individual who was Subject A would place his bet first. He would wait until the white signal light came on in his row (i.e., the row labeled Subject A) and then choose any one of the four horses which were to run in the race by pressing one of the buttons numbered 1–4 on the bottom of the apparatus. When he pressed one of these buttons, one of the four yellow lights in his row would light up, thus indicating his horse for that race. Immediately after that, either the red light labeled "lose" or the green light labeled "win" would come on in his row. These lights would indicate whether his horse had won or lost the race. It was further explained that in order to provide Subject B with some feedback concerning the accuracy of the judgments he had made about Subject A in the first part of the study, Subject A's choices and outcomes would be shown to Subject B on each race.

The experimenter then explained that after Subject A had finished making his bet on each race, Subject B would make his bet. He would wait for the white signal light to come on in his row (i.e., the row labeled Subject B), and would then make his bet by pressing one of the four buttons on bottom of the apparatus. Immediately after that, he would be informed of the outcome of the race by the red and green lights in his row. It was further explained that in order to provide Subject A with some feedback concerning the accuracy of the judgments he had made about Subject B in the first part of the experiment, Subject B's choices and outcomes would be shown to Subject A on each race.

In reality, both subjects were informed that they were Subject B, and the choices and outcomes for Subject A were supplied by the experimenter according to a prearranged schedule. This schedule was designed so that within each of four blocks of 20 trials, Subject A appeared to choose each of the four horses equally often. In addition, the apparent success (i.e., competence) of A was manipulated by the experimenter. In the high model's competence (HMC) condition, A's choices were followed by the green "win" light on 75% of the trials, and by the red "lose" light on 25% of the trials. In the low model's competence (LMC) condition, A's choices were followed by the green "win" light on 25% of the trials, and by the red "lose" light on 75% of the trials. Subjects were rewarded (i.e., presented with the "win" light) when they imitated the choices of the model. Pilot data suggested that consistent reinforcement for imitation led to extremely rapid acquisition of a tendency to match the behavior of the model. Thus, an attempt was made to slow down the learning of imitation by reducing the probability of reinforcement for this behavior. The value found to be most suitable for use in the present study was 60% reinforcement for imitation. Thus, in each block of 20 trials, subjects' choices were followed by the red "lose" light on eight trials regardless of whether they imitated or not.

The general procedures described above were adapted from those devised by Rosenbaum and Tucker (1962). However, it was decided to employ the four-choice situation described above rather than the two-choice situation employed by these authors in order to be able to study the learning of imitation over a somewhat wider range of possible scores.

After completion of the 80 training trials, the experimenter distributed a postexperimental questionnaire to the subjects. This questionnaire obtained a second measure of attraction toward the model, as well as information regarding the subjects' estimate of the success (i.e., competence) of the model.

RESULTS

MANIPULATION OF ATTRACTION TOWARD THE MODEL. In order to determine if the manipulation of attraction toward the model was successful, an analysis of variance was performed on the sum of the ratings of the model made by subjects on the last two questions of the IJS. The results of this analysis indicated that subjects in the HA groups rated the model as significantly more attractive than subjects in the LA groups ($F = 30.54$, $df = 1/44$, $p < .001$). The means for the HA and LA groups were 11.83 and 8.08, respectively. Thus, the manipulation of attraction toward the model appeared to be successful.

IMITATIVE BEHAVIOR. Figure 1 presents the mean number of imitative responses made by subjects in the four groups in each of four successive blocks of 20 trials. Inspection of this figure suggests that subjects in all four groups learned to match the choices of the model over trials. In addition, it appears from Figure 1 that model's competence and attraction toward the model interacted in influencing the level of imitation shown by subjects. Thus, subjects in the HMC-HA group made more imitative responses than subjects in the HMC-LA group in all blocks of trials, while subjects in the LMC-HA group made fewer imitative responses than subjects in the LMC-LA group. The results of an analysis of variance on these data are shown in Table 1.[2] As can be seen from this table, imitative behavior was not significantly influenced by attraction or model's competence. However, as suggested by Figure 1, the interaction between these factors was highly significant. The only other significant effect was that due to trials.

---

[2] Sex of subjects was included as a factor in an initial analysis performed on these data, and was found to have no effect upon imitative behavior. Thus, it was not included as a factor in subsequent analyses.

Table 1 | ANALYSIS OF VARIANCE OF NUMBER OF IMITATIVE RESPONSES IN FOUR BLOCKS OF TRIALS

SOURCE	df	MS	F
Between Ss	47		
Attraction (B)	1	59.63	2.07
Model's competence (C)	1	103.55	3.59
B × C	1	388.17	13.47*
Error	44	28.82	
Within Ss	144		
Trials (A)	3	174.89	28.77*
A × B	3	1.48	.24
A × C	3	7.73	1.27
A × B × C	3	13.13	2.16
Error	132	6.08	

  * $p < .001$.

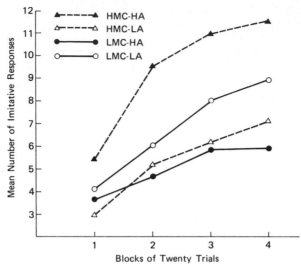

Figure 1 | MEAN NUMBER OF IMITATIVE RESPONSES MADE BY SUBJECTS IN FOUR TREATMENT CONDITIONS AS A FUNCTION OF SUCCESSIVE BLOCKS OF 20 TRIALS.

Thus, all groups showed an increase in the frequency of imitative responses over trials, but the rate at which subjects in the four groups learned to imitate the model was not influenced by attraction or model's competence.

In order to examine the effects of attraction and model's competence on the acquisition of matching behavior more closely, separate analyses were performed on the data for the first two and last two blocks of trials. The results of the analysis of variance performed on the data for the first two blocks of trials are presented in Table 2. As found in the previous analysis, the effect of trials and the interaction of model's competence with attraction were both significant. In addition, the main effect of attraction, and the interaction of model's competence with trials, also attained significance. The main effect of attraction indicates that subjects in the HA groups made more imitative responses than subjects in the LA groups during the first two blocks of trials. The interaction of model's competence with trials indicates that subjects in the HMC groups learned to match the behavior of the model more rapidly than subjects in the LMC groups during these blocks of trials.

The results of the analysis performed on the data for the last two blocks of trials indicated that only the interaction between model's competence and attraction was significant ($F = 9.79$, $df = 1/44$, $p < .01$). Thus, as suggested by the results of previous analyses, a high level of attraction toward the model facilitated imitation only when the model was competent in performing the experimental task.

POSTEXPERIMENTAL QUESTIONNAIRE. The first two questions on the postexperimental questionnaire were a repetition of the last two questions on the IJS. Thus,

Table 2 | ANALYSIS OF VARIANCE OF NUMBER OF IMITATIVE RESPONSES IN THE FIRST TWO BLOCKS OF TRIALS

SOURCE	df	MS	F
Between Ss	47		
Attraction (B)	1	38.76	4.41*
Model's Competence (C)	1	33.84	3.85
B × C	1	110.51	12.56**
Error	44	8.80	
Within Ss	48		
Trials (A)	1	133.01	34.81***
A × B	1	2.34	.61
A × C	1	19.26	5.04*
A × B × C	1	14.26	3.73
Error	44	3.82	

     * $p < .05$.
   ** $p < .01$.
  *** $p < .001$.

a second measure of attraction toward the model was attained in this manner. An analysis of variance performed on the sum of the ratings of the model made by subjects on these two questions indicated that subjects in the HA groups rated their partner as more attractive than subjects in the LA groups ($F = 55.99$, $df = 1/44$, $p < .001$). The means for the HA and LA groups were 12.33 and 7.50, respectively. Thus, the differences in level of attraction toward the model established in the first phase of the experiment were still apparent at the end of the experimental sessions.

The postexperimental questionnaire also required subjects to estimate the percentage of the races (i.e., the trials) on which their partner made successful predictions. An analysis of variance performed on these data indicated that subjects in the HMC groups estimated that their partner was significantly more successful than subjects in the LMC groups ($F = 135.96$, $df = 1/44$, $p < .001$). The means for the HMC and LMC groups were 78.38% and 26.42%, respectively. Thus, subjects were able to estimate their partner's success (i.e., competence) on the experimental task with a high degree of accuracy.

DISCUSSION

The results of the present experiment indicate that level of attraction toward the model and model's competence interact in influencing adult imitative behavior. It was found that a high level of attraction toward the model facilitated imitation when the model was successful in performing the experimental task (i.e., was high in competence), but interfered with imitation when the model was unsuccessful in performing this task (i.e., was low in competence). These findings agree with the results of previous studies (e.g., Bandura & Huston, 1961; Mischel & Grusec, 1966) in suggesting that variations in level of attraction toward the model on the part of observers produce specific rather than generalized effects upon imitative behavior. The results of the present study indicate that one factor determining the direction of these effects is the level of competence shown by the model.

The hypothesis that level of attraction toward the model would influence the rate at which subjects learned to match the behavior of this individual was not confirmed. Attraction failed to interact with trials in any of the analyses performed. In view of the fact that the manipulation of this variable appears to have been successful, this finding suggests that level of attraction toward the model may fail to influence the rate at which subjects learn to match the behavior of another person. However, further research (perhaps employing different magnitudes and schedules of reinforcement for imitation than the present study) must be conducted before any definite conclusions concerning the effects of this variable on the learning of imitation can be reached.

In view of the fact that the manipulation of attraction involved variations in the apparent degree of attitude similarity between subjects and the model, the results of the present study may be regarded as providing information on the effects of perceived similarity to the model on adult imitative behavior. Previous experimental evidence concerning the effects of this variable has been conflicting. Several studies (e.g., Burnstein, Stotland, & Zander, 1961; Rosekrans, 1967) have reported that subjects imitate the behavior of similar models more readily than that of dissimilar models. However, several additional studies (e.g., Epstein, 1966; Hicks, 1965) have reported that subjects may match the behavior of dissimilar models more readily than that of similar models. The results of the present experiment suggest that the effects of perceived similarity to the model on adult imitative behavior are strongly influenced by the competence of the model. Under conditions where the model was highly successful in performing the experimental task (i.e., was high in competence), a high degree of apparent similarity to this individual facilitated imitation. However, under conditions where the model was relatively unsuccessful in performing the experimental task (i.e., was low in competence), a high degree of apparent similarity interfered with imitation. This later finding is not consistent with the suggestion made by Kagan (1958) that identification with the model is reinforced (i.e., strengthened) by the subject's perception of similarity to this individual. Further research is necessary in order to investigate more fully the conditions under which a high degree of apparent similarity to the model may facilitate or interfere with overt imitative behavior.

The hypothesis that model's competence would influence the rate at which subjects learned to imitate was only partially confirmed. Results indicated that subjects learned to imitate a competent model more quickly than an incompetent model only during the first two blocks of trials. One possible explanation for this relatively weak effect of model's competence may lie in the fact that the incompetent model performed at exactly the level which could be attained by chance on the experimental task (i.e., correct responses on 25% of the trials in a four-choice situation). In view of the fact that this task was described to subjects as involving gambling behavior, it is possible that they perceived the chance-level performance of the incompetent model as indicating moderate rather than low competence as intended. The fact that previous studies which have found relatively strong effects of model's competence on adult imitative behavior (e.g., Rosenbaum & Tucker, 1962) employed incompetent models who performed at less than chance levels (i.e., correct responses on 20% of the trials in a two-choice situation) lends support to this suggestion. Future experiments may investigate this possibility by varying model's competence over a wider range than that employed in the present study.

SUMMARY

Forty-eight undergraduate students (24 males, 24 females) participated in an experiment designed to investigate the effects of attraction toward the model and model's competence on adult imitative behavior. Attraction was manipulated by varying the apparent degree of attitude similarity between subjects and the model, and the favorability of ratings about subjects ostensibly made by this individual. It was predicted that both attraction and competence would influence the rate at which subjects learned to match the behavior of the model. Results indicated that attraction produced no effect upon the learning of imitation, while model's competence influenced the acquisition of matching behavior only during the first two blocks of trials. The two independent variables interacted so that a high level of attraction facilitated imitation when the model was relatively successful in performing the experimental task (i.e., high in competence), but interfered with imitation when the model was relatively unsuccessful on this task (i.e., low in competence).

REFERENCES

Bandura, A., Grusec, J. E., & Menlove, F. L. Some social determinants of self-monitoring reinforcement systems. *Journal of Personality and Social Psychology*, 1967, 5, 449–455.

Bandura, A., & Huston, A. C. Identification as a process of incidental learning. *Journal of Abnormal and Social Psychology*, 1961, 63, 311–318.

Burnstein, E., Stotland, E., & Zander, A. Similarity to a model and self-evaluation. *Journal of Abnormal and Social Psychology*, 1961, 62, 257–264.

Byrne, D. Interpersonal attraction and attitude similarity. *Journal of Abnormal and Social Psychology*, 1961, 62, 713–715.

Byrne, D., & Griffitt, W. Similarity versus liking: A clarification. *Psychonomic Science*, 1966, 6, 295–296.

Byrne, D., & Nelson, D. Attraction as a linear function of proportion of positive reinforcements. *Journal of Personality and Social Psychology*, 1965, 1, 659–663.

Byrne, D., & Rhamey, R. Magnitude of positive and negative reinforcements as a determinant of attraction. *Journal of Personality and Social Psychology*, 1965, 2, 884–889.

Chalmers, D. K., Horne, W. C., & Rosenbaum, M. E. Social agreement and the learning of matching behavior. *Journal of Abnormal and Social Psychology*, 1963, 66, 556–561.

Epstein, R. Aggression toward outgroups as a function of authoritarianism and imitation of aggressive models. *Journal of Personality and Social Psychology*, 1966, 3, 574–579.

Flanders, J. P. A review of research on imitative behavior. *Psychological Bulletin*, 1968, 69, 316–337.

Grusec, J., & Mischel, W. Model's characteristics as determinants of social learning. *Journal of Personality and Social Psychology*, 1966, 4, 244–252.

Hicks, D. J. Imitation and retention of film-mediated aggressive peer and adult models. *Journal of Personality and Social Psychology*, 1965, 2, 97–100.

Kagan, J. The concept of identification. *Psychological Review*, 1958, 65, 296–305.

Kanareff, V. T., & Lanzetta, J. T. Acquisition of imitative and opposition responses under two conditions of instruction-induced set. *Journal of Experimental Psychology*, 1958, 56, 516–528.

Kanareff, V. T., & Lanzetta, J. T. Effects of task definition and probability of reinforcement upon the acquisition and extinction of imitative responses. *Journal of Experimental Psychology*, 1960, 60, 340–348.

Lanzetta, J. T., & Kanareff, V. T. Effects of a monetary reward on the acquisition of an imitative response. *Journal of Abnormal and Social Psychology*, 1959, 59, 120–127.

Mischel, W., & Grusec, J. Determinants of the rehearsal and transmission of neutral and aversive behaviors. *Journal of Personality and Social Psychology*, 1966, 3, 197–205.

O'Connell, E. J., Jr. The effect of cooperative and competitive set on the learning of imitation and nonimitation. *Journal of Experimental Social Psychology*, 1965, 1, 172–183.

Rosekrans, M. A. Imitation in children as a function of perceived similarity to a social model and vicarious reinforcement. *Journal of Personality and Social Psychology*, 1967, 7, 307–315.

Rosenbaum, M. E., & Tucker, I. F. Competence of the model and the learning of imitation and nonimitation. *Journal of Experimental Psychology*, 1962, 63, 183–190.

16 | Frustration and Aggression

16.1 | A STUDY OF CATHARSIS OF AGGRESSION*
Shahbaz Khan Mallick and Boyd R. McCandless[1]

BACKGROUND TO THE PROBLEM

Many of those interested, theoretically or practically, in personality theory, therapy, or general social psychology, for that matter, believe that aggressive acting-out behavior reduces aggression and hostility. Most theory of play therapy is still based on this hydraulic notion: the frustrated, angry, hostile child behaves aggressively, and this aggressive behavior reduces his level of hostility and aggression. Many parents and teachers accept the dictum that it is well to allow their children to blow off steam. Boxing, wrestling, and other intramural athletics are considered by some to provide catharsis for hostile aggression (Miller, Moyer, & Patrick, 1956). Freud spoke of Thanatos or a death instinct constantly working to return the organism "to the quiescence of the inorganic world [Freud, 1959, p. 108]." Libido interacts with the death instinct, neutralizing its effects on the person, by directing it outward as destruction, mastery, and will to power, concepts which may be subsumed under the general term *catharsis*.

Dollard, Doob, Miller, Mowrer, and Sears (1939) consider that inhibiting aggression is frustrating, and that aggressive behavior reduces the instigation to aggression (is cathartic in its effects). Buss (1961) also believes that violent aggression (and perhaps any violent activity) diminishes anger level following frustration and results in feelings of satisfaction about the acting-out behavior. Similarly, Berkowitz (1962) argues that a person whose anger has been aroused will tend to express it and that this expression will give him feelings of satisfaction similar to those obtained upon completing any motivated task.

* SOURCE: Mallick, S. K., & McCandless, B. R. A study of catharsis of aggression. *Journal of Personality and Social Psychology*, 1966, 4, 591–596. Copyright 1966 by the American Psychological Association and reprinted by permission.

[1] The authors are extremely grateful to Arthur Oestreich, director of the University Schools, Bloomington, Indiana; Lawrence Read, superintendent of schools, the Bloomington Metropolitan School System; and the principals and teachers of the three elementary schools in which the present research was conducted for permission to carry out the research, and for their cooperation in its conduct. Special thanks are due to the studies' sixth-grade confederates and third-grade subjects.

The research evidence about some form of counteraggression or catharsis as an aggression-reducing behavior is neither voluminous nor convincing. Thibaut and Coules (1952) find that subjects prevented from responding to the experimenters' confederate reduced friendly expressions toward the confederate significantly less than for subjects who were allowed to respond, and that those who were delayed in response increased in hostile responses more than those allowed to respond immediately.

Feshbach's (1955) well-known study using college students as subjects suggests that fantasy aggression may be cathartic. Hornberger (1959), in a partial replication of Feshbach's study, failed to obtain similar results. In another paper, Feshbach (1956) used children as subjects, and failed to find that aggressive free play reduced aggression: indeed, the boys (but not the girls) in his study who were initially low in aggressive behavior showed a significant increase in overt hostility after a series of permissive free-play experiences.

Hokanson (1961), like Feshbach (1955) and Hornberger (1959), used college students as subjects. His 80 male subjects were studied according to whether they were high or low in "test hostility," threatened or not threatened by the experimenter with retaliation, and frustrated or not frustrated. A variety of measures were employed, of which number and vigor of aggressive *behavioral* responses made toward the experimenter and *ratings* of hostility toward the experimenter are most relevant for the present study.

Hokanson's subjects gave both more and more vigorous "shocks" to the experimenter following frustration, but the more vigorous the shocks given, the less hostility they rated themselves as holding toward the experimenter following their "punishing" him. Hokanson thus finds that frustration increases *behavioral* aggression, using at least one measure similar to the one employed in the present study, and has a subfinding suggesting that behavioral expressions of aggression to the frustrator reduce or are at least associated with less intense verbal ratings of hostility toward him.

HYPOTHESES

Their interest in frustration-aggression-catharsis theory led the authors to set up and test the following five hypotheses, using children as subjects:

1. Angry aggression directed toward an inanimate object is not cathartic.
2. Aggression, unmotivated by anger or hostility, has no cathartic effect but may, instead, lead to an increase in aggressive responses, particularly in a socially permissive atmosphere.
3. Positive and reasonable verbal interpretation of a frustrating situation to the subject who has been frustrated has cathartic value in that it reduces hostility toward the frustrator.
4. Verbal aggression against a frustrator of the same sex does not reduce the hostility toward him (does not serve as catharsis).
5. United States girls, presumably because of cultural forces, will show less open aggression than boys. (*a*) However, in a permissive situation where privacy is assured, sex differences in open expression of aggression will be reduced.

Three experimental studies, the first a pilot study, the third an almost exact replication of the second, were conducted to test these hypotheses.

STUDY I

METHODS AND RESULTS.   In the first study, 30 male and 18 female children from two third-grade classes in a middle- and lower-middle-class public school were selected randomly from the total third-grade population and assigned randomly, 5 boys and 3 girls to each of 6 treatment conditions. Their ages ranged from 8 years, 4 months, to 9 years, 5 months, with a mean of 9 years.

Two sixth-grade children, one boy and one girl, were selected as confederates by nomination by class teachers and the school principal as "the most cooperative and dependable children in their grade." They were taken into the experimenter's full confidence.

The study followed a $2 \times 3 \times 2$ factorial design. There were 2 treatments—frustration and nonfrustration—and 3 types of interpolated activities—shooting a play gun at different targets on which were drawn figures either of a boy, girl, man, woman, cat, or dog; shooting at targets blank except for a bull's-eye; and solving simple arithmetic problems. The boy-girl dimension formed the third facet of the design.

The first phase of the study lasted for 5 minutes. In the frustration condition, the sixth-grade confederate "inadvertently and clumsily" prevented the subject from completing any of five moderately simple block construction tasks. The experimenter had promised the subject a nickel for each task completed within a time limit. The confederate also interspersed his interference with a predetermined set of six sarcastic remarks, such as "Ha! I see! You really need money. Let's see how you get it." No subject was allowed to complete any task.

In the nonfrustration condition, the confederate (always the same sex as the subject) helped subjects to complete their tasks (all subjects were allowed to complete all tasks), and no reward was promised or given, other than the experimenter's verbal comment, "Very good," at the end of each task.

The second, or activity interpolation phase, immediately followed the treatment phase and lasted for 8 minutes.

In the third phase, each subject was shown his partner (the same-sex confederate), who was sitting outside the experimental room with his hands in contact with electric wires which were apparently attached to a shock apparatus installed in the experimental room. The experimenter casually reminded each subject in the frustration condition of the confederate's uncooperative behavior, and told him that he could "get even" by pushing a button, thus administering shocks (which would not hurt the frustrator very much, but would make him uncomfortable). They were further told that the frustrator would not know who was shocking him. No limit was set on the number of "shocks" that could be administered. The number of shocks ostensibly given to the confederate was taken as a measure of his hostility.

Subjects in the nonfrustration treatment were also shown the confederate, no mention of noncooperation was made, but they were told they could administer shocks if they wanted to and that the confederate would not know who had shocked him.

At the end of the study, the nature of the experiment was discussed with all subjects. Without exception they thought it funny.

A large number of subjects made a response of one shock only, but only a few gave a large number. The distribution of scores was thus extremely skewed, and a log $(X + 1)$ transformation of scores was used.

The analysis of variance of the transformed aggression scores is shown in Table 1. Frustrated subjects manifested greater hostility than nonfrustrated subjects, but neither the sex of the subject nor the type of interpolated activity resulted in differences in amount of hostility.

STUDY II

METHOD. Thirty male and 30 female third graders from a school with a principally middle- and upper-class population were randomly selected from four third-grade classes and randomly assigned to five experimental conditions, six boys and six girls to each condition. Confederates were six boys and six girls, nominated as cooperative and dependable by their teachers and principal. Each worked with five subjects of the same sex, completing one unit of the five experimental conditions. As in Study I, they enjoyed the experimenter's full confidence.

The experimental tasks and the subjects' frustration or nonfrustration by the same-sex confederate were similar to those in Study I, except that subjects were given five nickels in advance. One nickel was taken from him after he had "failed" each of the five tasks, so that he ended the 8-minute frustration period penniless. At the end of this phase, each subject was asked to check a simple 5-step "like-dislike" scale ranging from 1, "I like him/her very much," to 5, "I really don't like him/her [the confederate] at all."

The second 8-minute experimental phase for one group each of frustrated and nonfrustrated subjects consisted of shooting guns at a target on which was placed a picture of an 11-year-old child of the same sex. The second pair of groups (one frustrated, one nonfrustrated) engaged in social talk (moderately standard for all subjects) with the experimenter for 8 minutes. The third frustration group was

Table 1 | ANALYSIS OF VARIANCE OF THE TRANSFORMED AGGRESSION SCORES IN STUDY I (FIVE BOYS AND THREE GIRLS IN EACH CONDITION)

SOURCE	df	MS	F
Frustration (F)	1	1.15566	15.10**
Activities (A)	2	.16679	2.18
Sex (S)	1	.00153	<1
F × A	2	.07398	<1
F × S	1	.00306	<1
A × S	2	.24056	3.14
F × A × S	2	.12031	1.57
Error MS	36	(.07651)	

** $p < .01$.

Table 2 | SCHEMATIC PRESENTATION OF THE DESIGN OF STUDY II

1ST PHASE (8 MIN.)	2ND PHASE (8 MIN.)						3RD PHASE (2 MIN.)
Initial treatment	*Play with guns and targets*		*Social talk*		*Reinter-pretation*		*Measure of residual hostility*
	BOYS	GIRLS	BOYS	GIRLS	BOYS	GIRLS	
Frustration	6	6	6	6	6	6	
Nonfrustration	6	6	6	6	0	0	

administered social talk plus interpretation (beginning in the third minute of conversation) to the effect that the frustrator was sleepy, upset, and would probably have been more cooperative if the subject had offered him two of the five nickels. At the end of the second phase, each subject was again asked to check the 5-point like-dislike rating of his/her confederate.

Phase 3 of Study II lasted for 2 minutes. Each subject was shown a "response box." He was told that the experimenter would go to an adjoining room and ask the confederate to do the same set of block-building tasks the subject had done. The subject could slow the older sixth grader's work by pushing one button, or help him by pushing the other. He could not push the button more than 20 times, although he need not count, as the experimenter would flash a signal light after the twentieth push. The experimenter then left the room, presumably to work with the confederate. The hostility criterion (aggression score) was the number of times the "slowing" button was pushed.

Upon completion of Study II, all subjects were told the nature of the experiment and, like the subjects in Study I, thought it great fun.

Table 2 is a schematic representation of Study II.

RESULTS.   Table 3 summarizes the analysis of variance of the aggression scores (number of pushes of the slowing button). Scores were transformed into log scores, using a log $(X + 2)$ transformation. Only the treatments effect was significant.

Table 3 | ANALYSIS OF VARIANCE OF AGGRESSION SCORES AMONG THE EXPERIMENTAL CONDITIONS OF STUDY II

SOURCE	*df*	*MS*	*F*
Treatments (T)	4	1.11387	9.49**
Sex (S)	1	0.3049	<1
T × S	4	.02982	<1
Error *MS*	50	(.11739)	

** $p < .01.$

Multiple comparisons were made among the total aggression scores of subjects in the different treatments, using Duncan's multiple-range test. The results of these comparisons are given in Table 4. Mean aggression scores for the aggressive play and social talk treatments did not differ significantly from each other either for the frustrated or nonfrustrated subjects. However, for each of these treatments, frustrated subjects had significantly higher mean aggression scores than comparable treatment groups of nonfrustrated subjects. These results are in line with those of Study I, where the frustration effect was highly significant, but the effect of interpolated activities was not.

Comparisons involving the interpretation group reveal that subjects to whom interpretation of the confederate was given produced significantly fewer aggression responses than subjects in the other two frustration groups (p's for each of the two comparisons are less than .001), but this frustration group did not differ significantly from either of the two nonfrustration groups.

Like-dislike ratings, collected at the end of the first and second phases of Study II, are available for only 50 subjects. The first of these ratings was intended to reveal hostility engendered by frustration as opposed to nonfrustration, while it was hoped that the second rating would reflect the influence of the interpolated activity on attitude toward the confederate. The authors are doubtful about the success of their methods, since the correlation between the posttreatment and the postinterpolation rating was .90. For this reason, detailed tabular presentations of the two ratings and changes from the first to the second are not given. However, the following findings appeared:

Table 4 | MULTIPLE COMPARISONS AMONG TOTAL AGGRESSION SCORES OF THE EXPERIMENTAL TREATMENTS OF SECOND STUDY II[a]

TREAT-MENT	FRUS-TRATION-REINTER-PRETATION	NONFRUS-TRATION-SOCIAL TALK	NONFRUS-TRATION-AGGRES-SIVE PLAY	FRUS-TRATION-AGGRES-SIVE PLAY	FRUS-TRATION-SOCIAL TALK
Mean aggression scores	6.37391	6.52881	8.14602	13.40896	13.72438
Order	a	b	c	d	e

MULTIPLE COMPARISONS

	a	b	c	d	e
a	—	ns	ns	****	****
b		—	ns	****	****
c			—	***	***
d				—	ns
e					—

[a] $N = 6$ per cell in each treatment.
*** $p < .005$.
**** $p < .001$.

For the first rating, F for the frustration treatment was highly significant. (The three frustration groups disliked their same-sex confederates much more than the two nonfrustration groups, but there were no differences among the three frustration or the two nonfrustration groups.) Fs for sex and Frustration $\times$ Sex were also significant at the .05 level of confidence. Girls admitted to less dislike than boys, but only in the frustration condition.

The pattern was the same (as would be expected from the high correlation between the two ratings) for the rating following the interpolated activity. However, when change scores were computed, F was highly significant for treatments, but not for sex or Treatments $\times$ Sex. Subjects in the social talk and aggressive play interpolated condition did not reduce their dislike of their same-sex confederate, while those in the interpretation condition did (p for each comparison was less than .005). This finding is even more striking when the high correlation between the two ratings is considered.

As has been mentioned, the authors hoped the second like-dislike rating would reflect residual hostility affected by different interpolated treatments following frustration. As such, these ratings should be correlated with the behavioral aggression score (number of times the slowing button was pushed). This proved to be the case, as the second like-dislike rating and the aggression score correlated .51.

However, it is possible that the way in which the like-dislike ratings were introduced affected the behavioral expression of aggression. Study III was run to introduce the attitudinal measures as an independent variable.

STUDY III

Study III is an exact replication of Study II in terms of procedures and number, sex, and social classes of subjects except that like-dislike ratings were administered to only half the subjects in each treatment condition and omitted for the other half.

As in Study II, raw aggression scores (slowing button pushing) were transformed into log scores using log $(X + 2)$ transformation. A $2 \times 2 \times 5$ analysis of variance was performed (treatments—frustration, nonfrustration—*replications—where Replication 1 did* not *include like-dislike ratings, and Replication 2 included the ratings as described for Study II*—and interpolated activities—as in Study II).

Table 5 summarizes this analysis of variance.

Fs for treatments, replications, the Treatments $\times$ Replications interaction, and the triple-order interaction of Treatments $\times$ Sex $\times$ Replications were all significant. Total aggression scores for subjects who had been administered the like-dislike ratings were significantly greater than those of subjects who had *not* been given the ratings, suggesting that the x variable of being "asked to consider your enemy" may actually intensify the expression of aggression toward him. Main effects of sex and interactions of treatments and sex, and sex and replication condition were not significant.

Comparison of the broad pattern of findings of Study II with Study III reveals no significant differences in any dimension, despite the larger number of significant Fs in Study III. Hence, conclusions drawn from Study III may be considered to agree closely with those of Study II (or vice versa).

Table 5 | ANALYSIS OF VARIANCE OF AGGRESSION SCORES AMONG THE EXPERI-MENTAL CONDITIONS IN STUDY III

SOURCE	df	MS	F
Treatments (T)	4	1.0292	16.44**
Sex (S)	1	0.1986	3.17
Replications (R)	1	0.3640	5.81*
T × S	4	0.0679	1.08
T × R	4	0.1753	2.80*
S × R	1	0.0002	<1
T × S × R	4	0.2297	3.67*
Error	40	0.0626	

* $p < .05$.
** $p < .01$.

An interesting difference between the correlations of the second like-dislike ratings and the aggression scores for the two studies appears, however. For Study II, this r was .51, but for Study III it was —.01 (where $N = 30$). Of course, this may well be a chance variation. As in Study II, correlation between the first and second like-dislike ratings was high (.85 in Study III).

DISCUSSION

One of the hypotheses toward which the three studies reported in the main body of this paper were directed questioned the value of expression of aggression as a cathar-sis serving to reduce (in this case, frustration-produced) aggression or hostility. This doubt appears to have been justified, at least when expression of aggression is toward inanimate objects.

Another hypothesis suggested was that aggression without anger lacks cathartic value, but that aggressive play in the presence of a permissive adult may lead to in-crease in aggression. All three of the studies reported above support this hypothesis. Actually, nonfrustration-aggressive play subjects consistently showed higher aggression scores (as manifested by "shocking" or "slowing down" a same-sex confederate) than nonfrustration-social talk subjects. (The difference, however, was significant only when the behavioral expression of aggression was preceded by like-dislike ratings of the experimenter's confederates.)

Taken together, the findings suggest that aggressive play, with or without previous frustration, has no cathartic value.

A major thesis of the present paper is that reasonable, positive interpretation of the frustrating situation has a cathartic effect. Studies II and III, where the hypothesis was tested, strongly support it. Behavioral expressions of aggression were lower for frus-trated subjects to whom interpretations had been given, and greater reductions in "dislike" ratings occurred following interpretation.

Verbal expression of aggression (like-dislike ratings) seems to have no cathartic effect on aggression directed toward a frustrator. If anything, such an expression by rating appears to have the opposite effect. This finding, if repeated in other contexts and for other populations, has rather startling implications: Verbal expressions of hostility (in this case, ratings) may actually lead to an increase of aggressive behavior toward the subject of the hostile expression—malicious gossip may induce action? expression of hostile feelings in therapy may lead to aggressive behavior in real life?

There were, somewhat to the authors' surprise and despite their hypothesis, no signicant sex differences in behavioral expression of aggression toward frustrators. In other words, in a permissive situation where they are assured they cannot be detected, girls behave just as aggressively as boys. However, girl subjects gave more favorable like-dislike rating of their frustrators than boys. (This finding was statistically significant in Study II, but not in Study III.) This is contrary to the general conviction that girls *talk* (in this case, *rate*), while boys *act*. The finding may, of course, be due to the ages of the subjects, most of whom were 8- or 9-year-olds. Cultural stereotypes of what is sex appropriate may not be well established by these ages, although there is considerable literature suggesting the contrary.

SUMMARY

Sixth-grade confederates of the same sex as the third-grade Ss either frustrated (interfered with) or did not frustrate a total of 168 8- and 9-year-old children, about ½ of whom were boys, ½ girls. Treatments following either frustration or nonfrustration included aggressive play, social talk, and reasonable interpretation of the frustrator's behavior. Aggression was measured behaviorally (responses were allowed that presumably punished the confederate, whether he had or had not been a frustrator) and by like-dislike ratings. Data from the 3 studies reported are consonant in direction when the designs permit direct comparisons, and lead to the following conclusions: Frustration leads to heightened aggressive feelings, but subsequent aggressive behavior does not reduce the aggression. Aggression in the absence of anger is without cathartic value. Reasonable interpretation of a frustrator's behavior is strikingly effective in reducing both behavioral and verbal (rating) aggression toward him. Verbal aggression toward the frustrator does not reduce aggression directed toward him, but may actually increase it. In a permissive, confidential situation, girls *behave* as aggressively as boys, although their like-dislike ratings of frustrating confederates reveal less hostility than boys.

REFERENCES

Berkowitz, L. *Aggression: A social psychological analysis.* New York: McGraw-Hill, 1962.

Buss, A. H. *The psychology of aggression.* New York: Wiley, 1961.

Dollard, J., Doob, L. W., Miller, N. E., Mowrer, O. H., & Sears, R. R. *Frustration and aggression.* New Haven: Yale University Press, 1939.

Feshbach, S. The drive reducing function of fantasy behavior. *Journal of Abnormal and Social Psychology*, 1955, *50*, 3–11.

Feshbach, S. The catharsis hypothesis and some consequences of interaction with aggressive and neutral play objects. *Journal of Personality*, 1956, *24*, 449–462.

Freud, S. *Beyond the pleasure principle.* New York: Bantam Books, 1959.

Hokanson, J. E. The effects of frustration and anxiety on overt aggression. *Journal of Abnormal and Social Psychology*, 1961, *62*, 346–351.

Hornberger, R. H. The differential reduction of aggressive responses as a function of interpolated activities. Paper read at American Psychological Association, Cincinnati, Ohio, September 4, 1959.

Miller, F. A., Moyer, J. H., & Patrick, R. B. *Planning student activities.* Englewood Cliffs, N.J.: Prentice-Hall, 1956.

Thibaut, J. W., & Coules, J. The role of communication in the reduction of interpersonal hostility. *Journal of Abnormal and Social Psychology*, 1952, *47*, 770–777.

16.2 | INFLUENCE OF SYMBOLICALLY MODELED INSTRUMENTAL AGGRESSION AND PAIN CUES ON AGGRESSIVE BEHAVIOR[*][1]

Donald P. Hartmann

The catharsis hypothesis, whereby exposure to aggressive models reduces hostile impulses and consequently decreases the likelihood of future aggression, has been the subject of controversy at least since the time of the early Greeks. Whereas Aristotle contended that dramatic displays quieted the emotions, Plato maintained with equally strong convic-

[*] SOURCE: Hartmann, D. P. Influence of symbolically modeled instrumental aggression and pain cues on aggressive behavior. *Journal of Personality and Social Psychology*, 1969, *11*, 280–288. Copyright 1969 by the American Psychological Association and reprinted by permission.

[1] This study is partially based on a dissertation submitted to the faculty of the Graduate School of Stanford University, in partial fulfillment of the requirements for the PhD degree. An earlier abbreviated version of this paper was read at the 1967 meetings of the Western Psychological Association.

The author wishes to express his appreciation to Albert Bandura for his guidance throughout all phases of this research; to Keith Griffiths, Director of Research, California Youth Authority, for his assistance in acquiring subjects; and to David Geeting for his work in preparing the experimental films. This research was supported in part by Research Grant M-5162 from the National Institutes of Health to Albert Bandura.

tion that they ". . . arouse violent emotions and stir men to all sorts of passions . . . [Jones, 1952, p. 250]." The concept of catharsis entered psychological theory by way of psychoanalysis (Hendrick, 1948) and eventually found its way into modern behavior theory in the classical monograph by Dollard and his collaborators at Yale (Dollard, Doob, Miller, Mowrer, & Sears, 1939). Only recently has systematic research (Bandura & Walters, 1963a; Berkowitz, 1962) necessitated substantial revision of this hypothesis. According to recent revisions by Buss (1961) and Feshbach (1961, 1964), the cathartic function of modeled aggressive stimuli is obtained only under certain specified conditions. Exposure to aggressive events is assumed to reduce subsequent aggression in hostility-aroused observers, but to augment aggression in nonaroused viewers.

A host of studies varying considerably in the form of modeled aggression and in the type of aggressive responses measured have found that exposure to aggressive stimuli under nonaroused conditions increases aggressive behavior in young children (Bandura, Ross, & Ross, 1961, 1963a; Hicks, 1965; Kuhn, Madsen, & Becker, 1967; Larder, 1962; Lovaas, 1961; Mussen & Rutherford, 1961), as well as in adolescents and adults (Walters & Thomas, 1963). Research evidence in support of the cathartic function of aggressive modeling cues under aroused conditions is meager and disputed on methodological grounds (Bandura & Walters, 1963a). While Feshbach (1961) has reported supportive results with college students, Berkowitz and his co-workers (e.g., Berkowitz, 1962, 1964a, 1964b, 1965; Berkowitz, Corwin, & Heironimus, 1963; Berkowitz & Rawlings, 1963) have reported increased aggression in angered subjects following exposure to aggressive models.

Although results of the above studies have shed some light on the determinants of the behavioral effects resulting from exposure to aggressive models, the different stimulus elements contained within an aggressive sequence must be isolated and their effects measured if the influence process is to be fully understood. An aggressive response sequence generally contains two separable and important stimulus events, that is, the instrumental aggressive response of the agent and the pain cues exhibited by the victim of the attack. Although a number of investigators (e.g., Berkowitz, 1964a, 1965; Berkowitz et al., 1963; Berkowitz & Geen, 1966; Feshbach, 1961; Walters & Thomas, 1963) have reported changes in the viewer's aggressive behavior after viewing aggressive sequences containing both these stimulus events, no attempt was made to determine whether the depicted instrumental aggression or the pain cues are primarily responsible for the obtained changes. It is apparent from the work of Bandura and his collaborators (Bandura et al., 1961, 1963a, 1963b) that the observation of instrumental aggression in the absence of pain cues can result in the increased expression of aggression. The important question, then, is whether pain cues exhibited by the object of aggression augment (as suggested by the secondary-reward theory of Sears, Maccoby, & Levin, 1957) or counteract the disinhibiting and/or eliciting effects of the display of instrumental aggression. Pain cues might lower the likelihood of aggression by the observer through empathic or vicarious arousal of anxiety which would lead to aggression inhibition.

The present study was designed to test the revised form of the catharsis hypothesis, that anger arousal determines the function of aggressive stimuli, and to assess the effects of exposure to instrumental aggressive responses and pain reactions upon subsequent aggressive behavior.

To date most experimental investigations on the effect of film-mediated violence have used either young children or college students. Consequently, in view of the important social issue of the effects of televised violence on aggressive youngsters (Berkowitz, 1962; Klapper, 1960; United States Senate, 1964), and as a test of the generality of the previously obtained findings on film-mediated aggression, the present experiment was conducted with male adolescent delinquents.

The subjects participated with a peer who served as the experimenter's confederate in a study ostensibly concerned with the effectiveness of various instructional devices. In the first phase of the experiment anger was aroused in some of the subjects by having the fictitious confederate express derogatory remarks about the subjects' performance on an ego-involving task. Neutral remarks were made to the others. After this initial treatment, the subjects were assigned to one of three film treatments. Each film portrayed two adolescent boys playing basketball. The neutral control film depicted an active though nonaggressive basketball game. The two aggressive film displays portrayed an argument-fight sequence; the instrumental aggression film focused on the agent's aggressive responses, whereas the pain-cues film focused on the victim's pain reactions. Subjects were then provided with an opportunity to administer electric shocks to their anonymous provocateur, and the duration and intensity of electric shocks administered were measured.

Based on the theory advanced by Bandura and Walters (1963b) and Berkowitz (1962), it was predicted that subjects who had observed a film depicting instrumental aggressive responses would inflict shocks of greater magnitude and of longer duration upon the confederate than would subjects who viewed the neutral film. On the assumption that a person who serves as a source of anger will constitute a stronger stimulus for aggression than a person who has been associated with neutral experiences, it was also predicted that subjects who experienced prior anger arousal would likewise respond with more aggression than would subjects not so aroused.

Since there is no adequate a priori basis for estimating the effects of depicted pain cues, no predictions were advanced concerning the direction of the differences between subjects in the latter treatment group and those in the other film conditions.

METHOD

SUBJECTS. Seventy-two male adolescents who were under court commitment to the California Youth Authority participated in this experiment. All subjects had been detained in the institution for a minimum period of 6 weeks and were awaiting either transfer to a treatment institution or home discharge. They ranged in age from 13 to 16 years, with a median age of 15½ years. Of the subjects, 22% were institutionalized for highly aggressive offenses, for example, strong-armed robbery, assault, and fighting, while the remaining 78% had committed a wide variety of lesser crimes.

PROCEDURE.   The subjects were individually contacted within the institution and asked to participate in an experiment on the effectiveness of teaching machines and audio-visual displays. They were then taken to a cable-strewn experimental room outfitted with a projector, screen, microphone, speaker, and the teaching machine which was a large impressive-looking apparatus covered with switches and various colored lights. The room and instructions were designed to lead the subjects to believe that the cable connectors, microphone, and speaker led into an adjoining room containing a peer who would be performing related tasks. The subjects were assured that the communication system and location of the participants in separate rooms would insure anonymity. This "fellow participant" was, in fact, a fictitious individual whose presumed responses to the experimental subject were recorded on tape in the voice of a delinquent boy from another institution.

After the subject had been given preliminary instruction on how he was to operate the intercom system to report his answers to the test items, the experimenter left the subject's room, ostensibly to give instructions to the fellow participant.

Aggression arousal was manipulated through the confederate's evaluative statements about the subject's performance on a nine-item multiple-choice test presumably measuring his ability to exercise good social judgment. One-half of the subjects underwent the aggression-arousal manipulation in which they were the recipients of a tape-recorded series of unwarranted and critical statements presumably from the confederate. The evaluator's tone was "cool" and disparaging as he challenged the subject's intelligence, "sophistication," and general competence. The remaining subjects assigned to the nonarousal condition received essentially neutral feedback comments.

Following the arousal manipulation, the subjects were randomly assigned to one of three film conditions. The 2-minute films were 16-millimeter black and white with sound tracks. The first minute of running time, which was identical for the three films, portrayed two boys shooting baskets on a basketball court. For the remaining minute the boys in the control film engaged in an active, though cooperative, basketball game, whereas in the two experimental films the boys engaged in an argument that eventuated in a fist fight. The pain-cues film focused almost exclusively on the victim's verbal and gestural pain reactions as he was vigorously pommeled and kicked by his opponent. The instrumental aggression film, on the other hand, focused on the aggressor's responses including foot thrusts, flying fists, aggressive verbalizations, and angry facial expressions. The subjects were told that the purpose of viewing the films was to determine how attentive people are to various film content. In order to enhance attending behavior and credibility, the subjects were further informed that they would be questioned about the film after the completion of the experiment.

After exposure, subjects were asked to assist the experimenter in a study ostensibly on the effects of performance feedback on learning rate. This aggression-performance task and accompanying shock-delivery system were patterned after the "aggression machine" and task originally designed by Buss (1961). The apparatus contained a panel with 10 switches arranged in increasing intensity together with lights that signaled right or wrong responses presumably made by the subject's partner in the adjacent room. After the subject sampled several of the shock intensities to apprise him of the magnitude of the aversive stimulation associated with the different switches, he was asked to administer the pain-producing shocks to his partner whenever he made an error on an assigned learning task. The subject was free, however, to vary both the intensity (which varied from slightly above threshold to quite painful) and duration of shocks administered. During the series of 25 learning trials, the subject's panel signaled 10 errors according to a prearranged program controlled by the experimenter. The duration and intensity of shocks inflicted upon the partner for his incorrect responses were recorded by the experimenter in an adjoining room through the use of a standard electrical timer and signal lights wired in series with the subject's shock-intensity switches.

Immediately following the measurement of aggression, the subject answered a series of questions, some of which were specific to the avowed purpose of testing the subject's memory for the film material. Other questions attempted to elicit information concerning the credibility of the experiment and the participant's subjective response to the shock procedure. The relevant data will be described in detail in the Results section.

Before the subjects were returned to their living units, those individuals who had been criticized for their performance during the induction of aggression arousal were assured of the correctness of their responses on the test of social judgment. The experimenter also expressed amazement at the unreasonableness of their evaluator's comments.

RESULTS

EFFECTIVENESS OF THE AROUSAL MANIPULATION. One of the items in a questionnaire administered to the subjects at the conclusion of the experiment was designed to measure the effectiveness of the arousal manipulation; this item required the subjects to rate how well they liked their partners. It was expected that subjects in the aggression-arousal condition would express less favorable opinions of their partners than subjects in the nonarousal condition. Comparison of pairs of means between arousal conditions by the t test reveals significant differences in the predicted direction for each of the three film treatments ($p < .025$). Thus, the questionnaire data clearly indicate that the arousal manipulation was successful.

MEASURES OF PUNITIVENESS. The primary dependent variables used in this experiment were the intensity and Intensity $\times$ Duration of shocks administered by the subjects. Separate analyses were made for each of these two measures.

Intensity. The mean shock intensities administered by subjects in the six experimental groups are presented in Figure 1. An analysis of variance performed on these data indicates that both arousal ($F = 8.67, df = 1/66, p < .01$) and the film treatments ($F = 11.04, df = 2/66, p < .001$) are highly significant sources of variance. Comparison of pairs of means by the t test indicated that as predicted, subjects who viewed the instrumental aggression film administered shocks of significantly greater intensity than did subjects who viewed the control film under both arousal conditions ($p < .01$). Ex-

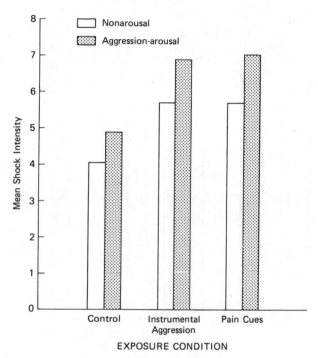

Figure 1 | MEAN SHOCK INTENSITY FOR SUBJECTS VIEWING THE CONTROL FILM, THE INSTRUMENTAL FILM, AND THE PAIN-CUES FILM.

posure to the pain-cues film similarly resulted in significantly more intense shocks than did exposure to the control film, again under both arousal conditions ($p < .01$). No significant differences were found, however, between the pain-cues and instrumental aggression film subjects ($t < .50$). Also, as predicted, aggression arousal enhanced the intensity of aggressive behavior. This effect was significant in both experimental film conditions ($p < .05$) and, though not significant, was in the predicted direction for subjects who observed the control film ($p < .15$).

Intensity $\times$ Duration. The means of Intensity $\times$ Duration[2] of shock for the various groups are presented in Figure 2. An analysis of variance performed on these data discloses significant arousal ($F = 11.64$, $df = 1/66$, $p < .01$) and film ($F = 8.70$, $df = 2/66$, $p < .01$) effects and a significant interaction ($F = 4.69$, $df = 2/66$, $p < .05$). Selected t test comparisons between pairs of means reveal differences similar to those found in the analysis of the duration measure. The predicted difference between the two arousal conditions was again significant, but only for the subjects who witnessed the victim's pain reactions ($p < .001$). This difference between arousal groups approached significance for the control film subjects ($p < .10$), but was extremely small for subjects who witnessed the instrumental aggression film. The expected difference between the in-

[2] Because the Intensity $\times$ Duration of shock scores were highly heterogeneous, all analyses involving these scores employed the $X' = 2$ arc sine $\sqrt{X/100}$ transformation.

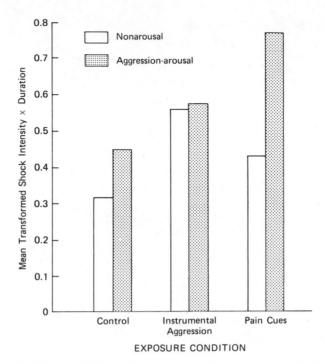

Figure 2 | MEAN TRANSFORMED SHOCK INTENSITY × DURATION FOR SUBJECTS VIEWING THE CONTROL FILM, THE INSTRUMENTAL AGGRESSION FILM, AND THE PAIN-CUES FILM.

strumental aggression and control-film subjects was significant under conditions of non-arousal ($p < .01$), but did not reach a satisfactory level of significance for the instigated subjects ($p < .10$). As was the case in the analysis of the shock-intensity data, subjects who witnessed the pain-cues film responded more punitively than did subjects who viewed the control film. These differences were statistically significant in the aggression-arousal condition ($p < .001$) and approached significance for subjects in the non-arousal condition ($p < .10$). A significant Film × Arousal interaction for pain-cues and instrumental aggression film subjects ($F = 8.70$, $df = 1/66$, $p < .01$) reveals that aroused subjects who had viewed depicted pain reactions administered more aversive stimulation than did similarly motivated subjects who witnessed the instrumental aggression film. The results were in the opposite direction for nonaroused observers; that is, instrumental aggression subjects expressed more punitiveness than subjects who witnessed the pain-cues film.

Offense record. Two additional analyses of variance were performed to test the expected relationship between the subjects' criminal history (severity and number of offenses) and their performance on the Shock Intensity × Duration measure. Subjects for whom the required case history data were available were divided into high and low groups on both offense variables. These two dichotomized variables were then placed into separate analyses of variance together with the film and arousal conditions. Because this procedure resulted in unequal cell frequencies, unweighted-means analyses were performed.

The 57 subjects who had institutional ratings of aggressive behavior based on case-history data as well as offense record constituted the sample for the first analysis. Of this sample, 31 subjects had no history of violence, while 26 had a history of some or extensive violence. Analysis of these data indicates a slight trend for the subjects with a history of aggressive behavior to inflict more aversive stimulation ($F = 2.82$, $df = 1/44$, $p < .06$—one-tailed test). The interactions involving the aggressive-history variable were not significant ($Fs < 1.75$).

For the second analysis the entire sample of 72 subjects was split at the median of the distribution of number of offenses and assigned to frequent and less frequent offender groups. Analysis of variance of these data reveals a significant main effect due to number of offenses ($F = 4.31$, $df = 1/60$, $p < .05$) and a significant Offense History $\times$ Film $\times$ Arousal interaction ($F = 5.04$, $df = 2/60$, $p < .01$). Neither the Film $\times$ Offense nor Arousal $\times$ Offense interaction was significant ($Fs < 1.25$). In order to illuminate the significant main and second-order interaction effects, means for the 12 Offense $\times$ Arousal $\times$ Film groups are presented in Table 1. As can be seen from this table, in four of the six comparisons between offender groups frequent offenders responded more punitively than less frequent offenders, though this difference was significant only for aroused subjects who observed the painful display ($t = 3.80$, $df = 60$, $p < .001$). In the case of the less frequent offenders, those who observed either the control film or the pain-cues film behaved less punitively than the comparable subjects who observed the instrumental aggression film, whether they had been aroused or not. By contrast, considering the frequent offenders who were angered, those who viewed the pain-cues film were substantially more aggressive than subjects in the remaining film conditions. To prevent the transformed scores from obscuring the meaning of the data, the mean of 1.0183 for the frequent offenders who were aroused and viewed the pain-cues film corresponds to mean shock intensity of 8.23 (maximum of 10.0) for an average duration of 3.05 seconds!

DISCUSSION

The results of the present investigation provide further evidence of the influential role of vicarious experiences in modifying human behavior. More specifically, they demonstrate the degree to which the observation of symbolic aggressive models, and aggression arousal, can enhance punitive behavior.

The findings cast considerable doubt on the validity of the catharsis hypothesis either as proposed by Dollard and his collaborators or the more recent revision by Buss and Feshbach. According to the latter authors, exposure to aggressive models should decrease aggressiveness in viewers experiencing anger arousal. This hypothesis would also lead one to expect that subjects who have been instigated to aggression and shown the control film would display greater punitiveness than equally aroused subjects provided with an opportunity to view highly aggressive behavior. Not only do the results of this study fail to support the foregoing prediction, but they are also directly

Table 1 | MEANS OF THE 12 OFFENSE FREQUENCY × AROUSAL × FILM GROUPS[a]

CONDITION	FILM		
	Control	Instrumental aggression	Pain cues
Aggression arousal			
Frequent offenders	.5020 (6)	.5307 (7)	1.0183 (6)
Less frequent offenders	.3850 (6)	.6350 (5)	.5550 (6)
Nonarousal			
Frequent offenders	.3816 (5)	.6373 (6)	.3934 (5)
Less frequent offenders	.3277 (7)	.4873 (6)	.4499 (7)

[a] Cell ns in parentheses.

contrary to it. Indeed, under conditions of arousal, subjects who observed displays of instrumental aggression behaved more aggressively than did subjects who viewed the control film. Exposure of angered subjects to pain cues also augmented punitive behavior. This latter finding is essentially in accord with the theory proposed by Sears et al. (1957). According to this theory, if signs of pain and injury resulting from a child's aggressive behavior have repeatedly been associated with the elimination of frustration for himself, they will acquire secondary-reward value. Pain cues, therefore, should serve as positive reinforcers to enhance aggressiveness. Additional support for this theory has recently been provided by Patterson, Littman, and Bricker (1967), who found that pain cues exhibited by a victim increase aggression in nursery-school-age children.

Although anger arousal generally increases punitiveness in subjects who have been exposed to aggressive models, it did not increase significantly the pain-producing behavior of subjects shown the control film. These findings suggest that the facilitative effects of arousal are dependent upon exposure to aggressive cues that may serve as eliciting or discriminative stimuli for aggressive behavior (Berkowitz, 1964a). The eliciting function of modeling stimuli as demonstrated in the present experiment with male delinquents corroborates the findings of other investigators with both younger and older subjects drawn from nondeviant samples (e.g., Bandura et al., 1961; Berkowitz, 1964a, 1964b; Berkowitz & Geen, 1966; Walters & Thomas, 1963).

A somewhat inconsistent finding that emerged from this study concerns the obtained interaction effects between arousal and the two experimental film conditions. Although no differences between the two aggressive-film groups were found on the intensity measure, the Intensity × Duration measure yielded a significant Film × Arousal interaction. A possible explanation for the differential results is that in the case of the intensity measure the subject deliberately selects a given shock intensity, and there is little ambiguity concerning his punitiveness. Duration of shock, on the other hand, represents a more ambiguous measure since the subject would find it more difficult to estimate accurately how long he kept the shock turned on. The lesser degree of cognitive control exercised with this measure may make it particularly sensitive to impulsive aggression following aggression arousal (Berkowitz & Buck, 1967).

It could be argued, however, that the combined measure which reflected both shock intensity and duration provides a more adequate measure of punitiveness, inasmuch as it includes the total amount of aversive stimulation administered. Justification for placing more confidence in the combined measure is provided by three subsidiary analyses. Correlations between mean scores on the two punitive measures indicate that both contribute unique variance to the Intensity $\times$ Duration composite. The average correlation for the six experimental groups equaled .44, with a range from —.25 for the nonaroused control film subjects to .80 for instigated subjects who viewed the pain-cues film. Second, intrasubjects analyses indicated that the two measures can, to a large degree, be viewed as compensatory; that is, 81% of the 68 subjects whose performance varied on both the duration and intensity measures over the 10 shock opportunities demonstrated a negative correlation between the indexes. Consequently, either measure taken by itself would not adequately reflect the amount of aggression displayed. A final attempt to evaluate the comparative worth of the aggressive-performance measures involved correlating them with institutional indexes of aggressiveness, that is, incidence of aggressive offenses and number of previous offenses. Although the correlations were generally low in magnitude and of borderline significance, correlations with the Intensity $\times$ Durations measure were generally highest in the three shock measures.

If confidence is placed in the Intensity $\times$ Duration measure, it would seem that when an individual is angered, particularly if he has a lengthy history of antisocial behavior, pain cues might serve as positively reinforcing stimuli (as suggested by Sears et al., 1957) and consequently augment aggressive behavior to an even greater extent than witnessing instrumental aggressive displays. This finding might also be interpreted as providing support for the hypothesis derived from the research of Bandura (1965) and his collaborators. According to Bandura's theory, the unpunished occurrence of aggression may not only convey permissiveness for aggressive actions, but it also may result in some degree of vicarious extinction of anxiety responses that are typically conditioned to intensive forms of physical aggression. Since punishment ordinarily follows an aggression-pain sequence with greater regularity than it does when aggression occurs without consequent injury to the recipient, it might be argued that the modeling of pain-producing aggression without any negatively reinforcing consequences to the agent may result in a greater degree of disinhibition.

In contrast, for individuals not aggressively aroused, exposure to instrumental aggressive responses produced more punitiveness than did exposure to modeled pain reactions. There was not a significant difference between the nonaroused subjects who observed pain reactions and those who viewed the neutral film. The former difference cannot be attributable to differences in implied permissiveness for aggression between the pain-cues and instrumental aggression films. Instead, it would seem that intense pain reactions, under conditions of nonarousal, produce an empathic response on the part of the viewers which results in aggression inhibition. Anger, therefore, would seem to raise the threshold for developing empathic inhibitory responses. Support for this interpretation is provided in a recent study by Feshbach, Stiles, and Bitter (1967). These authors found that shock to another person augmented pain-producing responses for insulted subjects; for noninsulted subjects the observation of pain cues resulted in a reduction in aggressive responding. Similar reductions in aggressive responding by nonaroused subjects following exposure to pain cues have also been reported by Buss (1966a, 1966b).

Based on the above reasoning, one might expect that increasing the intensity of depicted pain reactions would eventually produce a decrease in subsequent aggression; that is, the hypothesized relationship between pain cues and aggression is approximated by an inverted-U-shaped curve. Furthermore, it might be predicted that increased arousal would displace the gradient upward and toward the right, as would decreased socialization of aggression. Partial support for the hypothesized effect of decreased socialization of aggression can be found in the greater aggressive responses, particularly after observation of the pain-cues film, of aroused subjects with lengthy histories of antisocial behavior as compared with similarly aroused subjects with briefer criminal records. Further investigation of these hypotheses, as well as a functional analysis of pain cues for children of various ages, is currently in progress.

Although the specific relationship between the two types of aggressive cues and arousal must remain somewhat speculative as a result of this experiment, there is no doubt that a presumed "cathartic" experience did indeed enhance aggressive behavior.

SUMMARY

This study investigated the independent and interactive effects of anger instigation, aggressive displays, and pain cues on subsequent interpersonal aggression. Adolescent delinquents were initially subjected either to anger-arousing or nonarousing experiences. They then viewed a nonaggressive control film or one of two films depicting a fight sequence: the pain-cues film, which focused on the victim's pain responses, or the instrumental aggression film, which high-lighted the agent's aggressive behavior. The dependent measures were the duration and intensity of shocks that the subjects ostensibly administered to their provocateur whenever he made errors on an assigned learning task. The results revealed that (a) regardless of arousal level, subjects who witnessed the modeled aggression behaved more punitively than did subjects who had observed the same models behaving nonaggressively; (b) aroused viewers generally responded more punitively than did nonaroused viewers; (c) angered subjects who witnessed modeled pain reactions responded more punitively than did observers exposed to modeled instrumental aggression—for nonaroused subjects this difference was in the reverse direction; and (d) subjects with longer records of antisocial behavior delivered more aversive stimulation than subjects with less extensive records, particularly when they were angered and observed displays of pain. The overall findings contradict the catharsis hypothesis in both its classical and revised versions.

REFERENCES

Bandura, A. Vicarious processes: A case of no-trial learning. In L. Berkowitz (Ed.), *Advances in experimental social psychology*. Vol. 2. New York: Academic Press, Inc., 1965.

Bandura, A., Ross, D., & Ross, S. A. Transmission of aggression through imitation of aggressive models. *Journal of Abnormal and Social Psychology*, 1961, 63, 575–582.

Bandura, A., Ross, D., & Ross, S. A. Imitation of film-mediated aggressive models. *Journal of Abnormal and Social Psychology*, 1963, 66, 3–11. (a)

Bandura, A., Ross, D., & Ross, S. A. Vicarious reinforcement and imitative learning. *Journal of Abnormal and Social Psychology*, 1963, 67, 601–607. (b)

Bandura, A., & Walters, R. H. Aggression. In H. W. Stevenson (Ed.), *Child psychology: The sixty-second yearbook of the National Society for the Study of Education.* Part 1. Chicago: National Society for the Study of Education, 1963. (a)

Bandura, A., & Walters, R. H. *Social learning and personality development.* New York: Holt, Rinehart and Winston, 1963. (b)

Berkowitz, L. *Aggression: A social psychological analysis.* New York: McGraw-Hill, 1962.

Berkowitz, L. Aggressive cues in aggressive behavior and hostility catharsis. *Psychological Review*, 1964, 71, 104–122. (a)

Berkowitz, L. The effects of observing violence. *Scientific American*, 1964, 210, 35–41. (b)

Berkowitz, L. Some aspects of observed aggression. *Journal of Personality and Social Psychology*, 1965, 2, 359–369.

Berkowitz, L., & Buck, R. W. Impulse aggression: Reactivity to aggressive cues under emotional arousal. *Journal of Personality*, 1967, 35, 415–424.

Berkowitz, L., Corwin, R., & Heironimus, M. Film violence and subsequent aggressive tendencies. *Public Opinion Quarterly*, 1963, 27, 217–229.

Berkowitz, L., & Geen, R. G. Film violence and the cue properties of available targets. *Journal of Personality and Social Psychology*, 1966, 3, 525–530.

Berkowitz, L., & Rawlings, E. Effects of film violence on inhibitions against subsequent aggression. *Journal of Abnormal and Social Psychology*, 1963, 66, 405–412.

Buss, A. H. *The psychology of aggression.* New York: Wiley, 1961.

Buss, A. H. The effects of harm on subsequent aggression. *Journal of Experimental Research in Personality*, 1966, 1, 249–255. (a)

Buss, A. H. Instrumentality of aggression, feedback, and frustration as determinants of physical aggression. *Journal of Personality and Social Psychology*, 1966, 3, 153–162. (b)

Dollard, J., Doob, L., Miller, N., Mowrer, O., & Sears, R. *Frustration and aggression.* New Haven, Conn.: Yale University Press, 1939.

Feshbach, S. The stimulating versus cathartic effects of a vicarious aggressive activity. *Journal of Abnormal and Social Psychology*, 1961, 63, 381–385.

Feshbach, S. The function of aggression and the regulation of aggressive drive. *Psychological Review*, 1964, 71, 257–272.

Feshbach, S., Stiles, W. B., & Bitter, E. The reinforcing effect of witnessing aggression. *Journal of Experimental Research in Personality*, 1967, 2, 133–139.

Hendrick, I. *Facts and theory of psychoanalysis.* New York: Knopf, 1948.

Hicks, D. J. Imitation and retention of film-mediated aggressive peer and adult models. *Journal of Personality and Social Psychology*, 1965, 2, 97–100.

Jones, W. T. *A history of western philosophy.* Vol. 1. New York: Harcourt, 1952.

Klapper, J. T. *The effects of mass communication.* New York: Free Press, 1960.

Kuhn, Z. K., Madsen, C. H., & Becker, W. C. Effects of exposure to an aggressive model and "frustration" on children's aggressive behavior. *Child Development*, 1967, 38, 739–745.

Larder, D. L. Effect of aggressive story content on non-verbal play behavior. *Psychological Reports*, 1962, 11, 14.

Lovaas, O. I. Effect of exposure to symbolic aggression on aggressive behavior. *Child Development*, 1961, *32*, 37–44.

Mussen, P., & Rutherford, E. Effects of aggressive cartoons on children's aggressive play. *Journal of Abnormal and Social Psychology*, 1961, *62*, 461–464.

Patterson, G. R., Littman, R. A., & Bricker, W. Assertive behavior in children. *Monographs of the Society for Research in Child Development*, 1967, *32*(4, Whole No. 113).

Sears, R. R., Maccoby, E. E., & Levin, H. *Patterns of child rearing.* New York: Harper & Row, 1957.

United States Senate, 88th Congress, Second Session. *Television and juvenile delinquency interim report of the subcommittee to investigate juvenile delinquency.* Washington, D.C.: United States Government Printing Office, 1964.

Walters, R. H., & Thomas, E. L. Enhancement of punitiveness by visual and audiovisual displays. *Canadian Journal of Psychology*, 1963, *17*, 244–255.

16.3 | EFFECTS OF THWARTING ON CARDIAC RESPONSE AND PHYSICAL AGGRESSION[*][1]

Brendan Gail Rule and Lynn Stewart Hewitt

The notion that frustration leads to aggression has not been well supported, especially in situations where an overt aggressive response follows the frustration but does not facilitate attainment of some nonaggressive goal (Berkowitz & Le Page, 1967; Buss, 1963; Epstein & Taylor, 1967; Loew, 1967). The effects which have emerged in the study of the frustration-aggression hypothesis led Buss (1966) to contend that insult is the major antecedent of aggression and Berkowitz (1965) to propose that frustration, defined as interference with ongoing goal responses, is most likely to result in aggression in the presence of strong, aggressive cues (internal or external). Geen and Berkowitz (1967) have argued specifically that frustration produces a readiness to respond aggressively, a predisposition which, with appropriate cues, leads to aggression.

Does this readiness manifest itself in increased tension or physiological activation? Hokanson and his colleagues (Hokanson & Burgess, 1962; Hokanson & Shetler, 1961)

[*] SOURCE: Rule, B. G., & Hewitt, L. S. Effects of thwarting on cardiac response and physical aggression. *Journal of Personality and Social Psychology*, 1971, *19*, 181–187. Copyright 1971 by the American Psychological Association and reprinted by permission.

[1] This research was supported by a Canada Council Grant to the first author. Thanks are extended to David Rehill for collecting the data.

have demonstrated that a condition involving harassment and failure increased physiological activation, but they did not examine the effects of frustration alone on activation. Furthermore, they did not demonstrate changes in aggressive responding concomitant with physiological changes (Hokanson & Burgess, 1962).

Epstein and Taylor (1967) found that a partner's perceived aggressive intent, but not defeat alone, in a game intensified aggressive and physiological responses. Because the notion that frustration predisposes a person toward aggression is a part of current theory (Berkowitz, 1969), the possibility of concomitant physiological activation demands continued exploration. The purpose of this study was to examine the effects of three thwarting conditions, two involving frustration and one involving frustration plus insult, on cardiac response and subsequent aggression. It was expected that insult would enhance both overt aggressive and physiological responses, whereas frustration would intensify only physiological activity.

METHOD

SUBJECTS.   The subjects were 90 men, who participated for $1.50 or one experimental credit toward an introductory psychology course requirement. Seven other subjects also participated, but their data were discarded because of their suspicion.

PROCEDURE.   The subject was taken to the experimental room by a male experimenter and seated at a table. The subject was led to believe that another subject, who was presumably seated in the adjoining room, would be his partner. This other subject was fictitious. His remarks and responses were tape-recorded and played back by the experimenter via a silent foot pedal at the appropriate times.

The experimenter explained to the subject that his heart rate would be recorded throughout the experimental session. Two active and one ground electrode were then placed on the subject's chest, and a 2-minute recording of the subject's heart rate was taken on a Sanborn 51 Viso-cardiette. Although Lacey, Kagan, Lacey, and Moss (1963) have argued for the inclusion of galvanic skin response as a measure of arousal because of directional fractionation, especially when the subject is relaxed, heart rate was used for several reasons. Heart rate is less subject to artifacts than galvanic skin response and is more reliable than surface blood pressure measures. It has reflected stress and arousal effects (Blatt, 1961; Corfield, 1969; Malmo, 1965; Schnore, 1959) and, more relevant to this study, activation effects (Elliott, 1969).

After returning to the experimental room, the experimenter moved behind a curtain which shielded him from the subject's view. From this position, the experimenter read the initial instructions and operated the tape recorder and Viso-cardiette.

The subjects were told that the experimenter was interested in the effects of different kinds of reinforcement upon learning, and in order to control the influence of extraneous variables, such as gestures or facial expressions, they had been placed in separate rooms. The subjects were told that they could communicate with each other by means of a loudspeaker system connecting the two rooms. To justify the recording of heart rate, the subjects were informed that the experimenter was also interested in the physiological responses which occur during learning.

The subjects were instructed that in the first part of the experiment, the critical subject would serve as the learner, while the other subject would serve as teacher; in the second part of the experiment, the subjects were to exchange roles. The experimental task involved either teaching or learning a list of 10 nonsense syllables. The teacher was to read the list to the learner, who would then repeat as many of the syllables as he could remember. The teacher was then to reinforce the learner by giving feedback. In the first part of the experiment, the teacher was to give the critical subject verbal feedback, relating to the subject how well he had done. Subjects were told that the method of reinforcement for the second part of the experiment would be described later. The subjects were instructed to continue the learning trials until they were signaled by the experimenter to stop.

Following the instructions, the thwarting manipulation was introduced. One-third of the subjects learned a list of easy nonsense syllables, selected from Glaze's (1928) lists having higher association values (low thwarted), while another third attempted to learn a list of difficult syllables, selected from Glaze's lists having lower association values (moderately thwarted). All of these subjects received neutral comments (e.g., "Well, that's O.K.—let's do it again") as feedback on their performance from their partner. The remaining third of the subjects attempted to learn the same difficult list, but received very critical comments on their performance from their partner (high thwarted). The comments, delivered after each trial, were as follows:

[Trial 1] O.K. I think we're going to be here for a long time. But let's try it for the second time.

[Trial 2] You still haven't got them all right—I'll read the list again, and *this* time try and *concentrate* a little more. It's really not very hard.

[Trial 3] God! At the rate you're going, we're never going to get finished! I really don't think there's much point in continuing with this, do *you? Try harder* this time so that we can get out of here! *All right* . . . I'm going to read them once more and this time, I'm going to read them so *slow* that even *you* can get them.

Considerable pilot work was done to obtain the desired affective tone for these comments and to ensure credibility.

For all subjects, the experimenter then moved a previously concealed shock box, a modified version of Buss's (1961) aggression machine, to the table at which the subject was seated.

The experimenter explained to the subject that in the next part of the experiment, he would assume the role of teacher and administer physical feedback (reinforcement) to his partner, who would assume the role of learner. The subject was also told that he could vary the intensity, number, and duration of shocks received by his partner. Intensity could be varied by adjusting the large center dial to the desired level (0–330 volts) and by then pressing the shock-delivery button. Eight descriptive labels indicated to the subject the approximate severity of shock associated with the varying voltage levels: slight shock = 0–55 volts; moderate shock = 56–110 volts; strong shock = 111–170 volts; very strong shock = 171–225 volts; intense shock = 226–280 volts; extreme intensity shock = 281–335 volts; danger = 336–400 volts; severe shock = 401–450 volts.

To decrease the likelihood of suspicion, a governor was attached to the shock box which prevented the subjects from turning the dial beyond the 330-volt level. Subjects were instructed that a maximum of 330 volts was available for their use. The number of shocks could be varied by pressing the shock-delivery button more than once; the duration of shocks could be varied by depressing the button for varying lengths of time. The delivery button was connected to two shunt-clock timers, one visible to the subject and the other visible to the experimenter behind the curtain. The shock-box dial was connected to a meter, visible to the experimenter, which indicated the intensity levels set by the subject.

The subject was given a sample of shock of 45 volts to increase the realism of the situation. The experimenter then gave a list of 10 syllables to the subject and left the room, presumably to wire the partner to the shock apparatus. The list differed from the one previously learned by the subject, and no indication of its difficulty level was given by the experimenter. After 2 minutes, the experimenter returned, and the learning task commenced. The subject administered shock to his partner following each of three learning trials. In all conditions, the partner reported 3 syllables on the first trial, 5 syllables on the second trial, and 8 syllables on the third trial, for a total of 16 syllables.

The experimenter terminated the task at this point and asked the subject to rate his partner on a series of thirteen 7-point bipolar scales and to complete a questionnaire about the experiment. The questions included checks on the effectiveness of the thwarting manipulation, the subject's perception of the painfulness of shocks received by his partner, and the subject's suspiciousness. Following completion of the questionnaires, the subject remained quietly seated while 2 additional minutes of heart rate were recorded. The experimenter then removed the electrodes and thoroughly debriefed the subject.

RESULTS

SUMMARY OF EXPERIMENTAL DESIGN.   Ninety subjects were run in this 3×3 repeated-measures design, with 30 subjects in each cell. Dependent measures were (*a*) intensity, number, and duration of shocks; (*b*) changes in heart rate during the experiment; and (*c*) questionnaire ratings of the partner at the end of the experiment.

To assess the difficulty of the learning task, an analysis of variance was carried out on the subjects' actual learning of the syllables in the first half of the experiment. A significant main effect for thwarting emerged ($F = 12.39$, $df = 2/87$, $p < .005$). Low-thwarted subjects repeated more syllables than both high-thwarted subjects ($p < .001$, Duncan's multiple-range test) and moderately thwarted subjects ($p < .005$, Duncan's multiple-range test), thus providing a successful check on the manipulation of task difficulty. Moderately thwarted subjects tended to repeat more syllables than high-thwarted subjects ($p < .10$, Duncan's multiple-range test). The mean number of syllables (summed over trials) given by the low-, moderate-, and high-thwarted subjects was 20.40, 18.17, and 16.87, respectively.

The major dependent aggressive responses were the intensity, number, and duration of shocks, each of which was analyzed separately.

INTENSITY. Only the trials effect was significant ($F = 3.32$, $df = 2/174$, $p <$ 0.5) in this analysis. More intense shocks were given on the second shock trial than on the first trial ($p < .05$, Duncan's multiple-range test). Mean shock intensity on the third trial did not differ significantly from the other means. The means for the first, second, and third trials were 84.72, 101.89, and 95.39, respectively.

NUMBER. The thwarting main effect was significant ($F = 4.47$, $df = 2/37$, $p < .025$). Moderately thwarted subjects gave fewer shocks than both low-thwarted subjects and high-thwarted subjects ($p < .05$, for both comparisons, Duncan's multiple-range test). Subjects in the low- and high-thwarted groups did not differ from each other in the number of shocks given. The mean number of shocks given by low-, moderately, and high-thwarted subjects was 1.70, 1.17, and 1.64, respectively.

The Thwarting $\times$ Trials interaction also reached significance ($F = 2.56$, $df = 4/174$, $p < .05$). Low- and high-thwarted subjects increased the number of shocks delivered from Trial 1 to Trial 2 and then leveled off on Trial 3, while moderately thwarted subjects tended to decrease the number of shocks delivered over all three trials. Figure 1 shows the significant Thwarting $\times$ Trials interaction.

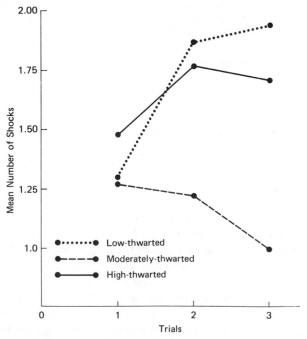

Figure 1 | MEAN NUMBER OF SHOCKS GIVEN BY LOW-, MODERATELY, AND HIGH-THWARTED SUBJECTS OVER TRIALS.

The absolute number of shocks administered by subjects in this experiment was quite low. Although the procedures (no feedback from victim and absence of the experimenter) were designed to facilitate display of aggression, the instructions may have inadvertently inhibited use of shock. Or, perhaps the instigation was relatively mild.

DURATION. None of the effects in this analysis yielded significant effects.

QUESTIONNAIRE DATA. Subjects rated their partners on a series of thirteen 7-point bipolar scales, with higher scores indicating more favorable ratings. An analysis of variance showed that the main effect for thwarting was highly significant ($F = 17.97$, $df = 2/87$, $p < .005$). High-thwarted subjects gave less favorable ratings to their partners than did moderately thwarted subjects or low-thwarted subjects ($p < .001$, for both comparisons, Duncan's multiple-range test). Ratings by moderately and low-thwarted subjects were not significantly different from each other. The mean ratings for high-, moderate-, and low-thwarted subjects were 4.26, 5.38, and 5.09 points, respectively.

Subjects responded to three postexperimental questions concerning anxiety, annoyance, and estimated painfulness of their partner's shock on 5-point scales. Analysis of the degree of annoyance felt during the experiment yielded a significant main effect for thwarting ($F = 7.66$, $df = 2/86$, $p < .005$). High-thwarted subjects indicated greater annoyance (mean rating of 2.67) than did low- and moderately thwarted subjects (mean ratings of 1.63 and 1.65, respectively, $p < .005$, extension of Duncan's multiple-range test to unequal replications; Kramer, 1956). The other two ratings did not yield significant effects.

PHYSIOLOGICAL DATA. For statistical treatment, the 60-second time interval just preceding the experimenter's reading of the instructions was used as an estimate of base-line heart rate. The degree of change occurring during various events in the experiment was calculated by subtracting the average of the subject's base level from his average reading for the event and reflected change in beats per 5-second interval. In order to provide a uniform counting record, conducive to subsequent exploratory analyses as well as for comparison with results of other studies, heart rate samples were based on 5-second intervals of time (Davis, Buchwald, & Frankmann, 1955). These samples were consistently taken from the first, last, and middle (if possible) portion of each event, so that no biased selection of intervals occurred.

Analysis of variance yielded no significant differences in base levels for the three subject groups ($F = .23$, $df = 2/87$). Changes in heart rate due to the independent variables were then tested by analysis of variance.

Thwarting manipulation. Cardiac response during this period was measured by counting and averaging the first three, middle three, and last three 5-second intervals of heart rate during the syllable presentation, along with the first two and last two 5-second intervals during the verbal reinforcement period, for each of the three learning trials. The thwarting manipulation (partner teaching and reinforcing the subject) resulted in nearly significant heart rate differences among the three thwarted groups for the thwarting period ($F = 2.52$, $df = 2/87$, $p < .10$). High-thwarted subjects showed greater increases, but did not differ significantly from the two other thwarted groups ($p < .10$, Duncan's multiple-range test, for both comparisons). The means, reflecting increases from base levels, were 1.16, .75, and .78 for high-, moderate-, and low-thwarted subjects, respectively.

Analysis of the thwarting event resulted in a highly significant trials effect ($F = 38.08$, $df = 2/174$, $p < .005$). Duncan's multiple-range test showed that heart rate increases were significantly greater ($p < .001$) on the first trial ($\overline{X} = 1.18$) than on the second ($\overline{X} = .77$) or third trial ($\overline{X} = .74$), thereby reflecting adaptation effects.

Shock instruction. Cardiac response during this period was measured by counting and averaging the first two, middle two, and last two 5-second intervals of heart rate during the instruction period. A significant thwarting main effect emerged in analysis of the shock-instruction event ($F = 6.91$, $df = 2/87$, $p < .005$). High-thwarted subjects showed significantly greater increases in heart rate for the shock-instruction period than did low-thwarted ($p < .005$, Duncan's multiple-range test) and moderately thwarted subjects ($p < .01$, Duncan's multiple-range test). The means, representing change from base levels, were .88, .35, and .23 for high-, moderate-, and low-thwarted subjects, respectively.

Presenting syllables. Cardiac response was measured by counting and averaging the first three, middle three, and last three 5-second intervals of heart rate for each of the three teaching trials. Analysis of the teaching event yielded a significant thwarting main effect ($F = 6.18$, $df = 2/87$, $p < .005$). High-thwarted subjects showed significantly greater increases in heart rate than both moderately thwarted ($p < .005$, Duncan's multiple-range test) and low-thwarted subjects ($p < .01$, Duncan's multiple-range test). The means for high-, moderate-, and low-thwarted subjects were .63, .08, and .16, respectively.

This same analysis revealed a significant trials effect ($F = 52.71$, $df = 2/174$, $p < .001$). Heart rate increases from base levels showed significant differences between the first ($\overline{X} = .49$), second ($\overline{X} = .27$), and third ($\overline{X} = .11$) syllable presentations ($p < .001$, for all comparisons, Duncan's multiple-range test).

In addition, a significant Thwarting $\times$ Trials interaction emerged ($F = 2.88$, $df = 4/174$, $p < .025$). Table 1 presents the means for this interaction. These means show heart rate adaptation effects, with slightly differing slopes for the three thwarting conditions.

Table 1 | MEAN HEART RATE CHANGE (SYLLABLE PRESENTATION LESS BASE LEVEL SCORES) FOR THWARTING × TRIALS INTERACTION

GROUP	TRIAL 1	TRIAL 2	TRIAL 3
Low-thwarted	.33	.13	.03
Moderately thwarted	.27	.01	−.05
High-thwarted	.86	.67	.35

Administering shock. Cardiac response was measured by counting the two 5-second intervals of heart rate during the shock-delivery period for each of the three shock trials. Analysis of heart rate change scores for the shock event yielded a significant thwarting main effect ($F = 3.93$, $df = 2/87$, $p < .025$). High-thwarted subjects showed greater increase from base levels than did moderately thwarted subjects and low-thwarted subjects ($p < .05$, for both comparisons, Duncan's multiple-range test). The respective means for high-, moderate-, and low-thwarted subjects were .67, .12, and .26. This same analysis yielded a significant trials effect ($F = 4.45$, $df = 2/174$, $p < .025$). Heart rate increases were significantly greater on the first shock trial ($\overline{X} = .60$) than on the second and third shock trials ($\overline{X} = .23$ and .22, respectively, $p < .05$, for both comparisons, Duncan's multiple-range test).

Postexperimental period. Analysis of heart rate during the postexperimental questionnaire period revealed no significant effects, nor did multiple-range tests reveal significant differences. Also, analysis of variance and multiple-range tests on heart rate during the final 2-minute recovery period yielded no significant effects.

Figure 2 depicts heart rate change from base line for each of the six events. Although adaptation effects are apparent after Event 2, the significant elevation of heart rate for the high-thwarted group, relative to the other two groups, is evident on Events 3, 4, and 5.

DISCUSSION

The three thwarted groups did not differ in cardiac rate increases during the thwarting period. However, when made aware of the opportunity to aggress, the

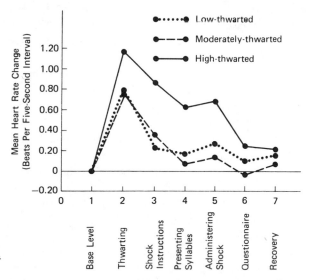

Figure 2 | MEAN HEART RATE CHANGE FROM BASE LEVEL OVER SIX EVENTS.

thwarted groups showed differential increases, with the high-thwarted group displaying greater elevation in heart rate than the other thwarted groups. This effect confirms Elliott's (1969) contention that heart rate might not reflect emotional tension level, except when responses can be initiated to cope with the arousal. The insulted subjects did not show significant increases over the other thwarted groups until they were told they could shock the other person, that is, that they could retaliate.

Differences among conditions were eliminated following shock delivery, thereby suggesting that cardiac recovery occurs only after the aggressive sequence has ended. While inconsistent with Holmes's (1966) findings that frustrated subjects maintain an elevated level of physiological arousal after aggressing, these results support Hokanson and Shetler's (1961) proposition that tension reduction takes place when a subject makes a response which is appropriate to the situation, as in overt aggression toward a frustrator. This study provides the additional information, however, that during the actual aggressive sequence, activation is high for insulted persons, as indicated by elevation of cardiac response throughout teaching and shocking the other person. As suggested by Elliott (1969), cardiac response seems especially sensitive to action instigation. An additional implication of these findings is that after terminating a series of aggressive responses, subjects who are then provided with an unexpected further opportunity to aggress may not be likely to express further aggression. Since their physiological tension has been reduced, strong aggressive cues or renewed drive arousal should be necessary to elicit aggressive responses.

Particularly relevant to the question posed in this study is the fact that moderately thwarted subjects, frustrated (operationally) by their failure on a task, did not differ from low-thwarted subjects in activation throughout the experiment. If these subjects were in a state of readiness, as proposed by Berkowitz (1965), it was not evident from their cardiac responses. What may be necessary for failure to serve as an activator is (a) a specific threat to self-esteem, as provided in the Geen and Berkowitz (1967) study, where subjects failed on a task which a peer had solved; or (b) the perception that the peer is the source of frustration (Dollard, Doob, Miller, Mowrer, & Sears, 1939; Lanzetta & Hannah, 1969).

In terms of aggressive responses, the low- and high-thwarted subjects delivered more shocks to their peer than did the moderately thwarted subjects. For the insulted subjects, the level of aggression was concomitant with increased heart rate and greater reported annoyance, so that their aggression seemed to reflect anger. However, the aggressive behavior of the low- and moderately thwarted persons must be understood in other terms. Apparently, their past performance on a similar task served as a comparison which led the subjects who succeeded (low thwarted) to expect that their peer could do well, and therefore shocked him to improve his performance, whereas those who failed (moderately thwarted) did not expect their peer to do well, and hence did not so reinforce him. This assumption is consistent with Lanzetta and Hannah's (1969) finding that attribution of ability to do a task because of competence led to increased shocks in a training task. These results suggest that although the amount of shock delivered in this situation may reflect aggression, in the sense of harming another person, it also reflects a tendency to use the shock as reinforcement for learning. Thus, experiments which are designed to measure aggression in terms of physical harm to another must include controls which will eliminate the operation of attribution effects. Furthermore, it is important to clarify the motivational basis for the delivery of shock in a situation, so that the *intent to injure*, rather than to help, the person can be unambiguously inferred. If one considers the amount of pain delivered by shock as a sufficient definition of aggression, then the results of studies so far demonstrate that insult, some types of task failure, and attribution increase aggressive responding. However, if one wishes to clarify whether the intent to physically injure is prepotent to the intent to teach or train, then experiments which unconfound these must be designed.

SUMMARY

This study examined the effects of various thwarting conditions on cardiac response and subsequent aggression. Subjects were asked to learn a list of nonsense syllables, with verbal reinforcement to be administered by a peer. Subjects received either an easy list with neutral comments from their peer, a difficult list with neutral comments from their peer, or a difficult list with derogatory comments from their peer. These conditions served to induce low-, moderate-, and high-thwarting conditions. The next phase of the experiment provided the subjects with the opportunity to reverse roles and teach their peer a list of syllables, with administration of shock as reinforcement. The results indicated that insult (high thwarting) enhanced both cardiac and aggressive responses, as expected. Low- and moderately thwarted subjects did not differ in physiological activation, thereby providing no support for the conjecture that frustration per se produces a physiological readiness to respond aggressively. The finding that low-thwarted subjects delivered more shocks to their peer than did moderately thwarted subjects was interpreted in terms of attribution theory. The need to specify conditions under which the motivation is to injure the other rather than to help the other learn (via aggressive responding) is emphasized. Several significant cardiac responses are discussed as supporting Elliott's notion that heart rate reflects activation or action instigation.

REFERENCES

Berkowitz, L. The concept of aggressive drive: Some additional considerations. In L. Berkowitz (Ed.), *Advances in experimental social psychology*. Vol. 2. New York: Academic Press, 1965.

Berkowitz, L. The frustration-aggression hypothesis revisited. In L. Berkowitz (Ed.), *Roots of aggression: A re-examination of the frustration-aggression hypothesis*. New York: Atherton Press, 1969.

Berkowitz, L., & Le Page, A. Weapons as aggression-eliciting stimuli. *Journal of Personality and Social Psychology*, 1967, 7, 202–207.

Blatt, S. J. Patterns of cardiac arousal during complex mental activity. *Journal of Abnormal and Social Psychology*, 1961, 63, 272–282.

Buss, A. H. *The psychology of aggression*. New York: Wiley, 1961.

Buss, A. H. Physical aggression in relation to different frustrations. *Journal of Abnormal and Social Psychology*, 1963, 67, 1–7.

Buss, A. H. Instrumentality of aggression, feedback, and frustration as determinants of physical aggression. *Journal of Personality and Social Psychology*, 1966, 3, 153–162.

Corfield, V. K. The role of arousal and cognitive complexity in susceptibility to social influence. *Journal of Personality*, 1969, 37, 554–567.

Davis, R. C., Buchwald, A. M., & Frankmann, R. W. Autonomic and muscular responses and their relation to simple stimuli. *Psychological Monographs*, 1955, 69(20, Whole No. 405).

Dollard, J., Doob, L., Miller, N., Mowrer, O., & Sears, R. *Frustration and aggression.* New Haven, Conn.: Yale University Press, 1939.

Elliott, R. Tonic heart rate: Experiments on the effects of collative variables lead to a hypothesis about its motivational significance. *Journal of Personality and Social Psychology*, 1969, 12, 211–229.

Epstein, S., & Taylor, S. P. Instigation to aggression as a function of the degree of defeat and perceived aggressive intent of the opponent. *Journal of Personality*, 1967, 35, 265–290.

Geen, R. G. Effects of frustration, attack, and prior training in aggressiveness upon aggressive behavior. *Journal of Personality and Social Psychology*, 1968, 9, 316–321.

Geen, R. G., & Berkowitz, L. Some conditions facilitating the occurrence of aggression after the observation of violence. *Journal of Personality*, 1967, 35, 666–676.

Glaze, J. A. The association value of nonsense syllables. *Journal of Genetic Psychology*, 1928, 35, 255–269.

Hokanson, J. E., & Burgess, M. The effects of three types of aggression on vascular processes. *Journal of Abnormal and Social Psychology*, 1962, 64, 446–449.

Hokanson, J. E., & Shetler, S. Effect of overt aggression on physiological arousal level. *Journal of Abnormal and Social Psychology*, 1961, 63, 446–448.

Holmes, D. Effects of overt aggression on level of physiological arousal. *Journal of Personality and Social Psychology*, 1966, 4, 189–195.

Kramer, C. Y. Extension of multiple-range tests to group means with unequal numbers of replications. *Biometrics*, 1956, 12, 307–312.

Lacey, J. I., Kagan, J., Lacey, B. C., & Moss, H. A. The visceral level: Situational determinants and behavioral correlates of autonomic response patterns. In P. H. Knapp (Ed.), *Expression of the emotions in man.* New York: International Universities, 1963.

Lanzetta, J. T., & Hannah, T. E. Reinforcing behavior of "naive" trainers. *Journal of Personality and Social Psychology*, 1969, 11, 245–253.

Loew, C. A. Acquisition of a hostile attitude and its relationship to aggressive behavior. *Journal of Personality and Social Psychology*, 1967, 5, 335–341.

Malmo, R. B. Finger-sweat prints in the differentiation of low and high incentive. *Psychophysiology*, 1965, 1, 231–240.

Schnore, M. M. Individual patterns of physiological activity as a function of task differences and degree of arousal. *Journal of Experimental Psychology*, 1959, 66, 297–333.

17 | Anxiety

17.1 | THE EFFECTS OF MANIFEST ANXIETY ON THE ACADEMIC ACHIEVEMENT OF COLLEGE STUDENTS*

Charles D. Spielberger

Acute shortages of trained professional and technical manpower have caused the academic mortality rate for college students to be a subject of considerable general concern to our society (Iffert, 1958).

There is a growing appreciation of the important role mental health and emotional factors play in the academic adjustment of college students.

Even apparently well-adjusted students have their share of emotional difficulties. Heath and Gregory (1946)—in a study of male college sophomores chosen on the basis of good health, satisfactory academic status, and overtly good social adjustment— reported that 90 per cent of their subjects raised questions or presented problems which were judged by the investigating staff as requiring professional aid for solution.

Rust and Davie (1961)—in assessing the nature, frequency, and severity of the personal problems of undergraduate college students—found that nearly 80 per cent of those who responded to their questionnaire reported that they had at least one personal problem during the current school year which bothered them "very often" or "fairly often"; 35 per cent of their sample indicated specifically that they had been troubled often by "nervousness."

These findings are consistent with general observations that late adolescence in the American culture is a time of "storm and stress" and a period of unusual difficulty in adjustment (Farnham, 1951).

Several recent studies (McKeachie, 1951; McKeachie et al., 1955) have demonstrated impressively that anxiety is manifested by college students in conventional classroom test situations to such an extent that the general level of academic performance

* SOURCE: Spielberger, C. D. The effects of manifest anxiety on the academic achievement of college students. *Mental Hygiene*, 1962, 46, 420–426. Copyright 1962. Reprinted by permission of the National Association for Mental Health, Inc.

is impaired. Strong motivations to achieve high grades appear to contribute directly to the adjustment difficulties of many students whose anxiety about failure is intensified by the academic situation.

Thus, it is apparent that college life is characterized by conditions and expectations which may heighten anxieties already present in students or may induce new anxieties. It would seem reasonable to expect that the stresses of college life are likely to have most serious effects upon those students who have developed pronounced tendencies to respond to threatening situations with anxiety and conflict.

But when investigations of the relationship between measures of student neuroticism or emotional adjustment and academic achievement are examined, the findings are equivocal and inconsistent.

For example, Thurstone and Thurstone (1930) have reported that less well-adjusted students tended to achieve higher grades, while Stagner (1933) has found that unstable and maladjusted students did less well than their more stable contemporaries. Other studies have reported no difference in the emotional adjustment scores of academic underachievers and overachievers (Rust & Ryan, 1953). Such inconsistencies have been attributed to inadequacies in the variety of personality tests which have been used, differences between the student populations which have been studied, and varying criteria of academic success (Harris, 1940).

Also, it has been noted that methods of data analysis have frequently not taken into account the possibility that a given personality variable may have different effects for persons with differing intellectual endowments (Spielberger & Katzenmeyer, 1959).

To this point Berger and Sutker (1956) investigated the combined effects of emotional adjustment and scholastic aptitude on the academic achievement of college students. Their measure of emotional adjustment did not by itself differentiate between academic successes and failures, but when used in combination with measures of ability, a larger number of the most able students with high conflict scores were academic failures than were students with equal ability but low conflict scores.

The purpose of the present study was to investigate the relationship between anxiety level and academic performance for college students when the student's ability is taken into account.

It was expected that college students with high anxiety would be more likely to perform less adequately throughout their college careers than would nonanxious students. Specifically, it was hypothesized that anxious students would obtain poorer grades and would be more likely to drop out of school because of academic failure than would nonanxious students.

METHOD

The measure of anxiety employed in the present study was the Taylor Manifest Anxiety Scale (MAS). This scale (Taylor, 1953) consists of 50 items from the Minnesota Multiphasic Personality Inventory which were judged by clinical psychologists to be consistent with Cameron's (1947) description of anxiety as manifested in chronic anxiety reactions.

The MAS was administered to all students enrolled in introductory psychology courses at Duke University at the beginning of each of six consecutive semesters from September, 1954, through June, 1957. The A.C.E. Psychological Examination for College Freshmen (1949 edition), which had been routinely administered as part of a battery of placement tests to all students entering the University as freshmen, served as the measure of scholastic ability.

Grade point averages (GPAs) for the *single* semester during which each student took the MAS served as one criterion of academic achievement. These were obtained from official University records. The student's GPA is the weighted average of his academic performance in course work where 4 points are credited for each hour of A, 3 points for B, 2 points for C, 1 point for D, and 0 for F.

Only male students were included in the present study, since it had been found previously that MAS scores for male and female college students may not have the same intellectual correlates (Spielberger, 1958). Eight students who obtained scores of 7 or higher on the Lie Scale of the MMPI were eliminated from the study.

Those male students scoring in the upper and lower 20 per cent of the MAS score distribution (raw scores of 19 and above and 7 and below) were designated as HA and LA respectively. After the data for the six semester subsamples were pooled, MAS scores, ACE scores and GPAs were available for a total of 140 HA students and 144 LA students whose Lie scores were below 7.

The long-term effects of anxiety on academic performance were evaluated in a follow-up study in which the graduation status of each of the HA and LA students was determined three years subsequent to the time the original data collection was completed.

For those students who had not graduated from the University by June, 1960, and who were no longer enrolled, their reasons for leaving and their cumulative GPAs at the time they departed were obtained from official University records.

Academic failure was defined for the purpose of the present study as: (1) having been dismissed by the University because of poor academic performance, and/or (2) having left the University with a grade point average below 1.75 (a GPA of 1.90 is required to graduate).

Both criteria were deemed necessary in that students who performed unsatisfactorily were often allowed to leave school for "personal reasons" so that the stigma of "academic failure" would not deter their acceptance at other institutions. Seventeen students, eleven HA and six LA, were either still enrolled in the University or had left with averages above 1.75. In evaluating the relationship between anxiety and dropouts resulting from academic failure, these students were eliminated from the sample; for this analysis there were 129 HA students and 138 LA students.

RESULTS

The students were subdivided into five levels of scholastic ability, on the basis of their ACE total scores. Each level consisted of approximately 20 per cent of the total sample. The lowest level of ability was designated I; the highest was designated V. The

ACE score ranges for levels I through V were 62–102; 103–116; 117–126; 127–137 and 138–174, respectively.

The GPAs of the HA and LA students were then compared for these ability levels. The relationship between manifest anxiety and grades for students of different levels of scholastic ability is depicted in Figure 1, where it may be noted that in the broad middle range of ability, the HA students obtained poorer grades than did the LA students. There appeared to be no differences between the HA and LA students at the extremes of ability.

These data were subjected to an analysis of variance [Lindquist (1953), factorial design]. The hypothesized main effect of anxiety was statistically significant ($F = 5.48$; $df = 1/274$; $p < .025$). The expected relationship between scholastic ability and GPA was also highly significant ($F = 5.60$; $df = 4/274$; $p < .001$).

Although the effects of anxiety and scholastic ability on grades appear to be inter-active, i.e., the effect of anxiety depends on the student's level of ability, the statistical test of this interaction was not significant ($F = 1.36$; $df = 4/274$; $p > 20$.

It may be noted in Figure 1, however, that the *observed* interaction is heterogeneous; failure to obtain a statistically significant interaction may result from the fact that analysis of variance tends to provide a relatively insensitive test of such interactions (Lindquist, 1953).

When the relationship between anxiety and dropout rate resulting from academic failure is examined, 8 of 138 LA students and 26 of 129 HA students were classified as academic failures, according to the previously stated criteria. The total number of students in the HA and LA groups at each level of ability and the number who dropped out of school because of academic failure are reported in Table 1.

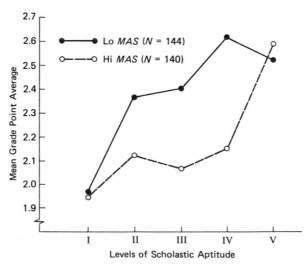

Figure 1 | MEAN GRADE POINT AVERAGES FOR HIGH AND LOW ANXIETY COLLEGE STUDENTS AT FIVE LEVELS OF SCHOLASTIC ABILITY.

Table 1 | HIGH AND LOW ANXIOUS STUDENTS AT FIVE LEVELS OF SCHOLASTIC ABILITY WHO DROPPED OUT OF SCHOOL CLASSIFIED AS ACADEMIC FAILURES

SCHOLASTIC ABILITY	HIGH ANXIOUS STUDENTS			LOW ANXIOUS STUDENTS		
	No.	No. Fail.	Per cent Fail.	No.	No. Fail.	Per cent Fail.
I	33	9	27.3	22	3	13.6
II	22	3	13.6	26	1	3.8
III	31	7	22.6	23	1	4.4
IV	21	5	23.8	37	0	0.0
V	22	2	9.1	30	3	10.0
Total	129	26	20.2	138	8	5.8

COLLEGE STUDENTS AT FIVE LEVELS OF SCHOLASTIC ABILITY. More than 20 per cent of the HA students failed, as compared to fewer than 6 per cent of the LA students. When students in Group 1, the lowest ability group, are excluded from consideration, nearly 18 per cent of the relatively able HA students are found to have left the University because of academic failure, as compared to only 4.5 per cent of the relatively able LA students.

DISCUSSION

The findings of the present study provide evidence of the detrimental effects of anxiety on college grades and dropout rates resulting from academic failure. The effect of anxiety on grades resulted from the fact that HA students in the middle ranges of ability did poorer than LA students of comparable ability (see Figure 1).

Although the obtained relationship was based on academic performance during a single semester, the data on dropouts indicated that the effects of anxiety on academic performance are not limited to a single semester. A larger percentage of the HA students were academic failures at all levels of ability, except the highest.

Moreover, when only the relatively able students are considered (those at ability levels II, III, IV and V), the percentage of HA students who failed was nearly four times as great as the percentage of LA academic failures. It is apparent that the loss to society of the creative abilities of potentially able students through underachievement and/or academic failure constitutes an important mental health problem in education.

The grades of low aptitude students were uniformly low, irrespective of their anxiety level; poor academic performance presumably resulted from their limited ability. However, since the dropout rate resulting from academic failure was approximately twice as high for the HA students at ability level I as for the LA students at this level, the combination of high anxiety and limited ability appears to have a more detrimental effect upon the performance of HA students over a period of time.

For the superior students, grades were high and apparently independent of anxiety level. It would seem reasonable to assume that college work was relatively easy for such students; their superior intellectual endowment made it possible for them to obtain good grades, irrespective of their anxiety level.

A more detailed analysis of the performance of students who scored in the highest level of academic ability suggests, however, that high anxiety may actually facilitate the performance of the most able students. For such students anxiety may provide increased motivation (Spence, 1958) which stimulates them to greater effort in their academic work.

For the purpose of examining this possibility, the GPAs for only those students in the highest ability group whose ACE scores were 150 or above were considered. The mean GPA for the very superior HA students ($N = 9$) was 3.01 as compared to a mean GPA of 2.70 for LA students of comparable ability ($N = 12$). This difference, however, did not reach a satisfactory level of statistical significance ($t = .90$; $df = 13$; $p > 05$).

Perhaps the most important implication of the findings of the present study is that it appears possible to identify members of the college population who, because of emotional problems, are not likely, under general conditions, to function at levels commensurate with their intellectual potential.

By identifying such students at the earliest possible time and offering them therapeutic opportunities, the academic mortality among able students who fail because of difficulties in their emotional adjustment could be reduced.

Ideally, such students should be identified at the beginning of their freshman year. The effects of anxiety on the academic performance of college freshmen might be expected to be more detrimental than for the students in the present sample who were predominantly sophomores and juniors.

The college freshman must adjust to demands for academic achievement under conditions of increased complexity of subject matter and heightened competition from his peers.

In addition, he is confronted with establishing a new set of social relationships in a strange environment. To the extent that freshmen with heightened anxieties can be identified early and offered therapeutic assistance, it is possible that academic casualties and, in some cases, emotional disorders can be prevented.

SUMMARY

In order to assess the effects of manifest anxiety on academic performance, the grades achieved by anxious and nonanxious college students for a single semester's work were examined.

The long-term effects of anxiety on academic performance were evaluated by determining—three years subsequent to the initial data collection—the number of anxious and nonanxious students who either had graduated or had left the University, classified as academic failures.

It was found that anxious students in the middle ranges of ability obtained lower grades and a higher percentage of academic failures than nonanxious students of comparable ability. Students of low ability earned poor grades irrespective of their anxiety level; however, a higher percentage of these students, with high anxiety, were academic failures than were the nonanxious students of limited ability.

For the very superior students (those with ACE scores above 150), it appeared that anxiety may have actually facilitated academic performance. To the extent that anxious students—likely to be underachievers or academic failures—can be identified early and offered effective therapeutic assistance, academic mortality rates resulting from emotional factors can be reduced.

REFERENCES

Berger, I. L., & Sutker, A. R. The relationship of emotional adjustment and intellectual capacity to the academic achievement of college students. *Mental Hygiene*, 1956, *40*, 65–77.

Cameron, N. *The psychology of behavior disorders: A bio-social interpretation.* Boston: Houghton Mifflin, 1947.

Farnham, M. L. *The adolescent.* New York: Harper & Row, 1951.

Harris, D. Factors affecting college grades: A review of the literature, 1930–1937. *Psychological Bulletin*, 1940, *37*, 125–166.

Heath, C. W., & Gregory, L. W. Problems of normal college students and their families. *School and Society*, 1946, *63*, 355–358.

Iffert, R. E., Retention and withdrawal of college students. Washington, D.C.: Office of Education, U.S. Department of Health, Education and Welfare, 1958. Bulletin No. 1.

Lindquist, E. F. *Design and analysis of experiments in psychology and education.* Boston: Houghton Mifflin, 1953.

McKeachie, W. J. Anxiety in the college classroom. *Journal of Educational Research*, 1951, *45*, 153–160.

McKeachie, W. J., Pallie, D., & Spiesman, J. Relieving anxiety in classroom examinations. *Journal of Abnormal and Social Psychology*, 1955, *50*, 93–98.

Rust, R. M., & Davie, J. S. The personal problems of college students. *Mental Hygiene*, 1961, *45*, 247–257.

Rust, R. M., & Ryan, F. J. The relationship of some Rorschach variables to academic behavior. *Journal of Personality*, 1953, *21*, 441–456.

Spence, K. W. A theory of emotionally based drive (D) and its relation to performance in simple learning situations. *American Psychologist*, 1958, *13*, 131–141.

Spielberger, C. D. On the relationship between manifest anxiety and intelligence. *Journal of Consulting Psychology*, 1958, *22*, 220–224.

Spielberger, C. D., & Katzenmeyer, W. G. Manifest anxiety, intelligence and college grades. *Journal of Consulting Psychology*, 1959, *23*, 278.

Stagner, R. The relation of personality to academic aptitude and achievement. *Journal of Educational Research*, 1933, *26*, 648–660.

Taylor, J. A. A personality scale of manifest anxiety. *Journal of Abnormal and Social Psychology*, 1953, *48*, 285–290.

Thurstone, L. L., & Thurstone, T. G. A neurotic inventory. *Journal of Abnormal and Social Psychology*, 1930, *1*, 3–30.

17.2 | CONTROL OVER STRESS, LOCUS OF CONTROL, AND RESPONSE TO STRESS*[,1]

B. Kent Houston

This study was conducted to investigate two factors which Lazarus (1966) asserts influence a person's perception of threat in potentially stressful situations. One factor is the person's belief about his capacity to counter or avoid threat in that situation, in other words, the person's belief about his control over the potential threat. The more control a person judges himself to have in a situation, the less threatening the situation will appear to him. Conversely, the less control a person judges himself to have in a situation, i.e., the more helpless he feels himself to be, the more threatening the situation will appear.

To support this proposition, Lazarus presents anecdotal material and describes two experiments. One experiment demonstrated that individuals prefer predictable punishment over unpredictable punishment (D'Amato & Gumenik, 1960). The other experiment (Pervin, 1963) indicated that it is less anxiety arousing for subjects to administer shock to themselves than for the experimenter to do it, and that predictable shock is less anxiety arousing than unpredictable shock. In two other experiments not cited by Lazarus (Champion, 1950; and Corah & Boffa, 1970), it was found that under certain circumstances, subjects exhibited less stress in a situation in which they believed they could terminate an electric shock than if they believed they could not terminate it. In none of these experiments, however, could individuals control threat in the sense of actually being able to counter or avoid the aversive stimulus, so to date there has been no direct experimental verification of Lazarus' proposition.

Lazarus' formulation was tested in this investigation by experimentally manipulating subjects' belief about countering or avoiding threat and assessing whether this differentially affected subjects' anxiety. In one condition (Unavoidable-Shock) subjects were led to believe that there was no way of avoiding an electric shock which would occur randomly while they performed a memory task. This condition was designed to encourage a person to feel helpless since he could not counter or avoid the threat. In another condition (Avoidable-Shock) subjects were led to believe they could avoid an electric shock by not making mistakes on a memory task. This condition was designed to encourage a person to feel that he possessed some control over the situation since he could

* SOURCE: Houston, B. K. Control over stress, locus of control, and response to stress. *Journal of Personality and Social Psychology*, 1972, 21, 249–255. Copyright 1972 by the American Psychological Association and reprinted by permission.

[1] Thanks are due to Ray Mulry for his suggestions on design of the study, to David S. Holmes for his generous assistance on the manuscript, and to Jay Fogelman for aid in scoring and analyzing the data.

counter or avoid the threat. It was predicted that subjects in the Unavoidable-Shock condition would be more anxious than subjects in the Avoidable-Shock condition.

Anxiety was evaluated in terms of self report and physiological arousal. Self report of anxiety was measured by Zuckerman's (1960) Affect Adjective Check List (AACL) and physiological arousal was measured by heart rate.

The second factor that Lazarus (1966) asserts influences perception of threat is a person's general belief about his control over the environment. Specifically, if a person generally believes that he lacks control (or is helpless), this should increase perception of threat, while the general belief that he has control should decrease perception of threat. In this study, general feelings of helplessness and control over the environment were identified by the use of Rotter's Locus of Control scale (1966). The Locus of Control scale is a measure of the extent to which an individual believes that reinforcements in his life are under his control and are contingent upon his behavior (internal locus of control, IC) as opposed to believing that reinforcements are not under his control and are not contingent upon his behavior (external locus of control, EC). It was predicted that EC subjects, since they generally feel more helpless, would be more anxious in both threat-of-shock conditions than IC subjects.

Independent of perception of threat, investigators have been interested in the relation between the internal-external control variable and task performance (Rotter & Mulry, 1965; Watson & Baumal, 1967). Typically, it has been found that an individual's performance is better in a situation in which there is congruence between his general belief about locus of control and his belief about the locus of control in that particular situation than is the case where there is incongruence in the general and situational beliefs. Therefore, in the present investigation it was predicted that IC subjects would perform better in the Avoidable-Shock condition where they thought they had some control over the situation while EC subjects would perform better in the Unavoidable-Shock condition where they did not think they had control over the situation. The task used to assess performance was a specially constructed digits backward test which is described below.

Watson and Baumal (1967) have hypothesized that the relationships between locus of control and performance in different types of situations are found because individuals in incongruent situations become anxious and the ensuing anxiety interferes with task performance. Unfortunately, the study by Watson and Baumal did not include a reliable measure of anxiety, independent of task performance, to properly evaluate this hypothesis. Therefore, an ancillary purpose of the present study was to test Watson and Baumal's hypothesis. Since subjects in the Avoidable-Shock condition were told that receiving or avoiding an electric shock was contingent upon their performance on a memory task, the situation was congruent with the generalized beliefs of IC subjects and incongruent with the beliefs of EC subjects. Therefore, on the basis of the hypothesis of Watson and Baumal, it would be expected that in the Avoidable-Shock condition EC subjects would be more anxious than IC subjects. Since subjects in the Unavoidable-Shock condition were told that there was no way of avoiding an electric shock which would occur randomly while they performed a memory task, the situation was congruent with the generalized beliefs of EC subjects and incongruent with the beliefs of IC subjects. Therefore, on the basis of Watson and Baumal's hypothesis, it would be expected that IC subjects would be more anxious than EC subjects in the Unavoidable-Shock condition.

In addition to the two threat-of-shock groups, a Non-Stress group was included in the design of the study for two reasons. One was to allow a check on whether subjects in the two shock groups did indeed experience stress. The second reason was to provide information on how IC and EC subjects would perform and how anxious they would become when not in a stressful situation. It was predicted that EC subjects would perform better than IC subjects in the Non-Stress condition since none of the subjects were led to believe they had control over the events in the situation and this would be congruent with the general beliefs of EC subjects. Applying Watson and Baumal's hypothesis, it was also predicted that EC subjects would be less anxious than IC subjects in the Non-Stress condition since the belief that the subjects had no control over the events in the situation would be congruent with the general beliefs of EC subjects.

METHOD

Sixty-six males fulfilling an introductory psychology experimental requirement served as subjects in this experiment. The subjects were assigned randomly, in equal numbers, to the three treatment conditions: Non-Stress, Avoidable-Shock, and Unavoidable Shock.

Subjects were run in individual sessions. After being told that the research was concerned with the relation between mood, physiological response, and performance on a verbal task, an EKG electrode was attached to each of the subject's wrists and a ground electrode was attached to the subject's right upper arm. The subject's heart rate (HR) was recorded on an E & M Physiograph (Model DMP-4A).

The session was divided into three parts: rest, assessment of limit for digits backward, and experimental. The procedures for the first two periods were the same for all subjects. Differential instructions given the two groups in the experimental period, described below, differentiated the groups into Non-Stress, Avoidable-Shock, and Unavoidable-Shock groups.

REST PERIOD. The subject was asked to relax for a period of approximately five minutes during which he completed Rotter's Locus of Control scale (1966). At the end of the rest period, the subject was asked to complete the Today form of the AACL by checking those adjectives that described how he felt *at that moment.* HR was recorded continuously during the rest period, but only the number of heart beats in a 30 second interval during which the subject was completing the AACL was used as the index of the subject's resting level. For subjects completing the AACL in less than 30 seconds, their HR for 30 seconds was extrapolated from the time they took to complete the AACL.

ASSESSMENT OF LIMIT FOR DIGITS BACKWARD. After completing the AACL, the Digits Backward Test from the WAIS was given with standard instructions (Wechsler, 1955, p. 41). The subject's limit was determined by the level at which he twice failed to repeat a set of a specified number of digits, and then he was given two practice sets of digits, each one digit less than his limit.

EXPERIMENTAL PERIOD. Subjects in the Non-Stress group were told they would be given some more sets of digits like the ones they had just done and then were given six sets of digits each one digit less than their individual limits. Subjects in both the Avoidable-Shock and Unavoidable-Shock groups were told that the experimenter was now interested in studying physiological response to electric shock and "shock" electrodes were placed on the index finger of the left hand. Subjects in the Unavoidable-Shock condition were told that they would be given some more sets of digits like the ones they had just done and that they would receive one or more painful electric shocks sometime during this period. The subjects were told that a shock machine was programmed to deliver shocks on a random basis and that there was no way of avoiding them. Subjects in the Avoidable-Shock condition were told that they would be given some more sets of digits like the ones they had just done and that they might receive a painful electric shock after every mistake they made in repeating the digits. The experimenter explained that he would depress a pedal on the floor after each mistake the subject made and the pedal activated a shock machine which delivered a shock on a random basis whenever the pedal was depressed. Therefore, the subject was told, he might or might not receive an electric shock after every mistake but surely he would receive a shock after some, if not all, of his mistakes. The experimenter went on to say, however, that the subject could avoid ever getting shocked by not making any mistakes. (Actually, none of the subjects in either threat-of-shock group was ever shocked.) The number of sets of digits the subjects repeated correctly (maximum of six) constituted the dependent measure of task performance.

At the end of the experimental period, the subjects were asked to complete the AACL according to how they felt *while repeating the last few sets of digits.* HR was recorded continuously during this period, but only the data for the last 30 seconds, during which subjects were repeating the last few sets of digits and for which the subjects indicated their feelings on the AACL, were used as the measure of HR during the experimental period.

RESULTS AND DISCUSSION

CONTROL OVER THREAT AND RESPONSE TO THREAT. Change scores (rest to experimental periods) derived for both AACL and HR scores[2] were used to determine whether the threat of shock was effective in stressing the subjects and to test Lazarus' hypothesis that belief about control over threat influences the perception of threat.

---

[2] As a check for the potential operation of the law of initial values (Lacey, 1956; Wilder, 1962), HR scores for the rest period were correlated with change in HR from rest to experimental periods. The correlation was significant, $r = -.37$, $df = 1/64$, $p < .01$, so a covariance adjustment was made on HR change scores for initial scores (McNemar, 1962).

Mean change scores for AACL and HR for the three treatment groups are presented in Table 1. For both the AACL data and the HR data, 3×2 analyses of variance were carried out comparing Treatment conditions (Non-Stress, Avoidable-Shock, and Unavoidable-Shock) and Locus of Control (EC—IC).[3] In these analyses, the sum of squares for treatments which has two degrees of freedom was partitioned into two components with one degree of freedom apiece. One component reflects the expected relationship between the treatment means (after Winer, 1962, pp. 65 and 70). Specifically, it was predicted that the mean AACL change scores and mean HR change scores for the Unavoidable-Shock condition would be greater than the mean for the Avoidable-Shock condition and both of these would be greater than the mean for the Non-Stress condition. The other component was the remainder sum of squares indicating how much of the Treatments sum of squares was not accounted for by the expected relationship between the treatment means.

For the AACL data, the special comparison for treatment means was significant ($F = .750, df = 1/60, p < .01$) while the remainder sum of squares was not significant ($F = .15, df = 1/60, ns$). These results and inspection of the data in Table 1 indicate that a) subjects in both stress conditions reported more negative affect than subjects in the Non-Stress condition thus providing evidence that the threat of shock was successful in inducing stress in the subjects; and b) that subjects in the Unavoidable-Shock condition reported more negative affect than subjects in the Avoidable-Shock condition.

When the HR data was analyzed, the results indicated that neither the special comparison for treatment means nor the component for the remainder sum of squares was significant ($F = 2.43, df = 1.60, ns$ and $F = 1.98, df = 1/60, ns$, respectively). However, inspection of Table 1 indicates that HR increased more for the threat-of-shock groups than for the Non-Stress group. This relationship approached significance ($F = 3.23, df = 1/60, p < .09$), a finding which provides additional evidence that the threat of shock was successful in inducing stress in the subjects. Inspection of Table 1

[3] Since a high score on the Locus of Control scale indicates a belief in external control, subjects in each condition who obtained a score above the median were assigned to an EC group and subjects who obtained a score below the median were assigned to an IC group. The median scores for the subjects in the three conditions are as follows: Non-Stress 9, Avoidable-Shock 9, Unavoidable-Shock 8. These medians are congruent with the measures of central value for the Locus of Control scale reported for various subject samples by Rotter (1966).

Table 1 | MEAN CHANGES IN AACL AND HR FOR THE THREE TREATMENT CONDITIONS

Change score	TREATMENT CONDITIONS		
	Non-Stress	*Avoidable-Shock*	*Unavoidable-Shock*
AACL	2.05	4.27	5.36
HR	0.94	3.91	2.38

also indicates that, contrary to prediction, HR increased more for the Avoidable-Shock group than for the Unavoidable-Shock group, which is opposite to the relation found for the AACL data. However, this difference did not reach statistical significance ($F = 1.18$, $df = 1/60$, ns). The greater increase in HR for the Avoidable-Shock than the Unavoidable-Shock group was probably due to the effort subjects in Avoidable-Shock expended in trying to get the digits correct in order to avoid the threatened shock. In other words, the subjects in Avoidable-Shock exhibited greater physiological arousal than subjects in Unavoidable-Shock because the subjects in Avoidable-Shock were making a substantial effort to achieve control over the situation. This interpretation is supported by the following considerations. Subjects in Avoidable-Shock were given the opportunity to avoid shock but were not led to expect it would be easy or definite that they could do so. They were in effect challenged to exercise control in the situation. Also, the digits backward task was difficult since it required performance near the limit of the subjects' ability. Therefore, it would take considerable effort to perform well enough not to make mistakes, and hence not to get shocked, as subjects in the Avoidable-Shock were encouraged to do. In a subsequent unpublished study in which subjects were questioned about their reaction to an avoidable shock condition, over 40% volunteered how hard they had tried to concentrate on, memorize, or remember the digits in order to avoid the threatened shock. The physiological arousal observed in Avoidable-Shock, then, appears to be due to a) apprehension about shock, which also influenced the increase in HR for Unavoidable-Shock subjects, and b) substantial effort to achieve control over the situation by performing the task well, which probably did not occur in Unavoidable-Shock since the subjects in this condition had been led to believe that control over the threat was not possible.

In summary, then, it was found that the possibility of receiving electric shock generally increased subjects' report of anxiety and level of heart rate. As predicted, the increase in report of anxiety was greater when the subjects thought they were helpless to do anything to counter or protect themselves from the shock than when they thought that their actions could lead to avoiding the shock. However, subjects increased more in physiological arousal when they thought they could avoid shock but the avoidant behavior was near the limit of their capacity than when they thought they were helpless to avoid shock.

The results indicate that a subject's response to a potentially threatening situation in which he may or may not have control is more complex than Lazarus (1966) proposed. Difficulty in achieving control, evidenced here by the effort required to exercise control, appears to be an important factor. When a person has to perform a difficult task to avoid an aversive event, a different pattern of response to the situation is found than might be expected if it were not difficult to make an avoidant response. For future theory and research, it appears necessary to not simply consider what effect control over a situation has on response to threat but to consider the effect of various kinds and conditions of control on response to threat.

LOCUS OF CONTROL AND RESPONSE TO STRESS. Watson and Baumal (1967) hypothesized that incongruence between subjects' general and situational beliefs about locus of control creates anxiety which may lead to performance decrement. On the basis of this hypothesis it was predicted that EC subjects would be less anxious than IC subjects in Unavoidable-Shock and Non-Stress and IC subjects would be less anxious than EC subjects in Avoidable-Shock. This prediction was tested through the use of the interaction terms from the 3×2 analyses of variance described in the previous section. The interaction between Treatments and Locus of Control was not significant for either the AACL data ($F = .35$, $df = 2/60$, ns) or the HR data ($F = 2.18$, $df = 2/60$, ns). The results of the present investigation therefore offer no support for Watson and Baumal's hypothesis. That is, subjects in incongruent situations (e.g., EC subjects in Avoidable-Shock) did not evidence greater anxiety as measured by AACL or HR increases than did subjects in congruent situations (e.g., EC subjects in Unavoidable-Shock).[4]

On the basis of Lazarus' (1966) formulation it was predicted that EC subjects would be more anxious in both threat-of-shock conditions than IC subjects. This prediction derives from the possibility that EC subjects generally feel more helpless than do IC subjects and therefore will perceive the possibility of shock in both threat-of-shock conditions as more threatening than IC subjects. Since no threat is involved in the Non-Stress condition, there is no reason to expect differences in anxiety between EC and IC subjects in this condition. Analyses non-orthogonal to the 3×2 analyses of variance described in the preceding section were made to test the expected relationship between means (after Winer, 1962, p. 65 and 70). Specifically it was expected that increases in AACL and HR would be greater for EC than IC subjects across both threat-of-shock conditions but there would be no differences between EC and IC subjects in Non-Stress. The analysis for AACL change scores was not significant ($F = .05$, $df = 1/60$, ns). Analysis of HR change scores and inspection of the data revealed a significant relationship among the means ($F = 9.47$, $df = 1/60$, $p < .01$). As expected, there was no significant difference between EC and IC subjects in change in HR in Non-Stress ($F = .12$, $df = 1/60$, ns). However, contrary to what was expected, it was found that IC subjects increased significantly more in HR than EC subjects across the two threat-of-shock conditions ($F = 9.47$, $df = 1/60$, $p < .01$).

It is clear, then, that these data do not support the prediction derived from Lazarus (1966) that people who generally believe they have control over the environment perceive situations as less stressful than persons who generally believe they are helpless in interacting with the environment, at least when general beliefs regarding control are

[4] This statement takes into consideration the possibility described earlier that increase in HR in Avoidable-Shock may reflect both apprehension and effort. One would expect from Watson and Baumal's hypothesis that EC subjects, who were in an incongruent situation in Avoidable-Shock, would be more anxious than IC subjects and therefore increase substantially in HR. Even if IC subjects, who were in a congruent situation in Avoidable-Shock, may have increased in HR as a result of expending effort in attempting to achieve control over the situation, one would expect that the increase in HR for EC subjects would at least approximate if not exceed the increase in HR for IC subjects. IC subjects, however, increased significantly more in HR than EC subjects ($F = 9.27$, $df = 1/60$, $p < .01$) which suggests that IC subjects may not only have expended more effort but were more aroused by threat than EC subjects.

measured by Rotter's Locus of Control Scale (1966). The data indicate that while IC and EC subjects do not differ in report of anxiety in stressful situations, IC subjects evidence significantly greater physiological response than do EC subjects.

A possible explanation for the difference between EC and IC subjects in response to stress is the following. EC subjects view forces outside themselves as being responsible for their fate and do not become very aroused when faced with threat because they resign themselves to the situation. IC subjects become highly aroused when threatened but they are reluctant to report anxiety, hence a significant difference in HR change scores but no significant difference in AACL change scores was found between IC and EC subjects across the threat conditions. The interpretation that IC subjects are defensive about reporting anxiety is supported by two research findings which indicate that IC subjects are more defensive and report less chronic anxiety than EC subjects. First, Tudor (1970) reports high correlations which indicate IC subjects scored significantly higher than EC subjects on both the MMPI Denial scale (Little & Fisher, 1958) and MMPI K scale. Second, Watson (1967) reports correlations between the Locus of Control scale and Manifest Anxiety Scale (Taylor, 1953) indicating that IC subjects report fewer characteristics of manifest anxiety than do EC subjects. The failure to confirm Lazarus' proposition then may be due to the possibility that the scale chosen to measure general beliefs about control over the environment also measures differences in the use of defensive maneuvers. Differences in the use of defensive maneuvers may have therefore obscured the expected relationships between general belief about control and response to threat.

LOCUS OF CONTROL AND PERFORMANCE.   To test the predicted relations between locus of control and performance, a 3 $\times$ 2 analysis of variance was performed on the digits backward data comparing Treatment conditions (Non-Stress, Avoidable-Shock, and Unavoidable-Shock) and Locus of Control (EC—IC).[5] In this analysis, the Locus of Control by Treatments interaction sum of squares with two degrees of freedom was partitioned into two components with one degree of freedom apiece. One component reflects the expectation that in the Avoidable-Shock condition the IC subjects would perform better than the EC subjects and that in the Unavoidable-Shock and Non-Stress conditions the EC subjects would perform better than the IC subjects. The other component of the interaction sum of squares is the remainder which is not accounted for by the predicted relations. The predicted interaction was significant ($F = 4.68$, $df = 1/60$, $p < .05$) while the remainder was not ($F = 1.28$, $df = 1/60$, ns). This result is consistent with previous findings (Rotter & Mulry, 1965; Watson & Baumal, 1967) and provides support for the hypothesis that subjects will perform better in situations in which there is congruence between their beliefs about locus of control in general and their beliefs about the locus of control in the particular situation in which they are working.

[5] See footnote 3 on page 364.

CONCLUSION

The results of this experiment reveal the following. 1) In general subjects found a threatening situation in which they had no control more anxiety provoking than one in which they had some control over the situation. 2) Subjects became more physiologically aroused (as measured by heart rate) when they thought they could exercise some control over the situation than when they thought they had no control. The greater arousal probably resulted from the effort subjects exerted in attempting to achieve control. 3) Subjects who characteristically see themselves as being in control of events in their lives (as measured by Rotter's Locus of Control scale) became more physiologically aroused under stress than those who see control of events in their lives as being external. This finding may be attributed to the possibility that the Locus of Control scale measures defensiveness. 4) Subjects performed better in situations in which there was congruence between their beliefs about locus of control in general and their beliefs about the locus of control in the specific situation in which they were working.

The results of this experiment suggest the following conclusions. 1) When investigating what effect control over a situation has on response to threat, it is necessary to consider the effects of various kinds and conditions of control. 2) The Locus of Control scale not only measures beliefs about control of events in a person's life but may also measure tendencies for use of defensive maneuvers. 3) The Locus of Control scale predicts task performance under conditions of certain reinforcement contingencies, but the data of this experiment offer no new evidence for the processes responsible.

SUMMARY

Lazarus proposes that the less control a person judges himself to have in a threatening situation, the more stressful it will be. Belief about control was manipulated by telling one group of subjects they could avoid shock by not making mistakes on a task and telling another there was no way of avoiding shock. Subjects in the latter group reported more anxiety but evidenced less physiological arousal than the former group. Lazarus also asserts that general beliefs about helplessness increase perception of threat. Contrary to expectation, external locus of control subjects (assumed to hold general feelings of helplessness) manifested less physiological arousal in stress than internal control subjects. Results congruent with previous findings were obtained between locus of control and task performance.

REFERENCES

Champion, R. A. Studies of experimentally induced disturbance. *Australian Journal of Psychology*, 1950, 2, 90–99.

Corah, N. L., & Boffa, J. Perceived control, self-observation, and response to aversive stimulation. *Journal of Personality and Social Psychology*, 1970, *16*, 1–4.

D'Amato, M. E., & Gumenik, W. E. Some effects of immediate versus randomly delayed shock on an instrumental response and cognitive processes. *Journal of Abnormal and Social Psychology*, 1960, *60*, 64–67.

Lacey, J. I. The evaluation of autonomic responses: Toward a general solution. *Annals of the New York Academy of Science*, 1956, *67*, 123–164.

Lazarus, R. S. *Psychological stress and the coping process.* New York: McGraw-Hill, 1966.

Little, K. B., & Fisher, J. Two new experimental scales of the MMPI. *Journal of Consulting Psychology*, 1958, *22*, 305–306.

McNemar, Q. *Psychological statistics.* (3rd ed.), New York: Wiley, 1962.

Pervin, L. A. The need to predict and control under conditions of threat. *Journal of Personality*, 1963, *31*, 570–587.

Rotter, J. Generalized expectancies for internal versus external control of reinforcement. *Psychological Monographs*, 1966, *80*(1, Whole No. 609).

Rotter, J., & Mulry, R. Internal versus external control of reinforcement and decision time. *Journal of Personality and Social Psychology*, 1965, *2*, 598–604.

Taylor, J. A. A personality scale of manifest anxiety. *Journal of Abnormal and Social Psychology*, 1953, *48*, 285–290.

Tudor, T. The concept of repression: The results of two experimental paradigms. Unpublished doctoral dissertation, University of Texas, 1970.

Watson, D. Relationship between locus of control and anxiety. *Journal of Personality and Social Psychology*, 1967, *6*, 91–92.

Watson, D., & Baumal, E. Effects of locus of control and expectation of future control upon present performance. *Journal of Personality and Social Psychology*, 1967, *6*, 212–215.

Wechsler, D. *Manual for the Wechsler Adult Intelligence Scale.* New York: Psychological Corp., 1955.

Wilder, J. Basimetric approach (law of initial value) to biological rhythms. *Annals of the New York Academy of Science*, 1962, *98*, 1211–1220.

Winer, B. J. *Statistical principles in experimental design.* New York: McGraw-Hill, 1962.

Zuckerman, M. The development of an affect adjective check list for the measurement of anxiety. *Journal of Consulting Psychology*, 1960, *24*, 457–462.

17.3 | FACTORS DETERMINING VICARIOUS EXTINCTION OF AVOIDANCE BEHAVIOR THROUGH SYMBOLIC MODELING*[,1]

Albert Bandura and Frances L. Menlove

It has been shown in a previous experiment (Bandura, Grusec, & Menlove, 1967) that avoidance behavior can be extinguished through observation of modeled approach responses without any adverse consequences accruing to the performing model. The basic mechanism underlying this phenomenon was assumed to involve vicarious extinction of mediating arousal reactions which motivate and exercise discriminative control over instrumental avoidance responsivity. The present study investigated variables that might be expected to facilitate vicarious extinction of conditioned emotionality by symbolic modeling procedures that lend themselves readily to psychotherapeutic applications.

The magnitude of vicarious extinction effects is likely to be determined, in part, by the number of modeling stimulus elements which are neutralized. That is, exposure to modeling displays depicting nonreinforced approach behavior by diverse models toward variant forms of the feared object should produce relatively thorough extinction of arousal reactions, and hence, extensive reduction in avoidance behavior. On the other hand, observers whose emotional responsiveness is extinguished to a restricted set of aversive modeling elements are apt to achieve weaker disinhibitory effects.

Under conditions where a series of aversive modeling stimuli is presented only once, certain observer characteristics might influence the extent to which emotional responses undergo extinction. Observers who are highly susceptible to emotional arousal would be inclined to respond to fear-provoking modeling stimuli with pronounced arousal reactions and might, therefore, show relatively strong resistance to vicarious extinction. In accord with evidence that high-anxious subjects do, in fact, show a slower rate of *direct* extinction than those who are relatively nonanxious (Spence & Farber, 1953), emotional proneness would be expected to serve as an additional determinant of the degree to which avoidance behavior is reduced through modeling procedures.

The above propositions were tested in an experiment involving vicarious extinction of avoidance behavior toward dogs. The modeling stimuli were presented in pictorial form because a secondary purpose of this program of research is to assess the therapeutic

* SOURCE: Bandura, A., & Menlove, F. L. Factors determining vicarious extinction of avoidance behavior through symbolic modeling. *Journal of Personality and Social Psychology*, 1968, 8, 99–108. Copyright 1968 by the American Psychological Association and reprinted by permission.

[1] This research was supported by Public Health Research Grant M-5162 from the National Institute of Mental Health.

The authors are grateful to Gail Brugler and Vonda Porter for their generous assistance in the conduct of this research.

efficacy of symbolic modeling techniques. One group of children observed a graduated series of films in which a fearless peer model exhibited progressively more intimate interactions with a dog. A second group of children was exposed to a similar sequence of graded modeling behavior, except that the films depicted a variety of models interacting positively with numerous dogs varying in size and fearsomeness. Children assigned to a control group were shown movies that contained no canine characters.

Evidence that deviant behavior can be modified by a particular method is of limited therapeutic significance unless it can be demonstrated that established response patterns generalize to stimuli beyond those encountered in treatment, and that induced changes endure after the therapeutic conditions have been discontinued. Therefore children were readministered tests for avoidance behavior toward different dogs following completion of the treatment program and again a month later. As a further test of the therapeutic efficacy of symbolic modeling, control children were administered the multiple-modeling treatment following completion of the main experiment.

It was predicted that both modeling approaches would reduce children's avoidance behavior, but that the diversified modeling procedure would achieve greater extinction effects. It was also hypothesized that low emotional proneness would favor relatively extensive vicarious extinction.

METHOD

SUBJECTS.   Thirty-two girls and 16 boys, varying in age from 3 to 5 years, participated in the experiment.

PRETREATMENT MEASUREMENT OF AVOIDANCE BEHAVIOR. All children enrolled in the Stanford Nursery School were administered a standardized test of avoidance behavior to identify those who were markedly fearful of dogs.

The test of strength of avoidance, which was identical to the one employed in an earlier experiment of vicarious extinction (Bandura et al., 1967), consisted of a graded series of 14 performance tasks in which the children were required to engage in increasingly intimate interactions with a dog. A female experimenter brought the children individually to the test room, where a brown cocker spaniel was confined in a playpen. In the initial set of tasks the children were asked, in the following order, to walk up to the playpen and look down at the dog, to touch her fur, and to pet her. Following the measurement of avoidance behavior to the dog in the protective enclosure, the children were requested to open a gate and remove the dog from the playpen, to walk the dog on a leash to a rug located at the end of the room, to remove the leash, and to turn the dog over and scratch her stomach. In subsequent items the children were asked to remain alone in the room with the animal and to feed her dog biscuits. The final and most difficult set of tasks required the children to climb into the playpen with the dog and, after having locked the gate, to pet her, scratch her stomach, and to remain alone in the room with the dog under the confining fear-arousing conditions.

The strength of the children's avoidance tendencies was reflected not only in the approach responses that they were able to perform, but also in the extent to which they could engage in the required behavior and the degree of vacillation, reluctance, and fearfulness that preceded and accompanied each approach response. Therefore, as in the previous study, children were credited 2 points if they fully executed a given task either spontaneously or willingly, and 1 point when they performed it minimally with considerable hesitancy and reluctance. Thus, for example, children who promptly stroked the dog's fur repeatedly when requested to do so received 2 points, whereas subjects who held back but then touched the dog's fur briefly obtained 1 point. In the item requiring the children to remain alone in the room with the dog, they received 2 points if they approached the animal and played with her, and 1 point if they were willing to remain in the room but avoided any contact with the dog. Similarly, in the feeding task children were credited 2 points if they fed the dog by hand, but a single point if they tossed the biscuits on the floor and thereby avoided contact with the animal. The maximum approach score that a child could obtain was 28 points.

Children were grouped into two levels of avoidance behavior and assigned on a stratified random basis to one of three treatment conditions. Although identical test procedures were employed, the children selected for the present experiment displayed considerably more severe phobic behavior than subjects in the first study, with approximately 70% receiving scores of only 7 points or lower.

APPRAISAL OF SUSCEPTIBILITY TO EMOTIONAL AROUSAL. In order to establish whether emotional proneness of observers is a significant determinant of vicarious extinction, mothers rated their children's fears on a questionnaire comprising 42 items, each represented by a five-interval scale describing increasing degrees of fearfulness. The items in this inventory were equally divided into the following three general categories: animal fears, interpersonal fears (e.g., physical aggression, peer rejection, separation, authority figures), and fear of inanimate objects or events (e.g., darkness, thunder, heights, unfamiliar places). In addition, the mothers were interviewed regarding the extent of their children's anxiety responsiveness, specific traumatic episodes that might have contributed to fearfulness of dogs, parental and sibling modeling of dog avoidance and apprehension, and the methods that the parents had employed in attempts to modify their children's avoidance behavior. The mothers of 14 dauntless children who, in the preliminary behavioral assessment, eagerly performed all the tasks in the avoidance test were also administered both the fear inventory and the interview to provide a basis for evaluating antecedent factors and the scope and magnitude of anxiety reactions exhibited by dog-phobic children.

TREATMENT CONDITIONS. In all treatment conditions children were shown a total of eight different 3-minute movies, two per day on 4 alternate days. Each session was attended by a group of three or four children who were seated facing a large screen in a semidarkened room. At periodic intervals during the movies the experimenter made simple descriptive comments about the events depicted on the screen in order to sustain a high level of attending behavior in the children.

Subjects who participated in the *single-model* condition observed a fearless 5-year-old male model display progressively bolder approach responses toward the cocker spaniel. The fear-arousing properties of the modeled displays were gradually increased from session to session by varying simultaneously the physical restraints on the dog and the directness and intimacy of the modeled approach responses (see Figure 3).

In the initial interaction sequences, for example, the model's behavior was limited to looking at the dog in the playpen and occasional petting. Subsequent movies showed the venturesome model walking the dog on the leash, grooming her, holding her in his arms, and serving her canine gourmet snacks. The feeding routines began with relatively nonthreatening amusing scenes in which the dog drank milk from a baby bottle and munched on a jumbo sucker held steadfastly by the model; later sequences depicted the dog vaulting toward hamburger patties and frankfurters that the model dangled in his hand. In the terminal set of movies the model climbed into the playpen with the dog where he petted her, fed her doggie bon bons and, as a finale, rested his head on his canine companion during a brief siesta in the overcrowded playpen. These modeled approach performances were interspersed with attention-sustaining segments in which the model attired both the dog and himself in colorful festive hats and oversized "Beatle" wigs.

Children assigned to the *multiple-model* condition observed, in addition to portions of each of the filmed sequences described above, several different girls and boys of varying ages interacting positively with sundry dogs ranging from diminutive breeds to larger specimens. The size and fearsomeness of this canine aggregation were progressively increased from small dogs that were nonthreatening in appearance to the more massive varieties. The films in the two modeling treatments were of equal length.

Children in the *control* condition were shown movies of Disneyland and Marineland for equivalent periods of time. This group provided a control for any direct extinction of avoidance behavior resulting from repeated behavioral assessments, as well as disinhibitory effects of extensive contact with amicable experimenters and increased familiarity with the person conducting the avoidance tests.

POSTTREATMENT MEASUREMENT OF AVOIDANCE BEHAVIOR.
On the day following completion of the treatment series, children were readministered the avoidance test consisting of the graded sequence of dog interaction tasks. In order to determine the generality of vicarious-extinction effects, half the children in each of the three conditions were tested initially with the experimental animal and then with an unfamiliar dog; the remaining children were presented with the two dogs in the reverse order. The testing sessions were separated by an interval of approximately 1 hour so as to minimize any transfer of emotional reactions provoked by one animal to the other.

The unfamiliar animal was a white mongrel, predominantly terrier, and of approximately the same size and activity level as the cocker spaniel. Both dogs elicited virtually identical approach responses from children tested in a separate study (Bandura et al., 1967) to evaluate the relative fearsomeness of the two animals.

FOLLOW-UP APPRAISAL.   A follow-up measurement of avoidance behavior was conducted approximately 1 month after the posttreatment assessment in order to determine the stability of modeling-induced changes. The children's responses were tested with the same performance tasks toward both animals, presented in the identical order.

After the experiment was completed, children who had participated in the modeling treatment were told that, while most dogs are friendly, before petting an unfamiliar dog they should ask the owner. This precautionary instruction was intended to forestall indiscriminate approach behavior toward strange dogs which might have unfriendly dispositions.

ASSESSMENT PROCEDURE.   The same female experimenter administered the pretreatment, posttreatment, and follow-up avoidance tests. To obviate any possible bias, the experimenter was furnished only minimal information about the study and had no knowledge of the conditions to which the children were assigned. The treatment and assessment phases of the study were further separated by the use of different rooms for each activity.

In order to provide an estimate of interscorer reliability, 25% of the behavioral tests, randomly selected from pretreatment, posttreatment, and follow-up phases of the project, were scored simultaneously but independently by another rater who observed the test sessions through a one-way mirror from an adjoining observation room. The two raters were in perfect agreement on 95% of the specific approach responses that were scored.

During the administration of each test item, the animals' activity was rated as either passive, moderately active, or vigorous, since the dogs' behavior may have some influence on the degree of avoidance exhibited by the children. These data disclosed that the dogs did not differ in their behavior either across experimental phases or between treatment conditions.

TREATED CONTROLS.   At the conclusion of the main experiment the efficacy of the symbolic modeling procedure was subjected to a further test based on an intrasubject design. Of the 16 children in the control group, 4 had left the San Francisco Bay area, but 12 were still enrolled in the nursery school. These children were shown the series of multiple-modeling films, after which they were administered the avoidance test with both animals.

RESULTS

Because the distributions of scores departed substantially from normality, and markedly so in the control group, the significances of differences were evaluated by non-parametric techniques.

Mann-Whitney U tests performed on approach scores for the total sample, and separately for each treatment condition at each phase of the experiment, disclosed no significant sex differences, and no effects due to the order in which the test animals were presented. Similarly, results of the Wilcoxon test reveal that children exhibited equivalent amounts of approach behavior toward the two dogs, indicating extensive generalization of vicarious extinction effects. The data were therefore pooled with respect to test order, dogs, and sex for evaluating the relative efficacy of the symbolic modeling treatments.

WITHIN-GROUP CHANGES IN APPROACH BEHAVIOR. The approach scores obtained by children in each of the three conditions at different phases of the experiment are shown graphically in Figure 1. A Friedman two-way analysis of variance disclosed highly significant phases effect ($\chi^2_r = 15.79$; $p < .001$). Separate comparisons of these scores for each condition by the Wilcoxon test indicate that the sizable phases effect is entirely due to the behavioral modifications produced by symbolic modeling. Control children showed no changes in their dog approach behavior during either posttreatment or follow-up assessments relative to their pretherapy behavior. By contrast, children in the single-modeling condition displayed significant increases in approach behavior after the completion of treatment ($T = 22$; $p < .01$), and 1 month later ($T = 9$; $p < .005$). Subjects who had observed the multiple modeling likewise achieved substantial gains as measured in posttreatment ($T = 13$; $p = .005$) and follow-up ($T = 6.5$; $p < .005$) phases of the project.

It is interesting to note that, whereas children in the single-modeling condition

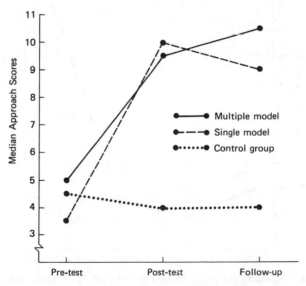

Figure 1 | MEDIAN APPROACH SCORES OBTAINED BY CHILDREN IN EACH OF THREE CONDITIONS AT DIFFERENT PHASES OF THE EXPERIMENT.

maintain their gains at the level achieved after treatment, those who had the benefit of multiple modeling became even bolder toward dogs in the follow-up period compared to their posttreatment behavior ($T = 10$; $p < .02$, two-tailed test).

DIFFERENCES BETWEEN CONDITIONS. The obtained differences between treatment conditions were not of statistically significant magnitude in the posttherapy assessment, although multiple-modeling subjects differed from the controls just short of the .05 significance level ($U = 87.5$).

A Kruskal-Wallis one-way analysis of variance computed on change scores between pretherapy and follow-up performances yielded a significant treatment effect ($H = 5.01$; $p < .05$). Comparisons between pairs of conditions, evaluated by the Mann-Whitney U test, showed that children who received the single-modeling ($U = 80.5$; $p < .05$) and the multiple-modeling ($U = 76$; $.025 < p < .05$) treatments achieved greater increases in approach behavior than did the controls. The two modeling conditions, however, did not differ from each other with respect to total approach scores.

TREATED CONTROLS. The approach scores obtained by control children in three pretherapy assessments and after they had participated in the multiple-modeling treatment are shown in Figure 2.

A Friedman two-way analysis of variance performed on these scores yielded a highly significant treatment effect ($\chi^2_r = 13.42$; $p < .01$). Wilcoxon tests computed between scores at different phases of the study revealed that the children's avoidance

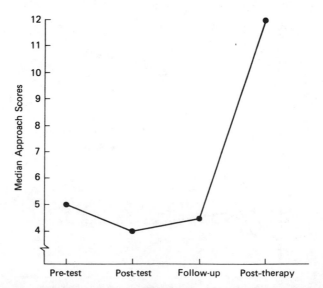

Figure 2 | MEDIAN APPROACH BEHAVIOR DISPLAYED TOWARD DOGS BY CONTROL CHILDREN DURING THREE TEST PERIODS AND AFTER THEY HAD RECEIVED THE MULTIPLE-MODELING TREATMENT.

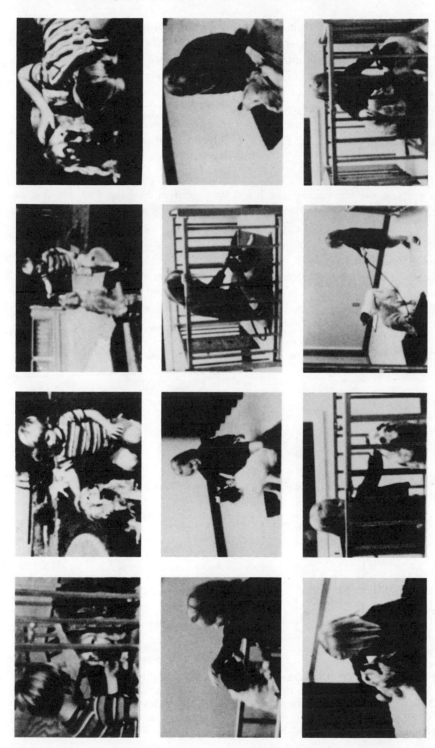

Figure 3 | PHOTOGRAPHS OF A CHILD WHO WAS APPREHENSIVE ABOUT DOGS ENGAGING IN FEARLESS INTERACTIONS WITH DOGS AFTER EXPOSURE TO THE SERIES OF THERAPEUTIC FILMS.

behavior remained unchanged throughout the control period. However, after exposure to multiple modeling of fearless behavior toward dogs, control children displayed a sharp increase in approach responses compared to their performance in the initial appraisal ($T = 3$; $p < .005$), the posttest ($T = 3$; $p < .005$), and the follow-up ($T = 0$; $p < .005$) assessments. The increased boldness of one of the control children who had been subsequently treated is portrayed in Figure 3. The top frames show the model's dauntless behavior; the lower frames depict the girl's fearless interaction with the animals, both of which she boldly corralled into the playpen after the formal test.

TERMINAL PERFORMANCES. The percentage of children in each condition who were able to perform the terminal approach task (i.e., remain confined with the dog in the playpen) is shown in Figure 4. Although the groups did not differ in this regard immediately after treatment, in the subsequent follow-up assessment twice as many children in the multiple-model condition completed the terminal task as did subjects in the other two groups ($\chi^2 = 2.73$; $p < .05$), which did not differ from each other.

The efficacy of the multiple-modeling treatment is further reflected in the substantial increase in terminal performances by treated controls from 17% in the follow-up phase to 50% after exposure to diversified symbolic modeling (Figure 4). Comparison

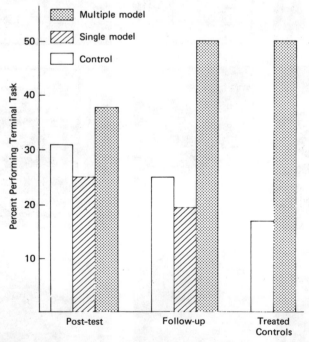

Figure 4 | PERCENTAGE OF CHILDREN IN EACH TREATMENT CONDITION WHO ACHIEVED TERMINAL APPROACH BEHAVIOR AFTER TREATMENT AND 1 MONTH LATER. (THE RECTANGLES ON THE RIGHT REPRESENT TERMINAL PERFORMANCES BY TREATED CONTROLS IN THE FOLLOW-UP PHASE AND FOLLOWING THE MULTIPLE-MODELING TREATMENT.)

of the incidence of terminal performances by children presented with the single-modeling display and all subjects who witnessed the multiple modeling shows the latter form of treatment to be superior ($\chi^2 = 2.98$; $p < .05$) for completely eliminating dog avoidance behavior.

VICARIOUS EXTINCTION AS A FUNCTION OF EMOTIONAL PRONE-NESS.

The rank-correlation coefficients between the various measures of avoidance behavior and emotional proneness are given in Table 1.

Severity of the children's avoidance behavior was unrelated to the degree to which they benefited from the modeling treatments; nor were the indexes of emotional proneness significant predictors of vicarious extinction for children who received the single-modeling treatment. On the other hand, in the multiple-modeling condition, which produced the more thorough extinction effects, susceptibility to emotional arousal was inversely related to degree of behavioral improvement. It is interesting to note, however, that emotional responsivity to potentially threatening interpersonal and inanimate events, rather than severity of animal fears, proved to be the better predictive measures.

ANTECEDENTS OF DOG-AVOIDANCE BEHAVIOR.

According to the questionnaire data the dog-phobic children have approximately twice as many animal fears ($t = 2.63$), which tend to be of greater intensity ($t = 1.99$), than children who displayed completely fearless behavior toward the test dog during the initial assessment.

Table 1 | DEGREE OF RELATIONSHIP BETWEEN DIFFERENT INDEXES OF EMOTIONAL PRONENESS AND VICARIOUS EXTINCTION

EMOTIONALITY VARIABLES	POSTTREATMENT CHANGE	FOLLOW-UP CHANGE
Single-modeling condition		
Total fears (inventory)	.09	.04
Animal	−.20	.06
Interpersonal	.04	−.09
Inanimate objects	.28	−.01
Total fears (interview)	.33	.41
Pretherapy avoidance behavior	.11	.18
Multiple-modeling condition		
Total fears (inventory)	−.61***	−.41*
Animal	−.30	−.21
Interpersonal	−.55**	−.26
Inanimate objects	−.58**	−.47**
Total fears (interview)	−.64***	−.48**
Pretherapy avoidance behavior	.37	.36

* $.05 < p < .10$.
** $p < .05$.
*** $p < .01$.

These two groups of children did not differ, however, with respect to their anxiety reactions to interpersonal and inanimate threats.

There is some evidence to suggest that parental modeling of fearful behavior is a significant contributory factor to children's fearfulness. Only one parent in the bold group reported any trepidation about dogs, whereas in 17 of the families of avoidant children one or both parents displayed such fears ($\chi^2 = 2.94$; $p < .05$). The data yielded no differences concerning peer modeling of dog-avoidance behavior and, although the incidence of specific traumatic episodes involving dogs was somewhat higher for fearful (35%) than bold children (21%), the groups did not differ significantly in this regard.

Perhaps the most interest finding in the interview data is that the majority of parents (56%) made no attempts to overcome their children's fears. Those who periodically tried remedial measures favored either explanations and verbal reassurances (12%), enforced contact with dogs (19%), or modeling of fearlessness (14%). However, the extinction and modeling endeavors rarely involved carefully graded presentations of threatening stimuli without which these techniques are not only likely to be ineffective, but may actually exacerbate anxiety reactions. A not uncommon domestic modeling scene is one in which a parent is busily petting a dog that is jumping about while simultaneously pressuring the child, who is clinging fearfully, to touch the bounding animal. By contrast, the present experiment, in addition to utilizing the principle of gradualism to reduce possible arousal of anxiety, involved concentrated exposures to modeling displays under protected observation conditions, and extensive variation of model characteristics, intimacy of approach behavior, and aversive properties of the feared object. Had the modeling sequences been presented in a widely dispersed and haphazard fashion and restricted to the more reserved petting responses by adults (whom the children are likely to discriminate as better able to protect themselves), the vicarious extinction outcomes might have been relatively weak and unpredictable.

DISCUSSION

The therapeutic effects of symbolic modeling appear sufficiently promising to warrant further development of this treatment approach. Highly fearful children who observed approach behavior modeled without any adverse consequences to the performer subsequently displayed stable reductions in avoidance behavior. Moreover, the extinction effects transferred beyond the stimulus objects encountered in treatment.

The vicarious extinction outcomes produced by the single symbolic model in this study appear to be somewhat weaker than earlier results with a subgroup of equally avoidant children who viewed live demonstrations of essentially the same approach responses by the same model. Although the single-modeling treatment effected reductions in children's avoidance responses, it did not sufficiently weaken their fears to enable them to carry out the threatening terminal approach behavior. There is evidence, however, that the diminished efficacy of symbolic modeling cues can be offset by a broader sampling of models and aversive stimulus objects. Children who received the diverse modeling treatment not only showed continued improvement in approach behavior, but also achieved terminal performances at rates comparable to equally avoidant children who, in the previous experiment, observed fearless behavior performed by a single real-life model.

The finding that high emotional proneness attenuates vicarious extinction indicates that modeling procedures must be further modified or supplemented with additional techniques to effect substantial reduction of avoidance tendencies in subjects who display a generalized pattern of anxiety. Such persons are unlikely to experience marked decrements in emotional responsiveness on the basis of a single exposure to a graded series of modeling situations. In a current adaptation of symbolic modeling for the treatment of phobias in adults, three factors have, therefore, been incorporated to further increase the therapeutic power of this method. First, clients are taught to induce and maintain anxiety-inhibiting relaxation throughout the period of exposure. Second, the rate of presentation of modeling stimuli is controlled by the client. Thus, if a particular modeling situation proves to be emotion-provoking the client reviews the threatening scene repeatedly until it is completely neutralized before proceeding to the next item in the graduated sequence. A self-regulated modeling treatment should permit greater control over extinction outcomes. Finally, clients who fail to attain terminal behavior are administered a powerful live-modeling–guided-participation form of treatment in which, after observing the most fear-provoking behavior repeatedly modeled without any adverse consequences, clients are aided through demonstration to perform progressively more threatening responses toward actual feared objects.

The phenomenon of vicarious extinction not only has important clinical implications, but it also raises interesting theoretical questions concerning possible mediational mechanisms governing the process of extinction itself. It is evident from results of both the present and the earlier study that performance of an overt response is not essential for its extinction. These findings question the generality of theoretical conceptualizations of extinction that rely heavily upon cognitive or physiological effects assumed to result from repeated evocation of effortful responses without reinforcement.

Both nonresponse extinction paradigms and explanations of vicarious effects (Bandura, 1965) are compatible with the dual-process theory of avoidance behavior. According to this view stimuli acquire, through their temporal conjunction with aversive experiences, the capacity to produce arousal reactions which have both central and autonomic components. It is further assumed that instrumental avoidance responses become partly conditioned to arousal-correlated stimuli. Suggestive evidence that arousal mediators may exercise discriminative control over avoidance behavior is provided by Solomon and Turner (1962). Animals first learned to make an avoidance response to a light stimulus. They were then skeletally immobilized by curare, and shock was paired with one tone while a contrasting tone was never associated with aversive stimulation. In subsequent tests the animals displayed the same degree of avoidance in response to the negatively valenced tone and the light, both of which evoked common arousal reactions, whereas avoidance responses rarely occurred to the neutral tone. Rescorla and Solomon (1967) provide additional evidence that classically conditioned effects exert mediating control over instrumentally learned behavior. The transfer is primarily achieved through central mechanisms rather than at the autonomic system level as is commonly assumed.

If conditioned arousal reactions are extinguished, both the motivation and internal controlling stimuli for avoidance responses are thus removed. It has been shown in a previous experiment (Bandura & Rosenthal, 1966) that conditioned emotional reactivity can be extinguished on a vicarious basis by having observers witness a model encounter aversive stimuli without experiencing any adverse consequences. A systematic test of this mediational theory of vicarious extinction would require simultaneous recording of autonomic and evoked electroencephalographic correlates of observational inputs involving modeled approach behavior toward feared objects.

Results of studies designed to extinguish naturalistically created avoidance behavior have bearing on another important issue in learning theory. Recent investigations of symbolic control of classical conditioning phenomena (Chatterjee & Eriksen, 1962; Fuhrer & Baer, 1965; Grings, 1965) demonstrate that only subjects who recognize the contingency between conditioned and unconditioned stimuli display autonomic conditioning. Moreover, subjects who are informed that the conditioned stimulus will no longer be accompanied by aversive stimulation show a prompt and virtually complete loss of emotional responses without experiencing any nonreinforced presentations of the conditioned stimulus.

The above findings provide strong support for the view that emotional conditioning and extinction, rather than representing a simple process in which external stimuli are directly and automatically connected to overt responses, are mediated through symbolic activities. However, precipitous extinction of laboratory-induced fears through informational means contrasts sharply with evidence of weak cognitive control of fears established under naturalistic conditions. Dog-avoidance responses were unaffected by informing children prior to the behavioral tests that the dogs were friendly and harmless. In fact, an initial procedure in which dog scenes were interspersed in absorbing cartoons had to be abandoned because the pictorial animals, although incapable of biting or otherwise hurting observers, nevertheless evoked strong aversive reactions so that many children promptly turned away from the screen whenever the canine characters appeared. Severe snake phobics likewise experience considerable emotional disturbance at the sight of a picture of a reptile while acknowledging that the agitation is groundless, since pictorial snakes cannot possibly inflict any injury. In the latter cases conditioned emotional responses are almost completely dissociated from accompanying cognitions. It would appear that principles regarding avoidance behavior established solely on the basis of responses created under laboratory conditions may, in some cases, have limited applicability to naturalistic phenomena the investigations are intended to elucidate.

SUMMARY

The present study was primarily designed to test the hypothesis that magnitude of vicarious extinction is partly governed by the diversity of aversive modeling stimuli which are neutralized, and by observers' susceptibility to emotional arousal. One group of children, who were markedly fearful of dogs, observed a graduated series of films in which a model displayed progressively more intimate interactions with a single dog. A second group of children was exposed to a similar set of graded films depicting a variety of models interacting nonanxiously with numerous dogs varying in size and fearsomeness, while a control group was shown movies containing no animals. Both the single-modeling and multiple-modeling treatments effected significant reductions in children's avoidance behavior, but only the multiple-modeling treatment weakened their fears sufficiently to enable them to perform potentially threatening interactions with dogs. Emotional proneness and degree of vicarious extinction were found to be unrelated in the single-model condition and negatively correlated for children who received the more powerful multiple-modeling treatment.

REFERENCES

Bandura, A. Vicarious processes: A case of no-trial learning. In L. Berkowitz (Ed.), *Advances in experimental social psychology*. Vol. 2. New York: Academic Press, 1965. Pp. 1–55.

Bandura, A., Grusec, J. E., & Menlove, F. L. Vicarious extinction of avoidance behavior. *Journal of Personality and Social Psychology*, 1967, 5, 16–23.

Bandura, A., & Rosenthal, T. L. Vicarious classical conditioning as a function of arousal level. *Journal of Personality and Social Psychology*, 1966, 3, 54–62.

Chatterjee, B., & Eriksen, C. W. Cognitive factors in heart-rate conditioning. *Journal of Experimental Psychology*, 1962, 64, 272–279.

Fuhrer, M. J., & Baer, P. E. Differential classical conditioning: Verbalization of stimulus contingencies. *Science*, 1965, 150, 1479–1481.

Grings, W. W. Verbal-perceptual factors in the conditioning of autonomic responses. In W. F. Prokasy (Ed.), *Classical conditioning: A symposium*. New York: Appleton, 1965. Pp. 71–89.

Rescorla, R. A., & Solomon, R. L. Two-process learning theory: Relationships between Pavlovian conditioning and instrumental learning. *Psychological Review*, 1967, 74, 151–182.

Solomon, R. L., & Turner, L. H. Discriminative classical conditioning in dogs paralyzed by curare can later control discriminative avoidance responses in the normal state. *Psychological Review*, 1962, 69, 202–219.

Spence, K. W., & Farber, I. E. Conditioning and extinction as a function of anxiety. *Journal of Experimental Psychology*, 1953, 45, 116–119.

18 | Defense

18.1 | REPRESSION OR INTERFERENCE? A FURTHER INVESTIGATION*[1]

David S. Holmes

The research strategy that has been most influential in offering support for the concept of repression was developed by Zeller (1950a). This approach has three major parts. First, experimental and control subjects learn and have their retention tested for a list of words. On this test, no differences are expected. Second, the experimental subjects are "ego threatened" (subjects are forced to fail on another task or are given negative personality feedback), while control subjects are not threatened. Then both groups are given a second recall test for the words. Since it is assumed that the anxiety introduced by the threat procedure will generalize to the words because they were learned in the same situation, and since it is also assumed that this anxiety will result in repression, it is predicted that on the second recall test the performance of the experimental subjects will be below that of the control subjects. Third, in an attempt to "lift the repression," the threat is eliminated (subjects are allowed to succeed or are debriefed), and the subjects are then given a third recall test on which it is predicted that there will be no differences in recall between the groups. Using this approach, numerous investigators have found results consistent with the predictions, and these results have been cited as empirical evidence for the existence of repression (Aborn, 1953; Flavell, 1955; Merrill, 1954; Penn, 1964; Truax, 1957; Worchell, 1955; Zeller, 1950b, 1951).

Recently, the interpretation of these findings as evidence for repression has been called into question by two investigations. D'Zurilla (1965) carried out postexperimental interviews with subjects who had participated in an experiment similar to the one discussed above and, contrary to what would be expected on the basis of repression, found that 62% of the experimental subjects thought about things related to the threatening

* SOURCE: Holmes, D. S. Repression or interference? A further investigation. *Journal of Personality and Social Psychology*, 1972, 22, 163–170. Copyright 1972 by the American Psychological Association and reprinted by permission.

[1] This investigation was supported by United States Public Health Service Grant 1 R01 MH20819-01.

task, while only 24% of the control subjects thought about things related to their task; that is, the experimental subjects attended to rather than avoided the threat. D'Zurilla went on to point out that the additional thoughts of the experimental subjects were irrelevant to the task of recalling the words, and he, therefore, speculated that the "increase in amount of conflicting cognitive events could have reduced the efficiency of recall [p. 256]" in the experimental group. In other words, he suggested that the reduced recall following ego threat might be due to response competition rather than to repression.

Holmes and Schallow (1969) attempted to experimentally test the question of whether reduced recall following ego threat was due to repression or response competition. In addition to the groups that received ego-threatening (experimental) or no (control) feedback, these investigators employed a third group which was shown a neutral movie (interference). After the experimental manipulation (negative feedback, no feedback, interfering movie), all of the subjects were tested for their retention of some previously learned words. They were then debriefed and tested again for retention. Consistent with the predictions based on the interference theory, the investigators found that while there were no differences among the groups prior to the experimental manipulation, after the manipulation, the control group performed significantly better than either the ego-threat or interference groups and, of most importance, that there were no differences between the performance of the ego-threat or interference groups. After the debriefing, which redirected the subjects' attention to the words, the recall test again indicated no differences between any of the groups. In reviewing their results, Holmes and Schallow (1969) pointed out that:

> If only the curves of the control and ego-threat groups are considered, the results of the present study can be viewed as a replication of the earlier work in which it was concluded that the ego threat had resulted in repression. However, the fact that in the present study the performance of the interference group differed from the control group but did not differ from the ego-threat group suggests that previous interpretations of differences between ego-threat and control groups as being due to repression could be called into serious question. . . . While it is impossible to prove the null hypothesis that the same process was operating in both the ego-threat and interference conditions, the inability to generate differential predictions which are supported by the data is certainly suggestive. It might, therefore, be that response competition rather than repression is responsible for the lowered recall performance found in the ego-threat condition of experiments of this type [pp. 150–151].

As the authors indicated, the fact that the interference and ego-threat groups performed in the same way does not necessarily prove that the same process was operating in both situations. This criticism is especially relevant since in their experiment the two hypothesized interferences were very different in origin and nature; that is, in the interference condition, the interference stemmed entirely from an extrinsic source (the movie) and was impersonal, while the hypothesized interference in the ego-threat condition was intrinsic to the individual (concerns about adjustment) and highly personal.

These are important differences, and they increase the conceptual distance between the conditions that the authors wanted to suggest as equivalent. If the interference that was hypothesized to be present in the two conditions had been more similar in source and nature, the authors would have been in a better position to suggest that repression was actually due to interference and response competition.

The present experiment was carried out in an attempt to overcome the problems noted above. Similar to the earlier experiment, the subjects in the control condition were given neutral feedback, while the subjects in one experimental condition were given negative "ego-threatening" personality feedback. In contrast to the previous work, however, in the second experimental group, an attempt was made to introduce interference by giving the subjects positive "ego-enhancing" personality feedback.

In this experiment the only difference between the ego-threatening and interference conditions was the fact that in one case the feedback was ego threatening, while in the other it was ego enhancing. This difference is, of course, crucial for the different predictions stemming from the interference and the repression theories. Interference theory ignores the threat versus enhancing nature of the feedback and suggests that the same type of interference (thoughts about the feedback) would be elicited and, therefore, would affect recall in both experimental conditions. Consequently, this position would not predict a difference in recall performance between the two experimental groups. Furthermore, since it was expected that less interference would be elicited in the control condition than in either of the experimental conditions, interference theory would predict that after the experimental manipulation, the recall performance of the control subjects would be superior to that of the experimental subjects. On the other hand, repression theory emphasizes the influence of ego threat and predicts a reduced recall only for those subjects exposed to an ego threat. That is, the repression position would predict that the performances of the subjects in the control and ego-enhancement conditions would be similar and that the performance of the subjects in these conditions would be superior to that of subjects in the ego-threat condition. These are the differential predictions that were under investigation in the present experiment.

Interestingly enough, with regard to postdebriefing performance, both theories predict an improvement. In the case of interference theory, the improvement would stem from the fact that after being debriefed, the subjects would no longer be distracted by the thoughts and concerns elicited by the feedbacks, while according to repression theory the improvement would stem from a return of the repressed made possible by the elimination of the anxiety.

METHOD

SUBJECTS.   Subjects in this experiment were 36 women from introductory psychology classes at the University of Texas at Austin. Subjects were run in groups of 2, and each subject was assigned to one of three conditions. During the experiment, each subject was seated in a chair facing a projection screen and was separated by a partition from the other subject. Attached to the arm of the subject's chair was a "response panel" which contained one green signal light and four switches labeled A, B, C, and D. The experimenter sat behind the subjects at a screened-off control center where he controlled the signal light and recorded which switches were thrown by the subjects.

PROCEDURE.   When the subjects arrived at the laboratory, they were assigned a seat and then told that the experiment would be run completely by a computer located in an adjoining room. The experimenter then threw a switch and took his place at the control center. Throwing the switch activated a concealed tape recorder which was supposedly running in conjunction with the computer and which was used to present all of the instructions. The subjects were first presented with a list of 40 words that was read twice. It was pointed out that these words would be used in a later part of the experiment and that at this point the subjects should "just listen to the words and become familiar with them." The words that were presented were the same ones used earlier by Holmes and Schallow (1969, p. 147, Table 1). After the words had been read, the subjects were asked to write down as many of the words as they could remember on a word familiarity check form. Supposedly, this was done as a check on their familiarity with the words, but actually it provided the premanipulation measure of recall for the words. After 2 minutes, the forms were collected, and the tape-recorded instructions went on to explain that the experiment in which the subjects were participating was a test "of a very sensitive and accurate test of personality . . . which can be used to predict future adjustment and performance in college women" and which was being adapted for use at the university. It was explained to the subjects that "the famous Rorschach Psychodiagnostic Inkblots" would be projected on the screen one by one, and that while each blot was on the screen, four nouns would be read aloud to them. The task of each subject was to decide which of the four nouns best described the blot she was looking at and to indicate her choice by throwing the appropriate switch on her response panel. They were led to believe that this would register their responses in the computer, which would then score the responses and give each subject feedback concerning each of her responses. Feedback was provided via the light on the response panel which flashed on and off one, two, or three times after the subject made each response. Each subject was told to count the flashes and record the number on the score sheet she had been given. The score sheets supposedly were going to be collected at the end of the session so that the members of the Psychology Department could evaluate the subjects' performance and determine whether the subjects "should receive future attention of any kind." Between recording their scores and being presented with the next inkblot, the subjects were told to use the number of flashes they had received as feedback after their preceding respones to look up the meaning of that response in the computer code books that they had been given. Each computer code book contained three response interpretations for each blot; one ego enhancing, one ego threatening, and one neutral. Each interpretation was printed on a separate page, and the pages were official-looking computer printouts. Each interpretation page had a tab on it identifying the blot and the number of flashes with which that interpretation was associated. Three different books were constructed so that the same number of flashes would result in three different feedbacks, depending on which book was being used. Consequently, in any one experimental session, the subjects in different conditions could be run despite the fact that the apparatus gave all subjects the same number of flashes for feedback. Subjects in the threat and enhancement conditions received negative or positive feedback after responding to Blots II, III, V, VI, VIII, and X. For example, after Blot VI, in the enhancement group, the subjects were informed that

> This response is indicative of outstanding leadership abilities. The leadership ability should enable this woman to assume positions of responsibility in large groups as well as in interpersonal relationships, and she should meet with considerable success.

After Blot X, they were informed that

> This response indicates that the individual is exceptionally well adjusted. This level of adjustment will enable her to function at a personal and academic level well above that of the average college student.

On the other hand, after Blot VI, the subjects in the threat group were informed that

> This response indicates the possibility that the individual has some under-lying personality problems. Either at the present time or in the near future this underlying maladjustment could cause serious difficulties for this person in her interpersonal relations with friends and superiors.

After Blot X, they were informed that "This response is suggestive of a high degree of pathology, and corrective steps must be considered." After responding to these blots, the subjects in the neutral condition received feedback indicating that their response had no particular significance. Feedback to all subjects after responding to Blots IV, VII, and IX indicated that "This response is consistent with previous responses thus confirming previous feedback. This response adds no new informa-tion." Subjects were not given feedback after responding to the first blot since the computer supposedly did not yet have enough information.

It is important to note that the words offered as response possibilities for the Rorschach inkblots were the same as those presented on the list at the beginning of the experiment and for which recall was tested. In this way, threat was directly associated with the material that was to be recalled.

After the subjects had looked up the interpretation of their last response, the score sheets and the computer code books were collected, and then the subjects were given the second 2-minute recall test using a word familiarity check form. This provided the measure of the subjects' postmanipulation recall for the words. After this recall test, the tape-recorded voice of the experimenter completely debriefed the subjects concerning the experimental manipulations. The subjects were then given a final 2-minute recall test using a word familiarity check form, and this provided the postdebriefing recall measure.

In summary, the procedure was as follows: learning task for 40 words; pre-treatment recall test for words (Test 1); Rorschach administration (previously learned 40 words as response alternatives) with subjects getting either ego-threatening, ego-enhancing, or neutral feedback; posttreatment recall test for words (Test 2); debriefing; postdebriefing recall test for words (Test 3). It should be noted that the procedure was almost completely automated and that the subjects were simultaneously run in different conditions, therefore reducing or eliminating any subtle experimenter effects. The high degree of automation in addition to the large amount of bogus technical information that the subjects were given concerning the test, its scoring, and the built-in safeguards to assure the reliability and validity of the feedback served to make the deceptions very believable.

RESULTS

The manipulations used in this experiment were evidently quite credible since only one subject (enhancement condition) indicated that she did not believe the instructions. The data from this subject and those of one other subject in the enhancement condition who did not follow the instructions were not used in the analyses. The recall data are presented graphically in Figure 1.

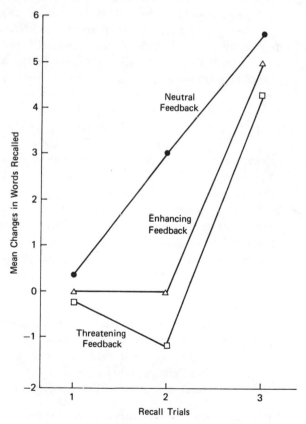

Figure 1 | MEAN CHANGES IN WORDS RECALLED BY THE SUBJECTS IN THE EGO-THREATENING, EGO-ENHANCING, AND NEUTRAL FEEDBACK CONDITIONS. (SINCE CHANGE SCORES WERE PLOTTED IN THIS FIGURE, ALL SCORES AT POINT 1 ARE ACTUALLY 0 AND WERE INCLUDED ONLY AS A REFERENCE POINT.)

EFFECT OF DIFFERENTIAL FEEDBACK ON RECALL.   A between–within analysis of variance comparing the recall performance of the three groups (neutral, enhancing, threatening) over the three trials (Recall Tests 1, 2, and 3) was carried out on the data. This analysis indicated that the groups effect was not significant ($F = .97$, $df = 2/31$), that the trials effect was significant ($F = 37.94$, $df = 2/62$, $p < .001$), and that the Groups $\times$ Trials interaction approached significance ($F = 2.20$, $df = 4/62$, $p = .079$). The important question to be answered, however, was which of the two rival hypotheses (i.e., repression or interference) was best able to account for the patterning of results. The repression hypothesis predicted that on the second trial the neutral and the enhancement groups would perform alike and better than the threat group. On the other hand, the interference hypothesis predicted that on the second trial the neutral group would perform better than the threat and enhancement groups and that these latter two groups would perform alike. Neither the repression nor interference hypothesis predicted differences between any of the groups on Trials 1 (before manipulation) or 3 (after debriefing). In other words, the hypotheses differed concerning whether on Trial 2 the enhancement group would perform like the neutral group (repression hypothesis) or whether it would perform like the threat group (interference hypothesis). The following procedure was used to statistically evaluate the rival hypotheses. The sum of squares for the Groups $\times$ Trials interaction (with 4 degrees of freedom) was partitioned into two components. One component (with 1 degree of freedom) reflected the extent to which the obtained means were congruent with what was expected from the particular hypothesis in question, namely, interference or repression. The other component (with 3 degrees of freedom) was the remainder sum of squares for the interaction not accounted for by the predicted relationships (after Winer, 1962, p. 65). The results indicated that the component of the Groups $\times$ Trials interaction predicted by the interference hypothesis was significant at the .01 level of confidence ($F = 7.27$, $df = 1/62$), while the F for the remainder was less than one and not significant ($F = .51$, $df = 3/62$). On the other hand, the component of the Groups $\times$ Trials interaction predicted by the repression hypothesis was significant at only the .05 level of confidence ($F = 4.03$, $df = 1/62$), while the F for the remainder was greater than one ($F = 1.59$, $df = 3/62$, $p < .25$). To decide how well data can be explained by a particular hypothesis, one should know how much of the data *can* be accounted for (the predicted component) as well as how much of the data *cannot* be accounted for (the remainder component). On both counts, the interference hypothesis was superior.[2]

That the performance of the groups conformed to what was expected by the interference hypothesis is further corroborated by the following subanalyses of the data. Between Recall Trials 1 and 2, the neutral group showed greater improvement in recall than either the enhancement or threat groups ($F = 2.79$, $df = 1/20$, $p = .107$; $F = 18.84$, $df = 1/22$, $p < .001$). Looked at in another way, the subjects in the neutral group

---

[2] It should be noted that these two sets of comparisons are not orthogonal and that the only difference between the two components revolves around one mean. Therefore, in view of that and the fact that the component of the interaction predicted by interference was significant at the .01 level, it is not surprising that the component of the interaction predicted by repression was significant at the .05 level.

improved in performance ($F = 66.00$, $df = 1/11$, $p < .001$), while those in the enhancement group remained the same, and those in the threat group deteriorated somewhat ($F = 1.73$, $df = 1/11$, $p = .213$). The fact that the subjects in the enhancement and threat groups performed in essentially the same manner and differed from the subjects in the neutral group could lead to the conclusion that feedback, irrespective of whether it was very positive or very negative, had the effect of interfering with recall performance, and that it was this interference rather than repression that resulted in the reduced level of recall.

One alternative hypothesis must be examined, however. It may be that the reduced recall on Trial 2 evidence by the subjects in the threat group was due to repression, while the reduced recall on Trial 2 evidenced by the subjects in the enhancement group was due to interference. That is, while the resulting overall performances were the same, the underlying processes may have been different. If repression was the underlying process, it would be expected that the reduced recall in the threat group resulted from a large decrement in recall of *response words* used by the subjects (i.e., those that the subjects selected as responses) because these were the words directly associated with threatening feedback. It would also be expected that there would be only a minimal decrement in the recall of the words that were not used as responses (i.e., those that were not selected) because these were not associated with threatening feedback. On the other hand, if interference were the underlying process, it would be expected that the reduced recall in the threat group resulted from a recall decrement distributed across all of the words (i.e., those that were and were not selected as responses and, consequently, were and were not associated with threatening feedback) because interference would influence all words equally. To test these alternative predictions, the proportions of response words recalled were compared across the three trials for the three groups. (Each subject's score was the number of her response words recalled on a trial divided by the total number of words that she recalled on that trial.) Data from the neutral and enhancement groups were used for comparison since it is clear that repression was not occurring in these groups. The mean proportions are presented in Table 1. Inspection and analysis of these data did not suggest that on Test 2 the subjects in the threat group recalled proportionally fewer response words than did the subjects in the other groups ($F = .22$, $df = 2/31$). Furthermore, a between–within analysis of variance comparing the three groups across the three tests did not reveal the interaction predicted on the basis of repression ($F = .25$, $df = 4/62$; that is, the subjects in the threat group did not evidence a relative reduction in their recall of

Table 1 | MEAN PROPORTIONS OF RESPONSE WORDS RECALLED

GROUP	TEST 1	TEST 2	TEST 3
Neutral	24	32	34
Enhancement	25	35	33
Threat	23	35	34

response words on Trial 2. With regard to this latter analysis, it might be noted that there was not a significant groups effect ($F = .92$, $df = 2/31$), but there was a significant trials effect ($F = 16.53$, $df = 2/62$, $p < .001$) which was due to the fact that in each case after words were used as responses (i.e., between Trials 1 and 2), the degree to which they were recalled improved relative to nonresponse words—a finding that would be expected on the basis of the increased attention that they had received as a function of being used as responses. In summary of these analyses, it is clear that no evidence was found for the predictions based on the theory of repression, and it seems reasonable to conclude that the reduced recall in both the enhancement and threat groups was due to interference caused by thoughts elicited by the feedback.

EFFECT OF DEBRIEFING ON RECALL.   A between–within analysis of variance comparing the performance of the three groups over the second and third recall trials revealed a strong trend in the direction of the predicted interaction ($F = 2.21$, $df = 2/31$, $p = .125$). Nonorthogonal analyses that were carried out to dscribe this interaction indicated that the subjects in the enhancement and threat groups evidenced about the same amount of improvement between the second and third trials ($F = .12$, $df = 1/20$, $p = .725$), while both of these groups tended to show greater improvements in performance than did the neutral feedback group ($F = 2.39$, $df = 1/20$, $p = .135$; $F = 3.58$, $df = 1/22$, $p = .069$). Since the enhancement group evidenced the same amount of improvement as the threat group, and since there was no evidence that repression was occurring in the threat group on Trial 2, it does not seem justified to conclude that this improvement in performance was due to a "return of the repressed," as it is usually interpreted. Rather, it seems that the general improvement in each of the three groups between Trials 2 and 3 was due to greater attention to the recall task after the debriefing which eliminated thoughts elicited by the previous manipulation and made the task more salient. The greater improvement in the threat and enhancement groups as compared to the neutral group occurred because the subjects in these groups were initially (Trial 2) more distracted and had lower levels of performance, and, therefore, the redirection of their attention had more impact both on their attention and on their subsequent performance. These findings are consistent with the interference explanation and inconsistent with the return-of-the-repressed explanation.

DISCUSSION

From the preceding results it seems clear that the presentation of salient feedback concerning the subject's personality interfered with recall performance on what seemed to the subject to be an unrelated task. Of most importance, however, is the fact that the effect was found regardless of whether the feedback was ego enhancing or ego threatening. The fact that ego-enhancing feedback had essentially the same effect as ego-threatening feedback raises serious questions concerning the interpretation used by many authors that the reduced recall after threatening feedback is due to repression. Similarly, it seems doubtful that the postdebriefing improvement in recall performance that has been noted by many investigators can be attributed to a return of the repressed. The conclusion that postdebriefing improvement cannot be attributed to a return of the repressed stems from the indication of the present experiment that repression was not occurring in the first place and from the finding that the same effect was noted in the ego-enhancing group in which there was no reason to expect repression, much less a return of the repressed.

The present results suggest that the recall decrements found in this experiment and in others of this type were due to problems with retrieval from long-term memory and that these problems were caused by attentional factors. More specifically, because the subjects were able to overcome the earlier recall deficit when their attention was focused on the critical material (i.e., after the debriefing), it must be concluded that the earlier recall deficit was due to poor retrieval of learned material stored in long-term memory. The poor retrieval apparently resulted from the subjects' attention to other (interfering) material. Interestingly enough, the attention-interference explanation is consistent with the results of Aborn (1953), who reported that when subjects were given a set to learn rather than incidental learning instructions, the recall decrement usually attributed to repression did not materialize. That is, when the subjects' set focused their attention on the critical material, there was no decrease in the recall, despite the presence of threat.

It should be noted that the present research is not the first instance in which the interference hypothesis has provided the most viable explanation for a performance deficit associated with personality factors. In their extensive reviews of the research on the performance deficit usually associated with schizophrenia, Buss and Lang (1965) and Lang and Buss (1965) concluded that interference was probably responsible for this deficit. It should be noted that these authors also pointed out that when the schizophrenics' attention and sets were properly focused and maintained, the deficit was eliminated. This effect is not dissimilar from the effect found in the present experiment when the subjects were debriefed and, as a result, had their attentions redirected. What is important here is not that interference impairs performance, because that effect has been known for a long time; what is important is the very strong possibility that the recall deficit that was previously thought to stem from repression is, in fact, a function of interference. This interpretation of the effects may find applicability beyond the research strategy considered in this paper.

It might be suggested that polarizing the question as "repression or interference" is inappropriate and that it would be more constructive to conceive of interference as the process by which repression occurs. With regard to this, however, it should be pointed out that the concept of repression already implies a process, and that process is very different from the interference process. Most important in this regard, however, is the fact that the unconscious plays a crucial role in the process traditionally associated with the process of repression, while it plays no role whatsoever in the interference process discussed here. This difference would result in widely divergent prescriptions for dealing with material that has been "repressed." In view of the theoretical confusions and conflicting implications that would result from the synthesis of these concepts, it seems desirable to maintain a clear distinction between them.

In reviewing the threat and enhancing feedback conditions employed in this experiment, it is important to note that in both cases the feedbacks were highly personal and that in both cases the interference that was hypothesized to result from the feedbacks (thoughts about the feedbacks) was produced by the subjects themselves. By using conditions that were so similar, the conceptual distance between the conditions was reduced over what it was in the previous work (Holmes & Schallow, 1969), thus making it easier to suggest that the same process was operating in both conditions when the groups in these conditions evidenced similar performances. Despite this, however, it still must be pointed out that it is impossible to prove the null hypothesis, and, therefore, the fact that the threat and enhancement groups performed the same does not necessarily prove that repression as it is traditionally conceived of was not occurring in the threat group. On the other hand, of course, neither can it be proved that interference was not taking place in the threat group. In considering the alternatives, it seems to the present author that parsimony as well as the weight of experimental evidence is in favor of the interference explanation. Independent of what actually was or was not occurring, and apart from theoretical speculations generated by this research, it must definitely be concluded that because of the alternative explanations for the data, Zeller's (1950a) paradigm cannot be used to provide evidence for the concept of repression. This leaves the concept of repression in a precarious position with respect to the necessary experimental verification.

SUMMARY

The experiment was carried out to determine whether the reduced recall usually observed in subjects after receiving ego-threatening information is due to repression or interference. Subjects learned a list of words, had their recall tested for the list, and then took a personality test in which the words were used as stimuli. Subjects were then given either ego-threatening, ego-enchancing, or neutral feedback. Following this, they were tested for recall again, debriefed, and tested for recall once more. Subjects receiving threatening and enhancing feedback performed alike and showed poorer recall on the postfeedback test than the subjects receiving neutral feedback. Since the subjects in the threat and enhancement conditions performed the same in terms of the number and nature of the words forgotten and since there was no reason to expect repression in the enhancement condition, it was concluded that postfeedback recall decrements were due to interference.

REFERENCES

Aborn, M. The influence of experimentally induced failure on the retention of material acquired through set and incidental learning. *Journal of Experimental Psychology*, 1953, 45, 225–231.

Buss, A., & Lang, P. Psychological deficit in schizophrenia: I. Affect, reinforcement, and concept attainment. *Journal of Abnormal Psychology*, 1965, 70, 2–24.

D'Zurilla, T. Recall efficiency and mediating cognitive events in "experimental repression." *Journal of Personality and Social Psychology*, 1965, 3, 253–256.

Flavell, J. Repression and the "return of the repressed." *Journal of Consulting Psychology*, 1955, *19*, 441–443.

Holmes, D., & Schallow, J. Reduced recall after ego threat: Repression or response competition? *Journal of Personality and Social Psychology*, 1969, *13*, 145–152.

Lang, P., & Buss, A. Psychological deficit in schizophrenia: II. Interference and activation. *Journal of Abnormal Psychology*, 1965, *70*, 77–106.

Merrill, R. M. The effect of pre-experimental and experimental anxiety on recall efficiency. *Journal of Experimental Psychology*, 1954, *48*, 167–172.

Penn, N. Experimental improvements on an analogue of repression paradigm. *Psychological Record*, 1964, *14*, 185–196.

Truax, C. The repression response to implied failure as a function of the hysteria-psychasthenia index. *Journal of Abnormal and Social Psychology*, 1957, *55*, 188–193.

Winer, B. *Statistical principles in experimental design.* New York: McGraw-Hill, 1962.

Worchell, P. Anxiety and repression. *Journal of Abnormal and Social Psychology*, 1955, *51*, 201–205.

Zeller, A. An experimental analogue of repression: I. Historical summary. *Psychological Bulletin*, 1950, *47*, 39–51. (a)

Zeller, A. An experimental analogue of repression: II. The effect of individual failure and success on memory measured by relearning. *Journal of Experimental Psychology*, 1950, *40*, 411–422. (b)

Zeller, A. An experimental analogue of repression: III. The effect of induced failure and success on memory measured by recall. *Journal of Experimental Psychology*, 1951, *42*, 32–38.

18.2 | AVOIDANCE LEARNING OF PERCEPTUAL DEFENSE AND VIGILANCE*[1]

Don E. Dulany, Jr.

Those who argue for a perceptual defense mechanism analogous to repression and those who believe that the adaptive value of sensitization to threat suggests a vigilance mechanism can both find support in a wealth of controversial data (Eriksen, 1954; Lazarus, 1954)—as well as can those who would deny both views (Howes & Solomon,

* SOURCE: Dulany, D. E., Jr. Avoidance learning of perceptual defense and vigilance. *Journal of Abnormal and Social Psychology*, 1957, *55*, 333–338. Copyright 1957 by the American Psychological Association and reprinted by permission.

[1] This article is based on a doctoral dissertation submitted to the Department of Psychology, University of Michigan. I wish to express my gratitude to Dr. E. L. Walker for his generous advice and guidance as chairman of my doctoral committee.

1951; Postman, 1951, 1953). Much of the confusion has resulted from the use of linguistic stimuli whose significance to the subject is a matter of dispute. So long as the history of the subjects' commerce with the stimulus materials remains uncertain, convenient assumptions permit any of the several views to be salvaged in the face of most data. The chief object of the present study is to produce experimentally the learning of perceptual defense and vigilance, and in so doing, to relate the mechanisms to antecedent experimental procedures.

Knowing that a stimulus is anxiety arousing does not in itself permit us to predict the perceptual reaction to that stimulus. Lazarus, Erikson, and Fonda (1951) have demstrated both perceptual defense and vigilance reactions to the same hostile or sexual, and presumably threatening, material; which reaction occurs is predicted from diagnostic categories. Encountering stimuli with sexual or hostile meaning is no novelty to the adult subject, who has had ample opportunity for learning to handle any anxiety they engender. We might guess that one kind of subject has learned to defend against threatening stimuli because with his particular experiences and personal economy that reaction has somehow been to his advantage. Another has learned perceptual vigilance because that reaction served him well. The specific learning mechanism involved has not been made clear. Hence, a second purpose of this study is to offer an account in terms of behavior theory of how perceptual defense and vigilance may be learned and to test two hypotheses derived from that account.

This analysis extends to perception a two-stage conception of avoidance learning that is essentially in agreement with the views of Mowrer (1944) and of Solomon (1953). Once an anxiety response has been classically conditioned to a previously neutral stimulus, any number of perceptual reactions are theoretically possible—vigilance and defense, as well as many qualitative distortions. The convenience of certain psychophysical methods has led to great experimental interest in two such reactions along the single dimension of recognizability. We may think of these potential perceptual reactions to a threatening stimulus as ordered in a hierarchy of probability of occurrence. There is some evidence that perceptual vigilance holds the dominant position in an initial hierarchy of perceptual reactions to threat. Pustell (1955) produced perceptual vigilance experimentally by classically associating an electric shock with a number of neutral geometric figures. Lazarus and McCleary (1951) classically conditioned GSRs to nonsense syllables, obtaining their threshold measures under threat of further punishment, but failed to find a significant difference between thresholds for their shock syllables and a number of nonshock syllables. Could a reluctance to name the shock syllable have cancelled out a primitive vigilance reaction? Lysak (1954) replicated their finding, then in another experiment removed the electrodes before obtaining threshold measures and found thresholds for his shock syllables to be lower than those for nonshock syllables. These findings suggest that perceptual vigilance is dominant in an initial hierarchy of perceptual reactions to a threatening stimulus, although response suppression may obscure the effect when there is a continuing imminent possibility of punishment. The superior adaptive value of such a mechanism is obvious.

Whatever perceptual reaction is initially dominant, it should be possible to realign this hierarchy by introducing selective reinforcement. The perceptual reaction that is instrumental to the avoidance of punishment and reduction of the conditioned anxiety should be strengthened. In the course of ordinary experience, perceptual defense and vigilance occur in the presence of varied and competing stimuli. They name two kinds of imbalance among a set of competing perceptual responses. If one perceptual response is punished while competing perceptual responses are instrumental to the avoidance of punishment and a reduction in anxiety, perceptual defense should be learned, since competing perceptual responses should tend to crowd out the critical perceptual response. On the other hand, perceptual vigilance should be learned when one perceptual response is instrumental to avoidance of punishment while competing perceptual responses are punished. Specifically, the following hypotheses are tested: (a) When one perceptual response is followed by punishment and competing perceptual responses are instrumental to avoidance of punishment, the punished response becomes weaker as compared with the competing perceptual responses; (b) When one perceptual response is instrumental to avoidance of punishment and competing perceptual responses are punished, the avoidance response becomes stronger as compared with the competing perceptual responses.

METHOD

SUBJECTS

The Ss were 32 undergraduates at the University of Michigan, evenly divided between the defense and vigilance training procedures. They were randomly assigned to the two procedures, the only requirement being that an equal number of men and women participate in each. All Ss were volunteers, and none was aware of the purpose of the experiment.

STIMULUS MATERIALS

Four rather meaningless, emotionally neutral figures—a circle, diamond, square, and triangle—were cut from black Munsell paper and mounted on white cards. The figures were arranged top, bottom, left, and right, on each of four cards, so that each figure appeared in all four positions. Hence, if each of the four cards was presented to the S an equal number of times, each figure would appear an equal number of times in each of the four positions. In this way, positional (Ohrbach, 1952) and frequency effects were controlled. Prior to this experiment, the figures had been roughly equated for discriminability by Thomas Pustell.

APPARATUS

A Gerbrands tachistoscope, designed for individual use, was adjusted for a constant exposure interval of .12 sec. throughout all experimental series. With a pre-exposure field of 6.29 ft. lamberts, an exposure field of 0.425 ft. lamberts, and geometrical forms of less than one inch diameter, this exposure time produced a level of awareness too low for the figures to be readily named.

The electric shock applicator contained four pairs of electrodes spaced about an inch apart and was designed to be strapped to the leg of the S just above the ankle. In order to discourage adaptation and at the same time prevent burns, the shock could be sent through first one pair of electrodes and then another from trial to trial. The shock circuits and applicator were designed by Dr. Carl Brown.

DEFENSE TRAINING EXPERIMENT

Level of awareness series. The experimental session began for each S with an assessment of his level of awareness. A particular exposure duration, together with illumination level, does not define a single level of awareness for more than one S. To ascertain whether level of awareness was related to the amount and character of the experimental effect, the S was given a simple discrimination task. A forced-choice technique developed by Blackwell (1953) and modified by Blum (1954) was selected for its sensitivity in measuring discrimination without awareness. It has the additional value of permitting a number of stimuli to be presented at once, a condition that more truly represents most perceptual situations.

The S was informed that he would be shown a number of cards, but that they would be flashed too briefly for him to see much. On each trial, E asked S to "Find the square" or "Find the diamond," etc. The S responded with "Top," "Bottom," "Left," "Right," depending on where he thought he saw the figure. He was instructed on each trial to focus on the fixation point in the center of the field. Sixty-four trials were run, and S's level of awareness was measured by his percentage of correct identifications.

Baseline series. Although the figures were roughly equal in recognizability for a group collectively, individuals find one figure or another more salient because of their peculiar perceptual histories and predilections. For this reason an empirical baseline of recognizability of each figure was obtained for every S. The procedure for this series was like that of the preceding in every way except that the S was instructed to "tell me on each trial which figure is *clearest*—which one is most *recognizable.*" He was again asked to convey his choice by saying "Top," "Bottom," "Left," or "Right," and to follow his hunch whenever uncertain. Any experimental effect produced by the following training procedure should register as a departure from this empirical baseline.

Training series. The defense training procedure was essentially like the baseline series, with the important difference that reinforcement was introduced. One of the geometrical figures, selected arbitrarily, was designated the critical stimulus. Each of the figures was the critical one for four of the 16 Ss. As in the preceding series, S was instructed to report on each trial which of the four figures was most recognizable by indicating its position. When the critical stimulus was selected, an electric shock followed two seconds after exposure of the figures and lasted another two seconds. Selection of one of the other three figures as most recognizable resulted in avoidance of the shock.

Circuits were designed so as to permit S's pressing of one of four buttons to reveal his choice of figures and control presentation of the shock. The critical stimulus, of course, varied in position from trial to trial, and therefore no single one of the four responses was always punished. The E noted the position of the critical stimulus before each trial, and adjusted a commutator, thereby determining which of the four buttons would activate the shock circuit.

For the purposes of this experiment it was imperative that the shock be punishing. It was necessary that it be decidedly unpleasant, even painful for best results, but short of incapacitating. Since individual pain thresholds for electric shock vary so widely, the intensity of shock was set at a subjective level for each S. After he had been assured that the shock was quite harmless and encouraged to take as much as he could stand, the shock was set at the level each S judged to be "just this side of beyond endurance." By phenomenological consensus of 32 Ss, the shock was decidedly unpleasant, even painful, and like the jab of a hot needle.

Sixty-four trials were run, approximately one every 10 seconds. After each block of 16 trials, S rested briefly.

Assessment series. Immediately after the training series, S was allowed to remove the shock applicator and was assured that there would be no more shock. The instructions and procedure for the assessment series were identical with those for the baseline series. The same cards were presented for 64 trials, and on each trial S indicated which figure was most recognizable. Finally, he was questioned for any knowledge of the rule by which he had been shocked.

VIGILANCE TRAINING EXPERIMENT

The vigilance training experiment repeated the defense training experiment with one important difference: the reinforcement prescription was reversed. When S selected one of the three noncritical stimuli as most recognizable, he was shocked; when he selected the critical stimulus, he avoided the shock.

RESULTS AND DISCUSSION

Relative perceptual response strength for each figure was measured by the frequency with which that figure was judged clearer than competing stimuli. The Ss of the defense training procedure should, if the first hypothesis is correct, select the critical figure less frequently in the assessment series, after training, than they did in the baseline series. Amount of shift in frequency of response ranged from 0 to —14 with a mean of —5.8. In order to evaluate the group shift, it was noted that 14 of the 16 Ss shifted in the predicted direction while two remained unchanged. By the sign test this shift is significant with a $p < .01$.[2] These findings confirm Hypothesis I.

Hypothesis II leads to the contrary expectation that Ss of the vigilance training procedure should select the critical stimulus more frequently during the assessment series than during the baseline series. Magnitude of shift ranged from —7 to +36 with a mean of +7.0. Thirteen of 16 Ss shifted in the anticipated direction, and this shift

---

[2] Since the direction of experimental shift was predicted, one-tail p values are reported.

is significant by the sign test with a $p < .025$. Thus the second hypothesis is supported.

We would also like to know what progressive changes take place throughout the training series, whether these changes follow a typical learning curve, and whether there is any sign of extinction in the assessment series. Consequently, pooled frequency of selection of the critical stimulus was graphed as a function of trials.

For the defense training group (see Fig. 1), frequency of selection drops precipitously from the baseline to the early part of the training series. Apparently the learning takes place very rapidly, although the abruptness of the drop may be partly due to a chance increase in frequency toward the end of the baseline series. In the vigilance training series, frequency of selection increases throughout the training series in a manner strongly suggestive of a learning curve. Since an anxiety reaction is very probably conditioned early in both training series, or even earlier, when the shock is adjusted to the appropriate subjective level, there is some reason to expect the instrumental learning of defense to proceed more rapidly than the learning of vigilance. Theoretically, vigilance is acquired as a single, critical, perceptual response, strengthened by anxiety reduction attendant upon shock avoidance; this is the kind of learning that ought to be describable by a familiar learning curve. The learning of perceptual defense, however, proceeds as the three competing perceptual responses are strengthened, by anxiety reduction, at the expense of the critical perceptual response. There is less basis for anticipating the function for this kind of learning. That the learning of defense did occur more rapidly than the learning of vigilance might be explained by the greater probability of reinforcement in the defense series. It is also likely that the greater number of shocks in the vigilance series produced a higher level of

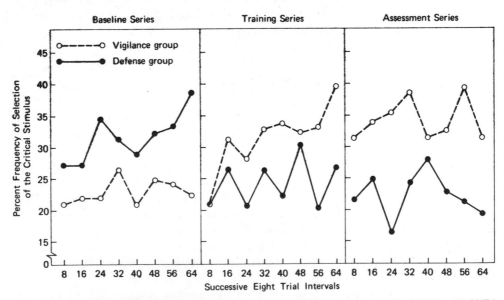

Figure 1 | MEAN PERFORMANCE OF THE DEFENSE AND VIGILANCE GROUPS THROUGHOUT EACH EXPERIMENTAL SERIES.

anxiety in the vigilance group. Conceivably, level of anxiety drive could be related to the rapidity and course of learning. Finally, for neither procedure is there any evidence of extinction in the assessment series; and in view of the well-documented resistance to extinction of avoidance responses (Sidman, 1955; Solomon, 1953) this is not too surprising.

A problem of interpretation arises from the fact that the empirical baseline values differ somewhat from their expected value of 25%–31.6% for the defense group and 23.0% for the vigilance group. While there is no reasonable alternative but to attribute this disparity to sampling fluctuation, it is important to distinguish two possible sources of error. Have two deviant samples been drawn from a population of responses that mark the baseline? Or have such deviant samples been drawn from a population of Ss varying in perceptual sensitivity to the critical stimuli? In the former case, we should expect some regression toward the value of 25% in the assessment series, quite apart from any effect of the training procedures. If the latter possibility is the case, then there is no problem, and the experimental effect is the more impressive for having over-ridden figure preferences. It is possible, for purposes of analysis, to eliminate those four Ss with the highest frequencies at the defense baseline and the three Ss lowest at the vigilance baseline, leaving the two baseline means approximately equal. Of the 12 Ss remaining in the defense group, 10 selected the critical stimulus less frequently during the assessment series than at the baseline. By the sign test this shift is significant with $p < .025$. Ten of the 13 Ss remaining in the vigilance group shifted in the predicted direction ($p < .05$). It seems clear that the regression hypothesis cannot account for these results.

How justified is the interpretation that these training procedures have changed the strength of perceptual responses rather than S's disposition to make a report that has invariably brought him a painful electric shock? If S at any time discerned a connection between pressing the button for a square and being shocked, it would be only prudent for him to take a good look on each trial, then press one of the other buttons. For a number of reasons this suggested process cannot account for these results. Only two of 32 Ss could name the critical figure or verbalize the rule by which they had been shocked. Typical of their replies when questioned were, "Maybe there was a pattern to it, but I don't know what it was" and "I didn't know what I did or saw would have anything to do with it." This is, in fact, learning without awareness. Moreover, if the S were deliberately falsifying his report, then during the assessment series, after the shock applicator had been removed, he should have abandoned this tactic; frequency of selection of the critical stimulus would have returned to what it was at the baseline. It is evident from the data that this did not happen. Furthermore, the greater his awareness, the more information he has to act on and the more successful he should be; yet no relation was found between level of awareness and magnitude of experimental effect.

If the theoretical assumptions of the study are correct, something like the following occurred. An anxiety reaction produced by the shock was conditioned to the stimulus figures. It seems likely that anxiety attached to all four figures rather than just to the critical figure because of their low discriminability at a low level of awareness.

Upon presentation of the stimulus, S tensed, gasped, or wrapped a leg around the chair, regardless of which figure was selected. The total conditioned stimulus was probably even more complex, consisting of a stimulus presentation plus a lapse of time of two seconds. Generally, anxiety reduction is assumed to follow upon withdrawal of the cues eliciting the anxiety. However, termination of the exposure period brought no visible end to the S's malaise. It was not until two seconds had elapsed and no shock had occurred that signs of relaxation or a relieved and grateful sigh appeared. In the absence of any good measure of momentary changes in the anxiety level it is reasonable to think anxiety drive reduction and reinforcement of the prior perceptual response occurred at this point.

This interpretation, which holds that the punished response is "weakened" only because competing responses are strengthened is advanced because it has worked well in describing the avoidance learning of skeletal responses (Mowrer, 1944; Solomon, 1953). Logically, of course, the shift in relative perceptibility of these figures could be credited either to sensitization to the nonpunished stimuli or desensitization to the punished stimuli, or both. The data prove only that at least one of these reactions must have occurred. This ambiguity is shared, however, with studies in which a single stimulus is presented by the ascending method of limits. In studies following the latter design, the assessed strength of the veridical percept is relative to the strength of competing perceptual hypotheses (Postman, 1953). The forced-choice procedure simply delimits the range of competing perceptual responses to a high priority few. Until the evidence for sensitization and desensitization is less equivocal, perceptual vigilance and defense can legitimately be identified only with shifts in balance among competing perceptual responses, in the one case toward a critical percept, and in the other case against it.

This study supports the view that perceptual defense and vigilance are learned reactions to anxiety arousing stimuli. It is consistent with Postman's recent statement that "the facts which give rise to this concept [of perceptual defense] can better be subsumed under other, more general, principles of perception" (1953, p. 298); the same could be said for vigilance. Both concepts, it is suggested, may be subsumed under more general principles of perceptual learning, but this statement is not to be construed as asserting that perceptual defense and vigilance are therefore explained away. Though the mechanisms appear to follow more general principles of learning, they nevertheless retain some identity as mechanisms.

SUMMARY

This study experimentally produces the learning of perceptual defense and vigilance and proposes a behavior theory analysis of the learning process. According to this analysis, perceptual defense is learned when the perceptual response to a threatening stimulus is punished and competing perceptual responses are instrumental to anxiety reduction. Competing perceptual responses when reinforced are strengthened at the expense of the critical perceptual response. Perceptual vigilance is learned when the perceptual response to a threatening stimulus is reinforced by anxiety reduction and competing perceptual responses are punished.

Avoidance learning procedures were employed to change the comparative recognizability of four geometrical figures presented simultaneously below the threshold for awareness. Sixteen Ss underwent defense training, another 16 vigilance training. Before each training series, the comparative recognizability of the four figures was assessed for each S by a forced-choice technique. In both training series, S reported on each trial the position of the figure he found clearest. During defense training, if he selected the critical figure, he was shocked. If he selected one of the other three figures, he avoided the shock. During vigilance training, selection of the critical figure was instrumental to shock avoidance while selection of any of the other three figures incurred the shock. After each training procedure, comparative recognizability of the figures was assessed again. Fourteen of 16 defense Ss found the critical figure less recognizable after training than before. Thirteen of 16 vigilance Ss found the critical figure more recognizable than before training. Learning in both cases proceeded in the absence of awareness.

REFERENCES

Blackwell, R. Psychophysical thresholds: experimental studies of methods of measurement. *Eng. res. Bull. No. 36*, University of Michigan, 1953.

Blum, G. S. An experimental reunion of psychoanalytic theory with perceptual vigilance and defense. *J. abnorm. soc. Psychol.*, 1954, *13*, 94–99.

Eriksen, C. W. The case for perceptual defense. *Psychol. Rev.*, 1954, *61*, 175–182.

Howes, D. H., & Solomon, R. L. Visual duration threshold as a function of word probability. *J. exp. Psychol.*, 1951, *41*, 401–410.

Lazarus, R. S. Is there a mechanism of perceptual defense? A reply to Postman, Bronson, and Gropper. *J. abnorm. soc. Psychol.*, 1954, *49*, 396–398.

Lazarus, R. S., & McCleary, R. A. Autonomic discrimination without awareness: a study of subception. *Psychol. Rev.*, 1951, *58*, 113–123.

Lazarus, R. S., Eriksen, C. W., & Fonda, C. P. Personality dynamics and auditory perceptual recognition. *J. Pers.*, 1951, *19*, 471–482.

Lysak, W. The effects of punishment upon syllable recognition thresholds. *J. exp. Psychol.*, 1954, *47*, 343–351.

Mowrer, O. H. On the dual nature of learning—a reinterpretation of "conditioning" and "problem solving." *Harvard educ. Rev.*, 1944, Spring, 102–148.

Ohrbach, J. Retinal locus as a factor in recognition. *Amer. J. Psychol.*, 1952, *65*, 555–562.

Postman, L. On the problem of perceptual defense. *Psychol. Rev.*, 1951, *58*, 113–123.

Postman, L. The experimental analysis of motivational factors in perception. In *Current theory and research in motivation: A symposium.* Lincoln, Neb.: University of Nebraska Press, 1953.

Postman, L., Bronson, W. C., & Gropper, G. L. Is there a mechanism of perceptual defense? *J. abnorm. soc. Psychol.*, 1953, *48*, 215–225.

Pustell, T. Cue and drive aspects of anxiety in relation to perceptual vigilance and defense. Unpublished doctoral dissertation, University of Michigan, 1955.

Sidman, M. On the persistence of avoidance behavior. *J. abnorm. soc. Psychol.*, 1955, *50*, 217–221.

Solomon, R. L., & Wynne, L. C. Traumatic avoidance learning: Acquisition in normal dogs. *Psychol. Monogr.*, 1953, 67, No. 4 (Whole No. 354).

Solomon, R. L., Kamin, L. J., & Wynne, L. C. Traumatic avoidance learning: the outcomes of several extinction procedures with dogs. *J. abnorm. soc. Psychol.*, 1953, *48*, 206–216.

19 | Self-Control

19.1 | COGNITIVE AND ATTENTIONAL MECHANISMS IN DELAY OF GRATIFICATION*, [1]

Walter Mischel, Ebbe B. Ebbesen, and Antonette Raskoff Zeiss

As early as 1890, William James contended that attentional processes are at the very core of the self-control phenomena usually subsumed under the term "will" or, since James's time, under the concept "ego strength." According to James (1890): "Attention with effort is all that any case of volition implies. The essential achievement of will is to attend to a difficult object . . . [p. 549]." In contrast, psychoanalytic theories of self-control emphasize unconscious processes and motivational dynamics, as well as internalization of values and intrapsychic conflicts to explain self-control phenomena. In spite of this shift in emphasis away from attentional to psychodynamic interpretations of self-control, some strands of evidence suggest possible links between attentional processes and self-regulatory mechanisms.

In particular, beginning with Hartshorne and May (1928), a few correlations have been found between indexes of moral behavior and measures of attention or resistance to distraction on mental tests (e.g., Grim, Kohlberg, & White, 1968). On the basis of such correlations, it has been suggested that the individual's ability to resist temptation may be facilitated by how well he attends to a task. In most experimental "resistance to temptation" paradigms, yielding to temptations, such as cheating, depends on the subject's being distracted from the main task to which he is supposed to be attending. In those situations a subject's ability to resist distraction may automatically make it easier for him to refrain from temptations such as cheating (Grim et al., 1968).

Using experimental rather than correlational methods, Mischel and Ebbesen

* SOURCE: Mischel, W., Ebbesen, E. B., & Zeiss, A. R. Cognitive and attentional mechanisms in delay of gratification. *Journal of Personality and Social Psychology*, 1972, 21, 204–218. Copyright 1972 by the American Psychological Association and reprinted by permission.

[1] This research was supported by Research Grant MH-6830 from the National Institutes of Health, United States Public Health Service. Portions of this paper were presented by the first author in an invited address, "Personality and Cognition," at the meeting of the Western Psychological Association, Los Angeles, April 1970.

(1970) have explored a different link between attention and self-control in the context of the delay-of-gratification paradigm. In that study, preschool children sat waiting for a preferred reward which was available at a later time. At any moment the children could signal to terminate the waiting, thereby obtaining a less preferred reward, while forfeiting the more desired one. The experiment investigated the effects of attention to the goal objects on the length of time that the children actually waited. Specifically, while the children waited, they were given the opportunity to attend to the delayed and/or to the immediately available reward or to neither reward.

In accord with several previous theories discussed by Mischel and Ebbesen (1970), it had been expected that attention to the delayed reward would facilitate delay of gratification. In part it was expected that making the reward objects salient might facilitate "time binding" by permitting the subject to engage in self-persuasion and anticipatory gratification. For example, he might sustain his delay by imagining how satisfying the preferred outcome would be (e.g., how good it would taste) when it became available. In fact, the findings obtained by Mischel and Ebbesen were exactly opposite to the predictions. It was found that if the child could attend to either or both of the rewards, he waited much less than if he could attend to neither reward during the delay period. In addition, the length of time which the children waited with only the immediate reward available for attention was similar to the time they waited with only the delayed reward available. Finally, when both rewards were available, children waited a slightly shorter time. Thus, children waited most readily when neither the delayed nor the immediate reward was available for attention during the delay period, and they waited a relatively short time when any reward was available.

Observation of the children's spontaneous behavior during delay of gratification suggested that the mechanism used by many youngsters to sustain their voluntary delay involved suppressing rather than enhancing attention to the rewards. The children seemed to reduce the subjective aversiveness of delay of reward by engaging in covert and overt distracting responses such as staring at the mirror, covering their eyes with their hands, and talking to themselves. These responses seemed to divert their attention away from the frustration-inducing rewards. Furthermore, self-induced distractions seemed to be fairly easy to maintain in the condition in which no rewards were facing the children, but seemed very difficult to maintain when any of the rewards were facing the children. Apparently, the children were able to delay longer when neither reward was available for attention because in this condition it was easier for them to avoid or suppress cognitions about the rewards.

Post hoc, the obtained results become most understandable if delay of gratification is seen as a frustration situation. Indeed, the essence of frustration is a delay or interruption in an expected and desired outcome (Mandler, 1964). The necessity to delay in order to obtain a more gratifying reward may be determined externally by physical barriers or other people. In self-control and voluntary delay of reward, this delay is self-imposed. If a person desires the delayed outcome, he must impose the frustrative waiting situation upon himself, foregoing the immediately available outcome for the sake of the more desirable but delayed alternative.

As Amsel's (1958, 1962) "frustrative nonreward theory" has suggested, frustration involves an actively aversive effect. It follows that any conditions that enhance the aversiveness of frustration should make it harder to wait. Although Amsel's work with frustration effects in animals has concentrated on the scheduling of prior reinforcement, it seems reasonable that any cues that enhance attention to what one wants but cannot have should increase the aversiveness of frustration. This interpretation of the frustration effect suggests that attending to the rewards cognitively, rather than helping to bridge the delay period, may make it more aversive to delay gratification, and therefore lead to shorter waiting time. The present three experiments were designed to test this proposition.

If our speculations regarding the frustrative effects of delay are correct, then delay of gratification should be enhanced when the subject can readily transform the aversive waiting period into a more pleasant nonwaiting situation. This line of reasoning suggests that voluntary delay of reward should be enhanced by any overt or covert activities that serve as distractors from the rewards. Through self-distraction, the subject should be able to suppress or avoid the aversiveness of wanting gratification but not having it, and thus convert the frustrative delay-of-reward situation into a psychologically less aversive condition. Therefore, it was expected that overt activities and internal cognitions and fantasy which could help the subject to distract himself from the rewards would increase the length of time which he would delay gratification.

To investigate the role of attention and cognition in delay of gratification, we gave each subject either an overt activity, a cognitive activity, or no activity to engage in during the delay period. The overt and cognitive activities were designed to reduce the probability that the subjects would be attending to the reward during the delay period. We then assessed how these alternatives affected the subjects' voluntary delay time, in comparison to the group of subjects which was not supplied with a distractor. Consistent with our extension of frustrative nonreward theory, we predicted that voluntary delay of gratification should be increased by any covert or overt activities that distract the subject from the anticipated outcomes and, conversely, should be diminished by attention to the rewards during the delay period.

EXPERIMENT I

To test our expectations, a study was designed with a delay-of-gratification paradigm in which aversive frustration was deliberately made high. For this purpose, preschool subjects were faced with both the immediately available and the more preferred but delayed reward during the delay period.[2] All children could signal at any time to

[2] This attentional condition was used because it presumably would provide maximum frustration cues. When the subject attends to the immediate reward and is tempted to take it, he is frustrated by remembering the contingency that attainment of the reward now prevents his getting the preferred reward later. When the subject attends to the delayed reward, he is frustrated by the fact that he wants it now but cannot have it yet. When he attends to both objects, both of the above aversive frustrations occur, and, hence, delay should be most difficult for him. Indeed, this attentional condition, in which both rewards are present, was the one that has produced the shortest waiting time in a previous study (Mischel & Ebbesen, 1970).

terminate the waiting period, thereby forfeiting the more preferred gratification but attaining the less desirable one immediately.

METHOD

Design.   The independent variable in this study was a manipulation designed to permit the subject to distract himself from the reward objects for which he was waiting. In all conditions, while the subjects waited, the immediate and delayed rewards were both physically available for direct attention. The dependent variable was the length of time the children remained alone in the room before they rang a bell and thereby ended the delay period.

Two methods of self-distraction were used. One technique involved an external activity; in the other method, instructions were given to generate internal cognitive activity. In the external activity, the child was given the opportunity to play with an attractive toy while he waited. In the cognitive activity group, instructions were given to increase the probability that the child would think pleasant and distracting thoughts while he was waiting. A control group was designed to determine how long the children would wait for the delayed reward without either the external or the internal distractors provided by the experimenters. To control for the effects of playing with an attractive toy or thinking pleasant thoughts *independent of waiting* for the delayed reward, two additional control groups of children were given either the toy or the cognitive sets but no delayed reward contingency.

Thus, a total of five groups were employed: Group 1: waiting for delayed reward with external distractor (toy); Group 2: waiting for delayed reward with internal distractor (ideation); Group 3: waiting for delayed reward (no distractor); Group 4: external distractor (toy) without delay-of-reward waiting contingency; Group 5: internal distractor (ideation) without delay-of-reward waiting contingency.

Subjects.   The subjects were 50 children (25 boys and 25 girls) from the Bing Nursery School of Stanford University. They ranged in age from 3 years 6 months to 5 years 6 months, with a mean age of 4 years 6 months. Six additional children began but did not complete the experimental procedures because they did not comprehend the instructions. Five males and 5 females, equated for mean age, were randomly assigned to each of the five conditions. One male and one female served as experimenters. Specifically, within each condition, the male experimenter ran 3 male and 2 female subjects, and the female experimenter ran 3 female and 2 male subjects.

Procedure.   The experimental room and setting was similar to that previously described (Mischel & Ebbesen, 1970). An addition was a barrier, behind which the experimenter, but not the children, could see and reach. Behind this barrier was placed a "Slinky" (a toy spring) and an opaque cake tin. Under the cake tin was a small marshmallow and a stick pretzel. A box of attractive battery-

and hand-operated toys was on a second table next to the barrier. A table and chair were against one wall, and on the table was a desk bell.

When the experimenter escorted a child to the experimental room, he first showed the child the box of toys and explained that they would play with the toys later on in the session. After finishing a brief demonstration of one or two of the toys, the experimenter escorted the subject to the table with the desk bell and asked the child to sit in the chair in front of the table. The experimenter then introduced and practiced the child's use of the bell signal. They played a "game" in which the experimenter repeatedly stepped out of the room, closed the door, but returned as soon as the child signaled. Every time the bell was rung, the experimenter thus immediately returned to the room. The procedure was the same as the one previously described (Mischel & Ebbesen, 1970), with the exception that in the present study the signal was a bell. Thereafter, the experimenter consulted a concealed slip of paper which informed him by a prearranged random schedule of the condition to which the child was to be assigned.

Delay-of-Gratification Contingency Instructions.   For subjects assigned to the three delay-of-gratification conditions (Groups 1, 2, and 3), the experimenter next removed the cake tin from behind the barrier and placed it on the table in front of the child, giving these instructions:

> Let's see what's under here. I'll bet it's a surprise. Oh boy, look at that. A marshmallow and a pretzel. Which would you like to eat? You can eat either the marshmallow or the pretzel. [At this point the child chose which one he wanted to eat.] Oh, you know what? I have to go out of the room now, and if you wait until I come back by myself then you can eat this one [pointing to chosen object] right up. But, you know, if you don't want to wait you can ring the bell and bring me back anytime you want to. But if you ring the bell then you can't have this one, but you can have that one (pointing to the unchosen object). So, if you ring the bell and bring me back then you can't have the _____, but you can have the _____.

The experimenter then assessed the child's comprehension by asking three questions: "Can you tell me, which do you get to eat if you wait for me to come back by myself?" "But if you want to, how can you make me come back?" "If you ring the bell and bring me back, then which do you get?" As previously mentioned, six children were eliminated from the study. Four failed to pass these questions, and the other two subjects were lost because one ate the food objects while the experimenter was out of the room, and the other one refused to ring the bell during training.

In one of the three delay-of-gratification conditions (Group 3), subjects did not receive either the thinking or the toy activity distraction instructions, but they did receive the foregoing waiting contingency instructions. In this condition, after the subjects answered the three comprehension questions correctly, they were simply told: "I have to leave the room now. And if you want to you can ring the bell whenever you want to and bring me back. When I come back, whether you ring the bell or wait for me to come back by myself, we'll play with all my toys."

In Groups 4 and 5—the two conditions with no delay-of-reward contingency

—the foregoing instructions of course were not given. Instead, the experimenter, after stating that he would have to leave, merely looked at some papers, while telling the child that he had to "check something" before he left and then shuffled through the papers for approximately as long as it would take to give the waiting contingency instructions.

Distraction through Overt Activity Instructions. In the two overt distraction conditions (Groups 1 and 4), the child was left alone in the room with a potential distracting activity that involved playing with a toy (the Slinky). In Group 1 each subject was also given the delay-of-gratification contingency instructions and thus was waiting with the possibility of getting the preferred food object if he waited long enough, and the less preferred object if he did not delay long enough. In Group 4 the child was left alone merely to play as long as he wished. In both of these groups, prior to leaving the room, the experimenter placed the Slinky on the floor and informed the child that he could play with the Slinky on the floor for as long as he wanted, that he could ring the bell whenever he wanted to bring back the experimenter, and that, regardless of whether the child rang the bell or waited, he could play with the toys when the experimenter came back.

Distraction through Cognition-Inducing Instructions. In Groups 2 and 5, before leaving the room, the experimenter gave the subject instructions designed to encourage the child to generate his own thoughts and covert cognitive activities while waiting. He said: "Oh, while I'm gone you can think of anything that's fun to think of, for as long as you want to, if you want to. Can you tell me something to think about that's fun?" (The experimenter paused for the child's examples and said "Yes" no matter what the subject said.) The experimenter then added other examples: "You can also think about singing songs, or think of playing with toys or anything that is fun to think of." His final departing instructions were identical to those given in the other groups.

Recall that Groups 2 and 5 differed in that only the children in Group 2 expected to get a reward if they waited long enough, although both groups could remain alone and "think about fun things" for as long as they wished before terminating the delay by signaling.

In all groups, when the experimenter returned he asked the child "What happens now?" No child failed to respond correctly (either verbally or by eating the proper food reward spontaneously). In all conditions the session ended with the experimenter and child playing with the toys as had been promised.

Sequence. To review, the order of events were as follows: (*a*) The experimenter demonstrated some toys to the child. (*b*) The child was taught how to bring the experimenter back into the room (by ringing the bell). (*c*) In Groups 1, 2, and 3, the children were presented with the delay contingency, and comprehension questions, while in Groups 4 and 5 the experimenter merely explained that he had to leave the room and that the children could bring him back whenever they wished to. (*d*) The overt distractors were presented in Groups 1 and 4, and the covert, in Groups 2 and 5. (*e*) Finally, all children were reminded that no matter what they did (ring the bell or not) when the experimenter returned, they would play with the toys.

RESULTS

Delay of Gratification.   The mean length of waiting time was computed for each condition (Figure 1). The first result to note is the extremely low mean delay time found in the delay-of-reward condition in which no distractor was available. In this condition, since both the chosen and unchosen rewards were present, and no distractor was available, the attention paid to the rewards should have been fairly high. The low mean delay time of less than ½ a minute found for this group replicates the low mean waiting time found in the previous comparable study when children also waited with both rewards present, and no distractor was available (Mischel & Ebbesen, 1970).

As can be seen in Figure 1, the mean length of time which the children waited was much greater when they had available either an external or a cognitive distractor during the delay period, the mean delay times in the latter two conditions being 8.59 and 12.12 minutes, respectively.

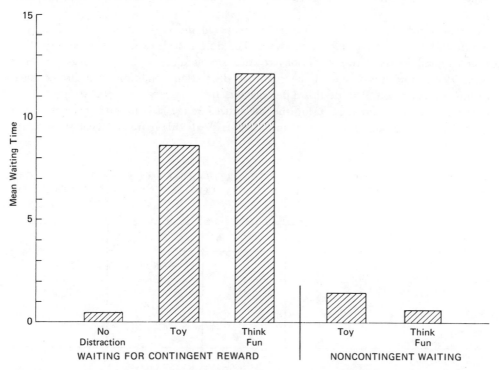

Figure 1 | MEAN NUMBER OF MINUTES OF VOLUNTARY WAITING TIME FOR EACH CONDITION IN EXPERIMENT I.

Table 1 presents a one-way analysis of variance for the mean waiting times and four orthogonal contrasts (Winer, 1962). The overall effect of conditions was highly significant ($p < .001$). Orthogonal contrasts were computed to determine the exact sources of this effect and to test specific hypotheses about the effect of distractors on the length of voluntary delay of reward.

The first orthogonal contrast (C_1 in Table 1) compared the three delay-of-gratification contingency conditions (Groups 1, 2 and 3) with the two conditions in which this contingency was absent (Groups 4 and 5). This contrast yielded a highly significant effect ($p < .001$), indicating that giving the children a reward for which to wait greatly increased the length of time which they spent alone in the experimental room.

It was also predicted that waiting would be long only in those conditions in which a chosen reward was contingent on delay *and* a distractor was available. As Figure 1 reveals, the availability of the desired but delayed gratification yielded a mean delay time of less than ½ a minute when the subject had no overt or cognitive distractions available to reduce or avoid frustration while he was attending to the rewards. The second contrast (C_2 in Table 1) was computed with only the three contingent delay-of-gratification conditions. This contrast compared the two distraction conditions (Groups 1 and 2) with the one no-distraction condition (Group 3). The F for this contrast was highly significant ($p < .001$) and strongly confirmed the prediction that children would wait longer for rewards if a distractor from the rewards were available during the delay period.

The third contrast (C_3 in Table 1) compared the two distraction conditions in which children were waiting for a reward. The difference between the mean length of times waited in these two conditions reached significance at the .05 level: a longer mean delay time was found in the cognitive distraction condition than in the overt distraction condition. Because this difference was not very great, a more stringent statistical test was also computed, using the studentized range statistic and the Tukey (a) procedure for a posteriori t tests (Winer, 1962). With this more stringent statistic, the

Table 1 | ANALYSIS OF VARIANCE AND ORTHOGONAL CONTRASTS FOR MEAN WAITING TIMES AS A FUNCTION OF DELAY CONTINGENCY AND DISTRACTION CONDITIONS

SOURCE	df	MS	F
Between	4	289.1	19.21**
C_1	1	428.2	28.46**
C_2	1	655.1	43.54**
C_3	1	62.7	4.18*
C_4	1	3.6	<1
Error	45	15.1	

* $p < .05$.
** $p < .001$.

difference between the toy distraction and the cognitive distraction when children were waiting for a reward did not approach significance ($t = 2.87$).

A fourth contrast (C_4 in Table 1) compared the two conditions in which reward was not contingent on delay (Groups 4 and 5). It was not significant ($F < 1$).

Another index of waiting behavior is the number of children who waited the full 15 minutes (i.e., until the experimenter returned by himself). These results (Table 2) were in the same direction as those reported for the mean waiting times. A chi-square compared the number of children waiting to criterion with the number who did not in the three contingent delay-of-gratification conditions, and yielded a significant effect ($\chi^2 = 8.18$, $df = 2$, $p < .025$). When delay of gratification was attempted in the presence of rewards and no distractors were available to suppress attention from them, not a single child waited to criterion. When distractors were available cognitively or overtly, half of the subjects waited to criterion. Moreover, when the distractors were available, but rewards were not contingent on waiting, not a single subject waited to criterion.

Before discussing the present results, two additional experiments will be described. These studies are intended to clarify further the cognitive and attentional mechanisms that seem most crucial for effective voluntary delay of gratification.

EXPERIMENT II

The effects found in the first study were strong and in accord with theoretical expectation. The results clearly supported the hypothesis that effective delay behavior is greatly enhanced by the avoidance or reduction of the frustrative aspects of delay of gratification. Such reduction presumably was achieved when the subjects shifted atten-

Table 2 | NUMBER OF CHILDREN WAITING OR NOT WAITING TO THE CRITERION (15 MINUTES) AS A FUNCTION OF DELAY CONTINGENCY AND DISTRACTION CONDITIONS (EXPERIMENT I)

WAITING TO CRITERION	WAITING FOR CONTINGENT REWARD[a]			NONCONTINGENT WAITING[b]	
	No distraction	*Toy as distraction*	*Thinking fun things as distraction*	*Toy as distraction*	*Thinking fun things as distraction*
No	10	6	4	10	10
Yes	0	4	6	0	0

[a] $\chi^2 = 8.18$, $df = 2$, $p < .025$.
[b] $\chi^2 = ns$.

tion away from the potential gratification and instead distracted themselves with competing cognitions or with overt activity.

The findings concerning the potency of the instruction-induced cognitive distractions seemed especially provocative. It also would be important to determine how the substantive content of cognitions (as generated by various types of instructions) affects subsequent delay behavior. A second experiment was designed to explore this topic.

It was assumed that the effects of instruction-produced cognitive content on voluntary delay would parallel those found by manipulation of external stimulus objects. Therefore, it was predicted that delay of gratification would be short when the frustration was made high by directing the children to think about the rewards. We also expected that the content of thoughts could influence their effectiveness in bridging the delay-of-reward period. Thus, we anticipated that aversive cognitions, as in "thinking sad thoughts," should be relatively ineffective compared to such positive cognitions as ideating about "fun things." Such a result could be expected for several reasons; first, aversive thoughts might be avoided and not employed effectively as distractors. Alternatively, if sad thoughts were generated by the children, the additional aversiveness might lead them to terminate the already aversive waiting situation. Consequently, it was predicted that delay of gratification would be longer when the cognitions were affectively positive distractors and shorter when the cognitions were affectively negative.

METHOD

Design.   A three-condition study was designed which varied the types of instructions given to the subjects just before they began to wait for rewards. The instructions were intended to induce in the subject various types of ideation during the delay-of-gratification period. One condition was a replication of a previously run cell: Subjects here were instructed that they could think about fun or happy thoughts while waiting. In a second condition the subjects were told that they could think unhappy or sad thoughts while they waited. In the final condition the children were instructed that they could think about the reward objects. In all conditions both rewards were again present during the waiting period. The dependent variable was the length of time that the children waited for their more preferred reward before terminating and settling for the less preferred outcome.

Subjects.   Thirty-two children from the Bing Nursery School of Stanford University were the subjects in this study. Six of them were lost because of incomplete understanding of the instructions or because they ate one of the reward objects while waiting for the experimenter. The subjects in the final analysis ranged in age from 3 years 9 months to 5 years 3 months, with a mean age of 4 years 9 months. The final data were based on 10 subjects in each of the two new conditions and 6 subjects in the replicated condition. Sex ratios and ages were equated across groups.

Procedure.   The initial procedure in the three conditions of this study was identical to that in Groups 1, 2, and 3 of Experiment I, in which the children were waiting for reward objects. The only differences came after the child had answered the usual three comprehension questions correctly. As in the earlier studies, after the child answered these three questions, the experimenter was informed as to which one of the following three sets of instructions he was to give; the decision had been determined randomly. The *"think fun"* distraction instructions were identical to those described for the equivalent group in Experiment I.

In the *"think sad"* distraction instructions, the key phrases as the experimenter started to depart were "Oh while I'm gone you can think of anything that is sad to think of, for as long as you want to, if you want to. Can you tell me something that is sad to think of?" (The experimenter paused for the child's examples and said "Yes" regardless of the answers.) The experimenter then added other examples: "You can also think of falling down and getting a bloody knee which hurts a lot, or you can think of crying with no one to help. You can think of anything that makes you unhappy."

The *"think food reward"* instructions directed attention to the reward objects. Therefore, the experimenter simply mentioned both reward objects as things the child could think about while the experimenter was gone: "Oh, while I'm gone you can think of the marshmallow and the pretzel for as long as you want to, if you want to." This thought was repeated several times in reversed order and rephrased form, with the experimenter noting that the child could think anything he wanted to about the pretzel and the mashmallow for as long as he wanted to.

In all groups the final departing instructions were identical and the same as described in Experiment I; thus, they emphasized that the child could ring the bell or wait, and in either event the experimenter and child would play with all the toys at the end.

RESULTS

The mean number of minutes waited in the three conditions ("think fun," "think sad," and "think food") is summarized in Figure 2. A one-way analysis of variance of these data is summarized in Table 3. It can be seen that most of the between variance is accounted for by the comparison between the think fun condition and the other two

Table 3 | ANALYSIS OF VARIANCE AND ORTHOGONAL CONTRASTS FOR MEAN LENGTH OF DELAY OF GRATIFICATION AS A FUNCTION OF VARIOUS THOUGHT-INDUCING INSTRUCTIONS (EXPERIMENT II)

SOURCE	df	MS	F
Between	2	176.1	5.47*
C_1	1	348.9	10.84**
C_2	1	3.3	<1
Error	23	32.2	

* $p < .05$.
** $p < .01$.

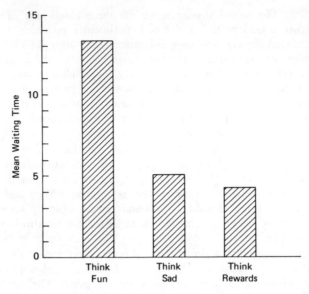

Figure 2 | MEAN NUMBER OF MINUTES OF VOLUNTARY WAITING TIME FOR EACH CONDITION IN EXPERIMENT II.

conditions, think sad and think food. This finding is exactly in accord with the prediction. The direction of the difference was as expected: namely, children waited longer for a reward when they presumably were distracted by thinking "fun things" than when they were thinking about the food rewards or than when they were thinking "sad things."

As Figure 2 indicates, instructions to think about the food rewards and instructions to think about sad things produced similar delay times. It is also interesting to compare the delay times in these two conditions with the delay time in a similar condition but without any ideation instructions—namely, Group 3 from Experiment I.

To compare these three conditions, the distribution of waiting times for subjects was dichotomized at the median. A chi-square comparison among conditions on this dichotomy did not approach significance ($\chi^2 = 3.2$, $df = 2$), suggesting that delay times in the three conditions were essentially similar. Thus, instructions to think about the rewards, or to think sad, did not significantly facilitate delay of gratification when compared to a no-ideation condition. Instructions to think about fun things, however, produced waiting times well above either of the two other think groups and also greater than the comparable but uninstructed delay-of-gratification condition (Group 3 from Experiment I). In this regard, note that the "think fun" group of Experiment II closely replicated the long mean waiting time found in the comparable condition of Experiment I.

EXPERIMENT III

Experiments I and II involved distraction manipulations when the subjects were waiting for delayed rewards that were always visually present and directly available to attention. It is conceivable that under conditions in which delayed gratifications are not physically available for direct visual attention, their mental representation in the form of images or ideas does have a "time-binding" function and would facilitate voluntary delay. Indeed, that expectation is one that might follow from Freud's (orig. publ. 1911) formulation of primary process and the development of delaying ability. Freud implied that delay capacity begins to develop when the child provides himself with mental representations or images of the delayed object, but *only* when he cannot see it externally. That is, some discharge of tension may be achieved by cathecting an image of the reward objects, but only when they are physically unavailable for direct attention. For example, the hungry child may achieve some gratification by hallucinating the mother's breast when it is absent. If one tested that hypothesis in the present paradigm, one would have to predict long delay times when subjects were instructed to ideate about the rewards but the rewards were physically obscured from view. On the other hand, a focus on the frustrativeness of nonreward predicts that such instructions would produce short delay times. Experiment III was designed to test which expectation was correct.

METHOD

Design. The previous experiments were undertaken to determine the effects of distraction from the reward objects on delay of gratification. This experiment was designed to direct the subjects' attention to the reward objects cognitively when the objects themselves were physically obscured during the waiting period. One experimental condition and two control groups were run. In all three groups both the immediate and the delayed rewards were obscured from the sight of the children during the waiting period. The groups differed, however, in the instructions given to the subjects. In the experimental condition, the subjects were instructed that they could think about the reward objects while waiting. In the two control conditions, the subjects were either told nothing or they were instructed that they could think about "fun things" while waiting. The dependent variable was the length of time that the children waited for the delayed reward before terminating by settling for the less preferred, but immediately available, outcome.

Subjects. Sixteen subjects were run in this study. The subjects ranged in age from 3 years 5 months to 5 years 6 months, and their mean age was 4 years 6 months. There were 11 males and 5 females. Half of the subjects were assigned to the experimental condition (which directed the children's attention to the reward objects). The remaining 8 subjects were equally divided between the two control conditions ("think fun" and no ideation). The sex ratios and the mean ages of the subjects were similar across conditions. One male experimenter tested all of the subjects.

Procedure. All procedural aspects of this experiment were identical to those in the previous two experiments except for the following modifications. In the previous experiments both of the reward objects were directly available for attention during the delay period. In this study it was necessary to remove the reward objects from the child's visual field. If the experimenter took the rewards with him when he left the child waiting in the room, he might affect the child's trust that the promised rewards would ultimately be returned. Therefore, the reward objects were placed under an opaque cake tin and put under the table at which the child sat so that they could not be seen by him during the waiting period. The children were told that this operation would keep the food objects fresh while the experimenter was out of the room. The rewards were obscured in this fashion after the child had passed the comprehension questions. Thereafter, the experimenter was informed of the condition in which the subject was to be run.

In the experimental condition the experimenter gave the subjects the "think food rewards" instructions used in Experiment II. These instructions were designed to direct the children's attention to the reward objects during the delay interval. In one control condition, the experimenter merely left the room; in the other control condition, the experimenter gave the identical "think fun" instructions that were used in Experiments I and II. After completing these instructions, the experimenter left the room.

RESULTS

All of the means are depicted in Figure 3. The "no-ideation" group mean was 12.86 minutes, and the "think fun" condition mean was 14.48 minutes. It is interesting to note that these means are very close to the "think fun" means found in Experiments I and II, which were 12.12 and 13.33 minutes, respectively. In the experimental condition ("think

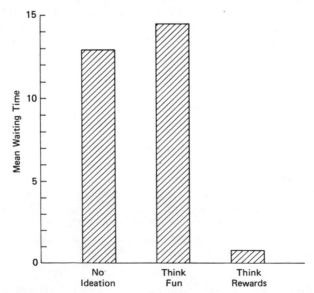

Figure 3 | MEAN NUMBER OF MINUTES OF VOLUNTARY WAITING TIME FOR EACH CONDITION IN EXPERIMENT III.

rewards") in which the children were directed to think about the physically obscured reward objects, the mean waiting time was only .78 minute. These results utterly contradict the belief that ideating about the reward objects in their absence enhances voluntary delay of gratification for them.

Mean delay times in the two control groups ("no ideation" and "think fun") obviously did not differ from each other, and, consequently, they were combined and compared with mean waiting time in the experimental condition. The resulting t test was highly significant ($t = 11.93$, $df = 14$, $p < .001$). Moreover, of the eight children in the experimental group, not a single one waited more than 2 minutes; in contrast, five of the eight control children waited the full 15 minutes ($p = .05$, two-tailed by Fisher's exact test). Thus, even when the rewards are not visually present, ideating about them and attending to them cognitively serves to substantially decrease, rather than to enhance, the duration of delay of gratification for the sake of attaining the preferred reward.

DISCUSSION: EXPERIMENTS I, II, AND III

Considering all three experiments together, it seems remarkable how well our brief cognition-inducing instructions seemed to work with our young subjects. The present seemingly simple techniques may provide a fruitful methodology for studying cognition and attention experimentally in young children. By manipulating cognition-inducing instructions and visual presence of rewards, extremely powerful effects on delay time were obtained.

To provide an overview of all the results, the main findings from the present three experiments are summarized in Figure 4. As Figure 4 shows clearly, effective delay of gratification depended on cognitive avoidance or suppression of the reward objects during the waiting period. This conclusion is based on several sets of data. First, when the subjects were waiting for the preferred but delayed reward with the reward objects in their attentional field, delay of gratification was minimal. In contrast, delay was dramatically facilitated when the subjects engaged in affectively pleasant cognitive distractions ("think fun" conditions) during the delay period. That result was replicated in the second experiment.

Second, and completely consistent with these findings, are the results from Experiment III, in which the rewards were not externally available for attention during the delay period. As Figure 4 shows, under these conditions the "think fun" group again yielded extremely long periods of delay of gratification. In contrast, cognitions about the rewards (induced by the "think rewards" instructions) resulted in an average delay time of less than 1 minute. Thus, when the children thought about the absent rewards, it was as difficult for them to delay gratification as when the rewards were directly in their attentional field (the no-ideation condition of Experiment I). Note also that when the rewards were not available for direct attention, uninstructed subjects (no ideation) found it relatively easy to delay gratification, waiting no less than the "think fun" children. These findings in the two no-ideation conditions essentially replicate those from

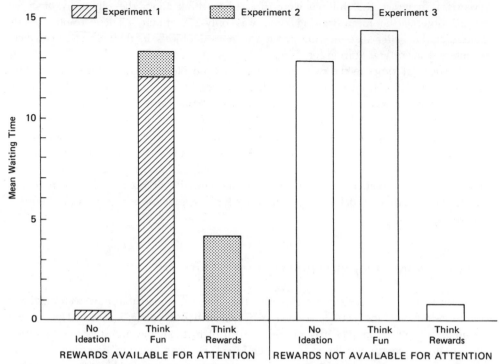

Figure 4 | MEAN NUMBER OF MINUTES OF VOLUNTARY WAITING TIME FOR TREATMENT CONDITIONS IN EXPERIMENTS I, II, III, COMPARING DIFFERENT IDEATION INSTRUCTIONS WITH CONTROLS.

comparable conditions in a previous study (Mischel & Ebbesen, 1970). In that study it was found that delay of gratification was exceedingly difficult when the youngsters faced the reward objects (either the delayed one, the immediate one, or both, with no differences between these conditions). However, just as in the present Experiment III, when the children waited with no reward objects in their attentional field, they were able to substantially delay gratification in order to attain the preferred but delayed reward.

The present data may be relevant to psychodynamic theorizing regarding delaying capacity. Predictions from psychodynamic theory concerning the development of delay capacity are complex since the process is seen as one that involves transitions from primary process to secondary process thinking. According to Rapaport's (1967) elaboration and clarification of Freudian theory, delay capacity begins with "the emergence of a hallucinatory image of the need-satisfying object when tension rises to the point where discharge should take place but the need-satisfying object is not present [pp. 315–316]." This part of the theory seems to suggest that instructions designed to help subjects imagine or ideate about absent but desired delayed gratifications should facilitate voluntary delay time. Clearly, the present data do not support such a view and therefore might be interpreted as undermining the Freudian position.

But Rapaport (1967) goes on to state that this image of the need-satisfying object does not provide "more than a minute opportunity for discharge [p. 316]." He therefore argues that delay is further developed by transition from primary process hallucinatory images to secondary process reality testing. In this phase of the development of delay capacity, discharge is postponed "until external reality conditions have been found suitable [p. 318]." Psychodynamic theory (as interpreted by Rapaport) thus suggests that effective delay begins to occur when the ego can divert energy away from images of delayed rewards and toward reality consideration and instrumental activity. Rapaport noted that internal impulse control requires "countercathexes" as in repression. This part of the psychodynamic formulation of delay seems to imply that removing attention from the delayed rewards might enhance effective impulse control. Rapaport correctly comments that "Little is known about the nature of the process by which these counter-cathexes arise [p. 219]." Future research needs to explore more closely the exact conditions that moderate the relations between specific cognitive activity and delay behavior.

The research thus far demonstrates that effective delay, rather than being mediated by consummatory fantasies, probably depends on suppressive and avoidance mechanisms that reduce frustration. This interpretation is congruent with the "Satan get thee behind me" approach to self-control recognized by Skinner (1948) in *Walden Two*. In his novel, Skinner described children learning to control themselves by learning to physically and mentally remove temptations. This approach emphasizes that one may effectively resist temptations by engaging in activities (overtly or covertly) that prevent one from attending to them. Obviously, not just any cognition serves as an effective distractor from aversive frustration or temptation. As the second experiment indicated, "think fun" is better than "think sad," whereas "think rewards" increases frustration most, hence making continued delay most difficult.

Observations of the children, in the reward-absent delay conditions, lend further credence to these interpretations. When the distress of waiting seemed to become especially acute, children tended to reach for the termination signal, but in many cases seemed to stop themselves from signaling by abruptly creating external and internal distractions for themselves. They made up quiet songs ("Oh this is your land in Redwood City"), hid their heads in their arms, pounded the floor with their feet, fiddled playfully and teasingly with the signal bell, verbalized the contingency ("If I stop now I get _____, but if I wait I get _____)," prayed to the ceiling, and so on. In one dramatically effective self-distraction technique, after obviously experiencing much agitation, a little girl rested her head, sat limply, relaxed herself, and proceeded to fall sound asleep.

These observations and the results from three experiments suggested that the ease with which subjects can cope with the frustration depends on the overt and covert response alternatives available to them during the imposed delay. The manipulations of the present experiments may be construed as having provided subjects with various types of planned alternative responses for coping with that frustration. The more the available response directed the child's attention away from the frustration, the better he was able to continue the delay and substitute a new adaptive activity during the frustration; in the present paradigm that activity could have been anything that kept him waiting without ideating about the goal objects.

It would be interesting to know if preschool subjects such as those in the present experiments were aware of the principle of "Satan, get thee behind me" before they actually began waiting. That is, given a choice of waiting for the preferred reward, with the rewards obscured or available for attention, would subjects make the right choice? To answer this question, 29 preschool children were administered the previously described instructions for the delay-of-gratification paradigm. Just before the point at which the experimenter would usually leave the child waiting alone in the room, she picked up an opaque cake cover and gave the subject the choice of covering with it either the rewards, or another set of comparable but irrelevant objects also lying on the table, or simply placing the cover over another fixed spot on the table. The results showed that the children chose the place to cover quite randomly before commencing their voluntary delay. That is, they did not seem aware that obscuring the relevant rewards would facilitate their ability to wait for them. Thus, young children do not seem to have insight into the role of cognition and attention in self-control, at least prior to actually waiting.

The data from the main experiments seem to contradict James's (1890) belief that "the essential achievement of the will" requires one to bear up and force oneself to maintain directed attention to the difficult or boring. Rather than trying to maintain aversive activities such as delay of reward through "acts of will" and focused attention, effective self-control may hinge on *transforming* the difficult into the easy, the aversive into the pleasant, the boring into the interesting, while still maintaining the task-required (reward-contingent) activity. Such transformations may occur either by engaging in the appropriate overt distracting activity (e.g., the "toy" condition) or changing one's own mental content and ideation so that it functions as a covert distractor.

It is important to recognize, however, that the mental transformations and distractions which occur during delay do not erase or undo the role of the reward contingencies in the waiting situation. This is evident in the data from Experiment I, which show how little persistence there was in "thinking fun" or playing with a toy when there was no waiting contingency. The distracting activity itself, while pleasant and distracting enough to maintain waiting for a contingent reward, did not in itself keep the children in the room for more than a minute. Additional evidence that the contingency was available mentally throughout the waiting period is that the children easily reproduced, verbally or by appropriate action, the contingency at the end of the waiting period. Children who had been busily distracting themselves for the full 15 minutes, playing with a toy or singing songs, immediately and spontaneously ate the appropriate food reward when the experimenter returned. Obviously then, the transformation of the aversive waiting into a pleasant play period does not efface the task-oriented purpose of the behavior, and presumably the two processes somehow coexist. Subjects were guided by their goals, even when seemingly absorbed in distractions designed to obscure them. Just how the contingency was operating is an interesting point for speculation. The contingency may have been available but never reproduced mentally until the end of waiting; even more likely, subjects may have reminded themselves of the contingency episodically throughout the waiting period. As mentioned previously, verbalizations of the contingency often occurred when the subjects momentarily left their distracting play and seemed about to terminate the waiting period. It is as if the subject periodically reminds himself of the goal for which he is waiting, distracts himself from it to make delay less frustrative, and then repeats the process.

Extending these speculations further, a good way to master the difficult or aversive may be to think or do something that is pleasant, while still performing the necessary task-relevant response (e.g., waiting, working). Rather than "willing" oneself to heroic bravery, one needs to perform the necessary "difficult" response while engaging in another one cognitively. The principle involved here seems similar to the one underlying "counterconditioning" of aversive emotional reactions in behavior therapy. To master a snake phobia, for example, the subject needs to deal with the problematic stimulus while engaged in a fear-incompatible positive internal response (e.g., relaxation); whereas in delay of gratification one must perform a difficult or problematic response while engaged in ideation of stimuli that are positive or distracting. In either case, it is easier to do something difficult if one also does something easy or pleasant at the same time.

The findings from the present studies seem extremely reliable, being based on several replications and diverse convergent data. However, one obviously cannot generalize from them to the role of cognition in forms of self-control other than the delay-of-gratification paradigm. For example, it might be adaptive to ideate about desired or needed but currently unavailable goal objects, but only in situations in which the subject's actions can be potentially instrumental in producing the desired outcome. Thus, when attainment of a positive outcome is contingent on the subject's own problem-solving behavior, it might help him to think about the goal object while seeking means for achieving or reaching it in reality. In contrast, in the present delay-of-gratification paradigm, attainment of the preferred goal required only passive waiting: beyond delaying, there was absolutely nothing the subject could do to influence the occurrence of the desired outcome. Moreover, even his delay behavior (while a necessary condition for attainment of the preferred outcome) could in no way influence the time at which gratification would ultimately occur.

Data relevant to the dilemma, in which subjects cannot do anything to attain a desired but unavailable outcome, may be found in studies of "defensive perception." Our studies on attention in delay employ a design, which, in a way, seems the reverse of these classic "new look" studies. In the latter the subject was, first, frustrated or pained and was then asked what he thought or perceived most readily (on projective measures). In contrast, in the present methodology, the subject is given the "thoughts," and then their effect on what he does is noted; specifically, his ability to sustain goal-directed delay behavior and to cope with frustration are measured. Consistent with our data, findings from perceptual defense studies indicate a tendency to avoid painful stimuli cognitively and perceptually when nothing can be done by the subject to cope with them instrumentally (e.g., Reece, 1954). It also has been reported that in response to projective material, sleep-deprived subjects showed *fewer* sleep-related ideas and themes than did controls (Murray, 1959). Likewise, food ideation is less when subjects are severely food deprived than when they are not hungry (Lazarus, Yousem, & Arenberg, 1953). Similarly, Clark's

(1952) pioneering experiments on Thematic Apperception Test (TAT) sexual imagery compared the amount of sexual responses in TAT stories written by sexually aroused and nonaroused males. He found less sexual imagery and also less "sexual guilt" in the stories of sexually aroused subjects. Clark attributed his results to a simultaneous, predominating increase in sexual guilt which he suggests was evoked by the sexual arousal and is "sufficient to inhibit the expression of sex with a consequent lowering of guilt [p. 398]." But a more parsimonious interpretation in terms of the present experiments is that the Clark results could reflect cognitive avoidance of all sexual thoughts (including those scored as "guilt") under conditions that made sexual thoughts highly frustrative, that is, sexual arousal with no opportunity for satisfaction.

Thus, when subjects cannot cope with aversive stimuli instrumentally (e.g., by going to sleep when sleepy, by finding food when hungry, by avoiding painful shock, and by obtaining sexual release when aroused, they may engage in cognitive avoidance of those stimuli. To decrease frustration, subjects may generate their own distractors and avoid the aversive stimuli cognitively, if possible, as we observed repeatedly in our studies. This conclusion—that aversive stimuli are avoided cognitively—may be restricted, however, to paradigms in which the subject believes that thinking about the aversive stimulus cannot change the contingencies in the situation.

The overall results of the present experiments help to clarify some widespread basic theoretical misconceptions regarding self-control. In particular, following dynamic formulations, it has been customary to construe voluntary delay of reward as involving the *ability* to defer immediate gratification. This ability has been viewed as an enduring trait of "ego strength" on which individuals differed stably and consistently in many situations. In fact, as the present data indicate, under appropriate motivational and attentional-cognitive conditions, virtually all subjects, even young children, could manage to delay for lengthy time periods.

Taken collectively, research on delay of gratification permits us now to speculate about a two-part process in delay of gratification. First, one must consider the determinants of the *choice* to delay for the sake of more preferred delayed outcomes. This choice is influenced mainly by the subject's expectations concerning the probable consequences of his choice. These consequences include the relative subjective values of the immediate and delayed outcomes themselves as well as other probable reinforcing outcomes associated with each alternative. As previous research has shown, expectancies relevant to these outcomes depend on the subject's direct and vicarious past experiences and trust relationships, modeling cues, the specific contingencies in the choice, and so on (e.g., Mischel, 1966).

Second, once the choice to delay gratification has been made, effective delay depends on cognitive and overt self-distractions to reduce the aversiveness of the self-imposed frustration. For this purpose, the subject needs to "tune out" on the goal objects and generate his own distractions while maintaining the contingent behavior for goal attainment.

Thus, the subject can wait most stoically if he expects that he really will get the deferred larger outcome in the waiting paradigm, and wants it very much, but shifts his attention elsewhere and occupies himself internally with cognitive distractions. Any conditions that shift attention from the delayed objects appear to facilitate voluntary waiting times appreciably. In order to bridge the delay effectively, it is as if the subject must make an internal notation of what he is waiting for, perhaps remind himself of it periodically, but he must spend the remaining time attending to other less frustrative internal and external stimuli.

SUMMARY

Three experiments investigated attentional and cognitive mechanisms in delay of gratification. In each study preschool children could obtain a less preferred reward immediately or continue waiting indefinitely for a more preferred but delayed reward. Experiment I compared the effects of external and cognitive distraction from the reward objects on the length of time which preschool children waited for the preferred delayed reward before forfeiting it for the sake of the less preferred immediate one. In accord with predictions from an extension of frustrative nonreward theory, children waited much longer for a preferred reward when they were distracted from the rewards than when they attended to them directly. Experiment II demonstrated that only certain cognitive events (thinking "fun things") served as effective ideational distractors. Thinking "sad thoughts" produced short delay times, as did thinking about the rewards themselves. In Experiment III the delayed rewards were not physically available for direct attention during the delay period, and the children's attention to them cognitively was manipulated by prior instructions. While the children waited, cognitions about the rewards significantly reduced, rather than enhanced, the length of their delay of gratification. Overall, attentional and cognitive mechanisms which enhanced the salience of the rewards shortened the length of voluntary delay, while distractions from the rewards, overtly or cognitively, facilitated delay. The results permit a reinterpretation of basic mechanisms in voluntary delay of gratification and self-control.

REFERENCES

Amsel, A. The role of frustrative nonreward in noncontinuous reward situations. *Psychological Bulletin*, 1958, 55, 102–119.

Amsel, A. Frustrative nonreward in partial reinforcement and discrimination learning. *Psychological Review*, 1962, 69, 306–328.

Clark, R. A. The projective measurement of experimentally induced levels of sexual motivation. *Journal of Experimental Psychology*, 1952, 44, 391–399.

Freud, S. Formulations regarding the two principles in mental functioning: 1911. In *Collected Papers*. Vol. 4. New York: Basic Books, 1959.

Grim, P. F., Kohlberg, L., & White, S. H. Some relationships between conscience and attentional processes. *Journal of Personality and Social Psychology*, 1968, 8, 239–252.

Hartshorne, H., & May, M. A. *Studies in the nature of character*. Vol. 1. *Studies in deceit*. New York: Macmillan, 1928.

James, W. *Principles of psychology*. New York: Holt, Rinehart and Winston, 1890.

Lazarus, R. S., Yousem, H., & Arenberg, D. Hunger and perception. *Journal of Personality*, 1953, *21*, 312–328.

Mandler, G. The interruption of behavior. *Nebraska Symposium on Motivation*, 1964, *12*, 163–219.

Mischel, W. Theory and research on the antecedents of self-imposed delay of reward. In B. A. Maher (Ed.), *Progress in experimental personality research.* Vol. 3. New York: Academic Press, 1966.

Mischel, W., & Ebbesen, E. B. Attention in delay of gratification. *Journal of Personality and Social Psychology*, 1970, *16*, 329–337.

Murray, E. J. Conflict and repression during sleep deprivation. *Journal of Abnormal and Social Psychology*, 1959, *59*, 95–101.

Rapaport, D. On the psychoanalytic theory of thinking. In M. M. Gill (Ed.), *The collected papers of David Rapaport.* New York: Basic Books, 1967.

Reece, M. M. The effect of shock on recognition thresholds. *Journal of Abnormal and Social Psychology*, 1954, *49*, 165–172.

Skinner, B. F. *Walden two.* New York: Macmillan, 1948.

Winer, B. J. *Statistical principles in experimental design.* New York: McGraw-Hill, 1962.

19.2 | TRAINING IMPULSIVE CHILDREN TO TALK TO THEMSELVES: A MEANS OF DEVELOPING SELF-CONTROL[*][1]

Donald H. Meichenbaum and Joseph Goodman

The development of the functional interaction between self-verbalization and nonverbal behavior has received much attention (Luria, 1961; Piaget, 1947; Reese, 1962; and see especially a review by Kohlberg, Yaeger, & Hjertholm, 1968). Two general research strategies have been employed to assess the influence of self-verbalizations on behavior. The first strategy is characterized by *S*'s performance on a task and *E*'s subsequent inference as to the presence or absence of specific cognitive activities. In general, this approach has used the concept of "deficiency" to explain poor performance. Reese (1962)

* SOURCE: Meichenbaum, D. H., & Goodman, J. Training impulsive children to talk to themselves: A means of developing self-control. *Journal of Abnormal Psychology*, 1971, 77, 115–126. Copyright by the American Psychological Association and reprinted by permission.

[1] This work was supported by the Ontario Mental Health Foundation Grant 120.

The authors wish to thank Dale Willows for her assistance in the collection of the data and Richard Steffy for his many constructive comments.

has suggested a mediation deficiency hypothesis; Flavell and his co-workers (Flavell, Beach, & Chinsky, 1966; Moely, Olson, Halwes, & Flavell, 1967) have offered a production deficiency hypothesis, and most recently Bem (1970) has suggested a comprehension deficiency hypothesis. The developing child is characterized as going through stages during which he (*a*) does not mediate or regulate his overt behavior verbally; (*b*) does not spontaneously produce relevant mediators; and (*c*) does not comprehend the nature of the problem in order to discover what mediators to produce. Thus, problem solving is viewed as a three-stage process of comprehension, production, and mediation, and poor performance can result from a "deficiency" at any one of these stages. The deficiency literature suggests that a training program designed to improve task performance and engender self-control should provide explicit training in the comprehension of the task, the spontaneous production of mediators, and the use of such mediators to control nonverbal behavior. The present cognitive self-guidance treatment program was designed to provide such training for a group of "impulsive" children.

The other strategy, which is designed to assess the functional role of private speech in task performance, directly manipulates the child's verbalizations and examines resulting changes in nonverbal behavior. Vygotsky (1962) has suggested that internalization of verbal commands is the critical step in the child's development of voluntary control of his behavior. Data from a wide range of studies (Bem, 1967; Klein, 1963; Kohlberg et al., 1968; Lovaas, 1964; Luria, 1959, 1961; Meichenbaum & Goodman, 1969a, 1969b) provide support for the age increase in cognitive self-guiding private speech, and the increase in internalization with age. These results suggest a progression from external to internal control. Early in development, the speech of others, usually adults, mainly controls and directs a child's behavior; somewhat later, the child's own overt speech becomes an effective regulator of his behavior; and still later, the child's covert or inner speech can assume a regulatory role. The present studies were designed to examine the efficacy of a cognitive self-guidance treatment program which followed the developmental sequence by which overt verbalizations of an adult or *E*, followed by the child's overt self-verbalizations, followed by covert self-verbalization would result in the child's own verbal control of his nonverbal behavior. By using this fading procedure, we hoped to (*a*) train impulsive Ss to provide themselves with internally originated verbal commands or self-instructions and to respond to them appropriately; (*b*) strengthen the mediational properties of the children's inner speech in order to bring their behavior under their own verbal or discriminative control; (*c*) overcome any possible "comprehension, production, or mediational deficiencies"; and finally (*d*) encourage the children to appropriately self-reinforce their behavior. We hoped to have the child's private speech gain a new functional significance, to have the child develop a new cognitive style or "learning set" and thus to engender self-control.

Two studies are reported which apply the cognitive self-guidance treatment regimen to impulsive school children. The first study, using second-grade children who had been assigned to an "opportunity remedial class," provided four ½-hr. individual training sessions over a 2-wk. period. The effects of training on performance measures and classroom behavior is reported. The second study examines the modification value of a particular component of the treatment regimen, namely modeling, which is designed to alter the child's impulsive cognitive style in one treatment session as assessed on Kagan's (1966) Matching Familiar Figures (MFF) Test. The impulsive Ss in the second study have been selected from kindergarten and first-grade classes as assessed by their failure to follow an instruction to "go slower" on a preassessment of the MFF test. Both studies indicate the general treatment regimen designed to train impulsive children to talk to themselves, a possible means of developing self-control.

STUDY I

METHOD

Subjects

The Ss were 15 second-grade children (8 females, 7 males) whose ages ranged from 7 to 9 yr. with a mean of 8 yr., 2 mo. and who had been placed in an "opportunity remedial class" in a public elementary school. The children were placed into the opportunity class because of behavioral problems such as hyperactivity and poor self-control, and/or they had low IQs on one of a variety of school-administered intelligence tests. The cutoff point on the IQ measures was 85, but for several Ss the last assessment was several years prior to the present research project. The children's behavior both in class and on performance measures was measured before and after treatment as well as in a 1-mo. follow-up assessment described below. Following the pretreatment assessment, Ss were assigned to one of three groups. One group comprised the cognitive self-guidance treatment group ($N = 5$). The remaining two groups included in the study were control groups. One control group met with E with the same regularity as did the cognitively trained Ss. This attention control group ($N = 5$) afforded an index of behavioral change due to factors of attention, exposure to training materials, and any demand characteristics inherent in our measures of improvement. In addition, an assessment control group of Ss who received no treatment was included. The assessment control group ($N = 5$) provided an index of the contribution of intercurrent life experiences to any behavioral change (e.g., being a member of the opportunity remedial class). Assignment to these three groups was done randomly, subject to the two contraints of (a) equating the groups on sex composition and (b) matching the groups on their prorated WISC IQ performance scores taken prior to treatment.

Treatments

Cognitive training group. The Ss in this group were seen individually for four ½-hr. treatment sesions over a 2-wk. period. The cognitive training technique proceeded as follows: First, E performed a task talking aloud while S observed (E acted as a model); then S performed the same task while E instructed S aloud; then S was asked to perform the task again while instructing himself aloud; then S performed the task while whispering to himself (lip movements); and finally S performed the task covertly (without lip movements). The verbalizations which E modeled and S subsequently used included: (a) questions about the nature and demands of the task so as to compensate for a possible comprehension deficiency;

(*b*) answers to these questions in the form of cognitive rehearsal and planning in order to overcome any possible production deficiency; (*c*) self-instructions in the form of self-guidance while performing the task in order to overcome any possible mediation deficiency; and (*d*) self-reinforcement. The following is an example of *E*'s modeled verbalizations which *S* subsequently used (initially overtly, then covertly):

> Okay, what is it I have to do? You want me to copy the picture with the different lines. I have to go slow and be careful. Okay, draw the line down, down, good; then to the right, that's it; now down some more and to the left. Good, I'm doing fine so far. Remember go slow. Now back up again. No, I was supposed to go down. That's okay. Just erase the line carefully. . . . Good. Even if I make an error I can go on slowly and carefully. Okay, I have to go down now. Finished. I did it.

Note in this example an error in performance was included and *E* appropriately accommodated. In prior research with impulsive children, Meichenbaum and Goodman (1969b) observed a marked deterioration in their performance following errors. The *E*'s verbalizations varied with the demands of each task, but the general treatment format remained the same throughout. The treatment sequence was also individually adapted to the capabilities of the *S* and the difficulties of the task.

A variety of tasks was employed to train the child to use self-instructions to control his nonverbal behavior. The tasks varied along a dimension from simple sensorimotor abilities to more complex problem-solving abilities. The sensorimotor tasks, such as copying line patterns and coloring figures within certain boundaries, provided *S* with an opportunity to produce a narrative description of his behavior, both preceding and accompanying his performance. Over the course of a training session, the child's overt self-statements on a particular task were faded to the covert level, what Luria (1961) has called "interiorization of language." The difficulty level of the training tasks was increased over the four training sessions requiring more cognitively demanding activities. Such tasks as reproducing designs and following sequential instructions taken from the Stanford-Binet intelligence test, completing pictorial series as on the Primary Mental Abilities test, and solving conceptual tasks as on the Ravens Matrices test, required *S* to verbalize the demands of the task and problem-solving strategies. The *E* modeled appropriate self-verbalizations for each of these tasks and then had the child follow the fading procedure. Although the present tasks assess many of the same cognitive abilities required by our dependent measures, there are significant differences between the training tasks and the performance and behavioral indexes used to assess improvement. It should be noted that the attentional control group received the same opportunities to perform on each of the training tasks, but without cognitive self-guidance training.

One can imagine a similar training sequence in the learning of a new motor skill such as driving a car. Initially the driver actively goes through a mental checklist, sometimes aloud, which includes verbal rehearsal, self-guidance, and sometimes appropriate self-reinforcement, especially when driving a stick-shift car. Only with repetition does the sequence become automatic and the cognitions become short-circuited. This sequence is also seen in the way children learn to tie shoelaces and in the development of many other skills. If this observation has any merit, then a training procedure which makes these steps explicit should facilitate the development of self-control.

In summary, the goals of the training procedure were to develop for the impulsive child a cognitive style or learning set in which the child could "size up" the demands of a task, cognitively rehearse, and then guide his performance by means of self-instructions, and when appropriate reinforce himself.

Attention control group. The children in this untutored group had the same number of sessions with E as did the cognitive training Ss. During this time, the child was exposed to identical materials and engaged in the same general activities, but did not receive any self-instructional training. For example, these attentional control Ss received the same number of trials on a task as did the cognitively trained Ss, but they did not receive self-instructional training. An attempt was made to provide both the experimental and attention control groups with equal amounts of social reinforcement for behavioral performance on the tasks.

Assessment control group. This untreated control group received only the same pretreatment, posttreatment, and follow-up assessments as the cognitive treatment and attention control groups.

Instruments

Two general classes of dependent measures were used to assess the efficacy of the cognitive self-guidance treatment regimen to improve performance and engender self-control. The first class of measures involved performance on a variety of psychometric instruments which have been previously used to differentiate impulsive from nonimpulsive children. The second class of measures assessed the generalizability of the treatment effects to the classroom situation. The female E who performed the pretreatment, posttreatment, and follow-up assessments on the performance measures and the two female Es who made classroom observations during pretreatment and posttreatment periods were completely unaware of which children received which treatment.

Performance measures. Three different psychometric tests were used to assess changes in behavioral and cognitive impulsivity during the pretreatment, posttreatment, and follow-up periods. Several investigators (Anthony, 1959; Eysenck, 1955; Foulds, 1951; Porteus, 1942) have demonstrated that the Porteus Maze test, especially the qualitative score which is based upon errors in style and quality of execution, distinguishes between individuals differing in impulsiveness. Most recently, Palkes, Stewart, and Kahana (1968) have reported that hyperactive boys significantly improved on Porteus Maze performance following training in self-directed verbal commands. Thus, the Porteus Maze performance provided one indicant of behavioral change. Because of the length of the assessment (some 45 min.), only years 8–11 of the Porteus Maze test were used. On the posttest the Vineland Revision form of the Porteus Maze test was used.

A second measure which has been used to assess cognitive impulsivity is Kagan's (1966) MFF test. The S's task on the MFF test is to select from an array of variants one picture which is identical to a standard picture. The tendency toward fast or slow decision times and the number of errors are used to identify the degree of conceptual impulsivity. Further support for the use of the MFF test in the present study comes from research by Meichenbaum and Goodman (1969a), who have reported a positive relationship between a child's relative inability to verbally control his motor behavior by means of covert self-instructions and an impulsive conceptual tempo on the MFF test. Parallel forms of the MFF test were developed by using six alternate items in the pretreatment and posttreatment assessments, with the pretreatment MFF test being readministered on the follow-up assessment.

The final set of performance measures was derived from three performance subtests of the WISC. The three subtests selected were Picture Arrangement, Block Design, and Coding. Respectively, these subtests are designed to assess (*a*) the ability to comprehend and size up a total situation requiring anticipation and planning; (*b*) the ability to analyze and form abstract designs as illustrated by *S*'s performance and approach to the problems; and (*c*) the child's motor speed and activity level (Kitzinger & Blumberg, 1957; Lutey, 1966; Wechsler, 1949). The results from the WISC subtests are reported in scaled scores and as a prorated IQ performance estimate.

In summary, the performance measures were designed to assess the range of abilities from sensorimotor, as indicated by qualitative scores on Porteus Maze and Coding tasks on the WISC, to more cognitively demanding tasks such as the MFF test, Block Design, and Picture Arrangement subtests.

Classroom measures. Two measures were used to ascertain whether any of the expected changes would extend into the classroom. The first measure behaviorally assessed the 15 children on their appropriateness and attentiveness within the classroom setting. We used a time-sampling observational technique (10 sec. observe, 10 sec. record) which was developed by Meichenbaum, Bowers, and Ross (1968, 1969) to rate inappropriate classroom behavior. Inappropriate classroom behavior was defined as any behavior which was not consistent with the task set forth by the teacher, that is, behavior which was not task specific. The children were observed for 2 school days 1 wk. before and immediately after treatment. The second measure involved a teacher's questionnaire which was designed to assess each child's behavioral self-control, activity level, cooperativeness, likeability, etc. The questionnaire consisted of 10 incomplete statements, each of which was followed by three forced choice alternative completions. The teacher filled out the scale immediately prior to treatment and 3 wk. later at the conclusion of the posttreatment assessment.

RESULTS

The relative efficacy of the cognitive self-guidance treatment program was assessed by means of a Lindquist (1953) Type I analysis of variance which yields a treatment effect, trials effect (pretreatment and posttreatment assessments), and a Treatment $\times$ Trials interaction. The results from the 1-mo. follow-up measures were analyzed separately. Multiple *t*-test comparisons (one-tailed) were performed on the change scores for each of the dependent measures. Figure 1 presents the performance measures.

The analyses of the three WISC subtests revealed only a significant Group $\times$ Trials interaction on the Picture Arrangement subtest ($F = 4.56$, $df = 2/12$, $p = .033$) and a strong trend towards significance on the Coding subtest (Group $\times$ Trials $F = 2.87$,

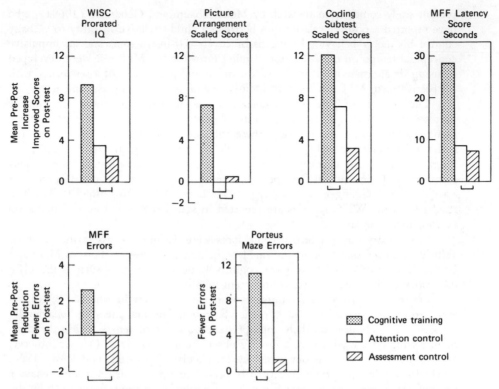

Figure 1 | MEAN CHANGE SCORES FROM PRETREATMENT TO POSTTREATMENT ON PERFORMANCE MEASURES. (GROUPS NOT CONNECTED BY SOLID LINE ARE SIGNIFICANTLY DIFFERENT AT .05 LEVEL.)

$df = 2/12$, $p = .10$). The performances on the Block Design subtest did not yield any significant groups, trials, or Group $\times$ Trials interactions. When the performances on the three WISC subtests were combined to yield a prorated IQ score, the relative efficacy of the cognitive training procedure is further revealed in a significant Group $\times$ Trials interaction ($F = 3.97$, $df = 2/12$, $p = .05$). The cognitive training group improved 8.3 IQ points ($SD = 3.8$), from an IQ of 88.4 to and IQ of 96.7. In comparison, the attention control group and the assessment control group improved, respectively, 3.4 ($SD = 4.1$) and 2.2 ($SD = 3.0$) IQ points. Multiple t comparisons indicated that the cognitive training group was significantly different ($p < .05$) from the attentional and assessment control groups on the Picture Arrangement and Coding subtests, and on the prorated IQ scores, whereas the two control groups did not significantly differ from each other on the WISC measures.

Further evidence for the efficacy of the cognitive training is derived from the measure of cognitive impulsivity, namely, the MFF test. A significant Group $\times$ Trials interaction ($F = 9.49$, $df = 2/12$, $p = .004$) was found on the initial decision time or latency score on the MFF test. The cognitive training group increased its mean total decision time for the six MFF items from pretest to posttest by 27.4 sec. ($SD = 10.3$), in comparison to the attention and assessment control groups who, respectively, increased their total posttest decision times by 7.4 sec. ($SD = 3.8$) and 6.8 sec. ($SD = 9.9$). The differential increase in response time indicates that the impulsive Ss in the cognitively trained group took significantly longer before responding on the posttest. The analyses of the error scores on the MFF test did not yield any significant differences, although the trend of the results did suggest differential effectiveness for the cognitively trained Ss. The cognitively trained Ss had a group total decrease on the posttest of 8 errors in comparison to the attentional control Ss, who had a group total decrease of only 2 errors on the posttest, and the assessment control Ss, who had a group total increase of 10 errors on the posttest. The absence of statistical significance on the error scores may be due to the relative ease of the MFF test for this age level and the use of a shortened version of the test in order to develop parallel forms (i.e., 6 items were used instead of the usual 12-item test). The potential usefulness of the cognitive training procedure in altering cognitive impulsivity was examined in the second study which is described below.

An analysis of the performance on the Porteus Maze test indicated a significant Group $\times$ Trials interaction ($F = 5.52$, $df = 2/12$, $p = .02$), with the cognitive training and the attentional control groups making significantly ($p < .05$) less errors on the posttest than the assessment control group. The mean change scores indicated that (a) Ss who received cognitive training improved most with 10.8 ($SD = 4.3$) less errors on the posttest; (b) Ss in the attentional control group made 7.8 ($SD = 6.8$) less errors on the posttest; and (c) the assessment control group made 1.2 ($SD = 47.$) more errors on the posttest. Both the cognitive training group and the attentional control group decreased errors on the posttest by cutting fewer corners, crossing over fewer lines, lifting their pencils less frequently, and producing fewer irregular lines. Palkes et al. (1968) have reported a significant improvement on the Porteus Maze test for a self-directed verbal command group relative to an assessment or no-treatment control group, but they did not include an attentional control group. The present results indicated that an attentional control group which received only practice on a variety of sensorimotor and cognitive tasks also significantly improved their performance on the Porteus Maze test. The inclusion of such an attentional control group is thus necessary in order to exclude alternative hypotheses.

The analyses of the Ss' classroom behavior by means of time-sampling observations and by teachers' ratings did not yield any significant differences. The absence of a significant treatment effect in the classroom may be due to a lack of generalization because of the limited number of training sessions and/or the lack of sensitivity of the assessment measures. The analyses of the 4-wk. follow-up assessment revealed that the cognitive training group maintained their improved performance on the test battery, relative to the attentional and assessment control groups. The analyses of the follow-up test performances relative to the pretreatment performance indicated that on the Picture Arrangement subest, the WISC prorated IQ score, and the decision time on the MFF, the cognitive training group was significantly different ($p < .05$) from the two control groups. The analysis of the qualitative performance on the Porteus Maze test indicated that both the cognitive training group and the attentional control group maintained their improved performance relative to the assessment control group.

The results of the first study proved most encouraging and suggested that a cognitive self-guidance training program can significantly alter behavior of impulsive children. The purpose of the second study was to examine the differential contribution of the various components of the treatment program in modifying impulsive behavior. The cognitive training procedure involved both modeling by E and subsequent self-instructional training by S. In this study a comparison is made between the relative efficacy of modeling alone versus modeling plus self-instructional training in modifying cognitive impulsivity as measured by the MFF test. Kagan (1965) has defined cognitive impulsivity as a conceptual tempo or decision-time variable representing the time S takes to consider alternate solutions before committing himself to one of them in a situation with high response uncertainty. Kagan and his associates (Kagan, 1965, 1966; Kagan, Rosman, Day, Albert, & Phillips, 1964) have shown that performance on the MFF test has high stability and intertest generality and is related to performance on visual discrimination tasks, inductive reasoning, serial recall, and reading skills. Most recently, investigators have been interested in the modification of cognitive impulsivity. Kagan, Pearson, and Welsh (1966) have attempted to train, in three individual sessions, inhibition to impulsive responding by requiring the child to defer his answer for a fixed period of 10 to 15 sec. During this period the child was encouraged to study the stimuli in the task and to think about his answer, but he did *not* receive training in more efficient procedures to emit during this interval. Significant changes in latency or decision time occurred, but no corresponding significant change in errors was evident. Debus (1970) examined the usefulness of filmed modeling of reflective behavior and found a decrease only in decision time, and, like Kagan, Pearson, and Welch (1966), no corresponding change in errors. The studies by Kagan et al. (1966) and Debus (1970) have concentrated on increasing latency times without paying sufficient attention to inducing improved cognitive and/or scanning strategies in the impulsive child. Siegelman (1969) and Drake (1970) have demonstrated that different attentional and cognitive strategies seem to underlie the performance of impulsive and reflective Ss. The data from Siegelman and Drake indicate that the impulsive child on the MFF test (*a*) displays a greater biasing of attention both in extent of scanning and in number of alternatives ignored; (*b*) is simply in search of some variant that globally resembles the standard and is not very discriminating or analytic in his viewing. In comparison, the reflective child seems to follow a strategy designed to find explicit differences among alternatives and then to check the standard for verification. The impulsive child's approach or strategy on the MFF task results in many errors and quick decision times. The purpose of the present study was to examine the usefulness of the cognitive self-guidance training procedure in altering the attentional strategy of the impulsive child on the MFF test. The efficacy of the self-instructional training procedure in modifying cognitive impulsivity is compared with a modeling-alone procedure. An attentional control group which received exposure to the practice materials but no explicit training was included for comparative purposes.

STUDY II

METHOD

Subjects

The 15 impulsive children who received training were selected from a larger group of kindergarten ($N = 30$) and first-grade ($N = 30$) public school children on the basis of two behavioral criteria. All of the children were individually tested on parallel forms of six items each of the MFF test. Interspersed between the two MFF forms the instruction "You don't have to hurry. You should go slowly and carefully" was given to all *S*s. The 15 impulsive *S*s (4 male and 4 female kindergarteners and 4 male and 3 female first graders) were selected on the basis of the *S*'s initial performance on Form I of the MFF test and the absence of any appreciable improvement in performance on Form II of the MFF test. Thus, the selected impulsive children were initially cognitively impulsive, and they did not significantly alter their style of responding even though they were instructed to do so. The use of an instructional manipulation to select *S*s is consistent with Vygotsky's (1962) suggestion that a child's capabilities are best reflected by his response to instructions.

Following Session 1, the 15 selected impulsive *S*s were randomly assigned to one of the treatment groups (viz., modeling alone or modeling plus self-instructional training) or to the attentional control group, subject to the constraint of comparable age and sex representation in each group. One week later in a second session, each of the impulsive *S*s was individually seen by a different *E* (female), who conducted the treatment, after which *S*s were tested on a third form of the six-item MFF test by the first *E* (male) who had conducted the testing in Session 1. The *E* who administered the three forms of the MFF test was thus unaware into which group *S* had been placed. The training materials consisted of the Picture Matching subtest from the Primary Mental Abilities (PMA) test and items from the Ravens' Matrices test. These materials elicit similar task abilities to the MFF test and provide a useful format for modeling reflective behaviors. The training procedure which lasted some 20 min. consisted of *E* performing or modeling behavior on one item of the practice material and then *S* doing an item. There were in all eight practice trials.

Treatments

Cognitive modeling group. The *S*s in this group ($N = 5$) initially observed the *E* who modeled a set of verbalizations and behaviors which characterizes the reflective child's proposed strategy on the MFF test. The following is an example of *E*'s modeled verbalizations on the PMA Picture Matching test:

> I have to remember to go slowly to get it right. Look carefully at this one (the standard), now look at these carefully (the variants). Is this one different? Yes, it has an extra leaf. Good, I can eliminate this one. Now, let's look at this one (another variant). I think it's this one, but let me first check the others. Good, I'm going slow and carefully. Okay, I think it's this one.

The impulsive child was exposed to a model which demonstrated the strategy to search for differences that would allow him successively to eliminate as incorrect all variants but one. The E modeled verbal statements or a strategy to make detailed comparisons across figures, looking at all variants before offering an answer. As in the first study, E also modeled errors and then how to cope with errors and improve upon them. For example, following an error E would model the following verbalizations:

It's okay, just be careful. I should have looked more carefully. Follow the plan to check each one. Good, I'm going slowly.

After E modeled on an item, S was given an opportunity to perform on a similar practice item. The S was encouraged and socially reinforced for using the strategy E had just modeled, but did not receive explicit practice in self-instructing. This modeling-alone group was designed to indicate the degree of behavioral change from exposure to an adult model.

Cognitive modeling plus self-instructional training group. The Ss in this group were exposed to the same modeling behavior by E as were Ss in the modeling-alone group, but in addition they were explicitly trained to produce the self-instructions E emitted while performing the task. After E modeled on an item, S was instructed to perform the task while talking aloud to himself as E had done. Over the course of the eight practice trials, the child's self-verbalizations were faded from initially an overt level to a covert level, as in Study I.

Attentional control groups. The Ss in this group observed the E perform the task and were given an opportunity to perform on each of the practice items. The E's verbalizations consisted only of general statements to "go slow, be careful, look carefully," but did not include the explicit modeling of verbalizations dealing with scanning strategies as did the two treatment groups. The Ss were encouraged and socially reinforced to go slow and be careful, but were not trained to self-instruct. In many ways this group approximates the methods teachers and parents use to demonstrate a task in which they make general prohibitions, but do not explicate the strategies or details involved in solving the task. This group can be considered a minimal modeling condition or an attentional control group for exposure to E and practice on task materials.

An attempt was made to provide all three groups with equal amounts of social reinforcement for their performance. At the completion of the modeling session, all Ss were told, "Can you remember to do just like I did whenever you play games like this? Remember to go slowly and carefully." The E who conducted the training departed, and the first E then administered Form III of the MFF test.

RESULTS

Selection of Ss

Table 1 presents the performance of reflective and impulsive Ss on the initial MFF test (Form I) and on the MFF test (Form II) which was administered immediately after the instructions to "go slower." Of the original 60 Ss tested, 45 were classified into either the reflective or impulsive groups, based on the S's response time and errors relative to the performance of the same age and sex peer group. The instructions to go

Table 1 | IMPULSIVE AND REFLECTIVE Ss' PERFORMANCE ON INITIAL MFF TEST (FORM I) AND ON THE MFF TEST (FORM II) ADMINISTERED AFTER INSTRUCTIONS TO "GO SLOWER"

Ss	MFF PERFORMANCE			
	Form I		Form II	
	$\overline{X}$	SD	$\overline{X}$	SD
Reflectives ($N = 20$)				
Total errors	6.3	3.5	7.7	4.0
Total decision time	99.8	6.5	123.8	10.5
Impulsives ($N = 25$)				
Total errors	16.4	3.8	11.4	7.0
Total decision time	42.9	5.5	58.1	7.6

slower resulted in a significant ($p < .05$) increase in the mean total response time on initial decisions for reflective Ss (i.e., from 99.8 to 123.8 sec.), but no comparable change in errors. The later finding may be due to a "ceiling effect" and/or a slight decrement in performance resulting from anxiety. Several reflective Ss indicated that they interpreted E's instruction to go slower as an indicant that they were not performing adequately. Ward (1968) has reported that anxiety over failure played a greater role in the performance of reflective children than it did in the performance of impulsive children. The impulsive Ss demonstrated a marked variability in how their performance changed as a result of the instructional manipulation. This variability permitted selection of the 15 most impulsive Ss whose performance changed minimally. In a second session, these impulsive Ss were provided with treatment. Table 2 presents the performance scores for the impulsive Ss who were selected for treatment and those impulsive

Table 2 | A BREAKDOWN OF IMPULSIVE Ss' PERFORMANCE ON FORMS I AND II OF THE MFF TEST

Ss	MFF PERFORMANCE			
	Form I		Form II	
	$\overline{X}$	SD	$\overline{X}$	SD
Impulsive Ss selected for treatment ($N = 15$)				
Total errors	15.2	3.5	12.2	4.6
Total decision time	42.8	5.3	51.2	5.9
Impulsive Ss *not* selected for treatment ($N = 10$)				
Total errors	17.6	4.2	10.5	5.4
Total decision time	43.0	6.0	65.0	8.3

*S*s who significantly improved their performance from the minimal instructional manipulation.

In summary, from a group of 60 kindergarten and first-grade children, 15 *S*s were selected who were most cognitively impulsive on initial testing and who minimally altered their response style when explicitly given the instruction to do so.

Analysis of Treatment Efficacy

Figure 2 presents the performance of the modeling group, modeling plus self-instructional group, and the attentional control group for the three six-item forms of the MFF test. The analyses of the decision times and error scores on Forms I and II of the MFF test yielded no significant group, trials, or Group $\times$ Trials interaction, indicating that prior to treatment the three groups performed comparably on initial performance and in response to instructions to go slower. The differential efficacy of the treatment procedures is indicated in the analysis of Form III of the MFF test which was administered immediately after treatment. On the decision time measure, the two treatment groups significantly ($p < .05$) slowed down their decision time on Form III relative to

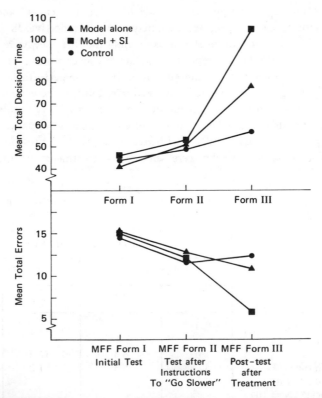

Figure 2 | MFF PERFORMANCES OF IMPULSIVE *S*s WHO WERE IN A MODELING-ALONE GROUP, A MODELING PLUS SELF-INSTRUCTIONAL TRAINING GROUP, AND AN ADDITIONAL CONTROL GROUP.

their own prior performances on Forms I and II and relative to the control groups performance on Form III. The modeling plus self-instructional training group which slowed down the most was significantly different ($t = 8.10$, $df = 8$, $p < .001$) from the modeling-alone group on Form III. The analyses of the error scores indicated that *only* Ss who received modeling plus self-instructional training significantly ($p < .05$) improved their performance relative to the other two groups and relative to their own prior performances.

In summary, the results indicated that the cognitive modeling plus self-instructional group was most effective in altering decision time and in reducing errors. The modeling-alone group significantly decreased decision time, but did not significantly reduce errors. The efficacy of the self-instructional component of the training procedure in fostering behavioral change is underscored by the fact that three of the five Ss in the self-instruction group spontaneously self-verbalized on Form III of the MFF test, whereas none did so in the other two groups. Similarly in Study I, several Ss in the self-instructional training group spontaneously self-verbalized in the posttest and follow-up sessions. It does appear that self-instructional training can bring an impulsive child's overt behavior under his own verbal discriminative control. At a macroscopic level, the impulsive children, after self-instructional training, do seem to be approaching psychometric tasks differently, taking their time, talking to themselves, and improving their performance. Research is now underway to explore the generality, persistence, and behavioral changes that result from self-instructional training.

DISCUSSION

The results of the two studies indicate that a cognitive self-guidance program which trains impulsive children to talk to themselves is effective in modifying their behavior on a variety of psychometric tests which assess cognitive impulsivity, Performance IQ, and motor ability. The results of Study II indicate that the addition of explicit self-instructional training to modeling procedures significantly alters the attentional strategies of the impulsive children and facilitates behavioral change. The impulsive children were taught to use their private speech for orienting, organizing, regulating, and self-rewarding functions with the consequence of greater self-control. The present self-instructional procedure seems applicable to the culturally deprived child, who has been described by Bereiter and Engelmann (1966) and Blank and Solomon (1968, 1969) as having a "central language deficit," namely, the inability to relate what he says to what he does. The deprived child does not spontaneously use language to direct his problem-solving behavior, especially when specific demands to do so are removed, nor does he exhibit normal capacities for self-control. An examination of the usefulness of the present self-instructional training procedures over a prolonged period of time with such deprived children is now underway.

The present studies indicate that the therapist can now attempt to modify not only the patient's overt behavioral response, but also the antecedent and/or accompanying cognitions. For example, cognitive self-guidance training procedures may be used to influence the attentional and cognitive strategies patients emit in a variety of situations. The possibilities of using self-instructional training procedures to alter (*a*) the "attentional deficit" in schizophrenics (Lang & Buss, 1965); (*b*) psychophysiological reactions of psychiatric patients (Grings, 1965; Schachter, 1966); and (*c*) cognitive styles in general (Ellis, 1963) are most promising. The application of the self-instructional procedure to operant conditioning programs with human Ss, especially children, also seems worthwhile. We suggest that having S self-verbalize, initially aloud and subsequently covertly, the contingencies of reinforcement will result in greater change and more generalization. Reinforcement can be made contingent upon not only the emission of the desired behavior, but also S's self-verbalization of what he must do to secure reinforcement. The literature on awareness (see review by Bandura, 1969) provides further support for the possible efficacy of having S learn to self-verbalize the correct reinforcement rules which influence his subsequent responding.

With the cognitive training procedure, the response chain to be modified is broadened and may thus be subjected to such modification techniques as modeling, reinforcement, and aversive consequences. We have explored in a series of studies the use of behavior modification techniques to alter the self-verbalizations of such patients as phobics, schizophrenics, smokers, speech- and test-anxious Ss, as well as impulsive children (Meichenbaum, 1970, 1971; Meichenbaum, Gilmore, & Fedoravicius, 1971; Steffy, Meichenbaum, & Best, 1970). In each case, therapeutically attending to the patient's self-verbalizations, as well as his overt maladaptive behavior, has led to greater behavioral change, greater generalization, and greater persistence of treatment effects. In each of these therapy studies the goal has been to bring S's overt behavior under his own discriminative control, a means of developing the self-regulatory function of private speech.

In conclusion, a *heuristic* assumption underlying the present line of investigation has been that symbolic activities obey the same psychological laws as do overt behaviors and that private speech is teachable. Thus, behavior modification techniques which have been used to modify overt behaviors may be applied to cognitive processes. Only future research will indicate the validity of this assumption, but the by-products, in terms of the development of new treatment techniques, will be sizable.

SUMMARY

The efficacy of a cognitive self-instructional (SI) training procedure in altering the behavior of "impulsive" school children was examined in two studies. Study I employed an individual training procedure which required the impulsive child to talk to himself, initially overtly and then covertly, in an attempt to increase self-control. The results indicated that the SI group ($N = 5$) improved significantly relative to attentional and assessment control groups on the Porteus Maze test, Performance IQ on the WISC, and on a measure of cognitive impulsivity. The improved performance was evident in a 1-mo. follow-up assessment. Study II examined the efficacy of the components of the cognitive treatment procedure in altering the impulsive child's performance on Kagan's measure of cognitive impulsivity. The results indicated that cognitive modeling alone was sufficient to slow down the impulsive child's response time for initial selection, but only with the addition of SI training was there a significant decrease in errors. The treatment and research implications of modifying S's cognitions are discussed.

REFERENCES

Anthony, A. Normal and neurotic qualitative Porteus Maze performance under stress and non-stress. Unpublished PhD thesis, Columbia University, 1959.

Bandura, A. *Principles of behavior modification.* New York: Holt, Rinehart and Winston, 1969.

Bem, S. Verbal self-control: The establishment of effective self-instruction. *Journal of Experimental Psychology*, 1967, *74*, 485–491.

Bem, S. The role of comprehension in children's problem-solving. *Developmental Psychology*, 1970, *2*, 351–358.

Bereiter, C., & Engelmann, S. *Teaching disadvantaged children in the preschool.* Englewood-Cliffs, N.J.: Prentice-Hall, 1966.

Blank, M., & Solomon, F. A tutorial language program to develop abstract thinking in socially disadvantaged preschool children. *Child Development*, 1968, *39*, 379–389.

Blank, M., & Solomon, F. How should the disadvantaged child be taught? *Child Development*, 1969, *40*, 47–61.

Debus, R. L. Effects of brief observation of model behavior on conceptual tempo of impulsive children. *Developmental Psychology*, 1970, *2*, 22–32.

Drake, D. M. Perceptual correlates of impulsive and reflective behavior. *Developmental Psychology*, 1970, *2*, 202–214.

Ellis, A. *Reason and emotion in psychotherapy.* New York: Holt, Rinehart and Winston, 1962.

Eysenck, A. J. A dynamic theory of anxiety and hysteria. *Journal of Mental Science*, 1955, *101*, 128–151.

Flavell, J. H., Beach, D. R., & Chinsky, J. M. Spontaneous verbal rehearsal in a memory task as a function of age. *Child Development*, 1966, *37*, 283–299.

Foulds, G. A. Temperamental differences in maze performance. *British Journal of Psychology*, 1951, *42*, 209–217.

Grings, W. W. Verbal-perceptual factors in the conditioning of autonomic responses. In W. F. Prokasy (Ed.), *Classical conditioning: A symposium.* New York: Appleton, 1965.

Kagan, J. Impulsive and reflective children: Significance of conceptual tempo. In J. D. Krumboltz (Ed.), *Learning and the educational process.* Chicago: Rand McNally, 1965.

Kagan, J. Reflection-impulsivity: The generality and dynamics of conceptual tempo. *Journal of Abnormal Psychology*, 1966, *71*, 17–24.

Kagan, J., Pearson, L., & Welch, L. The modifiability of an impulsive tempo. *Journal of Educational Psychology*, 1966, *57*, 359–365.

Kagan, J., Rosman, B. L., Day, D., Albert, J., & Phillips, W. Information processing in the child: Significance of analytic and reflective attitudes. *Psychological Monographs*, 1964, *78* (1, Whole No. 578).

Kitzinger, H., & Blumberg, E. Supplementary guide for administering and scoring the Wechsler-Bellevue. Intelligence Scale (Form I). *Psychological Monographs*, 1951, *65*, (10, Whole No. 319).

Klein, W. L. An investigation of the spontaneous speech of children during problem solving. Unpublished doctoral dissertation, University of Rochester, 1963.

Kohlberg, L., Yaeger, J., & Hjertholm, E. Private speech: Four studies and a review of theories. *Child Development*, 1968, *39*, 691–736.

Lang, P. J., & Buss, A. H. Psychological deficit in schizophrenia: Interference activation. *Journal of Abnormal Psychology*, 1965, *70*, 77–106.

Lindquist, E. F. *Design and analysis of experiments in psychology and education.* Boston: Houghton Mifflin, 1953.

Lovaas, O. I. Cue properties of words: The control of operant responding by rate and content of verbal operants. *Child Development*, 1964, *35*, 245–256.

Luria, A. R. The directive function of speech in development. *Word*, 1959, *15*, 341–352.

Luria, A. R. *The role of speech in the regulation of normal and abnormal behavior.* New York: Liveright, 1961.

Lutey, C. *Individual intelligence testing: A manual.* Greeley, Colo.: Executary, 1966.

Meichenbaum, D. Cognitive factors in behavior modification: Modifying what people say to themselves. Unpublished manuscript, University of Waterloo, 1970.

Meichenbaum, D. Examination of model characteristics in reducing avoidance behavior. *Journal of Personality and Social Psychology*, 1971, *17*, 298–307.

Meichenbaum, D., Bowers, K., & Ross, R. Modification of classroom behavior of institutionalized female adolescent offenders. *Behavior Research and Therapy*, 1968, *6*, 343–353.

Meichenbaum, D., Bowers, K., & Ross, R. A behavioral analysis of teacher expectancy effect. *Journal of Personality and Social Psychology*, 1969, *13*, 306–316.

Meichenbaum, D., Gilmore, J. B., & Fedoravicius, A. Group insight versus group desensitization in treating speech anxiety. *Journal of Consulting and Clinical Psychology*, 1971, *36*, 410–421.

Meichenbaum, D., & Goodman, J. The developmental control of operant motor responding by verbal operants. *Journal of Experimental Child Psychology*, 1969, 7, 553–565. (a)

Meichenbaum, D., & Goodman, J. Reflection-impulsivity and verbal control of motor behavior. *Child Development*, 1969, *40*, 785–797. (b)

Moely, B., Olson, F., Halwes, T., & Flavell, J. Production deficiency in young children's recall. *Developmental Psychology*, 1969, *1*, 26–34.

Palkes, H., Stewart, W., & Kahana, B. Porteus Maze performance of hyperactive boys after training in self-directed verbal commands. *Child Development*, 1968, *39*, 817–826.

Piaget, J. *The psychology of intelligence.* London: Routledge, 1947.

Porteus, S. E. *Qualitative performance in the maze test.* Vineland, N.J.: Smith, 1942.

Reese, H. W. Verbal mediation as a function of age level. *Psychological Bulletin*, 1962, *59*, 502–509.

Schachter, S. The interaction of cognitive and physiological determinants of emotional state. In C. D. Speilberger (Ed.), *Anxiety and behavior.* New York: Academic Press, 1966.

Siegelman, E. Reflective and impulsive observing behavior. *Child Development*, 1969, *40*, 1213–1222.

Steffy, R., Meichenbaum, D., & Best, A. Aversive and cognitive factors in the modification of smoking behavior. *Behavior Research and Therapy*, 1970, *8*, 115–125.

Vygotsky, L. S. *Thought and language.* New York: Wiley, 1962.

Ward, W. C. Reflection-impulsivity in kindergarten children. *Child Development*, 1968, *39*, 867–874.

Wechsler, D. *Manual: Wechsler Intelligence Scale for Children.* New York: Psychological Corporation, 1949.

19.3 | INTERNAL-EXTERNAL CONTROL AND THE ATTRIBUTION OF BLAME UNDER NEUTRAL AND DISTRACTIVE CONDITIONS* [1]

E. Jerry Phares, Kenneth G. Wilson, and Nelson W. Klyver

Internal-external control of reinforcement (I-E) is a generalized expectancy construct that has arisen from Rotter's (1954) social learning theory. It is viewed as a continuum of individual differences that cuts across need areas, and it refers to the extent to which one believes that reinforcements occur as a function of one's behavior (internal) or a function of luck, chance, powerful others, etc. (external).

A wide variety of construct-validity data is available (Rotter, 1966). Much of the research suggests the superiority of internals in both dealing with their environment and in their activity level in attempting to manipulate their surroundings (e.g., Davis & Phares, 1967; Gore & Rotter, 1963; Phares, 1968; Seeman, 1963).

Other studies, however, have begun to focus on the potentially defensive aspects of the I-E dimension. For example, Efran (1963) noted that externals showed less forgetting of failures than did internals. There is a suggestion here that an external orientation may provide less need to defend against the unpleasant thought of failure, since that orientation gives one a less threatening explanation of failure—forces outside oneself are responsible. Lipp, Kolstoe, James, and Randall (1968) found that pictures of physically handicapped persons, when shown tachistoscopically, resulted in lower recognition thresholds by handicapped externals than by handicapped internals. Thus, again, there appeared to be less denial on the part of externals. Finally, a study by Phares, Ritchie, and Davis (1968) showed that following psychological interpretations of their personality, external subjects recalled more of the negative interpretations than did internal subjects. Again, it appeared almost as if an external orientation provided ready access to a defense, and thus relatively less need to invoke forgetting as a response.

In the present study, we proposed to test the hypothesis that internals are less prone than externals to blame forces outside themselves for task failure. Indeed, by definition, an internal is one who believes that forces under his control are responsible for the occurrence or nonoccurrence of reinforcements. With such a generalized expectancy, it seems only reasonable to suggest that an internally oriented subject would show a greater proclivity for the self-attribution of blame than would an external subject. Thus, the present study simply suggests that if an internal subject shows a greater

* SOURCE: Phares, E. J., Wilson, K. G., & Klyver, N. W. Internal-external control and the attribution of blame under neutral and distractive conditions. *Journal of Personality and Social Psychology*, 1971, *18*, 285–288. Copyright 1971 by the American Psychological Association and reprinted by permission.

[1] This research was supported by Grant GS 2406 from the National Science Foundation.

tendency than an external subject to state general beliefs that reinforcements are a function of forces under his own control, he should also, therefore, show a greater tendency to be less blaming of forces outside himself following failure in a *specific* situation.

In an effort to show also how situational considerations can interact with generalized personality variables, the following specific hypotheses can be described. In a situation that does not provide any very explicit cues that external forces may have affected one's performance, it was anticipated that generalized I-E expectancies would operate in accordance with the analysis in the preceding paragraph. However, in a situation which does provide very explicit, distractive cues, it was expected that individual differences in I-E would recede in importance, and that these situational considerations would carry the bulk of the predictive weight. Briefly, when there are very *explicit* cues present, they should arouse specific expectancies regarding the locus of blame. When such cues are absent, ambiguous, or relatively weak, then the subject should place greater reliance on expectancies generalized from past experience—in this case, I-E.

Therefore, the specific hypotheses of this study were: (*a*) Following failure, internals will be less prone than externals to attribute blame to forces outside themselves. (*b*) However, this difference will appear only under relatively neutral or nondistracting conditions; when distraction is clearly present, it was expected that there would be no differences between internals and externals. (*c*) When they experience failure in a nondistractive situation, both internals and externals will attribute significantly less blame to other forces than they will in a distractive situation.

METHOD

SUBJECTS.   The I–E Scale (Rotter, 1966) was administered to 646 male students in several large introductory psychology classes at Kansas State University. Scored in the internal direction, the mean was 13.76 with a standard deviation of 3.48. Internals were defined as those scoring at or above one standard deviation from the mean, while externals were those with scores at or below one standard deviation from the mean. From these categories, 32 internals and 32 externals were drawn on a volunteer basis and given credit toward their final grade.

PROCEDURE.   Internal and external subjects were randomly tested in groups of from four to eight. There were two experimenters present at all times. They were seated far enough apart so they could not observe each other's work. They were told that the study was designed to determine whether there was any relationship between the Social Reaction Inventory (I–E Scale) which they had filled out earlier in class and several intellectual abilities. After these brief introductory remarks, the following instructions were read:

> Let me describe the Anagrams Test. This is a measure of verbal IQ. It measures speed and depth of thought processes. It indicates your ability to deal with symbols and also taps skills in the analytical reasoning area. This test is in-

cluded in many verbal IQ tests, as well as being an interesting parlor game. Obviously, it is more than just a game, however. We find that the average score is around 17. A poor score is 12 or less.

A test booklet was then presented. It contained 25 items, and a time limit of 10 minutes was imposed. However, in order to induce a sense of failure, only 12 of the anagrams were soluble. Thus, every subject was forced to fail, at least in terms of the norms provided.

Following the 10 minutes, all booklets were collected, scored, and the face sheets returned to the subjects. On the face sheet was printed a 5-step scale from excellent to poor. Every sheet had the word "poor" circled in red ink to reinforce the notion of failure. The experimenter made certain that each subject read his score.

Next, the Word Location Test was distributed, and the following verbal instructions were provided:

> The Word Location Test taps your ability to concentrate and to solve problems that involve breaking down a complex stimulus into parts. In addition, it relates to perceptual and analytical ability.
>
> In this case, your job is to locate 20 states which are embedded in a block of letters (15×15). You will have 10 minutes to complete this task. We have found that the average college student is able to get between 13 and 15 correct. A score of 8 or below is poor.

Again, the task was structured so that each subject received a poor score as before. Failure on both tasks was induced in order to provide a rather strong failure experience.

Two levels of distraction were also incorporated. Sixteen internals and 16 externals were assigned to each condition, making a total of 64 subjects. In the nondistraction condition, the two experimenters remained silent during the test-taking period and were active only during the reading of instructions and the scoring and distribution of the booklets.

Under the distraction condition, however, the following procedure was followed. Each 10-minute test period was divided into two 5-minute segments. The experimenters presented a different distraction during each of the four 5-minute segments. Four types of distractions were used: (a) the experimenters' reading aloud to each other letters to the editor in the college newspaper; (b) a discussion of an apparatus problem; (c) discussion of a statistics problem with accompanying use of the blackboard; (d) discussion of a recent football game. Each distraction lasted about 2 minutes and was carried on in a moderate but clearly audible manner.

At the conclusion of the experiment, each subject was given a form to fill out. This form was entitled "Experiment Evaluation Form." The nature of the form was explained to the subjects by the following printed instructions:

> Institutions that conduct these kinds of studies are required to carefully evaluate (1) the attitudes of those participating in experiments, (2) the experimental facilities used, and (3) the adequacy of the experimental methods. In view of this requirement, your cooperation on the following questionnaire will be extremely valuable. Not only will your frank responses fulfill a requirement that we request feedback from you but they will also help to improve

the quality of future experiments and enable the principal investigator to better understand and interpret the performance of subjects in the experiment. We hope you will be as frank as possible so that this research will be more meaningful than it otherwise might be.

The form consisted of 26 statements, each of which was to be rated on a 7-point scale (—3 to +3) from strongly agree to strongly disagree. In general, the items were of three classes: (1) adequacy of the experiment and its methods; (2) adequacy of the physical surroundings; and (3) the current state of the subject. Two examples of each class are as follows:

1. (a) The words used in the Anagrams Test do not appear frequently enough in daily usage to be good indicators of average ability. (b) I thought the instructions could have been more clear.
2. (a) The other people taking the tests were distracting. (b) Despite the age of this building, it is still quite adequate for the present kind of research.
3. (a) I had other things on my mind, such as school work, which prevented me from concentrating as well as I can. (b) The idea of being in a psychology experiment reduced my ability to concentrate.

The scale was constructed on a priori grounds specifically for this study and for the particular stimulus conditions associated with the study. Each item finally included was judged unanimously by the three authors as being (a) relevant to the blame dimension and (b) particularly associated with the tasks and conditions of this study. Three independent judges likewise agreed unanimously on how to score each item as regards the direction of blame. Finally, the scale was scored in such a way that positive numbers indicate blame attribution and negative numbers indicate a lack of blame.

In conclusion, we should add a few words about the nature of the distraction. We used distractions applied by the experimenters because such distractions were simple and easy to utilize and control. Originally, we included items in the blame-attribution scale which related to the experimenters' distractive behavior. However, in the beginning of the study it became apparent that the subjects were extremely loathe to mark items in any way that suggested criticism of the experimenters. At that point, it seemed either that the subjecs did not want to get the experimenters into trouble or else were afraid that the experimeners would note their criticism

Table 1 | BLAME-ATTRIBUTION SCORES FOR INTERNALS AND EXTERNALS UNDER DISTRACTIVE AND NONDISTRACTIVE CONDITIONS[a]

CONDITION	INTERNALS	EXTERNALS
Distraction	—7.69	—5.75
SD	12.17	12.78
Nondistraction	—17.13	+.25
SD	11.63	18.24

[a] n = per cell (total N = 64).

and take punitive action. In either case, the result was the same. Therefore, we discarded any attempts to use such items.

In deciding to continue to use the experimenters as a distraction, the reasoning was that to do otherwise might be too obvious. Thus, we wished to provide explicit cues for blame attribution without, at the same time, making the cues terribly blatant. For example, to heat the room to 90 degrees and then ask the subjects whether it was too hot seemed rather obvious and could discredit the whole situation.

RESULTS AND DISCUSSION

As noted earlier, the 26-item attribution of blame scale was scored so that positive numbers connoted blame attribution. The possible range of scores was from —78 to +78. Table 1 presents the basic data of this study. An analysis of variance showed the main effect of I-E to be significant ($F = 6.90$, $df = 1/60$, $p = .025$). The distraction-nondistraction main effect was, however, not significant ($F < 1.00$, $df = 1/60$). The I-E $\times$ Situation interaction was significant ($F = 4.41$, $df = 1/60$, $p < .05$). These analyses suggest: (a) internals are significantly less blaming than externals across both situations; (b) blaming behavior of subjects does not differ in a distractive condition as compared to a nondistractive one; (c) the pattern of blaming behavior was different for internals and externals in the distractive and nondistractive situations.

To further determine the significance of the foregoing analyses, several two-tailed t tests were performed. Under nondistractive conditions, internals were significantly less blaming following the failure than were externals ($t = 3.29$, $p = .005$). In the distractive condition, the differences between internals and externals did not approach significance. In addition, internals were significantly less blaming in the nondistractive condition than they were in the distractive situation ($t = 2.25$, $p < .04$). For externals, there were no significant differences under the distractive versus nondistractive conditions ($t = 1.07$).

As predicted, then, internals tended to resort to blaming behavior after failure to a lesser extent than did externals. Previous research has shown greater forgetting or distortion of threatening material on the part of internals. The present results provide a significant demonstration of differential attribution of blame following failure, and thereby suggest a reason for the internal's tendency to show more forgetting or distortion in the previously cited research. That is, less tendency to resort to blaming behavior may require more forgetting and distortion as a means of reducing discomfort following failure or threat.

Also as expected, the above differences between groups appeared in the nondistractive condition, but not when distraction was present. When the situation is *clearly* distractive, specific expectancies are apparently aroused which become the major determinants of conceptual behavior, thus diminishing the role of individual differences such as I-E. In line with the latter rationale, it is reasonable that internals were significantly less blaming in the nondistractive situation than they were in the distractive situation.

Externals, however, departed from this latter pattern. Their attribution of blame was not significantly different in the two situations. Particularly noteworthy were their scores in the nondistractive situation. Indeed, it appears a bit curious that externals should even exhibit a trend toward less blame in the distractive condition than in the nondistraction condition. It could be, however, that an external (out of defensive considerations) feels under some pressure to make strong use of his external orientation to account for failure when no apparent distractions are present. For example, previous research (Watson, 1967) suggests that externals are generally more anxious than internals. Being generally more expectant of failure, then, they might be more likely to utilize their external orientation and be less likely to accept responsibility for failure in a situation that itself offers no immediately apparent reasons for that failure. When failure occurs in the face of obvious distractions, however, the external may not feel compelled to be particularly defensive—indeed it may provide a rare opportunity for him to be safely self-denigrating (knowing full well that in this case it is not true).

In conclusion, a major contribution of this research seems to be the demonstration that following failure in a specific situation, internals and externals utilize greater or lesser blaming tendencies in a way that is predictable from their I-E orientation. Such a demonstration can, thereby, help us to better understand the previously noted link between I-E and processes such as differential forgetting and retention of threatening material by internals and externals.

SUMMARY

Internal and external subjects were failed on two tasks described to them as measuring intellectual functions. Half of the subjects were failed under distractive conditions and the other half under nondistractive conditions. Following this procedure, all subjects completed a blame-attribution scale. As predicted, under nondistractive conditions, internals were significantly less prone to use blaming behavior than were externals, while there were no differences between the groups in the distractive condition. Also as predicted, internals were less blaming in the nondistractive condition than they were in the distractive one. Contrary to prediction, the latter result did not obtain for the externals.

REFERENCES

Davis, W. L., & Phares, E. J. Internal-external control as a determinant of information-seeking in a social influence situation. *Journal of Personality*, 1967, *35*, 547–561.

Efran, J. Some personality determinants of memory for success and failure. Unpublished doctoral dissertation, Ohio State University, 1963.

Gore, P. M., & Rotter, J. B. A personality correlate of social action. *Journal of Personality*, 1963, *31*, 58–64.

Lipp, L., Kolstoe, R., James, W., & Randall, H. Denial of disability and internal control of reinforcement: A study using a perceptual defense paradigm. *Journal of Consulting and Clinical Psychology*, 1968, *32*, 72–75.

Phares, E. J. Differential utilization of information as a function of internal-external control. *Journal of Personality*, 1968, *36*, 649–662.

Phares, E. J., Ritchie, D. E., & Davis, W. L. Internal-external control and reaction to threat. *Journal of Personality and Social Psychology*, 1968, *10*, 402–405.

Rotter, J. B. *Social learning and clinical psychology.* Englewood Cliffs, N.J.: Prentice-Hall, 1954.

Rotter, J. B. Generalized expectancies for internal versus external control of reinforcement. *Psychological Monographs*, 1966, *80* (1, Whole No. 609).

Seeman, M. Alienation and social learning in a reformatory. *American Journal of Sociology*, 1963, *69*, 270–284.

Watson, D. Relationship between locus of control and anxiety. *Journal of Personality and Social Psychology*, 1967, *6*, 91–92.

20 | Self-Concepts

20.1 | PERSONAL CONSISTENCY AND THE PRESENTATION OF SELF*

Kenneth J. Gergen

I

The world of social perception tends to be a stable one. Through our abilities to conceptualize, the complex flux is simplified and rendered comprehensible. As a person is exposed to facts about another, such facts are ordered and assimilated. Noting a person's abrasive speech or brusque treatment of others, for example, may lead one to conceptualize this person as "aggressive." The concept is thus used to encapsulate a series of observations, and the conceptualization of a body of observations forms the cornerstone for what we know as "understanding" of the other. Once such judgments are formed they tend to remain intact and unchanging. On the one hand, new information about a person may simply be assimilated into the already existing conceptual structure. As often demonstrated in a laboratory setting, the initial information received about another may substantially color the interpretation one makes of facts revealed at a later time. On the other hand, if later information grossly violates the once crystallized judgment of the other, it may be either distorted or misperceived. Research has shown, for example, that when persons receive contradictory information about another, they often misperceive entire sets of facts in order to develop an internally consistent view of the person (Gollin, 1954). In these ways, persons tend to be seen as stable and consistent. One may say that David is friendly and kind, that Charles is domineering and unsympathetic, and the words or concepts used to describe these persons operate as if to indicate something about their personalities across time and across situations.

Once conceptions of another are developed, they also form the basis of social expectancy. If on a given day David were "unfriendly" or "unkind," such behavior would be surprising and one might be inclined to wonder why David was "not himself today."

* SOURCE: Gergen, K. J. Personal consistency and the presentation of self. In Gordon, C. & Gergen, K. J. (Eds.), *The self in social interaction.* New York: Wiley, 1968. Pp. 299–308. Copyright © 1968 by John Wiley & Sons, Inc. Reprinted by permission.

In effect, we come to perceive, expect, and assume personal consistency on the part of others in our social environment. One may well ask, however: How accurate is this assertion of personal consistency? What are its consequences in social life and in the behavioral sciences? . . . [Here] we take a close look at such issues, for they are intimately linked to the notion of the self and to the development of human potentiality.

CONSISTENCY AND THE BEHAVIORAL SCIENCES.   The conceptual bracketing of an individual's personality is no less true in the arena of everyday life than it is in the laboratory of the behavioral scientist. Research in personality, for example, largely rests on the assumption of personal consistency. If a person fills out a questionnaire in a particular way or judges a stimulus configuration in a given manner, he may be classified as having certain personality characteristics. Certain responses are said to be indicative of high self-esteem, others of a strong achievement orientation, and so on. On the assumption that the person acts consistently, and that the personality traits found in the testing situation universally characterize the person's style of life, predictions are made and tested concerning the person's behavior under a variety of conditions. This research tactic is, of course, a quite common one and lies at the heart of the "trait" approach to personality. As MacKinnon has pointed out, in its extreme form this approach assumes that behavioral traits, "operate as fixed attributes of an organism as stable and unchanging as a finger print or birthmark" (MacKinnon, 1944).

Theorists interested in the self-concept have largely supported this conception of personality. Even the term "self-concept" implies that a person has a singular way of conceiving of himself, and that he may view all his actions as either confirming or being inconsistent with this concept. Carl Rogers has suggested, for example, that "all perceptions of the qualities, abilities, impulses, and attitudes of the person, all perceptions of himself in relation to others are accepted into the organized conscious concept of the self" (Rogers, 1947). We find a similar approach in theories on personal identity. Erikson, Allport, and others, for example, equate the notion of identity with inner sameness or continuity. It is often supposed that the universal question for the person is "who am I," and the grammatical form of the question itself suggests that the answer should be in a singular form.

Over the past decade personal consistency has also come to play a cardinal role in models developed to explain processes of social influence. Festinger's (1957) model of cognitive dissonance is a good case in point, inasmuch as the entire theory rests on the premise that a person continuously strives for consistency among his thoughts. Inconsistency is said to produce discomfort or to be noxious, and many of the experiments in this tradition have attempted to demonstrate the irrational measures taken by persons in reducing inconsistency. It should also be noted that the consistency assumption has proved to be an empirically useful one in research on both personality and social influence.

THE CONSISTENCY ETHIC.   Perhaps one reason for the viability of the consistency assumption is that the ethical sanctions in Western culture tend to reinforce consistent behavior. That such sanctions do exist might be inferred from such Biblical statements as, "a double-minded man is unstable in all his ways," and, "no man can serve two masters" (Allport, 1961). In his *Outline of Western History*, H. G. Wells also remarks on the foibles of man by noting that "not one is altogether noble nor altogether trustworthy nor altogether consistent; and not one is altogether vile" (Wells, 1961). It may be said that we not only see people as being all of a piece, but we treat them as if they are, and we often punish them if they are not. If a person is seen acting in ways that violate our conceptions of him, we may often disdainfully characterize his conduct as "a facade," "superficial," or "insincere." A study conducted by Gergen and Jones (1963) demonstrated, for example, that over a variety of conditions a predictable person comes to be liked and an unpredictable one produces a negative reaction. The concept of "trust," with all of its evaluative loading, is in part based on one's being able to assume that a person will not contradict that which he *seems* to be. Similarly, the common exhortation to be "true to self" may largely rest in the desire to have others act in ways that are consistent with that we conceive them to be. The longstanding odium attached to the acting profession or to that of the politician may stem from the fact that inconsistency is often an occupational hazard or necessity for persons thus employed. It also seems plausible that the great fear evoked by masks in many primitive cultures may result from the fact that the mask itself casts doubt on the validity of the wearer's outward visage.

And there is certainly good reason for the social value placed on consistency. For one, it is simply less taxing and perhaps less anxiety-provoking if the social environment is not in constant and capricious flux. More important, to a large extent we base our behavior toward another on our conceptions of him, and the adaptiveness of this behavior may be in direct proportion to the correctness of these conceptions. "Correct" conceptions depend on another's acting consistently. Personal security is also based on the behavioral coherency of others. On a broad social level one might even say that social order is to some extent dependent on consistent behavioral patterns among members of a society. If all acted spontaneously and unexpectedly from moment to moment, chaos would soon erupt.

THE ETHIC IN THE BEHAVIORAL SCIENCES.   Behavioral scientists themselves are products of their culture, so it is no surprise to find in their work a certain moralistic cast placed on personal consistency. William James was perhaps the first to lend a strong voice in this direction. He differentiated between the basically healthy person whose inner constitution is "harmonious and well balanced from the outset" and the "sick souls" whose "spirit wars with their flesh, they wish for incompatibles, wayward impulses interrupt their most deliberate plans, and their lives are one long drama of repentance and of effort to repair misdemeanors and mistakes" (James, 1958). For James the only salvation for these "divided selves" lay in the "normal evolution of character," which consisted of the "straightening out and unifying of the inner self." Whereas the *Zeitgeist* of objectivity later reduced the occurrence of such baldly ethical statements, the implicit ethic has nevertheless remained in various forms. In Prescott Lecky's work (1945) we find, for example, that the "normally" functioning human being strives for consistency in all aspects of his life. Mental imbalance and suffering are equated with blockage of consistency-striving, and therapy is largely envisioned as a tool to remove such blocks. The value of "inner sameness" has also been stressed by theorists discussing identity formation. Rogers has stated that integration of various aspects of the person into a unified concept of self "is accompanied by feelings of comfort and freedom from tension" (Rogers, 1947), and again unity becomes a goal of psychotherapy.

It has thus far been pointed out that behavioral scientists have found the assumption of personal consistency a highly useful one, and that as cultural exemplars they, too, may value consistent behavior. One may well question at this point the possibility of a causal link between these two tendencies. Is it possible that the utility of the consistency assumption is based not so much on its reflection of inner needs and overriding personal dispositions as on the fact that consistent behavior is sanctioned no less forcibly in the psychological clinic or research laboratory than in other realms of daily life? In effect, the demands for consistency in such settings may well engender behavior that validates the basic assumptions. Personal consistency in these settings may itself be fostered by the social situation in which the behavioral scientist plays a significant role.

To illustrate the plausibility of this argument, let us consider first the case of the individual who has been classified as mentally ill. Such a person may, in fact, be capable of much normal behavior. However, the classification of "mentally ill" may itself be encapsulating in that it serves to orient the behavior of others toward him. Perceiving the person as "sick," the attendant in a mental institution may effectively reinforce "sick" behavior and fail to encourage conduct that is inconsistent with this perception.[1] In a challenging description of the "moral career" of the mental patient, Goffman points out that "the setting and the house rules press home to the patient that he is, after all, a mental case who has suffered some kind of social collapse on the outside, having failed in some over-all way, and that he is of little social weight, being hardly capable of acting like a full-fledged person at all" (Goffman, 1961). Of course, the goal of the institution is ultimately to bring the person into a "well" status, but the current conception of recovery from mental illness is that it is a gradual process, and this conception may have self-fulfilling properties.

The influence of the consistency assumption may be no less operative in the social psychological laboratory. Dissonance theory, as a case in point, is almost entirely based on laboratory research, and a noteworthy study by Aronson and Carlsmith (1962) may serve to illustrate the present argument. In this particular experiment, subjects were caused to fail continuously in a task and then suddenly to find that they had succeeded. Based on the assumption that sudden success would be dissonant with the person's continued failure, it was predicted that in order to restore a consistent state, subjects would purposely engage in behavior which would cause them to fail once again. The prediction was verified. It might be asked, however, what function the experimenter served in the experimental situation? The test on which the subject had continuously received a low score was one that the experimenter had publicly proclaimed to be a valid indicator of

[1] Interesting in this regard are recent findings communicated to me by Dr. Murray Melbin, to the effect that mental patients demonstrate greater symptomology during those times when a greater number of hospital staff members are within range of observation.

social sensitivity. Was it possible that the subject, feeling that the experimenter would be disappointed if his test failed to yield consistent results, attempted to do poorly in order to prevent the experiment's discomfort? A later study (Ward & Sandvold, 1963), in which the experimenter denigrated the validity of the social sensitivity test, failed to replicate the original findings, and strongly suggests that experimenter sanction of consistent behavior does produce effects.

To recapitulate the basic line of reasoning up to this point, it has been said that in daily life the assumption is often made that persons are basically consistent, and that this assumption is buttressed by ethical sanctions. It has further been pointed out that this assumption has been widely adopted and equally sanctioned in the behavioral sciences, and that such sanctions may produce the very behavior predicted on other grounds. It is now appropriate to take a more critical look at the assumption of personal consistency. To what extent is it supported by current evidence? How valid is it in describing or explaining social interaction? What limitations must be placed on its generality? And what problems are created for the person by the existing ethic? The remainder of this paper attempts to treat such issues and their relevance to the self. The empirical evidence is first reviewed with particular focus on recent studies in the psychology of self-presentation. Finally, we will be in a position to return to the question of the ethical underpinnings of personal consistency.

II

Empirical work tending to embarrass an assumption of behavioral consistency has been on the scene for a good many years. One of the earliest and most extensive studies in this line was that of Hartshorne and May (1928). Utilizing a large sample of school children, correlations among a variety of measures designed to assess tendencies toward being deceitful were found to be quite meager. In effect, a child who lied was neither more nor less likely to engage in other deceitful forms of behavior than one who avoided lying. The conclusion was thus reached that these various behaviors represent situationally specific habits rather than general or consistent traits. Unfortunately, the study leaves unclear whether the lack of correlation among measures was due to the subjects' lack of personal consistency or to the insensitivity of the measures employed. The data have also been criticized on a number of other grounds. Allport has pointed out that dishonesty, for one, may not be a general trait, and that children may also constitute a poor sample for demonstrating consistency (Allport, 1961).

Many other studies attempting to reveal behavioral inconsistency have emerged in the area of public opinion and attitude assessment. The classic in this realm is La Pierre's 1934 study in which the amount of anti-Chinese prejudice expressed by restaurant and hotel-motel owners on a mail out questionnaire was found to be far less than that found when they were actually confronted by a Chinese couple. In the same vein, it has been found that interviewers who "look" Jewish and have Jewish names elicit fewer anti-Semitic attitudes than those who don't appear to be Jewish (Robinson & Rohde, 1946). Katz reports that middle-class interviewers are more likely to elicit pro-conservative responses from low-income respondents than are working-class interviewers (Katz, 1942). Many similar findings are reported in Hyman's (1954) penetrating discussion of bias in the survey interview.

Although such findings serve to document inconsistency on the level of overt behavior, inconsistency on the covert or psychological level is yet another matter. These findings initially suggest that attitudes, conceived as psychological dispositions, have little cross-situational generality. However, such a conclusion seems unwarranted on the basis of this type of evidence alone. As Campbell has correctly pointed out, attitudinal dispositions vary in strength, and the public espousal of a position that seems discrepant from underlying feelings may simply reflect the fact that the feelings are not sufficiently intense to be expressed regardless of circumstances (Campbell, 1963). That an anti-Semite will not admit his feelings to a Rabbi, for example, may only mean that he does not feel strongly enough about his convictions to risk censure in such a situation. It does not mean that his underlying feelings are necessarily inconsistent with each other.

The same reasoning is also germane to the notion of the self-concept. Everyone is probably aware of circumstances that are inimical to his behaving as he truly feels himself to be, and responding to the dictates of such situations does not necessarily imply an inconsistent self-picture. Of course, this as well as the earlier examples have dealt with situations in which the person is attempting to avoid punishment. However, the preceding arguments apply equally to behavior stemming from what have been termed pro-active motives, or motives directed toward a positive goal state. For example, almost anyone who has worked in a new or different occupation has no doubt experienced a peculiar alienation from his behavior, an alienation fostered by the discrepancy existing between his time-worn conceptions of self and his current role-adoptive behavior. In essence, the attempt to achieve a desired goal has caused the person to behave inconsistently with his basic feelings about self. However, one may not infer on these grounds alone that his conceptions of self are contradictory.

Inconsistencies such as those described seem relegated to rather unusual or novel circumstances. Under normal conditions a person shuns those situations in which active dissimulation is required either in order to avoid punishment or to achieve a goal. What about the "average" sorts of events in a man's life, those which predominate in the day-to-day world of social relationships?

Perhaps the most sensitive and compelling treatment of the inconsistencies of everyday life has been provided by Erving Goffman (1959). Working from his own experiences and from a wide number of literary sources, Goffman underscores the subtle and often hidden variations in a person's behavior as he moves from one social situation to another. The picture of man resulting from these sketches is not a particularly laudible one. The Goffmanian man is a perpetual mummer, and all social relationships are made up of performances well calculated by the actor to achieve optimal returns. Certainly the ingredients of the "normal" personality, as served up by personality theorists discussed previously, could stand a dash or two of this robust flavor. However, for present purposes Goffman's treatment is insufficient. Goffman provides a discerning view of the chameleon-like behavior of individuals, but little attention is given to the ramifications of such behavior for underlying psychological structure. Essentially, in Goffman's work there is little in the way of a subjective sense of self for the person to present or reveal in behavior. His analysis also tends to place too heavy an emphasis on consciously calculated performances, while giving short shrift to behavior felt by the person to be "authentic." In addition, literary allusion and personal observation provide a shaky ground on which to establish conclusions. The case must ultimately rest on the controlled demonstration of both the antecedents and consequences of inconsistency.

SELF-PRESENTATION RESEARCH.   Over the past several years a number of experimental studies of self-presentation have been conducted, and inroads have been made into a number of the issues we have discussed. For present purposes we can confine ourselves to a brief description of several investigations which demonstrate the effects of (*a*) other persons, (*b*) the interaction environment, and (*c*) motivation, on the self-picture provided to others. First an attempt is made to show that behavioral inconsistencies can be elicited in rather systematic fashion. In most instances, such studies have involved the assessment of the same individual's behavior under two differing conditions. However, as noted earlier, contradictions in overt behavior may not be indicative of inconsistency in underlying feelings about self. Thus the central focus is on evidence dealing with covert feelings about oneself and one's presentation to others.

THE OTHER PERSON.   As a person moves from one relationship to another, he is exposed to others who vary widely in behavioral style and disposition. Is it possible to maintain a consistent stance in a constantly changing social environment? For example, how does one react when confronted by a person who is boastful and egotistical as opposed to one who emphasizes his shortcomings? In a study conducted by Gergen and Wishnov (1965), subject groups found themselves interacting with just such persons. Subjects had filled out a series of self-ratings almost a month prior to the experiment. During the experiment they again described themselves along the same dimensions, but this time for a partner who was perceived to be either egotistical or humble. In terms of expressed level of self-esteem, subjects paired with the egotist became significantly more positive; subjects confronted by humility began to emphasize their own shortcomings. In other words, level of expressed self-esteem did not remain stable, but changed in either direction depending on the characteristics of the other person in the situation.

Since these results demonstrate changes in overt presentation only, subjects were also asked about how honest and open they felt they had been during the information exchange. Over two-thirds felt they had been completely open or that responses during the exchange were essentially no different from those of the prior testing session. Further, when ratings of honesty were correlated with amount of self-esteem change, virtually no relationship was found. In effect, the behavioral changes in the situation did not seem to depend on conscious precalculation but appeared to reflect habitual and unconscious modes of relation to others.

In addition to the other's personality, his *behavior* toward a person may also produce marked changes in social identity. As a prime example, G. H. Mead and the many who have followed in his footsteps have long maintained that a person's concept of self is primarily dependent on the expressed view of others toward the self. By and large, the literature in this area has discussed the self-concept as if it were a single entity representing the combined attitudes of several significant others toward a person. Such a position is, of course, quite compatible with the assumption of personal consistency. On the other hand, as a person moves through his social world he may encounter others who see him in strikingly different ways. The traits sought out and reinforced by an employer, for example, are probably not those with which a man's children will resonate. Do a person's underlying feelings about himself shift along with his behavior as he moves from one relationship to another? A second study strongly suggests that they do.

In this instance (see Gergen, 1965) female undergraduates rated themselves on a large number of items designed to tap self-esteem. Several weeks later they were interviewed by a trainee in a large interviewing project. They were told that the trainee's major task was to learn to be honest and spontaneous with the respondent. During the interview the subject was asked to respond to the same self-esteem items administered earlier. As the subject rated herself on each item, the interviewer, a confidante of the experimenter, subtly began to indicate her feelings toward the subject. She smiled, nodded her head, and gave minimal verbal reinforcement each time the subject rated herself positively; she displayed minimal signs of disagreement whenever the subject gave a negative self-opinion. During the interview, the subjects' overt level of self-esteem underwent a marked increase, an increase substantially higher than that occurring in a control group of nonreinforced subjects.

In order to shed light on the relationship between the overt expression of self-esteem and the covert feelings, additional self-esteem tests were administered after the interview. Subjects were told to be as honest as possible in completing these measures, and that the interviewer would not have access to their answers. The results showed that the enhanced level of self-esteem, produced by the reinforcement procedure, carried over into the postexperimental period and remained significantly above the level found in the control group. It seems, then, that the interaction was successful in producing at least temporary changes in the way the subject viewed herself in the situation.

THE INTERACTION ENVIRONMENT.   Judgments of another's behavior are seldom unaffected by the environmental context in which they are made. A person's smile may be interpreted quite differently if others in the situation are suffering as opposed to sharing in the conviviality. In the same way, the environmental context of a relationship offers many cues which may affect one's presentation of self. Results from two studies serve to illustrate such effects.

In most social relationships the participants are aware of and may be affected by the apparent duration of their acquaintanceship. A relationship which is seen to be short-lived, for example, may sometimes allow greater freedom of action and spontaneity than one in which behavior may have long-term consequences (Thibaut & Kelley, 1959). In the Gergen and Wishnov study, one group of subjects faced a partner who was neither egotistical nor humble, but who attributed to herself strong as well as weak points. Half the subjects interacting with this person were led to anticipate a long-term relationship with the partner; the remaining half were told that after the interchange the circumstances would not allow a continued acquaintanceship. In subsequently describing themselves to their partners, subjects who anticipated further interaction became significantly more self-revealing, whereas those who did not expect a further relationship described themselves in essentially the same way they had a month earlier. While these findings demonstrate the effects of perceived duration, they of course raise questions about the "greater freedom of action" supposedly found in short-lived relationships. However, subjects in both conditions predominantly felt honest and unchanged, and the intensity of these feelings was unrelated to their actual behavior.

A second study attempts to isolate differences in self-presentation stemming from variation in task demands (Gergen & Gibbs, 1965). In what way, it asks, is a person's social identity altered by a task in which productivity is the major goal as opposed to one in which social compatibility or solidarity is stressed? In order to answer this and other questions, members of a naval training program participated in an experiment in which half were confronted with the former type of task and half with the latter. In the task emphasizing productivity, subjects were to work on maneuvering a mock ship out of danger when confronted by much complex information. In the solidarity task, the primary objective of the subjects was to be compatible and understanding in working out some maneuvering arrangements. Each participant was further led to believe that he would be working with a person who was either higher or lower in rank than himself. After one of the two tasks had been explained, he was asked to describe himself to his partner. The results revealed that regardless of the relative rank of the partner, subjects in the productivity condition became significantly more positive in their ratings of self, whereas those attempting to be compatible began to emphasize more negative aspects of self. When subsequently asked about their honesty in the situation, over three-quarters of the subjects indicated that they felt their self-ratings to be virtually the same as those made along the same dimensions a month earlier. In terms of subjective experiences of the subjects, these results quite closely parallel those of the Gergen and Wishnov study previously described.

MOTIVATION. It was reasoned earlier in this chapter that changes in self-presentation resulting from active goal seeking do not necessarily bear on the issue of internal consistency. However, a number of studies have demonstrated ways in which a person will alter his social visage in order to gain another's regard, and results from two of these shed important light on the problem of internal consistency.

In the first of these investigations (Jones, Gergen, & Davis, 1962), females were to be interviewed by a trainee in Clinical Psychology. Prior to the interview, half were asked to describe themselves during the interview in any way they saw fit to gain the interviewer's favor, while the remainder were told to be as honest as possible during the proceedings. Self-ratings made during the interview indicated, as expected, that self-description in the former group was significantly more positive than that found in the latter. More important, after the interview had been completed half the subjects in each of the groups found that the interviewer had reacted favorably toward them, whereas the remainder were led to believe that the trainee had been unimpressed. Subjects were then asked to assess the honesty of their self-ratings during the interview.

The results revealed that those subjects who had both engaged in dissimulating and been favorably received felt their self-descriptions had been quite honest. Their honesty ratings did not differ from those made by subjects who had originally been asked to be honest, and differed significantly from the ratings made by the ingratiating subjects who had incurred disfavor. In essence, the findings strongly suggest that one's perception of his own identity in a situation may be quite affected by extrinsic influences. In this case, subjects seemed to distort their feelings about what constituted authentic behavior in a highly pragmatic way. That which produced the more positive results was felt to be the "real self."

A second study (Gergen & Gibbs, 1965) penetrated such influences more directly. In this case, subjects were asked to formulate a talk about themselves which would gain the positive regard of a prospective employer. They were further encouraged to inflate this self-picture as much as needed in order to be successful. Half the participants subsequently delivered these speeches, and the others remained silent. Following the speech-making (and active role-playing for half the subjects) all were asked to rate themselves as honestly as possible on a self-esteem measure. This measure had also been administered some weeks prior to the experiment. An examination of self-esteem change revealed that both groups experienced an equally enhanced state of self-esteem, and for both groups such changes exceeded those found in a nonspeech-making control group. In effect, the subjective rehearsal of a given presentation, whether or not buttressed by active behavior, may alter a person's feelings about himself in a situation.

Scanning the results of the various studies described, what common threads can be identified? In light of the arguments developed in earlier sections of this paper, the work on self-presentation would strongly suggest the following:

1. The prevalent view that the normal behavior of individuals tends toward consistency is misconceived. If anything, the studies cited indicate the extreme ease with which a person can be caused to contradict himself. And we are not speaking here of differences in kind or type of behavior. A person's dishonesty in one situation is not necessarily inconsistent with his affability in another, nor does his occupational role necessarily contradict his role as father. Rather, we have seen that along the single and very central dimension of self-esteem, a person will shift in either a more positive or negative direction depending on situational influence.

Of course it is quite possible that our daily perceptions of others as consistent are not entirely erroneous. It seems quite likely, however, that to some degree we perceive consistency because with most social relationships we provide a constant stimulus value. Depending on the way we perceive a given person and the circumstances surrounding the relationship, we may provide a self-picture which remains relatively stable and coherent. This self-picture may have constant effects on the other's behavior. Remembering that an identical process may characterize the other's behavior at the same time, relationships may be subject to a process of mutual jockeying and crystallization of social identities. Once out of the relationship, however, the "personality" of each participant may be unrecognizable.

2. The view that a person has a consistent and stabilized image of himself, and will always recognize behavior which is discrepant from this image as alien, is in need of modification. To be sure, there are instances in which a person may discern that his actions and feelings are incompatible. However, the circumstances provoking such experiences may have to involve rather dramatic social dislocation.

The above research does suggest that transitions from one relationship to another may be accompanied by a process of *self-adaptation*. Such a process would cause a person's subjective feelings of identity to become adapted to and cohere with the circumstances of any new relationship. The person's own behavior, his thoughts about his behavior, and reinforcement received from others may all contribute to this type of adaptation. The net result is a reduction in the potential discrepancy between covert feelings and overt behavior, and thus of alienation from behavior. Such a process would allow for behavioral inconsistency without parallel feelings on the subjective level.

3. The popular notion of the self-concept as a unified, consistent, or perceptually "whole" psychological structure is possibly ill-conceived. Such a notion is simply not supported by the findings related to the above described process of self-adaptation. A revision of the construct of self seems in order, and such a revision might profitably be directed toward a theory of *multiple selves*. In lieu of the self-concept, a process of self-conception will ultimately be necessary.

III

Having reviewed a body of evidence which strongly suggests that consistency, either in thought or action, does not constitute the normal state of affairs, we are now in a better position to return to the problem of ethics. As pointed out earlier, both people in general and behavioral scientists in particular are prone to view consistency as a desirable state, and to reward others' behavior accordingly. What costs are incurred through the perpetuation of such an ethic? What are the repercussions of such sanctions for the psychological state of the individual? Several considerations loom as important.

For one, a demand for thoroughgoing consistency would fly in the face of a major mode of social adaptation. It would essentially freeze the individual personality in such a way that the person would fail to meet the requisites of a changing social environment. To be continuously serious, light-hearted, understanding, domineering, or the like, will reduce one's option for behavior and limit his potential for being within situations which require the opposite characteristics. Ludwig (1965) has even pointed out that active dissimulation and lying may be occasionally necessary and ethically permissible. And this is also to say that a prevailing need for achievement, need for positive regard, need for cognitive clarity, or any other of a host of needs or traits posited by personality theorists, will only be adaptive within a delimited set of relationships. Even the designation that a person is higher or lower on such and such a trait is mistaken if meant to imply that he does not often manifest the potential for the obverse of the designation.

It should be understood, however, that this is not to advocate a simple, chameleon-like approach to social interaction. Rather, it is to rely on the human capacity for rich and varied behavior, and on the fact that antithetical behavior may be enacted without losing one's feelings of honesty with self or with others.

It also seems that the more "natural" state of the organism is one which includes numerous disparities and contradicting tendencies. Freud came very close to making the same point in positing the *id*, that teeming repository of irrational and incompatible motives, as the basic given in personality structure. Of course, the argument need not be confined to a basic set of instincts. For any capacity possessed by the person, be it love, pain, lust, trust, nurturance, and so on, there exists the capacity and in some cases the need for its opposite. And too, polar capacities and feelings may exist coincidentally in the same relationship. From this point of view any strain toward consistency would appear to exist as an artificial overlay, fostered perhaps by a series of culturally specific learning experiences. Although being consistent may certainly be functional in some situations, in its most stringent form the overlay may well prevent the person from thoroughly partaking of the range and intensity of experiences potentially available to him.

If inconsistency can be considered a more intrinsically "natural" state, one wonders about the degree of frustration and emotional consternation generated in the attempt to bend oneself to the ethic. During the period of adolescence, for example, the individual may be particularly sensitive to the incompatibles in his life. Might it not be better to teach acceptance of the paradoxical than to require as a "mark of maturity" that the individual hang his identity on a limited set of his capacities for being? It also seems that internal demands and guilt feelings in the service of a consistency principle may constitute an appropriate context for generating repression. For example, it seems clear that the great anxiety many persons have about homosexuality is based on the assumption that one is *either* heterosexual *or* homosexual. If a person is unable to cope with or tolerate personal diversities, repression of its source could well result.

These arguments are, of course, quite tentative and should not be understood as advocating the abolishment of all consistent behavior. Of course, the commitment made to certain kinds of relationships demands consistency in certain realms of behavior. Many of a person's dearest experiences hinge on the establishment of trust within a relationship. And, as pointed out earlier, if every one were at all times acting unpredictably, what we know as "organized society" would cease to exist. However, personal consistency and stability may well be the by-products of most viable relationships—at least, within the relationships themselves. It is the expectation and demand for consistency across relationships which looms as most damaging to the individual. Quite probably persons vary with respect to their adherence to a principle of consistency. In light of these various arguments, future research might well be directed toward understanding the consequences of variations in this orientation.

REFERENCES

Allport, G. W. *Pattern and growth in personality.* New York: Holt, Rinehart and Winston, 1961.

Aronson, E., & Carlsmith, J. M. Performance expectancy as a determinant of actual performance. *Journal of Abnormal and Social Psychology,* 1962, 65, 178–182.

Campbell, D. T. Social attitudes and other acquired behavioral dispositions. In S. Koch (Ed.), *Psychology: A study of a science,* Vol. VI, New York: McGraw-Hill, 1963.

Festinger, L. *A theory of cognitive dissonance.* New York: Harper & Row, 1957.

Gergen, K. J. Interaction goals and personalistic feedback as factors affecting the presentation of self. *Journal of Personality and Social Psychology,* 1965, 1, 413–424.

Gergen, K. J., & Gibbs, M. G. Role playing and modifying the self-concept. Paper presented at the 1965 meetings of the Eastern Psychological Association.

Gergen, K. J., & Jones, E. E. Mental illness, predictability, and affective consequences as stimulus factors in person perception. *Journal of Abnormal and Social Psychology,* 1963, 67, 95–104.

Gergen, K. J., & Wishnov, B. Others' self-evaluations and interaction anticipation as determinants of self-presentation. *Journal of Personality and Social Psychology,* 1965, 2, 348–358.

Goffman, E. *The presentation of self in everyday life.* New York: Doubleday, 1959.

Goffman, E. *Asylums.* New York: Doubleday Books, 1961, 151–152.

Gollin, E. S. Forming impressions of personality. *Journal of Personality,* 1954, 23, 65–76.

Hartshorne, H., & May, M. A. *Studies in deceit.* New York: Macmillan, 1928.

Hyman, H. *Interviewing in social research.* Chicago: University of Chicago Press, 1954.

James, W. *The varieties of religious experience.* New York: New American Library, 1958.

Jones, E. E., Gergen, K. J., & Davis, K. E. Some determinants of reactions to being approved or disapproved as a person. *Psychological Monographs,* 1962, Whole No. 521.

Katz, D. Do interviewers bias polls? *Public Opinion Quarterly,* 1942, 6, 284–288.

La Pierre, R. T. Attitudes vs. actions. *Social Forces,* 1934, 13, 230–237.

Lecky, P. *Self-consistency, a theory of personality.* New York: Island Press, 1945.

Ludwig, A. M. *The importance of lying.* Springfield, Ill.: Charles C Thomas, 1965.

MacKinnon, D. W. The structure of personality. In J. McV. Hunt (Ed.), *Personality and the behavior disorders,* Vol. I, New York: Ronald, 1944, pp. 3–48.

Robinson, D., & Rohde, S. Two experiments with an anti-Semitism poll. *Journal of Abnormal and Social Psychology,* 1946, 51, 136–144.

Rogers, C. R. Some observations on the organization of personality. *American Psychologist,* 1947, 2, 358–368.

Thibaut, J. W., & Kelley, H. H. *The social psychology of groups.* New York: Wiley, 1959.

Ward, W. D., & Sandvold, K. D. Performance expectancy as a determinant of actual performance: A partial replication. *Journal of Abnormal and Social Psychology,* 1963, 67, 293–295.

Wells, H. G. *Outline of Western history.* Garden City, New Jersey: Garden City Books, 1961.

20.2 | THE INFLUENCE OF SELF-ESTEEM ON RATE OF VERBAL CONDITIONING AND SOCIAL MATCHING BEHAVIOR*[,1]

Donna M. Gelfand[2]

Recent years have witnessed an increasing interest in determining personality correlates of responsiveness to social influence processes. One variable which has received a good deal of research attention has been self-esteem, typically defined as a person's characteristic evaluations of himself and his accomplishments. Low self-esteem is characterized by feelings of personal inadequacy, guilt, shyness, and social inhibitons; high esteem reflects feelings of self-confidence and satisfaction (Hovland, Janis, & Kelley, 1953).

A person's characteristic self-esteem is believed to be a function of his reinforcement history (Cohen, 1959; Lesser & Abelson, 1959; Sears, 1942). The high esteem individual has presumably had a past history of chiefly positive reinforcement for his efforts, while a low esteem person has met with negative reinforcement in a variety of situations. It has been hypothesized that self-esteem is negatively related to social suggestibility on the assumption that low self-esteem and high persuasibility stem from the same type of previous experience, i.e., negatively reinforced instances of disagreement or discrepancy (Lesser & Abelson, 1959). Research done to date generally provides support for this theory (Hovland & Janis, 1959).

Since investigators interested in self-esteem have primarily been social psychologists, persuasibility measures such as opinion change (Janis & Field, 1959) and matching behavior (Abelson & Lesser, 1959) have been extensively studied. However, other measures usually employed by experimental psychologists (e.g., verbal learning) have not been investigated as they might relate to persuasibility and self-esteem. Furthermore, except for one or two studies (deCharms & Rosenbaum, 1960), measures of self-esteem have been largely response inferred (e.g., global ratings or personality questionnaires) rather than experimentally manipulated.

The purpose of the present study was to investigate the effects of both response inferred and of experimentally manipulated self-esteem upon social suggestibility as measured by a picture preference test involving matching behavior, and a measure traditionally used more by experimental psychologists, verbal operant conditioning.

* SOURCE: Gelfand, D. M. The influence of self-esteem on rate of verbal conditioning and social matching behavior. *Journal of Abnormal and Social Psychology,* 1962, 65, 259–265. Copyright 1962 by the American Psychological Association and reprinted by permission.

[1] This article is based on a dissertation submitted to the Department of Psychology of Stanford University in partial fulfillment of the requirements for the PhD degree.

[2] The author is greatly indebted to Albert Bandura for his advice and assistance in carrying out this research and in preparation of the manuscript for publication.

Children were assigned to high and low self-esteem groups on the basis of their scores on a self-concept questionnaire, and equal numbers of subjects from each group were then exposed either to a success or a failure experience designed to manipulate self-esteem. Following the esteem manipulation, subjects participated in a picture preference task with an experimental confederate and the subjects' tendency to match the behavior of the confederate was measured. Finally, subjects were administered a verbal conditioning task in which their responsivity to the experimenter's verbal reinforcement was measured.

Experimental hypotheses were derived from the theory proposed by Hovland, Janis, and their associates, that self-esteem and persuasibility are inversely related. It was predicted that in relation to high self-esteem subjects (high rated esteem subjects who succeeded), subjects low in self-esteem (low rated esteem subjects who failed) would be more inclined to match picture preference choices of the confederate and to condition reinforced verbal responses to a higher level. No predictions were advanced concerning performances of subjects whose experimentally mediated experiences contradicted their customary esteem expectations, i.e., subjects high in rated esteem who failed and subjects low in rated esteem who succeeded.

METHOD

SUBJECTS

Subjects were 60 fifth grade, public school children, 30 of whom were males and 30 females. Sixty additional children served as experimental confederates. Since there is some evidence that females are generally more persuasible than males (Hovland & Janis, 1959), subjects of both sexes were included in the study to check this finding.

DESIGN AND PROCEDURE

A 3 × 2 factorial design was used with two levels of self-esteem (high and low) and three experimental conditions (success, failure, and control). Subjects were first administered a self-concept test developed by Sears (1960). The test consisted of 100 questionnaire items covering 10 different areas of competence presumed important in children's self-evaluations. Subjects were asked to rate their ability on a five-point scale on each item. Self-esteem scores were the average of the subjects' self-ratings over the 100 items. On the basis of their test scores, subjects were dichotomized at the median into high and low self-esteem groups. One-third of each group was then randomly assigned to an experimental success manipulation designed to heighten self-esteem, one-third to a failure condition designed to lower self-esteem, while one-third constituted the control group which did not experience the experimental manipulations.

EXPERIMENTAL MANIPULATIONS

Failure Condition. Subjects were run in pairs in which one served as the experimental subject, while the other acted as an unwitting confederate. Subjects participated in four tasks in which the experimenter controlled results so that the confederate's performance was consistently better than the subject's.

The first task consisted of a 261-item arithmetic test involving addition, subtraction, and multiplication subtests, and was presented as a test of "arithmetic reasoning ability." In order to heighten the apparent importance of the test, it was prominently labeled Standard Arithmetic Reasoning Ability Test. Subjects were allowed 3 minutes to work on each subtest, and after 9 minutes, the experimenter ostensibly scored the tests and reported that the confederate completed twice as many problems correctly as did the subject. To emphasize further the success of the confederate, subjects were asked to record each other's scores on all tasks.

For the second task, subjects were asked to participate in a "test of physical power." Test apparatus consisted of a large, black box ($16'' \times 17'' \times 23''$) with a stirrup-type handle anchored on one side, a meter on another side, and a cord by which the experimenter could control the meter reading on a third side. The subject and the confederate were asked to take two turns each; while the subject was pulling, the confederate called out the meter reading and vice versa. Players received tied scores on this task because pretesting showed that having the confederate best on all four tasks made many subjects withdrawn or unduly upset.

The third task involved the use of materials from the Wisconsin Card Sort materials and was presented as a test of "problem solving ability." The task was arranged so the subject and the confederate could not see each other's sorts nor could they determine the correct criteria. Subjects were asked to sort the cards twice, and each time the confederate apparently achieved the solution much more quickly than did the subject.

The final task was a test of "hand-eye coordination." The equipment consisted of a miniature bowling alley ($36'' \times 12'' \times 6''$) with a runway at the end of which were three upright, doweled targets. The target area was screened from view by a fiberboard shield so the players had no way of knowing whether or not they struck a target. As a sign to the subjects that they had hit a target, a doweled marker dropped. The targets, however, were controlled with strings by the experimenter who was positioned at the side of the apparatus. The confederate and the subject each had two turns at bowling, and the confederate again won, receiving twice as high a score as the subject.

To further emphasize the differences in ability between the confederate and the subject, the experimenter instructed them to total scores obtained on all four tasks in order to establish the winner. The experimenter then congratulated the confederate on being the winner. For a detailed discussion of instruction and procedure see Gelfand (1961).

Success and Control Conditions. Experimental procedures in the success condition were identical to those described above, except the subject rather than the confederate was the successful partner. Control group subjects did not participate in experimental manipulations, performing only the two criterion tasks.

DEPENDENT VARIABLES

Two different criterion tasks were employed in this study. The first was a picture preference test consisting of 20 pairs of pictures representing a wide variety of subject matter and mounted on $11'' \times 14''$ white cardboard cards. A large pool of pictures was pretested on 60 fifth grade children and pairs of pictures were selected in which one picture was preferred by a three-to-one margin. The confederate was previously informed that this was actually a test to see whether children would follow a leader and that he would serve as leader. The confederate had first choice on each item and was asked to pick the picture the experimenter indicated for each pair. The experimenter held each card by one hand nearest the picture to be chosen. In each case, the confederate chose the picture less preferred by the pretest sample. To increase social pressure on the subject, the experimenter expressed agreement with the confederate's choices by saying "Good" after the confederate's response on each of the first five items. The score on this test was the number of unpopular pictures chosen by the subject.

Following the picture preference task, the experimenter remarked that the subject and the confederate had worked together on a number of tests and that now they would perform different activities. The confederate was given a neutral task (crossing out letters in a text) while the experimenter administered a modified Taffel (1955) verbal conditioning procedure to the subject. The subject was presented with a series of 100 3" × 5" white index cards on each of which was printed a verb in the past tense and the same six pronouns: I, We, He, You, She, and They. The subject was instructed to choose one of the pronouns on each card and say it aloud together with the verb.

The first block of 20 trials was used as a measure of operant level, and no reinforcement was given. For the following four blocks of 20 items each, the experimenter reinforced the subject's use of We and They with approving remarks such as, "That's a good one" or "Good one." The score on the conditioning series was the difference in number of We and They responses produced between operant level and the fourth reinforced block.

At the conclusion of the experimental session, the child who had previously experienced failure was given a success experience on the coordination task to heighten his feelings of self-esteem and thus counteract the reaction induced by the experimental failure condition.

RESULTS

EFFECTIVENESS OF ESTEEM MANIPULATION

As a check on the effectiveness of the esteem manipulation, subjects rated their performance before and after each task on a five-point rating scale ranging from 1—Very good to 5—Not very good. A median test (Siegel, 1956, p. 111) revealed no significant differences in initial self-ratings between Success and Failure groups ($\chi^2 = 0.05$, $p > .05$), but differences between groups were highly significant on final ratings ($\chi^2 = 25.83$, $p < .001$). The results clearly indicate that the experimental manipulations were successful in altering self-esteem so that subjects in the Success group rated themselves more favorably while subjects who failed evaluated themselves less favorably.

Additional evidence concerning the effectiveness of the esteem manipulations was provided by a check list completed by the experimenter on the subjects' behavior during the conditioning task. Subjects were rated on "anxiety" versus "confidence" behaviors. Behavior considered indicative of anxiety included speech regression, manual-oral contact, frequent sighing, reduction in response speed, drop in voice level, etc. Confident behavior included speaking in a loud, clear voice, increased speed in responding, and absence of fidgeting. In contrast to the High esteem-Success group which displayed 1 anxiety sign and 18 confidence signs, the Low esteem-Failure group yielded 18 anxiety and 5 confidence signs. Although these data were not analyzed statistically, it seems apparent that the Low esteem-Failure group exhibited considerably more overt anxiety than did the High esteem-Success or any other treatment group.

MATCHING BEHAVIOR ON PREFERENCE TASK

The first dependent variable measured was the number of imitative responses made by subjects in the picture preference task. Results of an analysis of variance performed on these data are summarized in Table 1. Because a Bartlett's test made on the residual error term indicated significant heterogeneity of variance ($\chi^2 = 59.13$, $df = 5$, $p < .01$), the .01 level of significance was adopted following Lindquist's (1953) recommendation. Variance of preference test scores was greater for Control subjects than for Success or Failure subjects. With this restriction, one main effect, the experimental esteem manipulation, proved significant. Subjects who experienced failure gave significantly more imitative responses than did subjects who experienced success. Neither initial self-esteem nor the interaction between initial and experimentally manipulated esteem significantly affected picture preference scores.

The results of a Duncan's multiple range test (Edwards, 1960) applied to these data are summarized in Table 2. Failure subjects were significantly more persuasible on the picture preference task than were Success subjects regardless of initial esteem level. Also, Control subjects high in self-esteem were more persuasible than were High esteem-Success subjects; a result not vindicated by the analysis of variance.

Table 1 | ANALYSES OF VARIANCE OF NUMBER OF MATCHING RESPONSES AND OF INCREASE IN REINFORCED RESPONSES ON CRITERION TASKS

SOURCE	df	MATCHING RESPONSES	REINFORCED RESPONSES
		F	F
Initial self-esteem	1	0.10	4.35*
Treatment conditions	2	17.29***	0.04
Initial esteem × Treatment	2	0.65	15.16***
Residual	54	(10.76)**	(18.77)**

  * $p < .05$.
  ** Error MS; significant heterogeneity of variance beyond $p = .01$.
  *** $p < .001$.

Table 2 | DUNCAN'S RANGE TESTS OF MEAN NUMBER OF MATCHING RESPONSES AND MEAN INCREASE IN REINFORCED RESPONSES*

SCORE	TREATMENT GROUP					
	Low-Fail	Low-Succeed	Low-Control	High-Fail	High-Succeed	High-Control
Matching responses	9.7$_c$	4.7$_{ab}$	7.4$_{abc}$	10.7$_c$	3.6$_a$	8.3$_{bc}$
Reinforced responses	5.0$_{ab}$	12.2$_c$	7.7$_{bc}$	9.7$_{bc}$	1.9$_{bc}$	6.3$_{ab}$

* Conditioning and picture preference test data were analyzed separately. Within each row, any two means bearing the same subscript are not significantly different at the $p = .01$ level.

VERBAL CONDITIONING RATE

The second dependent variable measured was the number of reinforced responses produced in the verbal conditioning task. An analysis of variance performed on the 20-trial operant series revealed that the treatment groups did not initially differ significantly in production of the reinforced class of responses. Neither initial esteem ($F = 0.86$, $df = 1/54$), experimental manipulations ($F = 0.20$, $df = 2/54$), nor the interaction ($F = 0.32$, $df = 2/54$) significantly affected operant level of production of We and They responses.

An analysis of variance of the conditioning data is summarized in Table 1. A Bartlett's test indicated significant heterogeneity of variance ($\chi^2 = 14.30$, $df = 5$, $p < .01$); therefore, only F ratios with probability of occurrence beyond the .01 level were accepted as significant. The variance of High esteem-Success subjects' scores was small while variance of scores for Control subjects was considerably larger. With this limitation, only the interaction term proved significant. An analysis of variance applied to a logarithmic transformation of these data to reduce heterogeneity of variance yielded the same results as the analysis of the original scores.

Table 2 shows the results of a Duncan's multiple range test applied to the conditioning data. Initially low esteem subjects who experienced success were significantly more conditionable than were initially low esteem subjects who experienced failure. Conversely, initially high esteem subjects who experienced failure conditioned to a significantly higher degree than did initially high esteem subjects in the Success condition. Control subjects initially low in esteem were significantly more conditionable than were High esteem-Success subjects.

Initial self-esteem was related to conditioning performance in a rather complex fashion. Because of the strong interaction effect between initial esteem and experimental manipulations, correlations between rated esteem and conditioning scores differed among treatment groups. For the Success and Failure groups, product-moment correlation coefficients of $r = -.77$ ($t = -5.12$, $df = 18$, $p < .01$) and $r = .43$ ($t = 2.02$, $df = 18$, $.10 > p > .05$), respectively, were obtained, while the correlation was not significant for Control subjects ($r = .17$, $t = -0.73$, $df = 18$). Only in interaction with experimental manipulations did initial esteem affect conditioning.

Contrary to the majority of previous findings by Hovland, Janis, and their associates (1959), male and female subjects did not differ significantly in their performance on any of the experimental measures.

DISCUSSION

The significant group differences in persuasibility found in this study partially confirm the Hovland and Janis hypothesis that self-esteem and persuasiblity are negatively correlated. An inverse relationship between self-esteem and persuasibility was obtained on both dependent measures, but it was experimentally manipulated esteem which affected scores on the picture preference task while the interaction between rated and manipulated esteem was the variable related to verbal conditioning scores. The High esteem-Success group proved least suggestible on both criterion tasks as predicted, and the high suggestibility of the Low esteem-Failure subjects on the picture preference task also followed prediction. However, the minimal responsivity of the Low esteem-Failure group on the conditioning task clearly contradicted the experimental hypotheses.

Differences in relative persuasibility of groups between the two criterion tasks may have been due to any or all of a number of factors:

1. The persuasion source was a peer, the confederate, in the picture preference task while the experimenter served as persuasive agent in the conditioning situation.
2. The status of the source was varied in the preference task while status remained relatively constant for the experimenter as source.
3. The preference measure was temporally closer to the experimental esteem manipulation than was the conditioning measure.
4. The measures differed in complexity. The subject chose between many alternatives in the conditioning task while only two alternatives existed in the preference test—to follow or not to follow the confederate in making a choice.

The influence of the first three of these factors can only be surmised, but there is some experimental evidence concerning operation of the fourth factor. Several experimenters have reported the finding that high anxiety facilitates learning simple tasks, but interferes with performance on complex tasks (Montague, 1953; Sarason, Davidson, Lighthall, Waite, & Ruebush, 1960; Taylor & Spence, 1952). The experimenters' ratings of subjects' behavior during the conditioning task provide some evidence that treatment groups differed in overt manifestations of anxiety. Groups which displayed moderate amounts of "anxiety" *and* "confidence" behavior (Low esteem-Success and High esteem-Failure) received the highest conditioning scores, while the Low esteem-Failure group which appeared the most anxious scored relatively low in conditioning. Since a high level of anxiety interferes with learning complex tasks (Taylor & Spence, 1952), there is reason to believe that the conditioning performance of the Low esteem-Failure group was affected by their anxiety and tension. Conversely, the high level of performance of Low esteem-Failure subjects on the relatively simple preference task could also be due to their high anxiety which facilitates performance on simple tasks.

Although evidence for facilitating and interfering effects of anxiety is mostly indirect in this study, the available data are consistent with this formulation.

A finding of considerable interest is the high responsivity to verbal conditioning of subjects exposed to experiences inconsistent with their customary self-evaluations (High esteem-Failure and Low esteem-Success groups). While there appears to be no ready explanation for these results, one might speculate whether the high rate of conditioning in these groups may reflect the effects of intermittent reinforcement. Since self-esteem is assumed to be a function of past success and failure experiences (Cohen, 1959), subjects in the High esteem-Success group could be viewed as having experienced a very high schedule of positive reinforcement, both previous to and during the experiment. Low esteem-Failure subjects, on the other hand, experienced a very low schedule of reinforcement, or negative reinforcement for their efforts. There is considerable evidence that schedules of partial reinforcement produce high rates of response (Ferster & Skinner, 1957). If it can be assumed that the experiences of the High esteem-Failure and Low esteem-Success subjects constituted a form of partial reinforcement, then the high level of conditioning exhibited by these groups would be expected.

deCharms and Rosenbaum's (1960) findings that rated, but not manipulated self-esteem was associated with matching behavior are at variance with results of the present study. This discrepancy in findings may be due to differences in potency of experimental manipulations. deCharms and Rosenbaum's esteem manipulation was relatively superficial in nature, in that adult subjects were simply instructed that they were either high or low in leadership potential. In contrast, the manipulations in the present experiment involved several tasks performed by young children who tended to be highly competitive with each other. Since a series of success or failure experiences was involved, the cumulative effects were very powerful. Differences in subjects' ages may also have contributed to the discrepancy in results obtained in the two studies. Adults may be more influenced by internal norms based on an extensive reinforcement history, while children may be more dependent on external feedback concerning the adequacy of their performance.

Finally, the results of the present study may partially explain the finding of Kanfer and Karas (1959) that prior success and failure experiences did not affect verbal conditioning performance. Such negative results might be due to an unassessed interaction effect between initial self-esteem and experimental manipulations. When initial, rated self-esteem is not considered, conditioning data from the present experiment yield results similar to those obtained by Kanfer and Karas. Since success and failure interact with initial self-esteem to affect social suggestibility, it is clear that a study utilizing only one type of esteem measure may produce somewhat misleading results. Therefore both rated and manipulated esteem should be considered in designing future suggestibility studies.

SUMMARY

The present study was designed to investigate the effects of response inferred and of experimentally manipulated self-esteem upon social suggestibility in children. Experimental hypotheses were derived from Hovland and Janis' (1959) theory that self-esteem and persuasibility are inversely related.

A personality inventory measure of self-esteem was administered to subjects who were assigned to high and low initial esteem groups on the basis of their test scores. Equal numbers of subjects from each group were then exposed either to an experimental success manipulation designed to heighten esteem or to a failure condition designed to lower esteem. Social suggestibility was measured by a picture preference task and a verbal operant conditioning procedure.

Results obtained were as follows:

1. Subjects who experienced failure exhibited significantly more matching responses on the picture preference task than did subjects who experienced success. Matching behavior, however, was not influenced by rated self-esteem.
2. A highly significant interaction was obtained between rated and experimentally manipulated self-esteem on performance in the conditioning procedure. Subjects exposed to experiences inconsistent with their customary self-evaluations (High esteem-Failure and Low esteem-Success groups) showed significantly more verbal conditioning than did subjects whose experiences were consistent with their self-attitudes (High esteem-Success and Low esteem-Failure groups).

Overall results were generally in accord with the theory that self-esteem and persuasibility are negatively correlated.

REFERENCES

Abelson, R. P., & Lesser, G. S. The measurement of persuasibility in children. In C. I. Hovland & I. L. Janis (Eds.), *Personality and persuasibility*. New Haven, Conn.: Yale University Press, 1959. Pp. 141–166.

Cohen, A. R. Some implications of self-esteem for social influence. In C. I. Hovland & I. L. Janis (Eds.), *Personality and persuasibility*. New Haven, Conn.: Yale University Press, 1959. Pp. 102–120.

deCharms, R., & Rosenbaum, M. E. Status variables and matching behavior. *J. Pers.*, 1960, *28*, 492–502.

Edwards, A. L. *Experimental design in psychological research*. (Rev. ed.) New York: Holt, Rinehart and Winston, 1960.

Ferster, C. B., & Skinner, B. F. *Schedules of reinforcement*. New York: Appleton, 1957.

Gelfand, Donna M. The influence of self-esteem on rate of conditioning and social matching behavior. Unpublished doctoral dissertation, Stanford University, 1961.

Hovland, C. I., & Janis, I. L. (Eds.), *Personality and persuasibility*. New Haven, Conn.: Yale University Press, 1959.

Hovland, C. I., Janis, I. L., & Kelley, H. H. *Communication and persuasion*. Princeton, N.J.: Princeton University Press, 1953.

Janis, I. L., & Field, P. B. Sex differences and personality factors related to persuasibility. In C. I. Hovland & I. L. Janis (Eds.), *Personality and persuasibility*. New Haven, Conn.: Yale University Press, 1959. Pp. 55–68.

Kanfer, F. H., & Karas, Shirley C. Prior experimenter-subject interaction and verbal conditioning. *Psychol. Rep.*, 1959, *5*, 345–353.

Lesser, G. S., & Abelson, R. P. Personality correlates of persuasibility in children. In C. I. Hovland & I. L. Janis (Eds.), *Personality and persuasibility*. New Haven, Conn.: Yale University Press, 1959. Pp. 187–206.

Lindquist, E. F. *Design and analysis of experiments in psychology and education*. Boston: Houghton Mifflin, 1933.

Montague, B. K. The role of anxiety in serial rote learning. *J. exp. Psychol.*, 1953, *45*, 91–96.

Sarason, S. B., Davidson, K. S., Lighthall, F. F., Waite, R. R., & Ruebush, B. K. *Anxiety in elementary school children*. New York: Wiley, 1960.

Sears, Pauline S. The pursuit of self-esteem: The middle childhood years. Paper read at American Psychological Association, Chicago, September 1960.

Sears, R. R. Success and failure: A study of motility. In Q. McNemar & Maud A. Merrill (Eds.), *Studies in personality*. New York: McGraw-Hill, 1942. Pp. 235–258.

Siegel, S. *Nonparametric statistics for the behavioral sciences*. New York: McGraw-Hill, 1956.

Taffel, C. Anxiety and the conditioning of verbal behavior. *J. abnorm. soc. Psychol.*, 1955, *51*, 496–501.

Taylor, Janet A., & Spence, K. W. The relationship of anxiety level to performance in serial learning. *J. exp. Psychol.*, 1952, *44*, 61–64.

20.3 | EFFECTS OF SELF-ESTEEM, PERCEIVED PERFORMANCE, AND CHOICE ON CAUSAL ATTRIBUTIONS[*][1]

Gordon Fitch

Heider (1958) described a model of the cognitive process people use in structuring their environment through causal attribution. In Heider's model, a person engaged in an activity attributes the outcome to one or more internal or external causal sources. Current research suggests a number of personality and situational variables which may affect a person's causal attributions, including self-esteem, perceived performance, and choice.

The high-self-esteem person has been conceptualized as liking or valuing himself,

* SOURCE: Fitch, G. Effects of self-esteem, perceived performance, and choice on causal attributions. *Journal of Personality and Social Psychology*, 1970, *16*, 311–315. Copyright 1970 by the American Psychological Association and reprinted by permission.

[1] This study is based primarily on a dissertation submitted to Purdue University in partial fulfillment of the requirements for the PhD degree.

as well as seeing himself as competent in dealing with the world he perceives (Cohen, 1959; Combs & Snygg, 1959). The low-self-esteem person is seen as disliking, devaluing himself, and in general perceiving himself as not competent to deal effectively with his environment.

Two partially contradictory hypotheses may be derived from self theory. The first is that persons are motivated to perceive events in a way which *enhances* chronic self-esteem. The second is that persons are motivated to perceive events in a way which is *consistent* with chronic self-esteem. These two contradictory hypotheses regarding self-esteem and interpretation of event outcomes may be integrated with Heider's concept of causal attribution. Self-esteem could be enhanced by attributing success outcomes to causal sources within the person and by attributing failure outcomes to casual sources outside the person. The attribution of success outcomes to internal sources should both enhance self-esteem and be consistent for the high-self-esteem person.

However, the prediction is different for the low-self-esteem person, depending on whether he is motivated to enhance self-esteem or maintain consistency with self-esteem. If he is enhancing self-esteem, the prediction is that he attributes causality for success to internal sources to a greater extent than causality for failure. If on the other hand he is motivated to maintain consistency with a low level of self-esteem, he should internalize the causality for failure to a greater extent than the causality for success. Support for the latter hypothesis was found by Silverman (1964): "The interpretation offered by these authors is that low self-esteem persons can only assimilate information relating to themselves which is consistent with their general self concept [p. 116]."

Cognitive dissonance theory (Festinger, 1957) has generated research which suggests the efficacy of volition or commitment in inducing cognitive dissonance (Brehm & Cohen, 1962). Brehm and Cohen concluded that people experienced dissonance to the extent that they freely chose to engage in an action discrepant with their private attitude. A logical derivation is that these subjects may have experienced dissonance only to the extent that the free choice of attitude-discrepant behavior led to a cognition that they were personally responsible for their behavior. Thus, it was predicted that degree of choice is positively related to the degree of attribution of event outcomes to internal causal sources.

The purpose of the present experiment was to resolve a discrepancy in the literature with respect to whether people interpret event outcomes in a way consistent with chronic self-esteem or in a way which enhances chronic self-esteem. A secondary purpose was to determine whether a person's degree of choice in participating in the experiment influenced his interpretations of event outcomes. Interpretation of event outcomes was operationally defined in terms of Heider's causal attribution theory.

METHOD

SUBJECTS.   The subjects were 135 undergraduate business students in classes taught by the experimenter. These students volunteered to participate in the experiment in return for a small reduction in required class work.

TASK.   The task was taken from Wyer (1967). The subjects viewed slides projected on a screen for a period of 3 seconds. Each slide contained a number of dots randomly distributed over its area. After viewing the slide for 3 seconds, the subject responded with an estimate of the number of dots on that slide. Each subject viewed 10 slides. The number of dots on each slide were 17, 48, 28, 37, 29, 38, 20, 40, 23, and 50. All subjects saw a sample slide with 7 dots before beginning the series.

INDEPENDENT VARIABLES.   Self-esteem was measured approximately 1 month before the subjects engaged in the experimental task with the Tennessee (Department of Mental Health) Self-Concept Scale (TSCS; Fitts, 1964). The TSCS was chosen primarily for ease of scoring, widespread availability, and ease of administration. Research on the reliability and validity of this scale has been summarized by Fitts (1965).

There were two manipulated independent variables, degree of choice and perceived performance. When the subjects were recruited, they were told they would have a choice of four experimental tasks. When the subjects reported to the experimental session, high-choice subjects were told that while there were originally four experimental tasks available, all necessary data had been obtained on three of the four tasks, and that therefore they had a choice of working on the remaining task or not participating at all, with full credit being given either way. Low-choice subjects were told that while there were originally four experimental tasks available, the procedure had been changed, and they had been randomly assigned to one particular task. Subjects in all experimental conditions worked at the dot-estimation task.

The perceived performance manipulation occurred through false performance feedback given to the subjects after they had completed their estimation of the number of dots on the series of slides. The subjects in failure conditions were told that they had scored at the 23rd percentile in comparison with comparable subjects. The subjects in the success conditions were told that they had scored at the 83rd percentile in comparison with comparable subjects. The choice of 23rd and 83rd percentiles for the false performance feedback was arbitrary. Intended perceptions of poor or good performance were further reinforced by expressions of sympathy or congratulations by the experimenter.

DEPENDENT VARIABLE MEASURE.   The primary dependent variable, causal attribution, was measured with a questionnaire which each subject completed after judging the series of 10 slides and receiving the false performance feedback. The question allowed the subject to distribute causality for his outcome over four possible causal sources, two defined by the experimenter as lying within the person and two lying outside the person. The two within-person sources were ability and effort. The two external sources were luck and the person's physical or mental condition during the period while he was performing the task. Subjects were instructed to distribute their responses over the four causal sources such that the total causality added to 100%, with no restriction as to the proportion of causality attributed to any one source. While there are methodological reasons for not restricting the subjects' responses to a limited set of categories, Heider's (1958) theory specifies the reciprocal nature of within-person and outside-person causal attributions. In order to be consistent with Heider, it was felt necessary to restrict the subjects' responses. It would have been desirable in testing the external validity of Heider's conception to allow free responses and determine if the responses did in fact align themselves into categories suggested by Heider.

DESIGN.   The basic design of the experiment was a 2 × 2 × 2 factorial, with 2 levels of self-esteem (high and low), 2 levels of action outcome (success and failure), and 2 levels of choice (high and low). The total design consisted of 8 experimental conditions, with 15 subjects per cell, plus one control group of 15 subjects. Subjects were assigned to experimental conditions as follows: After 120 subjects were administered the self-esteem measure, they were divided at the median into high- and low-self-esteem groups, with 60 subjects per group. Each group was then subdivided into four groups matched for mean, range, and standard deviation on the self-esteem measure, with the result of four high-self-esteem groups of 15 subjects each and four low-self-esteem groups of 15 subjects each. Two of the four high-self-esteem groups were randomly designated high-choice groups, and two were designated low-choice groups. Similarly, one of the two high-choice groups was randomly assigned to the success-feedback condition and one, to the failure feedback. An equivalent procedure was used for the four low-self-esteem groups.

There was also one control group of 15 subjects chosen at random from the original pool of 135 subjects. No independent variable measurements or manipulations were made for this group, which performed the task and immediately completed the dependent-variable questionnaire. The primary reason for including this group was to determine if causal attributions would be evenly distributed over the four causal sources in the absence of independent-variable manipulations.

PROCEDURE.   When the subjects reported to the experimental session, the appropriate choice manipulation was made, and the task was explained. After the subjects saw a sample slide with seven dots, they were asked to estimate the number of dots on each of the 10 slides after viewing each slide for 3 seconds. No time limit was imposed on making estimates. After completing the series, the experimenter purported to score the subjects' answers and completed the success-failure manipulation. Subjects were then administered the dependent-variable questionnaire and requested not to discuss the experiment with classmates until all sessions had been completed. All subjects were debriefed thoroughly in later class sessions.

RESULTS

The primary dependent variable was the subject's attributions of causality to the four available causal sources. These data are summarized in Table 1. The data in each row of Table 1 represent the mean percentages of causal attribution to each causal

Table 1 | DISTRIBUTION OF CAUSAL ATTRIBUTIONS OVER FOUR CAUSAL SOURCES

CONDITION			MEAN ATTRIBUTION TO CAUSAL SOURCES (%)			
			Internal		*External*	
SELF-ESTEEM	CHOICE	PERCEIVED PERFORMANCE	ABILITY	EFFORT	CHANCE	S'S PHYSICAL OR MENTAL CONDITION
High	High	Success	46	24	18	12
		Failure	29	24	31	16
	Low	Success	40	29	15	16
		Failure	34	18	23	25
Low	High	Success	32	28	21	19
		Failure	28	28	27	17
	Low	Success	36	30	22	12
		Failure	43	24	16	17
	Control		26	25	26	24

source by the 15 subjects in that experimental condition. (These percentages add to 100% in each row.) Control-group attributions were distributed evenly over the four causal sources, indicating lack of any inherent propensity to favor one causal source over another.

In order to fit the data into the Heider model, attributions to ability and effort sources were aggregated and designated internal. Attributions to chance and the subject's mental and physical condition were combined and designated external. It should be noted that the failure and success conditions refer to the false feedback given the subject by the experimenter, and not to the subject's actual performance.

An initial test of the self-esteem enhancement hypothesis tended to confirm it. A two-tailed t test demonstrated that success-feedback subjects attributed significantly ($p < .05$) more causality to the two internal sources ($\bar{X} = 66.3\%$, $n = 60$) than did the failure feedback group ($\bar{X} = 57.4\%$, $n = 60$; $t = 2.8$).

To provide further evidence, an analysis of variance was computed, with the dependent variable of combined internal attributions. Homogeneity of within-treatment variances was tested with Cochran's C statistic (Winer, 1962). The analysis of variance summary for attributions to combined internal sources is shown in Table 2.

It may be seen in Table 2 that neither measured self-esteem nor choice significantly affected attributions. The main effect of performance feedback was complicated by the significant ($p < .05$) Self-Esteem $\times$ Performance interaction. The Self-Esteem $\times$ Performance interaction was evaluated with an analysis of simple effects, that is, self-esteem at high and low levels of perceived performance (see Table 3).

Low-self-esteem subjects who received failure feedback attributed significantly ($p < .05$) more causality to internal sources ($\bar{X} = 62.1\%$) than did high-self-esteem subjects who received failure feedback ($\bar{X} = 52.7\%$), thus supporting the self-esteem consistency hypothesis.

Table 2 | SUMMARY OF ANALYSIS OF VARIANCE OF ATTRIBUTIONS OF CAUSALITY TO COMBINED INTERNAL SOURCES

SOURCE	df	MS	F
Self-esteem (A)	1	.85	<1
Perceived performance (B)	1	24.03	8.12*
Choice (C)	1	5.50	1.86
A × B	1	18.02	6.09*
A × C	1	6.12	2.07
B × C	1	.35	<1
A × B × C	1	.47	<1
Error (within)	112	2.96	

* $p < .05$.

Table 3 | SUMMARY OF ANALYSIS OF SIMPLE EFFECTS OF SELF-ESTEEM (A) AT LEVELS OF PERCEIVED PERFORMANCE (B)

SOURCE	df	MS	F
A at B_1	1	5.50	1.86
A at B_2	1	13.20	4.46*
Error (within)	112	2.96	

* $p < .05$.

However, this effect did not hold for success-feedback subjects. High-self-esteem subjects who received success feedback did not attribute significantly more causality to internal sources than low-self-esteem subjects who received success feedback. Thus, there was support for the self-esteem consistency hypothesis for low-self-esteem subjects receiving failure feedback, but not for low-self-esteem subjects receiving success feedback. On the basis of these data, it must be concluded that there is some evidence for *both* the self-esteem enhancement and self-esteem consistency hypotheses. Neither can be definitely accepted or rejected.

A final hypothesis was that persons attribute causality for an action outcome to internal causal sources, to the extent that they freely choose to engage in the action. Table 1 shows that the choice variable did not significantly affect attributions to internal causal sources, so this hypothesis was not supported.

CHECK ON INDEPENDENT VARIABLE INDUCTION. Postexperimental questionnaire responses indicated that the success-failure manipulation was successful. Subjects who had received success feedback felt significantly more comfortable after receiving the feedback than did subjects receiving failure feedback ($p < .05$). Success-feedback subjects reported significantly higher expectations of future success than did failure-feedback subjects ($p = .05$). Success-feedback subjects also reported that they thought they had done better than "most others" to a significantly greater extent than did failure-feedback subjects ($p < .05$). Mann-Whitney U tests (Siegel, 1956) were used on all questionnaire data.

There is a question as to whether the choice variable was successfully manipulated. Choice subjects indicated significantly ($p < .05$) greater perception of freedom to leave than did no-choice subjects. However, no subjects in the choice condition chose to leave without participating in the experiment. Many dissonance experiments have demonstrated the difficulty of manipulating this variable. Since none of the choice subjects actually chose to leave, the safer conclusion is that the effect of this variable on causal attributions was not validly tested.

DISCUSSION

These results support the hypothesis that self-esteem enhancement influences subjects to attribute success outcomes to internal sources to a greater extent than failure outcomes. There was also partial support for the hypothesis that self-esteem consistency affects causal attributions. That is, low-self-esteem subjects who received failure feedback attributed significantly more causality to internal sources than did high-self-esteem subjects who received failure feedback. However, the obverse of this prediction did not hold, that is, high-self-esteem subjects who received success feedback did not attribute significantly more causality to internal sources than did low-self-esteem subjects who received success feedback.

A somewhat speculative conclusion is that while high-self-esteem subjects tend to "internalize" success but not failure outcomes, low-self-esteem subjects tend to internalize both success and failure. This conclusion is at odds with one result obtained in the present experiment, but not previously discussed. When the subjects in this experiment originally completed the self-esteem measure, they were also administered the I-E control scale. Rotter (1966) described the I-E control scale as measuring the extent to which persons view the reinforcements they receive as being internally controlled, presumably regardless of the positive or negative nature of the reinforcement. A logical hypothesis would be that since the results of the present experiment suggest that low-self-esteem subjects internalize failure to a larger extent than high-self-esteem subjects and internalize success to about the same extent as high-self-esteem subjects, they might be expected to score more in the internal direction on the I-E control scale. The author's data do not support this hypothesis. There was actually a low (.23) but significant ($p < .05$) positive Spearman rank-order correlation of I-E control with self-esteem. That is, low-self-esteem subjects tended to score toward the external end of the I-E control scale. Unfortunately, I-E control was not an independent variable in the present experimental design, and the effects of I-E control on causal attributions cannot be directly assessed. Clearly, further research is needed to explicate the relationship between I-E control, self-esteem, and causal attribution.

SUMMARY

Subjects attributed causality for performance in a dot-estimation task to internal and external causal sources. Subjects were found to attribute significantly more causality to internal sources for success outcomes than for failure outcomes, supporting a self-esteem enhancement prediction. Low-self-esteem subjects who received failure feedback attributed significantly more causality to internal causal sources than did high-self-esteem subjects, who received failure feedback, thus supporting a self-esteem consistency prediction for low-self-esteem subjects. The prediction of a positive relationship between degree of choice in engaging in the task and internal attribution of causality was not supported. A significant Self-Esteem $\times$ Perceived Performance interaction is discussed, as is an unexpected relationship between internal-external control and self-esteem.

REFERENCES

Brehm, J. W., & Cohen, A. R. *Exploration in cognitive dissonance.* New York: Wiley, 1962.

Cohen, A. R. Some implications of self-esteem for social influence. In C. I. Hovland & I. L. Janis (Eds.), *Personality and persuasibility.* New Haven, Conn.: Yale University Press, 1959.

Combs, A., & Snygg, D. *Individual behavior.* (Rev. ed.) New York: Harper & Row, 1959.

Festinger, L. *A theory of cognitive dissonance.* New York: Harper & Row, 1957.

Fitts, W. H. *Tennessee (Department of Mental Health) Self-Concept Scale.* Nashville: Counselor Recordings and Tests, 1964.

Fitts, W. H. *Manual, Tennessee (Department of Mental Health) Self-Concept Scale.* Nashville: Counselor Recordings and Tests, 1965.

Heider, F. *The psychology of interpersonal relations.* New York: Wiley, 1958.

Rotter, J. B. Generalized expectancies for internal versus external control of reinforcement. *Psychological Monographs,* 1966, *80*(1, Whole No. 609).

Siegel, S. *Nonparametric statistics for the behavioral sciences.* New York: McGraw-Hill, 1956.

Silverman, I. Self-esteem and differential responsiveness to success and failure. *Journal of Abnormal and Social Psychology,* 1964, *69,* 115–119.

Winer, B. J. *Statistical principles in experimental design.* New York: McGraw-Hill, 1962.

Wyer, R. S., Jr. Behavioral correlates of academic achievement: Conformity under achievement and affiliation-incentive conditions. *Journal of Personality and Social Psychology,* 1967, *6,* 255–262.

AUTHOR INDEX

SUBJECT INDEX